TOTTENHAM HOTSPUR

AUDERE·EST·FACERE

HAMLYN

TOTTENHAM HOTSPUR

1882-1997

The Official Illustrated History

PHiL SOAR

PREFACE BY
GARY MABBUTT

FOREWORD BY ALAN SUGAR

ACKNOWLEDGEMENTS

The statistics for the first two editions were prepared by Ray Spiller, Chairman of the Association of Football Statisticians, with the late Morely Farror and Alex Wilson. The statistics for the years from 1985-1997 were prepared by Andy Porter.

Additional text and contributions from Pat Collins, Jonathan Culverhouse, Martin Tyler, Richard Widdows and Peter Arnold.

Art Director: Keith Martin
Design Manager: Bryan Dunn
Original Design: Brian Thomas
Jacket Design: Martin Topping and Vivek Bhatia
Design: Leigh Jones and Paul Webb
Picture Research: Maria Gibbs
Publishing Director: Laura Bamford
Editors: Adam Ward and Trevor Davies
Assistant Editor: Tarda Davison-Aitkins
Production: Mark Walker

EDITORS' NOTE

The editors would like to thank John Fennelly for his assistance in helping Gary Mabbutt put his thoughts about Spurs into words so skilfully, to Martyn Oliver for his assistance with the new documentary photography for this edition, to John Moulding, Ashley Weller and Andy Porter for their co-operation at various stages of the book's production, to Juliette Butler for her help on this project.

First published in Great Britain by Hamlyn Publishing in 1982 under the title *And the Spurs Go Marching On . . .* This edition published in 1996 by Hamlyn an imprint of Reed International Books Limited, Michelin House, 81 Fulham Road, London SW3 6RB and Auckland, Melbourne, Singapore and Toronto

A catalogue record for this book is available from the British Library

ISBN 0 600 59265 0

Produced by Butler and Tanner
Printed in Great Britain

PHOTOGRAPHIC ACKNOWLEDGEMENTS

All pictures by Action Images / Tottenham Hotspur Football Club except the following:

Action Images: 157 top, centre, below, 166 below, 168, 169 top left, 174 top, 178, 183 top, centre, below, 185 top, 188 top, below, 190 top, 191 top, below; Mick Alexander / Sportsimage: 123, 125 top, 127, 133; David Allen: 25, 34;

Allsport: 6, 142, 186 top, below, 187 top, 170, 171, /Stu Foster 195 right, /Gary M. Prior 196 top, /Ben Radford 193, 195 left; Danny Blanchflower: 73, 76, 77, 78, 79, 82, 83; Hedley Bull: 10, 14; Carleton Photographic Services: 125 below; Central Press: 61, 89, 92, 93, 126 below; Colorsport: 42, 43, 117, 120, 139, 141, 180, 181 top, centre, below, 184, 187 below, 190 below, 192 top, 192 below, 194, 196, 196 below, 197; Fox Photos: 63, 64, 65, 75, 98; Ray Green: 70, 71, 121, 122, 136;
Hulton Getty: 20, 27, 36, 37, 39, 40, 41, 44, 45, 47, 50, 51, 53, 54, 56, 57, 58, 128; Keystone: 67, 92; Mark leech: 182; Marshall Cavendish: 144; Popperfoto: 69, 84, 85, 96, 97, 100, 102, 103, 104, 105; Press Association: 104, 105, 119; Sport & General: 80, 105, 114, 115; Sunday Times Newspaper: 158 top; Syndication International: 87, 94, 95, 100, 103, 108, 110, 111, 112, 116, 124; Tottenham Hotspur F.C.: 8, 148, 149;
STW: 9, 10, 12 top, 17, 18, 19, 20, 21, 22, 23, 24, 26, 28, 29, 30, 31, 32, 33, 35, 38, 39, 45, 47, 47, 49, 59, 60, 66, 80, 89, 90, 91, 93, 94, 95, 107, 129, 130, 131, 134, 135;

Contents

Preface
by Gary Mabbutt

Tradition plays its part in making any Club great and there is no doubt that Tottenham Hotspur possesses that vital quality in abundance. Money, success, influence . . . they are all obviously important but it is tradition that makes a Club something special.

There will always be an exceptional aura about White Hart Lane that lives on despite the stadium developments of recent years. Indeed, the current new look to our famous ground has retained the unique atmosphere and I still receive a special 'buzz' whenever I drive through those black and gold gates.

I still recall how arriving here sent a shiver down my spine when I transferred from Bristol Rovers back in the summer of 1982. I had just turned 21 when I was invited up to London for pre-season training – the majestic presence of the place struck me from the beginning.

And then there was the dressing room! Not the ambience nor the fixtures and fittings - this time it was the quality of the players, with so many household names that I was quite staggered. Spurs had just retained the FA Cup and were regulars in European competition at the time. The team, led by Steve Perryman, reflected that success and ambition: Glenn Hoddle, Ossie Ardiles, Steve Archibald, Ray Clemence, Garth Crooks, Graham Roberts, Tony Galvin, Ricky Villa . . . there was quality and strength in depth in every department.

No wonder then that I was to adopt a utility role and play in just about every outfield position before settling in midfield and then moving back to central defence. And how apt, playing in that company, that my Spurs debut should come at Wembley! It was the Club's Centenary season, and since then, there have been many glorious years. Throughout them all, that distinctive sense of tradition has perpetually shone through.

The history of the Club is so important to everyone at White Hart Lane, and I quickly became aware of Spurs' proud past. When I arrived, there had already been seven FA Cup triumphs, plus the glorious 'Double' of 1961 (the year of my birth). Spurs were the first non-League side to win the Cup; the first British club to win a major European competition; the first to win the League Cup twice; the first English club to play in three major European Finals . . . the list of 'firsts' goes on and on, making you feel both honoured and under pressure from the moment that you signed!

From a personal point of view, I have achieved many milestones and as I have reached each of them I have looked back with pride. Playing in Europe - and helping Spurs lift the UEFA Cup in my second season - made me reflect back on those famous 'Euro Nights' at White Hart Lane and we've certainly had a few more since! I was only a baby when we won the European Cup Winners' Cup in 1963 but the individuals in Bill Nicholson's great side were known throughout the country in the years that followed and will long be revered and remembered. It was humbling to follow in the footsteps of such greats as Danny Blanchflower, John White, Dave Mackay and so many others and even more incredible when you look through the pages of this book and appreciate the great names associated with the Club since those early days more than a century ago.

It was the same when I was appointed captain in 1987. I felt immense pride when I considered the marvellous Spurs captains who had gone before me. And when I led the side to that record eighth FA Cup win of 1991, I was so aware of my predecessors who had climbed those Wembley steps in a Spurs kit to claim that same elusive prize. And yes, before the letters arrive, I *am* aware that our first two FA Cup Final wins were not at Wembley!

Our Wembley win over Nottingham Forest was all the more rewarding for the fact that we had lost 2-3 to Coventry City just four years before when I had scored at both ends in yet another final that had gone to extra time. So to play such an important part in our winner over Forest, when the unfortunate Des Walker conceded an own goal as I challenged for the ball, went a long way towards helping me forget that Coventry agony. I also felt so sorry for my England team mate Des because I obviously knew exactly how he felt.

Since then there has unfortunately been a great deal of trauma and uncertainty off the field that has seized the spotlight in this corner of North London. But Chairman Alan Sugar has steadied the ship, bringing in manager Gerry Francis to give us fresh impetus and optimism.

So having started this preface with the word 'tradition,' I now conclude with 'optimism.' We again have a team packed with internationals and the ability to succeed. As with all Spurs fans, my dream is the Championship, the ultimate accolade to ability, consistency, courage, stamina . . . plus a bit of good fortune.

This book represents the 'Ghost of Seasons Past.' The present and future promise just as much . . . and more.

Foreword

by Alan Sugar

As Chairman of Tottenham Hotspur I am delighted at this opportunity to play even a cameo role in the compilation of this important work because of my immense pride in this great club.

Such historical productions are important because clubs such as Spurs have almost an immeasurable history and that journey through time has helped shape the club into the institution that we have today.

As with all aspects of life, we can understand the present that much more by appreciating the past and the pages that follow are our tribute to those who have gone before and played a part, no matter how small, in giving the name Tottenham Hotspur the international perspective that it currently enjoys.

Of course there is another aspect of this book – to highlight the success that has marked our history and to unashamedly wallow in the memories of cups and goals, great games and great players. We have so much to be proud of and true Spurs fans can enjoy this nostalgia in the certain knowledge that I am determined that such glories will again be re-visited before too long.

Tradition is the quality that emanates from this book and so few clubs can claim that title. We have it in abundance at White Hart Lane and our fortunes are followed in the hearts of so many who are unable, for so many reasons, to actually watch our games.

We appreciate that we have an immense family of loyal supporters throughout the world and once this club is in your blood you never change. As a youngster, I still remember with clarity my father bringing me to watch Spurs at White Hart Lane and from that moment this was my club.

All my family and friends were Spurs fans and I am delighted to say that that passion continues today.

And this club continues to belong to everyone because, as I have said before, I see myself as a trustee of an institution that is not set in bricks and mortar but in the hearts and souls of all those who share my devotion.

True, it must also be a business because without that logic, attention and application, it could all tragically cease to be. But at 3pm on a cold winter's afternoon there is an intangible wisp of enchantment that settles on us all – and I could not now live without it.

Enjoy these pages. This is the story of our club. A club built on the dreams of little boys under a gas lamp in the High Road just outside our main gates.

Inevitably so much has changed and even now we continue the work to make our stadium second to none and a fitting home to lead us into the next century. Our optimism burns as brightly as ever – and may that never be extinguished.

Alan Sugar.
White Hart Lane.
June, 1995.

Early Days

If you have been watching Tottenham Hotspur play on some sunny September afternoon and are leaving White Hart Lane, pause a while. Instead of heading for your car, or for White Hart Lane station, turn left outside the ground and walk south down the High Road towards the City. Not far, just until you reach the traffic light on the corner of Park Lane. Stop there, and try to imagine that scene as it was one hundred years ago. Imagine, if you can, a group of perhaps a dozen or so boys in their early teens gathered there. Of course, in those days it would have been a delicate gas-lit lamp and not the sturdy traffic signal that we see today. Underneath it were not badly dressed boys, for they all came from relatively good homes around Northumberland Park. Not poorly educated boys either, for nearly all of them attended either St John's School (a local Scottish Presbyterian institution run by a Mr Cameron) or Tottenham Grammar School, now part of The Somerset Comprehensive School on White Hart Lane.

In the way of boys of all nationalities and ages, they would have answered to two nicknames – the 'Northumberland Pups' or the 'Saints' (after their school). The local rivals, who were soon to resent their pretensions in running a formal football club, were the 'High Road Cads', sons of shopkeepers on the main street, and 'Barkers' Bulldogs', from a rival school apparently run by a Mr Barker.

The Pups had probably been playing cricket down by the River Lea on Captain Delano's farm. He was the uncle of two of the boys under that lamp-post – the Thompson brothers – and he didn't mind them and many of their friends playing cricket on his land. If he, or any of their parents, were aware of the name they

The earliest picture of a Spurs team, probably taken before the club's first ever competitive match, a London Cup tie against St Albans on Saturday 17 October 1885. The team was (back row l to r) W. C. Tyrell, F. Lovis, Jack Jull, John Ripsher (President), Hedley Bull (who kept this print), Sam Casey and (front row l to r) T. W. Bumberry, R. Amos, Bobby Buckle, Billy Mason, Billy Harston and Frank Cottrell. The team is wearing its new blue and white strip, after Blackburn Rovers.

TOTTENHAM HOTSPUR FOOTBALL CLUB.

(ESTABLISHED 1880.)

PROGRAMME

OF FIRST GRAND

ANNUAL ATHLETIC MEETING

(Under A. A. A. Laws), held in the Grounds of

BRUCE CASTLE, TOTTENHAM,

ON SATURDAY, JUNE 13, 1891,

During Loan and Industrial Exhibition,

Commencing at 3.30 p.m.

OFFICIALS.

Referee (Pink Rosette)—HARRY LOOMAN, Esq. (Hon. Sec. S.C.C.C.A.)

Judges (Blue & White)—A. E. MARTIN, Esq., H. W. MILES, Esq. (Finchley Harriers), H. V. STARBUCK, Esq., J. TURNBULL, Esq., and S. A. MORRIS, Esq. (Tower A.C.)

Clerks of the Course (Red)—Messrs. A. E. BROADBERRY. R. BUCKLE, T. W. BUMBERRY, H. D. CASEY, J. M. DEXTER, F. DEXTER, H. GODDARD, J. C. JULL, W. MASON, A. S. PETTER, E. RUDSTON, H. R. STEPHENS, and F. S. WALFORD.

Starter (White)—F. J. MACKIE, Esq. (Tower A. C.)

Timekeeper (Yellow)—H. H. COOPER, Esq. (Tower A.C.)

Handicappers – Open Events—HARRY LOOMAN, Esq. (S.C.C.C.A.) Members Events – Messrs H. GODDARD (Tower A.C.) and F. G. HATTON.

Sports Committee—Messrs R. BUCKLE, T. W. BUMBERRY, H. D. CASEY, J. C. JULL, F. J. MACKIE, H. R. STEPHENS.

Hon. Sec. Club (Badge)—Mr. R. BUCKLE, White Cottage, White Hart Lane, Tottenham.

Hon. Sec. Sports (Shield)—Mr. F. G. HATTON, 3, Richmond Villas, Park Lane, Tottenham.

PRICE TWOPENCE.

PRINTED BY E. H. CRUSHA, "HERALD" OFFICE, TOTTENHAM.

gave themselves, the Hotspur Cricket Club no doubt they were amused by such airs and graces. September is the time that the cricket season comes to an end, so discussion no doubt turned to what to do during the winter. And in such simple fashion was born one of Britain and the world's greatest soccer clubs.

The boys decided to form a football club to be called, naturally enough, the Hotspur Football Club, and to play to association rather than rugby rules. Despite the fact that the Football Association had been in existence nearly 20 years, there was still no single set of soccer rules, though this was to be rectified within months at the first formal meeting of the four national associations. The date of formation of the Hotspur Football Club is usually given as 5 September 1882, the day

ABOVE: The first programme known to have been issued by the club, for an athletic meeting in 1891. Note that the date of establishment is given as 1880, almost certainly when the cricket club came into being but two years before football was adopted. RIGHT: Hedley Bull's membership card, dated 17 September 1887. Note that the annual subscription was 7s 6d (37p) and that the club gave its ground as the Marshes. The cards were coloured navy blue and this is thought to be the oldest existing memento of the club.

that subscriptions to the new club were first received. That day was actually a Tuesday.

There were, appropriately, just 11 founder members – E. Beaven, Bobby Buckle (the club's first captain), Fred Dexter, Stuart Leaman (the first goalkeeper), E. Wall, the brothers Anderson (J. and T.), the brothers Casey (L. and Ham who was sometimes nicknamed Sam) and the brothers Thompson (Jack and Peter), whose uncle loaned them that cricket pitch. Another eight members were to join during the year and, as all wanted to play, this was thought more than enough for the time being.

How exact are the date and details of the club's foundation cannot now be determined, but the basic facts were related as late as the mid-twentieth century by Charlie Denyer, who joined the club soon afterwards, and by L. R. Casey, the club's first treasurer. Casey's father had provided the club's first set of goalposts, symbolically painted blue and white, and it was an older Casey brother who had given the club its first ball and had, apparently, been the man responsible for suggesting the name Hotspur for the cricket club.

Harry Hotspur, immortalized in numerous history books and by Shakespeare in Richard II and Henry IV Part I, was the teenage son of the Earl of Northumberland. Sir Henry Percy, to give Hotspur his correct title, died leading rebel forces against the usurper King Henry IV at the battle of Shrewsbury in 1403. Henry IV had come to power just four years before by deposing Richard II, whom he later had killed in Pontefract Castle. The Northumberland family are better known as the Percys, the lords of the Scottish border who dominated northeast England for centuries as if it were their personal kingdom. From their great castles at Alnwick and Warkworth they controlled the main route to Scotland and were arguably the most powerful family in the land after the crown. They came to own lands in North London and part of that area later became known as Northumberland Park.

One of the football club's earliest bases, the YMCA, was called Percy House and they were to use the Northumberland Arms intermittently as a changing room for several years. The lives of the club's founders, then, were regularly touched by the history of the Percys, so what better name for their creation than Hotspur, a name so redolent of youth and glory. We have cause to be grateful to brother Casey for his suggestion. Along with the likes of Sheffield Wednesday and Nottingham Forest, Tottenham Hotspur is one of those romantic names which breaks up the dull litany of Citys, Towns and Uniteds on a Saturday evening.

EARLY MATCHES

The Hotspurs' first serious game was apparently against neighbours Latymer, but it was not until the following season, 1883–84, that their fixtures could really be described as at all formal. By this time they had asked a John Ripsher to place the club on a more permanent footing. Mr Ripsher was a prominent local figure both at All Hallows Parish Church and at the YMCA. Several of the team attended his bible classes and he had helped earlier with the cricket club. Such church connections

ABOVE LEFT: The site of what was once Captain Delano's farm, where the young Hotspurs started playing cricket in 1880. The ground is still marshy and the River Lea is beyond the tree-lined bank in the right distance.

ABOVE: This traffic light, which has replaced the street lamp on the corner of the High Road and Park Lane, now marks the site where the Hotspurs are reputed to have decided to form a soccer club. In the distance are the Red House, their headquarters from 1886 to 1891 and now adorned with a cockerel, and the White Hart pub, from whch the ground draws its name.

11

were not rare at the time; Everton and Southampton sprang from similar origins. Ripsher used the YMCA as the team's first base and, at what could be called the club's first Annual General Meeting in August 1883, 21 boys turned up.

Among the first rules were that all club members should attend scripture classes at All Hallows Church on Wednesdays, and that a rota should be established to determine which boys should carry the goalposts on Saturdays.

They had carried on playing soccer close to where they played cricket, on some marshy ground between the Great Eastern Railway and the River Lea, and the stationmaster at Northumberland Park allowed them to keep the posts in the station during the week. No doubt the players of the time were pleased that there was no crossbar to carry, only a tape. The Marshes (as the area has always been called locally) were already the home of two other clubs; University College Hospital played rugby there, while Park FC (later to be absorbed by Hotspur) played soccer.

The organiser of that first AGM was a clerk in Edmonton County Court named Jim Randall. He had joined the Hotspurs from local rivals the Radicals and was elected the new captain with Billy Harston as his deputy. Harston had an amazing career with the club. He partnered Bobby Buckle on the left wing for ten years, remained behind the scenes afterwards as assistant secretary and, over sixty years after being elected vice-captain, was still to be seen at home games as press box steward.

The Hotspurs did not stay at the YMCA long. During one scratch game in the basement of the building, a YMCA councillor investigating the noise was hit in the face by a ball, while other minutes mention the propensity of some boys to 'play cards and sample the mulberries at the end of the garden'. Having been ejected from Percy House, the club moved briefly to Dorset Villas and then on to the Red House in the High Road, which was used as headquarters for six years (1886–91). By remarkable chance this building, adjacent to the present ground, was later purchased by the club and is now used as their administrative offices with the address 748 High Road; truly a return to their roots. They did not actually get changed at the Red House, which was nearly a mile away from their pitch, but hired rooms in pubs closer to the Marshes, usually the Milford, the Park, or the Northumberland Arms.

The first game the club completed which was actually recorded anywhere was that match against Latymer. Playing on Saturday 6 January 1883, our young heroes lost 8–1! Matters improved and, over the next two seasons, 1883–84 and 1884–85, the Hotspurs were reported to have played 47 games, of which they won 27 and drew 4. One must treat these reports with caution, however, for it is impossible to gauge the quality of the opposition or even if they were playing first elevens. By this time it appears that only four of the founding fathers, Bobby Buckle, Fred Dexter, Sam Casey and Stuart Leaman, were still regular members of the first team.

Particular interest was always taken in that local derby against Latymer. It was the Spurs v Arsenal clash of its day and the history of

TOP: A picture of the whole club, also taken before the game with the City business house club St Albans in 1885. Back row, left to right, L. Brown, T. Wood, T. W. Bumberry, John Anderson, John Ripsher, Ham, known as Sam, Casey (the first secretary); middle row, left to right, R. Amos, W. Tyrell, Frank Lovis, Jack Jull, H. E. Goshawk, H. Hillyer, Stuart Leaman (the club's first goalkeeper), A. Bayne, Jim Randall, organizer of the first AGM and club captain; bottom row, left to right, Jack Thompson Jnr, Billy Randall (Jim's brother), Bobby Buckle (the first captain), G. Burt, G. Bush, P. J. Moss, Billy Mason, Billy Harston, the deputy captain and still press box steward as late as 1946, Frank Cottrell and Hedley Bull. Though the club's badge was supposed to be a large 'H', close examination shows that, at this stage, it was a Maltese Cross. This photograph was taken on the banks of the River Lea and, if the photographer had turned round, he would have seen the view below.

BOTTOM LEFT: Displaced in time by a century. There is nothing remaining to suggest that football was ever organized on the Marshes, but it is probable that the Hotspurs played where the allotments are today. White Hart Lane is about a mile in the distance and Alexandra Palace, where a joint ground with Arsenal was proposed in the mid-1970s, is over to the far left.

Mr. H Bull

159 Birkbeck Rd

Tottenham

✦ TOTTENHAM ✦ HOTSPUR ✦ F.C. ✦

→✦←

R. BUCKLE,
WHITE COTTAGE.
WHITE HART LANE, TOTTENHAM.

H. D. CASEY,
SHERWOOD LODGE,
PARK, TOTTENHAM.

Date as Post Mark.

Dear Sir, *v. Coldstream Guards (replayed Cup Tie)*

You have been chosen to play in the above Match on Saturday

next, at *Park*

Should you be unable to play, please advise us at once.

Yours faithfully,

R. BUCKLE,
H. D. CASEY, *Joint Hon. Secs.*

DRESSING ROOM

3 o'c 2.45 Sharp

In the club's early days, players were informed that they had been selected by postcard. This one was sent to Hedley Bull on 11 November 1891 and asked him to turn out at Park (meaning the Northumberland Park ground) at 3pm on the following Saturday, 14 November. Their opponents were Coldstream Guards in a replayed Luton Charity Cup match, which Spurs went on to win 7–2. As can be seen from the printed card, Bobby Buckle and Sam Casey were still running the club, nearly 10 years after they had founded it.

contests between the two clubs makes delightful reading. On 27 December 1883, Latymer turned up with only five players, though two arrived later. At the end of the match the teams could not agree on the score (Hotspur said it was 2–0 in their favour) and it remained unprinted in the *Tottenham Weekly Herald*, though that paper did remark that Latymer had suffered much verbal abuse from Hotspur supporters. Next time round the *Herald* got even more irate, pointing out that the club captains had submitted completely contradictory reports and that the paper would not print any more until they sorted things out. Then, as now, local papers relied on the clubs to give accurate reports of what transpired. Latymer attempted to overcome these various hurdles the next season by playing with twelve men, until the ruse was discovered at half-time. They tried the same thing in a reserve match soon afterwards but the Hotspurs had got wise to such ungentlemanly conduct by their neighbours and the fixture with the Edmonton club was dropped.

At the end of the 1884–85 season came another significant change. Sam Casey, the secretary, had been receiving mail addressed to another club called London Hotspur. As a result the Hotspurs decided to change their name to Tottenham Hotspur and distinguish themselves from this other side – which presumably soon passed out of existence after its brief appearance on the stage of football

history. At the same time the club decided to change its strip from all blue to blue and white. This was the result of a visit to Kennington Oval to see the 1885 Cup final. Blackburn Rovers, in their familiar blue and white, won the Cup for the second consecutive year by beating Glasgow's Queen's Park 2–0, and so impressed the Tottenham lads that the latter paid their own tribute. In case anyone should mistake them for the Rovers, the Tottenham shirts had a large 'H' near the left shoulder, though on the very first team picture, taken in October 1885, the badge appears to be a Maltese cross. For a few seasons in the 1890s the team bedecked itself in red shirts and navy blue shorts, even changing for a time to the then Wolves strip of chocolate and gold. It was not until 1900, after playing Preston North End in the Cup, that the Preston colours of white shirts and navy blue shorts were adopted and they have remained the same to this day.

A CHANGE OF HOME

Despite their relative success, life for the club was nothing if not impermanent. The marshland between the River Lea and the railway was public ground and the club had no more right to play there than a dozen kids who happened to turn up with a ball made from old rags. Fights over who could use a marked out pitch were not uncommon. The club had no control over any spectators who turned up, nor could it charge them anything. As the side became more established things did become a little easier – they were recognised as the best in the district and no longer had to fight for their pitch – but matters could not be said to be satisfactory.

P. J. Moss, who played for the club around this period, wrote about the last season on the Marshes in *The Football News* in 1900: 'In some of the games, with absolutely no gate money, it is no exaggeration to say that 4,000 spectators surrounded the field. They were not always considerate of the feelings of visiting teams and I well remember some East End Cup ties in which the visitors were pelted with mud, rotten turnips and other vegetable refuse.'

In 1888 Bobby Buckle, Sam Casey and Jack Jull (the club's best player, who had appeared whenever he was home from school right from the earliest days) found a pitch for hire just off Northumberland Park (which is actually a street running off the High Road, not a patch of open ground). It was an area shared by Foxes FC and was used for tennis in summer. The rent was £17 per annum. The first match there was reported to be a reserve game versus Stratford St John's early in September 1888 and the takings were a heady 17 shillings (85 pence). At the time there was much muttering locally about the club overreaching itself and getting 'too big for its boots' and it must be remembered that this really still was a group of ex-schoolfriends, few out of their teens, playing friendly matches every Saturday. In essence it was not so different from thousands of weekend pub teams around the country today.

In their later years on the Marshes, Spurs had begun to entertain some not undistinguished guests. In October 1885 they played their first ever competitive match in the first round of the London Cup. A crowd estimated at 400 saw them beat St Albans (not the current side of that name but a club based in the City of London) though the second round was something of a let-down as they crashed 8–0 to mighty Casuals at Wandsworth. Still, even to play the Casuals was something – in 1894 that club was to reach the final of the first ever Amateur Cup. The following season Spurs also entered the East End Cup and reached their first final, where they played another side to scale the heights of amateur football in later years, the Caledonians. The final was decided on the Marshes on Saturday 16 April 1887, but Tottenham were to lose by the only goal of the game, a low shot which skidded through their goalkeeper's legs. Hotspur were to find Cup finals rather easier in years to come.

THE ARRIVAL OF ARSENAL

One last game on the Marshes must be mentioned, Spurs first ever against Royal Arsenal. The game took place on 19 November 1887 and Spurs were leading 2–1 when the game was abandoned 15 minutes from time. Apparently Arsenal had turned up late, scored an early goal, defended for the rest of the match and were saved by the fall of darkness. Nonetheless, it was an auspicious start for Spurs in what was to become one of the greatest of all derby fixtures.

The first season at Northumberland Park proved a great success and the club even made a profit of £6. On Saturday 13 October 1888 the Old Etonians had come to Tottenham in the first round of the London Senior Cup, winning 8–2 with five of their goals scored by Arthur Dunn, a great Corinthian who was to give his name to the annual Public Schools Cup. The significance of the fixture could only be seen retrospectively. Just six years earlier Old Etonians had won the FA Cup. For nearly two decades it was felt that they may have been the last Southern side ever to do so – but who could then have believed that

THE WEEKLY HERALD, FRIDAY, April 30, 1886.

ANNUAL DINNER OF THE TOTTENHAM HOTSPUR FOOTBALL CLUB.

The first annual dinner of the above Club was held at the Milford Tavern, Park-lane, Tottenham, on Tuesday, the 20th inst., when 40 members and friends sat down to an excellent repast provided by the host (Mr Reeves), who deserves great praise for the perfect arrangement of all the details. John Ripsher, Esq., president, occupied the chair, and J. H. Thompson, Esq., one of the vice-presidents, the vice-chair.

After the cloth was cleared the chairman gave the usual loyal toasts, which were received with great enthusiasm, followed by Mr A. E. Broadberry giving the well-known song "Football." The Chairman then gave the Army, Navy and Reserve Forces, to which Mr S. H. Casey responded in a few well-chosen words, after which Mr A. Kemp sang "Too Late," which created a great impression, and in response to an encore gave a comic song "Right before the Missus too." The Chairman in rising to propose the toast of the evening "Success to the Tottenham Hotspur Football Club," said that football was now running a close race with cricket as the national pastime of this country, and it had been proved that football was played in England nearly 600 years ago. Many rulers had endeavoured to stop the playing of the game, notably Queen Elizabeth and King James 1st for various reasons, but football had survived through all, and he would as an instance point out to Lancashire where it is estimated that 100,000 people are either players or spectators at football every Saturday afternoon. He (the chairman) believed that the abuses to which football was subjected had entirely disappeared under the present scientific mode of playing the game, and he therefore called upon the gentlemen present to rise and drink "Success to the Tottenham Hotspur Football Club." The toast was drunk with three times three. Mr W. Mason, hon. sec., in responding, gave a sketch of the Club's career this season. He said that taking everything into consideration they had had a very successful season, much more so than they anticipated, for the fixtures were much stronger than those of previous seasons. They entered for the London Association Challenge Cup and had, to their surprise, succeeded in getting through the first round defeating their opponents (St. Albans) by 3 goals, the score being 5 to 2, but in the second round they were drawn against a club, viz. the Casuals, which proved too strong for them and were defeated by 8 goals to nil. With regard to the other matches they had been very successful, they had played 37, won 24, lost 11 and drawn 2; won 111 goals and lost 53. (Cheers.) There were 20 matches scratched mainly in consequence of the severe weather, otherwise their results most probably would have been better. Mr Mason also said that they had played 8 local matches and had only lost one, and that a 2nd xi fixture which was played with 4 men short, and he therefore thought that they had a right title of the first local club (cheers), but he was not certain they had played every local club, he was sure that they would not refuse to play any other should they think fit to challenge them. He said he had nothing further to say, but hoped the Club would still be more prosperous in their engagements next season. (Cheers.) Mr F. C. Hobbs now gave a song entitled "The Old Brigade," which was heartily received, and as an encore, gave "The Powder Monkey."

The Vice-Chairman (J. H. Thompson, Esq.), after referring in a few touching remarks to the high estimation in which Mr Ripsher was held by everyone in the Club, proposed "The President of the Club" which was drunk with musical honours. Mr Ripsher, in response to the toast, said it was five years ago that he was asked to fill the post of President, and he might say that during the whole of that time he had been always courteously treated by every member of the Club, and he hoped that the time was far distant when his connection with the Club would cease.

The toast of "The Vice-Presidents" was next proposed by Mr J. Jull, and drank with musical honours, and responded to by J. H. Thompson, Esq., who said it gave him great pleasure to fill the post as a Vice-President of The Tottenham Hotspur Football Club, and he would be pleased to do anything in his power to further their success.

Mr Mason now read letters of regret which he had received from the other Vice-Presiden s, viz., Joseph Howard, Esq., J.P., M.P., John Robson, Esq., and W. A. H. de Pape, Esq., who were unable to be present.

The Chairman next proposed "The Visitors," which was responded to by Mr F. C. Hobbs in a very humorous speech.

In giving the last toast of the evening, viz., "The Host," the Chairman took occasion to thank Mr Reeves for the perfect manner in which everything was carried out, and hoped, that although this was their first dinner, it would not be the last.

A long list of songs followed, and a most enjoyable evening was brought to a close by singing "The National Anthem" and "Auld Lang Syne."

LEFT: The Herald's report of the club's first annual dinner, held at the Milford Tavern on Tuesday 20 April 1886.

FAR LEFT: The Milford Tavern on the corner of Park Lane and Somerford Grove as it appears today. The annual dinner would have been held in the upstairs rooms, which were also often hired by the club as changing facilities before their games on the Marshes in the 1880s. The Tottenham that we know today was not the Tottenham of the club's founders. As late as the 1870s a traveller wrote: 'Tottenham has many outlying farms and much of the land is under plough . . . flowers are grown for the London market in the numerous nurseries.' It was, indeed, one of those nurseries (Beckwith's) which was to become White Hart Lane. The population of the area was much smaller. In 1881 there were only 23,000 people living in Edmonton, but the next twenty years saw new housing throughout North London, and Edmonton had grown to 62,000 by the time Spurs won the Cup in 1901.

Spurs would emulate this achievement within a dozen seasons?

In 1889 the club joined the Football Association as a full member. Crowds were increasing (reaching 3,000 for another appearance by the Casuals in the London Senior Cup in 1893) and the team was taking on more and more of what we would now call a professional appearance. Bobby Buckle resigned as secretary in the same year, leaving only Jack Jull of the early club members still playing. Jull had been a fixture at right-back from 1883 and was club captain for many years, also becoming the first Spurs player to win representative honours when he was selected for Middlesex in 1889. He died aged only 53 on 22 December 1920 and the *Weekly Herald* carried a glowing obituary, by chance alongside the first instalment of their 'History of Tottenham Hotspur'. Sam Casey remained as assistant secretary, and Bobby Buckle and Jack Thompson Jnr (his father, Jack Snr, had helped the club in its early days) were still on the committee.

PROFESSIONALISM ARRIVES

Obviously by this stage the club was looking for something better. It could continue arranging friendlies for ever, but the players were more ambitious. There were, nonetheless, obstacles. Soundings had already been made by the same Royal Arsenal who had come to the Marshes in 1887 about setting up a Southern League, with the implication that at least some of the teams would be professional. In 1892 a meeting of interested clubs had been held and 12 sides were provisionally elected. Spurs had tried to join but came bottom of the poll with only one vote, presumably their own. As it happened, nothing came of this meeting anyway. Most of the senior sides had been scared away by the intransigent attitude of the London FA, which made it quite clear that it would suspend any member club which embraced professionalism in any form.

This was a problem which was to continue for some years, finally reaching its bitter conclusion with the founding of the Amateur Football Alliance by the London, Middlesex and Surrey FAs in 1907. Arsenal had decided to ignore the threats and joined the Football League in 1893. Other senior clubs (and Spurs were, at the time, only in the second rather than first rank of these) faced worsening problems. They were experiencing the same difficulties as had the major Northern and Midland clubs before the formation of the Football League – namely that repetitive friendlies were not very attractive to crowds and that games had to be cancelled or rearranged at short notice when opponents found themselves engaged in the later stages of numerous cup competitions. At the same time, lack of organised fixture lists and unpredictable crowds meant that they were unable to sign the very best players, who went to Football League clubs. Spurs solved this problem, albeit temporarily, by joining the newly founded Southern Alliance with Erith, Slough, Windsor and Eton, Polytechnic, Old St Stephen's and Upton Park (not the current West Ham). They lost only three games in this league in its only season, and reached the fourth round of the London Senior Cup before losing again to old rivals Casuals. All in all, a satisfactory season, if one which consisted largely of marking time.

The same year saw the comical incident which led to the club becoming professional. It became known, melodramatically, as 'The Affair of Payne's Boots'. The gentleman in question was one Ernie Payne, a left-winger who had not played for Fulham's first team for some time when, at the beginning of the 1893–94 season, Spurs offered him a game. At the time both clubs were amateur and, if a player could not get a game with one club, he was perfectly free to move where he could. For some reason, however, Payne's move to Spurs was not appreciated by some at the Half Moon (where Fulham then played) and, on the morning of his first game for Spurs (21 October 1893), he found his kit had disappeared. Spurs thus had to kit him out. As they had no spare boots which fitted he was given ten shillings to buy a pair. Fulham heard about this and presumably still annoyed by the incident, complained to the London FA that Spurs were guilty of poaching and professionalism. A week later Spurs were found guilty of paying inducements to Payne, though they were found not guilty of poaching the player.

Payne returned the ten shillings to the club and it was argued, not unconvincingly, that if a club official, rather than Payne himself, had run out to buy the boots then the charge would not have held water. At the end of the day Spurs were suspended for a fortnight, and Payne for one week – actually rather a light

THE WEEKLY HERALD, FRIDAY, October 19, 1894.

The 'Spurs have got through the first round of the qualifying stage of the English Cup, but victory was only achieved after a very hard struggle. The attendance was the largest the 'Spurs have had this season, over 2,000 persons being present.

The local team was the same that beat the Casuals with the exception that Julian played instead of Dickie. Jull, contrary to anticipations filled his old position at back, and Monk kept goal. Elliott and Burrows were absent, the former thinking it better to go over to Notts Forest, whilst the latter aided the Arsenal Reserves. Elliott's re-instatement apparently, was of little good. Stanley Briggs looked like an old warrior with his head bound up.

West Herts were handicapped by the absence of two or three of their prominent men, including Weeler, but their eleven included footers of considerable ability. Their team was as follows: S. King (goal); L. S. Lidderdale and J. R. Paul (backs); J. Penney, F. C. Robins and G. E. Green (half-backs); H. R. L. Wright, S. C. Hobbs, J. O. Anderson, S. S. Taylor and R. M. Strout (forwards.)

Play was commenced very punctually, Mr Bisiker tootling the whistle at half past three exactly. West Herts forwards showed pretty combination. Julian having fouled, the ball was sent into the net without touching any body and directly after Monk was called upon to save, which he did, although at the expense of a corner. Goodall cleared and in turn either goal was visited. The locals attacked, and Payne was conspicuous for tricky play. After the Herts forwards had again been stopped, Hunter gave to Cubberley who put in a clinker but Lidderdale mullified. Jull brought up the visiting forwards and Payne had a chance of scoring. Instead, he shot yards over.

'Spurs were pressing. Archie Cubberley was tricking the Herts defence again and again, and sending in some fine shots. Taylor, by a splendid effort put the home citadel in danger but his shot was too feeble to get past Monk. Anderson also kicked over. Eccles transfered play to the other end. Payne secured and passed to Hunter who headed the ball into the net amidst great cheers.

'Spurs attacked almost continuously from now to half time. It was only occasionally that the Herts forwards could get away. King was a tower of strength to his side. Frequently had he to use his fists in expelling the sphere from the goal mouth, and right well did he acquit himself. Eccles, Payne, Cubberley and Goodall each shot but they found King invulnerable. At last the latter got the ball by the custodian and so was able to place his team two on.

Upon the sphere being set in motion, Welham had to repulse an attack of West Herts, and then the 'Spurs again gave their opponents defence a warm time of it. There was only one team in it now, the locals doing pretty well as they liked, except that they could not get the pilule past King. At half-time no more goals had been scored.

Having had four-fifths of the game with the slope against them it was naturally expected that the 'Spurs would be the superior lot in the second half. But how often does the unexpected happen. Whether they had been dosed with some wonderful physic during the interval, I can't say, but, West Herts now played with the utmost vigour. A corner was obtained directly after the restart, and Wright directed the ball into the net, cheers from the visitors supporters—of whom, by the bye, there were several—greeting such a successful re-commencement. Herts again looked dangerous but the home defence interposed with success. Julian shot across to Payne, who sent in a clinker, King stopped and fell to the ground with the ball. A general scuttle ensued at the goal mouth, the poor custodian remaining on the ground; at last he got the sphere away, being loudly cheered. It was more like a bit of Rugby.

West Herts again pressed. Strout passed to the right wing, and Hobbs headed a second goal for his side, thus making the scores equal. All was now suspense, and excitement ran very high. The visitors still hung round the home goal, and Monk and Jull in turn saved. Then Cubberley relieved, and Hunter tried King without effect. Roused by the cheers of their supporters the home team showed better combination. The sphere reaching Goodall from Cubberley he balked the West Herts defence. King ran out to meet him, but was not in time and Donald was able to score a third point with an easy shot.

Thundering were the cheers that followed. Directly after the locals all but scored again. West Herts were not dismayed and getting up placed Monk's charge in jeopardy. Shephard just managed to clear. Hands against 'Spurs was followed by Payne sending in a splendid centre which Goodall should have—but did not—converted into a goal. Eccles tried his luck, and it appeared that the ball went under the cross-bar, but the referee ruled otherwise. The visitors, although trying hard, friled to equalise and so the 'Spurs won by 3 goals to 2.

OPPOSITE TOP: *The Park Hotel beside Northumberland Park station, another of the local pubs whch players used as changing rooms during the 1880s. They would then use the level crossing on the left to reach their pitch, which was just a piece of common ground open to the public. The stationmaster at Northumberland Park allowed the club to keep its blue and white striped posts in the station during the week, thus saving the mile-long walk back to the High Road.*
OPPOSITE BOTTOM: *The Northumberland Arms on Northumberland Park; the club's first official ground was on playing fields behind this pub. When League Champions Aston Villa came down from the Midlands to play a friendly on Saturday 11 April 1896 they refused to get changed at the ground and hired the Northumberland Arms instead.*

LEFT: *The Herald's report on Spurs' first FA Cup match, against West Herts, on 13 October 1894. Spurs won 3–2, but note the reference to the ball going under the crossbar but the referee disagreeing. They reached the fourth qualifying round that year before being knocked out by Luton Town – a highly creditable performance. West Herts were the forerunners of Watford FC.*

RIGHT: White Hart Lane was ready for use in September 1899 and the opening first team match was a friendly against Notts County on the evening of Monday 4 September. County, who were fifth in the First Division the previous season, were well beaten, 4–1. The ground had no official name at the time and the report carefully avoids mentioning a title. The substitute goalkeeper who so impressed everyone, Walter Bull, was later to join Spurs.

OPPOSITE: The critical decision to go professional, made on Monday 16 December 1895. The committee obviously tried to stage-manage the meeting and push the proposal through. Several of the players opposed the move, and expecting to find themselves without a first team place if it succeeded. They were quite right; within three months only Stanley Briggs (the club captain and its best player, who refused to come to the meeting) and Ernie Payne remained in the side. The other nine were all new professionals.

A Knock for Notts.
THE LAMBS LOSE.

Fresh from their splendid victory over Derby County in the League, Notts County came South to give the Spurs their first game on the new ground on Monday evening. They altered their team in one or two respects, the most interesting of the changes being to substitute Montgomery, the old Spurs' back, for Prescott. The Spurs gave Morris a run in place of Stormont, but otherwise the eleven was the same as against Millwall. To add some semblance of dignity to the opening proceedings, Mr. C. D. Roberts, the chairman of directors (in the absence of Col. H. F. Bowles, M.P., who had been invited to perform the function) set the ball rolling.

In spite of the warmth, the first half was very spiritedly contested, and the play was decidedly interesting...

SPURS 4, NOTTS 1.

Tottenham Hotspur:—Clawley; Erentz and Tait; Jones, McNaught and Morris; Smith, Pratt, Copeland, Cameron and Kirwan.

Notts County:—Suter; Lewis and Montgomery; Ball, Bull and Lowe; Hadley, Macconochie, McCairns, Fletcher and Chalmers. **Referee:** C. D. Crisp.

---

punishment. G. Wagstaffe Simmons, later vice-chairman of the club, wrote that: '. . . the London FA issued a series of findings that staggered the football world . . . in their naked absurdity . . .' Bobby Buckle was rather more relaxed about it. He told Julian Holland some sixty years later that the committee of the time never had any doubts that the club would be suspended and were just unlucky to be caught breaking the extremely strict rules of the time.

But out of disaster can come strength, and so it was with Tottenham Hotspur. The Payne affair had drawn attention to the club and they were popular opponents everywhere; for instance, over 6,000 turned up to see them at Southampton St Mary's a month or so later. The committee had also begun to seriously doubt the wisdom of remaining within the control of the London FA, given its almost fanatic obsession with professionalism. This attitude is a difficult one to convey today, perhaps the only comparable modern example being the Rugby Union's censure on anyone who has ever played rugby league. It might also be recalled that Corinthians, the premier amateur club of the day who were twice chosen en bloc (in 1894 and 1895) to represent the *senior* England side in a full international, had an article in their constitution stating that they could not enter any organised competition of any kind.

Spurs, though without any conspicuous competitive success, had clearly exhausted the possibilities open to them as an amateur club. The move towards change was helped by the election of a new president in 1894. John Oliver, a carpet manufacturer in the City who was able to offer his players jobs, had been responsible for founding the Southern Alliance. He must have seen the potential that Spurs presented and was soon dragging them, some kicking and screaming, towards professionalism. It was a course that had already been adopted in the south by Woolwich Arsenal, Millwall Athletic and Luton Town.

He quickly erected the first stand at Northumberland Park and though it fell down in a gale soon afterwards it was a move in the right direction. By autumn 1895 the critical decision had been made and the club voted to go professional on Monday 16 December 1895. Only one member, a Mr Roynan, voted against, though there was much dissension at the meeting and a fair number of fans apparently transferred their allegiance to the still amateur London Caledonians over in Tufnell Park. Stanley Briggs, probably the club's best player at the time, was also against and refused to attend the meeting at The Eagle. He was the only amateur to continue playing for the side on a regular basis after professionals had been added to the staff.

AMATEUR CUP FROLICS

Tottenham had been having a successful time on the field. The previous season they reached the fourth qualifying round (roughly equivalent to the last 64) of the FA Cup and the second round of the Amateur Cup. Spurs' career in the Amateur Cup was short but not without incident. They had been invited, along with 80 other sides, to institute the competition in 1893 and their first game was in the second round (having got a bye in the first). That was on 11 November 1893, when Vampires were beaten 3-1 at Northumberland Park. Unfortunately Spurs were unable to play Clapham Rovers, 1880 FA Cup winners, in the next round because of their suspension after the Payne's Boots affair.

The next season saw a strange juxtaposition of events. On 13 October 1894 Spurs played West Herts in their first ever FA Cup match, winning 3-2. A week later, they were contesting the Amateur Cup and crushed Old Harrovians 7-0. One Peter Hunter scored in both games. The next two rounds of the Amateur Cup also saw impressive results; 6-1 against City Ramblers and 8-0 away at Romford. The fourth qualifying round was tougher – 1-1 and 3-3 draws against London Welsh (not the rugby club) followed by a 4-2 win at the Spotted Dog, at the time the home of the Upton Park club. By this time Peter Hunter had scored nine goals in the competition. Nottingham club Beeston were the next to go down, 2-0 at home, in the first round proper. The second goal, the last ever scored by Spurs in the Amateur Cup, was Hunter's tenth in the competition.

On 16 March 1895 Spurs entertained Amateur Cup holders Old Carthusians at Northumberland Park in the next round and crashed 5-0 before a massive 5,000 crowd. The Carthusians line-up had five full England internationals, including the immortal centre-forward G. O. Smith and the Walters brothers, A.M. and P.M. Full-back partners for many years, they were inevitably nicknamed Morning and Afternoon. Carthusians remain one of only two clubs ever to win both the FA and Amateur Cups. Spurs also progressed well that year in the FA Cup, reaching the fourth qualifying round before losing a replay to Luton Town.

The next season, 1895-96, Spurs were allowed to go through to the first round proper of the Amateur Cup, where they were drawn against Chesham. The game was never played, for as the *Weekly Herald* plaintively commented on 20 December 1895: 'Had not the Spurs adopted professionalism last week they would have had to play Chesham after Christmas. The Spurs are now drawn against Stoke in the first round of the English Cup (the name commonly used for the FA Cup at the time) on 1 February. The Spurs have certainly had no luck in the draws this season . . . it is not likely any effort will be made to induce Stoke to come to Tottenham to play their tie.' How different from the 1981 competition, when Spurs won the Cup after leaving London just once in nine matches.

Tottenham's first game as a professional club was actually against the old enemy, the Casuals, on 21 December and they won 3-1. No declared professionals were allowed to play against amateur teams like the Casuals.

ABOVE: The two men who ran Tottenham Hotspur for almost half a century; secretary Arthur Turner (left), whose arrival spelt the end of the Cameron era, and Charles Roberts, who was chairman from 1898 until his death in 1943. It was Roberts who decided in 1898 that the club must become a limited company and needed a better ground. RIGHT: Roberts proposed the formation of a company at a meeting in the Red Lion pub on the High Road on 2 March 1898. This picture, taken 83 years later before the 1981 FA Cup final, is a good indication of how close the club has always been to its locality and how its roots have remained on the High Road throughout its history.

the leading clubs in the land in friendlies (Notts County beat them 5–1, mighty Aston Villa, unarguably the best of them all, won 3–1 on 11 April 1896) but Spurs clearly needed the stimulus of competition. In July 1896 they applied to join the Southern League, created by Millwall Athletic's persistence two years earlier, and were elected straight to the First Division. A month earlier they had applied to join the Football League, where they were resoundingly rejected, coming bottom in a poll of ten clubs with just two votes. The actual voting was Blackpool 19, Walsall 16, Gainsborough 15, Burslem Port Vale 10, Luton 10, Crewe 4, Fairfield 3, Glossop 3, Macclesfield 2 and Tottenham 2.

THE SOUTHERN LEAGUE

Because of Spurs' dramatic rise to fame at the turn of the century, it is often assumed that the club was a great success in the Southern League days. It is true that they never finished lower than seventh during their twelve-year stint, but generally there were no more than half a dozen good sides in the League at any one time (usually Southampton, Portsmouth, Fulham, Millwall, the two Bristols and Tottenham themselves). Apart from their Championship season of 1899–1900, with virtually the same team that won the Cup a year later, Spurs never looked like winning the Southern League. When they applied for membership of the Football League in 1908 they had finished only seventh in the Southern League, behind QPR, Plymouth, Millwall, Crystal Palace, Swindon and Bristol Rovers and could thus count themselves fortunate to be elected. None of the sides above them applied and, even then, Spurs finished fifth out of six in the first ballot.

During their Southern League career Spurs regularly fielded senior sides in other competitions – notably the Western League – and their first team fixture list was invariably crowded. An important Western League match one week might see most first team players involved, whereas the following Saturday might throw up a Cup tie and either a Southern League or a rearranged Western League match. In this case the Western League side would effectively be the second team. Other leagues, such as the United or Thames and Medway, were less important and, although they were always recorded as first-class fixtures, the reserve side must often have deputised. For this reason it is very difficult to chart the exact record of the Spurs senior team in these years. In 1899–1900 they supposedly played 67 senior fixtures, winning 49 and scoring over 200 goals (thought to be a record in a single season by a genuinely senior club) but it is simply not possible that Spurs were represented in all of these games by their best side. The League tables from these years are all included in the appendices, as are all games which could have been senior matches, but readers should beware of interpreting their standard absolutely literally.

The first competitive game as a professional club was that tie at Stoke on 1 February. It was not a memorable start – Stoke won 5–0.

The new professionals were paid between 15 and 25 shillings per week (75p to £1.25) and, amazingly enough, three months into 1896 only two of the side which had played for the club in December 1895 remained in the team. They were Ernie Payne, of boots fame, and Stanley Briggs, the tough centre-half who had joined the club in 1890. The founding fathers by now had virtually no influence on the club's direction, despite it being only thirteen years old. John Ripsher had become the patron and even John Oliver remained on the committee only until 1898 before fading from the scene.

Having turned professional Spurs had no formal fixture list and they took to entertaining

1901

**John Cameron • Southern League champions •
Percy Park or White Hart Lane • Charles Roberts •
The First FA Cup • Joining the League •
Promotion and Relegation • Sick as a Parrot**

There have been, perhaps, no more than a dozen great sides in English soccer history. Tottenham has produced at least two of these – the 1960–61 Double team, arguably the greatest of them all, and the 1901 Cup winners, who so astounded their contemporaries. For the origins of that earlier side, one has to go back a couple of years into the nineteenth century. Like 1908 and 1958, the year from mid-1898 is one of the most critical in Tottenham's proud history. The team performed only moderately on the pitch and at the next AGM the club declared a loss of over £500 but, firstly, the club turned itself into a limited company, secondly it moved to White Hart Lane and thirdly, and most importantly, it began its first, brief, flowering with the appointment of John Cameron as manager. It was, incidentally, also the season in which the club won its first ever trophy – the reserves heading the London League.

The first of these key events was formalised on Wednesday 2 March 1898 at the Red Lion in the High Road. Though the team was moderately successful on the field, attendances were not really up to expectations and the club was sliding slowly into the red. The club had plenty of time to consider off-the-field matters at the time as the ground had been closed and several players censured on 21 February after a mini-riot during a game against Luton. Spectators had invaded the pitch and assaulted three of the Luton team!

One Charles D. Roberts was a figure known in the northern home counties for fund raising via events like military tattoos. He had also, apparently, once been a baseball pitcher with the Brooklyn Dodgers in New York. He was

Sandy Brown (shaking hands on edge of goal area) has just equalized from a John Kirwan (on far side of field) free-kick in the 1901 Cup final against Sheffield United at Crystal Palace. His 25th minute header was his 13th goal of the competition that season and he went on to make it a record 15 in all. Sheffield United goalkeeper Billy Foulke, about to pick the ball out of the net, was the largest man ever to play first-class football. At this time he weighed around 21 stone.

approached by Spurs, probably with a view to organising a fund-raising event at Northumberland Park. Once he got involved, however, it became apparent to him that the club needed far more cash than a mere tattoo could raise and he recommended turning Tottenham Hotspur into a limited company as a means of both raising money and protecting the committee from taking personal risks. It was around this time that the major clubs in the land were doing the same thing. The major advantage of this step was that it encouraged clubs to take risks and invest in the game, without the individuals in charge having to fear that they would become personally responsible for the club's debts and failures.

Roberts' proposal was accepted by the members, 8,000 shares of £1 apiece were issued and subscriptions were invited. A new board of directors was appointed – consisting of Charles Roberts (who remained a director until his death in July 1943), John Oliver (who resigned in November 1898), Bobby Buckle (who remained on the board until 1900, the last link with the original Spurs), Jack Thompson (another original Hotspur, nephew

of Captain Delano, who resigned in 1899) and Ralph Bullock (who resigned on leaving the country in 1902). One can only speculate as to why four of the five original directors resigned so quickly – but Charles Roberts was apparently not noted for having a shy, retiring personality. To the evident surprise of the directors, the share issue did not go well. Twelve months later a mere 296 applications had been received for only 1,558 of the shares. This left over three-quarters of the shares unsold.

But while money may not have been coming in through shareholdings, it was beginning to accumulate through the gate. On 29 April 1899 Northumberland Park saw its greatest ever attendance – 14,000 for the game against Woolwich Arsenal. That was at least twice as many as could see the game in comfort (there were still very few banked terraces on English football grounds) and dozens of people climbed onto the roof of the refreshment bar. It couldn't stand the weight, collapsed and there were some minor injuries.

That accident, fortunately not serious, persuaded the directors that they should find better accommodation. They struck lucky, for just a few yards from where the club had been founded, and where the heart of its support had always been, was an undeveloped plot called Beckwith's Nursery. The only buildings on it were greenhouses and nursery sheds used for growing plants. The land had been bought by Charrington's Brewery as it was adjacent to their White Hart public house on the High Road. They were thinking of building some rows of terraces on the site, partially to provide custom for the pub.

The landlord of the pub had spread around a rumour that a football club was interested in taking the land, because his previous pub had been near the Millwall ground and had been worth a fortune to him. He was therefore extremely keen to attract another club to the open space behind his premises. Having heard the rumour, and discovered the landlord was basically flying a kite, Charles Roberts and Bobby Buckle then approached Charringtons. After considerable debate the brewers agreed to Spurs leasing the ground – asking only that the club guarantee 1,000 spectators at first team matches and 500 at reserve games.

In return, Tottenham have served only Charrington beers ever since. The stands (rather flimsy structures) were moved from Northumberland Park and the new stadium had undercover accommodation for 2,500 seated ticket holders. The ground was formally opened on Monday 4 September 1899 when Spurs beat the country's oldest professional club, Notts County, 4–1 in a friendly and 5,000 people paid a total of £115 to watch.

This was not actually the first game on the pitch. There had already been three 'Whites versus Stripes' trials and a game for schoolboy hopefuls. All four matches had been open for the public. Though before the First World War it was generally referred to as 'The High Road Ground', it has been known as White Hart Lane ever since – despite the fact that its address is 748 High Road and it is some distance from White Hart Lane itself. The White Hart Ground would no doubt be a better name but the club, having initially preferred Percy Park, were happy to accept any name popularly bestowed upon their new 30,000 capacity stadium. Within a decade improvements had taken the capacity up to

ABOVE: The crowd at Crystal Palace surrounds the grandstand as the Tottenham players go up to be presented to Sir Redvers Buller at the end of the game. The Cup was not, of course, being presented. Note the packed banks behind the stand.
LEFT: More of the hemmed-in crowd, no doubt all hoping to see Spurs become the first non-League club to lift the FA Cup. Although the Cup final was held at Crystal Palace between 1895 and 1914, the ground had no terracing in the sense it is understood today. Spectators gathered on the slopes of what was effectively a natural amphitheatre and, needless to say, few got a good view of proceedings.
BELOW LEFT: Fans from the banked seats invade the pitch at the end of the game. The old pitch markings with a penalty line and the two arcs drawn six yards from the goal-posts were changed a year later.

OPPOSITE: A series of cigarette cards issued by Ogden's at the time of the 1901 Cup final victory. They are shown here full size and were printed black and white. The players are (top) David Copeland and Harry Erentz; (middle) John Kirwan, George Clawley, Tom Morris, John Cameron, Jack Jones; (bottom) Alex Brown, Alex Tait, Edward Hughes and Tom Smith. The reversed card is that of Jim McNaught, who lost his place to Edward Hughes after being injured against Preston (by courtesy of David Allen Esq).
BELOW: What they all took home from Bolton, an FA Cup winners medal. This is actually John Cameron's; his name is engraved on the front.

40,000, easily large enough for all but FA Cup semi-finals.

In 1901, Roberts bought the freehold of the ground from Charringtons for £8,900 and, at the same time, purchased land and houses behind the northern end (then called the Edmonton goal) for another £2,600. To finance this he organised another share issue, but this proved no more successful than the last, raising only £2,000. Roberts borrowed the balance of the money and Charringtons helped him out by turning £6,500 of the purchase price into a long-term mortgage to be paid back over several years.

The game against Notts County was the first of the 1899–1900 season, the year that John Cameron's great team gelled. Cameron had joined the club in that critical autumn of 1898. A native of Ayr, he had played for his home town club and then for mighty Queen's Park, where he had won a Scottish cap against Ireland. He had moved to Liverpool, where he worked for Cunard and played for Everton as an amateur. It was not until Spurs asked him to come to London that he had ever been paid for playing football. He was a classic Scottish inside-forward in all except build, being a slim six-footer. As well as playing, he soon became secretary-manager and this remarkable man also took on the administration of the newly formed and ill-fated Players' Union. Within two years of his, and the club's, arrival at White Hart Lane together they had won both the Southern League and the FA Cup.

THE FIRST GREAT SIDE

What was truly remarkable about the 1901 Cup winning side was that none of the eleven had played for the club for more than four seasons and only four could recall playing at Northumberland Park just two seasons before the FA Cup win. How John Cameron got them to play as a team so quickly remains something of a mystery, if a massive compliment to his footballing genius.

The old-timer of the side was Jack Jones, who had joined the club in 1897, was captain of the Cup winning team and won 16 Welsh caps in all. A strong left-half, he formed the critical left-wing triangle with Kirwan and Copeland which was to create so many of Spurs' vital goals in the Cup run. Spurs were his sixth club – he had already played for Rhuddlan, Bootle, Stockton, Grimsby and Sheffield United. Harry 'Tiger' Erentz had been signed from Newton Heath (later to become Manchester United) at the same time as Cameron in 1898. A Scotsman, born in Dundee, he was the heaviest (13 stone) and toughest member of the side, a fierce tackling right-back who followed an elder brother on to Spurs' books. The fourth player from the pre-1899 era was Thomas Smith, who had also joined the club in 1898. Born in Maryport, he had played for Preston before moving south. Essentially a simple right-winger, his great strengths were his pace (he was a cup winning sprinter) and the accuracy of his crosses.

In 1899 Cameron was to add six more of his great side. George Clawley, born in the Potteries, came from Southampton to keep goal and he was to feature in a quite remarkable incident in the 1901 final itself. He broke a leg during his first season at White Hart Lane, but recovered in time to regain his place for the Cup run. Sandy Tait, the left-back, was perhaps the best of all Cameron's signings. He hailed from the famous village of Glenbuck, bordering Ayrshire and Lanarkshire and later noted for its junior team, the Glenbuck Cherrypickers, which brought on such names as Bill Shankly. Tait originally played for Motherwell, moving to Spurs via Preston.

Tom Morris, the right-half, had the distinction of being born in Grantham, which made him special in being born further south than any of the other ten and hence closest to Tottenham itself. The hard man of the team, he was signed from the Lincolnshire club Gainsborough Trinity, which had a brief spell in the League between 1896 and 1912. Edward Hughes was the surprise member. Standing only 5ft 6in, he took over the centre-half spot when team captain Jim McNaught was injured in the 1900–01 first round tie against Preston. He played so well that McNaught never regained his place. Another Welshman, Hughes had been a colleague of Cameron at Everton and eventually won 14 Welsh caps, the last in 1907.

Cameron showed a distinct liking for players with a similar background to himself and his inside-left, Davie Copeland, was even born in the same town, Ayr. He was the quiet one of the team, having had a fairly undistinguished career with Ayr Parkhouse and Walsall Town Swifts. Outside Copeland, Cameron added John Kirwan, a genuinely tricky winger who had also played with his new manager at Everton. Copeland and Kirwan, who won 16 Irish caps, developed a critical understanding on the left flank, often aided by Cameron holding back behind them to play as a scheming midfield man.

There was only one gap in this remarkable team, and this was not to be filled until the beginning of the 1900–01 season when Alexander 'Sandy' Brown joined the team as centre-forward from Portsmouth. Like the other 'Sandy', Alexander Tait, Brown was born

Winner's Medal   *Reverse*

A Series, No. 44.

PACKETS OF

OGDEN'S TAB CIGARETTES

Contain Photos of
GENERAL INTEREST.

Jas. R. McNaught – Tottenham Hotspur Association Football Club, Winners of English Cup, 1900-1901 Also Winners of Southern League, 1899-1900.

This Series contains 150 Photographs.

in Glenbuck. He had played for St Bernard's in Edinburgh before joining Preston, like Tait and Smith. He had gone to Portsmouth the season before and, so far in his career, had done little to suggest that he was suddenly to become one of the most talked about centre-forwards of all time and one whose record of 15 goals in one season's FA Cup competition still stands. His career with Spurs was quite astonishing. Despite his fame he played for the club for just twelve months – moving on to Middlesbrough in the autumn of 1901 before winning his one Scottish cap.

He was an excellent header of the ball and Cameron had clearly decided that he needed a target for the accurate crosses of Smith and Kirwan. Despite being a great trier Brown was never really skilful enough (a fact fully appreciated by the newspapers of the time,

if not by opposition defences) and Cameron was either remarkably perspicacious or remarkably lucky to fit him in at that particular time. Brown's brief flowering was astounding: he was to score in every round of the competition, the first man known to do so, and netted four in the semi-final. Given the run of the ball and the confidence of success, he had an excellent shot and was a fine header of the ball. And yet he was a relatively easy player to 'find out' and hence to mark out of a game. He did not have the all-round range of skills that a great centre-forward needs, nor the genuine speed. Spurs' relative decline after 1901 was in large part because Cameron never again had a player on song like Brown to convert the team's neat approach play into goals. Vivian Woodward, Brown's successor, was a great

ABOVE: After the massive
crowd for the first game the
replay at Bolton was almost
deserted, the attendance of
20,740 being the smallest
for a final this century. Here
Tom Morris takes a throw
for Spurs; John Cameron is
the furthest right of the
Tottenham players, while
Harry Erentz stands with
his hands on his hips. Note
the empty benches behind
the goal and the penalty line
which then extended across
the pitch.
BELOW: Another view from
the same goal as Sheffield
United clear a Spurs attack.
Bolton obviously did their
best for the occasion – the
stand is covered in flags
and bunting – but they were
never again awarded a Cup
final replay.

player, but was arguably not a great centre-forward, as Brown certainly had been for that one amazing year.

The coincidences in the team Cameron built are too glaring to be ignored. Five were Scots, four of them coming from Ayrshire and its Lanarkshire borders. Two were Welsh, one Irish and, of the three Englishmen, none was born within 100 miles of White Hart Lane. Three had played for Preston, three for Everton. Thus despite being brought together quickly, then, the team members did find much that was familiar at Tottenham and John Cameron was there, on the field and off, to build a remarkable side.

The club had already had its first taste of real Cup success in 1898–99, although only four of the 1901 team were playing at the time. In all Tottenham played 10 games in the competition that year, eventually defeating Wolverton, Clapton (after a replay), Luton (after two replays), Newton Heath (1–1 at home then a 5–3 win in Manchester) and mighty Sunderland (League Champions in 1892, 1893 and 1895) 2–1 at home before

12,371 fans. In the quarter-finals, however, they had to travel to Stoke and the Potters, just as they did in Spurs' first professional game, had little trouble eliminating them – this time 4–1. The following season Spurs were allowed to go through to the competition proper without contesting the qualifying rounds, but had the misfortune to be drawn away at Deepdale and went out 1–0 at their first hurdle. Imagine their concern, then, when in 1900–01 they were yet again drawn against Preston in the first round, albeit at home.

By that time, at least, Spurs did have the confidence of having won a major competition. In the 1899–1900 Southern League they won 20 and drew 4 of their 28 games, scoring 67 goals and finishing three points clear of Portsmouth. All in all they won 49 of their 67 first team matches, losing only 10. After the financial loss of the previous year the club made a profit – if only £71 18s 8p (£71.94). Even the reserves did well, finishing second in the London League, and the club was dubbed 'The Flower of the South' by the London newspapers. Support was beginning to grow fast, and the mood of the district is well summed up by a verse originally printed in the *Tottenham Herald* and repeated by Julian Holland in his book *Spurs*:

What care I of things South African,
Or whether the Boers will fight,
Or that France has ceased to know the way,
Between what is wrong and right?
I care not for things political,
Or which party's out or in,
The only thing I trouble about,
Is will Tottenham Hotspurs win?

Note that the club was still popularly referred to as Hotspurs at the time.

The references to South Africa related to the Boer War, then at its height. The local ardour cooled a little as the 1900–01 season got under way. By November Tottenham were well down the field, quite unable to reproduce the understanding of the previous season. But from then onwards things began to improve, too late to assist in the League, where they finished a mediocre fifth out of fifteen, but just in time for the Cup, which started as late as Saturday 9 February that year, delayed because of Queen Victoria's death. Like many sides before and since, Spurs were unquestionably helped by having only the Cup to think about for the second half of the season.

THE 1901 CUP RUN

Spurs did not start well in their Cup tie against Preston. Perhaps it was the blue and white stripes they had agreed to wear because of the colour clash (it was not until 1924–25 that the away side changed automatically). After 28 minutes a long shot by the Lancastrian full-back McMahon left Clawley unsighted and Preston, 1–0 up, retreated back into defence for the rest of the game. The tactic almost paid off. Peter McBride in the Preston goal was excellent while Sandy Brown, in his first Cup tie for Spurs, could barely do a thing right. The man Brown had replaced, Tom Pratt, had been transferred to Preston and was having by far the better game. Who could have guessed then what was to happen in the next three months? In the 82nd minute Kirwan broke clear and centred for Brown to throw himself at the ball and thus score what was, by all accounts, a remarkable goal. No doubt the 18,000 crowd would, by that time, have regarded any goal as remarkable. So the final score was 1–1 and the tie had to be replayed at Deepdale on Wednesday 13 February, where the home side were clear favourites. Surprisingly, large numbers of fans travelled from London, paying 21/9 (£1.09) return for the privilege. Spurs made two changes. Hughes came in at centre-half for the injured McNaught and Jack Jones returned at left-half in place of Stormont, taking over as captain from McNaught. The team was to remain unchanged throughout the rest of the Cup run.

The Lancastrian home crowd of 6,000 was soon disappointed. In quick succession Cameron and Brown (twice) scored for Spurs and the game was effectively over by half-time. In the second half Brown completed his hat-trick and Preston's two goals from Becton and Pratt, against his old club, were academic.

The Tottenham team with the Southern League Championship Shield at the end of the 1899–1900 season. The Shield is held by Jack Jones, the Welsh club captain.

Tottenham's reward for beating Proud Preston was an even tougher tie – against Cup holders Bury. The Lancashire club, known as The Shakers, was proof that, even in football, every dog has its day. Bury's day was around the turn of the century. At Crystal Palace in 1900 they had beaten Southern League Southampton 4–0 and, in the 1903 final, were to go two better by beating Derby County 6–0 for what remains the record Cup final victory. Bury had been drawn away in every round of their 1900 Cup run and had won their first round tie in 1901 away again, 1–0 at The Wednesday. No wonder, then, that 21,000 people turned up at White Hart Lane on Saturday 23 February. As they had against Preston, Tottenham started nervously and, within just two minutes, they were a goal down. For half an hour it looked as if Bury would overrun the home side but then a cross from Smith reached Brown and his shot beat keeper Thompson easily; 1–1 at half-time and Spurs had a chance. The second half saw just one goal, a rerun of the first with Smith centring for Brown to score his sixth goal of the competition so far. Spurs were into the quarter-finals of the FA Cup for only the second time in their history.

Tottenham were relatively lucky in the next draw – away to Southern League Reading on 23 March 1901. All the other six sides in the quarter-finals – including the West Midlands quartet of Small Heath (Birmingham), Villa, Wolves and West Brom – were in the Football League. Reading were a modest Southern League side, at the time ninth in the table, but they had home advantage and were known as a tough, hard-tackling team.

It is usually the case that the team which wins the FA Cup has one critical moment which can be ascribed to good fortune rather than skill – an incident on which their success is later seen to turn. In Spurs' case, this occurred in the last few minutes of their match at Reading. The score at the time was 1–1. For the third consecutive tie, Spurs had gone behind in the first half – this time to a 20-yard shot by Evans – and John Kirwan had

equalised in the second half. Then, in the dying minutes, a Reading shot dropped over Clawley's head and Sandy Tait dashed in to fist it behind just before it crossed the line. There does not seem to have been much doubt in the minds of anyone who saw the incident that it was a penalty. But the referee was unsighted and the linesman, who was consulted, had apparently not seen anything and a goal-kick was given. The 14,417 crowd, then the largest Elm Park had ever seen, was not well pleased and the officials were abused right up to the final whistle. Spurs fans, who had paid 3 shillings (15p) for a cheap-day return, were no doubt mightily relieved. It was an incident which, in retrospect, might not only have altered the course of 1901 for Spurs, but could have changed the club's whole history.

The teams met again at White Hart Lane on Thursday 28 March before a crowd of 12,000. This time things were completely different. Copeland and Brown (from another Smith cross) had scored by half-time and Brown got another (his eighth of the competition) early in the second half; 3–0 to Spurs and they were in the semi-finals for the first time ever.

The draw for the semi-final had already been made and Spurs were to meet West Bromwich. The West Brom directors had been at the replay and immediately approached the Tottenham board to suggest Villa Park as a semi-final venue, despite it being only three miles down the road from The Hawthorns. Surprisingly Tottenham had no objections, perhaps because they would be guaranteed the receipts from a massive crowd there, and the match was set for Easter Monday. At the time clubs could make their own arrangements with the FA's approval, which was forthcoming.

Spurs could not play on the Saturday as their Southern League opponents, Bristol City, refused to let them cancel that day's match, nor would the Southern League let Spurs put out a reserve team. City were annoyed because Spurs had sent a reserve team for the Western League fixture at Bristol on 27 March, before the first team played Reading, and the West Countrymen stood to lose part of a second large gate within two weeks if they again faced the reserves. As a result, the first team played against City, won 1–0, and went up to Birmingham for what is, as far as is known, the only semi-final initially scheduled for a Monday afternoon.

The game itself, on Monday 8 April, proved a massive anti-climax. Albion, though bottom of the First Division of the Football League, were favourites but Spurs, playing as well as the club had ever done in its history, were to win easily 4–0. As *The Sporting Life* said at the time, with considerable understatement: '. . . it is very difficult to single out any particular Spurs player for praise, but possibly Tottenham will regard Brown as the hero of the match. It really must be said that the centre-forward made the most of his opportunities . . .' In fact Sandy Brown scored all four goals, two with his head and two with his feet, one from 30 yards. This is an astonishing semi-final performance by any standards – and as far as can be ascertained from the records Brown remained the only man to score four goals at this stage until Fred Tilson did so for Manchester City in 1934.

Oddly all the goals came in the second half. Yet again it was the service Sandy Brown received from wingers Kirwan and Smith that broke Albion – the pattern of the previous games was sustained and Cameron's tactical planning had proved itself against yet another major side.

Because of the delayed start to the competition, the final followed just twelve days later, on Saturday 20 April at Crystal Palace. The enthusiasm and excitement were probably unprecedented before a Cup final. The reasons are not hard to find. Tottenham stood on the verge of a threefold triumph – that of becoming

the first southern club since 1882, the first London professional side, and the first non-Football League club since that body was created to win the FA Cup. It is certainly true that clubs like Wanderers, Old Etonians and Clapham Rovers were London, or at least Home Counties, based, but their organization and support were as far removed from those of Spurs as the Isle of Man League is from the German Bundesliga.

Tottenham was the first London club with a widespread support and with working-class origins to reach an FA Cup final, then unquestionably the event in the football calendar. They were not, incidentally, the first professional southern club to reach the final – Southampton had done that the year before only to lose 4–0 to Bury. After knocking out Preston, Bury and West Bromwich, London really believed that this could be Tottenham's year, and turned up in their tens of thousands to see it happen. Estimates of the size of the crowd vary, but the papers the following day gave it as 114,815 and this is not likely to be an over-estimate.

This was the first game in football history which attracted a crowd of over 100,000 and it remains the third largest crowd ever for a football match in England – the two higher attendances being for the 1913 and 1923 Cup finals. The press of bodies was so great that the Spurs team could not get in through the players' gate, so director Ralph Bullock took them round to the official entrance. Here, in an incident so beautifully symbolic of its era and of many of the attitudes behind the Football Association, the team were told they couldn't come in because they hadn't got the right tickets. Bullock, to his credit, did manage to persuade the officials concerned that their

The 1921 Cup winners banquet was also held at the King's Hall in Holborn and the 1901 side was invited. All attended except goalkeeper George Clawley, who had died the year before, and the two sides were photographed together.

attitude was a little short-sighted, but one wonders what significance was placed on the incident by the Tottenham players. It also begs the question of what those same officials thought the huge crowd of 114,815 people had turned up to see.

Their opponents were Sheffield United, though most of the crowd would have turned up just the same if it had been Penzance United. The Blades had won the League Championship in 1898, the FA Cup in 1899 and had beaten Sunderland, Everton, Wolves and Villa (all First Division clubs) on their way to the final. It was their semi-final defeat of the great Aston Villa which had made United favourites for the Cup, though they were only 14th in the League. They had a remarkably talented team. In goal was Billy Foulke, 6ft 2in and even then weighing 21 stone, the biggest man ever to play professional football. In the centre were Tom Morren, one of only two men to win both FA and Amateur Cup winners medals, and the incomparable Ernest 'Nudger' Needham. The forward line was equally famed – Bennett, Field (the only one of the 22 players born in London or anywhere near it), Headley, Lipsham and Fred Priest, who became one of only half a dozen men to score three goals in FA Cup finals and the first to score two in a final and still finish on the losing side.

ASSOCIATION FOOTBALL

AND HOW TO PLAY IT

By John Cameron

SECRETARY
PLAYERS' UNION

PRICE

1/=

Net

WITH
NUMEROUS
ILLUSTRATIONS

"HEALTH & STRENGTH," Ltd.
12, BURLEIGH STREET, STRAND, LONDON, W.C.

On form, history and individual flair United certainly deserved to be favourites. Jack Jones and Nudger Needham tossed just as the guest of honour, Redvers Buller, took his seat to, according to the papers, great public support. Buller has found lasting fame in the history books by failing to win a single Boer War battle but could do little harm at Crystal Palace. Needham won the toss and, sensibly enough, chose to play with the sun and wind at his back. Kicking off at 3.30 p.m. Spurs again started nervously, and after 12 minutes Fred Priest shot past Clawley from 20 yards. This was not so disheartening for the Londoners crowded on the shallow banks – Spurs had now conceded the first goal in four of their five ties, in each case early on in the game.

It took the inevitable Sandy Brown only 13 minutes to equalise. John Kirwan took a free-kick on the left, up went Brown for the header and Foulke could only pick the ball out of the net. The game was following the script of Tottenham's well rehearsed earlier ties. There was no further score at half-time but, six minutes after the restart, Brown popped up again for his 14th goal of the competition. Jones to Kirwan, Kirwan to Brown, an interchange of passes with John Cameron and Brown was away to finish the move with a rasping, high shot off the crossbar – 2–1 to the Londoners and the crowd went berserk.

Those who saw Jack Allen score the 'over-the-line' goal for Newcastle against Arsenal in the 1932 final will argue that it was the most contentious ever conceded in an FA Cup final. They are wrong. One minute after Spurs had gone ahead thirty-one years before, Sheffield United 'scored' the goal that never was. So certain was everyone concerned, and everyone watching, that the ball had never gone over the line, that it has never been decided to whom the goal should be credited. And the ultimate irony was that the referee, Derby-based Mr Kingscott, became the first (but by no means the last) official ever to be caught out by the camera; the game was the first ever to be filmed and the producers, realising they were sitting on a gold mine, rushed out prints of the incident the following week. The moving pictures, which still survive, support the view that the ball never went over the line, or even went within a foot of it.

What happened was that Bert Lipsham, on the United left, got in a shot that Clawley could not hold. As the ball bounced in front of

the goalkeeper, William Bennett rushed in but could only force it off Clawley behind the goal-line. Clawley appealed for a goal-kick, Bennett for a corner (a view which the linesman supported) and the referee gave a goal. For a time no-one could understand why, but Mr Kingscott eventually explained that he thought the ball had gone over the line when Clawley fumbled Lipsham's shot. The referee refused to consult his linesman, who clearly disagreed with the decision, and the goal stood. If it was any consolation to Tottenham, the fates were perhaps only taking back what they had so generously given earlier at Reading. After this the game was played in a slightly unreal atmosphere, Sheffield having the better of the play but neither side coming near to scoring, and the game ended at 5.12 p.m. as a 2–2 draw. It was not until 1913 that extra time was allowed if the scores were level after 90 minutes, so the teams shook hands and left the pitch contemplating a replay.

THE EMPTY REPLAY

The teams met again the following Saturday, 27 April 1901, at Burnden Park, Bolton. Yet again, the officials of the Football Association had failed to distinguish themselves with the arrangements for the replay, the first in a Cup final for fifteen years. They had originally proposed Goodison Park as the venue (the scene of the 1894 final) but Liverpool had protested as they were playing Nottingham Forest at Anfield, just a mile away, on the same day. Quite why the FA could not have chosen one of the Birmingham (Villa were away) or Nottingham grounds, quite convenient for both clubs, remains something of a mystery. Bolton was also patently a bad choice as the main railway station was being rebuilt and the Lancashire and Yorkshire Railway did not want hordes of soccer supporters invading the town. As a result they refused to offer cheap-day return tickets and the paying gate was only 20,740, easily the smallest at a Cup final this century (though pre-paid tickets and some Bolton season ticket holders probably pushed the figure over 30,000). Sad and sorry tales were told for years afterwards of pie salesmen having to throw away their uneaten wares, the expected exodus from London and Sheffield never having materialised. Spurs own receipts from the match were only £400. Eighty years later, the final and its replay eventually grossed over

ABOVE TOP: A packed crowd watches the first half of the second round FA Cup tie between Spurs and Aston Villa at White Hart Lane on Saturday 20 February 1904. At half-time, with Villa leading 1-0, the crowd, which had been allowed to sit round the edge of the pitch (note that the corner flag has almost disappeared), invaded the pitch causing referee Jack Howcroft to abandon the match. The Herald reported that gates had been broken down (or possibly inadvertently left open) and that there were far too many people inside the ground. The FA fined Spurs £350 and ordered a replay at Villa Park the following Thursday. Spurs went on to win this game (ABOVE) 1-0 but were knocked out by The Wednesday in the next round.

£1,500,000, a sum unthinkable in 1901, to be shared between the FA, the FA pool, Spurs and Manchester City.

It was a cold day, with occasional showers and a strong wind. This, combined with what one newspaperman called '. . . a peculiar ground, sloping from the centre to the touch lines . . .' made for a rather scrappy game. The teams were unchanged, Sheffield again displaying their nine internationals opposed to Tottenham's four. Five minutes before the interval Tottenham yet again went behind, for the fifth time in their Cup run, when an unchallenged Fred Priest banged the ball home. Only three players (in 1970, 1989 and 1990) have since scored two goals in a Cup final and ended with a losers medal as reward.

It took Tottenham until the 55th minute to equalise, via a John Cameron snap shot, and from this point onwards the Spurs midfield took control. Tom Smith scored a clever second after another Cameron shot had been blocked and the inevitable Sandy Brown back-headed a third from either a Cameron or Kirwan (the newspaper reports differ) corner with ten minutes left. It was his 15th goal in the 1900–01 FA Cup, scored in only five rounds (rather than the six today) and established a record that will surely never be beaten. It was also the last Cup goal he was to score for Spurs. Kirwan, for his part, grabbed the ball at the end of the game, took it home and kept it until his death.

The trophy was presented to Jack Jones by Lord Arthur Fitzgerald Kinnaird, the President of the FA. Appropriately for it was he, as captain of Old Etonians in 1882, who had been the last man to receive the Cup on behalf of a southern side. When he did so, standing on his head in front of the pavilion at The Oval in

celebration, Tottenham Hotspur FC had not even been formed.

Back in North London, the reserves were deputising for the first team in a Southern League fixture against Gravesend United (they won 5–0). Again, the Southern League had not allowed the game to be postponed. Needless to say, no-one was much interested in the result of that game, but the reaction of the crowd to the score from Bolton was a sight to behold. The team did not get back from Lancashire until 1 a.m. the following morning, but there was a massive reception on the High Road, with a band playing 'Hail the Conquering Heroes Come' and a firework display.

'Arbee', who had followed the Spurs faithfully in the Tottenham Weekly Herald for a decade and a half, quite lost control of himself in the following Friday's report. His piece, which ran to a full page, began: 'There are times in a man's life when he thinks a lot of things he can't give expression to, and that's just how I feel about last Saturday's magnificent accomplishment at Bolton. It really seems a hopeless task to adequately paint the picture in the way I would wish the Spurs supporters to read, mark, and learn. Our whole aim and ambition has been to bring that coveted trophy, the English Cup, to Tottenham, and yet their names are few who have ever thoroughly believed such would be the case. I know Bob Buckle was always very keen on seeing this happy state of affairs before he renounced active association with the team, and I can understand the feelings the same Bob, Jack Jull, Sam Casey, Jack Thompson, and Billy Mason must have had last Saturday evening. And again, one's mind turns to that little mound in Tottenham Cemetery, whereunder poor Frank Hatton (secretary of the club in the 1890s) sleeps, and deplores the fact that he wasn't spared to see the fruit blossom on the tree he did a deal to nourish and train. There are a whole flood of recollections come to one's mind in this hour of triumph. The early enthusiasm of our amateurs when men like Sykes, Briggs, Burrows, Jull, Cubberley, and Payne did their bit to push the club along, the subsequent advent of Jack Oliver with a wonderful wave of prosperity, and then the drastic change in our constitution by that big leap into professionalism. And after that! Well, dark days, but always a silver lining. We've had rare friends and staunch 'all weather' supporters like Mr Jull Senior, Mr Roberts, Harry Burton, T. Barlow, J. T. Thompson, and always the aforesaid Jack Oliver, and, to go further back, Johnny Ripsher – a name immortal to old Spurs. Yes, the management have been in tight corners financially. But that's a detail. Begone dull care! Let us live in the sunshine of the present and talk about what is more seasonable.'

The club held a celebration banquet a week later at the King's Hall in Holborn, where Bobby Buckle proposed the toast to the Cup winners and spoke of the club's history. No doubt he, like his listeners, found it astonishing that the boys' team he and ten others had founded a mere nineteen years before had just won the single biggest prize in the game. Charles Crump, a vice-president of the FA, responded by saying that he hoped the Cup would remain in the south. It didn't - indeed it was twenty years before it returned, and the team that was to bring it back was none other than Tottenham Hotspur.

THE JOINING OF THE LEAGUE

It seemed after the 1901 Cup success that Tottenham Hotspur must go from strength to strength and become one of the country's great sides. But, just as mysteriously as it had risen, so the Tottenham side declined. It was by no means a spectacular decline, rather a dull meandering without peaks or excitement. Cameron's failure to repeat his successes of 1900 and 1901 remains an enigma. Somehow it seems bound up with the departure of that remarkable talisman Sandy Brown. As has been mentioned before, the Southern League performances were acceptable, but in no way outstanding – second, fourth, second, fifth, fifth, sixth, seventh. The first team won the Western League (something of a misnomer as none of the premier division sides then came from further west than Bristol) in 1903–04 and the reserves had a particularly good season the year before, winning the top two divisions of the London League as well as the South Eastern League.

The Cup was unsatisfactory for the first eleven. In 1901–02 the holders, as many holders before and since, went out at the first attempt. It took three games for Southampton to dismiss them – the last one ending 2–1 in a snowstorm with the lines being continually re-marked as the game went on. Southampton were to go on to their second final, where they were beaten by Sheffield United. In the next six seasons Spurs reached the quarter-finals four times, but were to go no further until after the First World War.

Tottenham did figure in one interesting tie in that dull period, a second round match against Aston Villa at White Hart Lane. Spurs had won away at Goodison in the first round and, as a result, there was a feeling that this might again be Tottenham's year. The crowd for the Villa game was massive and the club put benches around the edge of the pitch to accommodate more people. Villa scored in the first half and, at half-time, a large part of the crowd invaded the pitch and refused to leave. It remains unclear quite what the purpose of the invasion was, but it seems likely that this was the first example of a crowd deliberately invading a pitch in the hope of getting a game abandoned because their team was losing. It has happened several times in recent years of course, notably at Newcastle. In this case the fans were remarkably successful. Referee Jack Howcroft could not get the pitch cleared and the game was abandoned. The FA ordered the match to be replayed at Villa Park the following Thursday (25 February) and fined Tottenham £350. To everyone's surprise Spurs won the replay 1–0, the goal being scored by Bristol Jones who was tragically to die of typhoid a few years later while still an active player. Having been transferred from Bristol Rovers, he was called Bristol to distinguish him from Jack Jones. Nowadays, no doubt, the FA would have awarded the game to Villa and fined Spurs much more severely.

At the time Spurs could afford the £350. They made a good profit every year between their first as a professional club (1898–99) and the First World War, when the finances of many clubs collapsed. The first six seasons in the League, 1908–14, were particularly profitable, the club making over £22,000 in all.

Money was, of course, a major reason for Tottenham's desire to join the footballing elite, but there was a stronger driving force. This was sheer frustration with the attitudes of the Southern League. Conservative would probably be far too kind a term for its approach to twentieth-century football. Matters had come to a head between 1905 and 1907. Chelsea in 1905, and then Clapton Orient in 1906, had applied for membership, been refused, and had gone on to join the far more powerful Football League, which was happy to have members from the capital. In 1907 Fulham, champions of the Southern League the two previous seasons, joined them.

All of this was very worrying for the remaining major London clubs – Spurs, QPR, Millwall, Crystal Palace and West Ham. Leading Football League clubs were much bigger draws than their regular Southern League opposition (sides such as Leyton, Reading, Bristol Rovers etc) and Spurs were beginning to suspect a movement of their support to the Football League clubs in the metropolis. It might be added that the club's relatively poor playing record in recent years hardly helped crowds either. Spurs did try to overcome any financial problems a little by organising a baseball league at White Hart Lane in the summer. In the 1906–07 handbook they comment: 'Many supporters have got quite enthusiastic over the game...anyone who is desirous of playing should apply for a trial next spring.' To the regret of their baseball pitching chairman the scheme was a failure.

*THIS PAGE: The programme from a London Challenge Cup tie against Chelsea on 10 October 1910, which Spurs won 3-0. This was the year in which the cockerel symbol became firmly established with the placing of bird and ball on the roof of the Main Stand, and this style of programme and newspaper illustration was common until after the Second World War. The caption 'I've got a terrible left!' presumably refers to the wing pair of Bert Middlemiss and Billy Minter which represented Spurs' major scoring threat at the time. Tottenham went on to win the London Challenge Cup (sometimes known as the London Charity Cup) this season, defeating Fulham 2-1 in the final at Stamford Bridge. It was, however, to be their last success in the competition until 1929.
OPPOSITE TOP & CENTRE: Two views of the players' social club, situated on the corner of the High Road and White Hart Lane, taken in 1904. Note the bar and the picture of the 1901 Cup winning team over the mantelpiece.
OPPOSITE BOTTOM: The home team changing room at around the same time; nearest the camera is Tom Morris, the most durable of the Cup winning team, who received two hefty benefits and was still playing for the first eleven at the start of the 1911-12 season.*

34

The Southern League refused to concern itself with the financial fears of its members and would not streamline its organisation or look to closer links with the Football League. It was a policy which was eventually to bring the Southern to a previously unimaginable low ebb in the 1920s. Spurs became so frustrated by all this that they decided to resign from the Southern in 1908. Queen's Park Rangers did the same. Unfortunately neither club had anywhere to go. QPR, then Southern League champions, changed their mind and asked to be readmitted, which they were but only on the financially crippling terms that they had to play all their home games in mid-week. Tottenham were rejected for Football League membership at the annual general meeting in summer 1908 (the voting was Grimsby 32, Chesterfield 23, Bradford Park Avenue 20, Lincoln 18, Spurs 14 and Burton United 1) but refused to go back cap in hand to the Southern. The result was that, as August approached, they had no fixtures except for friendlies and the FA Cup.

Fate smiled on them in a surprising way. Stoke (they did not become Stoke City until 1925) had been relegated to the Second Division in 1907 but found, after a season there, that crowds were not big enough to support the club. They decided on 17 June 1908 to resign from the League, a hasty move that the people of the Potteries were soon to regret. But, before doing so, the Stoke chairman got in touch with Charles Roberts to tell him of the decision. Some deal was struck between the clubs, possibly financial, and Stoke supported Spurs behind the scenes. By the time of the election, however, the Stoke board had changed its mind and decided to enter the new ballot. Nonetheless, a place had been created in the Second Division and Tottenham applied for it, as did Lincoln City. City's claim was good. They were founder members of the Division in 1892, had temporarily fallen on hard times being voted out in favour of Bradford PA in 1908, and were much closer geographically to most of the other clubs. Tottenham had only two advantages – they offered the potential of large crowds in London and they still had the mystique of that astonishing Cup win.

From a playing point of view Spurs had little or no claim – fifth, sixth and seventh in the last three Southern League seasons impressed no-one and they had lost in the first round of the Cup (1–0 at Goodison) the previous season. The voting could not have been closer: Tottenham and Lincoln tied twice (17 and 20 each) before the League Management Committee gave Tottenham their vote, 5–3. It was said later that it was the unspecified deal with Stoke which had swung the balance, but the reality is that nothing could ever compete with the lustre 1901 had added to Tottenham's name.

EARLY LEAGUE YEARS

Before the First World War, the football season began on the first day of September. On occasions the League treated that quite literally so, in 1908, Tottenham found themselves playing their first ever Football League game on a Tuesday afternoon, that day being 1 September. Their opponents could not have been more attractive, FA Cup holders

BELOW: Blackburn goal-keeper Arthur Robinson gathers the ball from Sandy Young during the FA Cup second round replay at White Hart Lane on Thursday 9 February 1911. Bob Steel, brother of cen-tre-half Dan, looks on anx-iously. Blackburn won the game 2-0. Note the unusual method reserve forward Young is using to hold up his shorts.

Wolverhampton Wanderers, and a crowd of 20,000 turned out despite the pouring rain. The Midlanders, whose old strip Spurs had once worn, had just become only the second Division 2 side to win the FA Cup, and they had beaten hot favourites Newcastle United 3–1 to do so.

But Wolves were to find Spurs far trickier opposition, and the Londoners recorded their first League victory, 3–0, at the first attempt, Vivian Woodward scoring their first ever League goal after just six minutes. The side was interesting in that it contained only one member of the 1901 Cup-winning team; it was Hewitson, Coquet, Burton, Morris, Dan Steel, Darnell, Walton, Vivian Woodward, Macfarlane, Bob Steel and Middlemiss. Tom Morris was the sole survivor, though Sandy Tait, the club captain, had played on until the previous season aged 34. A fierce tackler, deadly serious on the field but apparently charming off it, Tait was an Edwardian Nobby Stiles and, by all accounts, the favourite of the crowd. Dan and Bob Steel were brothers, both from Glasgow, and Bobby Steel eventually took over his brother's key centre-half role. In those days this was not solely a defensive position, instead rather the link between attack and defence. The star of the 1908 side was, of course, Vivian Woodward.

Among Woodward's other accomplishments, and apart from scoring Spurs' very first League goal, he was, at the time, on the board of directors of the club – a remarkable combination. He was capped 23 times for the full England international side, 67 times for the England and United Kingdom amateur international teams, and captained the United Kingdom Olympic gold medal winning teams of 1908 and 1912. In his 23 full internationals he scored 29 goals, a record not bettered until Tom Finney scored his 30th in 1958. Tall and slim, he was a great dribbler, his style as well as his attitudes in some way belonging to the 1870s rather than the 1900s. It was said that he was never paid even the cost of a tram ride to the ground — an admirable amateur position, though one he could afford to adopt.

It was a great disappointment to the club when he decided to turn out for Chelsea in the 1909–10 season. Woodward remained on the Chelsea playing staff until the First World War, by which time he had scored 50 goals in 133 League games. There cannot have been many directors of League clubs who have played, even after their resignations, for another League club. Woodward, arguably the greatest centre-forward the club ever had, was to die on 31 January 1954, the same day as his friend and fellow director G. Wagstaffe Simmons, the club's first biographer and a journalist on *The Sporting Life*. How strange that these two central figures in Tottenham's history should pass away on exactly the same day.

Wagstaffe Simmons' views about the game coincided closely with those one assumes Vivian Woodward held. In his 1946 *History of Tottenham Hotspur FC*, the first serious biography of the club since the *Tottenham Weekly Herald* had produced a series of articles in 1921, Simmons ranges far and wide over his own experiences as a referee and covers at great length the minutae of various contemporary political debates over entertainment tax and shareholder problems. It is interesting that in his section of 'Red Letter Events' he records such moments as '1924: First Annual Concert. Visit of T. R. H. Prince and Princess Arthur of Connaught' and '1926: Visit of H. R. H. Prince Feisal'.

With the deaths of Charles Roberts in July 1943, Arthur Turner in 1949 and Wagstaffe Simmons in 1954 it is clear that a whole era was put to rest. Between the First World War and the death of Charles Roberts in 1943 there was only one boardroom change, and that was caused by the death of one of the directors.

ABOVE: The Spurs side lines up at the Park Lane End before their first game of the 1912-13 season, versus Everton on 2 September. From left to right: Middlemiss, Darnell, Bliss, Tattersall, Rance, Collins, Lunn, Grimsdell, Lightfoot, Minter, Brittan. They lost the game 2-0 and did not win a League match until 23 November, after nine defeats and three draws. This remains Spurs' worst start to a League season, though they somehow ended it seven points clear of relegation.
LEFT: West Brom goal-keeper Pearson punches away a Spurs corner from the head of Billy Minter on 9 September 1911. Spurs won the game 1-0.

More than a whole generation of key Spurs figures was to be swept away soon after the Second World War.

Back in 1908–09, the first League season was a good one for Tottenham. They were unbeaten at home until 13 March, when West Bromwich won 3–1. With a week left Bolton, West Brom and Tottenham were neck and neck at the top of the division with just one game left each. By chance all three had to play Derby County! West Brom went first and lost; Spurs went second and drew 1–1 at the Baseball Ground; Bolton went third and won. So Spurs went up on goal average ahead of West Bromwich, who had led the table for most of the season, and Bolton were champions. But if Spurs had drawn 2–2 with Derby, rather than 1–1, they would not have been promoted, such was the closeness of the race and the idiosyncracies of the goal average system.

Promotion was a long awaited follow-up for the club, which was progressing in other ways. The old Main Stand, pulled down in 1980, took five years to build in all and was opened at the start of the 1909–10 season. It was on that stand that the cockerel and ball were first placed. These were transferred to the massive East Stand five decades later.

The origin of the cockerel symbol has never been satisfactorily explained. The Duke of Northumberland believes that Henry Percy became known as Hotspur because of the enthusiasm with which he led his troops into battle, digging his spurs deep into his horse's flanks to gain maximum speed. The spurs that were attached to the legs of fighting cocks (until the sport was outlawed) were very similar and the club's badge in the nineteenth century was actually a simple spur. It must be assumed that a link was made between the fighting cock and cockspur and the cockerel took over as the symbol. Certainly by the turn of the century newspaper cartoons were featuring Tottenham as a cock and this continued through to the early 1950s, when that kind of illustration began to die out.

SICK AS A PARROT
Winged symbols are not unique in football and Spurs might also lay claim to being the originators of the most ubiquitous of them all – the sickly parrot. This story begins at the same time as the cockerel and ball were put on the roof, and was told by G. Wagstaffe Simmons in his 1946 history. The club's first tour was to the Argentine in 1908. On the field things went successfully, the team losing only one game in seven, and that to fellow tourists Everton. Off the field things were less cosy. Several people were shot during a riot in a town where the team were attending a music hall, and during one game a troop of cavalry took to the pitch to beat back spectators with the flats of their swords. Apparently the gates had been broken down and the promoters wanted to drive the spectators out so that they would have to pay to get back in.

In those days, of course, journeys were by boat and it took weeks to reach South America. On the way home, one of the amusements the ship laid on for passengers was a fancy dress contest, which was eventually won by two of the Tottenham squad dressed as Robinson Crusoe and Man Friday. Suffering some

LEFT: Bert Middlemiss and Chelsea's Taylor appear indifferent to the ball during a First Division fixture at White Hart Lane on 27 December 1913. Chelsea won 2-1.
BELOW: Before that season's other fixture between the clubs (at Stamford Bridge on 6 September 1913) Spurs captain Tom Collins, his Chelsea equivalent and the referee appear to be asking a passing bird whether they can have their penny back. Spurs won this one 3-1.

understandable confusion with the story of Long John Silver, they borrowed the ship's pet parrot to make their efforts more authentic and, in recognition of their success, the talisman bird was presented to the club by the ship's captain.

It apparently survived happily on the High Road for ten years, dying, according to Wagstaffe Simmons, on the day Arsenal were given Spurs' First Division place in 1919. Is it just possible that, in this incident, we find the roots of British soccer's most mysterious incantation: 'Sick as a parrot, Brian.'

Twelve months after promotion in 1909, Spurs were engaged in another tense battle, this time at the foot of the table. Again their fate was not resolved until the last match of the season, against neighbours Chelsea. Chelsea had 29 points, Spurs had 30 and, when the teams met at White Hart Lane one or other had to go down with bottom club Bolton. The unlucky ones were Chelsea, with Tottenham scraping home 2–1.

In some senses Tottenham's survival was of little significance. The club meandered along until the First World War, never rising above the halfway mark in the League, and it was honestly not a period which warrants much recalling. The Cup provides no more fertile ground for a historian, but there were a couple of games that deserve their place in the records. In the first round of the 1912-13 competition, Tottenham drew 1–1 with Blackpool at White Hart Lane. The Lancastrians, a Second Division club, were attracting poor crowds at the time, and agreed to sell their right to a home replay to Spurs. As a result the second game was played at Tottenham the following week and Blackpool, with two men off the field injured, lost 6–1.

The following year threw up a far more remarkable first round draw – away at Second Division Leicester Fosse's Filbert Street (they changed from Fosse to City after the First World War). That game resulted in Tottenham's highest scoring first–class draw, 5–5! Spurs won the replay 2–0 but went out to Manchester City at that club's old ground, Hyde Road in the second round.

OPPOSITE PAGE: The Red House was the club's headquarters from 1886 to 1891. For many years it was a hotel and dining room and advertised in the Spurs' handbook as 'adjoining the Spurs ground'. The club eventually bought the building (on the right of the lower picture), turned it into administrative offices and raised the cockerel and clock. The cockerel, perhaps distressed that the club was about to move into the new stand, fell off the clock in November 1981. The annual handbook was first issued in 1897-98 and did not change format until the 1940s. It was usually written by C. Wagstaffe Simmons, a referee, journalist and director of the club (LEFT).

Spurs played an annual charity game against the Edwardian equivalent of a showbiz eleven before the First World War. This particular picture was taken prior to the game on Thursday 5 March 1914, when Tottenham won 3-0. Few of the names would be familiar today, but seated in the centre is the great music hall star Marie Lloyd.

Despite the declaration of war in August 1914, the League and Cup were to continue for another season. This was, sadly, not to Tottenham's benefit. The club lost a disproportionate number of players who volunteered for the forces and this, added to the fact that the squad had never really got on top of First Division football anyway, meant that the club struggled from the start. The season's results make depressing reading: Sunderland won 6–0 at White Hart Lane and 5–0 at Roker, Liverpool won 7–2 at Anfield and Middlesbrough also scored 7. In the latter case Spurs did manage 5 by way of reply. The one bright spot was a Cup win over that same Sunderland side, a 2–1 victory being some con-solation for all those League goals conceded. At the end of the season Tottenham finished bottom with 28 points, just one behind Chelsea and two behind Manchester United.

There was an interesting sequel to the season's final positions. Manchester United's last game of the season had been against Liverpool and it was later proved to have been fixed. When the League recommenced after the War this fact, plus Arsenal's intense ambition for First Division football, were to result in some very debatable manoeuvrings from which Spurs were clearly the losers. This story is told in full in the chapter on the North London rivalry, as is Arsenal's unwelcome arrival on Highbury Hill.

1921

Second Division records • Jimmy Seed • Peter McWilliam • Dimmock's goal • The Cup again • The Freak Season • Rise and Fall • Managerial merry-go-round • Northfleet nursery

Though it was not apparent at the time, Spurs' second great team was already largely built by the time British troops were fighting the first battle of the Great War, at Mons. Bert Bliss and Arthur Grimsdell had arrived in 1912, Jimmy Cantrell and Fanny Walden a year later, and John Banks, Bobby McDonald and Tommy Clay were signed before the outbreak of war. More important, Peter McWilliam, the Newcastle and Scotland half-back, became manager during the 1912–13 season. McWilliam had been left-half of that great Newcastle side which won three Championships and reached five Cup finals between 1905 and 1911. He was not a great tactical manager, but he was a good judge of men and of footballers. The story is told that, after the change in the offside law in 1925

(easily the most important alteration in the game this century), he held no team talks to work out new tactics. Rather he left Jimmy Seed, the team's key-man and scheming inside-forward, to drop back into midfield and work out the problem himself.

Interestingly, that first game under the off-side law was against Arsenal at Highbury on 29 August 1925. Seed worked it out, and Spurs won 1-0. Given the direction the two North London clubs went in the next decade and a half (Arsenal won five Championships and two FA Cups, Spurs won nothing), plus Herbert Chapman's famed central role in developing the third-back tactic to counter the new offside rule, the result of the very first game under that revised system has a certain irony.

The Spurs team leaves Stamford Bridge with the Cup after the 1921 FA Cup final. The rain having finally stopped, the open topped charabanc drove through the West End and up the Seven Sisters Road to White Hart Lane.

To today's ears McWilliam's lack of direction sounds vaguely unprofessional, but it was a structured era and one in which managers primarily picked men they thought could play and then let them get on with it. The manager was often also the secretary, though Tottenham had had a separate occupant of that position, Arthur Turner, since 1907. Turner had been one of the promoters of Rotherham Town FC and was a Yorkshire accountant. He remained at White Hart Lane for four decades, a critical influence behind the scenes.

The manager's skill was blending the right players into a particular pattern, as John Cameron did so successfully when he brought in Sandy Brown to complete his Southern League champions of 1900. Peter McWilliam was to do the same, only his key man was not a forward but a schemer, Jimmy Seed.

The parallels between Cameron's side and McWilliam's are uncanny. They both had a very brief flowering, spanning just three seasons. They both won a major League one season and the FA Cup the next. They both added a key member after winning the League but before embarking on their Cup run. But, on a less memorable note, neither really fulfilled their apparent promise and both sides faded, not spectacularly as some clubs do, but rather they gently subsided. Seed, always recognisable with his slicked-back, black hair

LEFT: A first team line-up from the record breaking Second Division season 1919–20. Standing (left to right); Archibald, Smith, Jacques, Grimsdell, Lowe, Brown, seated, McDonald, Banks, Seed, Cantrell, Bliss, Dimmock. Bert Bliss was the season's only ever present and scored 31 league goals. The team scored 102 goals and finished with a record 70 points.

ABOVE: Programmes from five of Tottenham's six Cup finals up to 1981, the 100th FA Cup final. Spurs have since appeared in the finals of 1982, 1987 and 1991. In fact all nine finals have been in years ending with 1, 2 or 7. They lost only one: in 1987.

was born in Durham but made his name with the Welsh club Mid-Rhondda. That unsung side was good enough to win the first ever Welsh League title after Seed had gone in February 1920, as well as one of the sections of the Southern League.

Jimmy Seed had been signed by his local club, Sunderland, at the start of the War but they released him after he had been gassed in France. Hence his arrival in Wales. After his playing career was over, he became manager of Clapton Orient, where he made headlines in his first managerial season. Arsenal were using Orient as something of a nursery club, guaranteeing debts and holding control over the player registrations. In 1931 the League ordered Herbert Chapman to stop this empire building and, as a result, Seed found himself managing a club without a single player on its books at the beginning of the next season.

Seed coped, and quickly moved on to humble Charlton Athletic. In 1935 Charlton were promoted as champions of Division 3 South. A year after that they were promoted straight through to Division 1, the first club ever to achieve this (only QPR have done it since). The following season Seed almost completed a spectacular treble when Charlton finished runners-up to Manchester City in Division 1. He took them to the FA Cup finals of 1946 and 1947 (when they beat Burnley 1–0) and, in all, he remained manager at The Valley for over 23 years, longer than any manager at any other English League club.

But to return to Spurs. After McWilliam had signed Seed he never again went scouting in South Wales without a wig and false beard, so violent had been the scenes when Seed's transfer was announced. After his last game for Mid-Rhondda, Seed had to address a crowd outside the dressing room, promising them that he was not being forced to leave. After this the crowd allowed the directors and players to leave the ground, though they missed Peter McWilliam, who was to be thrown into a nearby bog.

Jimmy Seed was at his best combining with Fanny Walden on the right wing. Walden, a tiny man who had first been signed by Herbert Chapman at Northampton, was capped in 1914 and 1922 but missed what should have been the most important game of his career through injury – the 1921 Cup final. He was also a county cricketer for Northamptonshire. Chapman, who unquestionably became the greatest manager in British football with Huddersfield in the 1920s and Arsenal in 1930s, had been on Spurs books (playing just 42 Southern League games) and his discovery joined Tottenham for £1,700 in 1913. Walden's place on the wing, after his injury in February against Arsenal, was taken by John Banks, a converted inside-forward, who took his chance well and ended with a Cup winners' medal to show for it. Apart from Seed, the team's other thinker was right-back Tommy Clay, who joined from Leicester Fosse in 1913.

On Saturday, February 5th –

Spurs v. Clapton Orient

LONDON COMBINATION. KICK-OFF, 3.0.

On Monday, February 7th—

England v. South

INTERNATIONAL TRIAL. KICK-OFF 3.0.

Second Round—ENGLISH CUP.
Kick-off 3.0.

TOTTENHAM HOTSPUR.

RIGHT WING.   LEFT WING.

GOAL
Jacques
1

BACKS

Clay   McDonald
2   3

Smith   HALF-BACKS   Grimsdell
4   Walters   6
                            5
Walden   Seed   FORWARDS   Bliss   Dimmock
7   8   Cantrell   10   11
                          9

Referee—Mr. H. RYLANCE.
Linesmen—Messrs. H. Miller and A. E. Betts.

12   13   14   15   16
Cook   Howson   Hibbert   Marsh   Bonl
                       FORWARDS
          17   18   19
       McIlvenny   Storer   Duckett
                       HALF-BACKS
          20   21
        Boocock   Petts

                        BACKS
                          22
                        Ewart
                        GOAL
LEFT WING.   RIGHT WING.

BRADFORD CITY.

ANY ALTERATION WILL BE NOTED ON THE BOARD.

English League.—Division 1.

Made up to January 26th.

	P.	W.	D.	L.	Goals. For	Ag.	Pts.
Burnley	24	16	5	3	53	19	37
Newcastle United	24	13	5	6	47	26	31
Bolton Wanderers	25	11	9	5	46	29	31
Manchester City	24	13	4	7	49	30	30
Everton	26	10	10	6	41	36	30
Liverpool	24	11	7	6	41	23	29
Middlesbrough	24	11	7	9	37	31	29
Tottenham Hotspur	24	11	4	9	53	35	26
Arsenal	24	9	8	7	36	35	26
Manchester United	24	10	6	8	42	41	26
Aston Villa	24	10	5	10	41	43	25
Preston North End	24	9	5	10	37	35	23
West Bromwich Albion	23	7	9	7	31	36	23
Chelsea	24	8	7	9	26	36	23
Blackburn Rovers	21	7	8	6	35	36	22
Sunderland	24	7	8	9	29	35	22
Bradford City	23	7	7	9	32	34	21
Huddersfield Town	25	7	6	12	20	30	20
Sheffield United	27	4	10	13	24	48	18
Oldham Athletic	24	3	9	12	24	58	15
Derby County	24	2	10	12	18	31	14
Bradford	24	4	5	15	26	49	13

THE BEST WAY HOME TO ALL PARTS OF LONDON

By Metropolitan Electric Trains from outside the ground to Finsbury Park Station and thence by

UNDERGROUND

BEWARE!

The public is cautioned against buying "pirate" programmes. They are in no sense official. Our boys outside the Ground will in future wear caps labelled "Tottenham Hotspur Programme."

Seats may be reserved for any League Match on application to the Secretary, at 750, High Road, Lower Tottenham, enclosing P.O. for 5s. No seats can be booked by telephone.

London Combination.

Made up to January 26th.

	P.	W.	D.	L.	Goals. For	Ag.	Pts.
West Ham United	24	14	6	4	52	33	34
Tottenham Hotspur	24	12	5	7	61	32	29
Fulham	23	13	4	7	39	26	28
Queen's Park Rangers	19	10	6	3	47	25	26
Millwall	19	8	4	7	30	21	20
Crystal Palace	23	8	5	10	50	53	21
Chelsea	21	6	7	8	32	28	19
Arsenal	21	8	0	13	41	45	16
Clapton Orient	20	6	4	10	37	52	16
Brentford	22	2	1	16	21	72	8

LEFT: The programme from what became known as Jimmy Seed's game – the second round tie in 1921 between Spurs and Bradford City on 29 January 1921. Seed got a hat-trick in the second half, a 45-minute spell which he later called the best display of his life. John Banks, who had replaced Fanny Walden on the right wing, got a fourth and Spurs won 4–0. Apart from Alex Hunter replacing Jacques in goal when the latter was injured, the side was the same as the one which won the Cup. The numbers beside the players' names were of little practical help. Despite the efforts of Spurs and Arsenal, numbering was not introduced in League games until 1939.

FAR LEFT: Spurs supporters parade the short distance between Fulham Broadway underground station (then called Walham Green) and Stamford Bridge on the morning of the 1921 Cup final.

BELOW: Jimmy Cantrell breaks through the Southend defence during the 1921 third round tie at the Essex club's old Kursaal Gardens ground (the funfair can be seen in the background). Cantrell scored Spurs' equaliser to make it 1–1, but Southend then missed a penalty before Tottenham pulled away to win 4–1 in the second half.

45

BELOW: Arthur Grimsdell holds the Cup outside Stamford Bridge; after the obligatory photo was taken Grimsdell handed the Cup to trainer Billy Minter and caught a train home to Watford, not taking part in any of the celebrations afterwards.

OPPOSITE TOP: Despite the quagmire of a pitch, both King George V and the future George VI (then Prince Albert, Duke of York) came out to meet the teams. Here King George is shaking hands with Jimmy Seed while full-backs Tommy Clay and Bobby McDonald wait their turn.

OPPOSITE CENTRE: An hour and three quarters later Arthur Grimsdell receives the FA Cup from the King.

OPPOSITE BOTTOM: A very wet Stamford Bridge during the final.

Not very quick, but extremely clever positionally, he was a great passer of the ball. Oddly, the abiding White Hart Lane memory of Clay was of a mistake. It was in the quarter-finals of the 1919–20 FA Cup, against old enemies Aston Villa. Spurs, running away with the Second Division title, were well fancied to achieve a rare double when Clay, faced with a harmless ball and in no particular danger, somehow sliced his clearance backwards into his own net. It was the only goal of the game and Spurs went out, 1–0. Nearly forty years later, Tommy Clay remembered it as the single most vivid moment of his career. The England Selection Committee obviously didn't consider it so important, for Clay was picked for his first international two days later and he won four caps in all.

No great side has eleven great players. Apart from Clay and Seed, the Spurs of 1921 had perhaps two other stars, the left side partnership of Arthur Grimsdell and Jimmy Dimmock. Grimsdell, club captain throughout the 1920s, was born in Watford and was the epitome of a scheming, attacking wing-half. Spurs' single, most basic, movement was a triangle formed by Grimsdell, Dimmock and Bert Bliss. Grimsdell would play the ball down the left wing to Dimmock, Dimmock would beat the back, reach the goal-line and pass it inside for inside-left Bert Bliss, or

centre-forward Jimmy Cantrell, to shoot home. Julian Holland said of Arthur Grimsdell: 'When he was injured he was sorely missed. He inspired his men, and he stamped his personality on them . . . he was a players' player. Not only did he know what to do in any given situation, he could also do it. He impressed players and spectators alike with the *efficiency* of his play . . . it was utilitarian football with an emphasis on craftsmanship and it made him the greatest half-back of the decade, if not of all time.'

Seed, the counterbalance, was used not so much as the creator but as the organiser. It was Seed who had to drop back to cover the space left by Grimsdell's constant foragings down the left in support of Dimmock. And it was Seed who had to drop back to play the linkman after the offside law change. When Spurs were not seeing enough of the game (unlike Arsenal they have never been a side content to absorb pressure and defend for long spells; teams from White Hart Lane have always sought out the ball, not just the result) it was Seed who had to drop back to try and win the ball more often.

Dimmock was the idol of the fans, a local lad from Edmonton who was not yet 21 when he won his first England cap and his Cup winners' medal. A classic flying left-winger, he was the fourth of the side to be first capped in the

Cup winning year and there were seven caps in all – Clay, Grimsdell, Seed, Dimmock, Bliss, Walden and Bert Smith. It should be remembered that, at this time, the home countries played only three games a year, and to be capped was a far rarer achievement than it is today when international sides usually play four or five times as many fixtures.

Bert Bliss, at inside-left, was another great crowd-pleaser, the trigger man. He was small (5 ft 6 in) and balding, a West Midlander from Willenhall by birth. His 'glory' was really reflected glory. He succeeded because of the service he received from Dimmock and Grimsdell, a constant stream of passes which he converted to hammer-shots towards the goal or, more often, well wide or over it. One can see why he was such a crowd-pleaser. The other Bert, Smith, was actually signed on Bert Bliss's recommendation while the former was playing as a forward with Huddersfield. He was tried at right-half and succeeded well enough to play against Scotland in 1921 and against Wales a season later.

The four less well known members of the Cup winning side were goalkeeper Alex Hunter, signed from Queen's Park as an amateur, who took over from 26 February 1921 when regular keeper Jacques was injured against West Bromwich. Another Scot, Bobby

McDonald, was Clay's partner at left-back and, like Hunter, was an amateur when he signed from Inverness Caledonian. Centre-forward Jimmy Cantrell came from Notts County in 1913 and performed as something of a dual spearhead with Bert Bliss. Heaviest (12½ stone) and biggest (5 ft 11 in) was centre-half Charles Walters. Yet another amateur when he joined Spurs, Walters had made his name playing for Oxford City. With the exception of Seed (who replaced Banks in midfield) this was the team which walked away with the Second Division Championship in 1920.

THE 1921 FA CUP RUN

When Tottenham's lack of success in the pre-war First Division is considered, it is arguable that the Football League did the club something of a favour by refusing to elect it to that division in 1919. The injustice felt by club, players and fans was the perfect spur to show all concerned that a major mistake had been made. Tottenham ran away with the Second Division from the start. They won their first seven matches, scoring 28 goals and conceding just four. They dropped just two points at home (draws with Blackpool and Birmingham) all season and lost just four games away. All in all, they accumulated 70 points, easily the highest up to that time for any club in a season and not surpassed until Doncaster Rovers managed 72 in Division 3N in 1946–47. Tottenham's 70 points remained a record for the division until the end of the two points for a win system in 1981, and the club's 32 wins is still the highest number ever obtained in Division 2. Only one English club (Doncaster) has bettered it in a 42-match season. Of the club's 102 goals, 31 were scored by Bert Bliss, 19 by Cantrell, 14 by Grimsdell.

Hence Spurs had recorded their lowest ever League points total (28 in 1914–15) and their highest (70 in 1919–20) in consecutive League seasons.

The following season, 1920–21, the side settled down well in the First Division, eventually finishing sixth, but, as in 1900–01, it was the FA Cup that drew everyone's attention. This time Tottenham went right through the six rounds without a replay and the first two of these proved relatively easy. First round opponents on Saturday 8 January 1921 were Third Division Bristol Rovers (there was only one Third Division at the time). A crowd of 35,000 saw Spurs win easily 6–2, Rovers being further handicapped by having to play with ten men for virtually the whole game. Seed, Clay, Smith, Walden, Cantrell and Bliss got the goals.

Three weeks later First Division Bradford City should have proved tougher opposition at White Hart Lane in the second round, but a 39,000 crowd saw an equally one-sided match. This was Jimmy Seed's game for he scored a hat-trick (two within the space of 30 seconds) and ran the match. John Banks got the fourth from a Dimmock corner. Banks had come back into the side for Fanny Walden after the winger had been injured against Arsenal. All four goals came in the second half and Seed later said that it was probably the best 45 minutes he ever played. After the match Peter McWilliam ticked Seed off over his third goal – a 35-yard screamer – saying he should have dribbled it in and not shown off.

LEFT: The sole picture known to exist of the only goal of the 1921 FA Cup final. Jimmy Dimmock (white shirt, directly in line with photographers) ran down the left wing almost from his own half, somewhat fortuitously beat two Wolves defenders on the way, cut into the penalty area and hit a half-powered shot from around 15 yards out. The ball skidded in the mud just in front of keeper George and slipped underneath his diving arms. The ball can be seen entering the net just beside the left hand post. The two well placed Spurs players in the area are John Banks and, beside the penalty spot, Jimmy Seed. The picture on page 47, which shows Dimmock attacking down the left, was taken from the block of flats in the centre distance. The winning team was Hunter, Clay, McDonald, Smith, Walters, Grimsdell, Banks, Seed, Cantrell, Bliss and Dimmock. As can be seen from the two photographs, Stamford Bridge had virtually no cover from the elements at that time. The Chelsea ground, originally the home of the London Athletic Club, was opened for football in 1905 and was chosen for the first three post-war Cup finals because it had the largest capacity of all the London soccer grounds at that time. The crowd was 72,805 and the receipts (£13,414) were the highest then recorded for any football match.

ABOVE: The diminutive
right-winger Fanny
Walden, a five-foot-tall
county cricketer with
Northampton. A regular for
five seasons after the War,
he missed the 1921 Cup
final through injury. Here
he is flanked by keeper
Jacques and Tommy Clay.
ABOVE: Bert Smith,
Grimsdell and Jacques,
plus a publicity conscious
Midland Railway porter,
pose before the team set off
from St Pancras for the FA
Cup semi-final against
Preston at Hillsborough on
25 March 1922. It was an
exact rerun of the previous
year's round – same
ground, score and oppo-
nents. The only difference
was that Preston won
this time.

The third round should have been easier than it proved. The draw took them down the Thames to Southend, then playing on their old Kursaal Gardens ground. It was a classic David versus Goliath Cup-tie – Southend running, harrying, tackling and putting Spurs off their game. The Londoners did not respond too well to the problems Southend set, and were a goal down within 15 minutes, scored for the Third Division side by winger Nicholls. This at least provoked a response and Cantrell quickly headed home an equaliser from a Banks corner. A quarter of an hour before the break Southend should have gone ahead. Smith fouled Nuttall on the goal-line and skipper Fairclough prepared to take the kick. The referee, however, had noticed that the ball was not on the spot and moved it himself. Fairclough walked up to reposition it (a nervous habit rather than anything else) but the referee would not allow him to touch it. After some arguing Fairclough took the kick and shot wide. That was the turning point and Spurs did not allow Southend to regain the initiative in the second half. Banks, Bliss

(with a 25-yard free-kick) and Seed settled matters at 4–1 and Tottenham were through to the quarter-finals. But what would have happened if Fairclough *had* scored from that penalty did not bear thinking about.

By an odd quirk of fate, Tottenham's quarter-final opponents were Aston Villa, who had put them out at the same stage the season before. And, as in 1919–20 and in that famous replayed game in 1903–04, there was only to be one goal in it. 52,000 fans paid £6,992 to see the game at White Hart Lane, both figures easily records for the club at the time and the receipts were actually the highest ever recorded for any club game (other than a Cup final) in England. Villa had won the Cup the year before and were favourites to become the first club since Blackburn in 1890 and 1891 to do so in consecutive years. The goal came from a Dimmock move on the left; he centred for Seed but the schemer dummied and allowed the ball to run through to his right for Banks to side-foot it home from a narrow angle. For a reserve winger Banks was remarkably effective. Seed said afterwards that he hadn't dummied at all, but had frozen and that Banks had had to kick both Seed and the ball to take advantage of the sudden confusion in the Villa defence. The shot had lacked power only because most of the force had been absorbed by Seed's back!

The semi-final was against Preston North End. The game was played at Hillsborough before a crowd of 44,668. It was actually a poor contest, Spurs being by far the superior team. In the first half they had two seemingly good goals disallowed (one when the referee, a Mr Forshaw of Birkenhead, brought play back to give Spurs a free-kick) and Dimmock hit the bar when he should have scored. Bert Bliss did better with two goals in the 51st and 56th minutes, both from moves set up by the magical Arthur Grimsdell. Preston replied once later in the game – an own goal off Tommy Clay's knee. Unlike his own goal against Villa the year before, this one fortunately didn't matter.

THE 1921 CUP FINAL

Crystal Palace, home of the Cup final between 1895 and 1914, had been requisitioned by the Army during the war as a munitions dump. No one had restored the ground after the war ended and the Football Association had to turn elsewhere for a venue. Indeed, Crystal Palace was never again used as a football ground; Selhurst Park, home of the current Crystal Palace club, has no connection with its far more famous predecessor. The FA chose Stamford Bridge, essentially because it had a bigger capacity than any other London ground. It nearly proved a big mistake, for Chelsea reached the semi-finals in 1920 and would have played the final at home had Villa not defeated them. In 1921 Spurs clearly enjoyed the advantage any London club holds in a Cup final – a shorter distance to travel and an inevitably friendly crowd. Their opponents were Wolves, the first club Tottenham had ever played in the Football League and semi-final victors over Cardiff City. They were a Second Division club, but so had they been when they won the Cup in 1908. The crowd for the final was 72,805, easily the biggest at the ground up to that time, and the receipts were the biggest for any football match in history (though they were easily surpassed at the first Wembley final two years later). The crowds were so great that they were let into the ground at 10.30 a.m., hours before the kick-off at 2.55 p.m. It was not until 1924 that the Cup final became all ticket.

The match is perhaps best remembered for the weather. It had rained all day and, apart from a brief spell of sunshine just before the kick-off, it continued that way. Pictures of the two Kings (George V and the future George VI) shaking hands with the teams appear to show the Tottenham eleven lost somewhere in a paddy field. The weather also kept the photographers away. Only one picture survives of Jimmy Dimmock's goal, and that was taken from the terraces. In honesty, the conditions turned the game into something of a farce. Spurs were (and remained so throughout the next 40 or so years) a club which played the ball on the ground. A certain amount of rain was no disadvantage for them as favourites – it made defending harder – but a tropical downpour was a disaster. Strength would clearly tell over skill.

The game does not bear much recounting. The players slugged away, slipping and sliding in the mud, and, in general, Tottenham were the better side with Wolves creating hardly any chances. Tottenham took just one of the few good ones they created. Jimmy Dimmock was generally regarded by the following day's newspapers as having had a poor game, but in the 54th minute, he took a pass near the halfway line from Bert Bliss. He ran the ball through the Wolves half, beat Gregory, but could not beat Woodward, who intercepted the ball. Unfortunately for the Wolves right-back, who had kept Dimmock quiet all afternoon, the ball bounced back off his legs before he could clear it and Dimmock was able to pick it up again. He cut into the penalty area and shot left-footed from about 15 yards. The ball skidded on the quagmire, kept artificially low, shot under the out-stretched arms of Wolves keeper George and just slipped inside the far post. Any goal that wins a Cup final is a good goal, but some are luckier than others and few can have been luckier than Dimmock's. It was also a selfish goal, for both Seed and Banks were well placed for a killing pass. On a good day Dimmock would probably not have beaten either Woodward or George, but then on a good day Spurs would probably have won in far more style and the fans would have been far better entertained into the bargain.

Wolves pressed but could achieve nothing, particularly with Charles Walters in inspired form at the centre of the Spurs defence. If it was anyone's match, it was his. In the very last minute, soon after Jimmy Dimmock had hit the crossbar, Wolves outside-left Brooks broke clear a few yards out. He should have equalised, but Walters got across fast enough to deflect the shot. Walters was never very creative, but he was very fast and that was his strength.

Keeper Herbert Blake and Bert Smith combine to clear a Cardiff attack during a third round FA Cup tie at White Hart Lane on 24 February 1923. Arthur Grimsdell (centre) looks unsure about Blake's punching abilities. Spurs won the game 3–2 but went out in the quarter-finals to Derby County.

51

So Spurs had yet again brought the Cup back to London, still the only professional southern side to win the game's greatest honour. It was a record they were to maintain until Arsenal won the 1930 final, though Cardiff City in 1927 might claim to be included. Celebrations were certainly different then. Captain Arthur Grimsdell, having collected the Cup from the King, handed it over to trainer Billy Minter and went back home to Watford. It was carried back to Tottenham, via Hyde Park, Camden Town and the Seven Sisters Road, in an open charabanc. Attached were the original ribbons from the rather more glorious moment of twenty years before. There was, as in 1901, a celebration dinner at the Holborn Restaurant. The whole of the 1901 team attended with the sole exception of goalkeeper George Clawley, who had died on 16 July 1920.

The Cup was paraded around the ground the following week, carried by groundsman John Over. Four decades earlier Over had laid out the pitch at Kennington Oval for the first England v Australia test match and had joined Spurs from Edmonton Cricket Club. No one was allowed to set foot on the White Hart Lane pitch while he remained in charge of it. Even stars like Seed and Grimsdell would be disciplined if they ignored this rule; it was even rumoured that Over had doubts about them trespassing on his pitch on Saturday afternoons. When he died, his son Will took over as head groundsman.

THE INTER-WAR DECLINE

When a club is only just over one hundred years old it may seem a little strange to concentrate only briefly on nearly a quarter of that whole period. But compared with what had gone before and, more significantly, what has happened since, the period from the 1921 FA Cup win through to Arthur Rowe taking over after the Second World War can only be called disappointing. The club reached the semi-finals of the Cup in 1921–22, and finished second in the League, but from here onwards it was down all the way. They did not finish above the halfway mark for the next six seasons and were relegated to the Second Division in remarkable circumstances in 1928. It took five years to get back again but, after a brief flowering in third place in 1933–34, Spurs went straight back down again. And there they stayed for another decade and a half until Arthur Rowe's push-and-run team took football by storm.

If the predominant reflection on Spurs' League performances in this period is one of mediocrity, then at least the Cup provided more than a little interest. A good run in the 1921–22 competition took Spurs to a repeat semi-final, against Preston at Hillsborough. It was a game that Spurs should have won. They were one up at half-time but Preston equalised after the break having (according to the Press) drunk champagne during the interval. Towards the end Bert Bliss scored with a blistering drive but, at the moment it entered the net, the referee blew for attention to be given to a Preston player near the halfway line. It was an odd decision, to say the least, and, according to Wagstaffe Simmons, the player was not even injured anyway. The incident threw Spurs and Preston got the winner near the end. Preston's

luck ran out in the final; they lost to Huddersfield after the referee gave a penalty against them for a tackle which was clearly outside the area.

Between 1922 and the Second World War, Spurs got no further than the quarter-finals, though they did that in three consecutive seasons (1935–36, 1936–37, 1937–38) while in the Second Division. There were certainly some interesting performances in that three-year spell. In the 1935–36 third round draw, Southend were drawn at White Hart Lane. Memories were revived of the same round in 1920–21, though this time Spurs' job was expected to be easier. It wasn't: Tottenham scored four goals just as they did in 1921 but, amazingly enough, Third Division Southend did the same. Spurs won the replay 2–1, this time at Southend Stadium, but lost 3–1 away at Bramall Lane to Sheffield United in the quarter-final.

The following season, 1936–37, saw one of the most exciting games the club has ever taken part in. In fact it is difficult to think of a more exciting match from the great days of the 1960s. It came in the fifth round. Spurs had been drawn away at Goodison. It was a poor game, which sprang to life in the last five minutes after Everton had been awarded a penalty for a foul on William 'Dixie' Dean. Dean took the kick himself, but his shot was saved by ex-Manchester United goalkeeper John Hall. Dean followed up on the loose ball, but Hall saved again and cleared downfield. Jimmy McCormick picked up the ball and Spurs, right against the run of play, were suddenly ahead. But that wasn't the end of it. Coulter equalised for Everton and the game was forced into a replay at White Hart Lane on Monday 22 February 1937.

This was the game that Joe Mercer later wrote about as the most memorable match he ever played in. Everton were leading 3–1 with just seven minutes left. It should have been 4–1 after a strange incident revolving around a throw-in by Mercer himself. The linesman flagged for a foul throw but the referee did not notice. Everton attacked down the left, winger Gillick was fouled in the area and Everton were awarded a penalty. At this point the referee spoke to the linesman – and decided to award Spurs a throw-in back where Mercer had taken his. While the referee's judgement on facts is always correct, of course, having let play go on so long the usual response would have been to continue as if the foul throw had never occurred. At the time it did not seem to matter but, with just six minutes left, centre-forward Jack Morrison made it 3–2. Two minutes later Joe Meek ran through to equalise with a solo goal. The relief on the terraces was enormous, but they had yet to witness the finale for, with the last kick of the game, Morrison got a fourth and Spurs had won a game (4–3) which was as unwinnable as any they had ever played.

Joe Mercer said afterwards: 'I stood there hardly able to realise that we had lost . . . Programmes were going up in the air, coming down and being thrown up again. Men and women and boys were dancing in circles, shaking hands and slapping one another on the back and throwing hats (which probably did not belong to them) in the air. I bet there were thousands of hats lost that day and I bet no-one cared. On the day it was played I hated

that game. Today it stands out as the greatest in which I ever took part, a belief in which I must be joined by everyone who was there.'

As Spurs had won a remarkable third round game away at Fratton Park (home of then highly rated Portsmouth) by a startling 5–0, hopes were understandably high for further progress. Sadly, there was no fairy story to follow, for Preston won 3–1 at White Hart Lane in the quarter-finals. It was the fourth time Spurs and Preston had met in the Cup since the First World War, and laurels had remained equal, a 2–1 and a 3–1 win each. 1938 saw another quarter-final, this time with considerably less drama. Spurs had struggled to get there, having been taken to replays by undistinguished New Brighton and Chesterfield. They were drawn against Sunderland at White Hart Lane in the sixth round, and the game drew the largest attendance in the club's history, 75,038. The technical capacity was even higher (78,000) but

this crowd will surely remain the largest ever to see a game on the High Road.

They were to be sorely disappointed, Sunderland winning 1–0. There was one odd incident in the game, however. Colin Lyman shot home for Spurs from an acute angle on the left and Alec Gibbons, sure that the ball was over the line, celebrated by punching it into the back of the net. The referee gave a goal, but a linesman flagged that the ball had not crossed the line when Gibbons handled it, though it was clearly on its way. It was a very strange incident indeed, and it probably cost Spurs a semi-final place.

Not all inter-war Cup matches were wine and roses. Lowly Crystal Palace beat Spurs 2–0 at Selhurst Park in 1923-24, while unlikely Reading did exactly the same in Berkshire five years later. Neither of these humiliations compared with the quarter-final tie at Huddersfield on Saturday 3 March 1928 however. The home side, League Champions in 1924, 1925 and 1926, and runners-up in 1927 and 1928, scored five goals in the first half and presumably let up only out of pity after the break. They eventually ran out winners 6–1 in a game best glossed over. The players were later to complain that they had been made to go out on long walks across the snow covered Derbyshire moors from their Buxton hotel and had all contracted colds.

Peter McWilliam had remained as manager of the club until February 1927, when Middlesbrough offered him £1,500 per annum to take over at Ayresome Park. Spurs were reputedly paying him only £850, but he would have stayed for £1,000. The Spurs board refused, for whatever reason, to give McWilliam that small rise and he left, only to be asked to return nearly a dozen years later.

THE SEED AFFAIR

Billy Minter, an inside-forward with the club in the pre-war years, had been trainer of the 1920–21 Cup winning side and took over as manager from McWilliam. It was soon afterwards that the club perpetrated perhaps its

A Tottenham Hotspur season ticket from their fiftieth season, 1931–32. The bearer simply showed the plastic disc and was allowed into the ground (by courtesy of Hugh Wrampling Esq).

biggest ever mistake on the transfer market. In recent years only the sale of Pat Jennings to Arsenal can remotely compare with Jimmy Seed's departure for Sheffield Wednesday.

Seed had been injured and a Welsh lad from the Northfleet nursery, Taffy (Eugene) O'Callaghan, had been promoted to the first team. O'Callaghan and Spurs colleague Willie Evans were later to be key members in Wales' Home Championship winning sides of 1932–33, 1933–34, and 1936–37. He was playing so well on the left side of the field, combining magnificently with the ex-Fulham forward Frank Osborne, that Seed could not get his place back from 'Boy Wonder' O'Callaghan. Of course a place should have been found for both of them, for no club finds players of their quality more than once or twice a decade. But Seed was given a transfer and went to apparently doomed Sheffield Wednesday.

Arthur Grimsdell had broken a leg in 1926 and missed nearly a whole season, after which he was never quite the same player as he had been in the early 1920s. The loss in such a short space of time of the two great orchestraters of the 1920–22 period (and remember that footballers' careers were much longer and took time to develop in those days), was too much for the club to bear. Seed, in his autobiography, said that he left Spurs basically because they reduced his wages from £8 per week to £7 while he played in the reserves.

It was unknown at the time, but Seed's departure was to have a far more immediate effect on Spurs' fortunes. He joined Wednesday during the 1927–28 season, when the Yorkshire side seemed certain of relegation from the First Division. With only ten matches left to play, they were five points behind the 21st club. But Seed's arrival rejuvenated them and, as Easter approached, they seemed to have a chance, if a faint one, of survival. Spurs, with just six games left to play, were in the top half of the table with 35 points. The League was so close that year that the players were thinking of perhaps just scraping into the 'talent money' places – the top four in the division where clubs were allowed to pay bonuses to their players over and above the maximum wage. It is doubtful that relegation had ever occurred to anyone at White Hart Lane, for in many ways the

season had been an encouraging one. Their best result was at Goodison where they had beaten League leaders Everton 5–2 and Taffy O'Callaghan had confirmed his continuing selection with four of the goals.

But Easter was to prove vital. Wednesday and Spurs had to play each other twice. On Good Friday, 6 April 1928, the Yorkshiremen won 3–1 at White Hart Lane. Seed scored. On Easter Tuesday, 10 April 1928, they also won, 4–2 at Hillsborough. Seed scored again. Wednesday could now save themselves. Spurs, still with no thought of relegation, finished their season earlier than most of the division (they were above the danger area) and went off to the Netherlands on a tour. They had drawn 2–2 at Burnley on 14 April, lost 4–1 at home to Bury on 21 April and lost again, 2–0 away at Anfield on 28 April. When they returned a few days later they were a Second Division club. The results had fallen in such a remarkable way that seven clubs had ended with 39 points. Tottenham had 38 and Middlesbrough 37, the highest points totals ever recorded by two relegated clubs from a 22-team division before the introduction of three points for a win.

The whole table was a complete statistical freak. Derby, who finished fourth, had just six more points than Spurs. A span of seven points covered all but three of the clubs in the division – and champions Everton managed only 53. Nothing like it had happened before nor has happened since. But it made little difference to Spurs – they were a Second Division club again. Wednesday and Seed had not only saved themselves, they finished a respectable 14th. The following two seasons, 1928–29 and 1929–30, Seed led Wednesday to the Championship. Taffy O'Callaghan and Spurs had done him a quite remarkable favour.

RISE AND FALL
Billy Minter's reign as manager did not last long. On the two previous occasions the club had been in the Second Division they were promoted at their first attempt But Spurs could finish only 10th in 1928-29 and 12th in 1929-30 (still the worst performance in the club's League history) and Minter, who remained as an assistant secretary until his death, was replaced by Bury manager Percy Smith. Smith rapidly remodelled the side – its most

notable members being centre-half Alf Messer from Reading, Taffy O'Callaghan at inside-forward, and Eddie Harper at centre-forward. Harper had been the First Division's leading scorer with Blackburn in 1925–26, and was capped against Scotland the same year. He had been bought from Sheffield Wednesday in 1929, and, though past his best, scored 36 goals in 1930–31. No Spurs player beat this in a single season until Jimmy Greaves got one more in 1962–63. Yet within 12 months Harper had been replaced by the 'Chesterfield Tough', George Hunt.

The last survivor from the great side of the early 1920s left the same season. That was Jimmy Dimmock, who now weighed 13½ stone and who had been having problems for some time. And while the older fans mourned his passing, they could not fail to be delighted by the very promising team that Percy Smith was building. George Greenfield, a local boy from Hackney, was really the greatest talent and the man who paved the way for promotion in 1933. But before that season was even halfway through he broke a leg at Fulham and his career never flourished again. Smith replaced him immediately with the remarkable Willie Hall, who was to find lasting fame with his five goals in 28 minutes for England against Northern Ireland at Old Trafford on 16 November 1938. Three of those goals came within 210 seconds and no other player has ever scored more than five for England in a single international.

He was playing inside-right for his country that day, and was obviously helped in no small way by Stanley Matthews' performance on the wing. Hall scored seven goals for England that season, only two less than he managed for his club! Hall, who came from Nottingham and had previously played for Notts County, was also remarkable for his build. The inside-right was only 5 ft 7 in tall but weighed 11½ stone. This rather rotund, muscular shape was easily distinguishable to crowds not yet assisted by numbers on the back of shirts. For that improvement, incidentally, they have Spurs to thank, for the club pushed the change through a previously reluctant League before the beginning of the ill-fated 1939-40 season. Hall, whose name has happily lived in the record books, had a less happy sequel to his distinguished career. He was afflicted by disease and eventually lost both his legs. The club gave him a testimonial in 1946 which raised a hefty sum for the times. After their unhappy five-year sojourn in the Second Division, Percy Smith's Spurs eventually fought their way back up on 29 April 1933. Their elevation was not very impressive and, though the highlight of a 25-year period, was rather in keeping with the mood of that quarter century. Spurs lost 1–0 at Upton Park on that day while their only challengers, Fulham, went down by the same score at home to Grimsby. Stoke were champions, just one point ahead of Spurs, who at least had the distinction of being the only team in the top two divisions not to lose at home. Tottenham had started the season appallingly and were in the relegation zone in October. But they lost only three of their last 35 games, didn't once lose at home, and slowly pulled themselves up through the table. To celebrate both promotion and the club's

OPPOSITE PAGE:
Managerial comings and goings at White Hart Lane during the late 1920s and early 1930s. Billy Minter resigned in November 1929, going onto the club's administrative side, and on 1 January 1930 greeted Percy Smith from Bury (right, top picture) to the club in his place. After Tottenham's relegation in 1935, Smith was replaced by Jack Tresadern (middle, centre picture). He was welcomed to White Hart Lane on Monday 1 July 1935 by trainer George Hardy (left) and chief scout Ben Ives (right). Three years later, at the start of the 1938–39 season, Billy Minter welcomed back Peter McWilliam to the club. McWilliam had been manager of the Cup winning side in 1921 and had left to manage Middlesbrough in February 1927.
ABOVE: One of the most dramatic matches Spurs ever contested was a fifth round FA Cup replay against Everton on 22 February 1937. Spurs scored three goals in the last six minutes to win 4–3. In the picture Everton goalkeeper Ted Sagar clears a corner from the threat of Spurs forwards Jack Morrison and Joe Meek.
ABOVE LEFT: Spurs supporters leaving Euston on Saturday 20 February 1937. for the first tie at Goodison.

50th anniversary, the 1933-34 handbook tells us that '. . . a Grand Concert was held at the Municipal Hall.'

The club's successful spell continued into the following season. George Hunt, not at all cowed by the First Division, scored another 32 League goals to add to his 32 of the previous campaign, Willie Hall and half-back Arthur Rowe received their first caps, and the side finished an excellent third. They were ten points behind Arsenal and it must be admitted that they never really looked like actually winning the Championship after losing first place on 25 November. Nonetheless, portents were good for the future.

Portents may have been good, performance was anything but. The side fell apart almost from the start of the following season, 1934–35. In 1933–34 the goal record had been 79–56. In 1934–35 it was virtually the reverse, 54–93. The problem was in defence, where Cecil Poynton had gone (to Ramsgate), club captain Frank Felton had been released, and Arthur Rowe was injured so badly that his career never recovered. Suddenly the Spurs defence found itself without enough experience and took on the properties of a sieve. In all, 36 players were tried in the team during the season, but the problems were never really solved. Arsenal beat them 5–1 at Highbury and 6–0 at White Hart Lane, one of the most humiliating results in the club's history.

Taffy Day (left) and the 'Chesterfield Tough', George Hunt, on their way from Kings Cross to Bradford for a fifth round FA Cup tie against Park Avenue on 15 February 1936. Spurs drew the game 0–0 and won the Monday afternoon replay 2–1. They then travelled back to Bradford the following Saturday and won 5–2 in the League – a rare trio of games in one week for the same clubs. In the background is Fred Bearman, who was chairman of the club during the Double season.

Between 26 December 1934 (when they beat Grimsby 2–1) and 19 April 1935 (when they beat Blackburn 1–0) Spurs did not win a League game. This run of 16 matches remains an unequalled spell of failure in the history of the club, though, oddly, they won two Cup games in January. The board and the manager had been squabbling all season, and Percy Smith's departure at the end of it was singularly ungracious, considering that he had taken them to third place in the League but 12 months before. But then these things often are.

It was hardly a good time to open the new East Stand, then easily the most impressive structure on any English League ground. The cost was a staggering £60,000, largely financed through the support of Barclays Bank. As an illustration of just what an investment that was, £60,000 was almost exactly the same amount as the club's total aggregate profits (meaning annual profits minus losses) since the First World War. The most they had ever made in a single season was £17,417 in 1921–22 and in 1934–35 the club made only £8,777. Of the previous ten seasons, Tottenham had lost money in four.

Jack Tresadern, manager of Crystal Palace, took over for three seasons. He is best remembered for captaining West Ham United at the 1923 'White Horse' Cup final. He complained after that game that, when David Jack had scored Bolton's first goal, he was trapped in a section of the crowd which had prevented him getting back on the pitch after he had taken a throw-in. Sadly, his three years at White Hart Lane produced little to compare with that famed occasion. Tresadern's most memorable decisions were the sales of George Hunt to Arsenal, where he found a place in that all-conquering club's First Division line-up, and Taffy

O'Callaghan to Leicester. O'Callaghan proved a critical factor in Leicester's subsequent promotion to the First Division a season later in 1937 but he, like Willie Hall, did not survive to celebrate a comfortable middle-age for he was prematurely dead within a decade. The shades of Seed and Jennings did not go unnoticed by the fans, who never forgave Tresadern for seeming to blame these two great performers for Tottenham's troubles. Their later successes hardly assisted the manager's cause either, and his departure was inevitable.

Peter McWilliam came back to his old job for the last season before the Second World War, but time was obviously too short to work the miracles of 1920 and 1921. There were parallels with that period, however. Just as the post-Great War team had been emerging before it, so it was with Arthur Rowe's push-and-run side. McWilliam had sensibly decided that the team he inherited would not do the job, and he began to promote youngsters from the Northfleet nursery through the combination side. Les Bennett, Ted Ditchburn, Bill Nicholson and Ron Burgess all had their first taste of senior football before the War. Arthur Rowe had gone (to take a coaching job in Hungary) but he would be back.

THE WARTIME YEARS

The War was a bleak period for most clubs. Spurs had already been in relatively poor financial straits – by 1940 they had lost money in as many years as they had made it since their loss of permanent First Division status in 1928. Indeed, in 1929–30 they lost over £10,000 for the first time ever. Secretary Arthur Turner organised the side during the War and the club had some fleeting success in reaching the semi-finals of the London Cup in 1941 (they lost to Brentford). Later on in the War the club was clearly finding its feet, winning the Football League South in both 1943–44 and 1944–45. In the latter season, Spurs lost only one of their 30 games. All in all, these wartime results should not be taken too seriously. They obviously reflected the availability of players and the particular skills and positions of key individuals – some clubs had more players in the forces than others for instance. It is no coincidence that Aldershot, with so many army bases nearby, were the best side of the period. We have, nonetheless, included all first-team results from this period in the appendix for they do make interesting reading. One other intriguing event in the war years was the expulsion of Spurs, among a dozen London clubs, from the Football League in 1941. These clubs had refused to travel long distances for some games arranged by the League (on the grounds that they could not get their players released from war duties for long journeys) and organised their own League instead. The breach was healed quickly enough, though it generated a remarkable amount of heat for a time.

1951

Arthur Rowe • Push-and-run • Semi-final blues • Eddie Baily • Second Division champions • Make-it-simple, make-it-quick • Champions at last • Danny Blanchflower

I n the annals of Tottenham Hotspur the immediate post-war era will always be associated with Arthur Rowe and 'push-and-run'. The phrase originated in Spurs style: push because it was a short, accurate passing game where the ball was pushed for exactness, run because the three-man triangle and 'wall pass' (often described as a 'one-two' or, in America, as 'give-and-go') were an integral part of the style and required the man passing the ball to run immediately into a new position to receive it back. As it happens, Rowe never liked the phrase 'push-and-run', thinking it descriptively inadequate.

The memory is often deceptive in football. It was, in fact, almost exactly four years after VE-Day that Arthur Rowe returned to Tottenham. Nor did he build that great team of the era; it was already there. He basically gave it confidence, moulded its talents, and directed its style of play. And within twelve months Spurs were back in the First Division.

The Second World War had brought changes to Tottenham. When first-class football emerged from the gloom in 1946, the club had a new chairman and a new manager. Chairmen can be remarkably important, equally they can be irrelevant. At White Hart Lane, Charles Roberts had been the dominant force for over four decades. He had taken over the club in the previous century, at a time when the balance sheet showed a deficit of £501 and there was great concern for its financial future. One wonders what he would make of the expenditure of £4,000,000 on a new stand.

His right-hand man for virtually the whole period had been secretary Arthur Turner, who was to die six years after Roberts in 1949. And while their era had begun so well, with the 1901 Cup win, the entry to the League and the excellent side of the post-Great War years, the subsequent quarter-century must have proved a great disappointment to them both.

The team that is always associated with push-and-run and the 1951 Championship; standing left to right: trainer Cecil Poynton, Bill Nicholson, Alf Ramsey, Harry Clarke, Ted Ditchburn, Arthur Willis, Ron Burgess and Arthur Rowe; seated left to right: Sonny Walters, Les Bennett, Len Duquemin, Eddie Baily and Les Medley. Missing from the picture is Peter Murphy, who made 25 appearances that season. No other players made more than seven.

Doubly so, one assumes, because of the astonishing success of neighbours Arsenal. The Gunners in the 1930s were the most successful team in soccer history and only Liverpool in the 1970s and 1980s can be said to have surpassed them domestically since.

And it was to Arsenal's memory that Spurs went for their first post-war manager — specifically to Joe Hulme. He had appeared in five Wembley Cup finals, for Arsenal and Huddersfield, a record only Pat Rice has equalled since. For Hulme, the club and football generally, the immediate post-war years were an unreal period. Though, unlike the Great War, few British players had actually died in the fighting, the disruptions to home life had been much greater, and the experienced, talented players of 1939 had lost their late twenties and early thirties to the war. The younger players had had no concentrated experience of first-class football, and in this context the younger players were now aged between 24 and 30.

Hulme never blended the old and the new quite well enough. Spurs were often in with a chance, but always flattered to deceive, finishing sixth, eighth and fifth in their first three post-war Division 2 seasons. The 1948 FA Cup semi-final was the bitterest moment. Spurs had fought their way past Bolton, West Bromwich, Leicester and Southampton to reach Villa Park for their first semi-final in nearly three decades. Blackpool were the opposition after a simpler trot past Leeds, Chester, Colchester and Fulham.

It was a semi-final Spurs seemed to have won in the 63rd minute when centre-forward Len Duquemin scored after a goalmouth melee. But with four minutes left that marvellous imp Stan Mortensen went past four defenders and goalkeeper Ted Ditchburn and squeezed the ball home from an impossible angle on the goal-line. In extra-time Mortensen scored twice more and Spurs' season collapsed. Mortensen scored in every round that year, though Blackpool lost the final to Manchester United, and then became the only man to score a Wembley FA Cup final hat-trick in 1953; Spurs were just one of the clubs whose dreams were shattered by the England centre-forward. In Julian Holland's beautiful metaphor: 'Their paws buttered, they slipped helplessly down the rungs of the League ladder. . .' They did not score in their next four games, and well founded hopes of promotion disappeared with the April winds.

That single moment was really the end of Joe Hulme's managership, though Arthur Rowe did not take over until the end of the following season, on 4 May 1949. To Hulme's credit, it must be pointed out that the great side of the early fifties was already playing for him. Eddie Baily, energetic, enthusiastic, perhaps the key man, and Les Bennett were at inside-forward, Les Medley and Sonny Walters were on the wings, Harry Clarke, at 6ft 3in, had joined as the solid stopper centre-half from Lovell's Athletic in the March (Spurs, despite their cultured traditions elsewhere, have no history of stylish centre-halves), Ted Ditchburn was in goal, Bill Nicholson and Ronnie Burgess firmly established at halfback, and Channel Islander Len Duquemin was a brave, tough and willing, if not skilful, centre-forward.

At the end of Hulme's last season, after the transfer deadline, assistant manager Jimmy Anderson went down to Southampton and brought back the final link. He was the latest in a long line of thinking Spurs full-backs, following in the pattern of Sandy Tait and Tommy Clay and he was later to make something of a name for himself as a manager – Alf Ramsey. At age 29 Ramsey might reasonably have assumed that his brief first-class career was not far from an end, but he was to have five marvellous years with Spurs and England and it must have been a spell that taught him much that he was later to put into practice at Ipswich and at Wembley.

We are now entering a period when it is possible at last to let the actors speak for themselves. Before this date today's historian has only written memories, newspaper reports, second hand conversations; the principals of this post-war era were still, happily, with us as this book was written and wherever possible, it is best to let them tell their own stories.

ARTHUR ROWE — ONE MAN'S SOCCER VISION

It was a handful of sugar cubes spread round a table in the dining car of a London-bound express that originally brought the speaker's point home. That scene was recalled by neat soft-spoken Arthur Rowe, folding back almost half a century as he tells you what happened: 'We were returning home from a match at Bradford Park Avenue and were all dead pleased at our £2 win bonus, talking over the game and the last-minute goal which had done the trick for us. I spread the sugar around, trying to map out the moves leading up to our goal. It was one to savour because there were about seven passes starting out from our own penalty area. I argued that if we could plan moves like that instead of just hoping for it to happen we would score more often.'

So spoke a man with a vision, a man born just 10 minutes away from White Hart Lane. Even in the thirties push-and-run soccer was taking shape in the mind of the Tottenham centre-half, the club captain who was honoured once by his country, against France, and in time was destined to retrace his steps and manage his old club, his only club as a player. When he arrived at White Hart Lane the prodigal was firmly on trial as the manager of his first League club. Rowe had done things and won things as the secretary-manager of Chelmsford City, had been a big success. But that was the Southern League. It had brought him recognition and awards, but had it geared him sufficiently for a much greater challenge?

He spent the close season of 1949 planning the spreading of the soccer gospel according to Arthur Rowe. Modestly he now says: 'Our style was basically the method of Spurs football taught down the years . . . with variations. Tottenham had always tried to play football to entertain. When you can get both, entertainment with effectiveness, you are on the right road. Push-and-run, that was the label they came to pin on our style although, quite honestly, I was never very fond of it. You often saw something like our style happening in a match, any kind of match; a side suddenly stringing together short, quick passes and players moving intelligently to give and take them. It's as if the game suddenly got an electric shock. The thing about the Tottenham side I had was that we tried to make it happen all the time.'

He makes a surprising admission: 'I never told anybody how to play, I just made suggestions on playing patterns, put up ideas. I'd ask players if they had ever tried a certain move, talk it over with them, get them to discuss between themselves...then we'd try it out.'

'Make it simple, make it quick' was the maxim Rowe endlessly pumped into his men. That was the content of a famous telegram Rowe sent to ex-Spur Vic Buckingham on the eve of an Amateur Cup semi-final. Buckingham was managing Pegasus, the intellectual Corinthians of the mid-twentieth century. Pegasus beat Hendon in the semi-final and then went on to win the final against Bishop Auckland. As Rowe says: 'I took our style back to the streets, the way we played it as kids – off the kerb, off the wall, taking the ball at different angles, enlisting the kerb as a teammate who let you have the ball back immediately after you had played it quickly . . . the quicker the better. And all the time you were tailoring your ideas, your hopes to the limits or the limitations of your players, not asking them to do the things they could not do.'

Arthur Rowe had stored admiring memories of an old rival, Clem Stephenson, the star of a Huddersfield Town which had won a hat-trick of League Championships in the 1920s. Said Rowe of Stephenson, whom the England selectors of the time also only remembered to honour once: 'He was great. I was enthralled when I played against him, he best illustrated the style I wanted my teams to play. He played everything off quickly, you didn't catch him in possession. He was like Alex James but did things faster. I saw how much trouble he caused and thought "What if you get them *all* playing it like that?"

'So many players wanted to show their individual skills in those days, but it's a team game, everybody had to come into it. I tried to build a side who would play for each other because that's what the push-and-run style demanded if they were to get the most out of it. Some players had greater skills than others but you had to try and make all of them feel that they had a big part to play. For instance, I asked Sonny Walters if he was prepared to work harder by coming back more into our half . . . not something wingers reckoned to do in those days. I told him that he would have to defend more but he would also get more of the ball. I put it to Alf Ramsey that while I knew he was brought up on using long, measured passes, these tended to leave him out of the action once he had played them. But had he ever thought how much more accuracy was guaranteed, how much more progress could be made, if he pumped 15 or 20-yard passes to a withdrawn Walters?

'The opposing left-back would hesitate to follow Walters back into the Spurs half, which was definitely no-man's-land to the full-back then, thus giving Walters the vital gift of space. And Sonny could also now make an inside pass if Alf followed up and made himself available. We had one more option; with Ramsey's precision, once advanced he could drive the ball down the right for Les Bennett, coming to the near post, to turn the ball inside with his head. And Bennett created numerous chances doing just that. Ramsey's advances would throw a heavier load in defence on Bill Nicholson but he was the ideal cover at half-back – sound, solid and a rattling tackler.'

Ramsey at the back and Bill Nicholson in front of him patrolled the right-hand side of the field and remain the best known of that great side. But they were arguably not the stars. Captain was Ronnie Burgess, the successor to the great Arthur Grimsdell, and also left-half and captain for his country, Wales. While Nicholson kept back, protecting the flank and allowing Ramsey more freedom, Burgess played the roving half-back. He was always happier in attack, utilising a remarkable burst of speed for a nominal defender, and it took years of coaching, first from Peter McWilliam and then Arthur Rowe, to persuade him to curb this tendency when it was in the team's best interests.

INTERNATIONAL HONOURS

Eddie Baily, at inside-left, was the crowd's favourite. A local from Clapton he was the effervescent enthusiast – always running, always willing, always involved. A great dribbler, a great passer of the ball, possessor of an excellent shot, perhaps his one fault was confidence – he could so easily lose it, become unsure of himself. But it was around him that Rowe really built his team, for 'push-and-run', or whatever nomenclature one may wish to use, was virtually Baily's natural game. He was to win nine England caps, scoring five times. Nicholson, oddly, won only one, though he scored against Portugal in the opening seconds of that game. Ramsey won 31 caps while with Spurs, and scored three times from the penalty spot for England. They were not the only members of that side to be capped; Ted Ditchburn eventually appeared six times for England, Les Medley the same number, and full-back Arthur Willis, not an absolute regular in the side, picked up a cap against France in 1951. Ron Burgess appeared for Wales on 32 occasions, as well as for Great Britain against the Rest of Europe in 1947. Billy Rees, another reserve, won a Welsh cap in March 1950 — making eight internationals in all, a remarkably high number for a club gathered together in the middle of the Second Division and with virtually no outside purchases.

The team also had its unsung members — particularly inside-forward Peter Murphy, signed from Coventry, who played 25 times in the Championship season and yet whose name is rarely remembered. Arthur Rowe knew the way he wanted to play the game and he longed to try out his ideas with good players. That chance came, but he never believed it would be his old club which gave it to him or that any club could provide such talent: 'Not just good players, I took over some *marvellous* players. Eddie Baily, a natural one-touch player. I never saw a man who could play a moving ball either way and with either foot as quickly or as accurately.

Ted Ditchburn's successor, Ron Reynolds, gathers a high ball under the watchful eye of Alf Ramsey. The opposition that day, Saturday 12 February 1955, were Blackpool and a massive crowd had turned out because of Stanley Matthews, who can be seen in the left distance. The other Tottenham defenders are Mel Hopkins, Tony Marchi and Harry Clarke and Spurs won the game 3–2. It was, however, a poor season. Seven days later they were knocked out of the Cup at Third Division York City and finished the League in only 16th position. Note the new design in the middle of the Main Stand and Spurs' strange socks.

Where would you find an inside-forward like him now? Then there was the skipper, Ronnie Burgess, brilliant, a great player. And I don't use that word easily. I wanted the ball moved at speed from the midfield and that is what this priceless pair did for me. Then there was Alf Ramsey who gave us our momentum . . . from the back.

There was no finer competitor than Ted Ditchburn in goal, nor did I think there was a better keeper to be found. Ditchburn, Baily, Ramsey and Burgess . . . they played as you wanted them all to play. They were the ones who most used their abilities to the full.'

Eddie Baily tells of the lead-up and the outcome of that first season under the new Spurs boss: 'There were a lot more instinctive players about then than now. That team just came together and you really didn't know why. When Arthur took us over he had players with a lot of natural ability. He was a kindly, amiable man who soon saw that they could play the way he wanted the game to be played, the way it ought to be played. So he gave us every encouragement.

'He would encourage the simple principles, on and off the ball and the urge to play this more exacting but much more exciting game took us along with the obvious enthusiasm of the man. There was no coaching to it, we improved and improvised as we went along. We just did things instinctively and being good players – and we were – we chose to do the

right things more often than not. Basically, we played our game in a series of triangles, moves involving three players at a time with each learning and getting to know each others' parts. The whole thing became very fluid, there were no attackers and defenders, in a given situation we all became defenders or attackers.'

This was most obvious with Ted Ditchburn. Today the tactic of retaining pocession by having the goalkeeper throw the ball to a full-back is commonplace. When Ditchburn and Alf Ramsey did it consistently in the 1950s it was a remarkable departure in approach. Ditchburn would rather deflate the budding tactician Ramsey when he was asked how the ploy developed: 'Simply because I was such an awful kicker,' he would explain.

'We changed things,' says Baily today. 'We gave the ball to the man who was marked. But other players slipped into support positions to give the man with the ball more options. That in turn depended on how the ball had been given and we had to guarantee that our man received it. It was the kerb or the wall game with players in support to allow the man in possession a choice of angles. It drew defenders, it got our rivals chasing as well. Fine players like Joe Harvey of Newcastle and Pompey's Jimmy Scoular, always tough competitors, would have a few choice words to say as they tried to close you down. Joe used to call across to me at the start of a game: "We'll get you today, you little —" It wasn't meant as a threat or any kind of intimidation, just part of the ribbing that went on in those days. But it also carried a note of respect for you and your side.'

SECOND DIVISION CHAMPS

Rowe's push-and-run stylists swept Spurs to the top. Nobody could have bargained for such a dramatic impact in the new manager's first season. There was a home stutter in a 2–3 defeat by Blackburn Rovers in their third match, after delighting supporters with 4–1 victories over both Brentford and Plymouth Argyle. Then Burgess and his boys powered away on an unstoppable run from the 2–0 return win at Plymouth on August 31 until Leeds United halted them with their 3–0 success at Elland Road on 14 January 1950, an unbeaten sequence of 22 League matches at the end of which was a Cup win over Stoke City to make it 23 games in a row.

It meant that from the beginning of September until the season closed for them on May 6, they stood astride the Second Division, a nine-month reign at the close of which their rivals only got within a distant nine points as the rampant Spurs eased down on the home straight. For over the regulation promotion course of 42 League matches from August to May, Spurs had jinked their way clear of all opposition to burst into the 1950s with a lead of ten points, and then went on to stretch it to a runaway thirteen as April brought its usual clutter of games before the close down. And

the crowds crammed into White Hart Lane as Rowe's side stormed on. Loyal fans were rewarded for their patience as Tottenham served out the end of the fifteen-year exile in the Second Division.

Lukewarm followers saw a light rekindled, others came in from the fringes of North London and beyond for the first time as Spurs and their winning ways became the capital's leading attraction. North London indeed had become the mecca of football with the Tottenham home gates for that glorious season returning an average of 54,405, an incredible figure as you look at it now, and the next highest in the League having been established across at Highbury where Arsenal had totalled 51,381. White Hart Lane attendances topped 50,000 on no fewer than 15 occasions; the Southampton visit on February 25 brought the season's biggest gate . . . 70,305; 66,880 came to the April match with Hull City and the meetings with Queen's Park Rangers, Chesterfield and Leicester City all passed the 60,000 mark. More than a million and a half customers passed through the Tottenham turnstiles that season, still a record for the club. The return to the First Division could not have been gained in more conclusive fashion. Spurs scored more goals (81) and conceded fewer (35) than any of their rivals in the Second Division. The fans' cheers were particularly sweet music for Arthur Rowe. Though injured for several

Confusion at the back as Ditchburn fails to gather the ball from West Brom right-winger Griffin and Nicholson and Ramsey prepare to clear the danger area. Spurs' 3–1 win in this 9 October 1954 fixture was more than welcome; it was their first for ten matches and only their second at home since the season began. Ted Ditchburn and Ron Reynolds shared the goalkeeper's jersey, rather unsatisfactorily, for the next four seasons.

THE GOAL

LEAGUE CHAMPIONSHIP

F.A. CUP

...WHILE THE SPURS GO MARCHING ON

ABOVE: The rather premature cartoon which appeared in the club programme on Tuesday 26 December 1950, showing Arthur Rowe dreaming of Ron Burgess leading the side to the Double. The dreams and hopes were to be shattered just a week and a half later at Huddersfield, on 6 January 1951, when Spurs went out of the Cup 2–0 at the first hurdle. But perhaps it was really a premonition of ten years later . . .

OPPOSITE PAGE: Ted Ditchburn at his best, diving to save a Burnley shot on 27 October 1956. He kept a clean sheet that day, Spurs winning 2–0 against a side which was to figure prominently in the dramas of the next few seasons. Ditchburn was the last survivor of the push-and-run side.

months, he had played 18 games fifteen years before in that last season in Division 1.

Now they were back – and with a bang. In the Cup they had taken on First Division opposition in beating Stoke in the third round. For Sunderland in the fourth round there was an enormous crowd of 66,246, and Spurs turned the tap full on.

Sunderland, good enough to end the season third in the League, were simply swamped in a breath-taking home display, especially in the second half. Coming up after the interval with a 2–1 lead Tottenham then bewitched, bothered and bewildered a Sunderland defence which was laboriously slow and had the fact rubbed home by the speedy switchings up front and the rapid change of the points of attack by quicksilver Spurs forwards. Sunderland were run ragged as Tottenham piled up a 5–1 win, Sonny Walters and Les Bennett having helped themselves to two goals apiece and Les Medley getting the other. But Goodison Park in round five saw Everton in no mood to share a fate as bad or worse than Sunderland's. The Liverpudlians retained their Cup interest by the only goal scored, and a disputed penalty at that. Big Harry Clarke was ruled to have handled in the early minutes. Spurs protested at the penalty award but it made no difference. And they bade their Cup farewell when Wainwright rapped in the spot kick.

The return to the First Division lifted the spirits of everybody and everything connected with the club. Now there was an expectancy, a feeling of things about to happen. The lengthening queues for advance ticket sales heightened interest and hopes. Baily harks back to the players' mood at that time: 'You felt that you couldn't get started quickly enough. Remember, none of us had sampled the First Division before. We didn't fear it, we knew we were a very good side now. But we were impatient to find out just how good.' All the time Arthur Rowe fed his players virtual 'Sunday school' tracts; 'Make it simple, make it quick'; 'A rolling ball gathers no moss'; 'He who stops is lost'. 'I said them so often the boys must have got sick of hearing them,' he admits. He even had them printed

and scattered around wherever the players might appear. Said Eddie Baily: 'It got so that we were making them up ourselves.'

But what could have sounded very much like children at school repeating parrot-wise after teacher was apparently very real to the Tottenham players. Baily readily admits to chanting them aloud as reminders in the hottest of practice matches. There were cartoons, too. Rowe had one printed which showed a burglar with customary swag-bag at the ready, hurling a brick through a jeweller's window. The inevitable policeman approaches and over the shattered window we read, 'If we make space'; down to the second cartoon and a judge proclaiming 'three years' over the burglar with caption, 'We get time', and the last strip shows our hero, arrowed suit and all, breaking stones in a vast wilderness which could only be Dartmoor and the final lesson: 'And time means space.'

Spurs had never been able to boast a League title when they set out in the 1950–51 season. Their best effort had been as runners-up to Liverpool in 1922, six points adrift. Rowe himself was in the 1932–33 team which won promotion to the First Division, a point behind Stoke City, and then the following season did well enough to take third place in the title race behind Arsenal and Huddersfield Town, the dominant teams of the era. Some thought that there might have been some cracks showing in the side after their finish to the 1949–50 campaign, given the fact that they lost four of their last five matches and drew the other. Were they too casual or too arrogant in believing they had already done their job, it was asked?

Arthur Rowe shrugged it off: 'We had won the Second Division with six or seven games to go and if we had finished the job in the manner in which we had been playing up till then we must have ended up with a record points total. I don't think the players knew, or felt, that they were easing up. And I don't think that I was aware of it either. It happened, and that was it. It wasn't that we just didn't care once the title had been won. But there was a lesson there for us.'

The summer which intervened between Tottenham's Second and First Division Championships had seen what still has to be regarded as England's greatest humiliation – the 1–0 defeat by the United States in Belo Horizonte, Brazil. Ramsey, Baily, Ditchburn and Nicholson were all part of that discredited squad and they returned home to a still soccer-obsessed nation which was asking just where English football went next. The answer was to White Hart Lane.

THE LEAGUE CHAMPIONSHIP

Spurs had marked the opening of the season with a 1–4 home deflation by Blackpool. It furrowed the brows of the faithful. Then things began to fall into a more fruitful pattern four days later with a similar score, this time in their favour at Burnden Park with Bolton as the victims. A 2–2 away draw with Arsenal, four more goals against the unfortunate Bolton side, another away point at Charlton and it left no doubts. Tottenham were well able to take care of themselves in this more rarefied football atmosphere and their slick, slippery soccer, their punchy pace, sent out danger signals to every team in the First Division.

Their hurricane broke with a run of eight straight victories between the very last kick of September and mid-November. It was devastating and deadly, nothing could stem its force. Everything came together at once in a sustained, co-ordinated spell unparalleled by even the best this now great side had shown up to then. At the end of it all, 28 goals had humiliated such teams as Aston Villa, Burnley, Chelsea and Stoke City, West Bromwich Albion, Portsmouth, Everton and Newcastle United. The eight opponents among them mustered a feeble six scoring efforts in reply. And felt as if they had been through a threshing machine.

Said Eddie Baily: 'I have been lucky to have been in the right place at the right time to give me a lifetime of football satisfaction, but this was something else again.' The centrepiece of it all was three consecutive home performances, virtuoso stuff which stunned Stoke City with six goals, then rattled home a further five past proud Portsmouth, League Champions in the two previous seasons, and finally flattened luckless Newcastle United, who were to win the FA Cup that season but

failed to raise a whisper of defiance when seven successful scoring attempts filled the net behind them.

Baily himself and left-wing partner Les Medley each helped themselves to hat-tricks from this harvest, and Eddie tried to keep the pride from his voice in remembering: 'Our style commanded a lot of respect from others because of its freshness, because of the way it was played and the men who played it. You felt that you were helping to lift the tone of the game and so you got that respect from crowds as well. Other players would quiz you on it, and discuss how they might combat a team which moved all the time and always seemed to have more men than they did . . . the true yardstick of a great team.'

Arthur Rowe, the quiet genius behind it all, swallowed hard at the recollection: 'I never had more pleasure from the game than that team gave me,' he stated. 'When it was flowing like that and all going right I would sit transfixed at some of the football they put on. I was jealous for them, anxious that they should do justice to themselves. That was the only pressure, the rest was sheer pleasure.'

Tottenham's programme for Boxing Day, 1950, and the home match with Derby County contained a cartoon of manager Rowe, surrounded by the seasonal festive drinks and eats and snoozing by the fire with his feet up. He's dreaming a dream which has Burgess and his men marching towards a twin goal of the League Championship and the FA Challenge Cup. Perhaps it was not a dream at all, but a premonition of ten years hence. Within a fortnight Huddersfield Town had brought a rude awakening to at least the Cup part of the dream. They tumbled Tottenham out with a 2-0 third round eclipse on their own Leeds Road pitch, seemingly always a bad ground for Tottenham.

The Town, in fact, paid scant respect to Tottenham's soaring reputation that season for they beat them in three straight sets, 3-2 in their first League meeting, 2-0 in the Cup (both at Leeds Road) then 2-0 at White Hart Lane to end another Spurs run of unbeaten games late in the season and so dilute and delay the Tottenham title hopes. Not that the Yorkshiremen were any great shakes themselves; they had all their work cut out to avoid relegation at season's end, finishing 19th in the table.

A look on the Tottenham line-ups of the time proves how successful was the youth policy of the club, begun in the old Northfleet nursery era and, it must be said, in the days when clubs appeared to be able to find the time to wait for youngsters to come through. The worth of such a policy together with a tight talent net spread locally by the club scouts meant that an astonishingly high proportion of seven first team players came from London, or within a few miles of the capital, and most of the others came up through the Spurs farm teams: keeper Ted Ditchburn came from Gillingham, Bill Nicholson was born in Yorkshire but at Northfleet from school, Charlie Withers (Edmonton), Alf Ramsey, bought from Southampton but hailing from Dagenham, Harry Clarke from Lovell's Athletic but first from Woodford, Ronnie Burgess, belonged to Cwm, Monmouth, but another nursery graduate, Les Bennett came from Wood Green, Sonny Walters from Edmonton, Eddie Baily was a native of Clapton and his wing twin Les Medley was another of the Edmonton crop.

And checking down the playing staff we find Vic Buckingham (Greenwich), striker Jack Gibbons (Charlton), dapper little Tommy Harmer (Hackney), George Ludford (Barnet), Tony Marchi – Edmonton once more, Sid McClelland, a Rowe buy from Poplar, reserve keeper Ron Reynolds, from Aldershot, and Sid Tickridge from Stepney in the East End. By any standards that was a tremendous haul of local and home-grown talent, both in quality and quantity, and said much for the alert coverage of the Tottenham scouts under the shrewd chief spotter, Ben Ives.

Baily talked of the great bond between the players fostered by Rowe which came to mean equally as much as any other part of the team's preparation. 'It meant so much to us all,' he said. 'We were always playing for each other, it was genuine team spirit. We gave and accepted criticism of our game, of ourselves that was honest and well-intended. You played with a pride in yourself and the team.'

And all that for a win bonus of two pounds.' He smiled wryly and added: 'You know I never had a car until I was 34 years old; the only players I can recall owning one then were Ronnie Burgess and Ted Ditchburn. I believe it was Ted who had a big old thing that came straight out of the American bootlegging days . . . we called it "Dillinger" because Ted looked for all the world like the gang leader Jack Dillinger when he set off in it . . .

'I lived in Clapton and on match days I used to walk up the road and queue with the fans waiting to catch a bus to our ground. On the journey you would have to settle playing queries, chat about football generally and then give an optimistic forecast of the afternoon's game, and often having to stand all the way. Then, because the crowds were so great, you would have to drop off some way down the High Road and try and thread your way along the jammed pavements. But, at the end of the day, you might be two pounds better off.'

ROWE THE PLAYER

Arthur Rowe himself came up through the ranks like most of his team. He went to, and through, the Northfleet nursery after joining Spurs as a teenager when Peter McWilliam was still manager. But with a young eye on security he kept up his apprenticeship as an upholsterer until he had passed out. At 20 he felt that his football career was not taking off fast enough and he asked the then manager, Billy Minter, about it. To which he was asked quickly: 'What do you mean, has somebody been getting at you?' Then thinking on, Minter added: 'Come and see me next week.' And that's how young Rowe forced through his ambition to become a Spur, which he did after signing on at White Hart Lane for £4 a week.

He got his League chance, and took it, in the 1931–32 season and Spurs won promotion in 1933, ascending to the First Division with their young, attacking centre-half now firmly established in a very good side. Rowe gained his one England cap on his native White Hart Lane pitch on 6 December 1933 against France, a match which the powerful English side won 4-1 with two goals coming from George Camsell, of Middlesbrough, one from dynamic Eric Brook, the Manchester City winger, and the other from Birmingham's strolling Tom Grosvenor at inside-right. Club-mate Willie Hall was in that same English side and the names of the rest of his colleagues that day sound like a roll of drums in soccer history . . . goalkeeper Harry Hibbs, uncommonly short of stature for a keeper, this Birmingham star, but rated by many as the greatest we have ever had; full-backs Roy Goodall, of Huddersfield, and Newcastle's Dave Fairhurst (Goodall, it transpired, was getting the last of his 25 caps that day while for Fairhurst, like Rowe, this was to be a once-in-a-lifetime appearance); Alf Strange, of Sheffield Wednesday, and the fearsome Wilf Copping played either side of new boy Rowe at right and left-half respectively.

Rowe played adventurously at centre-half in accordance with Spurs wont to take the fight to opponents; he was never shackled by plans or areas of the playing pitch, the whole arena was his domain. So when England began to over-run the struggling French, Rowe was

RIGHT: Another Cup tie against lowly Humberside opposition at newly elected Scunthorpe's Old Show Ground in the third round on 12 January 1952. Captioned 'the optimist' by photographer Ray Green, a lone Scunthorpe forward confronts the might of the Tottenham side; from left to right the Spurs players are Ted Ditchburn, Tommy Harmer (partly obscured), Harry Clarke, Bill Nicholson, Charlie Withers, Ron Burgess, Len Duquemin, Les Medley and Alf Ramsey. The only ones missing are Sonny Walters and Eddie Baily. Spurs won the game 3–0.

in close support to a raid down the right-wing, much to the amazement of Strange, then gaining what was to be the last of his 20 caps. 'What are you doing, coming over to my side of the field?' he demanded of England's new-comer. 'I came over to see if you wanted any help,' was the cheeky answer Strange apparently received. The following season Rowe and Hall both suffered cartilage operations and Spurs went back to Division 2 and stayed there until Rowe regained the reins.

Rowe's playing career ended in 1938–39 when he lost his battle against injuries. He had played more than 200 League matches for Tottenham and took up a coaching appointment in Hungary, thus following in the footsteps of pioneer Jimmy Hogan some years earlier. He thoroughly enjoyed his stay at a Budapest college and was in the process of negotiating a three-year contract to become Hungary's national coach when the war clouds blew up even more menacingly. He said: 'I felt I was lucky to have got away before someone blew the whistle on me. I would liked to have stayed under different circumstances but it was obvious by then that something was going to happen.'

So instead of helping to loose a stream of future Hidegkutis, Puskases and Bosziks on unprepared Englishmen, Arthur Rowe went off instead to the Army to become one of the many sportsmen organising training, recreation and entertainment for the troops and travelling extensively. With the war over and football literally trying to find its feet again, he landed his job with Chelmsford City, to the great advancement of himself and the non-League club. The City, under Rowe, began in stirring fashion, winning both the Southern League title and the Southern League Cup in their first season together. And so it was that he was recalled to White Hart Lane and a team that was already waiting for him. 'Watching them was nothing short of uplifting,' said Rowe. 'I used to wish that all teams could have played like it for the benefit of the game. The fans at White Hart Lane loved us and that was a crowd that was well educated because they had seen good football through the years. Fathers watched it and brought up their sons on it; that was the Tottenham tradition. And it's so good to have seen it happening again in more modern times. There was no thuggery in our game, it had no part. You played football and you won the ball by positional sense. You played them out of the game. We did it in style, no jealousies, all pals together. It would have been great to have had all those wonderful games on tape so that you could take them down when you wanted and enjoy them all over again.'

CHAMPIONS AT LAST

Among those on the shelf above the video machine would surely have been the highlights from that last third of the season, while Spurs were still in the championship foothills. They had gone to the top of the First Division on 30 December 1950, the first time for 17 years. Tottenham held on to a one-point lead over Middlesbrough going into February of 1951 and Manchester United were lurking on the premises. But Spurs had given off the glint of champions and were to save themselves for a finishing burst in true Lester Piggott fashion. With the Easter matches

included, they had to play seven matches in March, which meant them rounding off the month with four games in nine days, a stiff programme. Altogether they then had twelve matches left to play.

Taking a leaf from Lewis Carroll, they became football's March Hares as they scudded ahead of their rivals with a powerful surge which saw them whip through the month's seven barriers with hardly a falter. Playing as confidently and as consistently as prospective champions should they gathered in twelve of the fourteen points the month had offered, a fitting tribute to their skill and dedication. First Chelsea were set aside 2–1 at White Hart Lane, next Stoke City held 0–0 in the Potteries. West Bromwich Albion were crushed in the capital, Len Duquemin notching a hat-trick in a 5–0 romp, and Fulham were 1–0 victims on Good Friday at Craven Cottage. On the Saturday, Portsmouth were held to a 1–1 draw at Fratton Park, Fulham seen off again, this time 2–1 in the Easter Monday return fixture, before the curtain came down on a prolific month's work with a 3–0 home beating of Everton.

Against that Tottenham run of success, the strength of Manchester United's challenge is clearly shown by the fact of their getting within three points of the leaders with just two games left to play. And this even though Tottenham had taken nineteen points from their last dozen matches – eight wins, three draws and one defeat against, of course, their bogey team, Huddersfield Town. That three-point gap left Tottenham in the fortunate position of having to play both their last two matches at home, against Sheffield Wednesday and Liverpool, the very last on 5 May.

But on Saturday 28 April 1951, it mattered little to visiting Wednesday that Spurs were at home with a crowd that had turned out solely to cheer them on to their first title success. Wednesday had their own worries how to win so that they could stay in the First Division (they failed on goal difference). But they meant to sell the pass dearly. Duquemin ('Reliable Len we used to call him because when all the other forwards were off the mark it was usually old Len who saved our faces,' said Eddie Baily) looked to have set Tottenham on the right road when he gave them the lead in the first half. As the game went on, however, a one-goal lead seemed a none too safe anchorage as desperate Wednesday fought to save First Division football for Hillsborough.

Then, with a quarter of an hour to go, the Tottenham roar began to well up, slowly gaining in power and rising to a pitch as the crowd sent out an urgent 'Hold out' demand to their favourites. The roar was at its height when a massed case of heart failure was avoided with the final whistle. Seven decades after playing on the Marshes, the British game's ultimate prize had at long last found its way to White Hart Lane.

That defeat of Wednesday meant Tottenham still had three points more than Manchester United so there was nothing left to play for in the final game except the credit of a job well done. Ironically enough, as Spurs were making hard work of removing lowly Wednesday from their path, the United were ramming six goals past Huddersfield Town. Alas for Matt Busby's side, they were to finish as runners-up for the fourth time in five years, having previously had a hat-trick of near misses as they finished below Liverpool in 1947, Arsenal in 1948 and Portsmouth in 1949.

A week later, after Spurs had beaten Liverpool 3–1 to close the season, Arthur Drewry, President of the Football League, made the presentation to skipper Ronnie Burgess, as a year earlier he had done with the Second Division Championship Shield. And the most rewarding part of his short speech was again, as the year before, the President's reference to the manner of the title achievement. Said Mr Drewry: 'I not only congratulate them on having won it, but also on the manner in which they did so.'

SECOND AGAIN

Spurs were unable to maintain their momentum in the following season. They swapped places with Manchester United and finished second. There were those who were ready to make excuses and blame the very heavy pitches of the season's winter months for Spurs not being able to produce one more League title. There was substance in it but in truth football clubs, like people, get the weather they get and have to make the best of it.

That being said, it could be argued that, of all the major teams, Spurs, geared to a moving style and a ball coming through quickly, would most likely suffer when the ground was stodgy, as it most surely was in the last quarter of 1951. And those who so believed were able to chide: 'What did I tell you?' when they received the news that the White Hart Lane pitch, because of the difficulty of proper drainage through a hard topsoil, was to be ripped up. It duly happened at the 1951-52 season's end and 3,500 tons of what had, in many eyes, prevented a second title was borne off and dumped on Hackney Marshes to make way for 2,000 tons of special new topsoil and nearly 25,000 turves.

Nor were there the happiest of auguries for the season when the stolid, dependable Harry Clarke was missing for the start after being injured in a practice match. Clarke had not missed a game in the two previous seasons; this time he was out of action for nine matches. 'Harry was a miss because he was such a great fellow to have around', said Eddie Baily. 'He was one of the blokes who did so much to make up the real spirit of the side. Funnily enough he never believed he should have been in the team. He didn't think he was good enough. On the pitch he was a hard, determined player, off it he was an old sentimentalist. He was a much better player than he realised.' Arthur Rowe agrees with that assessment of the towering pivot, who was bought by Jimmy Anderson just before Rowe took over. 'He was a determined old-time stopper and we all believed in him. He was very strong on his left side and this helped him a lot because most centre-forwards tend to swivel to the right and in doing so they ran into Harry's stronger side . . . and knew all about it.'

During that shaky start Newcastle United put seven September goals past Spurs at St James' Park . . . sweet revenge for the seven slammed past them a year earlier at White Hart Lane. Rowe's famed team talks probably had some positive effect, but from the end of November, in worsening weather, until the first League games of February the results were appalling . . . of twelve matches played they won four, drew one and lost seven. They rallied but by now it was too late and they fell four short of Manchester United's winning total and pipped Arsenal into second place by decimals.

The season's end saw one remarkable game which is worth recalling. This was Tottenham's 1–0 defeat of Huddersfield Town on 2 April, which helped send the Yorkshire club down to the Second Division. That solitary goal caused all the trouble. Tottenham had struggled against a Town side desperate to win points and keep themselves in the First Division. It had been a tough tussle, without a goal from either side to show for it, when Tottenham won a corner almost in the last minute. Eddie Baily took the kick.

The referee, who had just ticked Baily off, was along the bye-line, between the kicker and Huddersfield's near post. Baily, curling the ball in, struck the back of the referee and the ball rebounded into the path of the Spurs' forward.

So Baily moved to the ball, centred into the Town goalmouth and there was the alert Duquemin to head the ball home. That's when the storm broke . . .

Huddersfield players rightly claimed that the goal should not stand because the same Spurs player had touched the ball twice without another player intervening. The referee consulted the linesman nearest to the happening and maintained his ruling of a goal to Tottenham. The Huddersfield chairman, a gentleman of considerable proportions, hurried angrily down from the directors' box to the referee's dressing room and brushed all the waiting reporters aside as they lined up to get the referee's account of the incident. 'You can all wait, I'm seeing him first,' he stormed.

The air around was blue and the Town chairman announced that he would appeal to the League to have the match replayed. Which he did and everybody interested – and that meant every soccer fan in the country – took their different sides. Eventually the Football League Management Committee turned down Huddersfield's request for a replay and the Town then went to a Board of Appeal set up by the Football Association for an inquiry into all the evidence regarding that goal. But this was turned down too . . . and Huddersfield in due course went down as well. The conclusions were relatively simple. The referee said that he thought another player had touched the ball before Baily centred, though, as he was presumably face down on the pitch, no-one explained how he could have seen this. The fact that he was incorrect was irrelevant. If he said he thought another player had intervened, then his judgement was final.

By 1952–53 the great Spurs side was beginning to show the same signs of decline as had the League winning sides of 1900 and 1920. Despite a very successful close-season tour of North America, during which Spurs beat Manchester United 5–0 and 7–1 on successive evenings, they could finish only tenth in the First Division. Meanwhile the Cup was to revive memories of that melancholy semi-final in 1948. Tottenham began with two games against Tranmere Rovers, about halfway up the Third Division North at the time, then two very tough ties with Preston North End, due to lose the League title only by decimals; next came a softer touch in turfing out Halifax Town, also of the Third North, at their Shay Ground and then three encounters of the closest possible kind in the sixth round against Birmingham City, finally concluded by a late Sonny Walters goal at Molineux.

RAMSEY'S SLIP

Blackpool in the semi-final was supposed to be a revenge performance for the tragedy of 1948. Eddie Baily, a central figure in the terrible conclusion for Tottenham, years later still found it difficult to talk about his greatest disappointment as a player – not getting to a Wembley final. 'I've been there seven or eight times with Spurs and West Ham since, but always to watch. Yet that was the time we should have made it, and we really thought we were going to . . .'

The story of this meeting, of course, was of the slip by the usually so immaculate Alf Ramsey, when his pass back to Ted Ditchburn was too short. Jackie Mudie nipped in, fastened

onto the chance and put Blackpool into the final for the third time in five years. Baily takes it up: 'We knew there wasn't long to go and we began to think about extra-time. I don't think any of us were worried about that because we felt that we had been the better team and would still pull it off. Alf took all the stick for us not making it — on TV and the radio, in the papers all over the weekend and for years afterwards. Everybody blamed him, every headline reminded him — him, an England full-back, a man of his experience, and so on. The fans laid the defeat unquestionably at his door.

'But he took it all marvellously, and he needn't have done really. There was no better student of the game than Ramsey. He could go over a match and tell you everything that had happened in it. He often did so in our dressing-room. And he did just that at Villa Park, where we must have been the most miserable bunch of players in football history. Without any recrimination or attempt to shift the blame he told me where I had gone wrong on that goal. He went over every sickening moment . . . how I, having conceded a free-kick and stood there disputing it, argued with the referee that I had not handled the ball. Then how Blackpool rushed the kick to Bill Perry on their left wing who in turn was challenged by Ramsey . . . then that back pass.

'Alf made his point, telling me that if I had not stopped to dispute the referee's decision I would have been back deeper in our half and helping provide cover against the free-kick. As it was, I left a gap. And, as he always was, he was right this time. That might not have prevented Mudie's goal but we asked for trouble by not maintaining field discipline. I accepted Ramsey's findings, just as the rest did. Just as we always did when we criticised each other. None of it was made because of the sheer frustration of losing. It was a hard and bitter lesson and it was the first time I'd seen that team with their heads down. They were down because of the manner of our defeat and because we realised that it could well be the last real Cup throw for many of the side.'

Baily was right about the last throw of the dice for the great side of the 1950s. The second semi-final was to be their last flirtation with greatness. The records simply say that Perry's first half goal put Blackpool in front, that Les Bennett made the leveller for Duquemin in the second and that Spurs then lost Bennett as an effective unit for the last half-hour after he had had to go off following a violent knock in the face. But the real story of that game was of Ramsey's back pass, and it will always be recalled as one of those matches that one side loses rather than the other wins. The team then broke up fast. Les Medley left to live in Canada, the appearances of the great names became fewer and fewer, the side struggled in a First Division dominated by the youthful Manchester United – 16th, 16th and 18th between 1953 and 1956.

Rowe took the gradual break-up of his ageing side to heart and suffered more than anybody realised for the men who had been through so much with and for him. The fifth round Cup defeat by Third Division York City in 1955 at Bootham Crescent was the final blow — he was a sick man and had to rest. It was his second breakdown. He never went back to White Hart Lane.

But just before Rowe handed over to long-serving Jimmy Anderson, with Bill Nicholson becoming club coach, Arthur Rowe completed the transfer of Robert Dennis Blanchflower from Aston Villa, his most inspiring, most successful transfer and a testimony to the historical continuity that has always been evident at White Hart Lane.

FROM ROWE TO ANDERSON
Blanchflower serves as the bridge between the fade out of the fifties squad and the re-found glories that the sixties were to bring. For now the push-and-run conquerors were moving out and moving on . . . after Medley's departure came that of the magnificent Burgess and that neat little left-back Arthur Willis, the pair joining Swansea; Bill Nicholson's role now was clearly to show others the way; Les Bennett went to West Ham. The two North London First Division clubs were the chief rivals for the signature of the slightly built Blanchflower and the late Tom Whittaker was favourite to bring him to Highbury and make amends for an earlier missed opportunity to sign the now 29-year-old Northern Ireland captain. This happened when a much younger Blanchflower was playing for his Irish club, Glentoran, but Highbury moved too slowly and he went to Barnsley instead.

Managers Rowe and Whittaker, firm friends for all the intense rivalry of their clubs' followers, also had a great professional respect for each other. Aston Villa were reportedly asking £40,000 for Blanchflower and the fee frightened off most clubs. But neither Rowe nor Whittaker had any intention of going so high and, because they wanted no part of an auction, the two came to a gentlemens' agreement that they would not go beyond £30,000 on any account. And if both clubs made the same offer then it would be left to the player to make his choice of a move. The managers agreed to keep in touch and to keep the fee at around £28,000. They had the field to themselves.

Rowe badly wanted to enrol the classic wing-half skills of the cultured Blanchflower. Equally he needed the leadership he was sure he would get if the lively, loquacious Irish star would take over the captaincy of a Spurs team struggling to regain an identity. Rowe had already realised that Blanchflower was a one-off, a midfield thinker probably without a parallel in the twentieth century. With this argument he won his case for increasing his club's bid by £2,000 to reach the £30,000 ceiling he and Whittaker had agreed. Then Rowe, incredibly by any standards today, rang the Arsenal manager and told him the position; that if Arsenal wanted to match Tottenham's bid of £30,000 then it would be up to the player himself. But Arsenal stuck on £28,000 and Blanchflower had to take what had originally appeared second best. He was the most expensive half-back in soccer history and he began his Spurs career on 11 December 1954, playing at Maine Road against Manchester City and helping his new club to gain a much needed point from the 0–0 draw.

'The first match I'd been able to enjoy for some weeks,' recalled Rowe. And the lift in Tottenham's form went on so that they lost only one of the first ten League matches in which the new man played. 'I got Danny

OPPOSITE PAGE: Tommy Harmer slots home a penalty against Chelsea keeper Bill Robertson with perfect economy of effort on Wednesday 20 February 1957. Spurs, who finished second in the League this season, lost the game 4–3. Possibly the most popular Tottenham player of the post-war era, Harmer played in every League game of this season and appeared to be developing an excellent relationshp with Blanchflower. The hopes were not, however, to be fulfilled, Harmer ultimately being thought too frail to cope week after week with heavy grounds and more than his fair share of tough tackling. Nicholson eventually replaced him with John White, a Scottish waif for a Cockney wisp. Harmer later moved to Chelsea, where he scored the goal against Sunderland in 1963 that took the Pensioners back to the First Division.

because the team was running down. I knew that we had to change the pattern; other teams had been latching onto our game and getting to know it too well. Nor had we the players left to carry on as we were even if we had wanted to keep the pattern going. The team I had in mind was Blanchflower at right-half with little Tommy Harmer at inside-left as the axis of another, somewhat different, side. Those two had the combined skills to carry us forward. I was ready to throw the responsibility on them to pull us round.'

Rowe had been criticised over Tottenham's slump in form. He was found guilty of being too loyal for too long, that he did not make changes, or at least not quickly enough. He was accused of not playing Harmer early or often enough. Nothing or nobody split the fans as much as the abilities of the little genius who looked on field for all the world like some white-shirted scarecrow that had been left there by mistake. He was an impish football conjuror, a frail, pale wisp of a man who scaled 9st. when wet through and could see over a five-barred gate if he stood on tip-

toes. 'Harmer the Charmer' he was dubbed and he could be sheer soccer magic to his supporters. Quiet, shy and nervous off the field, he could bestride a match like some colossus with touches to illuminate the bleakest winter afternoon. But his detractors thought otherwise, that he was too small, lacked the stamina for heavy grounds and the strength to resist cynical and calculated tough tackling.

Rowe thought the world of him but looking back was as firm in his conviction as he had been then: 'With Blanchflower in the same side another pattern of play might have been created . . . that was my hope. But I couldn't see Tommy in the other (push-and-run) side. That was unfortunate for him. It also caused more argument than enough with those who wanted him in and could not see why he wasn't playing regularly. I told him, "You can rest assured that if any clubs come in for you and you wish to go, you can – with my blessing. And if you go somewhere and don't like it there, I'll gladly have you back." He was a most gifted player and it was quite sad because he was such a lovely little fellow. In different circumstances he would have been your first choice. But, as it was, I never really got the Blanchflower-Harmer tie-up working before my health broke and I had to give up the Spurs altogether.'

Harmer had joined Tottenham as an amateur in 1945, turned professional in 1948 and made his League debut early in the 1951–52 season when he played 13 games; but over his first five seasons he averaged only ten League matches. Amid other disappointments his biggest was surely being dropped during the 1955–56 season and before the club's third post-war FA Cup semi-final, against Manchester City, a match which had fierce repercussions.

Manager Jimmy Anderson, a cheerful, popular man but perhaps now too old and too inexperienced tactically, was installed for his second and more prolonged term of office following Arthur Rowe's departure; Bill Nicholson was appointed his right-hand man. Alf Ramsey, who had been left out towards the end of the previous season made his move to fame, glory and Ipswich Town in the close season; Eddie Baily also went, to Port Vale, and Anderson bought Maurice Norman from Norwich City and Bobby Smith from Chelsea as 1955 drew to its end. Only Duquemin and Clarke survived in the first team from the push-and-run days.

Anderson had done virtually everything at Spurs except play. He had come to White Hart Lane before the club had even joined the League and, just before he left, a party was held to celebrate his 50 years service. The situation with Ramsey was an odd one. Within the club it was known that he was keen to go into management, but Bill Nicholson, who had considerable coaching experience during his army days and had kept it up by looking after the Cambridge University side, was firmly established as coach. There could never be room at that level for both of them but, even forty years later, it is easy to see what a difficult choice it would have been. There were Spurs with the two greatest English managers of the next decade, both hoping to be asked to make Spurs a great club again. Not only were they contemporaries and team-mates, they had played together for so long, the one in front of the other. It was a situation that was to add poignancy to the tactical Spurs v Ipswich clashes of the early sixties, when Nicholson and Ramsey were fighting each other for the Championship.

The League performances were moderate

enough for most of season 1955–56, but the Cup still stirred. Non-League Boston United were 4–0 home victims in the third round; Middlesbrough fell 3–1 at White Hart Lane in the fourth; Doncaster Rovers were beaten 2–0 on their Belle Vue ground and the short hop to Upton Park saw West Ham removed in the sixth after a 3–3 draw at White Hart Lane had seen Spurs pull two goals back in the dying minutes. So for Manchester City on 17 March, St Patrick's Day, and the semi-final at ill-omened Villa Park. After the West Ham triumph Spurs travelled with high hopes that they could reach their first final in nearly 40 years.

Micky Dulin was on the Spurs right wing for the Boston success, Dave Dunmore took over there when beating the Boro. Then Harmer was tried as a deep lying outside-right against Doncaster, proved a success, was there for a solid 4–0 League win over Chelsea and stayed for the victory over the Hammers. The tactic was to play Harmer in a withdrawn position, tempting the full-back forward. To have played him way up on the wing would have invited his disappearance from the game as well as some physical treatment from the era's backs. Blanchflower recalls how Anderson, following the League game before

the semi-final, had seen Harmer take enough tough tackling from Portsmouth to raise the manager's doubts about playing him against the likes of the Manchester City hard man, Roy Paul. He told his captain he was thinking of playing Alfie Stokes for his speed. But after a midweek reserve match in which both Dunmore and Stokes played, it was Dave Dunmore who got the vote, the dropping of Harmer clearly disrupting the team's rhythm. That semi-final provided a third defeat in eight years at Villa Park for the luckless Spurs, a Bobby Johnstone header deciding the game in City's favour. But there was no doubt in Tottenham ranks that they would have earned a draw if German goalkeeper Bert Trautmann had been penalised for holding the legs of George Robb as the left-winger was about to knock the ball into an empty City net. Blanchflower has told his own story of that dejected Villa Park dressing-room . . . of the gamble which failed in the last twenty minutes when he pushed big Maurice Norman up in attack, dropping Johnny Brooks back . . . then, still hoping to drive Spurs level in the last minutes, he sent Brooks forward again . . . of how he had tried and failed. It seemed that Spurs could never hope to break the Cup hoodoo

A worm's eye view of the end of the Anderson era as Spurs entertain Burnley in the 1957–58 season. Spurs players in the picture include Peter Baker, Cliff Jones, Ron Reynolds, John Ryden, Terry Dyson and Maurice Norman. On top of the East Stand sit the cockerel and ball, which had been transferred from the Main Stand at the time the first floodlights were erected. Manager Jimmy Anderson had served the club for over 50 years in virtually every capacity except that of player. During this season a special presentation was made to him in recognition of his service, which began before Spurs had even entered the Football League.

77

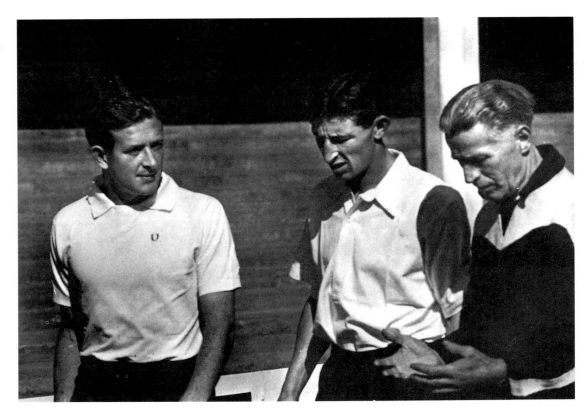

Dreams of a Double ... as 1960 approaches the hopes are real. Manchester United just failed to achieve it by a single game, in 1959–60 Wolves fail by the same margin. Blanchflower believes it will be done, Nicholson is prepared to admit it's possible. In 1959 Blanchflower, new goal-keeper Bill Brown, just signed from Dundee, and trainer Cecil Poynton dis-cuss the club's prospects.

that appeared to have settled on the Tottenham High Road.

In the League, Tottenham now needed a point from Cardiff and their final home match against Sheffield United, who in due course were relegated with Huddersfield, to be safe. But Blanchflower did not take part in the 0–0 draw with Cardiff, the result which meant safety. Manager Anderson gave out that he was injured, Blanchflower, when asked, said that he was fit. Manager and player discussed the captaincy before that last game with the Yorkshire club. Blanchflower said he could not be captain if he wasn't trusted with authority on the field. So the captaincy was taken off him for the game with Sheffield United. Harry Clarke started as captain the following season. Then Marchi, Bobby Smith and John Ryden took turns. But Blanchflower was still in the wings, waiting for his time to come.

Jimmy Anderson did almost every job there was to do at Tottenham in his fifty splendid years with the club. Twice he stepped into the breach when Arthur Rowe was ill, the second time for some three and a half years when he had to see off the rear end of the miserable 1954–55 season, with Spurs taking a moderate 16th place in the table. Despite the captaincy problems, Anderson was actually fitting the pieces well; Harmer and Blanchflower could work together and the pair of them turned in virtually a full complement of League matches

in 1956–57. This in itself was a great tribute to their staying powers, their skills having long been accepted and admired. But here they were, successful too as Spurs recovered and ended the season as runners-up again to Manchester United. Essentially Spurs were still an attacking side, and their century of goals was the first by any club in the First Division for two decades.

And that welcome improvement by the team was maintained sufficiently for Spurs to finish in third place a year later behind Wolves and Preston North End. It was a good return for Anderson in his second term of office (he had been in charge at the end of the War) but it took its toll. As with Rowe, the strain of big-time managership, and the need for the 24 hours-a-day application it brings, laid him low only weeks into 1958–59 when a familiar early season slump had settled in and the Tottenham defence was having one of its most harrassing times anybody could remember. Second and third in the League was hardly a disgrace, but it is also necessary to remember Anderson's good stewardship down the years, the manner in which he fashioned a side to trouble the best in those two previous seasons; besides which there were his shrewd signings... Maurice Norman ... Bobby Smith ... Cliff Jones ... Terry Dyson ... Terry Medwin ... Jim Iley ... John Ryden. Already the best side Spurs, and perhaps the Football League, has ever had was in the making.

1961

Remarkable though Bill Nicholson's managerial career at White Hart Lane was, nothing ever really matched his very first game in charge. At lunch-time on Saturday 11 October 1958, Nicholson was called to the Tottenham boardroom and appointed manager of the club in succession to Jimmy Anderson. In itself, this was no great surprise. He had been coaching the first team for three years and Spurs have ultimately always preferred to promote those they know (Minter, Rowe, Anderson, Burkinshaw to name other obvious examples).

The fixture that afternoon was not an attractive one. Spurs, with only nine points from eleven games, were sixteenth, a point clear of the bottom three. Everton were actually one of that bottom trio. What happened is history, for the game was to produce the biggest aggregate score of any ever played in the First Division – its 14 goals equalling a record set up when Aston Villa beat Accrington 12–2 a mere 66 years before. Spurs got ten of those goals and, as one paper reported: 'Tommy Harmer scored one and made nine.'

It was perhaps the peak of Tommy Harmer's amazing career, yet he had approached it with trepidation: 'All I can remember is feeling miserable that morning. I had been dropped for the previous four games and it was in the balance whether I'd get my place back.' Harmer's goal, Spurs' eighth, was as uncharacteristic as the day: 'The ball just bounced towards me and I hit it first time, on the half-volley, from 20 yards and it flew into the top corner of the net. I hardly ever scored from that range. It was just one of those days when everything goes in.'

A winning Spurs' side in the bath early in 1960. Clockwise from the top: Danny Blanchflower, Cliff Jones, Dave Mackay, Terry Medwin, Bobby Smith, Bill Brown and Mel Hopkins.

RIGHT: Bobby Smith heads home a centre from Alfie Stokes for the third of his four goals against Everton on 11 October 1958. It was Bill Nicholson's first game in charge and Spurs won 10–4, easily a record managerial debut. It also equalled the record aggregate score for any First Division game. Spurs' other goals were scored by Alfie Stokes (2), George Robb, Terry Medwin, John Ryden and Tommy Harmer. As the teams left the pitch Harmer commented to his new manager: 'We don't score 10 every week you know.' Alfie Stokes was a fine goalscoring inside-forward, finding the net 40 times in only 65 League games.

BELOW RIGHT: More mudlarking at White Hart Lane for Bobby Smith, who has just beaten Preston keeper Fred Else to make an easy goal for right-winger Terry Medwin. The game, on 18 January 1958, ended 3–3. Smith finished 1957-58 with 36 goals, equalling the club record in a season of League games. He eventually broke the club aggregate record as well, ending with 176 goals from 271 League appearances. This season was also to be Preston's last as a truly great club – they finished second, eight points ahead of Spurs, but within four years were playing Second Division football and the nostalgic clashes between two sides which had shared the same strip and contested so many dramatic Cup ties were to be no more.

Harmer's last comment probably sums the game up. For Spurs Bobby Smith got four, Alfie Stokes two, George Robb, Terry Medwin, the injured John Ryden and Harmer one each. For Everton Jimmy Harris joined the select band (possibly the only member) of those who have scored a hat-trick and still seen their team lose by six clear goals, and Bobby Collins got the fourth. Everton reserve keeper Albert Dunlop had let in four against a South African touring team in a friendly three days before; in one week he had thus picked the ball out of the net fourteen times. 'We must protect this man from lumbago,' wrote one witty Merseyside journalist on the Monday.

Harmer was nothing if not sanguine: 'We don't score ten every week you know,' he said to Nicholson as the sides left the field. Nicholson, as befitted his slightly pessimistic character, was equally cautious: 'I've been in this game long enough to know you can be in the clouds one minute and down to earth the next.' In this ease, he was quite right. The next Saturday, Spurs did almost as well, winning 4–3 at Leicester, but Nicholson was more interested in his defence's porousness than his attack's magnificence. In his first four games, including these two, they let in 15 goals and, after the Leicester match, won only one of their next 11 League fixtures. The phrase 'false dawn' could almost have been invented for Nicholson's managerial career.

FOOTBALL CORNUCOPIA
Though matters improved, the 1958–59 season was to all intents and purposes a write-off. It was an odd interlude in a period of dramatic success – their League positions went 2nd, 3rd, 18th, 3rd, 1st, 3rd, 2nd between 1956 and 1963, when the great days were to come to an end. Blanchflower and Harmer were dropped in turn, and with both of them out of touch Spurs were a pallid shadow of the side which had, for instance, taken two points away from pre–Munich Manchester United in a 4–3 thriller at Old Trafford, the first time a London club had won there for 19 years. Blanchflower had been a delight that previous season. As well as leading Northern Ireland to a highly improbable quarter–final place in the World Cup finals in Sweden, he had become the first Spurs player to be elected Footballer of the Year (he was to win the award again in 1961 and thus become, with Stanley Matthews, Tom Finney and Gary Lineker a near immortal). It is possible that Blanchflower was playing even better than in the Double year at this time. Julian Holland said of his displays in the 1957–58 season that: 'The football poured out of him in a ceaseless irresistable profusion, as though his genie had been taking lessons from the sorceror's apprentice. He was a footballing cornucopia . . . at this stage in his career he was the unfaltering dynamo tirelessly feeding the striving attack.'

But Blanchflower and Harmer were not the only ones suffering a few months later. Cliff Jones, the wonderful, direct winger from Swansea was finding it difficult to carry the game's most expensive player (£35,000) tag. Like his uncle Bryn, who had moved to Arsenal twenty years before for £14,000, Jones was thoroughly uncomfortable with the expectations this distinction carried. The Spurs crowd was not noted for its generosity to new signings

('I wouldn't say they were impatient' said Terry Venables a decade later, 'they wait till the third game before they give you the bird.') It was almost Jones' good fortune that he collided with Peter Baker in an early season practice match and broke a leg. He returned half–way through the season, when the crowd had forgotten his earlier fumblings, and he was allowed to develop, with Dave Mackay behind him, to become almost the definitive flying, goalscoring winger. Certainly it is hard to think of a better one since the Second World War. And while, strangely, Jones is somehow remembered as a left–winger, he wore the number seven shirt far more often than the eleven and rarely played for long on either wing anyway. Rather he was the most mobile of the prompting second line – starting anywhere and finishing anywhere.

To add to Nicholson's early season problems in 1958–59 Ted Ditchburn's career had been finished with a bad injury and reserve keeper John Hollowbread was in goal. Things were so difficult that Nicholson decided to put Blanchflower in the reserves where, at 33, the Irishman was trying, and failing, to raise any enthusiasm as a late developing inside–right. It was Nicholson's idea that he should try this out while the club tried to find a more defensive right–half for the League team in order to put a few more mines in the ever open pathway to the Tottenham goal area. The transfer request which followed, and Nicholson's solemn declaration that he would have the board turn it down, was in fact the end and the beginning of the matter. Blanchflower decided that he could work with, and for, the new Tottenham manager. There is no record of any real differences between the pair from that day forward. Their respect for each other and their close friendship remained till Blanchflower's death.

It was on 2 March 1959, before a drawn game at Wolverhampton, that Nicholson publicly acknowledged he needed Blanchflower. Spurs had not won one of their last four home matches. With the Irishman restored as captain they crushed Leicester 6–0 at home five days later. It was the turning point. From here onwards the only way was up.

Mel Hopkins was then injured on duty for Wales and this provided a long sought chance for the tidy Ron Henry at left–back. Hopkins had given fine service to Tottenham but soon the Baker–Henry full–back partnership took off and became one of the solid essentials in the Nicholson build–up.

Having squirmed through season 1958–59 the way ahead began to take on a more hopeful hue. Just before Easter Nicholson had set off on the sort of journey which was to become more frequent over the years, the kind of trip about which no–one knew anything but the closing of the door as Nicholson disappeared. This, one of his earliest, was supposed to have ended with him returning with Mel Charles. Instead of Charles, brother of the great John, the Nicholson capture came from over the other border, Dave Mackay from Hearts. At £32,000 he took over Blanchflower's mantle as Britain's most expensive half–back. It was the first of many transfers to be completed by Nicholson while others waited and wondered. Mackay and Blanchflower took to each other from the off. Spurs headed for the sixties with higher hopes than the previous season could substantiate. Eighteenth in the table was far from being the surest way of keeping the customers happy. Even less promising was a defence like a sieve which had 95 goals sunk past it, the worst defensive League offering anybody at White Hart Lane could remember. But Nicholson had begun to ring the changes. After Mackay he bought another Scot, another keeper to make a third along with Ron Reynolds and John Hollowbread, Scottish international Bill Brown of Dundee for £16,000. Tottenham had also bought back the commanding Tony Marchi from Italian football, where for two years he had effectively been on loan to Lanerossi Vicenza and Torino.

Outgoings there had to be to keep a balance and there was a warm, sentimental farewell to the last remaining players of the fabulous push-and-run team . . . Ted Ditchburn, twenty years with Spurs and with a club record of 418 League appearances, who went to Romford . . . gangling Harry Clarke, who left to enter management, and the 'quiet man', Len Duquemin, who left behind him a mark of 135 goals in League and Cup as he joined Bedford Town. These three left indelible memories and hard to follow standards. Other less significant actors were also to leave, Jim Iley to Nottingham Forest, Alfie Stokes to Fulham.

Blanchflower had been among the first to spot the new signs of hope in that past season, but few would have believed that the glory to be won would have much to thank for its lift-off to the playing fields of the USSR. Bill Nicholson himself was ever-grateful for the bond he was able to build in Russia between his players. Of that twelve-day close season tour he said: 'I was glad of the opportunity of getting the players together. I had said that we would go to see what it was like there. "It's a lot different," I had told the boys. There wasn't much chance for entertainment, so we had every day for training. We trained hard and we played three matches. I cannot overstate the value of that trip in terms of getting things together. And we still had a very enjoyable time, very enjoyable.'

Medwin scored the only goal against Moscow Torpedo, Johnny Brooks got two against Kiev (Spurs winning 2–1) and then he also got the only reply as the third game was lost 3–1 against a national squad in Leningrad. The full benefits of that Russian tour and of the understanding built up in advance of the new season came to fruition at the gateway to the sixties as Tottenham were caught up in a League title race with Burnley and the Wolves.

On 3 October 1959, Danny Blanchflower was in the Northern Ireland team which took a 4–0 home beating at Windsor Park, Belfast, from the Scots. In the Scottish side were his Spurs colleagues, Bill Brown and Dave Mackay. There was also a slim, pale youngster from Falkirk named John White, who scored one of those four Scottish goals. Blanchflower remembers his return from that debacle for the Irish and the greeting from Nicholson: 'What did you think about young John White?' Among the hints, the guesses and the crystal-bowl guidelines of the soccer gossip columns he had seen a vague reference connecting the youngster, unknown south of the border, and the Spurs.

When Nicholson filled in the gaps by telling his skipper that he could get White for a bar-

gain £20,000, Blanchflower told him to grab the next plane bound for Scotland. Mackay and Brown backed up the Irishman's high regard for their young countryman so that manager Nicholson was up and away and within the next 24 hours the signing was all but complete. All but, because ex-Scotland keeper Tommy Younger, the old Hibs and Liverpool favourite who was then managing Falkirk, having brought his player down to White Hart Lane to finalise the deal, saw that Nicholson was not happy with progress. He discovered the reason when he took White aside to ask him what was holding up the deal. He got the surprising answer: 'I'm not good enough for here, I'll never fit in with these players.' Younger said that he had never known a worse case of an inferiority complex: 'He had become a luxury for us because he was thinking two and three moves ahead and his passes were not being picked up,' understood the Falkirk manager.

And exactly as if to prey on those early fears of John White came Tottenham's first defeat of that 1959–60 season. It was Tottenham's 13th League match and was also White's debut, at Hillsborough against a powerful Sheffield Wednesday side . . . and Spurs were missing three regulars in Hopkins, Jones and Medwin, all playing for Wales that afternoon. White did manage to score the solitary Tottenham goal in their 2–1 defeat, but did little more. Two months later Nicholson swooped again to add striker Les Allen to his squad as Johnny Brooks crossed to Chelsea in an exchange deal. Allen and Bobby Smith were essentially similar – they were both goalscorers. Both could look clumsy out of the

penalty area, but they were part of a necessary mixture. A team cannot be composed entirely of John Whites. Swiftly, shrewdly, Bill Nicholson had, did we but know it, put together a collection powerful enough to tackle the world. It had taken him just a year and the mixture was now formed. For three months of 1959–60 – from December to March – Spurs led the way at the top of the First Division, their elevation coinciding with Allen's two-goal debut in the 4–2 Boxing Day success at Elland Road. In the return two days later Leeds' United hammered Spurs 4–1 at White Hart Lane; it didn't help the Yorkshiremen to avoid relegation, but it showed that Spurs did not yet have the consistency of a great side.

That was one shock result for Tottenham. Two more at Easter, just as big, ended any

The Double-winning side started the 1960–61 season in amazing style, beating their first eleven opponents. Hull City had set up a record with nine consecutive wins in the Third Division North from the beginning of a season in 1948–49 and Spurs were to surpass this on 24 September 1961 when Aston Villa came to White Hart Lane. 61,356 fans, then the biggest crowd of the season, crammed into the ground to see Spurs not only win their tenth consecutive game 6–2, but also record their highest score of the season. They reached six goals on only one other occasion during the Double year and never surpassed it. Bobby Smith (ABOVE) scored Spurs' second goal despite the efforts of Villa keeper Nigel Sims and centre-half Terry Morrall. The others were scored by Mackay, White (2), Allen and Dyson (in the background).

title hopes. Spurs had three Easter fixtures, then two more to complete their programme. But just as their own 3–1 win at Molineux was to rob Wolves of an historic League and Cup Double in the last but one match of the season, so did two unaccountable home beatings in 48 hours – 0–1 to Manchester City on Easter Saturday, and another 0–1 to Chelsea on Easter Monday – end any Tottenham title chance.

Tottenham lost the Championship by just two points, and they should have had them both against Manchester City. Cliff Jones' penalty, at the end of the first half, was well saved by goalkeeper Bert Trautmann but the Welshman, following up, tapped home the rebound. Unfortunately for Spurs, the referee had added time on for the penalty to be taken and the goal did not stand. Had it done so, they might have approached the second half differently and not conceded City's vital single goal. That being said, no team which loses its last two home matches deserves to win anything very much.

WOLVES AND THE DOUBLE

The Championship is always a matter of ifs and buts, never more so than in 1960 when Burnley's success was unquestionably unique. The Lancastrians never led the League until after their, and the Division's, final game, which they won at Maine Road. Burnley had actually lost 6–1 at Molineux only weeks before and, with just three weeks left, were little more than hopeful outsiders behind Spurs and Wolves. Wolves themselves had thrown away a

Championship which seemed to be theirs for the taking when Spurs came to Molineux on Saturday 23 April 1960. This was one of the truly critical games of Spurs' great years ranking alongside the Cup ties against Aston Villa and Sunderland, the European Cup semi-final with Benfica and the last gasp of the era, the European Cup Winners Cup final against Atletico.

Wolves were not only running strongly for the Double (and odds-on with the bookmakers to become the first team this century to achieve it) but were also on the verge of equalling Huddersfield's and Arsenal's record of a hat-trick of Championships. But even on the edge of such an achievement, it was clear to some that Molineux's great days were at an end – Wright, Swinbourne, Hancocks, Mullen and Wilshaw had all gone. Stan Cullis's long ball game remained, but the replacements were not as good as their predecessors. That being said, Wolves were now four points clear of Burnley and three clear of Spurs. If they beat Tottenham they had only Chelsea to overcome and the Championship was theirs. If Burnley did not get maximum points, then just beating Spurs would be enough. It did not seem too great a task for a team that was to walk over Blackburn Rovers in the Cup final two weeks later – particularly as opponents Spurs had lost their last two games, both at home.

But this was to be one of those moments when an observer can actually sense history turning. Spurs were relaxed, their chances of winning the League virtually gone. Blanchflower held his team talk in the middle of the pitch rather than in the dressing-room and, within two minutes, had created the first goal. Feinting to put Cliff Jones away on the right, he changed direction and centred for Bobby Smith. The centre-forward did the rest while the Wolves defence still covered the threat from Jones. Broadbent equalised but Mackay, with a rare header, put Spurs back in front. Their third, and final, goal was a classic: Terry Dyson flying down the left wing, a perfect cross and there was Jones with a full-length header.

Wolves did beat Chelsea at Stamford Bridge, 5–1, but Burnley pipped them anyway and the hat-trick and the Double had both gone. Wolves had been as baffled by Barcelona in the European Cup as they had by Spurs (who had also beaten them 5–1 at White Hart Lane). It was a decisive end to Wolves' great era. They have not won the League or Cup since.

Though everyone had hoped for better, third place behind champions Burnley and Wolves was still a boost for Bill Nicholson and Spurs. The rise from eighteenth in the table to third place a season later was improvement indeed. So was the performance of the defence, which had 45 fewer goals rattled past it this time. There was also proof that Tottenham were giving the fans what they wanted – they were the best supported home side in the country with an average of 47,948, a total only seriously challenged by Manchester United. It was also the season which brought the club's record victory . . . the 13–2 swamping of little Crewe Alexandra in an FA Cup fourth round replay in February 1960. Mighty Spurs had stuttered

and spluttered at Gresty Road. Blanchflower said that the Crewe supporters worked themselves up to a belief that they could provide a Cup shock and Spurs played so cautiously as to fumble over scraping a 2–2 draw in the first meeting. Only a shot which bounced back off a post saved Spurs from their fourth humiliation in six years – Third Division York, Bournemouth and Norwich already being in the record books.

The outcome of the Tottenham visit was a record 20,000 home gate for Fourth Division Alexandra, the reward for making Spurs play it again at White Hart Lane on the following Wednesday a massive 64,365 gate to share. But that and a rare look round the capital were all poor Crewe were allowed as Spurs turned cold killers under the arc lights to pile up the agony of a 10–1 half-time lead. Only a second-half easing down spared further torture for Crewe and unfortunate keeper David Evans, who had picked the ball out of his net 15 times (his only concession from fortune being two scores which were ruled out). Les Allen got five, Bobby Smith four, Cliff Jones three and Tommy Harmer the other goal. The story, perhaps apocryphal, is still told of how Crewe arrived on platform 2 at Euston and went home from platform 13. Poor Evans; he afterwards admitted to fearing seven or eight home efforts going past him, but 13! 'I don't know WHERE those other five goals came from,' he said, 'and I didn't feel too good about it.' But that was the end for Tottenham too, and on an off day in the next round Blackburn Rovers took away a 3–1 victory at the Lane.

ABOVE: A flying Bill Brown fails to connect with a Blackburn centre at Ewood Park on 27 August 1960. While Maurice Norman, now restored to his rightful centre-half spot, heads away, captain Danny Blanchflower appears to look on amused. Spurs won the game easily 4–1.

DREAMS OF A DOUBLE

Blanchflower, looking back, remembered how the team's new-found power began to give him ideas, how the all-round strength of the squad had increased, the force of 5–1 victories gained against Newcastle United at St James' Park, at Old Trafford when meeting Manchester United and of similar home wins over Preston and Wolves . . . days when everyone and everything moved in harmony. He could see only the Double, the Double which both Manchester United and Wolves had missed so narrowly in the past four seasons.

The 'impossible' Double was a far more common topic of football conversation then than it had been, say, thirty years before or was twenty years later. That was largely because both Manchester United and Wolves had come so close to achieving it within the space of three years. Both had failed by a single match – United in a Cup final they couldn't possibly lose, Wolves by conceding a home game to a side which had just lost two consecutive home matches. These amazingly close-run attempts had apparently proved one of two things to soccer journalists – that the Double certainly was possible or, alternatively, that it obviously wasn't. The latter school of thought quoted the psychology of the four-minute mile; that the mental barriers became so great in the home stretch that few athletes could break through them. But, up in North London, sat football's own squad of Roger Bannisters.

Joe Mercer recalled coming back from Sweden after the World Cup in 1958. On the plane, said Joe, Blanchflower could talk of little else to himself and Stan Cullis. It went on in the taxi from Heathrow. 'He told us over and over again that it was going to be done. "And we'll be the ones to do it," he had promised.' The Spurs captain repeated the vow when the elderly club chairman, Mr Fred Bearman, asked him what 1960–61 might bring for Tottenham. 'We'll get the Double for you this time . . . the League and the Cup,' came the confident answer. In fact Blanchflower had originally been confident about the Double before 1959–60. Looking back he said: 'We could have done it then, but we hadn't been there before, hadn't had the experience. The following season we were able to pace ourselves better.'

'That third in the League table was a boost,' said Bill Nicholson. 'We were getting it together, getting the team working and playing for one another and getting to know each other. Ron Henry for Mel Hopkins at left-back was an important change. Then Terry Dyson came in for Terry Medwin. I felt that we would have a good shout in the League, but in the Cup . . . well, who knows about the Cup? One afternoon on a strange pitch, an awkward ground, one or two little things going the opposite way and bingo! You're gone. It's different again, the Cup.'

Then, very firmly, he added: 'Anyway, I never did make predictions, it wasn't my job to. And it's not a thing I'd lend myself to, the game is so fickle. If Danny liked to say it . . . well, that was Danny. He should have known by then that teams often win games they don't deserve to win.'

Nicholson took a deep breath after this, as if trying to summon memories, those magical moments from perhaps the greatest single season in any English club's history, to feel for an echo of a sustained season of soccer classics and maintained at a pitch of performance no year had ever previously seen. Smooth, soft skills . . . perfect patterns . . . tenacity of purpose laced with hard discipline . . . still with a stylish swing to refresh their every game. And all the threads painstakingly pulled together by the stolid Nicholson, dependable as man and player, who had always performed within his own honest limitations, few as they were, forever pursuing excellence in his teams.

'I tried to keep our football as simple as possible,' he recalled. 'We had good players but I didn't want them to indulge themselves too much as individuals. "We've got to be effective, not exhibition players" I used to tell them. "You've got to involve other players like the 1950 side." You are always preaching involvement but the situations come on the field and the player has to do it himself. The good player will always know what it is best to do.

'In the 1950 side we played the short game. If you kick the ball any length there's a good chance the other side will intercept, and naturally you cannot be so accurate. It was so different from the long game favoured by the Wolves who lashed the ball from side to side and reckoned that long stuff to forwards, if not getting on the mark, did enough to unsettle defenders. Then they always had players coming through quickly, either to close down rivals or ready to snap up any half chances their assaults might have given them to feed on.

'In the 1960 side we had the skill to play balls first time, like the Rowe side did, but also the skill to play the longer game.' It is a theme he no doubt developed on many occasions, with him loyally insisting on including a salute for his old comrades in arms. 'Harry Evans, once the Aldershot manager, joined me as my assistant. He took a lot of work off to leave me free for the real job of preparing a team.' Unhappily, the popular Harry was to die in harness after a brief stay with the club, sorely missed by Nicholson.

GLORY, GLORY, HALLELUJAH

'I felt in 1960 that I had a side well prepared to do something. You cannot put it into words, it's a feeling you get. And I had this strong feeling around that time.' The result was that: Spurs became the first club to take the League and Cup Double this century; their 66 points total equalled the First Division record set up by Arsenal in 1930–31; their 33 away points also equalled Arsenal's of the same season; eleven consecutive victories from the start of the season bettered the record of Hull City, with their nine opening successes in 1948–49; the total of 31 winning matches was a First Division record, as was the 16 victorious away matches; Spurs achieved 11 doubles over their League rivals, which equalled the First Division performances of Manchester United (1956-57) and Wolves (1958-59); they attained 50 points in 29 games, faster than any club previously; and their 115 goals was a club scoring record for a season.

Statistics are a mundane wrap-around for a glorious season played out to the challenging background of 'Glory, Glory, Hallelujah', but they help us take in the picture more readily. Like the 31 points from the first 32 when only Manchester City's 1–1 draw at the Lane in October had temporarily stubbed a toe before sturdy Sheffield Wednesday ended that unbeaten run at Hillsborough on 12 November.

Spurs had opened up a seven-point lead over Wednesday, their nearest challengers, but the eight previous clubs that had journeyed to Hillsborough had not taken a single point away. Fittingly it was a giant of a match, tough, mean, abrasive with the 56,363 crowd stoking up a furnace-like atmosphere. Wednesday were nothing if not a defensive side. The strapping Peter Swan blocked the goal-path to Bobby Smith, who earlier in the season had hat-tricked his way against Blackpool into being Tottenham's best-ever goalscorer with 141 goals in his five years since joining from Chelsea. Alongside Swan, and soon to suffer with him in a bribery scandal, was red-headed firebrand Tony Kay. With burly Don Megson behind it was mainly these three who turned the tide against Spurs and their unbeaten record.

Billy Griffin's goal near half-time stilled the Tottenham roars. Maurice Norman set them off again when he equalised from a quickly taken Dave Mackay free-kick. But, with some 20 minutes to go, Megson attacked and crossed down the left for John Fantham to get the home winner. So Spurs had fallen at the 17th hurdle, after taking a record 31 points from the first 32. If anything, they were pleased. The tension of waiting for the inevitable defeat had been massive. It was a surprisingly cheerful team coach which left Hillsborough that evening, some of the players singing on the way to Sheffield Midland station. Long before this defeat they had earned a glowing tribute from that stern taskmaster Stan Cullis, manager of Wolves, after Spurs had buried them again, this time 4–0 on their own Molineux turf. 'They are the finest club side I've ever seen in the Football League – even better than the great Spurs of ten years ago.'

Three weeks later came the unforgettable meeting with Burnley, the reigning champions, an epic 4–4 clash which first established Tottenham as true heirs-apparent to the League throne and then fully proved that the crown

OPPOSITE TOP: Preston
keeper Fred Else gathers a
cross safely despite the
attentions of Bobby Smith.
Looking on are Preston
centre-half Joe Dunn and a
hungry Cliff Jones. This
game, on 19 September
1959, finished 5–1 in
Spurs' favour with Jones
getting two of the goals.
OPPOSITE BOTTOM: For
the following season's fixture at White Hart Lane, on
1 April 1961, Preston
changed their goalkeeper
but Eire international Alan
Kelly could do no better
than Else and Spurs scored
five again, this time without reply. Cliff Jones also
went one better, the flying
winger getting a hat-trick.
Julian Holland, in his book
SPURS — THE DOUBLE,
said of Jones: 'More than
anyone else, he made
Blanchflower's old age
comfortable,' refering to
Jones' tremendous speed
and willngness to run for
Blanchflower's long passes.

had been worn well, and not uneasily, by the Lancastrians.

Tottenham halted any early Burnley aggression on a miserable, rainy December afternoon, then struck three times in three minutes, first through Norman then with two breakaway efforts by Jones. And when Mackay came up with a fourth goal inside 40 minutes it was as certain as anything could be that Burnley were to be added to the list of Tottenham scalps. Even Bill Nicholson himself admits that he could not imagine soccer turning so fickle. But, before the interval, winger John Connelly strode through the home defence to pull one back and battle recommenced with Burnley drawing on pride and pedigree to push Blanchflower and company completely out of their stride. Next, Jimmy Robson, then the blond Ray Pointer, nipped in for Burnley goals and the noise was truly deafening when, with only a dozen minutes left, the elusive Connelly was again haring up the middle to present the crowd with an incredible draw. Few could quite remember the like of this remarkable match, or such a turnabout result. It was more a lesson for the prospective champions than the resilient title-holders but Bill Nicholson proved typically phlegmatic with his defence: 'We scored eight goals and still only drew,' he commented in the dressing-room.

Half way to the title finish there was no longer a bookmaker who would accept money on Tottenham. It was a one-horse race. The point and poise of the side was the Blanchflower-White axis, the wry, pale Scot having taken over Harmer's role ('Scottish waif for Cockney wisp' wrote one journalist) to add a more urgent, broader sweep to a side now better able to vary pace and power. Mackay, who seemed to play with a skirl of bagpipes in his game, was the ideal blend of flinty, foraging pirateer opposite his skipper, and the so brave Jones with his jet speed was a scimitar aimed at the heart of any defence. And now Smith and Allen were proving Nicholson's point, that with all the style in the world it was still goals which won matches in the end.

Little Dyson, small enough to be the son of his father, a leading northern jockey, had wrested the other wing place from Medwin with a bit more dash and unorthodoxy, while the defence had now bedded solidly down from keeper Brown and outwards to Baker and Henry, with Norman commanding in the air if occasionally reluctant to tackle on the ground. For the first three seasons after he had moved from Norwich, Maurice Norman had played at full-back, somewhat uneasily for much of the time. He was now in his prefered position in a defence which was, unlike the middle and front lines, built on extremely conventional principles.

In the 1960–61 season's first half they scored 21 more goals and gained 10 more points than they did in the second half. And they won five more games. The point is made for interest, not contention. By kinder weather alone the going should be more favourable, played mostly as it is in the autumn. But in any case, those who had been trying to pick the flaws in Tottenham's runaway leadership had seen ample evidence presented to them that the heavier going would not – and did not – really clog up the Tottenham works. But the fact was that they lost two of their first three League

games in the New Year, 0–2 at Old Trafford against Manchester United, then a 2–3 beating by Leicester City at White Hart Lane. They also finished their greatest ever season with another wobble, beaten 2–4 at Burnley and then by West Bromwich back at the Lane in two of their last three League matches. The West Brom game, played before 51,880 people on 29 April, was a particular disappointment. One more point would have broken Arsenal's First Division record. Instead, Spurs lost 2–1. But they were still masters enough of the First Division to bridge a ten-year gap in the club's history and reclaim the Football League Championship trophy for the Tottenham sideboard as they finished eight points ahead of Sheffield Wednesday and nine in front of Wolves. Appropriately the trophy was won by beating Wednesday.

It was against the Wednesday on 17 April that Spurs avenged their first defeat of the season with the same 2–1 scoreline, this time in their favour. But, as last time, it was no match for the faint-hearted and skill came second to all-out, full-blooded effort which had the smile freezing on the face of 'Smiler' Tommy Dawes, the Norwich referee. He booked both Mackay and Wednesday's Peter Johnson and Spurs fans were to suffer a slight case of shock when Megson, villain of the piece at Hillsborough, smashed home a first half free-kick to give his side the lead. The evening was one of roaring sound as 62,000 bayed for blood and goals; they had come to see Spurs win the Championship, not to appreciate a great football match. The home crowd, silenced momentarily, then set up even greater roars for Spurs to hit back. They did so almost immediately . . . twice. First Bobby Smith flipped the ball over England's Swan and slammed it home on the half-volley. And they were still acclaiming that goal when Blanchflower's free-kick was headed sideways by the lurking Norman and Allen thumped in a terrific, shoulder high volley. The match got even hotter in the second half; Smith charged Wednesday keeper Ron Springett into a post and the keeper was carried off, only to insist on returning within minutes. Some nail-biting moments for Tottenham's hopes ended with the crowd pouring onto the pitch at the final whistle and sheer pandemonium until skipper Blanchflower led out his players to take the crowd's thanks and appreciation.

'DANNY, DANNY'

The crowd had little doubt where the credit lay, calling specifically for 'Danny, Danny' to come out and take the victory salute. 'Footballer of the Year' for the second time in four years, the judgement of the fans was surely correct, though it is difficult to pin down exactly how Blanchflower made it all work. He was part of the team, but, probably uniquely, not of it; essentially he was the deputy manager. And while many managers would not (and did not) tolerate Blanchflower's insistence on having his own way, Bill Nicholson had the sense and the confidence to harness it rather than fight it. It was probably the best intuition Nicholson ever had. Blanchflower assessed his own contribution in relatively few words: 'I could change the rhythm, change the pace, slow it down if necessary, speed it up when we needed to. I also had the ball much more often than anyone else – so I should have done something with it shouldn't I? And I was a lot older than the rest – 34. I had learned how to play by then, and, at Villa, how not to play.

'Most of all I could read the team as players and as men. I think I knew how to bring out the best. I would never, for instance, direct Maurice Norman openly on the field – I'd ask Peter Baker or Ron Henry to talk to him. But with Dave Mackay you never had to worry about confidence or ego. I remember Terry Medwin getting injured once, being unhappy about staying on. Dave and I suggested Terry go out to the right-wing, where we used to put people who'd been in the wars, for a few minutes till he recovered. Five minutes later he came haring back: "Did you say go on the right-wing? I was on the right-wing!" I think I knew the team.'

Blanchflower had long since ceased to be a mere footballing figure and was a publicly feted 'personality'. His television advertisements for a breakfast cereal led to an Irish accented 'Hullo there' becoming a public catch phrase alongside such gems as Bruce Forsyth's 'I'm in charge'. His refusal to appear on *This is Your Life* (the programme's first such embarrassment) was front page news. 'I did it for personal reasons,' he said afterwards. 'If I told you what they were they wouldn't be personal any more would they?' Blanchflower, like many footballers, has remained unimpressed by television, questioning the apparent assumption that man's

BELOW: *Perhaps the single most worrying moment during the Double season, McPheat's shot flashes into the net for Sunderland to make it 1–1 in the FA Cup quarter-final. Playing at Roker on 25 February 1961, Spurs had taken an early lead through Cliff Jones but Sunderland eventually scored after four corner kicks in a row. The crowd invaded the pitch (BOTTOM) and this helped the players calm down. Blanchflower, seen about to pick the ball out of the net with Maurice Norman, told the referee: 'Let the fans work it off, we don't mind.' Spurs won the replay 5–0. Nicholson's greatest fear was just this sort of Cup upset: 'Who knows with the Cup? One afternoon on a strange pitch, an awkward ground, one or two things go the opposite way and bingo. You're out.'*

primary goal in life should be to appear on the small screen. His later career with such programmes as *Sportsview* was short-lived and not marked by outstanding displays of harmony with producers and directors who would not allow him the same creative freedom he enjoyed on the Tottenham pitch.

Bill Nicholson, the other half of this on-field/off-field relationship was blunter: 'In a poor side Danny was a luxury. That's why I dropped him. But in a good side his creativity, his unorthodox approach, was priceless – a wonderful asset.' Together they thought about the game and moulded that great side, the one that won the Double.

Nor did the Tottenham triumphs, or Tottenham-connected triumphs, end at that in 1961. With the FA Cup final still to come there was ex-Spur Alf Ramsey guiding his Ipswich Town side into the First Division for the first time in the club's history, plus Nicholson and Ramsey's mentor Arthur Rowe, thankfully back at work again, managing Crystal Palace from the Fourth to Third Division. And, not to be left out of the celebrations, the Spurs reserves were runners-up to Chelsea in the Football Combination and the third team romped away with the Eastern Counties League.

In achieving their League triumph, Tottenham spread their fire-power right across their attack; all five forwards were into double figures even before the halfway stage, proof that the canny Nicholson had the front blend about right. It pleased him that he was carrying on a Tottenham tradition in doing so.

'Supple and imaginative, that's how the game has always been played at Spurs. Or how they have always tried to play it over my years here. It's the man without the ball who is the most important. I can remember an old school-master who tried to show me the way. His words stuck and they always apply: "When not in possession get into position." I never forgot that phrase. You should never be just watching. I used to say when any of my players erred in this way, "If I catch you doing that again I'll charge you admission. If you want to watch, then you should pay".'

THE OTHER HALF

There was motivation enough for the Cup, the other leg of the impossible. They had eased the load by piling up the League points until that title was virtually assured well before the season was completed. From the New Year on the Cup trail opened up, with Second Division Charlton pressing Spurs, on an off day, far too close for comfort before going down 3–2 in the third round at White Hart Lane. Crewe Alexandra travelled down again in sheer terror for a fourth round set-to, and, although escaping the 13–2 annihilation of their previous visit, were not exactly flattered at 5–1.

A trip to their Cup bogey ground of Villa Park was the reward in February's fifth round draw. But the fixture list provided first a full dress rehearsal for that match in the shape of a League meeting between the clubs the previous Saturday. Spurs were happy enough with their League returns from Villa Park games (where they had not lost since Blanchflower moved down), distinctly not so when it came to the Cup, where they had, of course, been beaten in the semi-finals of 1948, 1953 and 1956.

The League match suffered from a lot of sparring and weighing-up by both teams trying to learn something for the more glamorous Cup tie ahead, and although there was effort enough there was not much more. Even so, Spurs made history by a 2–1 victory which took them to the fastest 50 points yet achieved. It was the barrel-chested Mackay who took the chief honours a week later in the Cup as Aston Villa went down again, this time 2–0, before an enormous 69,000 crowd. The goals, both from Cliff Jones and one in each half, were first a somewhat fortunate deflection off full-back John Neal, later Middlesbrough and Chelsea manager, the other an unstoppable drive to round off a smooth five-men Tottenham move. Julian Holland said of the astonishingly fast, direct Jones: 'More than any other player, it was he who made Blanchflower's old age comfortable.' No longer burdened by the most expensive footballer tag, Jones was now doing just what he had been bought for.

It was another Jones goal which held Sunderland to a 1–1 draw at Roker Park in the sixth round. Sunderland jolted Spurs out of their elegant stride in a rugged second half fight-back but later, with a packed 64,797 looking on at the White Hart Lane replay, the

Wearsiders were right up against it as five home goals poured past them without reply. And for conclusive proof that the Villa Park pitch held no more Cup terrors for them, Tottenham stilled a gusty, swirling wind sufficiently long enough to tame Jimmy McIlroy and the rest of the renowned Burnley team into a 3–0 submission in the semi-final. McIlroy and Blanchflower were close friends and shared the scheming role for Northern Ireland. The Burnley star was not, however, always entirely overwhelmed by his colleague's charms: 'People ask me why I often don't play as well for Ireland as I do for Burnley. It's simple – Danny always keeps me up all night talking.' Bobby Smith's two goals and a late one from Jones were the passport to a Wembley meeting with Leicester City in the final. The semi would have made a better final, and for Burnley the match was poorly timed, being just three days after their 4–1 European Cup defeat by Hamburg.

Unfortunately the final itself, on 6 May, was spoiled as a spectacle, or the spectacle it should be, by the injury to City's right-back Len Chalmers. He was hurt in a tackle by Les Allen in the 19th minute, a hard tackle but nothing more than a clumsy one, as Chalmers himself was quick to point out later. There are those who believe that in those early minutes, and with Chalmers still in action, Leicester looked the better bet as Cup winners; that Spurs did little justice to themselves as the heralded Team of the Century until the last twenty minutes of the match, and that was when tiredness had taken toll of a City side which battled helplessly against the odds of having Chalmers,

when he returned to the fray, limping bravely but ineffectively along the left wing.

Leicester could only hope to keep some self respect from the result. They did this by holding out until Smith, with a dummy, feint and cracking 67th minute shot which rocketed past young keeper Gordon Banks, and ten minutes later little Dyson, with a deliberately placed header from a precise Smith cross, enabled skipper Blanchflower to lead the way up to the Royal Box to redeem the pledge which he had made to his chairman at the start of the season – the League and the Cup. Forty-eight hours before he had received his second 'Footballer of the Year' award. It was a time for silverware.

Though it had to be whispered at the time, many found the final something of a disappointment. Everyone, except a few unfortunates from the Midlands, had wanted to see Spurs win, and win in style. At White Hart Lane, however, they remembered what had happened to Manchester United just four years before, when they were even hotter favourites for the Double. Certainly Leicester's chances in 1961 looked better than had Villa's in 1957, even if City had taken three appallingly poor games (0–0, 0–0, 2–0) to get past Sheffield United in the semi-finals.

For Spurs it had been a season of Cup finals; every side was desperate to beat them and the opposition raised its game time after time. This is why Blanchflower's ability to change the pace was so important – to slow everything down, absorb pressure, consolidate any gains they had made. In the 1970s, particularly with European teams away from home, such tactics became commonplace; in 1960

Before the great days began. From left to right: Peter Baker, Bill Brown, Dave Dunmore, Danny Blanchflower and a preoccupied Tommy Harmer, apparently concerned about his toes. Full-backs Peter Baker and Ron Henry were actually the only locally born members of the Double-winning team. At the beginning of the 1960–61 season Blanchflower had told chairman Fred Bearman that he thought the side could do the Double. 'In our last League match of the previous season at Wolverhampton we had been clearly better than the best of the competition, and this was the basis of my confidence,' Blanchflower was to say years later.

they were never really understood. Spurs approached the Cup final in 1961 in a more conservative frame of mind than for any other game they had played all season. It was, for instance, the only match during which Maurice Norman did not go up for corner-kicks. Certainly it is possible that Chalmers' injury was critical, Spurs only taking control in the last half hour when Leicester had been worn down by the combined burdens of knowing that, unlike most underdogs, they would not be popular winners, the understandable apprehension about their opponents, and, much the most relevant, playing with a man short.

Blanchflower felt the anticlimax as much as anyone in the stadium and made a more general point: 'I did not feel the same emotion before or after as I had with previous rounds. There were too many people there who did not care about the result and, at the end, I didn't have much heart for running around the stadium. I looked upon it as a duty rather than an enjoyment. For the player the reality of a Cup final can never live up to the dream, the promised land, anyway. The dreams are for the fan, not the player, for the lover of the game who will never know what it is like out there. Cup final day is the fans' day.'

Nicholson also mentioned disappointment before glories. 'Looking back now the Double was fabulous,' he said reflectively, 'but there was also disappointment for me when we did not put our Double feat right out of anybody's reach – remember that Arsenal caught up with us ten years later – by doing it for a second year in succession. Which we should have done.'

The key to this regret was his old colleague Alf Ramsey and one game in 1962.

IPSWICH AND RAMSEY

Nicholson explained: 'We were due to play Ipswich and in our team chat before the match I was keen that we should change marking tactics and have our wing-halves mark their wingers instead of the full-backs doing the job. This was because they had wily Jimmy Leadbetter pulling the strings back from deep and I believed that if our half-backs could do a smother-job it would enable us to raid forward while, we hoped, Blanchflower and Mackay throttled them before they could set up anything.

'But there was a disagreement about playing it that way and I conceded the point because I did not want them trying to play a tactical plan they were unhappy about. They beat us home and away, 3–1 on our own pitch. If we had beaten them 3–1 at White Hart Lane we would have done the Double again; it is just as simple as that. It was all a question of tactics.

'But the sequel is interesting . . . as Ipswich won the League title and we again won the Cup, we had to meet for the Charity Shield at the start of the new season, 1962–63. Alf Ramsey won the toss for the game to be played at Portman Road. There was no nonsense this time. I put my foot down and told them very firmly that we would play this one my way. Which we did and we beat them by 5–1.'

The tactics of these two clashes are worth a diversion, for they highlight the astuteness of Nicholson, the reasons why Alf Ramsey was able to win a World Cup and, more pertinently, the relative tactical illiteracy of most English managers at the time. Ipswich, newly promoted, had a mediocre squad at best. It is not too much of an exaggeration to say that Alf Ramsey won the Championship with just two strengths; one was the fact that hardly anyone in the division had met the Ipswich team before, the other was the use of slightly built Jimmy Leadbetter as a

withdrawn left-winger. Instead of pushing Leadbetter to the goal-line, Ramsey had him use the ball in a variety of ways, often slotting it diagonally into the penalty area from up to 50 yards out from goal. The opposing full-back, conventionally believing that the number 11 was nowhere near the danger-area, generally held off. But Leadbetter was a remarkably accurate kicker of the ball and his target was almost invariably the battering ram of a dual spearhead – Ray Crawford and Ted Phillips. Neither was at all subtle, but attacking the centre-half together (this was before the days of twin centre-backs and, remember, the full-backs had stayed wide) they were remarkably effective. Phillips scored 28 goals in his only First Division season of note (the next two years his tally dropped to 9 and then 4), Crawford 33. And no one really found them out until Nicholson revealed the simplicity of the tactic in that Charity Shield match. He brought the Spurs full-backs infield to outnumber Crawford and Phillips, and had the half-backs mark Leadbetter out of the game. Spurs won 5–1.

FIRST DIVISION 1960–61												
	P	W	D	L	F	A	W	D	L	F	A	PTS
Tottenham	42	15	3	3	65	28	16	1	4	50	27	66
Sheff Wed	42	15	4	2	45	17	8	8	5	33	30	58
Wolves	42	17	2	2	61	32	8	5	8	42	43	57
Burnley	42	11	4	6	58	40	11	3	7	44	37	51
Everton	42	13	4	4	47	23	9	2	10	40	46	50
Leicester	42	12	4	5	54	31	6	5	10	33	39	45
Man Utd	42	14	5	2	58	20	4	4	13	30	56	45
Blackburn	42	12	3	6	48	34	3	10	8	29	42	43
Aston Villa	42	13	3	5	48	28	4	6	11	30	49	43
WBA	42	10	3	8	43	32	8	2	11	24	39	41
Arsenal	42	12	3	6	44	35	3	8	10	33	50	41
Chelsea	42	10	5	6	61	48	5	2	14	37	52	37
Man City	42	10	5	6	41	30	3	6	12	38	60	37
Nottm F.	42	8	7	6	34	33	6	2	13	28	45	37
Cardiff C.	42	11	5	5	34	26	2	6	13	26	59	37
West Ham	42	12	4	5	53	31	1	6	14	24	57	36
Fulham	42	8	8	5	39	39	6	0	15	33	56	36
Bolton	42	9	5	7	38	29	3	6	12	20	44	35
Birmingham	42	10	4	7	35	31	4	2	15	27	53	34
Blackpool	42	9	3	9	44	34	3	6	12	24	39	33
Newcastle	42	7	7	7	51	49	4	3	14	35	60	32
Preston	42	7	6	8	28	25	3	4	14	15	46	30

OPPOSITE PAGE: The letter that changed, and made, Tottenham's history. Written by chief scout Ben Ives on 29 February 1936 it invited Bill Nicholson's parents to send their son down to White Hart Lane for a month's trial. While Ives mentions having had a chat with Nicholson, the future manager has no recollection of the meeting. The Mr Jones mentioned was the organiser of Nicholson's local team. The letter came as a complete surprise to the Nicholsons. 'My parents had never seen me play; they knew I was keen but had no idea whether I was any good or not. We weren't even exactly sure where Tottenham was,' says Nicholson. The letter goes on to reassure the 16-year-old's parents that. 'You need not fear about him as at present we have about 20 boys his age and we get them good lodgings with personal friends of mine . . . Mr Jones will put him on the night train at York and I shall meet him at Kings X, or should Mr Nicholson like to bring him down himself he would be welcome. The boy seems to be very bright and I am sure he will get on (here) and in any case I trust you realise that he must have a far greater chance of making headway in London than elsewhere.' Nicholson came and, 25 years later, so did the trophies. In the space of three years there were to be four of them.

LEFT TOP: Ron Henry and Peter Baker hold the Championship trophy and FA Cup respectively as the Double winners parade up the High Road.

LEFT BOTTOM: A year later the FA Cup, in the capable hands of Maurice Norman and Danny Blanchflower, takes the same route after Spurs had become only the fourth club in history to retain the trophy. They missed another Double by one game – when Ipswich beat them at home.

BOTTOM CENTRE: There'll be another bus along next year . . . this time carrying the Cup Winners Cup. Though the crowds couldn't know it, an era was at an end.

It was a vindication of manager Nicholson's tactical know-how and one could understand the disappointment of a man who had always aimed to be a winner. But it might also have been true to say that Tottenham took their eye off the ball over the last few laps of the League race. Five crucial home points were dropped in the last six matches to be played at White Hart Lane and that was definitely not championship form. Amazingly West Brom yet again beat them in the season's last home match – and again the score was 2–1. It was all too late when, faced with the most difficult ending possible to their programme, they rattled-off three away victories at Blackburn, Birmingham and Leicester. That only underlined what might have been. Ipswich and Burnley slugged it out in the final matches, both dropping points all over the place, but Ramsey clinched the title at the end with a convincing 6–2 win over the Lancastrians.

Almost as an afterthought, Spurs did win the Cup again – only the fourth club (after Wanderers, Blackburn Rovers and Newcastle United) ever to do so in consecutive years. The draw was not an easy one for them but they handled it in style. In the third round they drew 3–3 at St Andrew's and won the replay 4–2. The fourth round saw a 5–1 walkover at Plymouth, the fifth 4–2 at The Hawthorns. Spurs' only home draw was in the quarter-finals, when they beat Villa 2–0. Hillsborough, a favourite semi-final ground for the club (they were to win there in 1967 and 1981), was the venue for the penultimate round, and a relatively easy 3–1 defeat of Manchester United. It was a quiet campaign. Fans and Press were diverted by the drama of the European Cup and the intrigue of pursuing incomprehensible Ipswich in the League.

The final was a much better game than the previous year's, and brought together the best two teams of the period. Burnley, without an FA Cup win since 1914, were probably slightly favoured. Like Burnley when the clubs met in the previous season's semi-final, Spurs had just been knocked out of the European Cup (but by the odd goal only), and the general assessment was that Spurs were past their peak and coming downhill. The pundits were wrong. Jimmy Greaves, a member of the team for six months now, scored an early goal. Robson pulled one back but Smith scored an excellent second and Blanchflower made it safe at 3–1 with a late penalty, only the fourth ever given, and converted, in a Wembley final.

But, as in 1961, there was just a slight sense of anticlimax. Not because of the game, which was a good one this time, but because this wasn't really the Cup players and fans had

wanted to win. The 1962 FA Cup often appears as little more than a footnote to the Double because the real prize, the one that was never won, was the European Cup.

AND SO TO EUROPE

No British club has ever entered the European Cup with more confidence than did Spurs on 13 September 1961 against Gornik Zabrze of Poland. At no time were the supporters of Liverpool, Manchester United or Nottingham Forest ever as sure that this was their year as were the Spurs fans of 1961. This was not only because of the unquestioned excellence of their team, but also because the competition was, at last, wide open. Read Madrid had been beaten, by Barcelona, for the very first time the previous season. Benfica were the new champions – a good side to be sure, but surely not one to live with Spurs?

It was Tottenham's first trip to Europe, and their inexperience showed. Bill Nicholson told of his advance trip to Poland to have a look at the training facilities and hotels: 'They took me to this terrible place, and told me this is where we would be staying. I told them they would stay at the best hotel in England when they came to us, so I wanted Spurs to stay at the best hotel in Katowice (Gornik's home). They said this was the best hotel in Katowice. So we tried nearby Chorzow, but there were no decent hotels at all there, and Warsaw was hours away.' Spurs were one of the first British clubs to experience the total disorientation that trips behind the Iron Curtain can bring. Blanchflower told more of the story: 'There were prisoners in the streets digging up cobblestones, guarded by men with machine-guns. Going through the park leading to the Slaski Stadium we could see women, on their hands and knees, cutting the grass with what seemed to be large pairs of scissors. The stadium, massive, lit and tall like a distant castle, was the only welcoming thing about the whole place.'

Apparently no-one had told Gornik that this was Spurs' year for the European Cup. Within an hour the Poles were 4–0 up and Tottenham were as good as dead. 'I was bloody upset,' said Nicholson. 'We showed no determination or discipline.' But Jones and Dyson got two late goals back when the Poles let up and Spurs were in with a chance back home.

Perhaps the fondest memory of the great Spurs years of the early sixties is of the magical European nights. Twenty years later men from all over London still speak with damp eyes of those tremendous occasions — the first London had ever experienced and in an era, of course, when European Cup ties were not televised as a matter of course. It was not until these wonderful Wednesday nights that *Glory, Glory, Hallelujah*, the four-sided Tottenham wall of sound, really became established as the most individual and evocative of all English club tunes. As it happens, the club played *McNamara's Band* as the 'official' song at the time. 'The sound came from everywhere,' says Blanchflower, 'It was marvellous. When they sang, they all sang together fathers and sons, old and young. A local vicar used to complain that the whole thing was like a substitute for religion, and I suppose it was in a way. A century before those

OPPOSITE PAGE: The Double team. Standing left to right: Bill Brown, Peter Baker, Ron Henry, Danny Blanchflower, Maurice Norman, Dave Mackay; seated left to right: Cliff Jones, John White, Bobby Smith, Les Allen, Terry Dyson. This is the team that won the Cup in 1961. The following season's final saw Medwin and Greaves replace Dyson and Allen. At the end of the 1960–61 season Blanchflower paraphrased Nicholson's low-key approach saying: 'We've had what our manager might call a rather good year . . . '

fathers and sons would have sung in church together – but it wasn't in any way irreligious.' It was rather a sad reflection on all this that two decades later the Tottenham crowd at Wembley for the 1981 Charity Shield were singing 'Can you hear us on the box?' with barely a Glory, Glory to be heard.

To hear tell of it now, one could be excused for thinking that the great European nights went on for years. In actual fact there were really just two seasons and seven games (four in the European Cup and three in the Cup Winners Cup) and the legends that surround them really grew up from one particular game – the return leg against Gornik on 20 September 1961.

This was the night when the Poles found themselves outnumbered 60,000 to 11, when, as they admitted later, the noise from the crowd (who were much closer to the pitch than they were used to) battered them into submission. And yet they scored first through the appropriately named Pohl, and Tottenham, 5–2 down, were yet again up against the wall. The ferocity of their support drove them on – frightening the Spurs players almost as much as their opponents. Blanchflower got a penalty, and then the flood gates opened; three for Jones, two for Smith, one apiece for Dyson and White. At the end the crowd slumped back limp just from watching. Sitting or standing it had been an extraordinary experience and any-one who was there will talk about it with the same intensity today.

Nicholson's reactions to the first leg prob-lems were characteristic. Never again would Spurs be caught out that way. Preparations for away legs became intense, every detail was cov-ered, never again would Spurs players find themselves covered in flea bites from bug-rid-den beds, or bemused by the social conditions of the countries they had to visit. As Blanchflower repeated: 'You had to go there once, to experience it. It's difficult to win any-thing first time round.'

The next two legs were much easier. In nearby Rotterdam Feyenoord went down 3–1 (Dyson and young Frank Saul, with two, get-ting the goals) though Spurs disappointed their fans by playing safe for a 1–1 draw at home. Dyson again got the goal. In the quarter-finals Tottenham lost 1–0 in Prague to Dukla, play-ing much more cautiously than in Poland, and won 4–1 at home; Smith and Mackay both scored twice.

THE DREAMS DIE

In the semi-finals Spurs drew Cup holders Benfica. The other tie was between Real Madrid and Standard Liege. The prize, then, was as great as could be imagined – almost cer-tainly a final against Real in the Olympic Stadium in Amsterdam.

This is the fourth of those critical five games with which one can write the Spurs story of the early sixties. It is also the only one they lost and, in so doing, robbed the story of its expected denouement. When all is said and done Spurs did not, like Liverpool, Manchester United and Forest after them, reach the ulti-mate goal. They came as close as the wood-work on three occasions, and suffered almost certainly incorrect offside decisions twice, but that often tends to be the margin by which great stories are never told and by which great

prizes are never won.

Nicholson prepared himself well for the tie. He watched Benfica in Nuremberg and took the trouble to see Real beat Juventus in Madrid. 'Real were not the side they had been. I came back thinking that we would beat Real in the final if we could get past Benfica,' he remembers. Bela Guttmann, the Hungarian exile who was coaching that side of Portuguese and Mozambiquans and who had just acquired a young black player called Eusebio, agreed with Nicholson's assessment. He was proved correct – despite a Puskas hat-trick Benfica were to win one of the great finals, 5–3.

Nicholson's tactical planning was also more sophisticated now. For away games he would gen-erally play Tony Marchi as an extra defender. The player left out from the Double side was Les Allen, meaning Spurs had one less attack-er. Medwin, who could cover back better than Dyson, generally got the vote to play alongside Smith and Jones up front. Dyson, who had scored in each of the first four European Cup games, was never to play in that competition again. For the semi-final, however, Greaves was eligible, and he took the remaining place in Lisbon in a formation which was effectively a pioneering 4–3–3.

Tottenham always preferred to bring their opponents back to White Hart Lane for the second leg, knowing then what they needed to do. This allowed them to use the first match to get to know their opponents, the initial 45 minutes being played extremely cautiously. The whole scheme fell apart in Lisbon. Within 20 minutes Aguas and Augusto had put Benfica two ahead. Smith got one back, but Augusto headed his second to make it 3–1. The talk was not of the goals that were scored, but of the two that were disallowed – one by Greaves and one by Smith. Greaves, not a bad loser, says now: 'I reckon to this day the Swiss ref, Muellet, refereed us out of the final. I beat the full-back before I scored and was still given offside. Nine minutes from the end I crossed for Smithy to score and Muellet pointed to the centre-circle for 3–2. Then he saw the linesman flagging and disallowed the goal without even talking to him. But I was *ahead* of Smithy when I crossed.' Nicholson was brutal about the defeat: 'We gave away two vital goals because three players in a row made stupid mistakes.'

Spurs had already pulled back a two-goal deficit against Gornik and the crowd expected them to do so again. The ground was packed for the return leg on 5 April 1962, the noise terrifying. The average attendance for these four European Cup matches worked out at 60,430. Twenty years later David Miller of the *Daily Express* called the Benfica game '. . . the most electrifying ninety minutes of European football I have seen on an English ground,' and few who were there would ever question these sentiments. Bela Guttmann brought his extraordinary tactical and human know-how to succeed in one of his greatest tasks.

Guttmann himself deserves a diversion. He was a member of the Hungarian Olympic team in 1924, and went on to coach in America and the Netherlands before being imprisoned in a Second World War concentration camp. Having survived that, he took Ujpest to the Hungarian championship, coached Kispest

(who, renamed Honved, created something of a stir) and moved on to Italy. Here his AC Milan won the championship and were leading the Italian League when he was sacked for his pains, and he then took over the touring Hungarian side which had escaped the 1956 revolution. Having thus arrived in South America, he coached Sao Paulo to the 1958 Brazilian Championship, and almost certainly created the 4-2-4 system which Vicente Feola adopted for the Brazilian national squad in the World Cup in Sweden that year. Having thus learned to speak Portuguese, he ended up in Lisbon with Benfica.

Guttmann was a worthy opponent for Nicholson and Blanchflower. His gamesmanship was subtle but not extreme. He complained loudly about the physical excesses of Smith and Mackay, and the resulting Press comment seemed to intimidate Danish referee Aage Poulsen (certainly Guttmann thought it worked; he said afterwards: 'Yes, we got more than our share of free-kicks'). He knew the crowd would overawe his players, so he refused to let them warm up. They went straight out to the kick-off so that the atmosphere was not allowed to get to them before the game began.

Within 15 minutes a thoroughly underawed Aguas played a one-two with Simoes and slid the ball home across the rain-sodden six-yard box. Spurs were 4–1 down on aggregate. Then came a replay of one of the disallowed goals in Lisbon. White to Smith to Greaves, who, running between two defenders, scored from close in. The referee gave it, then consulted a linesman who had briefly raised his flag and the goal was disallowed. It was the third marginal decision that had gone against Spurs and it raised justifiable doubts afterwards.

After 38 minutes White finally made a goal for Smith, and then Blanchflower calmly converted another penalty four minutes after the break. Costa Pereira went the wrong way, Spurs were only one goal behind and there were 40 minutes left. History says they did not succeed, that their frantic attacks left them with no reward other than muddy woodwork – three shots that would have gone in another day came back off the posts and bar (though, to be fair, Aguas also hit the bar in the first half). Nicholson and Blanchflower both said afterwards that they thought Spurs were probably a goal better, over the two legs, but they wouldn't have changed their tactics if they had to do it again. 'I lost count of the near misses,' says Nicholson, 'but the one I'll always remember is when Dave (Mackay) hit the crossbar right at the end.' Blanchflower conceded Benfica's abilities: 'You have to remember that Pereira was magnificent against Bobby Smith and that Coluna was marvellous in midfield. I think Guttmann was sharper than we thought. All those years in Europe and South America, all that experience. He told me that Benfica would do it after the game in Lisbon.' Guttmann resigned the Benfica job after the final, eschewing a possible hat-trick, and moved to Penarol in Uruguay. He eventually went to live in Vienna where, so legend has it, he became a pool hustler. The destroyer of Spurs' most cherished dreams was to die there in August 1981.

Spurs themselves did not despair and the following season was to see them become the first British club to win a European trophy, the Cup Winners Cup. This was a new trophy, only three years old, and had yet to acquire its later status but Spurs were, nonetheless, impressive winners.

Nor was their League performance much behind when they finished runners-up to Everton for the Championship. They were six points in arrears of the Merseyside club with Burnley, always their close rivals, a further point behind. But the Lancashire side sampled some revenge for this and that Cup final defeat of the previous year by inflicting Tottenham's first FA Cup defeat for three years when they went to White Hart Lane for their third round meeting and came away clear 3–0 winners. No hat-trick here for Nicholson.

It was a season in which Spurs, with 111 goals, were the liveliest attackers in the Football League, Jimmy Greaves leading the way with a club record 37 goals which beat the jointly-held previous best of 36 by Ted Harper and Bobby Smith. This brighter if not quite as consistent Spurs side scored in each of their first 19 League games and it took new champions Everton to check them in the twentieth, when they earned a 0–0 draw from their visit.

THE CUP WINNERS CUP

In one glorious autumn seven game spree they averaged five goals a go, including nine rammed home against Nottingham Forest (Forest winger Trevor Hockey said afterwards: 'We scored first and last and they got nine lucky ones in between'), six against Manchester United, five against Leyton Orient away and the sharing of a 4–4 draw with Arsenal. They later hit West Ham for six, Liverpool for seven and Ipswich Town for five and Jimmy Greaves scored four goals against both Forest and Liverpool. The two Liverpool games were particularly entertaining. Having lost 5–2 at Anfield on Good Friday, Spurs won 7–2 at home on Easter Monday. But their failure to stay the course strongly, the 62 goals conceded, and the reallocation of matches following the worst hold-up which League football has ever experienced after the appalling 1962–63 winter, put paid to another title chance. From their last ten matches they took only eight points, winning three, drawing two and losing five of the games. It was the second consecutive season in which a terrible finish probably cost them the title.

The season was, in retrospect, one of hanging on for the final prize. The Cup Winners Cup final against Atletico Madrid in Rotterdam was the fifth and last of the era's critical games, partially because it was literally the last gasp of the Double side and the glory that had gone with their achievements.

The route to Rotterdam had not been a long or exhausting one, consisting of only three preliminary rounds for Spurs. Glasgow Rangers were poor opposition, going down 3-2 at home and 5-2 in London. Two of their defenders did, however, make their mark. A violent sandwich on Blanchflower damaged his knee and the cartilage came out. At his age (37) it took time to repair and he was to miss 22 games in all. John White's growing importance to the team is indicated by how well they played in Blanchflower's absence. The next round saw more Iron Curtain travels

OPPOSITE TOP: On 30 November 1961 Bill Nicholson made perhaps his best ever signing, bringing Jimmy Greaves back from Milan for £99,999. The fee was set at that figure so that Greaves would not have to carry the tag of being the first player to have cost an English club £100,000. Here the new boy listens with team-mates Blanchflower, Henry, Hopkins, Dyson, Hollowbread and Eddie Clayton to Nicholson's instructions at the Cheshunt training ground. Greaves' first senior game for the club was on 16 December 1961, against Blackpool. He got a hat-trick and maintained a record of scoring in every debut game of his career. OPPOSITE BOTTOM: Greaves and ball in a familiar position - the back of the net. The date is Saturday 24 November 1962 and Greaves has just put Spurs 1–0 ahead at Burnley, despite the efforts of defenders Brian Miller, Alex Elder and John Angus (number 2). The day was not to end happily for Spurs, however, Connelly and Pointer scoring in the second half to give Burnley victory. Seven weeks later the Lancastrians were to inflict Spurs' first FA Cup defeat for three years – 3-0 at the Lane.

with a match against Slovan Bratislava. By now Spurs were almost seasoned travellers in Eastern Europe, but Slovan were to pull them apart. Bill Brown, his nose all plastered up after one particularly brave dive at a forward's feet, kept them in the game. Spurs were lucky to keep the score down to 2–0. Blanchflower, from the previous year's experience with Gornik and Dukla, knew that Western Europe disorientated Iron Curtain sides even more than the reverse trip upset Spurs. 'We were never happy over there,' he says, 'but they couldn't believe their eyes when they came to London. We rarely had any trouble at home.' Blanchflower was right, Spurs scoring six without reply in the second leg.

The semi-final against OFK Belgrade was most notable for Jimmy Greaves being sent off – the first man in a Tottenham shirt to be dismissed since 27 October 1928. Greaves played at outside-right, John Smith moved to inside-forward and Maurice Norman turned out with an injured foot. Missing were Cliff Jones and Blanchflower when Tottenham arrived for the first leg in the Red Army Stadium, Belgrade. Greaves was sent off in the 55th minute for retaliation, and one man who could clearly remember the last time it happened, 35 years before, was Spurs trainer Cecil Poynton, for he was the unfortunate it had happened to. Greaves admitted later that he had taken a swing at Krivokuca, the home defender who had been trying to kick lumps out of him. Earlier there had been a free-for-all with the Hungarian referee roughly manhandled when trying to sort things out. The cause of it all was the senseless figure of wing-half Maric lying flat out in the home penalty area after a free-kick had been awarded against him for a horrific tackle on Smith. No-one in London had much doubt as to who had laid him out. Sixty thousand fans still gave ten-man Spurs a stirring

farewell as they left 2–1 winners through White and Dyson and thanks to heroic defence inspired by play-everywhere Mackay. Blanchflower returned for the second leg to make the first goal for Mackay . . . Belgrade pulled that back; then Jones and a Smith header meant the first one-legged European final for any English club on a 5–2 aggregate.

It was harsh on Nicholson that Dave Mackay, of all people, should miss the final against the holders, Atletico Madrid, in the Feyenoord Stadium in Rotterdam, a stomach injury keeping him on the touchlines. It was certainly not his week . . . he also came second to Stanley Matthews as 'Footballer of the Year'. Marchi made an admirable deputy for the Scot.

It was the prospect of Mackay's absence which troubled Spurs most as they waited for the final on 15 May 1963. 'With Dave in the team we feel we can beat anyone,' said Cliff Jones before the match. 'He makes things happen. He makes us go. Without him, the odds change.' The odds had changed and Mackay did not play, added to which Spurs lost their last domestic game 0–1 to already relegated Manchester City. Blanchflower was still not fit but, officially now assistant to the manager (not assistant manager), he preferred Bill Nicholson to make the critical decision. 'It's a simple choice', he said, 'either me on one leg or John Smith (a skilful reserve bought from West Ham) on two.' Nicholson ordered pain-killing injections for Blanchflower's knee and had him play. He was 37 and this, to all intents and purposes, was his last major match.

The Atletico match has gone down in folklore as the game Blanchflower won without kicking a ball. Nicholson, says David Miller, gave an almost funereal team-talk. 'Nick's confidence seemed to have gone,' said Jimmy Greaves afterwards, 'because we'd lost Dave Mackay and he was our best player. He just went through the Spaniards, player by player, pointing out their strengths. But he just made us worry whether they *were* as good as he had painted them.' Blanchflower took over from Nicholson and told them to listen to what *he* had to say. Greaves recalls the captain's own brand of team-talk: 'He said that if their centre-half was big and ugly then ours, Maurice Norman, was even bigger and uglier. That if they had a fast winger called Jones

OPPOSITE TOP: The goal that made the Double safe. In the 77th minute of the 1961 FA Cup final Bobby Smith (furthest left in picture) crossed for Terry Dyson to head past a despairing Gordon Banks.

OPPOSITE CENTRE: Ten minutes earlier Bobby Smith (just rising from ground) had feinted one way, turned the other and put Spurs 1–0 ahead against a Leicester City side reduced to ten men after an injury to Len Chalmers. Danny Blanchflower said that the final was probably Spurs' worst performance of the whole season.

CENTRE: The two scorers after the Cup win of 1961; Terry Dyson (left) and Bobby Smith, plus the photographer catching himself in the mirror and, also reflected in the mirror, John White bending over the table.

OPPOSITE BOTTOM: A year later and Bobby Smith scores a similar goal against Burnley after a John White run down the left. Smith's goal made the score 2–1.

THIS PAGE TOP: Jimmy Greaves (far left) scores the first goal of the 1962 final after just three minutes. This was the first medal Greaves had won – two more coming in the Cup Winners Cup and the FA Cup final of 1967.

THIS PAGE CENTRE: Jimmy Robertson (right) raises his arm in triumph as the ball hits the back of Peter Bonetti's net and opens the scoring in the 1967 final against Chelsea. In the 40th minute Alan Mullery's shot had rebounded off Chelsea defender Allan Harris and left Robertson with a clear opening from the edge of the penalty area.

THIS PAGE BOTTOM: After 67 minutes of the 1967 final Frank Saul put the result beyond reasonable doubt with a hooked shot inside Bonetti's near post. Saul, who was standing with his back to goal, is not in the picture, but looking on are John Boyle, Jimmy Robertson, Allan Harris, Jimmy Greaves and Marvin Hinton as Spurs' last Cup final goal of the decade buries itself in the net.

105

(which Atletico did – a strange coincidence), then ours was so fast he could catch pigeons.'

That pigeon-catching Cliff Jones played on the right-wing, Terry Dyson on the left, and it was to be Dyson's night. Spurs' first goal came in the 16th minute, a cross from Jones to the impeccable Greaves and into the net. Sixteen minutes later Dyson made it 2–0, but Ron Henry had to give away a penalty at the start of the second half and Collar made it 2–1. Spurs were on the ropes for perhaps twenty minutes, but were saved by a bolt from a highly unlikely source. Dyson, who had been having a good, teasing match against full-back Rivilla beat his man again and slung over a high, teasing cross. It went too close to the keeper, Madinabeytia, but somehow the goalie lost it in flight and it squeezed over his head at the near-post. Dyson claimed this fluke among flukes the result of his quick thinking when he saw the keeper move out two yards, but it certainly inspired the winger to believe anything was possible. Ten minutes from the end he sent over the cross from which Greaves made it four and then, in the 87th minute, Dyson made the night his by running 30 yards with the ball, dummying right and left and finishing with a 25-yard screamer. He had the immense satisfaction of playing the game of his career at the perfect time, a privilege few footballers ever enjoy. As the 5–1 victors walked back to the dressing-room Bobby Smith said to Terry Dyson: 'You'd better retire now, you'll never play better.'

THE OLD GUARD GOES

Dyson may not have decided to retire, but the next three years was not much more than the gradual dissolution of Nicholson's first great side.

· Little Harmer had departed the Tottenham scene just before Spurs hit their jackpot years. At 32 he had to abdicate in favour of the younger White after some 15 years at White Hart Lane, the longest-serving active member of a squad which had seen many changes under the demanding Nicholson. Many clubs were still ready to make room for him in their first teams when Spurs put a £6,000 transfer fee on his head, including his old team-mate Alf Ramsey at Ipswich. Harmer chose Watford, where he had worked in a print shop, but the move was not a success for the Third Division was not equipped to follow the advanced promptings of the wee fellow. His still bright talents were not being fully utilised until manager Tommy Docherty stepped in. He saw Harmer as the mastermind to lead his young Chelsea fledglings upwards and into the First Division. It proved to be a master stroke. Besides coaching and spreading his soccer lore around the Stamford Bridge dressing-rooms and training areas, he played in just five of that season's League matches, but was on the winning side every time to make a joke of the £3,000 fee he had cost Chelsea. And the one goal he scored came in the closing game of the season . . . to beat Sunderland, his club's nearest rivals for promotion, at Roker Park. He converted a centre into a goal with what might euphemistically be called his private parts. With that goal Chelsea went into the First Division, while Sunderland had to wait one more season.

There was satisfaction for Tiny Tom the fol-

lowing season when he went back to the Lane with Chelsea and had a leading part in both the Chelsea goals which brought a 2–1 away success over his old club. It's an echo of a favourite story of Eddie Baily about Harmer, his old colleague of the Arthur Rowe days and much later. According to Eddie: 'I thought I had been put out to grass when I was transferred from Tottenham to Port Vale. We played Nottingham Forest, then around the top of the Second Division, and we beat them 3–1. I must have impressed Forest's manager Billy Walker. I was told he wanted me to join him.

'Freddie Steele, the Port Vale manager, had me in his office and asked if I was willing to go. He received more than the £6,000 he paid for me . . . and a fair bit besides. We won promotion at Forest, I got a Second Division medal and so in no time I was back at the Spurs, in the First Division. We went to White Hart Lane leading the division in October 1957 and Tommy Harmer was in the Spurs team. I was then 36 and was captain for the day against many old pals I had left behind . . . I remember when the score was at 2–2 Tommy coming near to me and calling out, "I don't think much of your team, Eddie." But as we went off at the end I caught him up to tell him, "I think even less of yours, Tom" – we had won 4–3 and stayed top!'

In April 1964 the club lost a much-loved figure, its president, Fred Bearman, at the great age of 91. He had begun as a Spurs director 54 long years before, in 1910, was made chairman in 1943 and president in 1961 after retiring from the board. He had been a real tower of strength during his long association, a caring chairman. Three months later, just as the players were due to report back for pre-season training in July, came the tragic news of John White's death while sheltering from a storm during a round of golf at Crews Hill, Middlesex. It was a sickening blow to all who knew him. The pleasant, friendly, freckle-faced young Scotsman left a wife and young family and a great host of friends and admirers. In his near five years since joining from Falkirk he lit many of the fuses which set off the power drive of this great club side.

In a season in which he was to be tested by taking almost every bad knock that could be handed out, Bill Nicholson broke down and wept over the death of the slight 26-year-old young man of so many talents. He had been asked by the police to identify the body and had kept his feelings under his usual iron control until talking to his players after they had reported back.

He had already lost his right-hand man, Danny Blanchflower, who, at 37 and still feeling the recurring effects of that injury against Glasgow Rangers en route to lifting the Cup Winners Cup, had called it a day to switch sideways to reporting and talking football both in print and on television.

But the sad, bad news did not end there. Terry Medwin, on the summer tour of South Africa in 1963, had been injured in the very first match. That more or less ended the tour for him. But, worse for Nicholson's plans, he lost the services of the adaptable Welshman for the whole of 1963–64 season. Came December 1963 and their defence of the Cup Winners Cup. It did not last long, not even beyond the first challenge, despite the two-goal lead gained on the first leg of a domestic dust-up with Manchester United. A week later at Old Trafford the Nicholson furrowed brow took on another line of worry as United wiped out their two-goal deficit and finished 4–1 victors (4–3 on aggregate) to end any further Spurs interest in Europe. But they suffered a far deeper cut after only twenty minutes play when they lost Dave Mackay with a broken leg and inevitably, even though it was ironman Mackay, for the rest of the season. Within a year Nicholson had lost his whole midfield of White, Blanchflower and Mackay, that magical trio which had surely been the key to the Double. A month after Mackay's injury, Chelsea held a patched up Spurs 1–1 at White Hart Lane in the FA Cup, then put them out 2–0 in the Stamford Bridge replay.

Determined to get back in the senior line-up, Mackay put everything into his efforts to win the thumbs up for a return. He had been out of action for nine months when he turned out against Shrewsbury Town reserves . . . and that same left leg was broken again. And who else but the indestructible Mackay, with painful sweat pouring down his face, could beg his bearers, 'Don't let Bill Nicholson know, not yet,' thinking of the boss's preoccupation with first team troubles.

Nicholson had a special regard for Mackay, his first signing and the man he called the 'heart' of his teams. The loss of both Blanchflower and Mackay at the same time was like taking the works out of a watch; two players, two men who, in their own individual way, had meant so much and given so much to Tottenham and Bill Nick. He was interesting when he spoke about players like these: 'The character of a player meant as much to me as his skill,' he said. 'After all, he was going to represent my club and me. Most of my fellows were truly genuine. They were good to have around and ready to serve you fully. When the going became tough or rough you could still bank on them. That's when they proved you, and themselves, right or wrong. I pulled out of several deals for top players because I saw that I could not have them around this club. I like to think that I was consistent as a player, and I like consistency in players. You would have a job to go through my lot and say, "He was an inconsistent player."

'Danny Blanchflower was a fine captain. He was respected and could carry out any orders to the team. He was a class player and we always worked together very well. I admired him and still do, as a player and as a man. Dave Mackay was the complete professional, the heart-beat of a team with his fierce will to win in every game of every kind.'

BAILY RETURNS

Towards the mid-sixties Eddie Baily got the call from his old club. 'Bill Nick asked me to join him as coach and assistant manager. I got back just when the great Double side was beginning to break up. I've been so lucky to have been with clubs whose teams had been brought up in the best footballing traditions . . . Spurs, Nottingham Forest and West Ham. And I happened to be coach when manager Johnny Carey took Leyton Orient to their only season in the First Division back in 1962–63.

We went up with Liverpool and came down with Manchester City!'

He had a long ten-year partnership with Nicholson, his old playing colleague of the push-and-run days, before their break-up in September 1974. Baily was on the outside of the game looking in for two years during which time he worked as a games instructor, at a school in Enfield, teaching both football and cricket. He had been scouting for Chelsea along with the schools job, longing to get back, when Ron Greenwood rang to ask him if he would become West Ham's chief representative as that doyen of soccer scouts, Wally St Pier, was about to retire. When Greenwood took over the job of England manager, Baily was one of his first appointments as an observer, weighing up England's rivals in advance.

Later he would tell you: 'The game hasn't changed much, only people have. It's the same ball, same markings, the game's the same. One-touch football is what they are teaching and coaching now, we called it push-and-run so maybe we were a bit ahead of our time. We had forwards, now there are strikers, hit-men, target players; there are numbered formations, it's all done by numbers.' He was being more reflective than critical when he said it. 'Great players are players who haven't got the ball, the hardest thing in the game. But when they've got it, it is simply doing the right thing, picking the right thing to do, not the hard thing. Lesser players shun doing the simple thing.'

The Spurs break-up continued. Peter Baker went off to play in South Africa, Tony Marchi became player-manager of Cambridge City, unlucky Terry Medwin had to call it a day after that injury in South Africa, Terry Dyson joined Fulham, Les Allen went to QPR, where son Clive was to make a name for himself fifteen years later. 1965–66 was really the end of the old days. Bill Brown handed over to Pat Jennings, Ron Henry played just once, his place filled by the 'nice one, Cyril' Knowles, and the old-timer helped coach the reserves and the youngsters. A badly broken leg finished Maurice Norman's career, Cliff Jones found he could no longer catch pigeons and in 1968 contented himself with whatever feathered varieties they have at Fulham. Only Jones and Dave Mackay were left when the decade's final trophy was carried round Wembley, the FA Cup of 1967.

Mackay broke the final link in 1968, a good time to go: 'I could do nothing more for them, nor they for me. If I had stayed I would have got a share of the blame. It meant a new challenge.' He joined the star of the new generation, Brian Clough, at Derby. Far from being finished, he helped Clough bring Derby back to the First Division, and shared a long-deserved 'Footballer of the Year' award with Tony Book in 1969. On 20 September 1969, the Baseball Ground saw its largest ever crowd (41,826) and they saw Derby annihilate Tottenham 5–0. It was a magnificent moment for Mackay, who stayed around the East Midlands during that area's great decade, first to manage Nottingham Forest and then supersede Clough at Derby, where his side won the 1975 Championship, before Mackay drifted away from the limelight.

But all was not gloom and depression in the mid-1960s. Spurs did not cease to exist as a footballing force, and they maintained a respectable League position throughout these years of turbulent change – second in 1962–63, fourth in 1963–64, sixth in 1964–65 and eighth in 1965–66. The addition of Jimmy Greaves was, of course, the first, the most exciting and most significant change to the Double-winning side.

The addition of the goal-power of Jimmy Greaves towards the end of 1961 was simply a case of the alert Nicholson taking his chances as swiftly as the little striker himself took them on the pitch. 'He came in November, but his registration was held up for a time by the Football League,' said Nicholson. 'What a great player he proved for us and he seemed so happy here after the misery of his stay with AC Milan and his fall-outs with trainer-coach Rocco.

'I went for Jimmy because of something I had stored away in my mind, something he had said when I met him going to a dinner at the Cafe Royal. We got talking and it came up about his proposed transfer from Chelsea to a continental club. He told me that night that he would have loved to have played in our Double team. I stored that away. It wasn't too long after he went to Italy that we began to hear stories of how difficult he was finding trying to settle in Italy. How his game had suffered and that he was homesick. Then I heard he might be available for transfer and that's when I began to get things moving. He had such talent, such wonderful anticipation that he was on the right spot at the right time – the real art of the great striker. His timing was perfect and he was deadly. Once he lined up a goal in his sights the biggest certainty was that he would get it, he was such a deadly finisher.'

Greaves proved all this with his goal-a-game beginning with Tottenham and 20,000 turned out to see him score for the reserves at Plymouth. He hit a hat-trick in his first League match, a 5–2 home win over Blackpool, then went on to score 30 goals in the 31 games, League and Cup, he played in the second half of the 1961–62 season. His third goal against Blackpool was recently recalled by one national newspaper as being one of the greatest ever scored in post-war football, an overhead bicycle kick which made the £99,999 Nicholson had paid appear absurdly cheap. Greaves' goalscoring for Spurs in the next eight seasons was astonishing. His League tallies alone were 21 (in 22 games), 37, 35, 29, 15 (in 29 games), 23, 23 and 27. He led the First Division scorers an unprecedented six times between 1958 and 1969 and is the only man to have headed that list in three consecutive years.

There has not been another goalscorer like him in the post-war game, despite the effort and money the major clubs have put into trying to find a successor. Despite the goals, his relationship with Bill Nicholson was not always perfect. There is the famous story of a game during one of Tottenham's leaner spells. The manager was trying to get Greaves to come back and help the midfield more often, or to run into space more effectively. On one particularly lazy day Greaves' finishing was at its sharpest. He would score a goal, only to disappear for twenty minutes, and then pop up with another. After the game Nicholson was heard to comment: 'All he did this afternoon was score those four goals . . . ' Spurs now had three ex-Chelsea forwards – Allen, Smith and Greaves – and it was Allen who had to make way in the established first choice team.

During the mid-sixties there were other major additions. In 1966 Terry Venables also came from Chelsea, where Tommy Docherty had seemingly dismissed his key playmaker in a fit of disappointment after Chelsea had lost their second consecutive FA Cup semi-final. Venables, the only footballer ever to be capped at every international level for England (Schoolboy, Youth, Amateur, Under-23, Full), was essential to fill the creative hole in midfield, but he found the going difficult. At Chelsea he was in charge of a team of younger players who had been brought up on a faster, longer-ball game. The shorter, subtler Spurs style was not suited to Venables spraying long passes from the centre-circle and, though he won an FA Cup winners' medal against his old club, he never really fitted in as Nicholson had hoped. He and Mullery, signed from Fulham in 1964 for £72,500, suffered most at the hands of the Tottenham crowd and both had some cynical things to say about their experiences. It was their misfortune, of course, to have to try and step into the shoes of Blanchflower, White and, in Mullery's case later, those of the great Mackay. It is no disrespect to them both to suggest that this was simply not possible, that Spurs have never had, nor will probably ever have again, a centre-line quite like that one. No players in the

world could have filled that gaping hole and it was unfortunate that the crowd needed the enchantment of distance, via a few years, to appreciate the fact. 'It was bloody awful at the time,' says Mullery now. 'It took me at least two years to win the crowd over and get accepted and I'd have gone anywhere else for a time. I won them over in the end, but it was hard going.' Mullery recalls that he had gone to Tottenham because of Nicholson, and that the manager had predicted well ahead that Spurs would win the Cup again by 1967, which is one reason he had moved from Fulham.

The other major signings were Mike England, £95,000 from Blackburn Rovers to fill Maurice Norman's place, and the man with the three-penny bit shaped head, Alan Gilzean. Gilzean had starred in Dundee's surprise run to the semi-finals of the European Cup in 1963 when they beat FC Koln 8–1, Sporting Lisbon 4–1, and Anderlecht 4–1 away but went out to AC Milan at the penultimate stage. Gilzean had scored hat-tricks against Koln and Sporting, two against Anderlecht and the only goal of the home leg against Milan. His ability to head the ball in any direction was priceless, though Spurs did not reap maximum dividends from it until he was playing slightly behind Chivers in the early 1970s, a time when Gilzean's back header from a long throw into the penalty area might almost have been copyrighted. Like Blanchflower, Gilzean became an old war-horse, continuing until he was 36 in 1974.

There was a negative side to the transfer

market, both financially and domestically. Nicholson never found another really successful winger – going through the likes of Robertson, Saul, Morgan, Coates, Possee, Weller and Pearce. By the late 1960s, after Ramsey's 'penguin side' ('the wingless wonders' as parts of the Press had called them) of 1966 had sown its tactical seed, no major club was regularly playing more than one winger, and the one that remained was often having to double as a marking-back wide midfield man as well. Roger Morgan, one of celebrated identical twins from QPR, was the North London crowd's biggest disappointment. At £110,000 the fans thought they should have got Rodney Marsh (the joke on the terraces was that Rangers had wrapped Morgan in a paper bag and told Spurs they were getting Marsh, only they couldn't open the bag until they got home).

Domestically the problem was that youngsters were put off by Spurs image as the big-money club. Like Liverpool in the 1970s, it seemed that Spurs would always buy to fill the gaps – so what chance did youngsters have of coming through from the ranks? Nicholson denies it, but the fact is that only two of the 1967 Cup winning team (Jennings, Kinnear, Knowles, Mullery, England, Mackay, Robertson, Greaves, Gilzean, Venables and Saul) had come up through the juniors. Those two 'outsiders' were Kinnear and Saul, and the other nine had cost over half a million pounds. In present day terms that does not sound a lot but at the time no other club in the country could come near it. One of Spurs' problems

was their sheer success – buying a player a year used up the profits and brought the corporation tax bill down. Under the somewhat absurd Inland Revenue regulations, buying players was tax deductible whereas ground improvements were not, so while profits were good there was actually a need to buy expensive players.

1967 – ANOTHER FA CUP

The 1967 Cup win was a surprise, and all the more welcome for that. It is unusual for a club which has had such spectacular success to rebuild a team and come back for a major prize so quickly. Wolves did it in the 1950s, but the Spurs fans of 1967 appreciated the difficulty of the feat and the crowds that greeted the team and the trophy were even bigger than they had been in 1961 and 1962.

The third round draw was away at Millwall – actually a much harder prospect than it sounds. At the time the numbers came out of the hat Millwall had gone 59 League games at The Den without defeat, a record run that had lasted thirty-two months as they rose from the Fourth to the Second Division. As chance would have it, Millwall lost that record to Plymouth Argyle the Saturday before the third round, but Spurs had to weather a hard, goalless draw nonetheless. The replay was almost as tight, Gilzean getting the only goal.

The fourth, fifth and sixth rounds also threw up Second Division opponents. Gilzean got two and Greaves one to remove Portsmouth 3-1 and Bristol City then went down 2-0, both

OPPOSITE PAGE:
Saturday 29 April 1967 and Spurs are back in the FA Cup final. A 2–1 defeat of Nottingham Forest at Tottenham's favourite semi-final ground Hillsborough (where they won in 1921 and 1981) was inspired by a Jimmy Greaves snap shot in the first half and cemented by another from Frank Saul with 15 minutes left. Here Saul challenges full-back Peter Hindley while keeper Grummitt gathers the ball. Looking on are Alan Gilzean and Bobby McKinlay. It was the critical game on the road to Wembley for Spurs, Forest being favourites and finishing one place above them in the League.
BELOW: Jimmy Greaves after the game, talking with Terry Venables (left). Greaves was a constant nightmare to Forest, scoring 29 first-class goals against them in his career including four on no fewer than three separate occasions.

games being at White Hart Lane. Birmingham at St Andrew's in the quarter-finals was much tougher and Spurs were lucky to escape with a goalless draw. Despite Jimmy Robertson's speed on the right Greaves and Gilzean could do little that matched the winger's penetration, and all the good chances fell to Birmingham. The closest was when Jennings dropped a Fenton centre on the line and everyone joined in with their opinion as to whether it was over or not.

To their evident relief Spurs escaped with the draw and then crushed the Midlanders 6–0 on a White Hart Lane paddy field the following week. Venables scored straight from the off, unusually adding his name to the sheet, but soon added a second and Gilzean finally made use of one of Robertson's constant stream of crosses for a third before half-time. Birmingham got no better after the break and virtually gave up trying to control Greaves, who got two, with Frank Saul adding the sixth.

The semi-final at Hillsborough was the season's critical game. Nottingham Forest, second in the League and chasing Manchester United hard, were favourites, but they had lost Joe Baker in their classic quarter-final defeat of Everton and this was to disrupt their whole pattern of play. Despite having three other current or future England internationals up front (Hinton, Wignall and Storey-Moore), they depended on Baker's speed on the turn to win games no less than Spurs needed Greaves.

This game was, indeed, to produce one of Greaves' most memorable goals, a killing psychological blow as much as a single score because of his strange affinity for Forest. During his career Greaves scored far more goals (29) against Forest than any other club – including four on three occasions. Clearly he terrified the Nottingham club and his thirtieth-minute goal demoralised them so much that they lost a game they really should have won. As a goal it was probably not as classic a moment as three others that will always live in the memory – his bicycle kick against Blackpool in his first game for the club, his turn and dribble past four Manchester United defenders at White Hart Lane on 16 October 1965, and his run and shot past three Forest defenders when he never touched the ball but beat them simply by letting it run, dipping his shoulders and dummying left and right. But the semi-final goal was a great goal because of its context, because it got Spurs to a Cup final, because it was one of those goals that only Greaves seemed to be able to score, and because it was proof, if it was needed, that a single player can occasionally win for a team trophies that they would not otherwise have won. In recent years only Jimmy Greaves and George Best fall unquestionably into this category.

Greaves' goal came out of the blue at a time when Forest were clearly on top. A long clearance from Mike England was headed side-ways by Gilzean. As the ball bounced at Greaves' feet, he suddenly twisted and hit it left-footed on the half-volley from about 25 yards. The ball shot along the ground, snicked Grummitt's right-hand post and settled in the far corner of the net. The Forest defence never moved. With a quarter of an hour left Frank Saul robbed Terry Hennessey in the defender's half, set off for goal and whacked a magnificent shot into the net. Forest attacked frantically but could only reply once, from Hennessey himself, and Spurs were through. It was probably the best of all their semi-finals.

They found themselves facing Chelsea in the final; the Pensioners had, at the third consecutive attempt, managed to win a semi-final at last by beating Leeds 1–0. It was the first all-London professional final, which was excellent for the two competing sides but which somehow robbed the game of its national stage – the rest of the country was clearly indifferent to the whole thing. Deryk Brown wrote of the game: 'It was supposed to have been drab, which it wasn't, and supposed to have lacked atmosphere, which it did. This was Tottenham's fault only in that they were too good.'

Spurs did not break their routine at all. They trained as usual and spent just one night away. For the club it was not an overwhelming moment, being their fourth cup final in six years. For Chelsea's youngsters, however, it was rather too much; the Spurs players watched their opponents on television on the morning of the match and were delighted to observe nerve ends showing.

That Tottenham judgement on the Chelsea side was proved accurate; the younger team never settled, nor once looked like winning the game. Only Ron Harris, who kept Greaves out of things, enhanced his reputation. After 40 minutes Jimmy Robertson scored a well deserved goal. Mullery ran at the defence, his shot hit Allan Harris and Robertson buried the rebound from the edge of the area. After 67 minutes Frank Saul, with his back to goal, somehow hooked a shot into the corner of Peter Bonetti's net after a Dave Mackay throw. It was all over, Bobby Tambling's 85th minute header (Jennings effectively punched the ball at his head) barely even being a consolation for Chelsea. It was now Dave Mackay's turn to collect the silverware and Cliff Jones became the first substitute ever to collect a Cup final winners medal. It was more easily earned than his other mementos – he never left the bench.

The most significant benefit was, of course, that Spurs were back in the Cup Winners Cup. This time things did not end so happily. Their first rivals were the Yugoslav side Hajduk Split and they returned from the first leg with a 2–0 lead. It all seemed so easy. Then in the return the Spurs fans rejoiced as their team sailed on with a three-goal lead, then got another in the dying minutes. But not before the tough Yugoslavs had bounced back to grab three goals for themselves in a late rally which caused many palpitations.

Alan Mullery was sent off in a riotous second round away clash with the French club Olympique Lyonnais which saw Spurs defeated 1–0. The home side also lost their international centre-forward, Andre Guy, sent off in the scuffle with Mullery. A series of battles broke out round the terraces and spectators piled onto the pitch. The second leg resulted in a 4–3 success for Spurs but they went out on the away goals counting double rule. After 1962 and 1963 it was a terrible anticlimax.

The crowd, by now having got used to the fact that they were not going to be watching Blanchflower and White every week, were disappointed rather than depressed. Bill Nicholson remained the biggest critic having reached the summit it was hard for him to remain camped on the slopes.

A TOTTENHAM LEGEND
A hard man but a fair man was Alan Mullery's summary of Nicholson the manager at this time. There was little artistry but a lot of honesty in his game. But he always wanted to see his teams doing it in style. Ask him, looking at it as a player and a manager, did he enjoy football and he says: 'Enjoy . . . that is not a word I would think of using. You cannot do that, playing or watching with a direct interest, until after a match. As a player there is the preparation, the feeling of being keyed up, the bending of all your thoughts to the game. You carry these through any game. Same with a manager, there is too much else on when things are happening to say you enjoy it. Only if your side is playing exceptionally well and have gone well in front – very well in front – then maybe you might enjoy it as it happens. But enjoy . . .' and he leaves the thought in mid-air.

The stories of Tottenham Hotspur and Bill Nicholson are now so intertwined that it is virtually impossible to separate them. For the record, the future manager was born in Scarborough, one of a family of nine. His father was a groom and horse cab driver and Nicholson was a little special even then, passing scholarship examinations to go to Scarborough High School.

Leaving at 16 he went to work in a laundry and played soccer at weekends for a local team, the Young Liberals. He had no thoughts of becoming a professional footballer at this stage but, out of the blue, Spurs asked him to come for a trial in 1936.

'When the letter came no-one knew what to do. We weren't even sure exactly where Tottenham was. My mother and father had never once seen me play football. They knew I was keen, but they had no idea whether I was any good or not. I honestly had no idea what the world of professional football was about. Our heroes were the local Midland League side – none of my friends had even been to see Hull or York.'

Nicholson's opinion was that the local Spurs scout, based in York, had heard about him and Ben Ives, the chief scout, then took a trip to see for himself. Nicholson was probably introduced to Ives but retained no recollections of the meeting and certainly had no idea of what it might lead to. No other club had ever shown any interest, and from this point on his life in football was to be committed to the cause of Tottenham Hotspur.

He had a month's trial at White Hart Lane, and was taken on as a ground staff boy. 'We were cheap labour really,' he said later, 'I think I painted every single girder under those stands out there, eight to five we worked, every weekday. We trained two afternoons a week, including a lot of running round the pitch. There was no tactical discussion, just what we were able to organise ourselves. But it wasn't all bad, of course. I remember that Willie Hall, who was club captain at the time, was very kind and always took a great interest.'

Nicholson played for the nursery side, Northfleet, and signed as a full professional at 18, on the same day as Ronnie Burgess. The Welshman retained a warm spot in Nicholson's memory: 'If I had to pick out one player in all my time here, a player who had it all, I think I'd pick Ron Burgess. He could do anything. Once Arthur Rowe had sold Ron on his methods then he had no trouble with push-and-run. Convincing Burgess was the most difficult thing Arthur ever had to do, but once it was done, well . . . yes, if pushed I'd even put him above Blanchflower.'

Burgess and Nicholson had started to play odd games for the first team before 1939, but on the outbreak of war Nicholson joined the Durham Light Infantry. Because he was known to be a professional footballer, he was sent on a PE course and soon became a sergeant-instructor. He continued training new intakes throughout the War, eventually ending up in Italy where he took over a rest camp in Bari from Stan Cullis and then going on to Geoff Dyson's physical education headquarters at Udine.

He probably lost half his playing career to the War but doesn't regret it because he is convinced that it was those wartime experiences which made what came afterwards possible. 'It was invaluable. What I did for six years in the army taught me how to handle

OVERLEAF: Like virtually all other successful teams of the post-war era, Spurs great spell lasted just three years, during whch they won four trophies. The last was the Cup Winners Cup, photographed here with the squad at the beginning of the 1963-64 season. Standing left to right: Cliff Jones, Ron Henry, Mel Hopkins, Maurice Norman, John Hollowbread, Bill Brown, Bobby Smith, John White, Jimmy Greaves and John Smith. Sitting left to right: Frank Saul, Peter Baker, Dave Mackay, Danny Blanchflower, Tony March, Les Allen, Terry Dyson and Eddie Clayton. The only player from the great days not in this line up was Terry Medwin, who had been injured on a close season tour of South Africa and was never to play for the first team again. Within a year far worse was to have happened: John White was killed by lightning on a golf course, Dave Mackay was out having broken his left leg twice, Blanchflower had to retire after being given a terrible run-around by Denis Law at Old Trafford and Brown, Baker, Smith and Allen were no longer first choices.

people and how to talk to people. It obviously taught me how to get players fit, and I began to think about coaching routines – not in a very organised way, but how it could be done. After the War Freddie Cox asked some of the lads to go on a coaching course, and, with all those years in the army, I didn't find it too difficult. Gradually I got to think more about it.'

In 1946 he went straight into the Tottenham first team at centre-half for two seasons. He moved to right-half and stayed there until Danny Blanchflower took over the position in 1954. Nicholson had suffered a knee injury and had already said to Arthur Rowe that he felt the time had probably come to find a replacement.

They were good years for Nicholson, though not without their regrets. He was a member of the disastrous World Cup party in 1950 and won only one cap overall, basically because

Billy Wright held the right-half spot throughout Nicholson's career. That debut was as spectacular as his managerial one however; he scored against Portugal after just 19 seconds with his very first kick in international football.

Nicholson became the Spurs first-team coach in 1955. He had already helped Walter Winterbottom on England tours and courses ('He was a wonderful coach, taught me an enormous amount,' said Nicholson) and had trained the Cambridge University side for a time. He went with the England side to Sweden for the 1958 World Cup and, when Jimmy Anderson resigned a couple of month's later, the Tottenham board apparently asked the FA to help in making recommendations for the succession. It is possible that the board were just asking for confirmation of what they already knew. The reply soon came back, probably from Stanley Rous thought Nicholson, that the club had already got the very man at White Hart Lane, that they did not need to search any further and that Nicholson had already proved his abilities to the FA, never mind the club.

Bill Nicholson was regularly described as dour and pessimistic during his period as manager, adjectives which were impossible to apply and barely possible to believe talking to him later. The only hint of pessimism came when discussing the game's present state and prospects for the future: 'I go and watch Second and Third Division games nowadays and I think to myself: "How can even the managers of these teams bear to watch them 46 times a year?" It can be terrible. There's no point anyone pretending that the game has not lost a lot of what made it worth watching.'

Otherwise he was nothing if not positive, particularly about the 1980s side at the time of the interview. His pride also shone through when he spoke of the academic successes of his daughters and of his then five-year old grandson's enthusiasm for football, but, above all else, when he described how the Double side came together.

'People talk about the team's skills, rightly, but they don't seem to recall that the team succeeded because it was very fit and very well organised. That was almost disguised *behind* the skill. People used to come to Cheshunt from all over Europe to watch our training routines – stood there with stop watches and notebooks in their hands, writing it all down.'

When Nicholson became coach the players still often trained at the ground. When it rained they had to train under the stand where there were girders all over the place. 'Because of those years in the army, I could

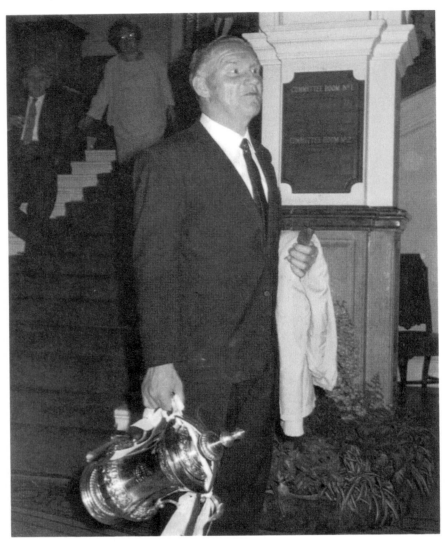

One man and his Cup; a contented Bill Nicholson carries the FA Cup away from Tottenham Town Hall on Sunday 21 May 1967, the day after Spurs had beaten Chelsea 2–1 in the first all-London professional Cup final. It was Nicholson's fifth trophy of the decade. 'People talk about the skills of Spurs' sides in that period,' Nicholson was to say, 'but they don't seem to recall that the side succeeded because it was fit and very well organised. That was almost disguised behind the skill.'

work out indoor routines where the girders didn't get in the way. But I pushed for the indoor training pitch (opened in the early 1960s) and that made a big difference.' Nicholson clearly loved the coaching; devising new routines, analysing how best to coach two-on-one situations, or how to tackle, making defenders play as forwards or vice versa, so that they could appreciate better their own roles. He would look at every facet of the game. Most things could be improved, could be broken down so that they could be coached; he would not accept that players either had or did not have certain skills and could not get better with the right routines.

'I was never a desk manager, like many were at that time. I would tell the directors that they could get me in the office before a quarter to ten. After that I would be out with the team, coaching'.

The side Nicholson took charge of already contained most of the Double side, but there were two or three vital additions to be made later. 'I'd been chasing Dave Mackay for some time but there seemed to be no chance; the club had enough money for a big signing, the directors wanted one and the transfer deadline was coming up. I went down to Wales to see Mel Charles. He wasn't sure and said he'd ring me at the weekend. Then, out of the blue, my sources in Scotland told me that Mackay might just be available. Only I couldn't do anything because of Charles – I couldn't buy them both

and I'd given my word and had to hope he'd say no. So I waited until Saturday night, when Mel Charles thankfully rang to say he wasn't going to sign. I got the sleeper to Edinburgh, signed Mackay from Tommy Walker at Hearts the following morning (which was the deadline) and brought him back. I remember the station-master at Edinburgh nearly went through the roof when he saw us together and realised what had happened. Nobody else got a whisper.

'With John White the problem was stamina. He seemed so frail I wasn't sure he was tough enough. Then someone – Danny, I think – mentioned that he was a cross-country runner. So I rang up White's army unit (he was on national service at the time) and talked to his commandant. "Yes, he's a bloody good footballer," said this officer, "but he'll not be playing football on Saturday. He'll be running for us in a race." We talked about John White and I soon discovered that he was an excellent cross-country runner. That convinced me.'

Les Allen's arrival was also a little different from the way it was reported at the time. 'Actually,' says Nicholson, 'Ted Drake [the Chelsea manager] rang me and said he needed Johnny Brooks. Ted was in trouble fighting relegation at the time, and I didn't really feel Brooks was the right man for his team then. But Ted persisted so I looked at their squad. Les Allen was in the reserves and it struck me as a good swap. Chelsea wanted money as well but I told them what they could do about that. What I liked about Les was that he could ghost into scoring positions, like Martin Peters.' Allen had already been on Spurs' books once, as an amateur, but had preferred to sign professional forms with Chelsea.

'So there was the Double side. There was no single secret to it, just as there's no school for managers where you can go and be told how to win things. The players in that side didn't get the rewards they should have though that wasn't clear at the time. I'm sorry about that, and that I was always too busy to appreciate the small things about people and about our success, which is a great pity.'

He still lived in the small house close to the ground which had been home to his wife Darkie (so called because she was the darker of twins) and himself for years and remained a positive presence at the club, without in any way casting shadows over the manager as Matt Busby did over his successors. Indeed, it was Keith Burkinshaw who insisted that Nicholson rejoin the staff in 1976. 'It's been my life, Tottenham Hotspur, and I love the club,' he readily agreed and he made the parallel between the Tottenham sides he served as a player and as a manager. Of the 1950 champions he said: 'Other clubs got to know our style . . . it was only for a short time. But the chief factor was that a lot of us went over the hill together. It was impossible to replace them. In a good side you can paper over the cracks with one or even two good players and the loss is not allowed to show too much. You can still play well and get by. But when it involves a lot of players going, then it's a real problem. It happened to me with the 1960 team . . . a lot of them finished at around the same time. That was the saddest thing, but I wouldn't have missed a moment.'

1971

**The Glory Game • Four seasons, four finals •
League Cups • Chivers and troubled times •
Rotterdam again • Nicholson resigns • Terry Neill
and Keith Burkinshaw • Relegation and renewal**

The seventies was the era of defensive football, the day of the spoiler. As the new decade opened in August 1970, with Spurs suffering their worst start since 1958–59, questions began to be asked as to whether they had players with the heart for this type of game.

After a 1–0 fourth round FA Cup replay defeat at Crystal Palace on 28 January 1970, Nicholson made sweeping changes. The Palace defeat was a watershed for Jimmy Greaves whose great goalscoring skills had rapidly gone into decline. It was his last game for Spurs, dropped along with Gilzean, Knowles and Kinnear. In March Nicholson moved into the transfer market in a deal which brought England World Cup star Martin Peters from West Ham for £200,000. The deal included Greaves in part-exchange. Sidney Wale, who

was in his first year as chairman following the death of his father, Frederick. wrote in the 1970–71 handbook: 'We shall always remember the joy and pleasure Jimmy gave us.' In just over eight years, Greaves scored 267 goals in senior matches, leaving behind him two club records which are still unbroken: his 37 First Division goals in a season (1962–63) and his aggregate League goals, 220 between 1961 and 1970. In his place, Nicholson went for experience rather than promise. Peters, still only 26, with his subtle ball skills and brilliantly timed blindside runs, was a goal-taker and goal-maker who had match-winning experience at the ultimate level.

Spurs finished the 1969–70 season eleventh in the First Division, their lowest for eleven years. They responded in the tradition set by their uncanny knack of winning major titles at

Alan Gilzean goes up with Denis Smith (right) and Alan Bloor of Stoke City during a League game in February 1972. Gilzean was signed from Dundee in 1964 and played for Tottenham for ten successful years, retiring at the age of 36. 'Football's not a job or a career – you're meant to enjoy it,' he said in 1972, 'I get paid to enjoy myself!'

OPPOSITE PAGE: The three goals which gave Spurs their two League Cup wins in 1971 and 1973. TOP: Martin Chivers scores the first goal of the 1971 final against Aston Villa. In the 78th minute keeper John Dunn could only parry Jimmy Neighbour's shot and Chivers followed up to break a rather poor, dead-locked game.

CENTRE: Just three min-utes later Chivers scored his second goal of the 1971 final and dispelled any hopes Third Division Villa's supporters might have clung to. Fred Turnbull (number 5) and Dunn could do nothing to stop a convincing run which had shown Chivers at his best. He had won his first cap just three weeks before, against Malta, and had finally recovered from the disastrous injury which kept him out of the game from September 1968 to August 1969. The length of time it took Chivers to regain his strength and confidence can be gauged from the fact that his first full cap came nearly four years after he won the last of his Under-23 selections. It can be argued that Spurs lost the best years of Chivers' career because of injury.

BOTTOM: Substitute Ralph Coates (far right) turns away after scoring the only goal of the 1973 League Cup final against Norwich City. In the 72nd minute a long throw from Chivers was touched on by Peters and Coates pushed the ball past keeper Keelan. It was probably the high-light of Coates' career with Spurs and it settled an extremely poor final throughout which Norwich, in their first Division 1 season, had been on the defensive. For Spurs it meant re-entry to Europe as well as becoming the first club to win the trophy twice. The winning side of 1971 was: Jennings, Kinnear, Knowles, Mullery, Collins, Beal, Gilzean, Perryman, Chivers, Peters and Neighbour. In 1973 England replaced Collins, Pearce replaced Neighbour, and Pratt replaced Mullery.

the start of a new decade. And their victory in the 1971 League Cup final heralded a revival in their fortunes. Spurs reached Wembley via four consecutive home ties and a semi-final against a Bristol City side struggling in the Second Division. Spurs' final opponents, too, weren't the most awesome in the world – Third Division Aston Villa.

Villa proved no pushovers, hitting the woodwork and forcing a goal-line clearance from Perryman. But with 12 minutes remain-ing and Villa holding a grip in midfield, Spurs broke the deadlock with two goals from Chivers to win 2-0.

With Chivers shaking off the effects of a bad knee injury, sustained three seasons earli-er, to produce his best form – 29 goals from 54 games – Spurs enjoyed a resurgence in the League and FA Cup too. Only an inspired performance by Ray Clemence in a quarter-final replay at White Hart Lane prevented them from reaching the FA Cup semi-final at the expense of Liverpool, while in the League a much improved defensive record (33 goals conceded against 55 the previous season) lift-ed them to third, their best position since 1967. How ironic that their last home game should have been against Arsenal, who were seeking a goalless draw or victory to clinch the Championship and first leg of their own Double exactly ten years on from Spurs' more historic achievement. From the glories of one-touch, the game had deteriorated to a monot-onous succession of high balls to a couple of big front-runners. Spurs came off second best when George Armstrong eventually found the head of Kennedy to give Arsenal the winning goal they needed to bring the title to Highbury.

The 1971-72 season saw Chivers continue his prolific goalscoring form – 44 goals in 64 matches – and Spurs create another British club record. On 17 May 1972, they won the new UEFA Cup, the successor to the defunct Inter-Cities Fairs Cup, thus becoming the first British club to win two of the European trophies. Only Liverpool and Manchester United have ever matched this feat. When the end came for Nicholson two years later, it wasn't Spurs' failure in Europe, the FA Cup or League Cup which was at the root of the problem, but their inability to win a League match. The anomaly was frequently remarked on but never satisfactorily explained, though chairman Wale said 'It was as if the players had got such a taste for Europe that it was the only competition in which they could raise their game.'

On a cold December afternoon in Bucharest, Spurs once again rose out of their League doldrums to inflict another impressive defeat on European opposition. Spurs beat Rapid 2-0 to finish 5-0 aggregate winners.

After Spurs' heady European campaigns, it was a bit of an anticlimax to be facing less than exotic Wolverhampton Wanderers in the UEFA Cup final itself. In a match the Press rightly dubbed 'The Forgotten Final', Spurs survived a tremendous Wolves onslaught in the second leg at White Hart Lane to emerge 3-2 aggregate winners.

"THE GLORY GAME"

The publishing of *The Glory Game* by Hunter Davies was a diversion in 1972. A minor sen-sation when it appeared, it remains the most controversial inside view of how any Football League club works. At the time journalist Michael Hart commented: 'The exposure is total and absolute. No one is spared. As one player put it to me: "He has dug his holes too deeply. I am surprised the club passed the transcript." Understandably the hierarchy at Tottenham were not happy with Mr Davies. The players, too, had a few choice phrases for him . . . (but) as one observed: "There's nothing we can do. It's all true".' But Mike Langley in *The People* said on 29 October 1972: 'The book has been scourged over the past few days by reviews of staggering naivety . . . it's been suggested that Chivers, Mullery and even Mrs Nick might make . . . a point of smashing Mr Davies's front teeth down his throat. But no one mentioned that he'd an arrangement with the club. That each player, and fan Morris Keston, read and approved his individual chapter. That the entire book was scrutinised . . . by club chairman Sidney Wale.' Langley went on to say that the man-agement and players were taking part of the profit from the book (implying that it was to their benefit to make it more spicy than usual) and concludes, interestingly, that: '. . . far from doing Spurs down I'd say he's glossed over a few sensitive details.' Twenty-odd years on, it actually reflects extremely well on the club that the author was allowed the freedom of a whole season with the side to write the book, and that the publishers were allowed to sell it without any of the devaluing censorship that so often accompanies anything written about football.

Up front Martin Chivers had his best sea-son to date in terms of goals scored, but he tended to have too many anonymous matches and was frequently the focal point of Nicholson's criticisms. Constant carping was the manager's way of trying to rouse and motivate the infuriatingly inconsistent, though talented, striker, ('He never stopped moaning' Chivers complains in *The Glory Game*).

However, the Spurs manager was faced with a player problem of a different nature as the 1971–72 season drew to a close. In an unprecedented revolt over pay, no fewer than nine first team players, including Chivers, were in dispute over their contracts. To the consternation of the board there were revela-tions in the Press about how poorly players were paid in comparison with the rest of the First Division (if not with the country at large) and, worst of all, that players at (admit-tedly highly successful) Arsenal were paid nearly twice as much. Led by Welsh interna-tional centre-half Mike England, the Spurs players optimistically demanded parity with their contemporaries at Highbury.

The UEFA Cup was a personal triumph for club skipper Alan Mullery. He scored a vital long range equaliser in the away leg of the UEFA Cup semi-final against AC Milan (Spurs drew 1–1 to win 3–2 on aggregate) and scored again, fairy tale like, in the 1–1 home draw against Wolves which clinched the Cup. It turned out to be a glorious swan-song for 'Mullers'. In the summer he made a perma-nent move back to Fulham.

WEMBLEY AGAIN

The following season repeated the pattern of 1971–72 – good cup performances contrasting

Kevin Keegan and Alan Mullery take off during a League game on 4 September 1971. Spurs won 2–0 with goals from Chivers and Peters. Nicholson said of Mullery: 'He was honest and dedicated and, of course, he was there at just the right time in 1972. It couldn't have worked out better for him.'

The result was that from a profit of £300,000 in their League Cup season of 1972-73, proceeds from the following season tumbled to a mere £35,000. Worse still, forecasts for the following season, 1974-75, when Spurs would be out of Europe for the first time in four years, were for a loss of £250,000. And the club was already committed to spending £200,000 on ground improvements.

August 1973, and for the second season in succession Spurs kicked off without a new signing. Unable to get the players he wanted, Nicholson decided to concentrate instead on his home-grown youngsters. Ray Evans established himself in the right-back position occupied for eight seasons by Joe Kinnear, Cyril Knowles was to make way for Terry Naylor and, in midfield, Nicholson gave an extended run to Chris McGrath, a promising young Belfast boy who had turned professional only 18 months earlier.

RIOTS IN ROTTERDAM

By March 1974, Spurs had won even greater admiration in Europe with a memorable fourth round UEFA Cup victory over West Germany's FC Cologne (2-1 away and 3-0 at home) while at home their image was being further tarnished by the threat of relegation. They recovered to finish eleventh in the League but Nicholson admitted: 'It was the most disappointing season since my first as manager. Had Spurs beaten Feyenoord in the UEFA Cup final in May 1974, Nicholson had intended to resign there and then.

But he was denied that coup de grace when, in a grisly sequel to the Battle of Bucharest, Spurs were traumatically beaten in the Riot of Rotterdam, their first defeat in ten major cup finals spanning 73 years. Feyenoord were formidable opposition. They had four internationals who, two months later, were to help take Holland to the World Cup final against West Germany.

Spurs needed a decisive home victory to stand any chance of maintaining their record of cup invincibility. With four minutes left and Spurs leading 2–1, de Jong stole a late equaliser. The writing was on the wall and everyone at White Hart Lane knew it. The 2–0 defeat at Rotterdam eight days later against a team of Feyenoord's quality was, on Sidney Wale's admission, no disgrace – that belonged to the so-called fans who brought mayhem to the match and to the streets of Europe's biggest port in a night of mindless violence and vandalism. Thousands of pounds worth of damage were caused to shops and cars during a rampage which resulted in 70 arrests and 200 injuries. Because Nicholson went out to talk to the crowd he was unable to give his usual half-time team talk. When Nicholson came back Steve Perryman thought he detected tears in the manager's eyes.

UEFA's punishment, ordering Spurs to play their next two European home ties at least 250 kilometres from White Hart Lane, was largely academic. There was no more Europe for Spurs in the 1970s, and in 1980 came UEFA's 25th anniversary amnesty.

NICHOLSON'S LAST STAND

Nicholson, his resignation plans temporarily shelved, returned to try and pick up the pieces. He faced problems on nearly all fronts, most of all with Chivers, who had finally made it clear

with poor league form. The difference this time was that the levels of achievement on all fronts were that much lower. They finished eighth in the League, two places lower than the previous season, were knocked out by Derby in the fourth round of the FA Cup (losing 5–3 in a home replay after leading 3–1 with five minutes to go), lost to Liverpool in the semi-finals of the UEFA Cup on the away goals rule (despite winning 2–1 at White Hart Lane), yet still managed to pull a rabbit out of the hat by lifting the League Cup for the second time in three years when they beat Norwich 1–0. The final was an individual success for Ralph Coates.

Events in football were now being influenced by the country's economic climate. Big pay packets and spiralling overheads were eating into or eradicating altogether the profits. Falling attendances throughout the game, as much a sign of the diminishing entertainment value of soccer as of the general effects of inflation and tight money, added to clubs' financial worries. And, for all their success, Spurs were as badly hit as anyone.

that White Hart Lane was no longer big enough for both of them. Nicholson replied: 'No one leaves until I've found replacements.' That was the rub. Replacements were proving almost impossible to find.

Nicholson's one transfer success in the summer of 1974 was persuading Alfie Conn, a young left-sided midfield player with hippie-length hair, to sign from Glasgow Rangers for £150,000. Nicholson had £500,000 to spend on new players but, as the new season opened with a series of calamitous defeats, Nicholson claimed that several top-class players were demanding five-figure sums 'under the counter' to move. It was Spurs' persistent refusal to pay these sums, as Sidney Wale confirmed, that lay behind Nicholson's failure to bring star names to White Hart Lane.

The breaking point for Nicholson came at the start of the 1974-75 season when Spurs, without a point, plunged to their fourth League defeat in their fourth match of the season at home to Manchester City. A crowd of 20,079 watched in dismay as Spurs lost 2–1. It equalled their worst ever League start 62 years before. For Nicholson defeat was the final straw. On the Saturday evening, after 38 years with Tottenham, the last 15 of them as the most successful manager in their history and as one of the most successful with any British club ever, he resigned.

Although Wale wouldn't say so publicly, there is no doubt that the contract dispute which upset Nicholson most was with Martin Chivers. Chivers' love-hate relationship with the club through this period was its most intriguing feature. Probably against his own wishes, Chivers became the dominant factor in its success. When he was playing well, and scoring goals, Spurs could win trophies. When he wasn't, they didn't. So his bad games were much more noticeable than those of other players, and he would receive much more criticism, both inside and outside the club, because of that.

The other strange factor about Nicholson's perceived problems at this point was that they had reached a cup final in each of the previous four seasons, and won three of them. Not to mention seven semi-finals in six seasons – surely enough to keep the most fickle fan interested.

Nicholson's first choice as successor was his assistant, Eddie Baily. After Baily he supported Blanchflower and Johnny Giles, either individually or as a team. The changeover might have been handled more smoothly if one or other of the alternative candidates had been given the job. Spurs didn't ask Nicholson's advice – they attempted to make the appointment as straightforward as possible by advertising the post. But they had to contend first with a massive Press campaign in favour of the man said to be the number one choice of the fans, and arguably the one everyone was expecting to take over, Double hero Danny Blanchflower. Immediately identified with the glory years, Blanchflower was a man who shared Nicholson's idealism but was still young enough, at 47, not to share his despair.

John Toshack tries to evade Alan Mullery in another Anfield clash of the early 1970s. Spurs did not win a match there for 73 years. Mullery joined the club from Fulham in 1964 and returned there eight years later, but not until after a fairy tale return to the side which saw him score a vital semi-final goal against AC Milan and another against Wolves in the final to help lift the UEFA Cup. Mullery suffered during his early days at the club by being compared with the great half-back line of the Double year: 'People always told me what Dave Mackay had done. Like telling me the wonders he performed after his injury. You wanted to say it's me, it's my injury, this is how I feel and I'm not putting it on.' Mullery, as Spurs' captain, lifted the club's second European trophy at White Hart Lane on 17 May 1972. It was also, as it happened, his last ever game for the club.

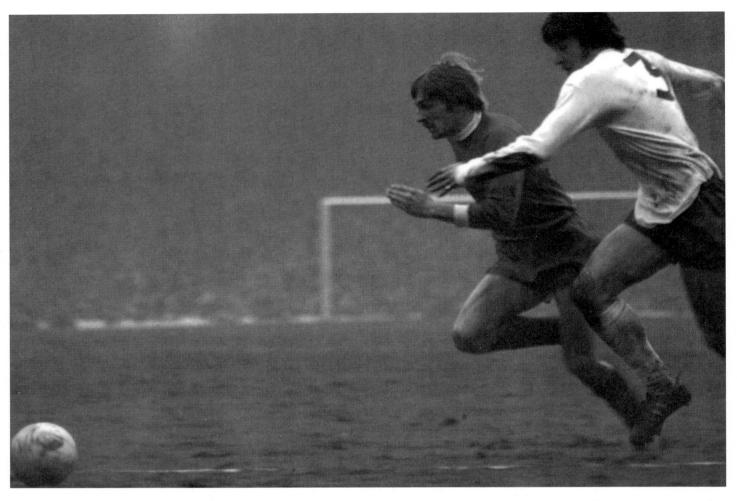

He had retired from the game in 1964 vowing never to go into management and spending the years instead trying to put an errant soccer world to rights from the platform of sports journalism in the *Sunday Express*.

'I know Bill wanted Danny to have the job,' said Wale, 'and I know they discussed it together. I told Bill that if he wanted Danny to be considered, Danny would have to apply like the others. He never did. It's as simple as that.'

Privately, the board feared that Blanchflower would challenge their authority as he had done constantly as a player and that he would ruffle the hitherto calm waters of White Hart Lane.

THE APPOINTMENT OF NEILL

In naming Hull City's Terry Neill the board had chosen someone with a good deal more in common with Blanchflower than with Nicholson; moreover, as a former and recent long-serving Arsenal player, Neill was among the very last people the fans wanted.

Capped a then record 59 times for Northern Ireland (thus beating the record held by Blanchflower and Billy Bingham), Neill had spent 12 years as centre-half at Arsenal before serving his 'apprenticeship' player-managing Second Division Hull and the Northern Ireland team. Like Blanchflower, Neill came from Belfast, shared the same energetic enthusiasm for the game, though not Blanchflower's brilliance, and had also captained club and country. And, while not as articulate as Blanchflower, he still had plenty to say for himself; indeed arguably rather too much, as

the Spurs board would find to their regret. He was 32 when he applied for the Spurs job, offering a happy-go-lucky football philosophy: 'If I fail, I've got a wonderful wife and two beautiful daughters to go back to.'

He took over as the First Division's youngest manager with a simple but daunting brief: to keep Spurs up. It was 13 September; Spurs were still bottom with just two points from their first six League games and had just been knocked out of the League Cup 4-0 at home by Middlesbrough.

Neill's relaxed approach ('I want you all to go out and enjoy yourselves' he started by telling his struggling team) brought mixed results, though helped by some points-earning goals from his new striker John Duncan, bought from Dundee on 19 October for £125,000. But questions began to be raised in the Press about Neill's apparently unconcerned attitude in the face of crisis. Neill was under constant fire from the fans, too. 'They made it clear they didn't want me from the outset,' he says. 'My every word and action was scrutinised for its level of devotion towards Tottenham Hotspur. It was a test of loyalty. In other words, what was I doing with THEIR club.'

For season 1974–75, the staff numbered 32 professionals and 13 apprentices, but by the end of the season those totals would be considerably fewer as Neill cleared the decks for his younger players to emerge and time caught up with the remaining stars from Nicholson's final days.

First to go of the old guard were Martin Peters and Mike England. Following a 3-0 home defeat by Leicester in February, which left Spurs even more firmly embedded in the relegation struggle, Neill sold Peters to Norwich for £40,000 – where he was to enjoy a renaissance under John Bond – while England walked out after a row, to retire from the English game at the age of 32. Spurs continued to live dangerously until the very last game of the season. The drama did wonders for the gates. For their penultimate home game against Chelsea, 50,998 watched Spurs win 2–0. A week later 43,762 were at Highbury for a 1–0 defeat by Arsenal which left Spurs needing victory in their last match, at home to Leeds two days later on Monday 28 April, to stay in the First Division. Anything less and they, not Luton, might be relegated. Neill's preparation included calling in a hypnotherapist to convince the team they were going to win. The idea worked, or rather it didn't fail, because in front of a 49,886 crowd Spurs stormed to a 4–2 win with two goals from a back-in-favour Cyril Knowles and one each from Conn and Chivers. But for Neill victory was a bitter sweet sensation. 'It was as if we'd won the Cup,' he says, 'but I'd worked 24 hours a day, seven days a week to keep Spurs in the First Division and I'd taken a lot of stick from the fans for my trouble. Yet here they all were chanting my name and calling for me to go out on to the pitch and acknowledge their cheers. Did I go? I went straight home. I'd paid my dues.'

BURKINSHAW'S ARRIVAL

Spurs fans don't thank Neill for very much these days but one of his appointments which must warrant their gratitude is Keith Burkinshaw, brought in as coach during the summer of 1975 (Neill's Hull coach, Wilf Dixon, who'd replaced Eddie Baily as assistant manager in the change-over, was moved to youth recruitment). The playing staff was strengthened by the arrival in September 1975 of a tall and powerful, if inelegant, central defender, Willie Young, who cost £80,000 from Aberdeen, and, two months later, striker Gerry Armstrong from Irish club Bangor. As essentially a players' manager, Neill had a cordial but distant relationship with the board. 'During the first 18 months they let me get on with the job without interference,' he said later. But events during the spring and summer of 1976 brought Neill's brief Tottenham reign to a swift and sour finale. On the morning of Sunday 25 April, the players prepared to set off on their close-season tour of Australia and the Pacific. Neill had promised a seat on the coach to Heathrow Airport for the only fan travelling with the party, 78-year-old retired bookmaker Mr Fred Rhye, a devoted follower who had missed only three of their matches in 40 years and was popular throughout the club. Yet Sidney Wale, for reasons which he went to some lengths to explain, chose the occasion to embarrass Neill by publicly countermanding his orders. Rhye was

Gerry Armstrong and Leicester's Steve Sims fight for the ball on 14 May 1977, Spurs' last day in the First Division for over a year. They won the game 2–0 with goals from Jimmy Holmes and John Pratt but it did them little good. They were already condemned to Second Division football for the first time in nearly three decades and eventually finished the season in bottom position. Armstrong had joined Spurs late in 1975 from Irish club Bangor but, with the arrival of Archibald and Crooks, was to move to Watford.

123

RIGHT: The clock at Molineux shows 8.40pm as Martin Chivers rises to meet a Mike England free-kick (one of Spurs' rehearsed moves), outjump Frank Munro and put the Londoners 1-0 ahead in the UEFA Cup final first leg. Wolves equalised from a McCalliog free-kick, but Chivers made it 2-1 with perhaps the best goal he ever scored for the club. Picking the ball up near the half-way line, he went past two defenders and shot on the run from all of thirty yards. The return leg was a perfect finale to the season for Spurs, the last game and the biggest crowd – 54,303. Mullery's headed goal made it 1-1 and the trophy was Spurs' – their eighth victory in their eighth cup final.

OPPOSITE TOP: Ralph Coates is hugged by an admirer at the end of the second leg of the UEFA Cup Final in 1972. Coates' arrival from Burnley was a matter of some secrecy and he actually signed for the club in the back of a car outside a Staffordshire hotel. At the time there was talk of Burnley wanting to keep Arsenal out of the bidding, but Nicholson insists that Burnley manager Jimmy Adamson was simply determined to honour his promise that Spurs could have first option on Coates.

OPPOSITE BOTTOM: Alan Gilzean and a very young Steve Perryman celebrate the 1972 UEFA Cup victory over Wolves.

told he would have to find alternative transport to the airport (he was paying his own way to follow Spurs) and Neill was left to hurriedly organise a taxi.

Neill won't admit to deliberately provoking the showdown which led to the final breach, but his actions at the end of the tour had that effect. As a reward for winning all nine matches, Neill promised some of his players and staff a bonus out of the proceeds of the tour, but the directors, and Wale in particular, were not prepared to sanction them. The party arrived back in England on 24 May and Neill handed in his resignation a fortnight later.

As soon as news of Neill's resignation reached Highbury, Arsenal chairman Denis Hill-Wood phoned Wale to see if the way was clear to offer Neill a job, and, within a fortnight of quitting Spurs, he was installed as Arsenal manager in succession to Bertie Mee.

Keith Burkinshaw had stayed well in the background throughout the Neill dispute. He had brief managerial experience at Workington and Scunthorpe and clearly had aspirations of his own, but his only experience in the transfer jungle, for instance, was spending three months trying to raise the £300 Workington needed to pay for a Scottish junior.

As one of the game's quiet men, Burkinshaw already had a lot going for him so far as Spurs were concerned. A workmanlike wing-half of moderate ability as a player, he had been rejected by Wolves before joining Liverpool. He made a handful of first-team appearances and spent most of his time in the reserves. He had just concluded a seven-year spell as a coach at Newcastle, the last four of them, between 1971 and 1975, in charge of the first team. In his final full season at St James' Park, Newcastle reached the FA Cup final – their first since 1955. His reward was the sack.

Burkinshaw believed that the good working relationship he had established with the Spurs players helped his claim to the managership. But what clinched the job for him was the impression he made on Sidney Wale during the fateful close season tour. 'On the tour I got the chance to get to know Keith,' said Wale. 'I found him hard-working, honest and I knew he was well-liked by the players. It was those qual-

ities which convinced the board when we considered his application.'

Spurs were playing with their backs to the wall from the moment they lost 3–1 at Ipswich in the first match of the 1976-77 season. Burkinshaw analysed the problem simply when he said: 'We just weren't good enough.' More specifically they were weak at the back and were beset by problems in attack. John Duncan, who had been top scorer for the previous two seasons, missed the first eleven games with a back injury which limited his first team appearances that season to just nine games, and in which he scored only four times. Defensively, the team started badly and then got worse. In consecutive away games they conceded 13 goals, including the club's then heaviest defeat when they went down 8–2 at Derby. The one defender who emerged with his reputation unscathed from the winter blitzkrieg was goalkeeper Pat Jennings. 'He didn't stand a chance,' said Burkinshaw.

Burkinshaw's early forays into the transfer market came before the full extent of the team's shortcomings were apparent. His first buy was £75,000 forward Ian Moores from Stoke in August. Peter Taylor, a winger of capricious skills who had played for England while still in the Third Division, and whom Neill had already tried to sign, came from Crystal Palace for £125,000 in September. When his defence crumbled, Burkinshaw imported John Gorman from Carlisle in November, but still the defeats piled up. On the cup front, the team suffered the ignominy of losing at home to Third Division Wrexham in the third round of the League Cup, and equally embarrassing was their exit at the first hurdle from the FA Cup when they lost 1–0 at Second Division Cardiff.

For the League game against Birmingham on 19 March Burkinshaw played his final card. Steve Perryman, club captain and mid-field ever present, was switched to the back four where Burkinshaw felt his leadership qualities, quick reading of the game and overall purposefulness could marshal a department which had lost all coordination and confidence. The move helped bring about 12 points from the last 13 League games of the season, but it came too late to save Spurs. The killer result was a 5–0 defeat at Manchester City in the penultimate match. Spurs were relegated for the first time in four decades.

If anyone's knives were out for Burkinshaw, Wale did a remarkably good job of keeping them out of his manager's back. 'I didn't expect the sack,' said Burkinshaw, 'but in view of our performance that season, they would have been justified in getting rid of me.'

Despite the setbacks of that season, Wale remained impressed by Burkinshaw's dedication and hard work. 'He showed many of the qualities of Bill Nicholson. Like Bill, he was never a publicity-seeker. He was honest, hard-working and, in short, more the sort of manager we'd been used to and we liked.'

THE JENNINGS THUNDERBOLT

Two decisions in his first year in charge, which were to prove of long-lasting significance, reflected Burkinshaw's awareness as a tactician, but his lack of experience as a manager. The single most contentious issue of the decade was, of course, Pat Jennings' sale to Arsenal, the repercussions of which rebounded on Burkinshaw with three-fold force. He had already sold Willie Young to Highbury in March 1976, and Jennings's departure was coupled with the sale, also to Arsenal, of defender Steve Walford. All three proved bargain buys for Terry Neill, none more so than Jennings, as Spurs fans were never to let Burkinshaw forget.

Young was sold right at the climax of the relegation battle because, despite his aerial strength, he possessed few ground skills and as a former player who perhaps shared Young's relative lack of natural ability, it was all the more important to Burkinshaw to create a team without such shortcomings.

The sale of Jennings was under very different circumstances. He was 31 at the time and the previous season had set a new club appearance record of 449 League matches, passing Ted Ditchburn's total of 418. He'd been voted Football Writers' Footballer of the Year in 1973, the Professional Footballers' Player of the Year in 1975–76 and had been made an MBE in the Queen's Birthday Honours List the same year. He was also Northern Ireland's most capped player, having passed Terry Neill's record of 59 caps in the 1975–76 season.

Standing 6ft tall with hands as big as frying pans, he was the complete goalkeeper, probably the best in Britain and perhaps the world throughout the 1970s. Bought from Watford by Bill Nicholson in June 1964, for a bargain £30,000, Jennings had spent twelve illustrious years at White Hart Lane, collecting an FA Cup winners' medal in 1967, League Cup winners' medals in 1971 and 1973 and a UEFA Cup winners' medal in 1972. 'Pat,' says Sidney Wale, 'had seen it all and done it all.' Although Jennings never asked for a transfer, it was almost an embarrassment for Spurs to have to ask a goalkeeper of his calibre to play in the Second Division. Understandably, he didn't want to leave the top division.

Spurs believed they had a capable deputy in Barry Daines, and adequate cover in Welsh Under-21 international Mark Kendall. A former Spurs apprentice, Daines was seven years younger than Pat Jennings and had stood in competently for him 19 times during the 1976–77 season when the senior player was injured. More to the point, Daines had told Spurs that he could see no future for himself at the club if Jennings stayed. Burkinshaw pointed out, with some justification, that the consequences of the Jennings' sale would not have rebounded so hard on him if Daines' progress as goalkeeper hadn't been hampered by injury. Said Burkinshaw ruefully: 'Barry never came near to fulfilling his potential, while Pat went from strength to strength.'

Burkinshaw's scheme to get Spurs out of the Second Division was founded on his faith in attacking football, a brave philosophy in the Second Division. To that end he retained the industrious Perryman in the back four and turned Terry Naylor and Jimmy Holmes into a couple of overlapping full-backs ready to attack down the flanks. 'Everyone was right behind it,' he said.

He didn't have to wait long to be vindicated. In their first match of the new season, Spurs beat Sheffield United 4–2 with goals from John Duncan, Chris Jones and two penalties from Keith Osgood. And that really was the story of their season. Spurs amassed 83 goals for their highest total since 1965, but their attacking style took its toll in defence where 49 goals were conceded. The result was that, despite being the Second Division's top scorers, Spurs

were involved in a nail-biting race for the promotion line with Brighton, Southampton and Bolton. The issue was not resolved until the last Saturday of the season, with Spurs playing at Southampton and needing a draw to be certain of going up at Brighton's expense. By a happy coincidence, Southampton also needed only a point to be sure of their promotion place so, with both teams content to defend, the match ended in the goalless draw. It was a result which drew more than a little cynical comment, particularly from along the South Coast at the Goldstone Ground.

So Spurs were back in the First Division at their first attempt. And their return was a triumph not only for Burkinshaw's tactics but for Spurs' attacking style of play. For far from playing to smaller houses in the Second Division, they maintained the upward trend in their gates that Burkinshaw had managed to accelerate even in their relegation season. From a home average of 27,836 in Terry Neill's last season, attendances rose to 30,173 in the season Spurs went down and were swollen by an extra 68,119 fans in the Second Division for an average of 33,417. It was a figure bettered by only six other clubs in the Football League and came at a time when attendances generally were falling fast. 'I suppose people must have liked something we were doing,' said Burkinshaw afterwards.

1981

Two Cup wins in succession • Steve Perryman • Glenn Hoddle • The new stand • Chris Waddle • The return of Venables • The beginnings of financial problems

'*Wherever Spurs play, whether it's Manchester, Malta or Mauritius, we're famous. Soccer is about big clubs and star names, but most of all it's about people. You can be playing for the biggest club in the world with the biggest stars in the game, but if you don't enjoy it, if you don't get on with the people around you, you're wasting your time. I enjoy Spurs because at this club everyone, from the humblest backroom boy to the highest-paid player, is treated with equal respect. They're all equally important to our success. That's what makes Tottenham Hotspur a great football club.*'

Steve Perryman, club captain in the centenary season.

The transfer market is as much part of the mystique of the soccer world as magical goals and memorable cup wins. In the seventies the outstanding memory is unquestionably the coup which Keith Burkinshaw pulled off in the summer of 1978. It was a time when virtually no foreigners played in the Football League, though no one who saw Argentina win the World Cup a month before could have failed to be impressed by the bewitching skills of their diminutive midfield player, Osvaldo Ardiles.

The first inkling that a sensational transfer deal was in the offing came in the few lines Fleet Street newspapers gave to a news agency report from Buenos Aires on Wednesday 28 June that Ardiles was to sign for Manchester United.

The next report to hit the teleprinters in Fleet Street came on the evening of Tuesday 4 July, nine days after the World Cup final.

Osvaldo Ardiles, Ricky Villa, Terry Yorath and Glenn Hoddle, four of the eight internationals on the club's books that season, line up against Crystal Palace on 6 October 1979. Villa scored Spurs' only goal in a 1–1 draw.

On 11 January 1983 Ossie Ardiles made his return to English football. The Falklands crisis had led to the midfielder being transferred to Paris St Germain but Keith Burkinshaw eventually brought him back from abroad for a second time. He made a cautious return – playing for the reserves against Luton at Cheshunt in front of a few dozen spectators.

Again, Spurs were not mentioned. Ardiles' club, Huracan, was reported from Buenos Aires as saying that he had been transferred to Sheffield United for £530,000. The same report quoted Ardiles' World Cup teammate, Ricardo Villa, as saying he had been transferred from Racing Club, Buenos Aires, to Manchester City for £315,000. It was not until three days later, on Friday 7 July, that the real news came out and this time it was on every front page. Ardiles and Villa were joining Spurs in what Jeff Powell in the *Daily Mail* called the most sensational deal in British soccer history. David Lacey summed up a common reaction when he wrote in *The Guardian*: 'When Keith Burkinshaw went shopping and brought back Ardiles, it was as if the janitor had gone out to buy a tin of paint and had returned with a Velasquez. Astonishment that the Argentinians were coming at all is equalled by the incredulity that they were going to play for Spurs, who seemed to have lost faith in major transfers following the muted success of such purchases as Coates, Conn and Taylor.'

How did it all come about? On the morning of Thursday 29 June, a few days after Argentina's 3–1 win over Holland, Bill Nicholson was sitting in his office just across the corridor from where Burkinshaw was having a meeting when the phone rang. It was the Sheffield United manager Harry Haslam on the line, asking to speak to Keith. Burkinshaw, who only minutes earlier had returned from giving his manager's report to the monthly board meeting, takes up the story. 'Bill came in, told me Harry was on the line and I had to go into his office to take the call. Harry told me

that both Ardiles and Villa were available for transfer and wanted to play in England. The tie-up was through Antonio Rattin the old Argentinian captain, who was acting as agent but who is obviously still best known here for being sent off at Wembley in 1966. He was a big mate of Harry's and Harry was phoning a few clubs to see if they were interested. Like everyone else I'd watched Argentina in the World Cup. You dream about having players like that in your side but you never think it could come off.'

Burkinshaw lost no time. He went straight back to the board meeting, which was still in progress, got the directors' blessing to fly out to Buenos Aires to pursue the deal and began to make the necessary preparations. The League ban on overseas players had been lifted a couple of seasons earlier, but Burkinshaw still needed to be certain that the necessary work permit could be obtained and one of his first calls was to the Department of Employment, who told him there should be no problem with a player of that ability. At that stage he was going with the intention of signing just Ardiles.

Burkinshaw caught the Friday night flight, arrived in Buenos Aires on Saturday morning and checked into the Hotel Libertador. Within a matter of hours he had his first meeting with Ardiles. 'It was one of those occasions when you immediately know something is right,' said Burkinshaw, 'there was an instant rapport. Within twenty minutes of meeting him, he'd agreed to sign.' Ardiles' next words took Burkinshaw by surprise. 'He told me he had a friend, Ricardo Villa, who also wanted to play in England. Could he come too?'

One of the reasons why Burkinshaw was able to win his board's immediate approval for the trip was because Haslam had told him that Ardiles could be bought for around £350,000 – a bargain price by English standards, even in 1978. With the bankrupt state of Argentinian soccer and the virtually permanent devaluation of the Argentinian peso, clubs were prepared to let their players go for under their international market value just to reduce debts. Perversely, it also meant that they wouldn't then go to any domestic rival. For their part, the players were so poorly paid that, even under the British taxation system, they'd be ten times better off than staying at home. Burkinshaw didn't know much about Villa except that he was the big, bearded player Cesar Menotti had twice sent on as substitute (once for Ardiles) to add some steel to the midfield in two crucial group matches. What he did know was that for around £700,000 he could have two leading members of the squad that had just won the World Cup. To put the figure in perspective, it was £250,000 more than Manchester United had just paid Leeds for Gordon McQueen, whom Burkinshaw had failed to sign earlier in the summer.

Back in England, on the Sunday morning, Sidney Wale was about to have a drink with his wife before lunch when the phone rang. 'It was Keith calling from Buenos Aires,' recalled Wale, 'He told me he had a bit of a problem. There was another player who wanted to come too. Well, we'd agreed as a board on one but since Keith wanted an answer straight away, I told him to hang on, and did some quick mental arithmetic. I worked out how much the bank would allow us on overdraft, how much extra we could expect to raise from season ticket sales with all the interest that was bound to be aroused, and I thought, we'll take a chance, so I gave Keith the go-ahead. We were both putting our heads on the chopping block. It was a big gamble to take, but looking back on it now, it was the best decision I ever made.'

Burkinshaw reached agreement with Villa even more swiftly than with Ardiles. 'Within a minute of meeting him, he'd agreed to sign,' said Burkinshaw.

By the time the new League season came around on 19 August, the soccer-going public's attention focused with excitement and eager anticipation on the debuts of Ardiles and Villa. And the two Argentinians couldn't have asked for a sunnier South American day on which to make their entry into British football. A crowd of 41,223 turned out on a magnificent summer's afternoon at the City Ground, Nottingham, to watch the new champions Forest do battle with the most talked-about team in the League, Tottenham Hotspur.

With 26 minutes gone, Spurs were trailing 1–0 to a goal by Martin O'Neill when Peter Shilton was drawn out to a low cross from Ian Moores. But with a deft skill which belies his massive stature, Villa teased the ball away from Shilton's grasp and flicked it past the outstretched leg of Archie Gemmill into the corner of the net.

Villa would have to wait almost three years to score another goal with such public acclaim. But this was more than enough to be going on with. Spurs collected a well-deserved point in their opening match back in the First Division,

BELOW: When he arrived in 1978 Osvaldo Ardiles, was heralded as the most sensational import to British football of the decade. 'If Spurs had bought Batman and Robin they could scarcely have created greater curiosity,' said Brian James in the Daily Mail. Surprisingly Spurs paid slightly less for Ardiles than for Villa and the two cost around £700,000 in total, arguably the best deal of the decade. Ardiles soon became known as one of the club's humorists. When asked whether Keith Burkinshaw gave him more or different tactical instructions than Cesar Menotti he quickly replied. 'It is the same in both countries. The only difference is that in Argentina I understood them.'

THIS PAGE TOP: Trainer Johnny Wallis, manager Keith Burkinshaw and physio Mike Varney in the dug-out before kick-off. Burkinshaw had a relatively undistinguished career as a professional, as he recalls: 'As a 15-year-old I went to Wolves. When you were 17 they decided whether or not they would take you on – they decided against me. So I went to a Midland League club called Denaby United for about 13 weeks when Liverpool took me as a full-time pro. I was also working down the pits at the time. I was at Liverpool for four years but still in the reserves so I asked for a transfer and went to Workington for eight years. Ken Furphy was manager and we got promotion. After he left I took over as manager for 3 or 4 months, but left after a disagreement with the club and went to Scunthorpe with Freddie Goodwin. After three years I ended up as acting manager but at 33 cartilage trouble made me quit as a player and I went to Newcastle as a coach for Joe Harvey.'

THIS PAGE CENTRE: Garry Brooke gets in a fierce left foot shot at Middlesbrough. A local player, born in Bethnal Green, he scored a vital goal against Hull in the fourth round of the tri-umphant 1980–81 Cup run, but was granted a free transfer at the end of the 1984–85 season.

THIS PAGE BOTTOM: Tony Galvin contests pos-session with Geoff Palmer of Wolves.

OPPOSITE TOP (INSET): The aggressive side of Glenn Hoddle; Ardiles' arrival was a great plus for the England midfield play-er. 'Glenn has shown greater maturity,' said Burkinshaw a few months later. 'He's really begun to turn it on. Ardiles thinks he's a must for England.' Hoddle was to win 53 caps, all but nine while a Spurs player.

OPPOSITE TOP : Hoddle brings the ball away from England colleague Bryan Robson, then with West Bromwich Albion.

OPPOSITE BOTTOM: Ricky Villa takes on Villa's Gordon Cowans.

the Sunday papers proclaimed the result with predictable headlines like 'Viva Villa', and already Spurs were rather prematurely being tipped to win the Championship.

But the honeymoon was soon over. Only four days later, Spurs were brought down to earth with a bump. Playing their first home match before a crowd of 47,892, who laid on a South American-style confetti welcome for their new heroes, Spurs were roundly beaten 4–1 by Aston Villa. A 2–2 home draw against Chelsea followed and then a result which in two words and two figures rudely shattered Burkinshaw's brave new world; Liverpool 7 Tottenham 0. It is the only time in their history that Spurs have been defeated by a margin of seven goals in a Football League match. But their fans did at least see the next League champions that September day – Liverpool. For Keith Burkinshaw, the problem of grafting South American skill on to the muck and nettles of English league soccer was only just beginning.

Looking back on that new era in Spurs' history, Burkinshaw explained the dilemma in which he found himself. 'Over there,' he said, metaphorically pointing to a distant corner of the globe, 'all the attackers attack, and the defenders defend. That means all your midfield players attack as well. Ossie and Ricky didn't know the meaning of the word defend when they first came here. It's a coach's nightmare when you've got five against three – and the three are yours because the midfield's in attack. That's what happened to us at Liverpool and they're the sort of team who punish you for it.'

Spurs continued to win friends, if not as many matches as they would have liked, throughout the season. The curiosity factor of Ardiles and Villa swelled gates wherever they played, making Spurs the top away attraction in the League. While Villa struggled to secure a regular first team place, Ardiles delighted fans with his darting runs, perceptive passing and use of space. Pictures frequently show him with the ball glued to his right instep, while his eyes are glancing about to see who's in space.

'It's his terrific skill combined with the ability to play with his head up which makes him a world-class footballer,' said Burkinshaw when Ardiles had settled in. 'He's 5ft 6in and weighs under ten stone. People said he would be knocked all over the place when the pitches got heavy here in winter. But he's proved them all wrong. He's hardly had an injury since he arrived. There's a very tough character inside that little frame.'

Indeed, it was Ardiles' ability to ride heavy tackles and still maintain his superb balance which won him almost as much admiration as his marvellous ball skills. But despite his individual success, Spurs finished a moderate 11th in their first season back in the First Division One. They reached the quarter-finals of the FA Cup before going out 2–0 to Manchester United in an Old Trafford replay, but overall their achievement fell short of the high expectations held for them after such a sensational summer. And Burkinshaw still hadn't solved the problem of how to make the best use of his new acquisitions.

Spurs skipper Steve Perryman summed up the problem: 'We'd come up from the Second Division using a winger and overlapping full-backs to provide crosses for tall front men who were good with their heads. But with Ardiles and Villa, we naturally channelled everything through midfield. We were playing shorter, quicker balls, changing our game to a style which our strikers just weren't used to. It was unfair to expect them to play that way.'

Spurs added the combative talents of Welsh international captain Terry Yorath to midfield for the 1979–80 season as they continued to juggle with the permutations. But even Yorath's ball-winning ability – a quality rather lacking in Spurs' armoury until then – failed to make much impression on their overall performance. Unlike the previous season, when their home form let them down, this time it was Spurs' away form which was disappointing, and the club slipped to 14th, scoring a meagre 52 goals while conceding 62.

The season was, however, memorable for one match: Spurs' third round FA Cup victory over Manchester United in yet another titanic struggle between the two clubs. United had beaten Spurs in the previous season's quarter-final replay, knocked them out of the current season's League Cup after two hectic second round legs, and here they were again, poised for their sixth cup meeting in two seasons after United had forced another 1–1 draw and another Old Trafford replay.

Ardiles had often been quoted about his dream of appearing in a Wembley final, but it seemed the chance had once again eluded him. And the prospect of a Spurs victory looked even more improbable when, midway through the Old Trafford match, goalkeeper Milija Aleksic, who had made a brilliant reflex save from Sammy McIlroy earlier in the game, was stretchered off with serious chest and head injuries after a collision with Joe Jordan. But after 'the save of the season', as Aleksic's effort was later voted by the BBC, came 'the goal of my life' by Osvaldo Ardiles.

With Glenn Hoddle in goal for the injured Aleksic, and the game heading for a second replay after 119 minutes without a goal from either side, Villa received the ball on the edge of the United penalty area. What happened next was a piece of South American magic, pure and simple. As Ardiles said: 'Most English players would have gone to the bye-line and crossed. But I knew Ricky's play. I knew he wanted to lay the ball back and I darted back to find space just inside the box. Just as I anticipated, Ricky saw me, rolled the ball back, and I looked up and with all my strength aimed for the top corner.'

The ball curled beyond the despairing Bailey and into the exact spot Ardiles had picked. Seconds later the whistle went and jubilant Spurs had won a match they were expected to lose. Victories followed over Swindon and Birmingham, but again the quarter-finals proved the bogey round. In a tense home game against Liverpool, they lost by the only goal, a typical opportunist effort from the edge of the box by Terry McDermott which won the BBC's 'Goal of the Season' award. Ardiles' dream would have to wait another season . . . but just another season.

Burkinshaw recognised that if his bold experiment was not to fizzle out in anticlimax, if his cherished vision of a truly great Spurs side was to be accomplished with his current

squad, time was running out. Ardiles and Villa each had just one more season of their contracts remaining, while Spurs' other prize possession, the richly gifted Glenn Hoddle, was also approaching the end of his contracted period.

Hoddle, so often an enigma with his breathtaking skills alternating with long periods of anonymity, had just enjoyed his most successful season. He increased his work-rate, conquered his frequently criticised habit of fading from matches well before the final whistle, and scored an impressive 22 goals in all. What was remarkable about Hoddle's feat was that not only did he score them playing from midfield, but that so many came from outside the penalty area. The point was never more clearly illustrated than when he scored on his England debut on 22 November 1979, with a superb 20-yard volley in the 2–0 win over Bulgaria at Wembley.

It was a dream start to an international career, but somehow Hoddle was unable to establish his England place, a fact that puzzled Burkinshaw as much as Hoddle's many admirers. 'He's so good that by now he should be among the world's best,' said Burkinshaw. 'Just talk to Ossie Ardiles. He says that Glenn is one of the best players he had come across in world football, and that's some accolade.'

In May 1980, with the backing of Spurs' new chairman, Arthur Richardson, Burkinshaw made the first of two new purchases that took Spurs' spending that summer to £1.5 million. Sidney Wale, who had surprised everyone at the club with his decision to resign from the board at the end of the 1979–80 season, admitted that the advent of the million-pound transfer was one of the reasons that caused him to retire from a soccer world he saw becoming increasingly inflationary. An accountant by profession and a sensibly cautious man with money, Wale liked to try to balance the books and he said: 'It alarmed and saddened me to see so many clubs going deeper and deeper into the red.' Ironically one of Wale's last decisions before his retirement and subsequent appointment as the club's life president was to sanction the building of Spurs' £4.1 million stand, an act he acknowledged, looking at the problems that clubs such as Chelsea, Sheffield United and Wolves had, could make or break Spurs.

But he said: 'We had little choice with the building of a new stand, although we could have settled for something a little less ambitious and grandiose. The original stand had wooden floors and was a potential fire hazard. The time had come when we had to do something.'

Whatever Wale's reservations about spending huge sums of money on new players, Arthur Richardson had no such inhibitions. Spurs reaped an instant dividend. Steve Archibald, bought in May from Aberdeen for £800,000, and Garth Crooks, a £650,000 August arrival from Stoke, struck up an explosive partnership which yielded 46 goals and helped the club to its first major title for eight years. Having correctly diagnosed Spurs' problems in attack, Burkinshaw had gone for two quicksilver strikers, essentially ground players

with the ability to play with their backs to goal, fit into the new midfield pattern, turn their marker, and, above all, score goals. In other words players who could profit from the split-second timing of Ardiles' short-ball game.

Archibald's name had been linked with Spurs for some time but the deal wasn't concluded until Aberdeen's shrewd manager, Alec Ferguson, had made certain of only Pittodrie's second Scottish League championship, and thus a hefty transfer fee for his twenty-goal star. England Under-21 striker Crooks had been a consistent scorer for Stoke over the previous three seasons with nearly fifty goals but, with the Potteries club anxious to pay off some of their debts and Spurs looking for a hunting partner for Archibald, a deal was swiftly concluded which meant that, in the best Spurs tradition, the club was once again starting a new season with a couple of exciting and expensive new stars.

Even skipper Steve Perryman, who saw so many big names come and go while making a record number of appearances for the club, admitted Spurs wouldn't be Spurs without their star signings. 'Our fans have come to expect it, I've come to expect it, I think most of the players have come to expect it,' he said. 'It brings an air of excitement to be club, fans talk about it, it brings them in each season and it means they know we're always trying to get things right.'

Crooks and Archibald got things right from the opening day of the season. Crooks marked his debut with a goal in the 2–0 win over Forest, and propelled by his August hat-trick in

Tottenham's somewhat fortuitous equalising goal in the 81st minute of the first game at Wembley in 1981. Just as Spurs' fans were beginning to believe that they were about to witness Tottenham's first ever FA Cup final defeat, their side was awarded a free-kick on the edge of the penalty area. As Hoddle stood over the ball, City winger Tommy Hutchison took up his appointed position on the left-hand edge (TOP) of the Manchester City wall. But as Hoddle took the kick (CENTRE) Hutchison ran behind the wall, presumably to cover any shot which might curl into the top right corner. In fact, at this stage, there was no danger; keeper Joe Corrigan had that side of the goal well protected and the free-kick was going wide. A few moments later (BOTTOM) the ball struck Hutchison on the angle of shoulder and head and was neatly deflected into the other corner of the net. Joe Corrigan had already made a safety dive and could do nothing. Hutchison thus became only the second man (Bert Turner of Charlton in 1946 was the other) to score for both sides in an FA Cup final, and at a time when he must have begun to think that his excellent first-half diving header had won the trophy for City.

the 4–3 win over Crystal Palace, Spurs led the First Division for the first time in nine years. But it was in the FA Cup that they enjoyed their finest hour. Said Perryman: 'We'd felt for a couple of seasons that our best chance of success was in the Cup. We knew our League form wasn't consistent enough to win the First Division but we thought we had the individual talent in the one-off games to go all the way.'

Tottenham began their Wembley odyssey without Ardiles, who had been given leave of absence to play for Argentina in the Gold Cup in Uruguay in January 1981. In a defensive match at Loftus Road, Spurs were held to a 0–0 draw by a Queen's Park Rangers side hoping to sneak into the fourth round on the break. Tottenham opened up their game at White Hart Lane and, though they were clearly not playing with much confidence, scored a decisive 3-1 victory. The game was a personal triumph for winger Tony Galvin, who scored on his return after a pelvis operation.

Spurs were next drawn at home to Hull, who, despite their Third Division ranking, held out for 84 minutes before succumbing. The match marked the return of Ardiles, though not without a ripple of controversy. In his absence Spurs had gone six games without defeat, including their first victory over Arsenal in four seasons. Ardiles didn't help his case by returning several days late from South America and promptly found himself dropped for the Arsenal match. The matter was quietly forgotten but Ardiles also sounded a warning about his personal future at the club: 'Spurs want me to stay and I want to play for them for another two years. But we can't agree on a new contract. We're not even close on the financial aspects.'

If Galvin was the success of the third round, it was 20-year-old Garry Brooke who was the star of the fourth. Demoted because of Ardiles' return, there was still room on the substitute's bench because of a knee injury sustained by Villa in the tie with Rangers. Brooke, a home-grown youngster with a deceptively powerful shot from a very short back-swing, broke Hull's resistance after coming on in place of Ardiles, shooting Spurs ahead in the 84th minute and laying on their second for Archibald four minutes later. Even Ardiles was impressed: 'He made the difference. I love the way he plays. He's a brilliant prospect.'

Spurs were drawn at home a second time with a fifth round tie against Coventry, a team much vaunted for having the youngest average age in the First Division. The result was never in doubt with Ardiles, Archibald and Hughton contributing to the 3–1 victory. Spurs were now in the quarter-finals, the round they'd stumbled at in the previous two seasons.

'We'd had Liverpool and Manchester United those times so we were due a bit of luck,' said Perryman. Spurs duly got it when the draw was made: a home tie with Third Division Exeter. 'We knew then that we could win the Cup,' said the captain. Conquerors of Newcastle and Leicester in the previous rounds, Exeter were no push-overs. Indeed it took a second half injury to midfield player Ian Pearson to throw Exeter's defence into sufficient confusion to allow Spurs to score. Graham Roberts headed them in front. Paul Miller completed what was then a formality and Spurs marched 2–0 victors into the semi-finals.

THE YEAR OF THE COCKEREL

For those who believe in omens, Tottenham Hotspur's progress towards the winning of the hundredth FA Cup was little less than inevitable. It was, after all, the 'Year of the Cockerel', thoughbeit in the Chinese calendar. The superstitious pointed to the catalogue of major trophies gathered to White Hart Lane in the first season of each new decade. Nevertheless Burkinshaw took nothing for granted, establishing some ground rules in the week leading up to the semi-final against Wolverhampton Wanderers at Hillsborough. One day, but one day only, was set aside for the requirements of television, radio and newspaper reporters, an exercise to protect the squad which was successfully repeated before the final.

At the Spurs training ground in Cheshunt on that final press day, Ricky Villa, an absentee from the Cup since an injury in the third round, confirmed his fitness to return; Steve Perryman chatted happily of his memories of significant Spurs victories over Wolves in the 1972 UEFA Cup final and 1973 League Cup semi-final, while Milija Aleksic pondered on the prospect of his first FA Cup tie since his shuddering, jaw-breaking collision with Joe Jordan at Old Trafford more than a year before.

Tony Galvin established the tone of a memorable semi-final with the first incisive break after just four minutes. From his cross Steve Archibald had only to stretch forward to turn the ball over the line for his 25th goal of the season. But, only minutes later, Wolves were level. Andy Gray guided down a header and Ken Hibbitt's low shot arrowed inside Aleksic's left-hand post. Yet by half-time Tottenham were back in the lead with a goal that generated some considerable heat. As Osvaldo Ardiles surged purposefully towards the extremities of the penalty area, George Berry's tackle sent him flying into the area. The Spurs appeals were for a penalty, the Wolves defenders believed the challenge to be fair. Referee Clive Thomas judged that a foul had been committed, but just outside the box.

Glenn Hoddle totally deceived Paul Bradshaw. The goalkeeper's awareness of the danger from a direct shot over the wall sucked him in right behind his-line of defenders. Hoddle deftly guided the ball into a vacant corner.

In the second half the tempo understandably dropped, only to reach a new crescendo in the final minute of normal time. Television's much-used replay of the central incident clearly showed that in a tackle on Hibbitt, by unlikely Hoddle of all ironies, the ball had been played well before the man if, indeed, the man had ever been touched at all. The tackle was entirely fair. Referee Thomas, without the aid of technological assistance and from a different angle, signalled dramatically for a penalty. Mayhem followed. Archibald and Ardiles argued their claims of injustice to such lengths that they might have been sent off, instead of merely becoming two of the game's eight cautioned players. Burkinshaw intervened to pacify his team before the start of extra time. Meanwhile Willie Carr had produced an unerring touch from the spot, remarkable circumstances for his first goal of the season.

Neither side could muster their flagging resources to settle the tie in the additional thirty minutes, but Tottenham's desperate disappointment was partially mollified by the venue for the replay. At Highbury, it was virtually a home match. Soon after the start, Garth Crooks picked up a ball that Wolves should have cleared and Tottenham established a lead that was rarely threatened. On the stroke of half-time the same striker settled the outcome in glorious fashion. Hoddle released a through pass of stunning accuracy and Crooks provided a sprinter's pace and a perfect finish. The final goal belonged to Villa, from a lazy swing of his left foot some thirty yards out that emphasised the latent power of the Argentinian, a power that was too often hidden. So uncertain was his future at the time, it could have provided an epitaph for his days in English football. As it turned out it was just a rehearsal for an even greater spectacular.

WEMBLEY AGAIN

Villa and Ardiles thus became the first two Argentinians to play in an FA Cup final, with Manchester City the opposition after surprising favourites Ipswich Town 1–0 in the other semi-final at Villa Park. Keith Burkinshaw kept faith with his semi-final selection, which meant a Wembley disappointment for important squad members like Don McAllister, Gordon Smith, the injured John Lacy and, particularly, Barry Daines in his testimonial year. So often playing the bridesmaid to victorious goalkeepers, in all those years he had still won nothing of note. The green jersey went to Milija Aleksic. Steve Perryman, unselfishly accepting any role if it suited the team, had now been switched to right-back and had just broken the club appearance record previously held by Pat Jennings. Chris Hughton, naturally right-sided, was happier at left-back, though he worried that his only attack of cramp had come at Wembley when playing for the Republic of Ireland fifteen months earlier.

The centre of the defence had come under continual scrutiny in a season in which Tottenham's attractive philosophies had often been at the expense of a vulnerability at the back. At twenty-two Paul Miller had risen from the ranks of the apprentices, and had won back his place just at the right time, before the third round. Alongside him Graham Roberts, a year younger, added a romantic note to the hundredth final. Thirteen months earlier he had been working as a fitter in a shipyard with only the memory of a 1973 appearance at Wembley to cherish . . . as a ballboy!

In midfield Osvaldo Ardiles was living out a dream held since he had watched the 1979 final between Arsenal and Manchester United, a sentiment that provoked a highly successful record which swelled the funds of the players' pool of commercial earnings from their achievements. References to Ossie going all trembly and Tott . . . ing . . . ham can probably bear omission from the story, though the demands of the players' pool did bring forth some unflattering comments; *The Observer* suggested that Ossie's knees had probably gone trembly at the thought of the demands (into four figures) for player interviews. Unlike Ardiles, Ricky Villa had not been selected for the 1978 World Cup final and, surprised that

he had bounded back so quickly from three months absence with injury, he described the prospect of the final as the greatest day of his career.

To the right in midfield of the two South Americans Glenn Hoddle could point to two unusual statistics. He had scored in both his Wembley internationals for England, and had contributed a goal in each of his last four games against Manchester City.

Tony Galvin attracted much less publicity than Hoddle as the final approached, yet his role in the pattern of play had become barely less important. His commitment and energy on the left showed no signs of a major groin operation at the start of the season, although it still gave him considerable pain. The younger brother of a professional, Leeds' and Hull's Chris Galvin, Tony had arrived in the big-time via a Russian degree at Hull University and Goole Town of the Northern Premier League – which was no doubt a unique combination.

For Steve Archibald and Garth Crooks, the Cup campaign provided a splendid climax to a season in which their talents had blended superbly. The substitute's shirt went to Garry Brooke, who had marked his first full league game in December with two goals against Southampton. Now twenty, his development had been aided by a spell on loan in Sweden, and coming off the bench he had already contributed a number of impressive performances.

The occasion was more significant than usual, for it was the 100th final and it was fortunate that the draw had brought together two of the game's greatest names and provided a London v Lancashire clash for such a historic match.

Manchester City had come alive since the November arrival of John Bond in the manager's chair. His side was also that which had won the semi-final: Joe Corrigan, Ray Ranson, Nicky Reid, Tommy Caton and Bobby McDonald, Tommy Hutchison, Steve Mackenzie, Gerry Gow and Paul Power, Dave Bennett and Kevin Reeves, with Tony Henry as substitute.

History will record that the one hundredth FA Cup final lived up to its billing, but not before it threatened to fall horribly flat. The events of Saturday 9 May lasted wearily for two hours with the most memorable experience being that of Tommy Hutchison, who became only the second man ever to score for both sides in a Cup final. On the half-hour, Hutchison's superb near-post header produced a goal in the same unlikely vein as that of Trevor Brooking's which had won the Cup for West Ham United a year earlier.

Keith Burkinshaw recalled the half-time discussion: 'We felt that they couldn't keep running like that. We had to make sure we played through the middle of the park. We didn't do it enough, though give credit to Manchester City – they didn't give us any space.' As Tottenham initiated some improvements in the second half, they clearly owed nothing to Villa, an anonymous figure to both his own dismay and to that of the millions watching the match live in Argentina. Brooke's arrival in his place offered a perkier alternative, and the replaced Argentinian sought to hide his disappointment in the dressing-room rather than watch the remaining minutes of what he was sure would be Tottenham's first FA Cup final defeat. His lonely and very public walk, which ended tearfully in the dressing-room, had reached the mouth of the tunnel when he checked to watch a free-kick ten minutes from time.

HODDLE'S FREAK GOAL

With one hand on the FA Cup, Manchester City lost that grip in a freak moment. Hutchison opted to move from his allotted defensive task to run behind the wall and cover the swerve round the outside of the line of defenders. His reading of Hoddle's intentions was exactly right, but with Corrigan covering any danger from the free-kick, the goalkeeper was left stranded as the ball spun off Hutchison's shoulder and into the other corner. Ten minutes from being crowned the hero, Hutchison's unnecessary intervention had made him at least part villain.

The most relieved player in the ground was the one who had just left the pitch. Gradually Ricky Villa swallowed his pride and, by extra time, had marched back to the bench. On the field the additional period produced little to remember, and John Bond lamented at the end of the affair: 'We could have had penalties, or even played until somebody scored, though it might have ended up two-aside the way everyone was dropping in extra-time. Everybody was wandering around not knowing what to do. I think that if a game of this importance, with a crowd of this size, ends in a draw, it is an anti-climax.' It was only the second Wembley FA Cup final ever to need a replay.

On the coach back to the post-match banquet at London's Hilton Hotel, Garth Crooks quickly broke the atmosphere by encouraging raucous renditions of *Ossie's Dream*. Graham Roberts, who had lost two front teeth in a collision with Chris Hughton, suffered further pain when an emergency stop by the bus induced a bout of cramp. At the front Keith Burkinshaw was already affirming, despite the poor form of Villa, that his side would be unchanged when the battle continued.

The first ever Wembley replay of an FA Cup final took place on Thursday 14 May, with a controversial edict from the Football Association that penalties would decide things if the match was again drawn after extra-time. Recharged, Tottenham Hotspur and Manchester City produced an enthralling contest, arguably one of the great finals.

This time both sides scored inside the opening ten minutes, the first from Villa, whose show of temperament at his substitution five days earlier had looked like a thoroughly unwise snub to his manager. But Burkinshaw's wise reaction to the affair could not have produced a better ending. Villa's goal had its roots in the work of Ardiles, whose attempted shot struck Archibald. The Spurs leading scorer, who was to have no personal good fortune in either match, swung quickly to shoot. The ball ricocheted off the body of Corrigan straight to Villa and, from just outside the six-yard box, he drove it straight into the unprotected net.

Steve Mackenzie's equaliser now lies buried among a welter of memories of this marvellous match. In the context of most other games it would have lived as the abiding memory. From just outside the Spurs' penalty area, Hutchison nodded the ball down and Mackenzie's right-footed volley sped past Aleksic.

Though Corrigan continued to be the busier

With Corrigan already committed, Garth Crooks slides home the rebound from a Steve Archibald shot and Spurs draw level again at 2–2 in the 1981 Cup final replay on Thursday 14 May. This was the first time that an FA Cup final replay had ever been played at Wembley. Indeed, it was only the second replay that had been necessary since the stadium was built nearly 60 years before. The players, left to right, are: Ranson, Perryman, Caton, Hutchison, Corrigan, Miller, Crooks and Archibald.

keeper, it was City who made the next inroad-early in the second half. Bennett's speed uncovered a soft centre in the defence and Miller and Hughton converged for a combined challenge that demolished the progress of the City striker. Referee Keith Hackett from Sheffield awarded only the fifth penalty in the history of Wembley FA Cup finals. Kevin Reeves joined the names of Mutch, Shimwell, Allen and Blanchflower and kept up the unfailing record by placing his shot to the goalkeeper's left with sufficient power, though Aleksic guessed the right way.

So lethargic in adversity in the first match, Tottenham now produced a response far more in keeping with the quality of their players. Hoddle had already enjoyed a much more productive game when he lit the flame under a grand finale. A controlled lofted pass caught City coming out and found Archibald onside. The Scot was not able to fully digest the offering but the defenders could not recover, and the crumbs were devoured by Crooks for his 22nd goal of the season. Twenty minutes left and two goals each.

What followed has now passed into the folk-lore of the competition; the same brooding, bearded Latin American figure who had sulked away to the Wembley dressing-room the previous Saturday was to place his name on that roll-call of legendary figures whose deeds will be remembered long after they have gone.

In the 76th minute Ricky Villa collected the ball on the Spurs left outside the penalty area, a long way from, and no direct threat to, Joe Corrigan's goal. Caton and Ranson were the defenders caught momentarily off their guard by the audacity of an Argentinian who was in no mood to settle for a safe square pass. The two young City players were entangled as Villa worked a magical web, with sure-footed changes of direction this way and that and which were coupled with the physical power that had always made him such a difficult player to knock off the ball. Corrigan advanced to try to halt the trail of devastation, but Villa retained his balance and took advantage of the goalkeeper committing himself: 3–2. Wembley roared its appreciation of a superb solo goal, and Villa raced away totally unstoppable in his triumph. It was not that it was just an outstanding goal – more, it was a courageous goal. To have the courage to hold onto that ball with 15 minutes of an FA Cup final replay left – that was the ultimate significance of the moment.

'It's great after last Saturday,' enthused Villa, whose command of English was now vastly improved from the silent days of his arrival in 1978 alongside the more talkative Ardiles. 'The ball seemed stuck to my feet. I don't know how many players I beat but the thrill was terrific when the ball went into the net. I just wanted to run anywhere. I say thank you to the manager. He took big chance on me for the semi-final. Before tonight I have not much luck in England, I think.'

Steve Perryman, who had begun to worry as to whether the side would ever win a major trophy under his leadership, collected the FA Cup from Princess Michael of Kent, a reward for his twelve years of unquestioned loyalty to Tottenham Hotspur. Keith Burkinshaw, controlled in the fashion of his native Yorkshire, had seen his team selection vindicated: 'How can you leave out a player of his quality? Ricky showed all his skill tonight. He was pleased that I had so much faith in him. But above all I am thrilled for our fans who have waited a long time for success and now they have their pride back. They did not desert us when we slipped into the Second Division. I hope we have repaid them for their loyalty.'

THE CENTENARY SEASON

The centenary season, 1981-82, started in tremendous style. Though attendances were dropping elsewhere in the country, Spurs had become the League's biggest drawing card. Their football was often a delight to watch. Patrick Barclay said in *The Guardian* after one of the season's first games, a Cup final repeat at Maine Road, that: 'If every team played like Tottenham Hotspur, football's only problem would be in pacifying the hordes of supporters unable to get into packed grounds. They bring beauty to the game, and people like that. If all the public wanted was to see one side win and another lose, they would go to the nearest park and save money.'

Spurs' two major signings before the season began had been the England goalkeeper Ray Clemence, for £300,000, and the Welsh international defender Paul Price from Luton.

Unfortunately Price was injured early on and Clemence took time to settle into a new defensive pattern, having left such a familiar one behind on Merseyside.

This was never clearer than at Wembley for the 1981 Charity Shield, when his uncharacteristically poor handling helped Aston Villa achieve a 2-2 draw they probably did not deserve. The clubs shared the trophy and Spurs continued their amazing Wembley record – this was the eighth game they had played there and they had yet to be defeated. Clemence also set up a personal record that day – it was his sixth appearance in the season's annual opener.

The Charity Shield was also notable for the display of a Spurs reserve, Mark Falco, who scored his side's two goals. Deputising for Garth Crooks, who had undergone a cartilage operation, Falco went on to score nine goals in the season's first twelve games, before suffering a ligament injury himself.

Falco's most notable performance was in Amsterdam, where he scored twice in the highly creditable 3-1 Cup Winners Cup win over once mighty Ajax. The club was concerned that its first European trip since the disaster at Rotterdam should be back to the Netherlands – it would have been preferable to play rather further away where fewer of the troublesome element could afford to travel. There was happily little trouble, though it is a comment on the current interpretation of the term that Jeff Powell could write in the *Daily Mail*: 'Thirteen arrests, mostly for window-breaking and car-scratching, one unconfirmed minor stabbing and the separation of two small groups of squabblers on the terraces were no more than a routine night's work for the Dutch police.'

The return at White Hart Lane was no less easy – Spurs winning 3-0. Little Dundalk, runners-up in the League of Ireland, proved far tougher opposition in the second round of the Cup Winners Cup, holding Tottenham 1-1 in Ireland and going down to a single goal from

Garth Crooks in the return. It was enough, however, to put Spurs through to the quarter-finals of the competition in March 1982.

Although Tottenham's signing of Ray Clemence received the summer's headlines, far more significant to the club was the fact that Hoddle, Villa and Ardiles had all renewed their contracts. Vice-chairman Geoff Richardson rightly pointed out that: 'In the current climate, with some players looking to European salaries and with others exercising their new freedom to move where they like at the end of a contract, this was as important as signing three new stars.'

CUPS AND MORE CUPS

As the centenary season settled down, it seemed to North London that Spurs were contesting one non-stop cup tie.

From the beginning of October through to the middle of February, when the League Cup finalists and FA Cup quarter-finalists were decided, Spurs played 25 games of which 12 were cup ties. They were already in process of establishing a record for modern times when, on February 13, they beat Aston Villa in an FA Cup fifth round tie to establish a run of 23 consecutive cup matches without defeat. This covered three competitions – the FA Cup, the League Cup and the Cup Winners Cup. At this stage their last cup set-back had been a League Cup tie at Upton Park on 2 December 1980. Far more remarkable, the last occasion on which Tottenham had been drawn away in a cup tie was in the third round at Queen's Park Rangers on 3 January 1981. They had obviously had to play two-legged matches and semi-finals away from White Hart Lane, but had not otherwise had to travel. Fortune indeed seemed to be favouring them.

The Centenary Year, 1982, could not have got off to a more dramatic start. After nearly one hundred years of almost totally ignoring each other in the FA Cup, Arsenal and Spurs were drawn together at White Hart Lane in the third round on 2 January. It was to be a one-sided game, Garth Crooks winning it with the only goal, as well as hitting a post and bar. It will always be remembered, however, for the manner of the goal. An Ardiles pass gave Crooks the chance of a weakly hit left-footed shot. Jennings, returning to his old stomping ground, had the ball well covered, but it somehow slipped under his arm and dribbled over the line. To make the day thoroughly forgettable for Jennings, he later suffered a groin strain in a wild chase and tackle outside the penalty area with Crooks, had to leave the field and was to be out of the game for months. He said afterwards, with no overstatement: 'It's the worst goal I've let in during the whole of my career.'

Spurs won just as easily in the next two rounds, against Leeds (Crooks again scoring the only goal) and against League Champions Villa. The latter game was yet another 1-0 home win, the goal coming from a Falco diving header after an excellent Paul Price run and a Crooks' centre.

Steve Perryman and Ossie Ardiles hold the FA Cup aloft after the 1981 Cup final replay against Manchester City. Spurs would win the Cup again the following year – also after a replay – but Ardiles would not be in the team.

For the moment though, attention returned to the League Cup, where the whole country was gearing up for perhaps the most attractive final ever in this previously poor relation of a cup competition. It was to be a clash of the country's best and most popular sides of the moment – Liverpool and Spurs.

Spurs had undergone a difficult path to Wembley. The home and away second round tie was against Manchester United.

In the first leg Steve Archibald scored the only goal; in the away return, before 56,000 people, Mike Hazard volleyed one in early on and it was all over. The next two rounds were easier – Second Division Wrexham succumbed 2-0 to Hughton and Hoddle goals, while Third Division Fulham conceded just one, again to Mike Hazard, but it was one too many for them. The fifth round, again at home, against Nottingham Forest was the toughest tie: it was Spurs against Peter Shilton, the only goal eventually being a mis-hit shot by Ardiles. The game's talking point was, however, a thrice taken penalty by Glenn Hoddle. Shilton saved Hoddle's first effort, diving to his right, but the kick was ordered to be retaken because Forest defenders had been encroaching; Hoddle succeeded with the next, to Shilton's left, but again had to retake it because Mark Falco had entered the area; Hoddle changed direction again, put it just inside Shilton's right-hand post – and this time saw the England keeper save it again. Hoddle's face was saved by Ardiles in the second half and it proved a happy day for the 6,000 fans who occupied the new West Stand for the very first time.

The League Cup semi-final was against West Bromwich, again another tight and hard fought tie and against a side Spurs had not defeated for three seasons. The first leg, in the Midlands, ended goalless after seven names had been taken and Galvin and West Brom's Jol were sent off in the closing minutes. Galvin was singularly unlucky to be dismissed for nothing much more than an arm wave of exasperation after he had been impeded. The second leg, a week later, was far more dignified. After 56 minutes Falco back-headed a ball from Hoddle and Mike Hazard added to his tally of valuable goals. Yet again a single goal won it and, with the same result removing Villa from the FA Cup three days later, Spurs had played their tenth domestic Cup game of the 1981–82 season without defeat. Far more remarkable was the fact that they had yet to concede a goal in either the FA Cup or League Cup. So far, ten games had seen ten goals for and none against; eight had ended 1-0, one 2-0 and the other was goalless. The decision to buy Ray Clemence was looking better by the Saturday.

The remarkable sequence of nine consecutive home ties was finally broken for the FA Cup quarter-finals. Even so Spurs still remained in London. They had played 29 cup matches since they had last been drawn to play outside the capital in a normal domestic single legged tie. That was way back on 26 January 1980 when they had drawn 0-0 at Swindon in the fourth round of the FA Cup. Of those 29 matches all had been played on London grounds except the first semi-final in 1981 against Wolves (at Hillsborough) and the away halves of the two legged League Cup ties against Manchester United and West Bromwich.

The FA Cup quarter-final against Chelsea was perhaps the most exhilarating of all their cup ties in a cup-packed season. Spurs went in for half-time having conceded their first cup goal of the season – a quite magnificent 25-yard free-kick from Mike Fillery. But the Pensioners' hopes were to be short-lived for, within a quarter of an hour of the restart, Spurs were 3–1 ahead. The goals came in quick succession from Archibald (after Francis failed to hold a Hoddle shot), Hoddle himself after a delightful cross-passing sequence from Archibald to Hazard to Hoddle, and then a third from Mike Hazard before Alan Mayes made it 3–2. A few days later Tottenham patiently awaited their chances in the first leg of the Cup Winners Cup quarter-final against Eintracht Frankfurt. Miller and Hazard took their openings late in the second half and Spurs had a two-goal lead to take to Germany for the second leg. Talk had now, a little late but the more insistently for that, turned to the apparent possibility of Spurs winning four prizes. Everyone at the club dismissed this as pure fantasy – it was only a few days before that view was to be confirmed.

THE RECORDS TUMBLE
On Saturday 13 March 1982 Spurs lost their first ever domestic Cup final, at the ninth time of asking; they lost for the first time at Wembley, also their ninth appearance; their run of 25 consecutive cup games without defeat came to an end, though it went into the

record books as the longest ever, beating Blackburn's run of 24 set up only four years after Spurs were founded; and, of course, they lost any chance they might have had of winning four trophies in a season.

It was Liverpool who were to get the cream at the end of the newly-named Milk Cup final, but not before Spurs had appeared to be on their way to a famous and uncharacteristic success until just three minutes from the end of normal time. The details of the game are easily told. Steve Archibald scored after just 11 minutes when he somehow managed to latch on to a lofted pass from Glenn Hoddle, persevere rather than dribble his way past the Liverpool defenders Thompson and Lawrenson, and then beat keeper Grobbelaar, who had already committed himself. For the next 76 minutes Spurs defended, getting behind the ball, bringing forwards back into midfield, closing down the Liverpool powerhouse.

But in that 87th minute concentration lapsed just long enough. Substitute David Johnson, on for McDermott, crossed from the right. Somehow or other the Spurs defence let it through, and there was young Ronnie Whelan, Liverpool's discovery of the season, to place it to Clemence's right.

From that moment on the result never seemed in doubt. Twenty minutes into extra time, Ossie Ardiles, clearly the best of the Spurs players on display, gave the ball away to Ian Rush near the penalty area. The ball passed quickly from Rush to Dalglish to Whelan and into the back of the net. Rush added a third in the dying seconds but by then it was all academic. The writing had been on the milk bottle from the moment Whelan scored his first goal. Spurs were brave in the unaccustomed role of vanquished; in a history lasting 99 years and 6 months there had never been the need to hand down lessons on how to be good final losers.

The Championship remained the most alluring, if certainly the toughest, of the three remaining prizes. Because of their run of Cup matches, plus exceptional problems during the winter's cold spell, Tottenham had spent most of the season four or five games in arrears of the other challengers. Theoretically they were almost always in a position to eventually head the League, but they would have had to win most of their games in hand to do so – a near impossible feat in modern times.

The attempt was to be a brave, if doomed, one. Excellent results such as a 3-2 defeat of Southampton, at a time when the Saints headed the League, a 1-0 Easter win over Ipswich, then second in the division, and a sweet 3-1 success at Highbury two days later, clearly left Spurs in with a chance. But inevitably they were occasionally erratic; a 1-0 defeat at The Hawthorns on 27 March was their first League setback away from home in six months, but a 2-2 home draw with Sunderland just after Easter was rather more crucial. The 1981–82 season was the first which awarded three points for a win, and to take only one point from the then bottom club in the division (particularly after being 2-0 up at half-time) was careless in the extreme.

By the time Spurs arrived at Anfield on 15 May, the last Saturday of the season, their chance had gone and, ironically, Liverpool needed to win to secure a record 13th Championship. Spurs had not won at Anfield for 70 years and this was no moment to break the sequence. A glorious Hoddle goal, from nearly 40 yards out and swerving left to right over Grobbelaar's head, provided a delightful memory but Liverpool won 3-1 and confirmed Keith Burkinshaw's prediction made ten games earlier. After a crucial 2-0 defeat for Spurs at Old Trafford he had said: 'Liverpool are such a good team for getting these 1-0 wins, aren't they? I can't honestly say we stand a great chance of catching them now.' And so it was to prove.

As 1982 progressed, injuries to his front runners meant that Burkinshaw had to be able to permutate Crooks, Archibald, Falco and Chris Jones almost game to game. In midfield things were even more fluid – a choice being made among Ardiles (before his return to Argentina), Villa, Hazard, Brooke, Hoddle, Perryman and Graham Roberts depending on who was fit. Roberts' play was a revelation. He proved that he was not only a strong, forceful centre-back, but also a rather subtle, hard-working midfield tyro when given the chance. Against Southampton he even contrived to score a hat-trick, all three goals coming from open play. This may well be the only occasion in first-class soccer history that a centre-back, playing in midfield, has scored a hat-trick – and against the League leaders.

Tony Galvin's role on the left was also perceived as more critical. With neither Archibald nor Crooks being a natural target man, Galvin's speed down the wing was the essential variety in a mix which would otherwise have depended too heavily on a skilful midfield pushing ground-balls through the middle to utilise the speed of the front-runners. The full-backs also proved themselves valuable overlappers. Chris Hughton had long performed that role, and scored the occasional goal into the bargain, but Steve Perryman's ability to read Glenn Hoddle's intentions became almost telepathic.

CUP WINNERS AND CUPS

If the Championship was to slip slowly from Spurs grasp, perhaps the single most likely prize – the European Cup Winners Cup – shot dramatically from that of Ray Clemence in one dreadful moment.

Tottenham had survived the quarter-final second leg away at Eintracht Frankfurt somewhat fortuitously. Two-nil up from the first leg, they conceded two goals very quickly to Eintracht's Borchers and the Korean Bum Kun Cha and seemed on the way out. However a slow, cautious recovery in the final 45 minutes was rewarded when, ten minutes from time, Hoddle delicately placed a 20-yard shot into the corner of the net to put the Londoners into the semi-final.

Initially they seemed fortunate to draw Barcelona in the last four, partially because it meant avoiding favourites Dinamo Tbilisi, but more relevantly, because Barcelona were to host the final in their own Nou Camp Stadium and it seemed preferable to face them over two games than in a single one on their own patch. As it turned out, that reasoning was defective. Standard Liege won both legs against Dinamo and Barcelona came to London obsessed by the need not to lose.

Playing the final at home would mean a full

During the 1981–82 season Spurs played 23 cup matches, all of which were in London except for semi-finals and the away halves of two-legged ties. For the second consecutive season they reached the FA Cup final having played only their semi-final outside the capital.

OPPOSITE TOP: Garth Crooks scores the only goal of the fourth round FA Cup tie against Leeds at White Hart Lane on 23 January 1982. The new stand (background) had been brought into use just five days before.

OPPOSITE CENTRE: Same competition, same place, same score but different opposition. After a magnificent run by Paul Price from his own half, Mark Falco heads the only goal of the fifth round against Aston Villa on 13 February. Looking on with differing hopes are Ken McNaught and Graham Roberts. This was Spurs' tenth domestic cup game of the season and they had still to be beaten, having scored ten goals and conceded none.

OPPOSITE BOTTOM: Paul Miller disentangles himself from the net after celebrating Steve Archibald's (second left) goal at Stamford Bridge in the FA Cup quarter-final on 6 March 1982. Chelsea keeper Francis had failed to hold a Hoddle free-kick and Spurs were level at 1-1. This game was Spurs 25th consecutive cup match without defeat and broke the long-standing record of 24 undefeated cup matches set up by Blackburn Rovers in 1886, just four years after Spurs were founded.

house for the Spaniards at Nou Camp extended to hold 120,000 spectators for the World Cup opening match being held there only a couple of weeks later – and almost one million pounds for the club. They therefore arrived in London with a succeed-at-all-costs attitude.

The result was 'the most cynical game I've seen for 10 years,' according to Frank McLintock. Barcelona manager Udo Lattek ('the match was sometimes too violent') had sent out a hit-squad very reminiscent of the bunch of Atletico Madrid thugs which disgraced Celtic Park in the 1974 European Cup semi-final. In both cases, the Spaniards did their job. Barcelona went home with a 1-1 result and only one man – Estella – sent off. He was later suspended for two matches (meaning he missed the final) while both clubs were fined, Barcelona much the more heavily.

Despite all this, Spurs might have survived had it not been for a terrible error by Ray Clemence, his first critical mistake since the Charity Shield eight months before. A speculative 35-yard shot from Barcelona full-back and captain Olmo was aimed straight at the keeper

and looked totally harmless. As Clemence stood and gathered the ball it somehow squirmed from his grasp and over the line. It should be said, in mitigation, that it was Clemence's excellent performance in Germany in the previous round that had kept Spurs in the competition at all. Graham Roberts popped up for a late equaliser but it was not to be enough. 'We didn't expect them to play like that,' said Keith Burkinshaw, 'we had heard so much about them being a good side technically, but it never showed through.' A fortnight later in Barcelona Spurs, who had thus far lost only four games away from home all season and hence had cause for some hope, went down 1-0.

After Spurs FA Cup quarter-final defeat of Chelsea the semi-final was against the side they had defeated in the Double-winning 1961 Cup final – Leicester City. Leicester were to go down by the same score as in the 1961 final – 2-0. Like the game at Wembley twenty-one years before, it could hardly be called a classic. The first half was tight, the most newsworthy item being the Leicester crowd's continual booing of Ardiles.

Argentina had invaded the Falkland Islands 24 hours before the game and there was considerable speculation about what would happen to that country's most popular exports to Britain – Ardiles and Villa. Ardiles was due to return to Buenos Aires the following day anyway but Cesar Menotti, the Argentine manager, had indicated that he might be prepared to let his key midfielder return to England for the Cup final. Menotti was quoted as saying: 'Keith Burkinshaw and all the people at Tottenham are my friends. Always Tottenham have said Yes, Yes and Yes again to Menotti. Now it is impossible for Menotti to say No if they need Ardiles for the Cup final. Ardiles will decide.' The crisis obviously put Ardiles' eventual return in doubt, as did an interview given at Buenos Aires airport on his arrival there.

But if the Villa Park semi-final threatened to be Ardiles' last game for Spurs, he certainly made his mark on it. In the 56th minute he moved towards Hoddle as the latter took a corner on the right. In a clearly set-piece move, Hoddle pushed the ball short to Ardiles, who, having lost his marker, was able to turn and put across a low centre for Crooks' to volley home from the six-yard line. Leicester's troubles mounted. In an incident reminiscent of 1961 (when they had lost right-back Len Chalmers for most of the final) an innocuous collision between Galvin and Leicester's current right-back Tommy Williams left the defender with a hairline fracture of the shin and his side with ten men.

Even more was to come. In the 76th minute, a Galvin cross went begging and was collected about 20 yards from his own goal by Ian Wilson. The Leicester man was under no pressure and had any number of options. He chose a back pass to Mark Wallington, but got too much of his foot under the ball and clipped it perfectly over the goalkeeper's head into the net. It was, if nothing else, one of the most memorable goals scored in a semi-final in years and it guaranteed Tottenham's tenth game at Wembley, their thirteenth cup final and a chance to equal the performances of 1961 and 1962 in retaining the FA Cup.

The 1982 final was an unexpected and unpredictable one against Second Division Queen's Park Rangers. Rangers run to the final – past Middlesbrough (winning 3-2 away after drawing 1-1 at home), Blackpool, Grimsby, Crystal Palace and West Bromwich – was impressive enough. Spurs knew they would face a tight midfield and a very committed defence. And as the club approached the 1982 FA Cup final there was a very real fear that Burkinshaw's side had peaked too early, that it had seen its period of excellence around the middle of what had been an over-long and over-strenuous season. Ardiles had gone back to Buenos Aires, Hoddle seemed prone to nagging injuries.

At the back the best combination had yet to emerge and any instability in the centre of the defence put even more pressure on the side's cornerstone and captain, Steve Perryman. Often referred to at the time as the best uncapped player in the country, Perryman at last won the recognition he deserved, when coming on as a substitute for England against Iceland in Reykjavik in June 1982.

Perryman had played his last game for England Schoolboys just days before joining Spurs as an apprentice in 1967. He progressed easily into the Under-23 team, winning 17 caps, and was undoubtedly being groomed for the senior team when a pair of unconnected events robbed him of his inheritance.

First Ramsey was sacked from the England job after the failure to reach the 1974 World Cup finals. Then Perryman had to switch positions as Spurs went through their relegation traumas in the mid-1970s. 'I won the Under-23 caps playing in midfield, then I changed to the back four. I realised then that if England wanted two big men at the back, capable of winning everything in the air, I'd never get a look-in,' Perryman reasoned.

Throughout his career, Perryman remained the eternal cherub. In 18 years at the club, he passed Pat Jennings' record of 472 League appearances and established the current record of 655, before joining Brentford as player-manager. When he signed as a professional in 1969, he joined names like Gilzean, Greaves and Mullery. 'Spurs were the team to play for then. I was in four finals in my first five years,' he recalls. Perhaps Perryman's greatest qualities were his versatility and durability. Keith Burkinshaw said he was one of the best speed-readers of a ball in the game, but his ability to play a variety of roles to great effect was probably a reflection of his tremendous staying power as much as anything else.

There were to be other tangible rewards as well. Two weeks before the FA Cup final he was voted Football Writers' Footballer of the Year, the third Spurs' player to win the award after Blanchflower and Jennings. Glenn Hoddle was a close second, reflecting the impression the Spurs side had made on the country through an excellent season. Perryman also joined Hoddle in Ron Greenwood's final forty for the World Cup finals.

In a sense, the real story of the 1982 Cup final had been told before a ball had even been kicked. Just as Spurs had played their semi-final the day after Argentina invaded the Falklands, so Keith Burkinshaw was faced with a decision whether or not to play Ricky Villa the day after the British task force had landed there. At 11.30am on the morning of the match Burkinshaw was forced to concede that both he and the player felt the situation had become too tense for Villa to play. In itself that was a terrible decision to have to make. What made it so ironic were the memories of a year before, of a Cup final replay in which Villa scored twice and won the match with perhaps the most memorable individual goal scored at Wembley since the War.

Villa himself stayed at home with his family to watch the game on TV – not to avoid the fans or his team-mates, but to try and keep away from insistent media pursuers. At the ground the fans chanted his name with affection and sadness, hoping that they had not seen the last of the two symbols who had so dramatically placed Spurs back on centre-stage four years before.

Sitting on the coach on the way to Wembley Burkinshaw must have been pondering on a fraught end to a strange season. Three months before Spurs might have won four trophies. Now here he was, having agreed a new three-year contract with the club the night before, forced to resign himself to the probable loss of the two talismen who had first brought him to managerial prominence, and also having to cope with three troublesome injuries to the players he did have left. Ray Clemence had a calf injury, Tony Galvin an uncertain knee after a month out of the game, and captain Steve Perryman, who had not missed a match all season, a pulled thigh muscle.

In the event all three took the field, the team having Clemence back in goal; Perryman, Price, Miller and Hughton at the back; Graham Roberts pushed into midfield to join Hazard and Hoddle, and the front runners were the season's first choices – Galvin, Crooks and Archibald.

The clubs may have only played each other once before in the FA Cup (in 1981) but the team members knew each other well enough. Mike Flanagan had played with Steve Perryman in the Spurs team which won the 1970 FA Youth Cup. Les Allen, Clive's father, was manager at QPR when Terry Venables followed him from White Hart Lane to Shepherd's Bush in 1969. Not surprisingly, young Clive had trained for a time at Spurs and had even scored a hat-trick in Tottenham colours when playing for London Schools against Coventry at the Lane.

Before the game David Miller said in the *Daily Express* that: 'Together Ardiles and Burkinshaw have made a statement of princi-

ple (about the game) which has possibly been the most important in English football since the era of Moore-Hurst-Peters at West Ham. At an admittedly lean time in the game, Burkinshaw has more than deserved his success and it is what he has done for the game as much as for Tottenham that we should be celebrating today.'

But as Danny Blanchflower said after the 1961 final, the talking was rather better than the playing. It was 0-0 after 90 minutes but Spurs eventually broke the deadlock with ten minutes of extra time left. Glenn Hoddle played a one-two with Graham Roberts, hit a low shot from 20 yards and saw it go through Tony Currie's legs, take a slight deflection, and beat Rangers' excellent keeper Peter Hucker. It seemed all over but, with just five minutes left, Spurs were suckered by a QPR set piece. A Stainrod long throw was back-headed by Bob Hazell and nodded in by an unmarked Terry Fenwick. It was the first goal ever scored from open play by a full-back in a Cup final.

So for the second year running, and for only the third time since the final moved to Wembley, there was to be a replay. And this time the problems were to be QPR's. Clive Allen's ankle injury ruled him out while Glenn Roeder was suspended after an earlier sending off at Luton and so Tony Currie captained the side. Gary Micklewhite and Warren Neill came into the QPR team while Spurs remained unchanged.

And, at 9.15pm on Thursday 27 May, only one thing really mattered; that was that Spurs had retained the FA Cup and won the trophy for the seventh time in seven appearances equalling the record then held by Aston Villa.

There was to be just one goal, scored after a mere six minutes before either side had settled. Graham Roberts set off on a surging run into the right side of the penalty area; three yards inside his legs were swept away by Tony Currie; it was a clear penalty, as QPR manager Terry Venables agreed at half-time. Glenn Hoddle took the kick without any preamble, placing it in the corner to Hucker's right. This time he didn't need a deflection. As an attacking force, Spurs' final virtually ended there. As on the previous Saturday, they looked like a team that had been playing flat out for months, as indeed they had. Not until the very last minute, when Steve Archibald was put through yet again and this time hit the post, did they look like scoring a second.

But the essence of football is that the better team is the one which scores more goals. The simple fact was that QPR, after attacking for the greater part of the match, did not manage to do so once. Nonetheless they seemed to have succeeded in the 43rd minute when a Gary Micklewhite shot was disallowed because Terry Fenwick was judged to have been offside for an instant. The decision was a let-off – the Spurs players had not protested and it was the sort of goal which would have been allowed on a different day. After 65 minutes QPR went even closer when John Gregory hit the crossbar with a beautifully volleyed chip and for most of the second half it was really a matter of Spurs holding out.

A strangely quiet Thursday night with the exhausted Cup holders hanging on to a one goal lead is not the archetypal image of the English season's dramatic conclusion. The air of unreality was highlighted by the empty spaces on the terracing. For the only time in the 60 years since the very first Wembley game in 1923, it had been possible to buy tickets at the gate for an FA Cup final. Even then, the stadium was not full.

But, at the end, there could hardly be a more fitting conclusion to the centenary season than the winning of a record seventh FA Cup. It is the FA Cup that has been Spurs' symbol, almost as much as the cockerel. It was their astonishing win in 1901 that gained them not only a place in the history books but a place in the Football League. It was the glory of 1921 which proved the answer to Arsenal's stealing of their First Division place. It was the moment in 1961 which placed the crown on the best club side the country had ever seen; it was 1962 and 1967 which saw Jimmy Greaves in his rightful place; and it was to be 1981 which left the game with the enduring memory of one glorious goal and two Argentinians.

So the 1982 Cup celebrations surely seemed a fitting finale to the centenary story and yet, at that very moment, events were in train to prove that no story ever ends. As the actual centenary date was reached, in September 1982, negotiations which were to have a far wider effect on the club than any FA Cup win were being quietly concluded.

The symbol and the spur had been the new stand. The intention to build it, declared in mid-1980, had already caused the resignation of one chairman, Sidney Wale. Wale had, however, remained the biggest shareholder.

Steve Archibald in action against Feyenoord in the second round of the UEFA Cup in the 1983-84 season. By beating Feyenoord 4-2 and 2-0, after 6-0 and 8-0 wins against Drogheda in the first round, Spurs registered 20 goals in two rounds. Archibald was their top scorer this season with 21 goals in 32 League games.

ABOVE: With just six min-
utes of the UEFA Cup final
against Anderlecht left on
23 May 1984, Graham
Roberts forces the ball over
the line and gives Spurs the
chance of extra time.

BELOW: As Tony Parks
makes his historic save
from Arnor Gudjohnsen's
penalty, the Spurs players
(from left to right) Ardiles,
Stevens, Roberts and
Hughton rush to congratu-
late their young keeper.
Spurs beat Anderlecht 4-3
in the penalty shoot-out.
Roberts and Stevens had
already scored penalties for
Spurs, as had Falco and
Archibald.

And while the building had gone reasonably to schedule, there was no disguising the fact that the father and son team of chairman and vice-chairman Arthur and Geoff Richardson were, despite their confident earlier assertions, increasingly worried about matching costs with revenues. A basic part of the plan had been to sell the 72 boxes for £30,000 each, covering a three-year lease. That would, in theory, have covered nearly half the cost of the whole enterprise. The problem was that, with the recession deepening and companies becoming very sensitive about visible directors' perks (this was the period when numerous chairmen's Rolls-Royces were quietly sold), the boxes were just not moving. Having set the price at £30,000, it also became very difficult to reduce this figure to create more interest. Those that had committed would, not unreasonably, expect a similar deduction. And, as the bills rolled in, it also became clear that the original estimate of £4 million had been somewhat unrealistic. When the final reckoning came to be made the overall costs were nearly £1 million higher, and the club was faced with interest and repayments on the loan of around £800,000 per annum. To make matters worse, despite reaching two Cup finals and taking £3 million in receipts (easily their highest ever), the club's profit on the 1981-82 season was only £200,000.

All of this was probably manageable, but it was seen to be combined with a standard of public relations and organisation off the field which bore no relation to that achieved by Keith Burkinshaw and the team on it. At a meeting to discuss the new stand, a prospective purchaser of a private box asked for confirmation that it would be available for European matches, a point which should have been rhetorical. Arthur Richardson seemed unsure, giving an answer that gave an impression of poor planning and even poorer salesmanship, and this was compounded by an unconvincing and uninspiring appearance on a televised brains trust on the future of football. The move into the new stand had thrown the ticket office and administration into ill-disguised chaos. Season ticket holders had first been moved out of the old main stand and then back again, but the new systems were poorly installed and numerous seats were double, and even treble, booked. Given the fact that this coincided with a run of big attendances and major Cup games, the organisation was clearly beset with problems.

Despite all this, the board still felt secure. There had never been a takeover attempt at the club, partially because of its traditions but largely because of the article of association which required that any share transfer had to be authorised by the board. The consequence was that this article of association (effectively a rule of the club) could only be overturned by a vote of the shareholders. But, and here was the catch-22, the board knew all the shareholders, controlled a large percentage of the shares itself and, by its veto, could theoretically prevent any outsider from buying any shares anyway.

The board's confidence was eventually shown to be misplaced in the face of a clever assault by two rich young fans, 31-year-old Paul Bobroff and 35-year-old multimillionaire property developer Irving Scholar. Scholar had approached the Richardsons back in 1980, genuinely worried about matters prior to the

stand being built, and offering his services as a property consultant free of charge. His motivations were concern for the club as a fan, but his interest was not reciprocated. Bobroff later also offered his company's computer facilities to sort out the problems in the ticket office, but this was not to be taken up either.

By February 1982, while Spurs ploughed on to two Cup finals on the field, matters were equally intense off it. Scholar and Bobroff had devised a plan to get round the problem of the articles of association. They could buy shares – the problem was that the board did not have to recognise the purchase. So, in addition to the shares, they also acquired the proxy voting powers of the previous owner. In other words, they could use the votes whether the board recognised the purchase or not. With half the shares, they could overturn the old rules at the next meeting. At the rapidly escalating share price (which reached £300 per share) it would cost around £500,000 to buy up enough, always assuming the owners would sell.

The critical moment was when ex-chairman Sidney Wale decided to sell. His son-in-law, Douglas Alexiou, was already on the board and was to become chairman when the coup was carried through. Wale had always disagreed with the building of the stand and, while too gentlemanly to bear a grudge, bore the current board little personal goodwill after his replacement as chairman. By November 1982 Richardson realised that Bobroff and Scholar had enough promises and proxy votes to call an extraordinary general meeting and unseat him. He had no choice but to resign and allow Bobroff to join the board. Scholar, the effective owner of the club with Bobroff, remained in Monte Carlo for the time being.

For the next year and a half Spurs made more news off the field than on it. Ossie Ardiles had, of course, gone back to join the Argentinian national squad before the 1982 World Cup, had supposedly commented at Buenos Aires airport that the Malvinas were Argentinian (a perfectly understandable sentiment for anyone of his nationality, especially so public a figure) and that he would never play in England again. As the Falklands War continued through the summer of 1982 it did indeed seem unlikely that he could ever return. Keith Burkinshaw arranged a year's loan to Paris St Germain, supposedly for £100,000, and it was assumed that that was the last of Ardiles.

Keith Burkinshaw's relationship with the Argentinians had always contained a large element of chance, and so it was to prove again. Spurs had invited the Luxembourg national team, who had just played England at Wembley, to come to the Christmas 1982 party at White Hart Lane. The Luxembourgeois interpreter also acted in the same capacity for Paris St Germain, and had been involved in the Ardiles transfer. He told Burkinshaw that Ardiles, who had not settled well, was prepared to return and that the French club would probably agree. Burkinshaw flew off again on his second Argentinian-chasing odyssey, concluded the deal, gave St Germain their money back, and Ardiles was at home in Hoddesdon by the New Year, 1983.

The Ardiles story did not continue quite so happily. In only his second game back in England he broke a leg. In a friendly six months later, shades of Dave Mackay, he sustained another fracture. A year later there was an operation for cartilage trouble. He was now 32, a difficult age to make a comeback after three such disturbing blows. But Ardiles himself was philosophical, as he told Brough Scott of the *Sunday Times*: 'Alas, people are entitled to think I can't come back. Maybe sometimes I think it myself. But I don't have economic problems and more than anything I love to play football. All my life, from six or seven, I can play very, very good, but they always say I am too small. Now they say I am too old. We'll see.'

Questions were beginning to be asked about the team and the direction the club was going in 1984, as the cold wind of the recession seemed to be affecting Spurs more than other major sides. While they tried to match the expenditure and the ambitions of Liverpool, Manchester United and Arsenal, the other members of the current unofficial elite, it did seem that Tottenham's base support fell below that of their rivals. Between mid-January and May 1984, with the club well out of the Championship race, there were only two gates above 25,000 and several below 20,000, well under the effective break-even point. It had become a simple truism that the club needed at least one good Cup run each season to hope to balance its books.

Happily, the overhang of financial worries had been largely solved by a brave and unique step taken by the new board. The decision was made to become the first club to take a full stock-market listing, which meant, simply enough, that absolutely anyone could buy shares in the club. The new board had already put £1,150,000 into the club early in 1983, and they then raised another £3,800,000 by selling shares to the public. The two injections of cash largely eliminated the bank borrowings, causing many people elsewhere in the game to ask why such a simple and relatively obvious idea had not been tried by other clubs in difficulty. Perhaps the answer was the massive depth of support for the club, particularly in relatively financially sophisticated North London.

Well before the end of the 1983-84 season it had become clear that Keith Burkinshaw would leave at its end. The reasons were complex. He had been in effective control for some time, had been conspicuously successful and was rightly noted as a man who spoke his mind and stuck by his own beliefs. The fall in attendances in 1984 was financially worrying, and the board's frank and publicly stated view was that the football team, while the necessary core of the whole business, was only part of the business and that other sectors, such as the development of the property on the High Road, were financially significant as well. Expenditures on the team had to be viewed in that light.

Burkinshaw also suffered a season-long running argument with his main striker, the unpredictable Scot Steve Archibald, who continued to play for the team having vowed at one point never to speak to the manager again. At season's end the club conducted a number of financially astute deals, especially in obtaining a remarkable £1¾ million by selling Alan Brazil (who had been bought from Ipswich in March

1983 for £500,000 without impressing) to Manchester United and Steve Archibald to Terry Venables in Barcelona where, it must be said, the Scotsman surprised everyone by leading the Spanish scoring list as Barcelona ran away with that country's League Championship. Peter Shreeves, the new manager, spent some of the cash in bringing Clive Allen from QPR. While Allen's early linking with the other new purchase, Notts County winger John Chiedozie, seemed encouraging, injuries and loss of form soon led to the striker being replaced up front by the old team of Falco and Crooks.

But this is to run ahead of the highlight of 1984, yet another trophy for the departing Burkinshaw. While domestic events had provided little cheer (Spurs going out to Norwich in a fourth round FA Cup replay and to Arsenal in the third round of the Milk Cup), there was always the UEFA Cup. Their run through the competition was not noticeably easy, though it started in style.

In the first round they amassed 14 goals without reply as the Irish part-timers of Drogheda were despatched 6-0 on their own ground and 8-0 at White Hart Lane. A superb performance by Glenn Hoddle, upstaging a much publicised return to the European arena by Johan Cruyff, paved the way to victory in the second round over Dutch side Feyenoord. Spurs couldn't stop Cruyff scoring, however, and their 4-2 home win was more precarious than it looked until Hughton and Galvin put the result beyond doubt in Rotterdam. Once again there were the same scenes of violence which had marred Spurs' previous visit to the Dutch port in the final of the same competition back in 1974. Tottenham fans left a trail of destruction and 30 injuries. In the event the club was probably fortunate to escape with an £8,000 fine by UEFA.

Spurs scored their most impressive victory in the third round. A goal by Michael Rummenigge gave Bayern a 1-0 home win. Steve Archibald levelled the scores in the home leg and Mark Falco, who was to score another vital goal in the semi-finals, hit their winner.

Security problems dominated the quarter-final tie against Austria Vienna, whose unprotected ground looked a sitting target for trouble-makers. Spurs gave themselves a comfortable 2-0 home lead and the away leg passed without incident except on the pitch, where the Austrians fought to a 2-2 draw after Brazil and Ardiles had inflicted further damage.

Spurs were frankly lucky to win their semi-final, against the perennial Yugoslav challengers Hajduk Split. Losing 2-1 on the Adriatic, Falco getting the priceless away goal, Tottenham crept through 1-0 at home when Mike Hazard hit a low, hard drive into the right-hand corner from 20 yards after just six minutes. Roberts, Miller and Garry Stevens all performed sterling roles in the middle of the field and at the back to close Split down for the remaining 84 minutes.

Tottenham's opponents in the final, the club's fourth in Europe, were to be the holders of the trophy, Anderlecht, with the first leg in Brussels. It was a hard game, with Spurs pleased to come away with a 1-1 draw. They were leading through a 58th-minute Paul Miller header – another vital away goal which

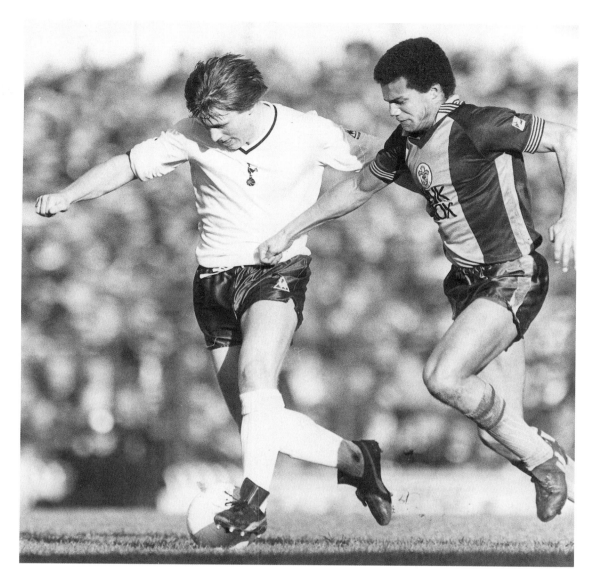

was to prove Spurs' passport right the way through the competition – and held on until six minutes from the end when Anderlecht forced an equaliser. Once more crowd trouble dominated the tie and a Spurs fan was shot dead in a Brussels bar after a disturbance.

The return, and Keith Burkinshaw's last game as manager of the club, was memorable essentially for its conclusion, yet another penalty shoot-out. Almost unknown prior to 1982, these events had become increasingly and irritatingly familiar after the France v West Germany World Cup semi-final that year. In 1984, two of the three European competitions (Liverpool defeated Roma in the Champions Cup the same way) went to the same unsatisfactory conclusion. The actual result after 120 minutes was again 1-1, but this concealed the fact that most independent observers thought Anderlecht the better team. 'Roberts, who scored the first penalty kick, as much as Parks and the rest of them hung on to beat a better team for Burkinshaw's sake,' said Jeff Powell in the *Daily Mail*. 'It may seem a little churlish to focus attention on the ugly character of Spurs' defensive play in their hour of triumph,' wrote Robert Armstrong in *The Guardian*, 'but there is no doubt that the London side would not have reacted with the same stoical fortitude shown by the Belgians, who declined to retaliate under extreme provocation. The fact that Spurs could muster only a single goal in two hours – and that from Roberts – indicates how fortunate they were to topple Anderlecht.'

The Belgians had actually gone ahead after an hour when Morten Olsen's beautiful through ball put Alex Czerniatinski away and the Polish miner's son flicked the ball past keeper Tony Parks, who had been standing in for the off-form Ray Clemence towards the season's end. Tottenham continued to battle. Roberts, captaining the side in Perryman's absence, was in the thick of everything, and was probably lucky the West German Mr Roth seemed to view his antics benignly. With the game increasingly looking all over for the home side, Burkinshaw made his very last decision as Tottenham manager – he sent on his talisman. Off came Miller and Mabbutt, on went Ally Dick and the man whose own career had been so closely linked to Burkinshaw's, Ossie Ardiles. As if by pre-arrangement with the gods, it worked.

Ardiles, with one of his earliest touches, hit the crossbar, the ball came back into a crowded penalty area and Roberts somehow forced it

ORDINARY SHARE CERTIFICATE

Tottenham Hotspur plc

(Incorporated under the Companies Acts 1948 to 1981. Registered in England No. 1706358.)

Number of Shares

ONE THOUSAND TWO HUNDRED AND THIRTY

Certificate No.
12552

Registration Date
13/02/85

Number of Shares
******1230

This is to Certify that

PHILIP WILLIAM SOAR ESQ

Joint Holder(s)

is/are the registered holder(s) of fully paid
Ordinary Shares of 25 pence each in
Tottenham Hotspur plc subject to the
Memorandum and Articles of Association
of the Company.

Given under the Seal of the Company.

No transfer of any of the Shares specified herein will be registered unless accompanied by this Certificate 08710350AR   PHILIWI/00

Transfer Office: Bourne House, 34 Beckenham Road, Beckenham, Kent BR3 4TU

Printed by Henry Jaffe Limited, London.

One thing that can make a Tottenham follower's lot a happy one compared to that of the supporters of many teams . . . a part ownership of the club. This modest share certificate is the author's.

home. There were just six minutes of normal time left and the teams were level on aggregate, 2-2.

The half-hour of extra time produced numbing tiredness but no goals, leaving 21-year-old Tony Parks to face the remarkably daunting task of penalties to decide the destination of the trophy. Roberts took the first and scored. Then the Anderlecht and Danish captain Morten Olsen struck his shot well to Parks left, but the young keeper surprised the whole ground by saving it. 'I could see in the Anderlecht player's eyes where he was going to go,' said Parks afterwards, 'so I just dived to the left.' Falco, Stevens and Archibald scored for Spurs, de Groote, Scifo and Vercauteren did the same for Anderlecht. That meant that if Danny Thomas, signed from Coventry the year before, scored from the fifth kick, the trophy was Spurs'. In the kind of moment which can live with a player for the rest of his career, full-back Thomas ran up, shot unconvincingly, and Munaron saved. It was now 4-3 on penalties and there was only one of the original 10 penalties left.

If Anderlecht scored it would be 4-4 and go to sudden death. Parks said later: 'I'd dived left for all four penalties so far, so I thought it was best to change my mind.' Icelander Arnor Gudjohnsen took the kick, Parks threw himself to his right and palmed it away. Up jumped the young reserve and hared off down the pitch. 'You read about this sort of thing in comics,' he said later. 'It's a lovely feeling. I started playing at nine on Hackney Marshes – now all this. I'm only 21 and not so long ago I thought I'd have to move to another club to get a chance.' It was very much Parks' night, and Burkinshaw's.

The manager was going out on a high note, winning a European trophy and having reached four finals in four years. The parallels with Bill Nicholson a decade before were uncanny. He too resigned after reaching four Cup finals in four seasons. He too won three of them, including the UEFA Cup. He too had spent a season in dispute with his principal striker.

Debate about a successor ranged far and wide. Terry Venables, David Pleat and Graham Taylor were favoured. In the end the club maintained its tradition of promoting from within. An intelligent new broom has the sense to preserve those ideals which have worked in the past. The man who got the job was Burkinshaw's assistant, Peter Shreeves. Like Burkinshaw, Shreeves had not had a particularly distinguished playing career – appearing or coaching at Reading, Chelmsford, Charlton and Wimbledon. At the tender age of 18 he was just three days away from a Welsh under-23 cap when he broke a leg playing for Reading. The chance never came again. He is Welsh because his parents were evacuated from Islington to Neath and he was born there during the Battle of Britain. Perhaps the most quoted fact about him is that he has been a taxi-driver, which he was while coaching Chelmsford in the late 1960s. He retired from playing at the age of 28 with cartilage trouble and had coached ever since, though John Pratt was by now (acting as) trainer of the Spurs first team. Terry Neill brought Shreeves to Spurs in 1975, as youth team coach, and one of the advantages he had was that many of his early charges had grown with him into the first team.

That was certainly something of benefit as the Spurs team went through a fair number of permutations in the first half of the 1984–85 season. Up front Allen, Falco, Crooks, Galvin and Chiedozie fluctuated without any set of three settling down. In midfield none of Hoddle, Stevens, Ardiles, Mabbutt or Hazard was exactly a permanent fixture. But this did not serve to greatly upset the way the team played. Though they were unexpectedly knocked out of the Milk Cup at home by Sunderland, and almost inevitably lost 1-0 at Anfield in the FA Cup, the League remained open and Spurs well placed in the top three. The fact that the League was, for perhaps the first time since 1981, of interest outside Merseyside was actually due to Liverpool starting the season very badly. The championship had gone to Liverpool in the three previous seasons, and in 1984-85 it certainly looked likely that the trophy would return to the said city, if not club. FA Cup holders Everton led the League from early on, with Spurs a steady second in a well-paced chase. The critical day could well have been Saturday 2 March. While Spurs won 1-0 at Stoke, Garth Crooks capitalising on a dreadful goalkeeping error by his old club, Everton let go a golden opportunity to keep the gap dangerously wide and effectively eliminate the third club, Manchester United, from the chase at the same time. With the score 1-1 at Old Trafford, and less than ten minutes left, Everton were awarded a penalty. Bailey saved from Sheedy and Everton got one point out of United rather than three. Suddenly the race was wide open and, almost as suddenly, Spurs were favourites. Ten of their remaining 15 games were at home.

Two weeks later the omens seemed to have gone into reverse. Having lost 2-1 at home to Manchester United in the interval, Spurs had to travel to a resurgent Liverpool. It was exactly 73 years to the day – 16 March 1912 that they had last won at Anfield. Early in the second half, with the score at 0-0, Hoddle nodded a subtle header to the edge of the penalty area, Mike Hazard hit a scorching volley to Grobbelaar's right, the keeper palmed the ball out but there, as he had been at Stoke, was Garth Crooks and Spurs were 1-0 up. Thanks to excellent Clemence goalkeeping that's the way the score stayed. Spurs were level top, had thirteen games to play and nine were at home. Everton, ahead on goal difference, had injury problems, and were still in the FA Cup and Cup Winners Cup while Spurs had nothing else to concentrate on. The attempt to retain the UEFA Cup had collapsed at the quarter-final stage. Opponents Real Madrid were thought to be little more than a shadow of their former glorious selves; but the only goal in the whole 180 minutes was an own-goal, Steve Perryman deflecting a shot past Ray Clemence in the first leg at White Hart Lane. Spurs were the better team in the Bernabeu Stadium two weeks later and suffered from a disgraceful refereeing decision when a Falco header was disallowed. With three minutes left the frustrations boiled over and Steve Perryman ended a tie he will hope to forget by being sent off for a dreadful tackle on Valdano. This time no one could argue with the referee's decision.

Sadly, in the space of five days on the cusp of March and April two disastrous home defeats left them clutching at straws rather than rungs on the Championship ladder. First came Aston Villa, an admittedly poor side lacking both their regular goalkeeper and central defender Allan Evans. Two breakaway goals, a frustrated Spurs attack and a 2-0 home defeat looked ominous. Five days later came the crunch – the visit of leaders Everton to White Hart Lane. Everton scored twice, from Andy Gray and Trevor Steven, and though both goals were aided by defensive errors they were very well taken and a late Roberts goal could not conceal the fact that Everton were by far the better side. In retrospect, it was probably the leg injury to Gary Stevens a month before which had been the turning point. Now virtually an England regular, his ability to play either as central defender or in midfield was invaluable to the team.

Spurs' loss of form was a huge disappointment to the club and its fans, but as it happened Everton had gone into one of those sequences which make a club unstoppable. Heading for an undefeated run of 30 matches, chasing three trophies and already well past the previous highest ever points total, they were uncatchable and clearly the best side in the country. Another year Spurs' efforts would have won them the Championship; this year Everton brooked no real contenders.

Club Chairman Irving Scholar was philosophical about the season's end: 'Ever since I first watched Spurs from the terraces in 1954 I've believed that if the club wins a trophy it is essential that it deserves to win it and is seen to deserve it. This is Everton's year – but it's also our best League performance for around 15 years. Don't forget that.'

Since his arrival at the club at the end of 1982, Scholar's main priority had been putting the financial side in order. He had already had informal discussions in the City about a public flotation prior to the takeover. As soon as there was a change of control he was quick to introduce an efficient computer-controlled ticket system (long Spurs' Achilles' heel) and arrange a testimonial for Bill Nicholson, who celebrated 50 years with the club in February 1986.

The biggest problem was paying for the stand, something Scholar's business career well suited him for: 'It is interesting that every club which has gone in for a major new stand since the early seventies has had major problems as a result. Chelsea and Wolves both nearly went out of business, Forest were fortunate to have the revenue from that amazing spell of theirs. Spurs were in a similar position. The reason is quite simple; a new stand is a capital asset and has to be paid for out of capital. A player isn't – you can pay for him out of profits and deduct the transfer fee before paying tax. Basically, if a stand costs, let's say, £5 million, then you need to make profits of around £10 million to pay for it. And who can make that sort of money in football nowadays? The reason we went public was very straightforward; money raised in a share flotation is capital. Hence it could all be used to pay for the capital cost of the building. It made perfect sense. '

Scholar was surprised no other clubs had followed Spurs' route: 'Every kind of business is represented on the Stock Exchange – why not football clubs? It's a conservative game, but the advantages are enormous; not least that you give the fans a chance to have a share, and, as a result, a say in *their* club.'

In May 1985 the club received permission to develop its valuable Cheshunt training ground, a plan which should be worth at least £3 million to Spurs. 'We may develop it ourselves,' said Scholar. 'Why not? It's very sensible for the club to have interests outside football because they provide other sources of income. Of course, football will always be the basis but if we can make money elsewhere then it is bound to benefit the club. The key is to do things gradually, steadily, not to rush major decisions. We are going to continue developing the ground, but a step at a time like Manchester United at Old Trafford.

'The traditions of the club are vital to me. I've always believed in the way the club plays the attacking game, the style, the fact that we have always been known as a *positive* club. That will never change while I'm chairman. The club must always come first and we only want players at White Hart Lane who want to play for Spurs. That's why we spend as much

time, more in fact, investigating a player *off* the field than on it when we make a new signing.'

In 1985 the problems of football were indeed rather more off the field than on it. While Spurs had certainly experienced a reasonably satisfactory season, the game itself was in turmoil. 1984-85 would not be remembered for Everton's Championship or Norman Whiteside's astonishing FA Cup final winner, rather it would go down in the history books as the year of Bradford and the ghastly culmination of so many ills at the European Cup final in Brussels.

For Spurs, the first thing to go was their hard-won place in Europe, not just for one season but perhaps for a footballing generation. As with the other major clubs, revenues from television, sponsors and, for that matter, week-by-week gates were suddenly also brought into question. Few major clubs could afford the consequences that loomed before them – Spurs alone would almost certainly be several hundred thousand pounds worse off than they had projected by losing European competition in one season alone. It induced a sense of real sadness in more than one way.

Only a year before Spurs had effectively won a European trophy in that very Belgian capital. Their return leg against Anderlecht had, unusually for an English club game, been televised live throughout Europe. While it lacked the quality of European matches two decades before, it certainly compared for excitement. 'It was a wonderful advertisement for the club and for the English game,' said Irving Scholar. 'It was fast, thrilling and tense. In many respects it was probably the best game seen at White Hart Lane since the legendary Benfica match.' It was sad that it would be many years before we could expect to see its like again.

After the horror of Heysel, Peter Shreeves began his second season robbed of the UEFA Cup place his third place had earned in May 1985. Following four successive years of European competition that involved 32 games and saw the likes of Barcelona and Real Madrid, Bayern Munich and Eintracht

Frankfurt, Ajax and Feyenoord at White Hart Lane, Spurs fans would have to be content with the fare offered by the domestic scene – a situation which put even more emphasis than usual on the two cup competitions.

It was especially galling for the talented Chris Waddle, 24 and already an England regular with eight caps when he signed from Newcastle for a tribunal-fixed fee of £590,000 in July. One of the most enigmatic players ever to wear the Spurs colours, Waddle was a unique amalgam of vision and waywardness, a combination that could send supporters, colleagues and managers into paroxysms of pleasure or the depths of despair.

Aptly named, Waddle cut an unlikely figure for a football hero, round shoulders hunched over ungainly gangling gait as he ambled, aimlessly it seemed at times, across the White Hart Lane turf. Even when he received the ball he hardly looked a 'natural': yet there were times, plenty of them, when there was no-one in England to touch him.

He had deceptive skill, a wicked change of both pace and direction, the ability to pass and cross with both feet – and, above all, vision. On his day he could leave bemused opponents helplessly in his wake or slit a defence open with a raking pass; on others, however, he would be a proverbial 'waste of time', exasperating fans by disappearing up blind alleys of his own making. Shy, taciturn and sometimes difficult, he struggled with lack of confidence, but gradually he won over the fans (his Spurs displays were invariably better than his patchy performances for England).

Waddle began his Spurs career in style, heading two goals on his League debut in a 4-0 drubbing of Watford at the Lane on the opening day of 1985–86 – the first having come from fellow debutant Paul Allen. But then came the first poor spell of what was (as so often with Tottenham) a season of baffling spells: four straight League wins in September, only one point from six games after Boxing Day, just one defeat in the last 12 matches, with 14 goals in the last three.

Though the late run took Tottenham to 10th place in the League, their chase for honours had finished back on 4 March when Everton – the only class opposition encountered in the cup competitions that season – beat them at White Hart Lane in the fifth round of the FA Cup in what proved to be captain Steve Perryman's last match for the club. It was the fourth year in a row that Spurs had failed to get past the last 16, and coming on top of a miserable League run – itself prefaced by a fourth round League Cup exit at the third attempt at the hands of Second Division Portsmouth – it undermined Peter Shreeves' tenuous position.

Shreeves had bought well, securing not just Waddle (second top scorer on 14 behind Mark Falco's 21), but also the hard-working, ball-carrying services of Paul Allen, snatched from West Ham under the noses of Arsenal and Liverpool for £400,000, again set by a tribunal. Paul was the third member of his family to sign for Spurs, following uncle Les and cousin Clive; Bradley, Clive's younger brother, was a junior prospect at the club as a 13-year-old but chose to join QPR.

Clive's continued absence until late November with a groin injury didn't help

Shreeves' cause, and put added pressure on the willing Falco to produce the goals; nor did the persistent injuries to Ossie Ardiles (only 20 League games) and John Chiedozie (13). He also made sensible deals in the transfer market, Micky Hazard moving to Chelsea for £310,000 in September 1985 after growing frustrated with failure to command a regular first-team place; he would return, after visits to Portsmouth and Swindon, in 1994.

A former player with Reading and, after injury, with Southern League sides Chelmsford and Wimbledon, Shreeves had moved up through the coaching ranks under Keith Burkinshaw and he stayed faithful to his predecessor's attempts to play flowing, attacking football. Indeed, his teams scored four goals or more seven times in 1984–85 and no fewer than 11 times the next season; with 14 of those 18 occasions at home, no fan could claim his sides didn't entertain.

But the board – and perhaps many supporters – wanted success. Although the players generally held him in high regard, at least as a coach, liking his emphasis on skill and invention in training, he was sacked.

If Peter Shreeves had been more of an entertainer himself he might have survived a good deal longer. Plenty of more vocal managers have had worse records and lived to tell the tale (as would Terry Venables), but Shreeves was no Allison or Docherty, no Atkinson or Clough, and he went across London to become assistant manager to Jim Smith at QPR. However, like Perryman, Ardiles and Hazard, he would be back.

PLEAT'S NEW APPROACH

Shreeves' replacement at White Hart Lane was somewhat different – a confident talker at home with players, coaches, directors and the media. David Pleat was chairman Irving Scholar's first choice, a tried and tested operator who for eight years had kept lowly Luton in the First Division by playing attractive, entertaining football, despite meagre resources and a continual leak of good players to bigger clubs. Friendly and amusing (he became a regular TV and radio pundit during his several subsequent spells out of management), Pleat took up where Shreeves left off – and added his own special ingredient.

The 1984-85 season began with a 4-4-2 system, with average results. Always willing to experiment, Pleat introduced a new approach at Oxford on 22 November, inspired by the French team in the 1984 European Championships and both France and Belgium in the 1986 World Cup, with a mobile five-man midfield supporting a lone striker of pace, Clive Allen. Allen scored twice and Waddle, played by Pleat in a roving role on the right rather than on the left or down the middle, notched the others in a 4-2 win. The display received rave reviews and though the day was marred by a hamstring injury to the recent £600,000 signing from Standard Liège, Nico Claesen, the system would bring Spurs a chain of good results – only four defeats in the next 19 League matches – with Paul Allen, Glenn Hoddle, Ossie Ardiles, Tony Galvin and recent England cap Steve Hodge (like Claesen 24 years old but costing £50,000 more from Aston Villa) the usual candidates for the five places.

Players also departed, Mark Falco going to Watford for £300,000 on Claesen's arrival and Graham Roberts moving to Glasgow Rangers in December for £450,000. While local product Falco (despite ceaseless endeavour and a respectable tally of 68 goals in 174 League games) had never won over the White Hart Lane crowd, Southampton-born Roberts had become a Tottenham folk hero, recalled as a ruthless ball-winner, the toughest tackler at Tottenham since the incomparable Dave Mackay. Roberts could dish it out, too: the challenge that put Arsenal glamour boy Charlie Nicholas into the Highbury stand on New Year's Day 1986 is set firmly in club legend.

Pleat's first major signing would eventually follow Roberts to Ibrox. Richard Gough of Dundee United was Scotland's regular right-back when he preferred Spurs to Chelsea for £750,000 in the close season, but he could play anywhere – and though he was not the manager's first choice for centre-back (that was Ipswich Town's Terry Butcher, who ironically went instead to Rangers), this was the position he filled to such effect. He formed a fine understanding with Gary Mabbutt – like many supporters, Pleat thought that centre-back was Mabbutt's natural position – and when Gough was appointed captain on New Year's Day Spurs fans imagined the 24-year-old had taken the job for several seasons to come.

With Ray Clemence in continuing good form and injuries blissfully absent – the trio missed only nine League games between them – the goals-against column was reduced to 43 in 42 First Division games. They were helped by solid performances from the three full-backs – Gary Stevens, Danny Thomas and Mitchell Thomas – and the cover of a five-man midfield.

Pleat's plan would work, of course, only if there was a striker of class to finish the job. And, unlike the luckless Peter Shreeves, he was blessed with a fit and on-song Clive Allen. The man had a phenomenal season, scoring 33 goals in the League (in 39 games), 12 in the Milk Cup (nine) and four in the FA Cup (six). Even without his seven penalties, the total would still have bettered Jimmy Greaves' record tally, though he couldn't touch the 37 League goals notched up by Greaves in 1962-63.

The 5-0 thrashing of West Ham in the fifth round League Cup replay at White Hart Lane on 2 February was perhaps the best of many fine team performances during the season. A semi-final with Arsenal was the prize and Spurs grabbed it with both hands; and even if the Hammers were hit by injuries, few teams could have lived with Tottenham that night.

With solid progress in the FA Cup, the treble wasn't out of the question. But while Allen would win both the FWA and PFA Footballer of the Year awards, he would end up with no winner's medal. Spurs failed, if that's a fair word, on all three fronts.

In the League Cup, having scored five goals in three earlier games, and despite Clive Allen netting in each of the three semi-final games against Arsenal, the Gunners nicked the 4 March replay at the Lane with a wicked deflection off Danny Thomas' heel that set up David Rocastle for the last-ditch winner. Over five hours of football, Arsenal had been ahead for just one minute – unfortunately it was to be the last minute.

Three days later the home crowd saw a tackle from Gavin McGuire of Queen's Park Rangers put an end to the footballing career of Danny Thomas, who had proved a great favourite since his move from Coventry for £250,000 in June 1983. A disappointing month ended on a sour note, the result of the 3-1 defeat at Luton being overshadowed by demonstrations aimed at both David Pleat and his club.

In the League, where Pleat raised the club's average home attendance by 5,022, Spurs were to prove the victims of a fixture backlog that saw them play 14 League and Cup games in five weeks, falling behind Everton and Liverpool during a run-in which gleaned only five wins in 13 matches. Indeed Spurs were later to be fined £10,000 for fielding what was effectively a reserve side against the new champions at Goodison five days before the FA Cup final.

CUP FINAL OWN-GOAL DEFEAT

It wasn't a year ending with a '1', but it was 20 years since Dave Mackay lifted the trophy when Spurs beat Chelsea. Their run had been comfortable (Scunthorpe, Crystal Palace, Newcastle, Wimbledon), but their semi-final opponents were Watford, then a respectable First Division side. At Villa Park, however, Tottenham hit top form, Steve Hodge grabbing two goals and the Allen boys one apiece to crush Graham Taylor's men (including Mark Falco and John Barnes) by 4-1. The Watford scorer was also an Allen – Malcolm.

Spurs were in their seventh final and their phenomenal unbeaten record looked unlikely to be broken. Their opponents, the journeymen from Coventry, had scraped through the last four with a 3-2 extra-time win over Leeds and, though they finished 10th in the table, they had won only three League games away from home all season. Yet while manager John Sillett looked to be enjoying every moment of the day at Wembley on 16 May, David Pleat (more used to being an underdog in big games with Luton) appeared strangely nervous.

He must have felt a lot better after just two minutes, when Clive Allen headed his 49th goal of the season, and a lot worse when Dave Bennett levelled nine minutes later. But when Spurs regained the lead at the perfect moment – skipper Gary Mabbutt claiming what's usually recorded in the football bibles as an own goal by Brian Kilcline – they were again firm favourites. But it wasn't to be: Keith Houchen brought Coventry back with a marvellous diving header, taking the final to extra time for the fifth time in seven years.

Substitutions of Claesen in place of Hughton and Stevens in place of Ardiles made little impact, and as so often at Wembley it was a bizarre goal that settled it, Lloyd McGrath's cross being firmly deflected over the despairing Clemence by Mabbutt's attempted interception. Poor Clemence: he had been beaten 16 years before by a deflected winner (albeit slightly) when Charlie George's fierce shot nicked Larry Lloyd's foot.

The immediate aftermath was at best muted, at worst acrimonious. Richard Gough, who had played well below par and had become the first Spurs captain to lead his team to defeat in an FA Cup final, stormed out of the dinner after a row with David Pleat. There were inevitably plenty of recriminations, not all of them so public. A massively promising season had finished in cruel anti-climax.

It would not be players who gave David Pleat grief the following season, however: it would be the tabloid press. *The Sun* began its

lurid allegations about his private life in July, but after his wife and family stood by him the paper's attention appeared to drift elsewhere. With several big changes at White Hart Lane – Glenn Hoddle moving to Monaco for £750,000, Chris Fairclough coming from Nottingham Forest for £500,000, along with former Real Madrid star Johnny Metgod for £250,000 – there was indeed much to talk about.

PLEAT HOUNDED OUT

It certainly looked as though 1987–88 was going to be a classic season for Spurs fans. Their side won six and lost two of their first 10 games, Nico Claesen matching Clive Allen goal for goal, and the 2-0 defeat of Sheffield Wednesday on 2 October set up a club record of 14 successive home League wins. A new era was looming.

But so was *The Sun* and the most scandal-seeking of the tabloids returned, visiting Pleat more than once at unreasonable hours and making fresh allegations. In his view, his position became untenable, and in the great tradition of British public figures he was obliged to step down, tendering his resignation at an emergency board meeting on the evening of 23 October.

The fans had seen Pleat as a permanent fixture, building on the near-misses of the previous season to lead London's assault on Merseyside (10 Championships in 12 seasons) and take Tottenham back into Europe. Despite the flagrant summer stories chairman Irving Scholar wasn't alone in still being stunned by events: 'I'd believed he was going to be the Spurs manager for many years to come. I went home [from the board meeting] and felt completely numb.'

Pleat's replacement was chosen for Scholar, not only by the clamour of the press and supporters but also by the League club bosses' recent 'agreement' not to approach contracted managers during the season. Thus there was no leading, proven coach available in England.

Terry Venables was on holiday in Florida when Pleat resigned, and Scholar flew out to sign him. It was good timing: despite huge success in Spain – he was hailed as a saint after taking Barcelona to their first League title for 11 years in his initial season and to the European Cup final the following year – the rapport with the Nou Camp crowd was long gone and the club was happy to release him by mutual consent, making room for Johan Cruyff. Thus on 27 October, in the American autumn sunshine, the man who had played for Spurs in their record triumph at Wembley in 1967, by now acknowledged as one of Europe's finest football thinkers and twice the unsuccessful target of approaches from Arsenal, agreed to become the manager of Tottenham Hotspur, to take over in December. It would be the start of the most traumatic, topsy-turvy period in the club's history.

By contemporary English standards Venables' terms were extremely generous: a three-year contract with a salary of £150,000 and a signing-on fee of £50,000. But he would have to earn it. After Pleat's departure assistant manager Trevor Hartley and coach Doug Livermore had taken over, with team selection somewhat confused and at times even passing to a coterie of senior players.

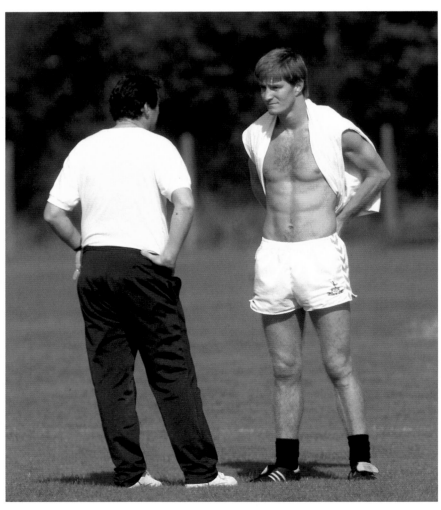

BELOW: Dundee United's robust defender Richard Gough was David Pleat's first major signing in the 1986 close season, with Irving Scholar helping him pip Chelsea's Ken Bates to the £750,000 prize. A versatile, combative player then playing right-back for Scotland, Gough made his mark at Tottenham as an attack-minded centre-back playing alongside Gary Mabbutt. Pleat had sensibly moved Mabbutt from midfield into the heart of defence. But Gough and Pleat didn't always see eye to eye: Gough walked out of the post-match gathering after the 1987 FA Cup final, having become the first Spurs captain to lose an FA Cup final. He returned to Scotland in October 1987, where he partnered Graham Roberts in Graeme Souness' highly successful Rangers side.

The team's form was by now quite appalling: having narrowly lost their last two League games under Pleat – the first of which saw the groin injury to Ray Clemence at Norwich which would end his career – they went down 3-0 at Forest the day after his resignation and then, five days later at Villa Park, the day after Venables had signed, they went out of the League Cup 2-1 to Graham Taylor's Aston Villa. Defeats by Wimbledon (3-0 away) and Luton, and draws with Portsmouth and QPR followed. Richard Gough, who had followed Graham Roberts to Rangers for £1.5 million in September for family reasons, and Chris Waddle, out with heel and hernia problems for much of the season, were being sorely missed.

TEL TAKES CHARGE

Though hardly a hero as a Tottenham player, 'Tel' was now seen as a managerial saviour and when he took over earlier than expected, White Hart Lane's best crowd since the visit of Everton in April 1985 (47,362) turned out on 28 November to witness his first match in charge, and the expected instant miracle – against a Liverpool side unbeaten in the League all season.

The game was a gross disappointment, Steve Hodge being sent off before half-time in a 2-0 defeat, and worse was to follow a fortnight later with a 1-0 home defeat by lowly Charlton. With Allan Harris alongside Venables, the slide was halted just in time for Spurs to finish in a deceptively comfortable 13th place. Hopes of Wembley had crashed at the end of January, when Third Division Port Vale beat a lacklustre team 2-1 in the Potteries, Spurs' goal coming from a raw 19-year-old called Neil Ruddock.

Goals were indeed hard to come by: Spurs scored only 26 in 25 matches that season under Venables, and the League total of 38 was the lowest since the club had joined the League in 1908. Clive Allen lacked support, touch and luck, Waddle was nagged by injury, Claesen slid in and out of form and favour, and Metgod's potential influence was restricted by injury to a dozen appearances, mostly as substitute.

While able to wield the chequebook, however, Venables opted for a cautious approach, encouraging youth (Vinny Samways, Brian Statham) as well as buying: goalkeeper Bobby Mimms from Everton (£375,000), Paul Walsh from Liverpool (£500,000) and, first and most controversial in December 1987, his old skipper Terry Fenwick from QPR (£550,000). Fenwick was not only a dodgy purchase in the eyes of most fans; he also persuaded Venables to agree to terms that radically pushed up the salary structure at White Hart Lane, with the utility player actually earning more than Chris Waddle. Meanwhile, in the spring of 1988, Venables loaned the 35-year-old Ossie Ardiles to Blackburn. Not for the first time, fans at a Venables club sometimes found the manager's strategy difficult to understand.

Though on the high side by the standards of the time, these transfers were merely a prelude to a summer of 'super signings' – 21-year-old Paul Gascoigne from Newcastle for a British record of £2 million and 23-year-old Paul Stewart from Manchester City for £1.5 million – though Mark Hateley had been first choice

here. Neither had yet been capped at full level by Bobby Robson, but for Gascoigne an England debut was imminent, and in a rather stale era his remarkable skills on the ball were a breath of fresh air for a flair-starved football public.

Some of this vast outlay was recouped with the sale of four players. Out of contract Clive Allen went to Bordeaux for £900,000 after a relatively poor tally of 13 goals in 37 games, and three players went 'home' – Nico Claesen to Antwerp for £550,000, Steve Hodge to his native Nottingham with Forest paying £550,000, and Dutchman Johnny Metgod to Feyenoord for only £175,000.

Fleet Street dubbed Venables 'Mr Moneybags'. On 28 July the *Daily Mail* said that 'no one in football has spent so extravagantly as Venables this summer,' and Spurs were regarded as big if not profligate spenders – in sharp contrast to neighbours Arsenal's highly geared youth system.

For Spurs fans, however, the prospect of the new season was mouth-watering, and the opener at home to Coventry couldn't come quickly enough. Unfortunately, they would have to wait because the East Stand was not ready in time. There was no alternative but to postpone the game.

Later, the three-man management committee of the Football League decided that Tottenham were guilty of breaching Regulation 24 and two points were to be deducted from their season's total. On appeal to the FA (on the grounds that the two-point penalty was not mandatory) these were reinstated – and Spurs ordered to pay a £15,000 fine. The stand was

Clive Allen celebrates yet another accolade. Following his 49 goal haul in 1986–87, the former QPR striker received both the PFA and FWA Player of the Year awards. He is seen here with the Spurs Supporters' Club Award.

ABOVE: Gazza strikes a pose after scoring on his home debut: 10 September 1988 against Arsenal no less. The looks on the fans' faces say it all – a footballing god has arrived at White Hart Lane – and Mitchell Thomas appears unsure whether he should actually touch him. However, the Waddle-Gascoigne-Stewart partnership hardly clicked straight away, and this 3-2 defeat was the second in a 10-match start that brought a paltry seven points.

RIGHT: Mellow yellows: Stewart, Howells and Waddle celebrate Stewart's winner against Wimbledon on 15 April 1989, towards the end of a marvellous run that began in February and registered nine victories in 13 League matches to take Tottenham from the edge of relegation to a respectable sixth place in the First Division. Waddle's form was devastating. For Venables, however, his main problem was a reliable scorer: Waddle himself topped the season's totals with 14 goals.

eventually reopened for the visit of Arsenal on 18 October, 1989, witnessing a 2-1 victory.

The refund of the two points was welcome news for a club that had made a dreadful start to the season, bottom of the table with just one win in 10 League matches – the worst performance for 13 years. A potentially prolific attack missed a genuine proven striker, while a defence that looked good on paper just leaked goals (22 in those 10 games, for example). Then in the 11th game, a 3-2 defeat of Wimbledon, Gary Stevens sustained a knee injury in a challenge from Vinny Jones which put him out for the rest of the season.

Gascoigne started well – both he and his pal Waddle scored on his home debut, a 3-2 defeat by Arsenal – but he would not really warm up until later in the season. A Spurs recovery in November was devalued by a poor performance in the League Cup, where after needing extra time in a replay to get past Blackburn they lost 2-1 to Southampton at The Dell. But worse, far worse, was to follow.

Gascoigne was unavailable for the awkward third round FA Cup tie at Second Division Bradford City on 7 January , a game that could either set Spurs on the way to Wembley or effectively finish their season. It would do the latter. On a day no Tottenham fan wants to recall Bradford won 1-0, a result that (coming a year after the ignominious defeat at the hands of Port Vale) had even the most committed Venables admirer questioning whether he should have stayed in Spain.

With no Cup run and the East Stand fiasco, money was short and clearly going to get shorter. At the board meeting a month after the

Bradford debacle Venables was understandably told he would have to sell before he could buy, whereupon the manager produced a list of candidates. Top of the pile to pay for his intended purchases – Coventry's midfielder Steve Sedgley, Sheffield Wednesday left-back Nigel Worthington and Wolves striker Andy Mutch – were Chris Fairclough (valued by Venables at £500,000) and Gary Mabbutt (£600,000), the latter's inclusion being baffling to the directors, most notably Scholar. Venables' obvious down on the captain's playing style had always puzzled observers (he considered Mabbutt sluggish and prone to positional lapses), and was yet another irritant in the deteriorating relationship between chairman and manager.

Scholar may have won the day (Mabbutt did not make the mooted move to Steve Coppell's Crystal Palace for £750,000), though Enfield-born Sedgley would finally move to Tottenham for that price in July. Fairclough went to Leeds, first on loan in March and later permanently for £500,000, and at Elland Road he reproduced the style he had shown as a youngster at Forest and which inexplicably deserted him at White Hart Lane and he became a key member of Leeds' Championship winning team. Bobby Mimms didn't move on until December 1990 (Blackburn Rovers for £250,000), making only four further first-team appearances. The reason was the the arrival of Erik 'the Viking' Thorstvedt, an extrovert Norwegian international who, after a disastrous televised debut against Forest on 15 January, conceded only 16 goals in 17 games to become a firm favourite of Lane loyalists. Another factor in Spurs' spring revival was the arrival of

'Nayim' (real name Mohamed Ali Amar, born in the Spanish enclave of Ceuta, on the Moroccan mainland) who added a continental dimension to midfield while on loan from Barcelona – a move made permanent in June.

These two, with Fenwick moving into the back four alongside Mabbutt, helped (yet again) to transform a miserable season into an encouraging one. From the fringe of relegation and a double cup exit the club clawed its way up the table, first to safety and then to what would have been, in normal circumstances, the fringe of Europe in sixth place. Between the 1-0 defeats at Old Trafford on 5 February and Loftus Road on 13 May, Tottenham won nine and drew four of their 14 matches, the only defeat in a sparkling sequence that registered a goal tally of 27-10 being at the hands of title-chasing Liverpool.

It was the sensational form of Chris Waddle that was the most salient feature of this run. In one three-game spell, especially, he was simply breathtaking, scoring four goals that Spurs fans will always savour: the dribble and angled drive against Norwich, the chip in the mud at Southampton, and the magnificent pair that sank Aston Villa at White Hart Lane. It was the kind of scoring power which, added to his consistent brilliance, drew the European scouts like bees round a honey pot.

Helped too by Gascoigne bubbling and Stewart starting to score, the climb up the table removed any danger of serious criticism of Venables. Still, it didn't take much to see that what he lacked was a genuine goalscorer. Waddle topped the list in 1988–89 with 14, one ahead of Stewart, but third was Fenwick, seven of his nine coming from penalties. Paul Walsh, while a tireless user of space, scored only six times in 37 games.

LINEKER COMES, WADDLE GOES

Venables found his striker all right: the best this country has managed since Jimmy Greaves and, arguably, the most lethal finisher in Europe since Gerd Müller. In June he signed Gary Lineker; after three years at Barcelona, England's favourite son was coming home. And at £1.2 million the 28-year-old must have been one of the bargains of the century.

The deal was a comprehensive coup for Venables but despite the modest fee it would trigger a series of unforeseen events in the boardroom. At the ratifying meeting Paul Bobroff, chairman of the public holding company, emphasised to his colleagues, including Venables, that the money had to be recouped as soon as possible: the first payment of £600,000 was due on 1 August, the balance a year later. But after the manager left the room, Bobroff announced there was no money at all for the deal, and Scholar had guaranteed the deal from his own resources. The truth, hidden from many at the club for a long time, was that Spurs were not just short of immediate funds, but in serious debt.

All this meant little to the ecstatic fans; to them the prospect of England stars Gascoigne, Waddle and now Lineker in the Tottenham team would represent no less than a holy trinity of talent in residence at the cathedral of cultured football. For Irving Scholar, however, the possibility lasted only days. Just minutes before the press conference for Lineker's arrival there came a phone call from a Paris middle man representing Bernard Tapie's Olympique Marseille, offering first £2½ million and then £3 million for Chris Waddle. While the chairman continued to play hard to get, the manager, somewhat characteristically, suggested a cheeky 'pay now, move later' deal.

LEFT: Former Spur Steve Hodge chases Chris Waddle. David Pleat paid £650,000 for the midfielder as a 24-year-old from Aston Villa in December 1986. Though his early performances were good, he never settled in London and his form inevitably suffered. Terry Venables recouped £550,000 from Forest (Hodge's first club) in August 1988. In 1992 Hodge was part of the Leeds Championship winning squad. Like Waddle, Hodge was an England squad regular and spent even more time on Bobby Robson's bench than his more talented colleague.

But Tapie wanted Waddle right then. And when Scholar later asked for £5 million (only Ruud Gullit had moved for more at that time), the Marseille boss didn't wince; he would certainly pay that for Waddle and Walsh, and £4 million for the one player. It was an offer Scholar simply couldn't refuse.

Waddle might object, of course, and most observers were surprised when the player, happy at Tottenham and with six years of a seven-year contract to run, jumped at the chance to hone his skills in the south of France. Spurs supporters were even more dumbfounded. Venables used the potential profits cautiously, signing only Sedgley and, just after the season's start, 28-year-old Welsh international left-back Pat van den Hauwe from Everton for £575,000. What later hurt the fans was that having bought Lineker at a bargain price, sold Waddle for a fortune and not spent in the interim, the club was still in deep financial trouble.

Back in July, however, the supporters were suffering from a shattered dream. They had seen the dawn of a new era, with Gascoigne, Waddle and Lineker to take Spurs to the apex of Europe. Now it had been blacked out, apparently by mismanagement, and seemingly by greed. The fans could not know how the cost of the new stand had restricted the club's ability to manoeuvre. And the feeling of anti-climax was deepened by a miserable start to the 1989–90 season, with only one win (against Luton) in the first six League matches.

While Lineker hit a hot streak, with eight goals in seven League and League Cup games, to ease Tottenham out of their embarrassingly lowly position in the autumn, success in the cup competitions would elude Venables for yet another season. The patience of supporters starved of European action was tested further. Nor did it help Venables' public relations that this year both exits were at home – a 3-1 humbling by new bogey team Southampton in the third round of the FA Cup on 6 January and then, at the end of a dire month in which they took only two points from three League games, a 3-2 defeat by a fast and skilful Forest side who made Spurs look pedestrian.

Indeed Spurs were somewhat fortunate to make it that far, because apart from a marvellous 3-0 win over Manchester United at Old Trafford in the third round they had really struggled, beating plucky Fourth Division Southend only on away goals in the second round and needing an own goal to gain a replay against Tranmere in the fourth round.

After another frustrating period on the slide it was left to Lineker to lift the spirits – and the club up the table. His seven goals led to a final flourish of eight wins in 10 games to take Tottenham to third in the table behind Liverpool and Aston Villa. In better times, and had UEFA relented, it would have meant the passport to Europe.

The role of Gary Lineker in saving Spurs' season, despite his involvement in England's World Cup build-up, cannot be overrated. With constant changes in personnel behind him (only some of which were enforced by injury), and often feeding only on scraps, he scored 24 out of Spurs' 59 League goals – Stewart was second with only eight, Gascoigne next with six – and he stayed remarkably free of injury trouble; indeed, he was the only player to complete the League programme.

1991

An eighth FA Cup • Extinction looms with bankruptcy • Sugar takes over • Gascoigne and Lineker follow Waddle abroad • Legal and financial strife • Sugar ousts Venables • Banned from the Cup • Ardiles and Francis • The year of Klinsmann

Tottenham kicked-off the 1990–91 season with essentially the same side; yet the campaign was to be the complete antithesis of 1989–90. Instead of starting badly, leaking goals, then pulling themselves up, they began with an unbeaten run of 10 games. But then came an almighty slide: in the 24 League games over the six months from December to May Spurs won just three (Luton, Derby, Southampton), with only their 10 draws keeping them in mid-table. Lineker, troubled by a rare injury in the spring, managed a relatively modest total of 15 League goals (three of them penalties).

The League Cup, too, had started in great style, with five goals against Hartlepool at the Lane, and progress was steady until they met Chelsea in January, with a goalless draw in the fifth round at Stamford Bridge in front of 34,178. Tottenham's humiliating 3-0 defeat in the replay was the seventh cup exit at home in the nine seasons since Spurs had last won silverware at Wembley. If ever a football manager needed a good run in the FA Cup, Venables needed it now.

ANOTHER YEAR ENDING IN '1'

And he got it – after all, it was a year ending in '1'. Stewart scored the goal that beat his old club Blackpool in Tottenham's voodoo scenario – away to a lowly club in the third round – and Oxford were duly despatched at home 4-2 in the fourth, a result significant for the rebirth of Gascoigne, whose League form had been patchy. Against Oxford he really turned it on, creating two goals and scoring two himself (one a beauty) and throughout displayed his extravagant skills.

In the fifth round Gazza again dazzled by scoring both goals to beat Portsmouth; in the quarter-final against Notts County he conceded the lead by failing to clear his lines, then won the match with a superb late hit. All this time he was carrying the burden of constant European club and press attention (partly a result of his famous World Cup tears in Turin) and, to cap it all, he was suffering from an injury that would need an operation before the semi-final with Arsenal, their first meeting in the FA Cup since Garth Crooks' goal won the third round in 1982. Top of the table with just two League defeats all season, Arsenal were chasing their second Double and were clear favourites against a Spurs side who had won only twice in the League that year.

In addition David Howells had been absent for 11 weeks, returning to the first team just four days before, in the match against Norwich, and Gascoigne had played only an

hour of that game following his operation. Both were risked from the start by Venables. The FA had both the common and commercial sense to stage the match at Wembley, the first ever semi-final there, and the 77,893 crowd was one of the highest ever to attend a semi-final. The Hillsborough tragedy was still fresh in everyone's memory and it wasn't until 1995 that the FA felt confident enough to return FA Cup semi-finals automatically to the provinces.

Though both League encounters between

In an era of big-name signings David Howells has been a reminder of football's past – the home-grown, loyal, one-club man, in his case one who could play up front, in the middle or at the back. Despite being dogged by injury, he was outstanding under Francis in 1995-96.

Tony Adams and Gary Mabbutt lead out their teams for the FA Cup semi-final at Wembley on 14 April 1991, the first semi ever held there. Sitting atop the First Division and defeated just once in the League all season, Arsenal were clear favourites against a Spurs side that had won just three of its last 18 League games. For Venables the match was crucial: early exits in three consecutive seasons (1988-90) had really put the pressure on to do well this time . . . in a year ending with a "1".

BELOW: Paul Gascoigne's (extreme left) free-kick is already there before David Seaman has had a chance to get either hand to the ball, and Spurs are ahead in the 1991 FA Cup semi-final after just five minutes. This early strike forced Arsenal to push forward, giving the Spurs five-man midfield the space and time to kill the game off.

the clubs had finished scoreless that season, the first goal came after just five minutes, when Paul Stewart was needlessly brought down 30 yards from goal by Anders Limpar. Gascoigne's free-kick was unstoppable; nobody, least of all David Seaman, who had confidently lined up a two-man wall, anticipated that he would strike the ball with such venom. Powerful, deadly accurate and with a slight bend, the ball flew into the top corner of Arsenal's net for one of Wembley's best strikes. It remains one of the most memorable goals of the 1990s.

It was a sensational start, and just four min-

utes later it was 2-0. A neat exchange of passes between Gascoigne and Allen ended with Allen's cross eluding Howells but finding the chest of striker Alan Smith, who had tracked Gary Mabbutt back to the six-yard box; his poor control near the line let in Lineker, who poked the ball home from close range. Arsenal had conceded only 16 goals in 31 games before the final; now they leaked two in 10 minutes.

Just before half-time, and very much against the run of play, Arsenal scored, Smith atoning by beating Mabbutt to a Dixon cross – though Thorstvedt had come and then, fatally, retreated. With Gascoigne and perhaps Howells bound to tire, Tottenham would be in for a tough 45 minutes.

Gascoigne went off on the hour to a tumultuous reception from the Spurs fans and the energetic Nayim came on. It was the cue for Tottenham to score again, Mabbutt winning the ball in the middle of the park to set Lineker off on a run against a retreating defence. Samways drew Steve Bould and Lineker had too much pace for Tony Adams; his shot entered the net via Seaman's hands.

A final Arsenal assault, including a brief scare when Campbell hit the bar and Paul Merson failed to net the rebound, was followed by elation: Spurs would be returning to Wembley on 18 May, and they had spiked their rival's Double.

As the Wembley final approached, Spurs supporters little realised that their treasured institution faced liquidation. Then, just days before the game, new bankers Midland (Bobroff had switched from the traditional Barclays) extended their facilities until the end of August.

The evening before the Cup final was to be taken up by negotiations on two fronts – firstly the efforts by Terry Venables to acquire the club, and secondly by the continuing saga of where Gascoigne would play in the future. With the players resting upstairs, it seemed almost certain that the Saturday would see Gascoigne play his last game for Spurs, and certainly possible that it could be the last game Spurs ever played as a first-class club.

Between 4.30 pm and 10 pm on Friday Irving Scholar and Terry Venables sat in the hotel trying to reach an agreement on the sale of Scholar's shares from chairman to manager. Gascoigne complicated the issue – Scholar had offered to sell at a lower price if Gascoigne could be kept at the club. Scholar's control had really disappeared; he was no longer on the board of the holding company, and, though still chairman of the football club, his influence now essentially extended to where and to whom he chose to sell his shares.

By 10 pm it was clear that there were no deals to be struck. And the prime asset had already gone. Gascoigne was the difference between a future and bankruptcy and, by the eve of the Cup final, he had already committed himself to Lazio.

In an interesting paragraph in his own book *Venables: The Autobiography*, the former manager notes that: ' . . . for once the team doctor was not required to fire his usual "tranquilliser dart" into Gazza to put him to sleep.' Venables goes on to say that Gazza never needed anyone to hype him up, and all of the efforts before the Cup final, in particular, were designed to calm him down, not wind him up. But, as Venables also says about Gascoigne that day:' . . . it looked like his mind was somewhere else . . . the transfer might have been on his mind . . . in any event he was not as hyped up as normal and certainly nothing like he had been before the semi-final.'

Wembley that was to be a breeding ground for memories that few finals provide. Forest were the emotional favourites – Brian Clough never having won the FA Cup and still being enormously popular. As the teams took to the field the Forest manager grabbed Venables' hand and held onto it. As Venables said later:

Context is crucial. Gazza, returning after an operation, produced his magic after just five minutes, against Arsenal and in front of almost 78,000 spectators at Wembley. Small wonder that he jumped for joy.
Running to congratulate him is man-of-the-match Vinny Samways, who had one of his best ever games for Spurs and looked the complete midfielder.

'He wouldn't let go, so I made him laugh, which at least made it look as if we were joking and not a couple of lovers.' As they reached the playing area, Venables brought his hand up as if to wave at someone and Clough was forced to let go.

UNPUNISHED FOUL

The game was just 90 seconds old when Gascoigne confirmed with his studs what everyone in the ground suspected - that he was hyped up to a level that was beyond anyone's control. Out on Spurs' right Gascoigne 'tackled' the Forest midfielder Garry Parker. As Parker moved towards him Gascoigne lifted his leg to the horizontal and simply kicked Parker at chest height. Parker went down in a heap. The reaction of everyone watching was identical: 'He'll be very lucky to stay on the field'. Terry Venables said afterwards that the tackle was vicious and his first thought was: 'Christ, that's him booked.'

It was the post-match consensus, and one which has grown with time, that Gascoigne's tackle on Parker was the worst ever seen in a Cup final and that Roger Milford's decision not even to book him was amazing. Gascoigne's madness was to strike again after just 12 minutes of the match. Forest's young

right-back Gary Charles ran right to left across the edge of the penalty area and was tackled by Gascoigne, who simply kicked him viciously on the right knee after the ball had gone. Charles got up without a murmur, Roger Milford chuckled and Gascoigne was treated for an apparent injury to his own knee.

Stuart Pearce took his trademark free-kick, left-footed into the top left-hand corner. Thorstvedt was even standing at that side of the goal knowing exactly where the ball would go, but could barely move as Pearce's shot rocketed past. As Forest celebrated, Gascoigne collapsed in the middle of the field clearly unable to play on. The players gathered around him, Venables came onto the pitch. Suddenly everything was in the balance – Gascoigne's future, Spurs' future, the fee for Gascoigne, Venables' future at White Hart Lane – even whether there was a future at White Hart Lane at all.

Nayim came on as substitute, but the reality was that Spurs should have been down to ten men. Roger Milford said later that he didn't feel it was necessary to take any action with Gascoigne because the Spurs player was clearly not able to continue.

After 25 minutes, Paul Allen put Gary Lineker through to score a classic sharp

Lineker goal. Lineker was clearly onside, but the linesman made the most public mistake of his career, and it was disallowed. Five minutes later Lineker was through again, this time from Paul Stewart. Mark Crossley, in the Forest goal, brought Lineker down and was arguably lucky not to be sent off himself. The penalty was indisputable and Lineker took it well, hitting the ball towards the corner to Crossley's left. Unfortunately for Lineker, Crossley guessed correctly and turned the ball away.

So at half-time Forest were 1-0 ahead and the 80,000 crowd had surely seen one of the most dramatic 45 minutes of football in the history of the competition. Venables spoke to Gascoigne, by now in a hospital bed. The medical team already knew that Gascoigne had torn his cruciate ligaments. He certainly wouldn't play for at least six months, Lazio would presumably not now pay for him, and it was quite possible he would never wear a football shirt again.

It took Spurs just seven minutes of the second half to equalise. Nayim put Stewart through and the midfielder capped what was surely his best ever performance for Spurs with a beautiful cross-shot goal. Forest, with Spurs keeping Nigel Clough well under control, did not have a clear-cut chance in the second half and, by the end of 90 minutes, the pendulum had firmly swung towards Tottenham.

Venables talked to his players before extra-time. 'We're back in the game and it's got "WIN" written all over it. The only thing that can stop us is if we stop ourselves. They're on their heels, they don't know if they have got anything left in them.' Brian Clough sat on the bench chatting to a policeman while Archie Gemmill and Alan Hill tried to inspire a flagging Forest in the five-minute break.

There was just the one goal in extra time. Nayim put in a corner from the right, Paul Stewart flicked it on and Mabbutt came charging in on the far post. In attempting to head the ball out for another corner, Des Walker managed to put it just inside the post, for an own goal. Mabbutt, the loser via his own

o.g. in 1987, went up to collect the trophy. Spurs thus became the first club to win the FA Cup eight times and no one had missed the fact that the year ended in a one. It was the first domestic trophy that Venables had ever won as a manager. The team and their wives got on to the club coach and took the Cup to hospital for Gascoigne to see. Gascoigne, whom Venables says was crying, received his medal in his hospital bed. That was the end of his Tottenham career.

FINANCIAL PROBLEMS MULTIPLY

The euphoria of the Cup final was soon to be replaced by the realisation that all the problems had not gone away. Indeed, they had suddenly got significantly worse. The new stand – having cost £9 million – still had largely to be paid for and there was no acquirer on the horizon who came close to being acceptable to the banks and the current shareholders.

With Lazio reducing the amount they were now prepared to pay for Gascoigne to £4.85 million (the actual sum was the subject of intense dispute later) and with no other bidders for the player even remotely likely, the Midland Bank became more crucial in the tempestuous mix. The pressure to conclude matters – one way or the other – was intense.

It was at this point that Alan Sugar stepped up on stage. He was 46 years old and his company, Amstrad, had been one of the success stories of the Thatcher years. His speciality was today's technology at tomorrow's prices – in other words, bringing the very latest electronic products to a mass market at affordable prices.

BELOW: Gary Lineker watches Paul Stewart's angled shot beat Mark Crossley to make it 1-1 after 52 minutes of the 1991 FA Cup Final. After the chaotic first half hour involving Gascoigne's tackles, Pearce's goal, Lineker's good 'disallowed' goal and Crossley's penalty save, the second half was almost calmness itself.

LEFT: Paul Allen (11) and Lineker congratulate the scorer. If Vinny Samways had enjoyed his best game for the club in the semi-final, Stewart reserved his for the big one. He would continue his good form through 1991-92, gaining full England recognition.
BELOW: The expressions of Stuart Pearce, substitute Steve Hodge and Nigel Clough need no explanation as Des Walker's attempted clearance goes into the Forest net. It was a remarkably sweet irony for Gary Mabbutt (arm aloft), whose own goal had given Coventry victory four years before.

He was not a soccer obsessive in the sense that Irving Scholar was, but his sons Simon and Daniel and his brother Derek were all fans. The first Amstrad offices had been in Tottenham, near the ground. Sugar and Venables had met some time before when Venables had taken part in an Amstrad advertising campaign. It is interesting that Venables said in his book *Venables: The Autobiography* (page 302) that: 'I had known

Sugar slightly for several years, but had taken an instinctive dislike to him...'

Alan Sugar contacted Terry Venables 48 hours after Spurs had won the trophy. Venables returned the call and within days the two were negotiating with Scholar and Bobroff. Venables declared himself prepared to invest £3 million in the club, which impressed Sugar, but Sugar was clearly going to be the financially senior partner and made it clear that he saw

Moments to savour for Gary Mabbutt as he holds the trophy aloft to celebrate Spurs' record eighth FA Cup win in 1991. Mabbutt had been club captain since 1987. An unsung stalwart for the club since 1982, Mabbutt helped Spurs win the UEFA Cup in his second season. He is a diabetic who has to suffer several insulin injections each day.

the arrangement as a business transaction. Alan Sugar said to Irving Scholar during their negotiations that Terry Venables saw himself as an entrepreneur, a view Sugar was not in agreement with. Nonetheless, Sugar was sensibly quite prepared to leave Venables to handle all the football aspects of their joint venture.

With Alan Sugar now a credible and wealthy bidder the Midland Bank were considerably more relaxed and, on 12 June, gave the club a year's extension on their £11 million overdraft. Sugar and Venables were negotiating to buy the stakes of both Scholar (who owned 26 per cent) and Bobroff (11 per cent). Together, while not 50 per cent, these two stakes would give them effective control of the company and the club. Right up to the very last minute Scholar was still talking to Robert Maxwell, who also still seemed to want to buy the club.

Eventually Sugar was able to persuade Paul Bobroff to sell his stake and Irving Scholar, who was in Monte Carlo, chose to sell to Sugar as well when it finally became clear that Maxwell would not be able to deliver.

Because Venables could not come up with his promised £3 million immediately, Sugar was obliged to finance the whole deal for the first 10 days. And while Sugar had funded his share from his own bank account, Venables had to borrow most of his £3 million. The two parties held 17.8 per cent of the shares each. On 6 December 1991, however, Tottenham decided to issue more shares to raise money as it still did not have the necessary funds to repay the overdraft. The consequence of this was that Alan Sugar's percentage of the company rose to 48 per cent while Terry Venables' increased to just 23 per cent. This was because Sugar could afford to buy any available extra shares while Venables could only buy a relatively small extra number. So, to all intents and purposes, it was now Alan Sugar's company.

SUGGESTIONS OF SLEAZE

In the next few years, an almost interminable series of television programmes and newspaper articles were to attempt to delve into the sources of Terry Venables' funds, the details of Paul Gascoigne's sale to Lazio and the decline and collapse of the relationship between Sugar and Venables. These programmes and articles became the subject of a number of lawsuits and libel actions and a level of animosity rarely seen either in sporting or in financial circles.

The details, in themselves, are ultimately not important to the story of Tottenham Hotspur. It is clear that the trust between Alan Sugar and Terry Venables broke down over a number of issues.

Matters came to a head at a board meeting on 6 May 1993. Though the club had been doing much better financially because of the sales of Gascoigne and Lineker and the arrival of the new Sky Television contract, on the field results had not been exceptional and attendances were down on 1991. At the conclusion of the board meeting Sugar handed Venables a letter which suggested for the first time that Venables sell back his shares, at their original purchase price, and resign as chief executive.

ABOVE: Gary Lineker scores his second against Porto in the Cup Winners' Cup match on 23 October 1991. It was a goal that represented Spurs at their best – a one touch move involving practically every Spurs' player. After six blank years Tottenham were back in Europe and they rose to the occasion: after three successive League defeats, two of them at home, they put themselves on course for the third round with a 3-1 win. RIGHT: Gordon Durie had scored three vital goals in six Cup Winners' Cup matches in 1991–92, but neither he nor any Tottenham player managed it in Rotterdam on 4 March against a defence superbly marshalled by sweeper and former Spur Johnny Metgod. It was revenge for the club Tottenham had beaten 6-2 on the way to taking the UEFA Cup in 1983–84.

Another board meeting was arranged for Friday 14 May at which the formal termination of Terry Venables' contract was discussed. The board voted two to one in favour of Venables leaving, with one director (Tony Berry) abstaining. Because of his personal interest in the issue, Venables was not allowed to vote.

Venables, who was portrayed in the popular press as the hero of the situation, went straight to the courts and won an injunction to keep matters as they were until the courts had decided whether his dismissal was proper and legal. Sugar, meanwhile, found himself continually intimidated by hate mail, death threats, demonstrations outside his home, obscene phone calls and abusive verbal attacks outside the court. In the end, Venables' decision to go to the courts was to prove to be a misjudge-

ment. Sugar never wanted a court battle.

After three days the judge observed that 'There was nothing to suggest that the board of directors did not have the normal right to hire and to fire the company's chief executive or that if Mr Sugar and Mr Venables should fall out, they were nevertheless bound to continue to support each other indefinitely.' He went on to later add that: 'Whether Mr Venables' dismissal was in the best interests of Tottenham is not a matter for the court to decide. That is a matter for the Tottenham board'. That was both a fair summation of the truth and the end of Terry Venables' association with Tottenham Hotspur. Soon afterwards, he sold his stake in Spurs for £3 million. By April 1994, he had been appointed coach of England. His personal financial affairs would continue to be a matter of speculation and will no doubt be so for a very long time.

Sugar was reluctant to press his attack personally or even in court. Any revelations which appeared critical of Venables would, almost by definition, be damaging to Spurs in both the short and long term and it was hard to see how Sugar or the club could gain from that. He did, however become irritated by where the credit for saving the club, and returning it to the black, was going: 'Terry Venables did not save this club. Twelve million saved this club. And I put up most of it.'

The legal and press battle seemed to have the stamina of Paul Allen in his prime – it just ran and ran. Venables' autobiography, published in September 1994, was another opportunity for old wounds to be opened, scraped and to have salt rubbed into them. Happily, a certain amount of humour was now creeping in. *The Sunday Times* asked Alan Sugar to review the book (his fee going to Great Ormond Street Hospital for Sick Children) and his two-page piece was a rare opportunity to enjoy the conflict and their jokes. His concluding line was also a delight: 'The book is certainly guaranteed an immediate sale of at least 10,000 copies because, with so many allegations lodged against so many people, I should imagine every law firm in the country will buy.'

A RETURN TO FOOTBALL

While all of this was going on, Tottenham had been playing football. Only days after his takeover, at the press conference of 22 June 1991, Alan Sugar stated: 'I will look after the £11 million at the bank, while Terry Venables will look after the 11 players on the pitch'. A neat line, and an assurance also given to Irving Scholar, but within weeks Peter Shreeves had returned as first-team coach and then manager, with Venables abdicating direct team responsibility on his appointment as chief executive of Tottenham Hotspur plc.

Shreeves, who since leaving White Hart Lane in 1986 had been assistant and then caretaker manager at QPR (then passed over for Trevor Francis) and later No. 2 to Steve Perryman at Watford, returned to take control of what was essentially Venables' 1990–91 squad but with two notable differences: Gascoigne had gone, laid up for more than 12 months before he could play for Lazio or England, and Gordon Durie had arrived, signed from Chelsea for £2.2 million (a million more than Lineker in 1989).

This Anglo-Scottish strike force began well, registering five wins in seven games and Lineker in a real purple patch with 11 goals, Durie chipping in with two. Then, inexplicably, a 2-1 defeat by Manchester United signalled a ghastly sequence of only five wins in 25 League games to leave Spurs in danger of relegation. To make matters almost intolerably worse was yet another home defeat in the third round of the FA Cup, the club relinquishing control of the trophy with a spineless 1-0 home defeat in a replay with Aston Villa. It was the home form that was crippling: 11 defeats in the League, plus that loss in the FA Cup and, on 1 March, another in the second leg of the League Cup semi-final against Forest, avenging their Wembley defeat of the previous year. Small wonder that Lane regulars were worried.

Without Lineker the Second Division would have been almost a certainty. But while Durie experienced a six-month goal drought in the League, and Stewart, Walsh and the rest registered no more than a handful each, the England striker struggled on magnificently, scoring 28 goals in 35 League games and five from as many matches in the League Cup. It was a phenomenal performance in a struggling team, recognised by the Football Writers' Association, who voted him their footballer of the year.

There was always the excitement of Europe to fall back on. With the UEFA ban now over Spurs found themselves with successive trips to Austria in the European Cup Winners Cup. First there was a faltering, early-season performance against Sparkasse Stockerau of Vienna

Return to Wembley: Spurs walk out for the FA Cup semi-final with Arsenal on 4 April 1993, two years after the club's classic victory in the same fixture. Six players (Thorsvedt, Edinburgh, Mabbutt, Howells, Nayim, and Allen) survived from that day, but this time there was no magic Gascoigne free-kick or Lineker double. Unable to score, Spurs surrendered the chance of a 10th final to a goal from Tony Adams.

in the preliminary round, goals coming in each leg from Durie and Mabbutt. Then there came more formidable opposition in the form of Hajduk Split, the Croatian side having to play in Linz because of the war with Serbia – and winning 1-0 in front of only 7,000 people. In the second leg, goals from Durie and defender David Tuttle, a fine drive, saw Tottenham through at White Hart Lane.

Three weeks later Spurs shrugged off their appalling League form to beat Porto 3-1 at White Hart Lane, with Durie and Lineker (2) reviving their earlier form, and a solid defensive display in Portugal for a goalless draw gave Spurs supporters some comfort during the long winter months, but when they played Feyenoord on 4 March they ran into two fine displays by ex-Spur Johnny Metgod, now 34, first in front of 48,000 in Rotterdam (1-0) and then when Feyenoord defended their lead with a goalless draw at White Hart Lane.

Spurs were left to aim for respectability in the League. After yet another defeat (2-1 by Liverpool), they won five out of their next seven games (nine goals for Lineker) and finished 15th. The fans remained loyal, at least to Lineker: his farewell home appearance before moving to Grampus 8 (a 3-3 draw against his old club Everton) pulled in a crowd of 34,630.

It was hard not to feel sympathy for Shreeves. If the team did well, it was Venables' side; if they performed badly, it was down to the coach. But although he was hampered by lack of money and forced to operate against a background of boardroom battles he was nevertheless guilty of being overcautious at times and some of his team selections baffled the most trusting of fans. A pleasant enough man, he did not have his tenuous one-year contract renewed in the summer of 1992 and, for the second time in six years, drifted away from White Hart Lane to other venues.

A TOUCH OF THE CONTINENT
After the rights issue in December 1991 which raised £7 million – Venables took a more active role in team affairs for 1992–93, creating a continental-style structure by appointing Doug Livermore (chief coach) and Ray Clemence (his assistant) as his right-hand men; he would remain in overall control of team affairs while they would be responsible for day-to-day matters – and team selection.

Paul Stewart, having come good in 1991 with a fine season capped by his FA Cup final goal, and consolidating his contribution with three England caps in 1991–92, was forced to move back north for family reasons and joined Liverpool for £2 million.

Icelander Gudni Bergsson came under increasing pressure, as Dean Austin, a classy attacking full-back, followed in Justin Edinburgh's footsteps from Southend for a fee of £375,000 in June, and decided to leave. Also arriving were centre-backs Jason Cundy (signed from Chelsea for £800,000 after a promising period on loan at the tail-end of 1991-92), and Neil 'Razor' Ruddock, back for a second spell for a tribunal-fixed £750,000 in May having shown growing maturity at Southampton.

All three moves were set up by Shreeves, as was the loan of Andy Gray from Crystal Palace, Steve Coppell getting a useful price of £900,000 in the summer of 1992. Even in goal

there were changes, Ian Walker continuing to chase Shreeves' estimation back in 1985 that he was 'the next Peter Shilton' by allowing the experienced Thorstvedt between the posts only when he was injured.

Despite the constant changes, not all of them enforced by injury, Spurs did well to finish eighth in the new Premier League and have a good run in the FA Cup. This time it was Arsenal's turn: the Gunners won their second semi-final with Spurs at Wembley, a crowd of 76,263 seeing a goal from Tony Adams putting his side through. Forest had earlier knocked Spurs out of the League Cup for the second year running – this time with a 2-0 win in the fifth round in December.

That Spurs had a reasonable season was due (as so often before) to the goalscoring exploits of one man. Bought just after the start of the season to do the impossible – follow in the formidable footsteps of Gary Lineker – Teddy Sheringham was a very different kind of striker, but at 26 he had learned to play both the long-ball game (at Millwall) and the short-passing game (at Forest). At Tottenham, after his £2.1 million move in August, he scored 21 goals in the 38 remaining League matches to lead the Premier League list, with four more in five FA Cup appearances and three in four League Cup ties (he didn't miss a game). And he did not just stop at chasing Lineker's club achievements: despite fierce competition he won a place in the England side.

Sheringham played 17 games alongside Gordon Durie but the partnership failed to flourish, first because the Scot's form faltered following allegations that he had feigned injury and, in the spring, through genuine injury.

Help for Sheringham up front came from a very different source – the 18-year-old Nick Barmby, a product of the FA's School of Excellence. Very unlike Sheringham in size, shape and style, Barmby complemented the No 10 nicely in a limited number of outings and his surprisingly mature play – his precocious talents were shown to good effect in the televised 2-0 win over Norwich in the fourth round of the FA Cup – had many critics hailing him as a future England star. In fact he would make his full debut under Terry Venables against Uruguay in March 1995 – as Peter Beardsley came off.

Both players benefited from the arrival of Darren Anderton, a rangy 20-year-old winger whose performances in Portsmouth's 1992 FA Cup run had persuaded Venables to part with £1.7 million – another signing that must have made Peter Shreeves seethe with envy. While he struggled with a nagging injury in the early weeks, his later form was confident, then at times sparkling after his return following a hernia operation around Christmas. He, too, would get an England call-up under Venables.

From the end of January these three and the rest of the side gelled as Spurs, playing the kind of exhilarating football for which the club is renowned, enjoyed six successive victories, five in the League and one in the FA Cup. Sheringham scored 10 of the 19 goals in that sequence, and it was his tally of 16 in the last 17 League matches that gave Spurs a respectable eighth place – comfortable if well outside Europe.

Given the relative success of an exciting side, with youngsters like Barmby, Anderton and Austin grafted on to the experience of Mabbutt, Allen and Samways (now a midfield regular), the future on the field appeared rosy. The positions of Livermore and Clemence seemed safe, too; but the next stage of English soccer's longest-running lager saga was straight out of a Jeffrey Archer novel.

ALL CHANGE AGAIN

Following a falling out on the eve of the FA Cup final, Venables was sacked by Alan Sugar as chief executive and overall manager in May 1993, a move that may well have had its roots in the very move which rescued Spurs' season. Venables became the subject of press allegations

about a 'bung' (illegal payment) arrangement with Forest boss Brian Clough over the transfer of Teddy Sheringham – a similar allegation would, ironically, lead to the eventual sacking of Arsenal manager George Graham in February 1995.

Venables finally lost his legal battle with Sugar on 14 June – and only five days later Ossie Ardiles was installed as team manager at the Lane. The situation was full of ironies: not only did West Bromwich Albion threaten to sue Spurs for poaching the Argentinian, but they appointed his assistant as manager at The Hawthorns. His name was Keith Burkinshaw.

By now Alan Sugar, also mindful of the need for experienced business management, had already strengthened the 'team behind the team' with the appointment of Claude Littner as Chief Executive. Littner, with his background in crisis management, had previously demonstrated a tough results-orientated approach as Managing Director of a number of Amstrad's European subsidiaries. His success in organising the management team and getting the financial side back on an even keel and into an extremely healthy position in such a relatively short time, was to provide the foundation for future multi-million pound deals and the continued development of the stadium, facilities and the business in general.

On 6 July Ardiles sacked Clemence and made Steve Perryman his assistant, with Pat Jennings coming in as goalkeeping coach. Livermore was retained as 'first team coach and chief scout'.

The first signals for Spurs supporters, who were split on the events, were very mixed, with the hosts beating Paul Gascoigne's Lazio 3-2 in the opener of the pre-season Makita tournament but then crashing 4-0 to Chelsea at home in the final. Ardiles, strangely, began in classic Venables signing style, taking Jason Dozzell from Ipswich for £1 million (later increased by tribunal to £1.75 million) and Colin Calderwood from Swindon for a tribunal-fixed £1.25 million (three times the amount Ardiles had offered his old club).

Despite losing Nick Barmby for the first couple of months of the season with shin-splint trouble and Anderton only appearing as a substitute in August, Tottenham started in promising form, winning five and drawing

LEFT: 'Razor' Ruddock tangles with Arsenal striker Kevin Campbell in the 1993 FA Cup semi-final at Wembley. After just two League games at Millwall the centre-back moved to Southampton, maturing in both play and attitude before being brought back to White Hart Lane for £750,000. But after only one season at Spurs, he chose to seek his fortune on Merseyside and was transfered to Liverpool for £2 million.

BOTTOM LEFT: Nayim comforts Justin Edinburgh after the 1993 FA Cup semi-final. The game triggered a strange end to the 1992-93 season: Spurs recovered to trounce Norwich 5-1 five days later and finished by beating Arsenal 3-1 at Highbury, but in between they lost four of their six matches, including a 6-2 defeat at Liverpool.

BOTTOM RIGHT: Doug Livermore and Ray Clemence had no chance to pursue their promising policies. Terry Venables' legal battle with Alan Sugar over his role at the club was resolved on 14 June 1993 and their positions as his protégés were untenable. Five days later Sugar appointed West Bromwich Albion boss Ossie Ardiles as manager and the Argentinian installed two former Spurs players on his staff: Steve Perryman (assistant manager) and, pictured here with Ardiles, Pat Jennings (goalkeeping coach).

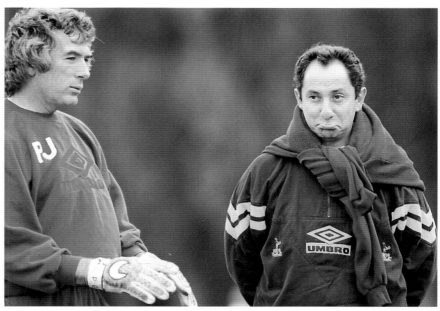

Danny Blanchflower, who retained a very special place in the affections of all Spurs fans, died on 9 December 1993, aged 67. Coming as it did only weeks after the demise of Arthur Rowe, manager of the great 'push and run' side of the 1950s, it seemed to symbolise a change of era. Now the game is dominated by sponsorship deals, multi-million pound transfers and live television, and seems a far cry from the days of brown balls, black white and photographs and the tactics and skills of soccer purists like Rowe and Blanchflower.
Blanchflower will always be associated with the Glory days and in particular the Double.

three of the first 10 League matches. The prolific Sheringham averaged a goal a game; he kept that up in the League Cup, too, scoring twice against Second Division Burnley. It was a remarkable sequence, beginning with an excellent win at Kevin Keegan's newly-promoted Newcastle and including a 2-1 success at Liverpool, where Spurs had won only twice in 81 years.

In statistical terms the most remarkable result was the 5-0 trouncing of Joe Royle's Oldham at White Hart Lane on 18 September, when Tottenham totted up what must surely be one of the fastest three-goal bursts in the League's history: Sedgley (5min 2sec), Sheringham (6min 48sec) and Sedgley again (7min 36sec) scored to record the team hat-trick time of 2 minutes and 35 seconds, grabbed during a frantic opening spell where two of the goals were gifted by misplaced clearances from poor Latics keeper Paul Gerrard. The down side of this thrilling match – Durie (his last goal for the club) and Dozzell (his first) scored the others – was the loss of the promising Dean Austin with a broken leg.

The run ended with a 2-1 defeat at champions Manchester United, a game that saw Teddy Sheringham carried off with a knee injury which, with complications, would keep him out for a crucial five months. Without his goals, and

his underrated general forward play, Spurs struggled, securing three points only twice in the next 18 League games and finding the going tough in both knockout competitions.

In the League Cup, 1-0 wins over Derby and title-chasing Blackburn (Barmby and Campbell the scorers) were followed by a home defeat by Aston Villa, the eventual winners.

In the FA Cup Spurs needed not only a replay but a 5-4 penalty decider to get past a plucky Peterborough side who would finish the season at the foot of Division 1 (the old Second Division). This was the first shoot-out at White Hart Lane since the UEFA Cup final of 1984, and like that one it was won by a Spurs save, on this occasion when Ian Walker shut out 16-year-old sub Andy Furnell. Spurs then crashed 3-0 at Portman Road to a pedestrian Ipswich team fighting relegation from the Premier League.

Thus Ardiles' first quest for honours finished on 29 January, and the complexion of Spurs' season had now radically changed. It wasn't until 2 March that Ronny Rosenthal, signed from Liverpool for £250,000 in January, secured the first point of the year in a 1-1 draw with Villa, following seven successive League defeats. Draws against fellow strugglers Sheffield United and Ipswich weren't enough to allay fears of the worst, and it took a gritty 2-0 win against a battling Oldham on 5 May (goals from Samways and Howells condemning the hosts to Division 1) to preserve Spurs' precious Premier League status – and, if in the record books 15th slot in the table now looks comfortable, the management, players and above all the fans knew just how tight the dog fight had been.

The season had been beset by problems, and supporters could only speculate on what might have been were it not for the injury to Sheringham and, later, the loss for long periods of Austin, Howells, Mabbutt, Thorstvedt and Calderwood, though Micky Hazard's return from Swindon helped compensate for the absence of Howells and the signing of Kevin Scott from Newcastle for £850,000 helped plug the hole at the back for the last vital stages.

The attitude of Gordon Durie didn't help, either. After the Coca-Cola Cup game with Burnley at White Hart Lane – when Caskey was sent off at 1-1 – Ardiles confirmed that he would fine the Scot the maximum amount for his abusive reaction on being replaced by substitute Howells (who scored), and later put him up for sale 'dissatisfied with his commitment'. Rangers paid £1.2 million in November to take him back to Glasgow.

The last thing Spurs needed around this time was a major problem at the back, but on 24 November their faltering season turned positively ugly when captain Gary Mabbutt sustained a fractured cheekbone from John Fashanu's elbow during a more than usual fractious clash with Joe Kinnear's Wimbledon. Later the same week (following a PFA decision to launch a campaign to outlaw the so-called 'lethal elbow'), Spurs officially reported the incident to the FA, accompanying their case by video evidence of a 'dangerous challenge'. Meanwhile, Wimbledon reiterated their observation that referee Keith Hackett awarded no foul and saw no reason to reappraise that decision having seen the replay.

Mabbutt, one of the most fair-minded

defenders in the game, was diagnosed as carrying no fewer than four fractures of the cheekbone and three fractures of his eye socket. It was not a pretty sight – and, to many football fans outside north-east London, nor was the prevarication of the FA. Their commission decided, after 4½ hours of videos and interviews, that they needed more time to consider whether to charge Fashanu with misconduct.

The next day – Christmas Eve, as Mabbutt prepared to undergo further surgery – the commission decided not to charge Fashanu because they could not be sure there was 'sufficient intent' – this despite the fact that referee Hackett now conceded there was 'a measure of intent'. It was hardly a seasonal gift for the Spurs skipper, but he did receive some comforting news the following week when he was awarded an MBE in the New Year's honours list. Mabbutt's absence was crucial, though Steve Sedgley filled in admirably before returning to midfield and scoring vital goals against Everton and Southampton. Wearing a 'phantom' mask to protect his appalling injuries, Mabbutt made a typically brave return in the reserves on 10 February and resumed his place in the first team 17 days later against Chelsea to help in the fight against relegation.

While one fine Tottenham captain was honoured, another – indeed perhaps the club's greatest – had died. Danny Blanchflower, one of the tiny handful flatly to refuse the unexpected invitation to parade his past on *This Is Your Life*, had passed away on 9 December. When approached by Eamonn Andrews with the words: 'Danny Blanchflower, this is your life,' Blanchflower simply replied: 'Oh no it

isn't,' and walked away. Coming only a month after the death of 'push and run' manager Arthur Rowe, aged 85, it seemed somehow to signal yet another aspect of a club in a state of change. New ownership, new management, an Argentinian manager – and, the following season, a veritable invasion of European stars.

Tottenham's bad luck – and poor form – continued into 1994, with Erik Thorstvedt ruled out for several weeks after damaging knee ligaments during a depressing defeat by bottom club Swindon on 22 January, the fourth match in a miserable sequence of seven consecutive League defeats. Not surprisingly, attendances at White Hart Lane began to fall, only 17,452 turning out for the visit of Villa on 2 March.

The season was bedevilled by events off the field, too, with the legal battles over management of the club becoming something of a football soap opera. On 2 September Venables resigned from the Tottenham board; a fortnight later a much-publicised *Panorama* programme was broadcast, containing allegations about his business dealings, the nub of which was the source of the money used to buy his stake in Spurs.

In January the police apparently cleared him of any illegal dealings in his business affairs – the move took him a vital step nearer the England job vacated by Graham Taylor, a choice supported publicly by Alan Sugar – but two days later Tottenham presented a petition to the High Court to wind up Venables' company Edennote in order to recoup the estimated costs of £350,000 caused by his previous legal action. Despite the allegations still hanging over his reputation, Venables took over as the national coach on 28 January.

Darren Anderton stretches out a long leg to score the final goal in Spurs' 3-0 win over relegation rivals Southampton on 23 April 1994. Dave Beasant is helpless and Paul Allen, returning to the Lane as a Saints player, can only look on and admire.

The petition was far from the first litigation of the season, involving Spurs. The FA charged Spurs with misconduct over the appointment of Ossie Ardiles – the day before the club announced profits for 1992–93 of some £3.3 million. In November Spurs were found guilty, fined £25,000 plus costs, severely censured and warned over 'future conduct in such matters'.

Even during the gruelling, nail-biting end to the season Tottenham's torrid affairs in court were far from over. While the hearing for the claim against Edennote was deferred, Tottenham were fighting a claim for £500,000 from the Inland Revenue over signing-on fees dating back to the 1980s and pursuing a claim against Bill Jenkins, architect of the £6million East Stand reconstruction, for £700,000 repair bills in respect of the dry-rot in the stand.

And hanging over the club was the big one: the array of tawdry allegations during the Scholar era first rumoured back in February. On 12 May, only five days after their last game (a rather prophetic 2-1 home defeat by Gerry Francis' QPR), and ironically the very same day that Edennote was finally wound up in the High Court by Sugar and Spurs, the FA formally charged the club with misconduct concerning alleged irregular payments to an array of players after studying documents handed over voluntarily by Sugar.

The charges didn't relate to 1993, nor even the 1990s: these 'interest-free' loans were said to have been made between 1985 and 1989. On 25 May the FA announced that if Spurs were found guilty and punished by demotion, relegated Sheffield United, who finished 20th, would take their place in the Premiership. It seemed that the FA were determined to make Alan Sugar pay for remarking, during his court

BELOW: *Alan Sugar and Jurgen Klinsmann announce the totally unexpected arrival of the German star (for a reported $3.3 million) on 29 July 1994.*

battle with Venables, that football is 'riddled with corruption'. The date of the inquiry was set for 14 June. The allegations concerned 40 charges of malpractice involving 15 players and a total of £545,000 between 1983 and 1989, the six most serious relating to alleged transfer rule breaches between 1985 and 1989 during the purchases of Paul Allen, Chris Fairclough and Mitchell Thomas. Despite Gascoigne being listed among the recipients, the biggest single sum involved was an interest-free loan of £75,000 to Paul Stewart.

Even in the build-up to the World Cup finals, this case was big news. On the whole the press was sympathetic, though on 12 June the *Daily Mirror* called Spurs 'the club that is dying of shame'. In the *Sun* on the day of the hearing Jimmy Greaves made a passionate plea for his old club to retain Premier League status, and for the real culprits to be brought to book. He was granted his first wish, but there was a massive price to pay: the FA not only deducted 12 points from the club's total for the coming season but also banned them from the FA Cup. The £600,000 fine, though a record, was almost an irrelevance considering the economic implications of the first two stipulations. Oh yes, and Spurs had to pay considerable legal costs.

The reaction was one of shock, almost disbelief: 'Sentence of Doom', 'Gutted', 'Sugar Caned for £7m', 'Cheating Spurs in Disgrace' ran the tabloid headlines, with the club dubbed Tottenham Dropspur and Tottering Hotspurs.

Former player Garth Crooks described the sentence as 'Draconian' and likely to 'blow the game apart. The FA have opened up a can of worms.' Gordon Taylor of the PFA claimed 'the FA have done everything but relegate them.' With four clubs facing the drop in 1995, it was seen as especially harsh. The players' reaction was predictably one of disbelief and dismay, with David Howells' observation that it was 'slow torture . . . worse than relegation' widely quoted. The club's share price plummeted on the Stock Market and the bookies lengthened the odds on Spurs winning the Championship from 50-1 to 250-1.

Sugar was understandably angry, stating: 'I'm not going to be intimidated by these archaic and barbaric methods.' The FA's stance represented a 'deliberate vendetta against our club and against me personally'. Despite the risks of a possible harsher sentence, Sugar received broad backing for his appeal to a three-man FA tribunal. For the hearing, at St Albans on 2 July, Sugar ditched his heavyweight team, conducted his own case – and came away with a substantial prize. In effect he clawed back six points at £150,000 apiece, the tribunal reducing the penalty from 12 points to six but increasing the fine from £600,000 to £1.5 million. However, the FA Cup ban was still in place. It was a crucial change, not least in trying to attract new players. Speculation had been rife ever since Sugar publicly promised the manager money to spend in early May (Richard Gough was then a candidate), but the 12-point penalty and then the World Cup finals had held things up.

Two days after the swingeing penalties on Spurs, Steve Sedgley's transfer to Ipswich had recouped a million and on 7 July Vinny Samways put in a transfer request. However, such domestic changes were overshadowed on 27 July when Ardiles' patient search was rewarded with the arrival of Ilie Dumitrescu, a leading light of Romania's run to the World Cup semi-finals, for $4.3million (US).

The quiet, intelligent forward signed for Spurs on 29 July, but his transfer was that day eclipsed by another – one of the most astonishing deals in the history of English football. A day before his 30th birthday, Jürgen Klinsmann became a Spurs player. For the second time in six weeks an event involving the club had rocked the football public. 'Alan Sugar pulled off English football's transfer coup of the decade yesterday by signing charismatic German World Cup star Jürgen Klinsmann for Tottenham,' led off Brian Scovell in the *Daily Mail*. The Spurs chairman was in Monte Carlo to finalize the $3.3million (US). capture of the former German Footballer of the Year.

'Most of the negotiations were conducted from the communications room of Sugar's yacht *Louisiana*,' continued Scovell. 'The White Hart Lane chief planned his holiday in

ABOVE: Klinsmann's first game for Spurs saw a marvellous 4-3 victory at Hillsborough, with the German scoring a classic headed goal from Anderton's cross. As a retort to all the observations in the English press about Klinsmann's 'diving', the Spurs forward line rushed across the pitch and threw themselves to the ground in a highly original parody of the accusations.

macy, first parried questions on the subject and then joked about it in near-perfect English, disarming both press and public.

This man was no 'over the moon' player. Fluent in four languages, a supporter of Greenpeace, driver of an ageing VW 'Beetle', impeccably behaved at all times, here was a refreshing antidote to the yobbish, spoiltbrat antics of many British soccer stars – both past and present. This was to be a new kind of football hero.

The level of interest was staggering. 'Since news of the signings was announced our phones have been jammed,' explained the ticket office. 'At the time of the punishments we were all down in the dumps. But this has given the place a spark. The news has tipped the balance and suddenly there is a wave of optimism.'

Meanwhile, and on the back of his brave fight against the FA's harsh punishments, the position of Sugar had changed dramatically with the signings. From being a hard-nosed businessman with no real passion for the game – let alone a love of the club so professed by his predecessor – he had for the supporters become a saviour, prepared to bend his holiday round the pursuit of his prey and commit his personal millions into the purchase of top players.

More column inches were devoted to Klinsmann than any other pre-season topic, including Manchester United. Everything from his impact on share prices (Spurs' rose 21% in the week after the double signing) to his ability to handle Vinnie Jones was considered, though for most football writers there was one key area. Mick Dennis caught the mood well in the London *Evening Standard* as early as 4 August: '. . . although Spurs supporters are salivating at the prospect of a glut of goals, the rest of the country wants to boo him.'

All eyes were on Hillsborough and its sell-out crowd on 20 August for the opener against Sheffield Wednesday. Ardiles did indeed play his five-man attack, answering critics' predictions of defensive frailty by deploying Calderwood in front of a back four that featured Stuart Nethercott alongside Sol Campbell in the middle. The line-up was completed by Ian Walker in goal, with David Kerslake and Justin Edinburgh filling the fullback positions; Micky Hazard and former captain Gary Mabbutt formed a venerable pair on the bench.

The Hollywood script – blighted only by the absence of Chris Waddle in the home team – continued to be written for Spurs as they beat Wednesday 4-3 in one of the finest games of the season. Four of Ardiles' 'famous five' scored, Klinsmann losing Des Walker to head in Anderton's cross and make it 4-2 before wheeling round and lurching into a studied dive along the turf – to be followed by Sheringham and the rest of the team, including Ian Walker. Remarkably, the vanquished home fans appreciated the parody, and when the striker hurt his face in an ugly clash of heads with Des Walker shortly afterwards, and was stretchered off with blood pouring from his mouth, the Yorkshiremen gave him a standing ovation. No mean feat: in less than 90 minutes he had become the most popular German in the north of England since Bert Trautmann.

The final exit: Ossie Ardiles leaves Spurs for the last time, the crushing 3-0 defeat at Division 1's bottom club Notts County leaving little room for any other outcome. 'Brazil in 1970 were the best team I have ever seen - and they had only one defensive midfielder. They showed what attacking teams can do,' said Ardiles correctly. Unfortunately his attacking formation had generated just 20 wins in 65 games. With Ardiles went Perryman, after an association lasting nearly 30 years.

the Mediterranean to ensure he would be in the right place at the right time to negotiate directly with the German, who steers clear of agents.'

The signing of Klinsmann and Dumitrescu gave the close season at Spurs, and indeed across the country, a fresh angle. A player of genuine international class, with 25 goals in 65 matches for his country (five of them in the recent World Cup), Klinsmann had been a huge success at both Inter Milan and Monaco after leaving VfB Stuttgart, but his reputation in England was shallow: here he was seen as a talented creator and masterful taker of goals who tarnished his performances with clever con-tricks to elicit free-kicks from less astute referees. And while mature fans might speculate on everything from the strengths of the potential Sheringham-Klinsmann strike partnership to the arrival of a blond German at a club with such strong Jewish associations, the newspapers just couldn't resist having a go; indeed several of them featured step-by-step diagrams on how to follow the Klinsmann 'dive'. Jürgen himself, full of charm and diplo-

What's more, his overall performance (full of commitment and free of con-tricks), his goal, his antics and his heroics – he was back after the match with 11 stitches in his lip giving interviews to the media – did much to endear him to the rest of the nation. Klinsmann's arrival was already giving the season a much-needed lift. It was a shame that only 25,553 could squeeze into White Hart Lane for the midweek visit of Everton. The unchanged team again delivered in dangerously exciting style, Klinsmann getting both goals (a volley and a header) in a 2-1 win, achieved despite a missed Sheringham penalty.

If Spurs supporters were ecstatic, the chairman was pretty pleased too. The next day the share price shot up 14p, adding £1.6million to the club's Stock Market value to take it past £20million. In the 27 days since the signings of Klinsmann and Dumitrescu the valuation of Spurs had gone up by £5million, and by some £8million since the initial FA decision to dock 12 points. But this, of course, is the real world: Tottenham had two wins in two games and were still at the foot of the table.

On the following Saturday a dull United still beat Spurs 1-0 to bring fans down to earth a little, that feeling helped by another missed Sheringham penalty. For many, however, this was merely a blip, the roller-coaster returning to the rails for a 3-1 win at Ipswich on the Tuesday for Spurs' first 'real' points, with Klinsmann notching two goals to take his tally to five in four games.

Spurs then lost twice in six days to lowly opposition: first Matt Le Tissier outgunned a below-par Klinsmann at the Lane to give Southampton their first win of the campaign and then, more worryingly, they went down 3-1 at Leicester. Klinsmann scored again, but the defence was looking increasingly leaky.

Any sane fan realised now that dreams of the League title were sheer fantasy, and that

Happy New Year: Gica Popescu carefully steers home his shot to score the only goal of the derby against Arsenal at White Hart Lane on 2 January 1995, his third goal for Tottenham. While Popescu had settled down well during Spurs' fabulous run – they were now sixth in the Championship and reinstated in the FA Cup – his compatriot Dumitrescu had gone the other way, playing well under Ardiles but fading in the Francis era and finally going on loan to Seville at the end of December. Popescu's goal would herald a bad year for Arsenal, who would suffer Paul Merson's drug problem, the scandal surrounding George Graham's departure, severe loss of form and, finally, defeat by Real Zaragoza in the European Cup Winners' Cup final to a magnificent goal scored by Nayim, a former Spurs player.

the League Cup was indeed a crucial lifeline. So when Spurs went behind to Watford after just 26 seconds at Vicarage Road in the first leg of the second round there was more than a little concern on the terraces. New boy Gica Popescu, signed from PSV Eindhoven for £2.9million and replacing Calderwood to play behind his countryman Dumitrescu, must have wondered what was happening. The other starters (Mabbutt for Nethercott, Hazard for Barmby) must have been nearly as perplexed. But it was all right: Spurs ran out 6-3 winners, with Klinsmann grabbing a hat-trick.

If Popescu was the last piece in Ardiles' jigsaw – Sugar revealed that he had invested £8 million of his own money over three years – there was little evidence of the finished article working well against Nottingham Forest at White Hart Lane on the Saturday. Indeed it was Dutchman Brian Roy, not Spurs' imported stars, who stole the limelight, and the 4-1 drubbing highlighted what the press had been saying since the season's start: a team needs to be solid at the back and winning the ball in midfield before it can exploit its rich diversity of talent in attack. With three successive League defeats and 12 goals conceded in four games, Ardiles' future was again put firmly on the line. Under mounting pressure he maintained his calm – 'I'm surprised by all the speculation surrounding my position' – as he looked to the match with Gerry Francis' QPR for his first home victory in five attempts.

It was hardly surprising that the team performed poorly in a scruffy 1-1 draw. The next game, Leeds away, elicited a more credible 1-1 draw, with Dumitrescu judged man of the match in spite of his almost total lack of comprehension at team talks. Ardiles, having been backed both by the PLC's Annual General Meeting and the local paper that week, could breathe a little easier.

Manchester City at Maine Road should have been a chance to consolidate, but it wasn't taken: Spurs lost 5-2 to a side for whom old

boy Paul Walsh did much of the damage, scoring two of the first three goals and making a couple more. For the tricky Coca-Cola Cup third round tie against Notts County the following Wednesday, Ardiles made three changes (Walker, Kerslake and Scott making way for Thorsvedt, Austin and Calderwood).

Despite the obvious pressure on this game – the League Cup was Tottenham's only realistic chance of a trophy and of entry to Europe – the manager remained in an upbeat mood. But if the matches against Forest and Manchester City had been embarrassing, the result against a County side propping up the Endsleigh League Division 1 was positively numbing. Not only did Spurs lose, but they lost calamitously, 3-0.

For County it was not so much giant-killing as taking candy from a big baby. For Spurs, playing a side who had not won at home in the League for six months, it was perhaps the most humiliating night in the club's history. The press had universally seen it as Ardiles' last-chance game, and they were right.

He was called to Sugar's Essex home on the Monday night, his contract was 'terminated with immediate effect' and he left the club the next day. If he blamed the grinding Venables-Sugar row for some of his troubles ('I was the pawn in the middle of their battles'), Ardiles left White Hart Lane as he had played and managed there, with dignity, honesty and a touch of humour.

Meanwhile Gerry Francis emerged as a clear favourite as Ardiles replacement. Having resigned from his job (apparently on the rumour of Rodney Marsh being installed as general manager) to put himself firmly in the frame, he eventually took on the mountainous task of reviving Tottenham's flagging fortunes. Interestingly, while Alan Sugar mused on winning the League within three seasons, Francis signed up only on a one-year 'rolling' contract. One result of his arrival and the choice of his back-up team was to be the departure of

Flying high: Ronny Rosenthal pictured during the game of his life at Southampton on 1 March 1995. In one of the most extraordinary performances ever seen in the history of the FA Cup, he came on as a substitute before half-time – with Spurs trailing 2-0 in a fifth round replay Rosenthal scored three times from three very different positions, twice in the second half and again in extra time. Spurs won 6-2 in the end, but it was Rosenthal's night and he would keep his place for much of the rest of the season. He would certainly relish the next tie – a quarter-final at Anfield against his old club Liverpool.

assistant manager and former captain Steve Perryman, whose association with the club had begun in 1967.

Francis' first match was a salutory lesson on Spurs' problems, a 4-3 home defeat by an Aston Villa side lacking a manager. Francis had reversed Ardiles' philosophy, playing five central defenders across the back and a sweeper (Popescu) in midfield.

However things now began to look up for Spurs off the field. On 25 November, just ten days after Francis' appointment, the FA announced following an arbitration hearing that a new commission would shortly review the club's summer punishments – widely interpreted as code for a likely reprieve on the FA Cup ban. Ossie Ardiles was entitled to feel a tad aggrieved.

It was Francis who had whatever luck was going. At Anfield the next day an own goal from old boy Neil Ruddock gave them an unwarranted 1-1 draw against Liverpool, and the new manager was relieved that the only goal his side gave away was a penalty.

Francis was hardly having easy opposition to start with. After Liverpool came Newcastle, and though weakened by injuries the visitors still posed a real test, notably through the probing of the irrepressible Peter Beardsley. The crucial 4-2 victory – another turning point in Tottenham's topsy-turvy season – owed much to a hat-trick from Sheringham, but there was the selfless work of Klinsmann, the guile of Anderton and a handsome performance in the defensive wedge by David Howells, who had found his niche for the rest of the season. With six points deducted, Spurs now moved a couple of places above the relegation zone.

The forthright Francis had been working mostly on defensive duties in training but, vitally, he had simply made the players fitter for football, too. 'I don't think it's something they've done here, that kind of running, for three or four years, if at all,' he said, referring to area-to-area sprints. "It's bloody hard work. There aren't too many players, if any, who want a ball afterwards. Mostly they want a basin.'

They would need champagne glasses for the next twist of fate; on 3 December they were drawn at home to Altrincham in the FA Cup, a clear signal that entry in the competition would follow. Six days later it did, with the arbitration tribunal going all the way, also reinstating the six deducted points in the League. The £1.5 million fine imposed at the July appeal remained – an average international's transfer fee being viewed as more than fair for a wealthy club guilty of illegal payments, even if the wrong directors were being penalised.

While most supporters had been unaware of the situation, this decision had been pursued by Alan Sugar and his lawyers and the matter had gone to arbitration. Indeed the tribunal's verdict on the FA's disciplinary committee was damning: the charges against Spurs were 'misconceived, bad in law and should not have been proceeded with . . . and it was irrational to impose any penalty other than a fine.'

Tottenham continued their improvement throughout December, moving up the table with two wins and two draws; amazingly, not a goal was conceded, and they finished the year with a 4-0 win at Coventry (their biggest away win for nearly two years) to move into sixth place in the Premiership. There was talk of Europe. A miracle was in the making. And Spurs were resurgent.

The only casualty of the new system had been Ilie Dumitrescu. An adventurous free spirit, he found it difficult to tie down a place in the first team and suffered most from the departure of Ardiles, finding the going tough in the high workrate policy of Francis, who preferred the reliable down-to-earth performances of Howells and, latterly, the committed power of Ronny Rosenthal. Just before Christmas he asked for a transfer and on 30 December he was sent on loan to Seville in the Spanish

From being banned from the FA Cup Spurs roared into the semi-final.
BOTTOM : Teddy Sheringham celebrates after his marvellous goal against Liverpool at Anfield in the 1994-95 quarter final – a beautiful arched shot around David James.
RIGHT: With just two minutes remaining, Klinsmann won the game for Spurs with a neat flick from Sheringham's pass. 2-1 to Spurs, at Anfield, and surely Tottenham's name was written on the Cup they started the season banned from entering.

League until the end of the season.

Next came perhaps the sweetest moment of the season: the FA Cup third round tie against Altrincham; goals from Sheringham, Nethercott and Rosenthal steered them safely through.

The following week they completed the double over West Ham with goals from Sheringham and Klinsmann, the German's first in seven games. A minor blemish (how times change) was a conceded goal – again the first in seven games. Gerry Francis' record, after a dozen games, was now nothing short of astonishing: P12, W7, D4, L1, F23, A9. It was Championship form.

If proof were needed of Spurs' resurgence – they had not played a club from the top five since early December – it came with the visit of League leaders Blackburn to White Hart Lane on 4 February. The eventual champions looked

LEFT: But an even greater suprise occurred in the semi-final at Elland Road. Here Matt Jackson scores the first of Everton's four goals on 9 April 1995. BOTTOM: Spurs' only reply in this remarkably disappointing day was to be a penalty from Klinsmann, who quickly rushed in to retrieve the ball from Neville Southall's net. But it was to be to no avail and the end of an unlikely fairy tale.

vulnerable to Spurs' snappy, accurate and imaginative first-time passing, and goals from Klinsmann, Anderton and Barmby completed a convincing 3-1 win that threw the title race wide open.

Here was the fusion of talent, toil and tactics that Francis was seeking, and the covering of Anderton and Barmby in defensive positions illustrated the approach to good effect. Barmby's reward was to be called into Terry Venables' England squad (along with Sol Campbell, and joining regulars Anderton and Sheringham) for the ill-fated game with the Republic of Ireland in Dublin, which was abandoned due to hooliganism. The experience of Colin Calderwood was much happier – he was in the Scotland team which earned a draw with Russia in Moscow in March, thus graduating from a man with an unsure future under Ardiles to an assured international in three months.

March was a spectacular month that kicked

off with a most remarkable Cup replay at The Dell. In a pulsating match it was an unsung journeyman, Ronny Rosenthal, coming on as a substitute, who kept Spurs' Cup dreams alive, scoring a stunning hat-trick that took them into the lead from being 2-0 down at half-time. It was the substitution of the season. In the 56th minute he swept in Barmby's awkward cross over the amazed Grobbelaar; two minutes later the keeper was non-plussed again as Rosenthal unleashed an angled shot from well out on the right; then, in the 11th minute of extra time, while moving down the inside-left channel, he let a shot go from over 25 yards that flew into the top corner of the Saints' net. Spurs added three more against a demoralised opposition, but it was the Israeli's night: he just couldn't put a foot wrong.

There was a growing feeling now, after the nature of this incredible comeback, that Tottenham's 'name was on the Cup'. Francis kept faith with the team that did so well against Southampton for the quarter-final away to Liverpool. Liverpool, beaten only once at home in the League, went ahead in the 38th minute through Robbie Fowler, but Klinsmann cleverly set up Sheringham to level on the stroke of half-time with a beautifully flighted shot into the corner. Spurs won on points in the second half, and with two minutes left – and Liverpool hanging on for the replay – Sheringham returned the favour with a deft flick and Klinsmann coolly finished the move in style. The strikers took the accolades – rightly so, when Anfield had been such a grave-yard for Tottenham in recent years – but the whole team played magnificently and no one better than Howells, who gradually wrested control of the game from Liverpool's powerful midfield. Klinsmann was tearful after the final whistle as he celebrated with thousands of ecstatic travelling fans at the Anfield Road end. And he was not alone in being moved by the generous ovation given his team by the Kop.

David Lacey in *The Guardian* was not alone either in applauding Francis' astonishing effect on the club since his arrival: 'It's possible to argue that, had Gerry Francis been organising the team from the start of the season, Spurs might now be heading towards a second Double. For consistent quality of performance they are now up there with Manchester United, Newcastle, Blackburn and, as this match showed, ahead of Liverpool.'

Yet that game was to prove the zenith of Tottenham's season. Over the next 11 days they would play goalless draws with both United (away) and Liverpool (at home), the matches sandwiching a laboured 1-0 win over bottom of the table Leicester. But with the teams above them making few mistakes these five points were worth little. Leeds slipped back into sixth place and the UEFA Cup became a receding target. All eyes were now on Elland Road – an unpopular choice of venue for both Spurs fans and for Francis, who quite rightly wanted the bigger stage of Wembley – and the FA Cup semi-final against Everton on 9 April.

For reasons that would frustrate Spurs fans for months – should Francis have really brought back Nethercott and Popescu after six weeks, for example? – Everton not only won but won fairly comfortably. They showed all the determination, industry and discipline brought to their play by Joe Royle since his arrival in November (and which they would demonstrate again in the final with Manchester United), and they didn't allow Spurs to play their flowing game. In addition, the defence gave away sloppy goals. Two late scores from substitute Daniel Amokachi sealed the victory – Royle admitted he was on the pitch in error – but Klinsmann's penalty had been little more than a token comeback. If any club's name was on the trophy in 1995, it was obviously that of Everton.

The dream had ended not with a thunderous climax but with a dark cloud. Only a week after the semi-final exit, allegations broke that Dumitrescu had pocketed some £550,000 from Steaua Bucharest on his move to Tottenham, and White Hart Lane grew increasingly impatient with the rumoured transfer of Jürgen Klinsmann.

While he was initially expected to stay for two seasons the German captain had stated on 27 March that he had turned down Inter Milan and Bayern Munich – but the latter 'only for the present'. In the first week of May it surfaced again and finally, after days of speculation, he announced on 11 May that he was indeed returning home to play for Bayern in the 1995–96 season.

Two days later Klinsmann bade farewell to 33,040 sad fans in his last game, failing to score in a 1-1 draw with Leeds; indeed he had been stuck on 29 goals for more than a month, and a missed penalty at St James's Park would have made it 30. But it wasn't that important. Sure, it would have been good to score, but Klinsmann had been making as well as taking goals all season, including a critical part in many of Sheringham's tally of 23. Now the formidable partnership was to be parted and with it, thought many Spurs fans, the best

chance of success in 1996.

Klinsmann had been the leading character in the most fascinating, twisting season in the club's long history – the Double notwithstanding – in a few months metamorphosing from a loathed cheat to a universally liked sportsman voted Footballer of the Year by the Football Writers Association.

The irony was not lost on the majority of caring football fans in England. During a season that saw their beloved sport riddled with almost endemic sleaze and corruption – endless stories of bungs, bribes, drugs, riots, assaults, dissent, poor administration and even the death of a fan – it took a previously distrusted foreigner to show us how to play and how to enjoy our national sport. Few footballers have made such an impact in so short a space of time as Jürgen Klinsmann did in England in 1994–95. Alan Sugar's sensational gamble paid massive dividends both for his club and for the game in general, and it very nearly brought off a miracle.

The sport must move on. And so must the club. On 22 May, Gica Popescu signed for Barcelona. All three foreign visitors to White Hart Lane, it seems – Dumitrescu, Klinsmann, Popescu – had been one-season wonders. But what a season.

INTERTOTO TROUBLE

The summer of 1995 involved Spurs in the UEFA Intertoto Cup, a competition which had been in existence for 34 years. It grew in importance when UEFA decided that the UEFA Cup would be expanded in 1995-96 and that two teams from the Intertoto Cup would proceed into the UEFA Cup first round.

The Premier League initially applied for three Intertoto Cup places and UEFA then insisted that three Premiership clubs enter the 60 club tournament.

At first all the clubs declined to participate. Then after it was forcefully explained that UEFA would ban all English Clubs from the competition unless three Premiership Clubs entered by the deadline date, Spurs, Wimbledon and Sheffield Wednesday conditionally volunteered to take part, subject to two conditions being agreed by the FA, The Premier League and UEFA.

First, no home matches would be played at the host ground and second that the clubs would be allowed to play weakened teams which would not include first team players. All the governing bodies accepted these terms verbally and in writing.

In spite of these elaborate precautions, Spurs and Wimbledon were subsequently barred for one season from any European competition they might qualify for within the next five years. In addition, England lost its 'fair play' place.

Led by Chairman Alan Sugar, Spurs produced a comprehensive and compelling Appeal that was ultimately successful. The ban was reduced to a fine which was shared between all the Premiership clubs.

Alan Sugar remained unimpressed, commenting 'There is still a black mark against our name with UEFA. We entered the Intertoto Cup to protect English football because UEFA threatened to impose punitive measures on all qualifying clubs. We don't see this as any kind of victory. We are simply in the same position

RIGHT: Ruel Fox joined Spurs from Newcastle in October 1995 and his bubbling play soon won over the fans. On the training ground with him is his new skipper Gary Mabbutt. BELOW: Chris Armstrong in action against Wimbledon in December 1995 by when he had settled into the Spurs front line as a fast-running partner to Sheringham and a striker who could operate well on the wings.

out of the way, Spurs began their preparation for the 1995–96 season with a tour of Scandinavia. But things did not go well. Gerry Francis' team won two and lost seven of their nine games, and picked up a number of injuries. As if this wasn't bad enough, they also began the new season with the chairman's relationship with Klinsmann taking on an acrimonious aspect with reports that Klinsmann had criticised Sugar for not being prepared to spend money to win the championship. An angry Sugar disclaimed this bitterly on television. In an early club programme for the new season he wrote a personal message to Spurs fans pointing out that Gerry Francis had been told he could spend £7.5 million, but that apart from Chris Armstrong he had been unable to get the players he wanted for the prices that they were worth. This was backed up by Francis, who said he had tried to buy Les Ferdinand, who eventually went to Newcastle, and Andrei Kanchelskis, who signed for Everton.

Armstrong was a £4.5 million signing from relegated Crystal Palace in June. He had had an unhappy season with Palace, his league goalscoring ability having apparently deserted him, and three months before his transfer he had been excluded from the League Cup semifinal after a January drugs test had revealed signs of cannabis. Many thought his acquisition was a gamble. The other notable pre-season signing for Spurs was that of out-of-contract Clive Wilson from Queens Park Rangers, reuniting him with his old boss, ex-Rangers manager Gerry Francis.

In July England international Nick Barmby, who was born in Hull, became homesick for the north-east and was sold to Middlesbrough for £5.25 million. A footnote to the Spurs departures was the decision of Ossie Ardiles to quit English football for a one-year contract as coach to Guadalajara of Mexico.

Spurs kicked off the new season with a newly acquired £4 million, four-season shirt sponsorship deal with the desk-top computer company Hewlett Packard. After failing to win any of their first four matches, Spurs were third from bottom of the table. Sugar's disenchantment with the England coach Terry Venables continued, and Venables was banned from the ground. However in September the Chairman relaxed the ban for the sake of harmony in England's bid to win the European Championship in 1996.

After their bad start, Spurs won six matches in a row, four of them in the League, the other two being both legs of the Coca Cola Cup first round tie with Chester, who were beaten 4-0 and 3-1. Much of the reason was the fine partnership built up by Sheringham as scorer-in-chief and Armstrong as provider. Sheringham scored in all six of these matches, ten goals in all, while Armstrong netted twice in one of the League Cup matches.

The third round of the League (now 'Coca-Cola') Cup saw the end of Spurs' interest. Two up and cruising at half-time at Coventry, they conceded a dubious penalty while temporarily reduced to ten men as Dean Austin received stitches to a cut above his eye. Coventry converted the spot kick and added two more to win 3-2.

Meanwhile Darren Anderton, impressive for England in the summer's Umbro Cup when he

as every other club in England - we have the right to qualify for Europe.'

With the distraction of the Intertoto Cup

scored one of the two last-gasp goals which earned a draw with Sweden, followed a pre-season hernia operation by picking up a pelvic injury in September which kept him out for much of the rest of the season. In October Francis bought Ruel Fox from Newcastle and he immediately impressed with his fast-running penetrative attacking performances on the right wing.

Spurs' forward line looked as sharp as any in the Premiership, especially when Armstrong began to score, and indeed take over the main scoring role for a while from Sheringham. The first Premiership match in which both scored was satisfyingly against Arsenal at White Hart Lane in November, and resulted in a 2-1 win. With Colin Calderwood at centre back playing with the authority that regular selection for Scotland encouraged, David Howells, who clocked up his 200th appearance in August, commanding in midfield and Ian Walker's performances earning a call-up into the England squad, Spurs defence was also solid, and the team had reached third place in the Premiership by Christmas. From 18 November to 23 December they did not concede a League goal for 602 minutes, beating their previous record of 576 set in 1987. It must have been very satisfying for captain Gary Mabbutt who enjoyed a testimonial centred on a pre-season match with Newcastle, and who passed two appearance marks during the season: 450 League games on 9 December against Queen's Park Rangers, and 600 senior games on 9 March, against Nottingham Forest in the FA Cup fifth round, which Spurs eventually lost on penalties in the rescheduled replay, at White Hart Lane.

This was as far as Spurs were to get in the Cup competitions. They started seven FA Cup matches without reaching the sixth round. Two games were needed to get past lowly Hereford in the third round (1-1 at Hereford, 5-1 at the Lane) and two more to pass Wolves in the fourth (1-1 at home, 2-0 away). The fifth round match at Nottingham Forest, which was televised, was abandoned at 0-0 after only 14 minutes as a blizzard struck the ground. The second attempt ended 2-2 and the replay at White Hart Lane 1-1, calling for a penalty shoot-out. Spurs scored only one penalty, lost 3-1 and manager Francis devoted two-thirds of his page in the next programme to the iniquities of the system, suggesting away goals counting double (which would have seen Spurs through) was better.

There were other changes in personnel in the New Year. Andy Sinton became the second player to play under Francis at Queens Park Rangers to rejoin him at Spurs, via Sheffield Wednesday, for £1.5 million, while Ilie Dumitrescu was transferred to West Ham (initially subject to a work permit, which took a ludicrously long time in coming, as the World Cup star had not played 75 per cent of Spurs' senior games). Darren Caskey, who had made his first appearance of the season in one of Spurs' best displays, a 4-1 beating of Manchester United on New Years Day, was transferred to Reading.

On 30 March, during the home match with Blackburn Rovers, Bill Nicholson, the club president, celebrated 60 years with the club, and was presented with a silver plaque by Alan Sugar.

It was the only significant silver any Spur was to acquire that season. The team failed to hold on to their third position in the table and a decline in form saw them finish eighth, outside the UEFA Cup qualifying zone. Ian Walker and Teddy Sheringham were the only two ever-presents in the League, with Chris Armstrong, Sol Campbell, Gary Mabbutt and Ronny Rosenthal being the only other players to appear in more than 30 matches. Darren Anderton, who returned as a substitute in a 0-0 draw at Highbury with only four matches of the season to go, played just five complete League games all season, and was sorely missed. In the second last match he netted two goals at Elland Road in a 3-1 defeat of Leeds, and everybody hoped this augured well for the following season. Of the 47 League goals coming from Spurs players, 16 were scored by

ABOVE: *Sol Campbell gets the better of Dennis Bergkamp in the goalless draw at White Hart Lane in February 1997. During a difficult season for Spurs, Campbell continued to improve his game and by the end of the season he had become a key player in Glenn Hoddle's England team.*

RIGHT: *The versatile Andy Sinton provided much needed goals (six in the league) as well as a good degree of industry during the 1996–97 season.*

Sheringham, 15 by Armstrong, and 16 by the rest put together, so Anderton's fire-power would be essential if Spurs were to make a challenge in 1996-97.

The big event in the football world in the summer of 1996 was the European Championship, held in England. Anderton and Sheringham were key players for England, and Anderton forced a save from Switzerland's goalie in the first minute of the first match at Wembley. The two Spurs men played in all England's group matches, Sheringham scoring twice in England's 4-1 victory over Holland. England finished top of their group and the two Spurs players played in the quarter-final (won on penalties from Spain) and the semi-final against Germany, which also went to penalties. Sheringham slotted the fifth penalty, to put England 5-4 up, but Southgate missed the sixth for England and Germany won 6-5. Ian Walker was also in England's squad but did not play.

There were encouraging signs for Tottenham during the summer. Allan Nielsen, a strong and versatile Danish international midfielder with a knack of scoring goals, was signed from Brøndby for £1.6 million, although Spurs had to wait until 4 September for his first appearance, as Brøndby insisted he play in their European Champions' League matches before joining Spurs. The 25-year-old had previously played for Bayern Munich and Odense in Switzerland. Espen Baardsen, an 18-year-old goalkeeper with Under-21 international caps for Norway, was also signed. Born in California, Baardsen previously played for San Francisco All Blacks and appeared for USA at Under-18 level. Two promising youngsters, Chris Day and Steve Slade, Under-21 internationals themselves for England, were allowed to leave for Crystal Palace and Queens Park Rangers respectively. As manager Gerry Francis pointed out, he would have liked to have kept them but clubs are unable to keep players who wish to go once their contracts have run out, and goalkeeper Day's prospects were limited with Walker established in goal, and Slade had Armstrong and Sheringham among his rivals in the forward positions. Another goalkeeper to leave the club was the long-serving Erik Thorstvedt, with 219 League and Cup appearances for the team. Given a free transfer, he joined Wolves. Perhaps the best news for the club was the two-year contract signed by Gerry Francis. It was the first time Francis had signed a contract in his managerial career.

In the last week in July the side left for a pre-season tour of Norway, where they won, lost and drew their three matches. In a 2-0 win at Hamar over Hamkam, Anderton and Armstrong scored and 17 players were used. New keeper Baardsen played throughout. Two days later, at Skien, Spurs lost 2-1 to Odd Grenland, Ronny Rosenthal scoring, with Walker, Clive Wilson and Nethercott getting on the pitch. The tour ended the next day with a 0-0 draw with Raufoss, Howells getting his first game, so 21 players had a kick. Baardsen had impressed, playing 135 minutes without conceding a goal.

Teddy Sheringham made his first pre-season appearance in the four friendlies Spurs played on the grounds of teams from the Football League. Spurs won them all: 3-0 over Brentford at Griffin Park, 1-0 over Reading at Elm Park, 3-1 over Southend at Roots Hall, and 3-1 over Charlton at The Valley. This last was a testimonial for Charlton's long-serving Colin Walsh. Half of Tottenham's ten goals in these games were scored by the old firm of Armstrong and Sheringham, who had performed so well the previous season, so the omens looked good.

Spurs had been busy with improvements in the close season, particularly at their new Spurs Lodge training ground at Chigwell, where five full-size pitches had been completely relaid on the 24-acre site. A new irrigation system and pavilion meant Spurs were one of the best-equipped clubs in the country for training facilities. At White Hart Lane itself the pitch had been totally renovated during the summer with the old undersoil heating system replaced and a new irrigation system installed to make for a superb playing surface. Around the pitch, the hospitality areas in the South Stand had been completed with all areas enjoying views on to the pitch and the West Stand had been improved with a new Press Lounge installed and refurbishment to many areas. Off the field everything was in place for Spurs to have a good season.

The 1996-97 season was notable for the number of top-quality imports into the Premiership from the continent, a result of two things: firstly, the Bosman ruling in the European courts – which gave out-of-contract players moving between EU countries the right to a free transfer – and secondly the huge wealth which Premiership clubs had acquired as a result of their contract with Sky Television. This allowed British clubs to compete so far as transfer fees and salaries were concerned with the previously much richer Leagues in Italy and Spain. Chelsea set the pace with their signing of the top-class Italian players Zola, Vialli and Di Matteo, and the

BELOW: Colin Calderwood gets in front of Alan Shearer to head the ball back to Ian Walker during the Premiership game with Newcastle at White Hart Lane. In a season dominated by injuries to key players, the powerful Scotland defender missed just three league games for Spurs all season – only Ian Walker and Sol Campbell managed more appearances in 1996–97.

Frenchman Leboeuf among others, while Manchester United had the Czech Poborsky and the Dutchman Jordi Cruyff. Even unfashionable Middlesbrough had the Italian Ravanelli and two Brazilians, Juninho and Emerson. Spurs, of course, had been the pioneers of importing exotic foreign talent with their bold signings of Ardiles and Villa in the 1970s and the equally stunning capture of Klinsmann in 1994.

The season got off to an excellent start for Spurs, whose first match was at Ewood Park, Blackburn. Dalglish's Rovers had been Premiership champions in 1994-95 and had done well in 1995-96. In fact they had lost only five home games in two seasons, conceding an average of only a goal a game. So Spurs' 2-0 opening win was a superb performance. Chris Armstrong got both goals and looked sharp, as did David Howells, who played a major part in both build-ups. But the victory was marred by serious injury to captain Gary Mabbutt, whose leg was broken in the 18th minute. Gary's bad luck seemed to be equalled only by his popularity, which allowed him to keep smiling even though 18 minutes was to be the sum of his football for the season.

Unfortunately the good start was not maintained in the first game at White Hart Lane against Premiership newcomers Derby County.

Spurs began where they left off against Blackburn, and Teddy Sheringham got himself on the scoresheet with a great free-kick, but Spurs' superiority waned in the face of a strong second-half fight-back and Derby scored an equalizer in the dying seconds. However four points from two games was not a bad start, and Spurs fans had something to celebrate the following day when new England manager Glenn Hoddle announced the names of four Spurs players in his squad for the World Cup qualifying match with Moldova: Walker, Campbell, Anderton and Sheringham. And young Spur Gerry McMahon was named for the Northern Ireland World Cup squad. With Colin Calderwood on Scotland duty in Austria, Ronny Rosenthal helping Israel beat Bulgaria, Allan Nielsen scoring for Denmark in a 2-0 win in Slovenia, and Espen Baardsen in Norway's Under-21 draw with France, August ended and September began with plenty of international action for Tottenham men.

However, things began to go wrong for Spurs in the Premiership from then on. They failed to score in their next two games, at home to Everton, which ended 0-0, and away to Wimbledon, when Allan Nielsen made his debut but could not prevent Spurs going down 1-0. But worse were the injuries. With Mabbutt and Austin, who had not yet played,

With six goals in 29 starts and many more assists – courtesy of a long throw – Allan Nielsen proved to be one of Gerry Francis' most shrewd signings.

194

out for months, the injury-prone Darren Anderton was forced to miss the Everton game and Chris Armstrong picked up an injury after half-an-hour. With Teddy Sheringham injured while training with England, Spurs went down to their first defeat of the season when both strikers, Armstrong and Sheringham, were unable to play against Wimbledon.

At this difficult juncture midfielder Andy Turner left for Portsmouth for £250,000 with provisos for additional fees according to number of appearances, international selection and sell-on fee. An Under-21 international for the Republic of Ireland, Turner had made 25 senior appearances since 1991.

With Armstrong back and Rory Allen making his full senior debut Spurs then went down 2-1 at home to the high-flying Newcastle United in front of over 32,000 fans. Spurs were a little unlucky to lose but had the satisfaction of seeing Allen score on his full debut. They then had the luck on their side at Southampton, winning 1-0 with an Armstrong penalty.

The Premiership programme was interrupted when Spurs went to Preston for a Coca-Cola Cup second round first leg tie and drew 1-1, Darren Anderton's first goal of the season, scored in the second minute, being cancelled out by another very late equaliser. Leicester City, the next visitors, were newcomers to the

Premiership and Spurs seemed to have an ideal chance to move up the table and impress Sky viewers in their season's first appearance live on television. Justin Edinburgh was making his 200th senior appearance for Spurs but pulled his hamstring in the first half to increase Spurs' injury problems. Without both Sheringham and Armstrong again, Spurs played Sol Campbell in attack, but a resilient Leicester came out on top 2-1, despite Walker saving a penalty. The Spurs younger set was further depleted when Gerry McMahon left to join Stoke, and Darren Anderton revealed he had a hernia problem similar to the one that had been so troublesome when he joined Spurs and that sooner or later another operation would be required. It was some relief for Spurs when, with Teddy Sheringham returning to the side, they beat Preston 3-0 in the second leg of the Coca-Cola Cup tie, and Rory Allen scored two. Anderton got the other but then decided to have his operation and was forced to miss the next six games.

On 21 September 1996 the Spurs Lodge training complex was officially opened and soon-to-be Prime Minister Tony Blair unveiled a plaque at the main entrance and then tested Ian Walker with some well-placed penalties.

A trip to Old Trafford to face Manchester United was unproductive, resulting in a 2-0

BELOW, LEFT: Rory Allen takes the game to Manchester United in the FA Cup tie at Old Trafford. The young striker showed immense potential to come into an injury hit team and contribute four goals in 16 appearances. The future certainly looks bright for the young Spur.

BELOW: Steffen Iversen was courted by a number of top European sides while playing in the European Cup for Norwegian champions Rosenborg. The young striker chose to join Spurs and managed six goals in 16 games before his season was ended prematurely by injury.

instituted against former manager Terry Venables was settled to his satisfaction.

A 3-0 win at Middlesbrough lifted Spurs to eighth in the table, with Sheringham scoring twice and Ruel Fox getting his season's first. Chris Armstrong, now restored to the side, netted as Spurs went forward in the Coca-Cola Cup at the expense of Sunderland, beaten 2-1 at White Hart Lane, and he scored again at Stamford Bridge, but Chelsea won 3-1 in a sad and very emotional match which followed the death in a helicopter crash of their young vice-chairman Matthew Harding. Spurs had offered to postpone the match.

Good home wins over West Ham and Sunderland lifted Spurs to seventh in the table, but a 3-1 defeat at Highbury by the old enemy Arsenal, who scored twice in the last two minutes to transform a very even match, was followed by a huge shock in the Coca-Cola Cup at First Division Bolton. Spurs had no excuses for a 6-1 thrashing that ended their interest in the tournament.

A Spurs defeat 2-0 by Liverpool at White Hart Lane was remarkable for Liverpool's second goal, a tame low shot from Steve McManaman that Walker had covered until it took a freak bounce just in front of him and leapt over him into the net. Walker could only sit and smile in bewilderment about it. Perhaps Spurs fans, too, could permit themselves a little smile over the publication of a national survey which announced they were the wealthiest fans in the country, although nobody could laugh at another injury to Chris Armstrong, the season's leading scorer, which looked like keeping him out for most of the season.

Two away games were quite satisfactory, a win at Coventry and a draw at Leeds. The side at Coventry included a new signing from Rosenborg, Steffen Iversen, a colleague of Espen Baardsen in Norway's Under-21 side. As with the signing of Nielsen earlier in the season, Gerry Francis had to wait for his man while he fulfilled a European commitment for his current club, in this case a European Champions' League match at AC Milan. Rosenborg pulled off a major European shock by winning 2-1 and qualifying for the knockout stage of the tournament, a quarter-final tie with

ABOVE: Swiss international Ramon Vega joined Spurs in time to make his debut in the league at home to Manchester United in January. Unfortunately injuries and suspension greatly diminished the impact made by the highly rated defender.

RIGHT: The emergence of young full-back Stephen Carr into a first-team regular was a major plus for Gerry Francis. The Republic of Ireland Under-21 also provided a great deal of attacking impetus down the right flank.

defeat, but Spurs played well and deserved more, with new captain David Howells having an opening 'goal' disallowed because the ball had struck his upper arm. In this match Colin Calderwood made his 650th senior appearance (123 for Spurs), and Teddy Sheringham his 500th (170 for Spurs).

Allan Nielsen netted his first goal for Spurs in a 1-0 home defeat of Aston Villa, in a game that made the news pages of the papers because of the extraordinary gesture of the Villa goalkeeper, the Australian Mark Bosnich. Barracked by fans who chanted 'Klinsmann' because of a controversial foul he had inflicted on Spurs' German player two seasons before, Bosnich put his finger under his nose to represent Hitler's moustache and gave the Nazi salute. It was a moment of madness for which he apologised profusely in all quarters afterwards, but could not avoid ultimate FA discipline and was fined £1,000. Alan Sugar gracefully accepted Bosnich's apology on behalf of Spurs, and a few days later Sugar was in the news again when a libel action he had

European champions Juventus. In the circumstances it was very sporting of Iversen to deny that he wished his transfer to Spurs could not have been postponed a little longer. Striker Iversen took over the number 18 shirt previously worn for Spurs by Jürgen Klinsmann, and modestly rejected suggestions that he would become a new Klinsmann.

After the Coventry match discussions took place with Liverpool's central defender John Scales to join Spurs, after it had seemed the former Wimbledon player was about to sign for Leeds, but as Scales was injured his debut had to wait.

Spurs had a traumatic time over Christmas and the New Year period. A 1-1 draw with Sheffield Wednesday at the Lane on the Saturday before Christmas was followed by a 3-1 victory over Southampton, again at the Lane, and notable for Iversen's first two goals for the club. The other was scored by Nielsen, the middle of three goals in successive matches. Then, with the New Years Day game at Leicester called off because of freezing conditions came a trip to Newcastle on 28 December which resulted in a 7-1 defeat. The two defeats, just over four weeks apart, by Bolton and Newcastle, were the worst in Gerry Francis's managerial career.

With Spurs now as near halfway in the Premiership as it is possible to be, tenth, the main interest left in the season was the FA Cup, but fortune was again not smiling on Spurs. Their injury list for their third round tie ruled out Sheringham, Anderton, Armstrong, Scales, Iversen, Dozzell, Baardsen and Mabbutt with Rosenthal ill. Their opponents were champions and cup-holders Manchester United – at Old Trafford! However the makeshift team put up a very spirited performance, and were somewhat unlucky to go down 2-0 with Neil Fenn making his debut.

Better news for fans was the signing of another continental international, the 25-year-old Swiss central defender Ramon Vega, for whom Spurs paid the Italian club Cagliari £3.75 million. By coincidence Spurs' next match was also against United, at the Lane, where Vega made his debut. United won again, 2-1.

Spurs then lost 2-1 to Nottingham Forest in curious circumstances. Andy Sinton was fouled, but without Spurs gaining advantage Forest broke away to score the winner, at which point the referee booked the player who'd fouled Sinton. As February arrived a run of three home games were won (Blackburn 2-1), lost (Chelsea 1-2) and drawn (Arsenal 0-0). Narrow defeats by relegation strugglers West Ham (4-3) and Forest again (1-0, with John Scales starting a match for the first time) dropped Spurs to a dangerous 13th in the table but a 4-0 away win at Sunderland, where Steffen Iversen recorded the season's first hat-trick for Spurs, brought them back to the tenth position from which they'd not strayed more than three places for five months or so.

By the last Premiership matches of the season Spurs were ninth, but they were then defeated at home by Coventry City in one of the most significant results of the season - it allowed Coventry to move up from 19th in the table to 17th and avoid relegation by a single point. Coventry won 2-1 and resisted a late effort by Spurs to force an equaliser. So Spurs finished tenth, their second worst in the Premiership. It had been an unlucky season, plagued again with injuries. Only five players appeared in both first and last matches. One of the big successes to emerge from the reserves in the season was Republic of Ireland Under-21 defender Stephen Carr who, after two senior appearances in 1993, came into the side as a substitute in the first home game of the season and kept his place.

Spurs hoped that the bad season of 1996-97 might be a turning point for them. Nothing was lacking for a return to the old glory – superb training facilities, a modern White Hart Lane, a reshaped, balanced side and a strong determination to win major honours. If they could be luckier with injuries – particularly to vital attackers Armstrong and Anderton – and the continental imports could realise their potential, then Spurs could be back at the top before the millennium.

Tottenham Hotspur is now an institution well into its second century. No one survives who can tell us about those days spent playing on the Tottenham Marshes, or even about the way the club eventually arrived at White Hart Lane. Few of us will be there to celebrate the Bicentennial in 2082. But there is one thing that we can be sure of: that as long as football continues to be played, then the Spurs will go marching on . . .

The Captain's armband passed to David Howells on several occasions during the 1996–97 season. In February, the long-serving midfielder skippered Spurs at Upton Park for a Premiership encounter and despite horrendous conditions and a recent family bereavement he played extremely well, scoring a breathtaking goal.

TOTTENHAM HOTSPUR –
the complete first class record

The Hotspurs did not have a recognised fixture list until their third season; the first official 'list' was published in the Weekly Herald on 24 October 1884. Between their formation in 1882 and season 1892–93, all games can be classified as friendlies except for a small number of appearances in local cup competitions, when the specific competition is mentioned. Between 1884 and 1892 only games which were included on the fixture list at the beginning of the season and were reported by the Herald have been included. For the other seasons prior to 1896–97, when the club joined the Southern League, only games covered by the Herald as first team matches have been included. The club obviously arranged other games on free Saturdays, but there are no means of distinguishing, at this distance, whether those games were first, second or third team fixtures. In seasons where the Herald gives the team's final record as including more games than were actually reported, then this fact has been noted. Again, it is probable that the paper included some second team matches in its summary. The Herald, incidentally, is referred to in various sources as the Weekly Herald, Tottenham Herald and Tottenham Weekly Herald but these are all the same newspaper. In 1882–83 only one game, against Latymer, was reported by the Herald and it is therefore more than likely that the team's other fixtures were against local scratch sides. The Latymer fixture was only covered because the Edmonton club was quite prominent at the time – otherwise the Hotspurs' first season would have been ignored completely.

In a number of cases in the first decade, games were definitely played but no record of the result remains. This is usually because the Herald did not cover the game, but occasionally it was because the result was disputed and the paper did not wish to offend either team by stating one result. At other times, games had to be called off because of bad light and, on at least two occasions, because the ball burst and there was no replacement.

Between 1896 and 1908, Spurs played in at least two first class leagues and sometimes in three. In theory all of these games were first class, for the reserve teams contested other leagues such as the South Eastern League and the London Combination (reserve leagues and games are not covered here). It does not seem possible, however, that all of the Thames and Medway League, United League, Southern District Combination or even Western League games can have been contested by the first team. They were, nonetheless, published as first team fixtures and have been included here. The same problem applies to friendlies, which are always difficult to classify. In general, friendlies where it is known that most of the first team turned out have been included, but the reader must assess for himself or herself how seriously these games would have been taken by the club.

Several discrepancies in the various league tables, particularly prior to 1900, have been identified but not always altered. These generally occur when the for and against columns do not add up (or do not correspond to those results which are known), or where some results are missing or are contradictory in different sources. While every effort has been made to ensure that the Spurs figures are correct, at this distance it is impossible to find the missing information, or to resolve contradictory scores and results for other clubs. Given the choice between leaving these tables out or reproducing them as published at the time, with their errors, we have chosen to do the latter. The same problems apply to early Southern League appearances and to goalscorers (who were occasionally not recorded as late as 1939). Even in the 1970s, there are goalscoring discrepancies between newspaper reports, club programmes and annual aggregates. These often arise through interpretation of what constitutes an own goal. We have tried to be as accurate as is now possible in all these cases but there are occasions where, for instance, early appearances do not add up to the required totals and there is no way of correcting the figures. In recent seasons substitutes have added a further complication, and our rule has been to include a substitute as having made an appearance if he actually came on the field. The appearances and goals columns apply only to Southern League and Football League matches throughout.

Key to Competitions

AC	Amateur Cup
CS	Charity Shield
CUP	Minor wartime cup competitions
EC	European Cup
ECWC	European Cup Winners Cup
EEC	East End Cup
f	Final (of a Cup competition)
F	Friendly
FC	FA Cup
FLC	Football League Cup
LCC	London Challenge Cup (sometimes referred to as London Charity Cup)
LCup	London Wartime Cup
LGC	Wartime League Cup
Lge	Football League (or, in wartime years, whichever League was operating [Football League South, London Combination, Regional LeagueSouth, London League] as shown by the League table that season).
LLge	London League
LnC	London Cup (known also as the London Association Cup and the London Senior Cup)
LPCF	London Professional Charity Fund
LSupp	London Supplementary Wartime Competition
LuCC	Luton Charity Cup
MC	Middlesex Cup
r	Replay (of a Cup tie)
SAll	Southern Alliance
SCC	Southern Charity Cup
SDC	Southern District Combination
SDCC	Southern District Charity Cup
sf	Semi-final (of a Cup competition)
SLge	Southern League
SLS	Sheriff of London's Charity Shield (occasionally referred to as Dewar Shield)
TEX	Texaco Cup
TLge	Thames and Medway League
U EFA	UEFA Cup
ULge	United League
VC	Victory Cup
WDC	Wolverton and District Charity Cup
WLge	Western League
WR F	War Relief Fund

Blank spaces in early years represent local friendlies the only sort of game at that time apart from occasional cup matches.

The columns in each league table are, in order, played, won, drawn, lost, for, against and points.

SEASON 1882/83

| 30 Sep | | * | Radicals | L | * |
| 6 Jan | | A | Latymer | L | 1-8 |

* Venue and score unknown, but lost by two goals

SEASON 1883/84

6 Oct		H	Brownlow Rvs	W	9-0
13 Oct		H	Evelyn	W	5-1*
20 Oct		A	Grange Pk	L	1-3
27 Oct		H	Leyton Rvs	W	1-0
10 Nov		A	Brownlow Rvs	W	1-0
24 Nov		H	Sekforde Rvs	W	2-0
1 Dec		A	Sekforde Rvs	W	1-0
8 Dec		A	Leyton Rvs	L	1-3
15 Dec		H	Claremont	W	2-0†
26 Dec		H	Oak	W	6-0
27 Dec		H	Latymer	W	2-0
29 Dec		H	Star	W	3-0
12 Jan		A	Woodgrange	L	0-1
19 Jan		A	Grafton	W	1-0
26 Jan		H	Albion	L	0-1
2 Feb		A	Clarence	W	1-0
9 Feb		H	Albion	W	3-0
16 Feb		H	Hanover Utd	L	1-2
23 Feb		H	Grange Pk	W	1-0‡
8 Mar		A	Hanover U 2nds	W	2-0
15 Mar		A	Latymer	W	2-0
22 Mar		A	Remington	W	2-0

* Hotspurs score recorded as 'five goals and one disputed goal'
† Game lasted only 60 minutes
‡ Grange Park played with only 10 men

SEASON 1884/85

27 Sep		*	J. Jull XI		5-4
4 Oct		A	Remington	W	4-0*
11 Oct		H	Abbey	W	1-0
18 Oct		H	Woodgrange	L	4-5
25 Oct		H	Grange Pk	W	4-0
1 Nov		A	Sekforde Rvs	W	4-0
8 Nov		A	Marlbro Rvs	W	1-0
15 Nov		A	Latymer	W	2-1
22 Nov		H	St Peters	W	3-2
29 Nov		H	Hadley		‡
6 Dec		H	Tottenham	W	4-0†
13 Dec		A	Woodgrange	D	0-0
20 Dec		H	Sekforde	W	5-0
26 Dec		H	Grove		‡
27 Dec		H	Enfield	W	3-0
3 Jan		A	Hadley		‡
10 Jan		A	Abbey	D	1-1
17 Jan		A	Grange Pk	L	0-1
24 Jan		H	Victoria	W	5-0
31 Jan		H	St Martins		‡
7 Feb		H	Fillebrook	W	3-0
14 Feb		H	Latymer	D	0-0
21 Feb		H	St Peters		‡
28 Feb		A	Bedford Rvs	D	1-1
7 Mar		A	Marlbro Rvs		‡
14 Mar		A	Victoria Wand		‡
21 Mar		A	Remington		‡
28 Mar		A	St Martins		‡
4 Apr		H	Mars		‡
11 Apr		A	Grove		‡

* Jack Jull's XI versus Billy Harston's XI
† Tottenham were a different side from Hotspurs
‡ Scores either unknown or disputed by the two clubs

SEASON 1885/86

3 Oct		A	Silesia Coll	W	4-3
10 Oct		A	Grange Pk	L	0-3
17 Oct	LnC	H	St Albans	W	5-2
24 Oct		H	Westmstr Rvs	W	*
7 Nov	LnC	A	Casuals	L	0-8
14 Nov		A	Fairfield	L	0-1
28 Nov		H	Dalston rvs	W	3-0
26 Dec		H	Bowes Pk	W	2-0
2 Jan		H	St Martins	W	3-0
9 Jan		A	Woodgrange Pk		*
16 Jan		A		L	0-2
6 Feb		H	Edmonton Ind	W	4-1
13 Feb		H	Grange Pk 2nds	L	0-3
20 Feb		H	Sth Hackney	W	8-0
27 Feb		H	Silesia Coll	D	1-1

6 Mar		H	Ilford	W	6-1
13 Mar		H	Rutland	W	5-0
20 Mar		H	Upton Excelsior		*
27 Mar		H	Enfield Lock	W	6-1
3 Apr		H	Park	W	8-0
10 Apr		H	Park	W	8-0
17 Apr		H	Hermitage	W	3-0

* Score not available

According to Tottenham Weekly Herald a total of 37 games were played at all levels this season, of which 24 were won and only 11 lost. Total goals for were 111 with 51 against. Nonetheless, the Herald only records the results of the 22 matches above.

SEASON 1886/87

2 Oct		H	Sth Hackney	W	13-1
9 Oct		H	Woodford Bdg	W	2-0
16 Oct	LnC	H	Upton Pk	L	0-6
30 Oct		H	Old St Pauls	D	1-1
13 Nov		A	Silesia Coll	L	2-3
27 Nov		A	Fillebrook	L	1-4
4 Dec		A	Iona	W	5-0
18 Dec	EEC	H	Phoenix	W	6-0
27 Dec		H	Dreadnought	W	6-0
22 Jan	EEC	H	Park	W	2-0
22 Jan		H	Foxes	W	2-1
5 Feb		A	Park	W	4-1
12 Feb		A	Fillebrook	W	3-0
19 Feb	EEC	H	St Lukes	W	2-1
5 Mar		H	Edmonton Ass	W	2-1
16 Apr	EECSF	H	Caldonians	L	0-1
23 Apr		H	Enfield Lock	W	6-0*

* Herald gives score as 'six goals and one disputed goal to nil.' The Herald gives the club's record for the season as played 20, won 14, lost 5, against 22. Results of two games against City Ramblers and another possibly against Silesia College were not recorded by the Herald.

SEASON 1887/88

1 Oct		H	Buckhurst Hill	W	6-1
8 Oct	LnC	A	Hendon	L	0-6
29 Oct		H	St Augustines	W	5-1
12 Nov		H	Nondescripts	W	6-1
19 Nov		H	Royal Arsenal	W	2-1*
3 Dec		A	Luton Town	W	2-1
10 Dec		A	Priory	W	3-0
24 Dec		H	Balmoral	D	1-1
31 Dec		H	St Martins	W	3-0
7 Jan		H	St Brides	W	3-2
14 Jan		A	Bowes Park	D	2-2
21 Jan		A	Old St Pauls	W	2-1
4 Feb		A	Royal Arsenal	L	2-6
18 Feb		A	Olympic	W	5-1
17 Mar		A	St Brides	W	3-0
2 Apr		A	Clapton	L	1-6

* Abandoned after 75 minutes because of bad light

SEASON 1888/89

22 Sep		A	Royal Arsenal	W	1-0
13 Oct	LnC	H	Old Etonians	L	2-8
20 Oct		H	Clapton	L	2-5
17 Nov		H	Millwall Rvs	D	1-1
24 Nov		H	Plaistow (Knt)	W	4-0
1 Dec		H	Old St Marks	W	5-1
8 Dec		H	Upton Excelsior	D	3-3
15 Dec		H	Plaistow	W	2-1
22 Dec		H	Bowes Pk	W	4-0
26 Dec		H	Orion Gym		*
10 Jan	MC	H	Civil Engineers	D	0-0
16 Jan		A	Windsor Phnx	L	1-2
19 Jan	MC	A	Civil Engineers	L	1-4
1 Mar		H	Windsor Phnx	L	1-2
9 Mar		H	Royal Arsenal	L	0-1
16 Mar		H	Edmonton	D	1-1
13 Apr		H	Orion Gym	W	6-1

* Result not available

SEASON 1889/90

21 Sep		A	Royal Arsenal	L	1-10
28 Sep		H	Westminster	W	13-0
5 Oct		H	Vulcan	W	5-1
12 Oct		H	Iona	W	10-0
19 Oct		A	Edmonton	L	2-3

2 Nov	LnC	A	Old St Stphns	L	0-4
9 Nov		H	Clapton	W	5-3
16 Nov		A	Finchley	D	1-1
23 Nov		H	Hampstead	W	1-0
30 Nov		A	Sutherland	W	1-0
4 Jan		H	Foxes	D	1-1
11 Jan		A	Romford	D	0-0
18 Jan	MC	A	Old St Stphns	W	4-2
1 Feb		H	Robin Hood	W	2-0
8 Feb		H	Vulcan	W	2-1
15 Feb	MC	H	Clapton	L	†
1 Mar		A	Swindon	L	1-2*
8 Mar		H	Unity	W	3-1
15 Mar		H	Edmonton	L	1-4
4 Apr		H	Dreadnought	L	0-1
5 Apr		A	Uxbridge	D	2-2
7 Apr		A	Maidenhead	W	3-2

† Score not available
* According to the Herald Swindon won by 'one goal and one disputed goal to one'. The Herald says that the club played 45 games in all this season, winning 22 and drawing 10, but they record only the results of the 22 above.

SEASON 1890/91

27 Sep		H	Hampstead	W	6-3
4 Oct		H	Grove House		*
11 Oct		A	Edmonton	L	4-6
18 Oct		A	Luton Town	L	1-4
25 Oct		H	Northumbrlnd Fusiliers	W	1-0
1 Nov	LnC	A	QPR	D	1-1
8 Nov	LnCr	A	QPR	W	2-1
15 Nov		H	City Ramblers	W	1-0
22 Nov		H	Barking	W	3-0
6 Dec		A	Unity	D	1-1
24 Jan	LnC	A	Barnes	W	1-0
31 Jan	LnC	A	Millwall Ath	L	1-5
7 Feb		H	Orion	W	7-1
14 Feb	MC	H	Clapton		*
21 Feb		H	Vulcan	W	6-0
28 Feb		H	Old St Stephns	W	3-0

* Result not available

SEASON 1891/92

26 Sep		H	Hampstead	W	6-2
3 Oct		H	Grange Pk	W	4-2
10 Oct	LnC	H	Calednian Ath	W	4-3
24 Oct		H	Clapton	L	1-2
31 Oct	LnC	A	Hampstead	W	3-2
7 Nov	LuCC	A	Coldstream	D	3-3
14 Nov	LuCC	A	Coldstream	W	7-2
21 Nov	LnC	A	City Ramblers	L	1-4
28 Nov		H	Old St Stphns	D	0-0
5 Dec	MC	A	Minerva	L	0-2
12 Dec		H	Forest Swifts	D	1-1
19 Dec		A	1st Scots Gds	L	0-4
26 Dec		H	Kings Lynn	L	*
2 Jan		H	Uxbridge	W	3-0
9 Jan		H	QPR	L	1-2
23 Jan		H	Westminster	D	2-2
30 Jan		H	Old St Lukes	W	3-1
6 Feb		H	St Albans	L	1-2
13 Feb		A	Clapton	D	1-1
20 Feb		A	City Ramblers	W	*
27 Feb		H	Grenadier Gds	W	9-0
12 Mar		H	Casuals	W	3-1
26 Mar		A	Luton	L	1-3

* Result not available

SEASON 1892/93

17 Sep		H	Paddington	W	10-0
24 Sep	SAII	A	Polytechnic	W	2-1
1 Oct		H	Royal Arsenal	W	3-0
8 Oct		H	Coldstrm Gds	W	6-0
15 Oct	SAII	A	Old St Stphns	W	3-0
22 Oct		H	Coldstrm Gds	W	3-2
29 Oct		H	2nd Scts Gds	L	2-4
5 Nov	SAII	A	Windsor	W	2-1
12 Nov		H	Clapton	L	1-2
19 Nov	SAII	H	Erith	W	3-2
26 Nov		H	Caledonian Ath	W	5-0
3 Dec	LnC	A	Polytechnic	D	2-2
10 Dec		H	Hampstead	D	1-1
17 Dec	LnC	H	Polytechnic	W	3-0
24 Dec		H	Coldstrm Gds		*
26 Dec		H	Edmonton		*

14 Jan	SAII	A	Erith	L	1-2
21 Jan	SAII	A	Slough	D	3-3
28 Jan	LnC	H	Casuals	L	1-2
4 Feb	SAII	A	Slough	W	5-2
11 Feb	SAII	H	Polytechnic	D	2-2
18 Feb		H	London Welsh	D	2-2
25 Feb	SAII	H	Upton Pk	W	1-0
4 Mar	SAII	A	Windsor	W	5-2
11 Mar		H	QPR	W	1-0
25 Mar	SAII	A	Old St Stphns	L	1-2
1 Apr		H	City Ramblers	W	1-0
8 Apr	SAII	A	Upton Pk	L	1-4
15 Apr	WDC	†	Smethwick	L	0-2
22 Apr		H	London Welsh	W	4-1

† Played at Wolverton

The Herald gives Spurs full first team record for the season as played 31, won 17, drawn 6, for 79 and against 46. They fail to record the results of five of these matches, however.

* Result not available

Southern Alliance 1892–93

1	Old St Stphns	12	10	1	1	44:15	21
3	**TOTTENHAM**	**12**	**7**	**2**	**3**	**29:21**	**16**

Only two other fixtures were known to have been played – Slough v Upton Park on 29 April and Windsor v Polytechnic on 23 April. The results of these games are not recorded and, as far as known, the league was left incomplete. The Southern Alliance was disbanded at the end of this season.

SEASON 1893/94

16 Sep		A	Enfield	L	1-5
23 Sep		H	Romford	D	2-2
30 Sep		H	Casuals	L	0-1
7 Oct		H	City Ramblers	W	2-0
14 Oct		H	London Welsh	W	1-0
21 Oct	LnC	H	Old St Marks	D	0-0
28 Oct	LnCr	A	Old St Marks	L	1-6
4 Nov		H	1st Scts Gds	L	1-2
11 Nov	AC	H	Vampires	W	3-1
18 Nov		H	London Welsh	W	2-1
9 Dec	LCC	H	Crusaders	L	2-5
16 Dec		H	Erith	L	0-1
19 Dec		H	Friars	W	2-1
23 Dec		H	Wolverton	D	2-2
26 Dec		A	Southampton	L	0-1
30 Dec		A	Uxbridge	L	0-1
13 Jan		H	3rd Gren Gds	D	1-1
20 Jan	MCr	H	3rd Gren Gds	L	0-2
27 Jan	WDC	H	Chesham	D	2-2
3 Feb		H	City Ramblers	D	0-1
8 Feb		H	London Hospital	D	1-1
10 Feb		H	Polytechnic	W	5-0
17 Feb		H	Highland Iftry	D	2-2
24 Feb	WDC	H	Chesham	W	3-0
2 Mar		H	Uxbridge	D	1-1
10 Mar	WDC	*	Smethwick	L	0-1
23 Mar		H	Scots Gds	W	3-1
24 Mar		H	Slough	W	3-0
26 Mar		A	N/Brompton	D	3-3
31 Mar		H	Polytechnic	D	0-0
7 Apr		H	Old St Stphns	D	1-1
14 Apr		H	Ilford	L	0-1
21 Apr		H	Crouch end	D	2-2

* Played at Wolverton

SEASON 1894/95

15 Sep		A	Uxbridge	L	0-2
22 Sep		H	Casuals	W	3-1
29 Sep		A	Lon Calednian	L	1-3
6 Oct		H	3rd Gren Gds	D	1-1
13 Oct	FC	H	West Herts	W	3-2
20 Oct	AC	H	O/Harrovians	W	7-0
27 Oct		A	Crouch End	D	2-2
3 Nov	FC	H	Wolverton	W	5-3
10 Nov	AC	H	City Ramblers	W	6-1
17 Nov		H	Hglnd Lt Ifnt	D	1-1
24 Nov	FC	A	Clapton	W	4-0
1 Dec		A	Romford	W	8-0
8 Dec	LCC	H	Crusaders	W	4-2
15 Dec	FC	H	Luton Town	D	2-2
22 Dec	AC	H	Lon Welsh	D	1-1
25 Dec		H	Sheff & Dist	W	7-1
26 Dec		H	Wst Liverpool	W	3-0

Season 1894/95 (continued)

Date	Comp	H/A	Opponent	Result
29 Dec		H	Vampires	W 4-1
5 Jan	ACr	H	Lon Welsh	D 3-3
19 Jan	ACr	*	Lon Welsh	W 4-2
26 Jan	LnC	H	Lon Welsh	W 5-0
23 Feb	AC	H	Beeston	W 2-0
2 Mar	LnC	A	Old Westmster	D 3-3
9 Mar	LnCr	H	Old Westmster	L 4-5
16 Mar	AC	H	O/Carthusians	L 0-5
19 Mar	LCC	H	O/Carthusians	L 0-3
23 Mar		H	Lon Calednian	W 5-1
30 Mar		H	City Ramblers	W 2-0
6 Apr		H	Casuals	L 1-2
12 Apr		H	Lpool Casuals	W 6-0
13 Apr		H	2nd Scts Gds	D 1-1
16 Apr		A	Bristl Sth End	W 7-0
25 Apr		H	Lon Calednian	W 2-0
27 Apr		H	Brimsdown	W 2-0

* Second replay at Spotted Dog Ground

SEASON 1895/96

Date	Comp	H/A	Opponent	Result
7 Sep		A	Royal Engs	L 0-3
14 Sep		H	Royal Scots	W 3-2
21 Sep		H	Casuals	W 3-2
28 Sep		H	Ryl Ordnance	W 2-0
5 Oct		A	Claptn Orient	L 4-5
12 Oct	FC	A	Luton Town	W 2-1
19 Oct		H	Ilford	W 2-0
26 Oct		H	Ryl Artillery	L 1-2
2 Nov	FC	A	Vampires	L 2-4*
6 Nov		H	Luton Town	L 0-2
9 Nov		H	Old Westmsters	W 2-1
16 Nov	FC	H	Vampires	W 2-1
23 Nov	FC	A	Ilford	W 5-1
30 Nov		A	Lon Welsh	W 3-2
7 Dec		H	Caledonian	L 0-3
14 Dec	FC	H	Old St Stphns	W 2-1
21 Dec		H	Casuals	W 3-1
25 Dec		A	Millwall Ath	L 3-5
26 Dec		H	Accrington	W 3-0
28 Dec		H	Freemantle	D 2-2
4 Jan		H	Reading	W 2-1
11 Jan		H	Millwall	D 1-1
18 Jan		H	Ilford	W 2-1
25 Jan		H	Notts County	L 1-5
1 Feb	FC	A	Stoke	L 0-5
8 Feb		H	Royal Scots	W 2-1
10 Feb		A	Luton Town	L 0-9
15 Feb		A	Ryl Ordnance	L 1-2
22 Feb		H	Clapton	W 4-0
29 Feb		H	Burslm Prt Vle	W 3-1
4 Mar		A	Gravesend	D 1-1
7 Mar		H	1st Scts Gds	W 8-0
9 Mar		A	Ryl Ordnance	L 1-3
14 Mar		H	Uxbridge	W 4-0
16 Mar		A	Woolwich Asnl	W 3-1
19 Mar		H	Ryl Ordnance	D 2-2
21 Mar		H	Manctr Reg	W 8-0
26 Mar		H	Woolwich Asnl	L 1-3
28 Mar		A	Lon Calednian	W 5-0
3 Apr		A	Reading	W 3-2
4 Apr		H	Ostwsle Rvs	W 4-0
6 Apr		H	Middlesbrough	W 5-0
7 Apr		H	Swindon	L 2-3
11 Apr		H	Aston Villa	L 1-3
15 Apr		A	Swindon	W 2-0
18 Apr		A	Southampton	L 1-4
22 Apr		A	Gravesend	D 1-1
25 Apr		H	Wellingboro	W 3-0
30 Apr		H	Woolwich Asnl	W 3-2

* Replayed because Vampires pitch was 'improperly marked'

SEASON 1896/97

Date	Comp	H/A	Opponent	Result
3 Sep	F	H	Rossendale	W 7-0
5 Sep	SLge	A	Sheppey Utd	D 3-3
10 Sep	F	H	London Caled	D 3-3
12 Sep	SLge	A	Wolverton	W 1-0
17 Sep	F	H	Casuals	W 4-0
19 Sep	ULge	A	Millwall	L 5-6
24 Sep	F	H	Luton Town	D 0-0†
26 Sep	F	A	Casuals	W 4-1
1 Oct	F	H	2nd Cold Gds	W 4-1
3 Oct	SLge	A	Gravesend	W 3-1
8 Oct	F	H	Royal Scts G	W 5-0
10 Oct	SLge	H	Chatham	L 2-3
17 Oct	SLge	H	Gravesend	W 4-0
24 Oct	SLge	A	Ryl Ordnance	W 2-1‡
29 Oct	F	H	Southampton	W 3-1
31 Oct	SLge	A	Chatham	W 2-1
2 Nov	ULge	A	Rushden	L 0-2
7 Nov	SLge	H	Sheppey Utd	W 3-2
9 Nov	ULge	A	Woolwich Asnl	L 1-2
14 Nov	SLge	H	Swindon	W 3-1
16 Nov	F	A	Luton Town	L 0-3
19 Nov	WDC	H	Gravesend	W 3-2
21 Nov	F	H	Blackpool	L 0-2
28 Nov	SLge	H	Millwall	L 1-3
5 Dec	SLge	A	Reading	L 1-2
12 Dec	FC	H	Old St Stphns	W 4-0
16 Dec	WDC	A	Wolverton	W 2-0
19 Dec	F	A	Clapton	W 2-1
25 Dec	SLge	A	Millwall	L 0-4
26 Dec	F	H	Vampires	W 4-0
26 Dec	F	H	3rd Gren Gds	L 2-3
29 Dec	F	H	Northfleet	W 4-0
6 Jan	FC	H	Maidenhead	W 6-0
9 Jan	SLge	A	Swindon	L 0-1
11 Jan	F	A	Chatham	L 1-2
16 Jan	FC	A	Luton	L 0-3
23 Jan	F	H	Aston Villa	D 2-2
28 Jan	F	H	Chatham	D 2-2
30 Jan	ULge	A	Wellingbro'	D 2-2
6 Feb	F	H	3rd Gren Gds	W 9-3
10 Feb	F	A	Gravesend	W 3-1
13 Feb	SLge	H	Northfleet	W 5-0
15 Feb	F	A	Southampton	L 0-2
20 Feb	SLge	A	N/Brompton	L 1-2
25 Feb	ULge	A	Woolwich Asnl	D 2-2
27 Feb	ULge	H	Loughbrough	L 1-2
4 Mar	ULge	H	Rushden	W 5-1
6 Mar	SLge	A	Northfleet	L 0-2
9 Mar	F	A	Eastbourne	W 1-0
13 Mar	ULge	A	Luton	L 1-2
15 Mar	ULge	A	Kettering	D 1-1
20 Mar	SLge	H	Reading	D 4-4
25 Mar	F	H	Gravesend	W 3-2
27 Mar	SLge	A	N/Brompton	W 6-0
29 Mar	SLge	A	Southampton	D 1-1
1 Apr	SLge	H	Wolverton	W 2-0
3 Apr	ULge	H	Millwall	L 1-3
5 Apr	WDCsf	*	Rushden	W 2-1
8 Apr	SLge	H	Southampton	D 2-2
10 Apr	ULge	A	Luton	L 1-2
16 Apr	F	H	Nottm Forest	D 1-1
17 Apr	ULge	H	Kettering	D 1-1
19 Apr	ULge	A	Wellingbro'	D 1-1
20 Apr	F	A	Blackburn	L 1-2
22 Apr	F	H	Everton	W 2-1
24 Apr	ULge	A	Loughbrough	L 2-3
26 Apr	F	A	London Caled	D 1-1
29 Apr	WDCf	A	Wellingbro'	L 0-2

* at Wellingborough
† abandoned
‡ void after Royal Ordnance resigned from Southern League

Player	SL App	Goals
Allen	9	
Almond	16	1
Ambler	19	
Briggs	7	1
Burrows	16	
Clements	20	10
Collins	2	
Crump	18	2
Devlin	20	1
Fleming	2	2
Hatfield	1	
Lanham	1	
McElhaney	19	8
Main	1	
Markham	3	
Milliken	19	7
Montgomery	20	
Newbigging	9	2
Payne	18	5
Robertson	1	3
Wilson	5	1

United League 1896–97

	P	W	D	L	F:A	Pts
1 Millwall Ath	14	11	1	2	43:22	23
8 TOTTENHAM	**14**	**1**	**4**	**9**	**25:34**	**6**

Southern League 1896–97

	P	W	D	L	F:A	Pts
1 Soton St Marys	20	15	5	0	63:18	35
4 TOTTENHAM	**20**	**9**	**4**	**7**	**44:32**	**22**

SEASON 1897/98

Date	Comp	H/A	Opponent	Result
2 Sep	F	H	Glossop	W 3-2
4 Sep	Slge	A	Sheppey Utd	D 1-1
9 Sep	F	H	Ryl S. Fuslrs	W 12-0
11 Sep	F	A	Chorley	W 3-1
16 Sep	ULge	H	Kettering	D 1-1
18 Sep	Slge	H	Southampton	W 2-0
23 Sep	F	H	2nd Scts Gds	W 4-1
25 Sep	Slge	A	Millwall	W 7-0
29 Sep	ULge	A	Loughbro'	W 2-1
2 Oct	Slge	A	N/Brompton	L 0-1
7 Oct	F	H	3rd Gren Gds	W 4-0
9 Oct	Slge	H	Gravesend	W 2-0
11 Oct	ULge	A	Luton	L 0-5
16 Oct	ULge	A	Millwall	D 0-0
20 Oct	F	H	Reading	W 2-1
23 Oct	Slge	A	Soutampton	L 1-4
30 Oct	FC	A	Southampton	L 1-4
2 Nov	F	A	Eastbourne	W 2-0
6 Nov	Slge	A	Reading	D 3-3
9 Nov	F	A	N/Brompton	W 3-0
13 Nov	Slge	H	Bristol City	D 2-2
20 Nov	FC	A	Luton	L 3-4
27 Nov	Slge	A	Bristol City	L 1-3
1 Dec	F	A	Gravesend	L 0-3
4 Dec	ULge	H	Wellingbro'	W 5-0
11 Dec	F	H	Kettering	D 1-1
18 Dec	Slge	A	Wolverton	L 2-1
25 Dec	ULge	A	Woolwich Asnl	W 3-2
27 Dec	F	H	Ilkeston	W 4-2
28 Dec	F	H	Stockton	W 3-0
1 Jan	ULge	A	Fushden	L 2-5
8 Jan	ULge	A	Rushden	W 3-1
10 Jan	ULge	A	Kettering	L 2-4
15 Jan	ULge	H	Northfleet	W 4-0
19 Jan	ULge	A	Southampton	D 2-2
22 Jan	Slge	H	Wilverton	W 7-1
27 Jan	F	A	Gravesend	L 1-2
29 Jan	F	A	Chatham	L 2-4
3 Feb	ULge	H	Luton	D 2-2
5 Feb	Slge	A	Swindon	L 0-3
9 Feb	F	A	Sussex	W 2-1
12 Feb	F	H	Sheff Utd	D 1-1
15 Feb	F	H	St Bernards	W 4-0
19 Feb	Slge	A	Northfleet	W 3-1
26 Feb	Slge	H*	Reading	D 1-1
28 Feb	F	A	Chesham	W 4-2
5 Mar	Slge	A	Gravesend	W 2-1
9 Mar	F	A	Tunbridge W	W 5-0
12 Mar	ULge	H	Millwall	W 3-2
17 Mar	ULge	A	Loughbro'	W 5-0
19 Mar	Slge	H	Sheppey Utd	W 4-0
24 Mar	ULge	A	Southampton	W 7-0
26 Mar	F	A	Sunderland	L 0-2
2 Apr	Slge	A	N/Brompton	W 3-1
8 Apr	ULge	A	Woolwich Asnl	W 1-0
9 Apr	Slge	A	Chatham	W 2-1
11 Apr	Slge	A	Swindon	W 2-0
12 Apr .	F	H	Lincoln	W 2-1
16 Apr	Slge	A	Millwall	L 1-3
29 Apr	F	A	Reading	D 3-3
23 Apr	ULge	A	Wellingbro'	D 2-2
25 Apr	F	A	Aston Villa	L 2-3
28 Apr	F	A	Woolwich Asnl	L 0-3
30 Apr	F	H	Bolton	D 2-2

* Game versus Reading played at Millwall as Northumberland Park suspended after attacks on Luton players

Player	SL App	Goals
Ambler	1	
Black D.	20	8
Briggs S.	1	
Burrows L.	9	
Cullen J.	21	
Crump	11	
Davidson J.	17	8
Downie	7	
Hall A.	21	
Hartley A.	15	7
Jones J.L.	20	1
Joyce W.	19	16
Knowles J.	19	
Madden K.	2	
Meade T.	10	5
Montgomery J.	16	
Stormont R.	22	3
Tannahill R.	11	3
Own Goal		1

United League 1897–98

	P	W	D	L	F:A	Pts
1 Luton	16	13	2	1	49:11	28
2 TOTTENHAM	**16**	**8**	**5**	**3**	**40:27**	**21**

Southern League 1897–98

	P	W	D	L	F:A	Pts
1 Southampton	22	18	1	3	53:18	37
3 TOTTENHAM	**22**	**12**	**4**	**6**	**52:31**	**28**

Thames & Medway League 1897–98

	P	W	D	L	F:A	Pts
1 N/Brompton	16	13	1	2	47:15	27
4 TOTTENHAM	**16**	**11**	**0**	**5**	**34:28**	**22**

SEASON 1898/99

Date	Comp	H/A	Opponent	Result
1 Sep	F	H	Gainsbro'	W 6-2
3 Sep	TLge	H	Thames Iron	W 3-0
5 Sep	ULge	H	Luton	W 1-0
10 Sep	Slge	A	Bedminster	D 1-1
12 Sep	F	H	Surrey Wandrs	W 5-0
17 Sep	Slge	H	Sheppey Utd	W 3-2
19 Sep	ULge	A	Luton	W 4-3
24 Sep	Slge	H	Warmley	W 7-1*
26 Sep	TLge	H	Sheppey Utd	W 3-2
1 Oct	F	H	Burton Wand	W 5-2
3 Oct	TLge	H	Gravesend	W 3-1
5 Oct	ULge	A	Brighton Utd	W 2-1
8 Oct	Slge	H	Chatham	W 2-0
10 Oct	ULge	H	Southampton	W 4-0
15 Oct	Slge	A	Bristol	W 1-0
17 Oct	TLge	H	N/Brompton	W 2-1
22 Oct	Slge	A	Millwall	L 2-4
26 Oct	TLge	A	Dartford	W 3-2
29 Oct	FC	A	Wolverton	W 4-0
2 Nov	TLge	A	RETB	W 6-2
5 Nov	Slge	H	Reading	W 3-0
9 Nov	ULge	A	Reading	L 0-1
12 Nov	ULge	A	Bristol City	W 2-1
19 Nov	FC	A	Clapton	D 1-1
23 Nov	FCr	A	Clapton	W 2-1
26 Nov	Slge	A	Ryl Artillery	W 3-2
3 Dec	Slge	A	Bristol City	L 1-2
5 Dec	ULge	A	Kettering	W 3-0
10 Dec	FC	H	Luton	D 1-1
14 Dec	FCr	A	Luton	D 1-1
17 Dec	Slge	A	Sheppey Utd	L 2-3
19 Dec	FC	A	Luton	W 2-0
21 Dec	F	A	Surrey Wandrs	D 1-1
24 Dec	Slge	A	Warmley	W 5-1*
26 Dec	Slge	A	Southampton	D 1-1
27 Dec	F	H	Ilkeston	W 5-0
31 Dec	Slge	A	Swindon	L 3-4
2 Jan	TLge	A	Chatham	W 5-0
7 Jan	Slge	H	Ryl Artillery	W 1-0
9 Jan	Slge	H	Chatham	L 0-4
14 Jan	TLge	A	Gravesend	L 2-4
16 Jan	TLge	H	Sheppey Utd	W 3-0
21 Jan	Slge	A	Brighton utd	W 1-0
23 Jan	ULge	H	Reading	D 1-1
28 Jan	FC	A	Newton Heath	D 1-1
1 Feb	FCr	H	Newton Heath	W 5-3
4 Feb	Slge	A	Reading	L 0-2
v6 Feb	TLge	H	Grays Utd	W 2-1
11 Feb	FC	H	Sunderland	W 2-1
15 Feb	ULge	A	Southampton	L 1-2
18 Feb	Slge	H	Bristol City	W 3-2
20 Feb	ULge	H	Rushden	L 1-2
25 Feb	FC	A	Stoke	L 1-4
27 Feb	ULge	A	Kettering	W 1-0
4 Mar	TLge	H	Millwall	W 1-0
8 Mar	TLge	A	Gravesend	W 3-0
11 Mar	ULge	A	WoolwichAsnl	L 1-2
13 Mar	Slge	A	N/Brompton	D 1-1
16 Mar	TLge	A	Thames Iron	W 3-0
18 Mar	Slge	H	N/Brompton	W 3-0
20 Mar	TLge	H	RETB	L 1-2
22 Mar	TLge	A	Grays	L 0-1
25 Mar	Slge	H	Brighton Utd	L 1-3

Date	Comp		Opponent		Result
27 Mar	ULge	A	Rushden	D	0-0
31 Mar	SLge	H	Southampton	L	0-1
1 Apr	SLge	H	Gravesend	W	3-0
3 Apr	SLge	H	Swindon	D	1-1
4 Apr	ULge	A	Brighton Utd	W	3-0
8 Apr	ULge	A	Chatham	L	0-1
10 Apr	TLge	A	N/Brompton	L	4-5
13 Apr	TLge	H	Dartford	W	9-0
15 Apr	SLge	A	Bedminster	L	0-1
17 Apr	ULge	A	Wellingbro'	L	1-3
22 Apr	SLge	H	Millwall	W	3-1
24 Apr	ULge	H	Wellingbro'	W	5-2
26 Apr	ULge	A	Millwall	L	1-3
29 Apr	ULge	H	Woolwich Asnl	W	3-2

* Warmley resigned from Southern League on
21 January 1899 so their results void

Player	SL App	Goals
Ambler	2	
Atherton	2	
Bradshaw	22	3
Cain R.	22	
Cameron J.	23	11
Cullen J.	19	
Downie E.	4	
Erentz H.	22	
Hall A.	2	
Hartley A.	3	1
Jones J.L.	14	
Joyce W.	19	10
Leach	4	2
McKay C.	17	4
McNaught J.	19	
Meade T.	5	
Melia J.	13	
Rule A.G.	3	2
Smith T.	24	5
Stormont R.	21	
Payne E.	1	
Waller W.H.	3	
Own Goals		2

United League 1898–99

1 Millwall Ath	20	14	3	3	42:19	31
4 TOTTENHAM	20	11	2	7	36:25	24

Southern League 1898–99

1 Southampton	24	15	5	4	54:24	35
7 TOTTENHAM	24	10	4	10	40:36	24

SEASON 1899/1900

Date	Comp		Opponent		Result
2 Sep	Slge	A	Millwall	W	3-1
4 Sep	F	H	Notts Co	W	4-1
9 Sep	SLge	H	QPR	W	1-0
13 Sep	F	A	Richmond	W	3-1
16 Sep	SLge	A	Chatham	W	3-2
18 Sep	SDC	H	Portsmouth	W	2-0
23 Sep	SLge	H	Reading	W	2-1
26 Sep	F	A	Clapton	W	4-1
30 Sep	F	A	Southampton	L	1-2
2 Oct	SLge	H	Gravesend	W	4-0
7 Oct	SLge	H	Brighton Utd	W	6-1†
11 Oct	SDC	A	Reading	L	1-2
14 Oct	SLge	A	Bedminster	L	1-2
16 Oct	SDC	H	Millwall	L	1-2
21 Oct	SLge	H	Bristol Rvs	W	1-0*
23 Oct	SDC	A	QPR	W	3-1
28 Oct	F	H	Southampton	W	4-3
30 Oct	SDC	H	Reading	W	3-0
4 Nov	SLge	H	Thames Iron	W	7-0
6 Nov	SDC	H	Chatham	W	8-0
11 Nov	F	H	Ilkeston	W	7-0
15 Nov	SDC	A	Bristol City	D	3-3
18 Nov	F	H	Bolton	W	4-0
20 Nov	SDC	H	QPR	W	3-1
25 Nov	F	H	Corinthians	W	5-1
27 Nov	F	H	Kaffirs	W	6-4
2 Dec	SLge	A	Swindon	W	2-0
4 Dec	SDC	A	Chatham	W	1-0
9 Dec	SLge	H	Bristol City	D	2-2
11 Dec	F	H	Players/South	W	3-2
16 Dec	SLge	A	Cowes	W	6-1†
18 Dec	F	H	HRBourkesXI	W	12-2
25 Dec	SLge	H	Portsmouth	W	3-0
26 Dec	SLge	A	Southampton	L	1-3

Date	Comp		Opponent		Result
30 Dec	SLge	H	Millwall	W	2-1
1 Jan	F	A	Middlesbro'	D	2-2
2 Jan	F	A	Sunderland	W	3-1
6 Jan	SLge	A	QPR	D	0-0
8 Jan	SDC	H	Southampton	W	3-2
13 Jan	SLge	H	Chatham	W	2-1
17 Jan	SDC	H	Portsmouth	D	2-2
20 Jan	SLge	A	Reading	W	1-0
27 Jan	FC	A	Preston	L	0-1
3 Feb	SLge	A	Sheppey Utd	W	4-1
5 Feb	F	H	Oxford Univ	W	7-2
10 Feb	SLge	A	Brighton Utd	W	3-0†
17 Feb	SLge	H	Bedminster	W	5-2
24 Feb	SLge	A	Bristol Rvs	D	2-2
3 Mar	SLge	A	Portsmouth	L	0-1
5 Mar	F	H	Stoke	W	6-0
10 Mar	SLge	A	Thames Iron	D	0-0
12 Mar	SDC	H	Bristol City	W	2-0
17 Mar	F	A	Corinthians	W	3-1
19 Mar	SLge	A	Bristol Rvs	W	5-1
24 Mar	SLge	H	N/Brompton	W	1-0
31 Mar	SLge	A	Gravesend	W	6-2
2 Apr	F	H	Thames Iron	W	3-0
7 Apr	SLge	H	Swindon	W	3-0
13 Apr	SLge	A	Southampton	W	2-0
14 Apr	SLge	A	Bristol City	L	0-3
16 Apr	SLge	H	Sheppey Utd	W	3-0
17 Apr	SDC	H	Woolwich Asnl	W	4-2
21 Apr	F	A	Aston Villa	L	3-4
24 Apr	SDC	A	Woolwich Asnl	L	1-2‡
26 Apr	SDC	A	Millwall	D	0-0
28 Apr	SLge	A	N/Brompton	W	2-1
30 Apr	SLge	A	Southampton	W	4-1

* Abandoned after 55 minutes

† Games void: Brighton United resigned from
Southern League on 10 March, Cowes
resigned from Southern League on 18
December

‡ Game not completed because of crowd
trouble

Players	SL App	Goals
Cameron J.	25	11
Clawley G.	7	
Copeland D.	24	12
Chapman	1	1
Erentz H.	16	
Haddow D.	20	
Hughes E.	1	
Hyde L.	6	2
Jones J.L.	18	
Kirwan J.	26	10
McNaught J.	24	
Melia J.	12	
Morris T.	20	4
Munro	1	
Pratt T.	26	19
Riley	2	
Rule A.G.	4	
Smith T.	24	6
Stormont R.	22	1
Tait A.	28	
Waller W.H.	1	
Own Goal		1

Southern League 1899–1900

1 Southampton	22	18	1	3	53:18	37
3 TOTTENHAM	22	12	4	6	52:31	28

Southern District Combination 1899–1900

1 N/Brompton	16	13	1	2	47:15	27
4 TOTTENHAM*	16	11	0	5	34:28	22

* Match between Woolwich Arsenal and
Spurs at Plumstead abandoned after 55 minutes because of crowd trouble (score stood
at 2-1). Never replayed.

SEASON 1900/01

Date	Comp		Opponent		Result
1 Sep	SLge	H	Millwall	L	0-3
3 Sep	F	A	Bristol Rvs	L	0-1
8 Sep	F	A	Southampton	W	3-1
10 Sep	F	H	Reading	D	3-3
15 Sep	F	H	Chatham	W	5-0†
17 Sep	F	A	Millwall	W	2-1

Date	Comp		Opponent		Result
22 Sep	SLge	A	Bristol City	D	1-1
24 Sep	F	H	Richmond Ass	W	8-0
27 Sep	F	A	Notts Co	L	1-4
29 Sep	SLge	H	Swindon	W	2-0
3 Oct	F	A	Reading	D	1-1
6 Oct	SLge	A	Watford	L	1-2
8 Oct	F	A	Notts Co	D	1-1
13 Oct	F	H	Corinthians	D	2-2
15 Oct	F	H	Millwall	W	1-0
20 Oct	SLge	A	QPR	L	1-2
22 Oct	F	H	Luton	W	3-1
27 Oct	SLge	H	West Ham	D	0-0
31 Oct	F	H	QPR	W	7-0
3 Nov	F	A	Portsmouth	W	3-1
5 Nov	F	H	Camb Univ	W	3-1
10 Nov	SLge	A	N/Brompton	W	2-1
12 Nov	F	A	Luton	L	0-1
17 Nov	WLge	H	Portsmouth	W	8-1
24 Nov	SLge	A	Reading	L	1-3
26 Nov	SLge	H	Bristol City	W	4-1
1 Dec	SLge	H	Kettering	W	1-0
5 Dec	WLge	A	Swindon	W	1-0
8 Dec	WLge	H	Millwall	D	1-1
10 Dec	WLge	A	Bristol Rvs	W	6-0
15 Dec	SLge	A	Millwall	W	2-1
17 Dec	F	H	Preston	D	1-1
22 Dec	WLge	H	Southampton	W	2-0
25 Dec	SLge	H	Portsmouth	W	4-1
26 Dec	SLge	A	Southampton	L	1-3
29 Dec	F	H	Newark	W	3-0
5 Jan	F	H	Clapton	W	3-0
8 Jan	F	H	German XI	W	9-6
12 Jan	SLge	A	Swindon	D	1-1
14 Jan	F	H	CWBrowns XI	W	4-2
19 Jan	F	A	Watford	W	7-0
26 Jan	SLge	H	Bristol Rvs	W	4-0
4 Feb	F	H	Oxford Univ	W	5-2
9 Feb	FC	H	Preston	D	1-1
13 Feb	FCr	A	Preston	W	4-2
16 Feb	SLge	A	West Ham	W	4-1
18 Feb	WLge	H	Reading	W	3-2
23 Feb	FC	H	Bury	W	2-1
27 Feb	SLge	H	Swindon	W	5-0
2 Mar	SLge	H	N/Brompton	W	2-1
6 Mar	WLge	A	Reading	D	1-1
9 Mar	SLge	A	Bristol Rvs	L	0-1
11 Mar	WLge	A	Southampton	D	1-1
16 Mar	SLge	A	Reading	W	1-0
18 Mar	WLge	A	QPR	D	1-1
23 Mar	FC	A	Reading	D	1-1
27 Mar	WLge	A	Bristol City	L	1-4*
28 Mar	FCr	A	Reading	W	3-0
30 Mar	SLge	H	QPR	W	4-1
3 Apr	SLge	A	Gravesend	L	1-2
5 Apr	SLge	H	Southampton	W	1-0
6 Apr	SLge	H	Bristol City	W	1-0
8 Apr	FCsf	‡	WBA	W	4-0
13 Apr	WLge	A	Millwall	W	1-0
15 Apr	WLge	H	QPR	D	2-2
17 Apr	WLge	A	Portsmouth	L	0-1
20 Apr	FCf	‡	Sheff Utd	D	2-2
22 Apr	WLge	A	Bristol Rvs	L	0-4
24 Apr	SLge	A	Portsmouth	L	0-4
25 Apr	SLge	H	Luton	W	3-2
27 Apr	FCfr	‡	Sheff Utd	W	3-1
27 Apr	SLge	H	Gravesend	W	5-0*
29 Apr	SLge	A	Luton	W	4-2
30 Apr	SLge	A	Kettering	D	1-1

* Reserves played these fixtures as first team
playing Cup tie

† Match void as Chatham resigned from
Southern League on 20 December 1900

‡ Semi-final played at Villa Park, Cup final at
Crystal Palace and Cup final replay at Bolton

Players	SL App	Goals
Anson	2	
Brown A.	20	10
Burton	3	1
Buckingham	5	
Cameron J.	21	6
Clawley G.	25	
Erentz H.	21	
Forthum	2	1
Haddow D.	3	
Hawley	3	2
Hudson	1	
Hughes E.	19	2

	SL App	Goals
Hyde L.	8	4
Jones A.E.	6	1
Jones J.L.	17	3
Kirwan J.	20	5
McNaught J.	18	
Melia J.	10	1
Moffat	5	3
Moles J.	3	
Morris T.	19	3
Pangbourn T.	2	
Smith T.	17	2
Stevenson	3	
Stormont R.	22	5
Tait A.	22	
Woodward V.J.	2	2
Own Goal		1

Southern League 1900–01

1 Southampton	28	18	5	5	58:26	41
5 TOTTENHAM	28	16	4	8	55:33	36

Western League 1900–01

1 Portsmouth	16	11	2	3	36:23	24
3 TOTTENHAM	16	8	5	3	37:19	21

SEASON 1901/02

Date	Comp		Opponent		Result
2 Sep	F	H	Hearts	D	0-0
7 Sep	SLge	H	Millwall	W	2-0
9 Sep	Wlge	H	Reading	W	4-0
14 Sep	SLge	H	QPR	W	2-0
16 Sep	LLge	A	Woolwich Asnl	W	2-0
21 Sep	SLge	A	Reading	D	1-1
23 Sep	F	A	Sheff Utd	L	1-3
28 Sep	WLge	H	Southampton	W	5-0
30 Sep	WLge	A	QPR	W	3-1
5 Oct	SLge	A	Bristol Rvs	W	2-1
7 Oct	WLge	H	Millwall	W	3-1
12 Oct	SLge	H	N/Brompton	W	3-1
14 Oct	WLge	H	West Ham	W	2-0
16 Oct	F	H	Rest Sth Lge	W	2-0
19 Oct	SLge	A	Northampton	L	1-3
21 Oct	WLge	H	Bristol rvs	W	4-1
26 Oct	SLge	H	Watford	W	8-1
2 Nov	SLge	A	West Ham	W	1-0
4 Nov	LLge	A	Woolwich Asnl	W	5-0
9 Nov	SLge	A	Wellingborough	W	1-0
11 Nov	WLge	H	Swindon	W	6-0
13 Nov	F	A	West Norwood	W	3-1
16 Nov	WLge	A	Portsmouth	L	1-3
18 Nov	WLge	A	Bristol Rvs	W	4-0
23 Nov	SLge	A	Swindon	W	3-1
2 Dec	F	A	Army Assoc	W	2-1
7 Dec	SLge	A	Kettering	W	2-0
9 Dec	WLge	H	QPR	W	3-2
14 Dec	F	A	Corinthians	L	0-3
16 Dec	LLge	A	West Ham	L	1-3
21 Dec	SLge	A	Millwall	D	1-1
25 Dec	SLge	H	Portsmouth	L	1-2
26 Dec	SLge	A	Southampton	L	0-1
28 Dec	SLge	A	QPR	W	3-0
1 Jan	F	A	Everton	L	1-3
2 Jan	F	A	Hearts	L	1-3
4 Jan	SLge	H	Reading	W	4-2
6 Jan	LLge	A	Millwall	D	1-1
11 Jan	WLge	A	Southampton	L	1-5
15 Jan	WLge	A	Reading	D	1-1
18 Jan	SLge	H	Bristol Rvs	W	1-0
25 Jan	FC	H	Southampton	D	1-1
29 Jan	FCr	A	Southampton	D	2-2
1 Feb	SLge	H	Northampton	W	1-0
3 Feb	FCr	*	Southampton	L	1-2
8 Feb	SLge	A	Watford	W	3-0
10 Feb	LLge	H	QPR	L	1-5
15 Feb	SLge	H	West Ham	L	1-2
17 Feb	WLge	A	Millwall	W	3-1
22 Feb	SLge	H	Wellingborough	W	3-0
1 Mar	SLS	H	Corinthians	W	5-2
8 Mar	SLge	H	Swindon	W	7-1
10 Mar	WLge	A	West Ham	D	1-1
15 Mar	SLge	A	Brentford	L	1-2
17 Mar	WLge	H	Portsmouth	D	0-0
22 Mar	SLge	H	Kettering	W	4-0
24 Mar	LLge	H	Millwall	D	1-1
28 Mar	SLge	H	Southampton	D	2-2
29 Mar	SLge	A	Luton	D	0-0
31 Mar	SLge	A	Portsmouth	L	0-1

Date	Comp	H/A	Opponent	Result
1 Apr	F	H	Sheff Utd	W 3-2
5 Apr	SLge	A	N/Brompton	D 0-0
9 Apr	WLge	A	Swindon	W 1-0
12 Apr	SLge	H	Luton	D 0-0
14 Apr	LLge	A	QPR	W 2-1
21 Apr	LLge	H	West Ham	D 2-2
23 Apr	SDCC	A	Woolwich Asnl	D 0-0
26 Apr	F	H	Brentford	W 3-0
28 Apr	F	H	Preston	L 1-2
29 Apr	SDCCr	H	Woolwich Asnl	W 2-1
30 Apr	F	A	Portsmouth	W 2-0

* FA Cup 2nd replay (at Reading FC)

Player	SL App	Goals
Barlow J.	3	1
Brown A.	26	18
Burton J.H.	2	
Cameron J.	24	13
Clawley G.	20	
Copeland D.	29	9
Erentz H.	30	
Fitchie T.T.	1	
Gilhooly P.	9	1
Griffiths F.J.	9	
Haig-Brown A.R.	2	
Hughes E.	22	1
Hyde L.	2	
Jones J.L.	26	1
Kirwan J.	28	10
McNaught J.	17	
Moles J.	1	
Morris T.	26	3
Soulsby T.	1	
Smith T.	23	4
Stevenson	1	
Tait A.	26	
Woodward V.J.	2	

Southern League 1901–1902

1 Portsmouth	30	20	7	3	67:24	47
2 TOTTENHAM	30	18	6	6	61:22	42

Western League 1901–1902

1 Portsmouth	16	13	1	2	53:16	27
2 TOTTENHAM	16	11	3	2	42:17	25

London League 1901–1902

1 West Ham	8	5	1	2	18:09	11
2 TOTTENHAM	8	3	2	2	15:13	9

SEASON 1902/03

Date	Comp	H/A	Opponent	Result
6 Sep	SLge	H	QPR	D 0-0
8 Sep	SCC	A	West Ham	W 2-1
13 Sep	WLge	A	Southampton	D 1-1
15 Sep	WLge	H	Millwall	W 4-3
20 Sep	SLge	H	Wellingborough	W 6-1
22 Sep	WLge	A	QPR	W 2-0
27 Sep	SLge	A	Bristol Rvs	L 2-3
29 Sep	WLge	H	Reading	W 2-1
4 Oct	SLge	H	Northampton	W 2-0
6 Oct	LLge	A	Brentford	W 5-1
11 Oct	Slge	A	Watford	W 2-1
13 Oct	WLge	H	Bristol Rvs	L 0-1
18 Oct	SLge	H	Brentford	W 3-1
20 Oct	LLge	A	West Ham	D 0-0
25 Oct	Slge	A	Millwall	L 0-2
29 Oct	WLge	A	Reading	L 0-3
1 Nov	SLge	H	West Ham	D 1-1
3 Nov	WLge	H	QPR	W 3-0
8 Nov	F	H	Portsmouth	D 0-0
10 Nov	F	H	Camb Univ	W 2-1
15 Nov	F	A	Corinthians	W 3-1
17 Nov	LLge	A	Woolwich A	L 1-2
22 Nov	SLge	H	Swindon	W 2-0
24 Nov	SCC	H	Reading	D 1-1
29 Nov	WLge	A	Portsmouth	D 2-2
1 Dec	LLge	H	Woolwich A	W 1-0
6 Dec	SLge	H	Luton	D 1-1
8 Dec	F	H	London FA	D 2-2
10 Dec	F	A	West Norwood	W 9-0
13 Dec	F	H	Corinthians	D 2-2
15 Dec	LLge	H	West Ham	W 4-0
20 Dec	SLge	A	QPR	W 4-0
25 Dec	SLge	H	Portsmouth	D 2-2
26 Dec	SLge	A	Southampton	W 1-0
27 Dec	WLge	H	Southampton	D 0-0
3 Jan	SLge	A	Wellingborough	W 2-0
5 Jan	SLge	H	N/Brompton	W 3-1
10 Jan	SLge	H	Bristol Rvs	W 3-0
12 Jan	LLge	H	Brentford	W 1-0
14 Jan	SCC	A	Reading	L 2-3
17 Jan	SLge	A	Northampton	L 1-3
22 Jan	F	A	Camb Univ	W 1-0
24 Jan	SLge	H	Watford	D 1-1
28 Jan	WLge	A	Millwall	D 1-1
31 Jan	SLge	A	Brentford	D 1-1
7 Feb	FC	H	WBA	D 0-0
11 Feb	FCr	A	WBA	W 2-0
14 Feb	SLge	A	West Ham	L 0-1
16 Feb	WLge	H	West Ham	W 1-0
21 Feb	FC	A	Bristol City	W 1-0
23 Feb	WLge	A	Bristol Rvs	L 0-2
2 Mar	LLge	A	Millwall	W 3-0
7 Mar	FC	H	Aston Villa	L 2-3
19 Mar	WLge	A	Brentford	D 0-0
14 Mar	SLge	H	Kettering	W 4-0
16 Mar	LLge	A	QPR	L 0-1
19 Mar	WLge	A	West Ham	D 0-0
21 Mar	Slge	A	Luton	L 0-3
23 Mar	LLge	H	Millwall	W 1-0
26 Mar	WLge	H	Brentford	W 4-0
28 Mar	SLge	H	Reading	W 2-0
30 Mar	LLge	H	QPR	W 3-0
4 Apr	SLge	A	Reading	D 0-0
6 Apr	F	H	QPR	W 1-0
10 Apr	SLge	H	Southampton	W 2-1
11 Apr	SLge	A	N/Brompton	L 0-3
13 Apr	SLge	A	Portsmouth	L 0-2
14 Apr	SLge	H	Millwall	W 2-0
22 Apr	SLge	A	Swindon	L 0-2
25 Apr	SLge	A	Kettering	L 0-1
30 Apr	F	H	Nottm Forest	W 2-1

Player	SL App	Goals
Barlow J.	4	1
Brown C.	12	
Burton J.H.	11	1
Cameron J.	14	2
Chalmers J.	4	
Clawley G.	30	
Copeland D.	28	8
Dryburgh T.	17	2
Erentz H.	25	
Fredericks	1	
Gilhooly P.	6	3
Haig-Brown A.R.	1	
Houston R.	9	4
Hughes E.	20	3
Jones J.	8	3
Jones J.L.	17	
Kirwan J.	26	7
Morris T.	27	1
Tait A.	25	1
Warner A.	20	8
Watson J.	13	
Woodward V.J.	12	2
Own Goal		1

Southern League 1902–03

1 Southampton	30	20	8	2	83:20	48
4 TOTTENHAM	30	14	7	9	47:31	35

Western League 1902–03

1 Portsmouth	16	10	4	2	34:14	24
4 TOTTENHAM	16	6	7	3	20:14	19

London League Premier Division 1902–03

1 TOTTENHAM	10	7	1	2	19:04	15

SEASON 1903/04

Date	Comp	H/A	Opponent	Result
5 Sep	SLge	A	Fulham	D 0-0
7 Sep	WLge	H	Reading	W 3-1
12 Sep	SLge	H	Millwall	L 0-1
14 Sep	SLge	A	Brentford	D 0-0
19 Sep	SLge	A	QPR	L 0-2
23 Sep	F	A	N/Brompton	L 0-3
26 Sep	SLge	H	Plymouth	L 0-2
28 Sep	SCC	A	Millwall	L 1-3
3 Oct	SLge	A	Reading	D 2-2
5 Oct	WLge	H	QPR	W 3-0
10 Oct	SLge	H	Wellingbro'	W 1-0
14 Oct	WLge	A	Reading	W 2-0
17 Oct	SLge	A	Bristol Rvs	L 0-1
19 Oct	F	H	N/Brompton	W 4-2
24 Oct	SLge	A	Brighton	D 2-2
31 Oct	WLge	A	Portsmouth	W 3-0
2 Nov	WLge	H	Brentford	D 1-1
7 Nov	SLge	H	Northampton	W 2-1
9 Nov	WLge	A	QPR	L 0-2
21 Nov	SLge	H	West Ham	W 2-1
28 Nov	F	H	Brighton	W 7-0
30 Nov	WLge	H	Bristol Rvs	W 2-1
5 Dec	SLge	A	Luton	L 2-3
7 Dec	F	A	Burnley	W 4-0
12 Dec	F	A	Corinthians	W 5-1
14 Dec	WLge	H	West Ham	W 4-1
19 Dec	SLge	A	Kettering	D 3-3
25 Dec	SLge	H	Portsmouth	L 0-1
26 Dec	SLge	A	Southampton	L 0-1
28 Dec	WLge	H	Southampton	W 1-0
2 Jan	SLge	H	Fulham	W 1-0
9 Jan	SLge	H	Millwall	W 1-0
16 Jan	SLge	H	QPR	D 2-2
23 Jan	SLge	A	Plymouth	W 3-1
30 Jan	SLge	H	Reading	W 7-4
6 Feb	FC	A	Everton	W 2-1
13 Feb	SLge	H	Bristol Rvs	W 5-1
20 Feb	FC	A	Aston Villa	0-1*
22 Feb	SLge	H	Swindon	W 1-0
25 Feb	FCr	A	Aston Villa	W 1-0
27 Feb	WLge	H	Portsmouth	D 1-1
29 Feb	SLge	H	Plymouth	W 5-1
5 Mar	FC	H	The Wednsdy	D 1-1
10 Mar	FCr	A	The Wednsdy	L 0-2
12 Mar	SLge	H	Brentford	D 1-1
19 Mar	SLge	A	West Ham	W 2-0
26 Mar	SLge	A	Swindon	D 0-0
28 Mar	WLge	A	Brentford	W 2-1
1 Apr	SLge	H	Southampton	W 2-1
2 Apr	SLge	H	Luton	D 1-1
4 Apr	SLge	A	Portsmouth	L 0-1
5 Apr	SLge	H	N/Brompton	W 1-0
9 Apr	SLge	A	N/Brompton	W 1-0
13 Apr	SLge	A	Brighton	W 2-1
16 Apr	SLge	H	Kettering	W 5-1
18 Apr	WLge	A	West Ham	W 1-0
20 Apr	WLge	A	Plymouth	D 0-0
23 Apr	WLge	A	Southampton	L 0-1
25 Apr	SLge	A	Northampton	W 1-0
27 Apr	WLge	A	Bristol Rvs	W 4-2
30 Apr	SLge	A	Wellingbro'	D 3-3

* Abandoned after crowd invasion. FA ordered replay to be played at Villa Park and fined Spurs £350

Player	SL App	Goals
Berry	3	
Brearley H.	16	3
Brown C.	2	
Burton J.H.	5	
Burton O.	15	
Cameron J.	3	
Chalmers J.	6	1
Copeland D.	32	5
Erentz H.	16	
Gilhooly P.	1	
Hughes E.	24	
Jones J.	25	15
Jones J.L.	20	1
Kirwan J.	28	4
Leach-Lewis A.	1	
McConachie A.	6	
McNaught J.	13	
Mapley	5	
Mearns F.	5	
Milton	1	
Morris T.	22	2
Quinn	1	
Tait A.	25	
Walton J.	12	4
Warner A.	17	3
Watson J.	17	
Williams C.	29	
Woodward V.J.	17	10
Turner A.D.	5	5
Own Goal		1

Southern League 1903–04

1 Southampton	34	22	6	6	75:30	50
2 TOTTENHAM	34	16	11	7	54:37	43

Western League 1903–04

1 TOTTENHAM*	16	11	3	2	32:12	25

SEASON 1904/05

Date	Comp	H/A	Opponent	Result
3 Sep	SLge	H	Fulham	L 0-1
7 Sep	WLge	A	Reading	W 1-0
10 Sep	SLge	A	Watford	W 1-0
12 Sep	F	H	Brighton	W 3-1
17 Sep	SLge	H	Plymouth	W 2-0
19 Sep	F	A	QPR	W 4-1
24 Sep	WLge	A	West Ham	D 0-0
26 Sep	WLge	A	Bristol Rvs	W 1-0
1 Oct	SLge	H	Reading	L 1-3
3 Oct	WLge	A	Millwall	L 2-3
8 Oct	SLge	A	Bristol Rvs	L 1-3
10 Oct	SCC	A	Woolwich Asnl	W 3-1
15 Oct	SLge	H	Northampton	L 0-1
19 Oct	WLge	A	Plymouth	L 0-5
22 Oct	WLge	A	Portsmouth	L 0-1
24 Oct	SLge	A	West Ham	L 0-1
29 Oct	SLge	H	Brentford	D 1-1
31 Oct	F	H	London FA	W 4-1
2 Nov	F	A	Littlehampton	W 7-0
5 Nov	SLge	A	QPR	W 2-1
7 Nov	WLge	H	Reading	D 2-2
12 Nov	SLge	H	Millwall	W 1-0
12 Nov	WLge	A	Fulham	D 0-0*
19 Nov	SLge	A	Brighton	D 1-1
21 Nov	WLge	H	Plymouth	W 2-0
26 Nov	SLge	A	Luton	L 0-1
28 Nov	F	H	Camb Univ	D 2-2
3 Dec	SLge	H	Swindon	W 6-3
5 Dec	F	H	G. Robey's XI	W 2-1
10 Dec	SLge	A	N/Brompton	D 1-1
17 Dec	SLge	H	Wellingboro'	W 8-1
26 Dec	SLge	A	Southampton	D 1-1
27 Dec	SLge	H	Portsmouth	D 1-1
31 Dec	SLge	A	Fulham	L 0-1
2 Jan	WLge	H	Fulham	L 0-5
7 Jan	SLge	H	Watford	W 2-0
9 Jan	SCCsf	H	West Ham	W 10-0
19 Jan	F	H	Corinthians	L 0-2
21 Jan	SLge	H	West Ham	W 1-0
24 Jan	F	A	Camb Univ	D 4-4
28 Jan	SLge	A	Reading	L 2-3
4 Feb	FC	A	Middlesbrough	D 1-1
9 Feb	FCr	H	Middlesbrough	W 1-0
11 Feb	SLge	A	Northampton	W 3-0
18 Feb	FC	H	Newcastle	D 1-1
22 Feb	FCr	A	Newcastle	L 0-4
25 Feb	SLge	A	Brentford	D 0-0
27 Feb	WLge	H	Millwall	W 4-1
4 Mar	SLge	H	QPR	W 5-1
6 Mar	WLge	A	Bristol Rvs	L 1-2
11 Mar	SLge	A	Millwall	W 2-0
18 Mar	SLge	H	Brighton	D 1-1
20 Mar	WLge	A	QPR	D 1-1
25 Mar	SLge	H	Luton	W 1-0
27 Mar	WLge	A	West Ham	D 1-1
29 Mar	WLge	H	Southampton	D 1-1
1 Apr	SLge	A	Swindon	L 0-2
3 Apr	WLge	A	Brentford	L 1-2
5 Apr	SLge	A	Plymouth	L 1-2
8 Apr	SLge	H	N/Brompton	W 2-0
11 Apr	WLge	H	Brentford	D 0-0
15 Apr	SLge	H	Wellingboro'	L 0-1
17 Apr	WLge	A	Portsmouth	L 0-1
21 Apr	SLge	H	Southampton	L 1-2
22 Apr	WLge	A	Southampton	L 0-1
24 Apr	SLge	N	Portsmouth	L 2-3
25 Apr	F	H	Sheff Utd	D 0-0
27 Apr	SCCf	N	Reading	D 0-0
29 Apr	SLge	H	Bristol Rvs	W 1-0
4 May	F	A	Hohen Warte	W 6-0†
7 May	F	A	Everton	L 0-2†
10 May	F	A	Vienna Ath	W 4-1†
12 May	F	A	Torna	W 7-1‡
14 May	F	A	Testgyakor	W 12-1‡
16 May	F	A	Everton	L 0-1‡
21 May	F	A	Slavia	W 8-1‡

* Reserve team appeared at Fulham † In Vienna ‡ In Budapest N at Fulham

Player	Lg App	Goals
Berry	8	
Brearley H.	19	3
Bull W.	26	2
Burton J.	9	
Chapman H.	3	1
Copeland D.	18	2
Eggett	27	
Freeborough	1	
George	3	1
Glen	19	11
Hughes E.	15	2
Kirwan J.	26	3
McCurdy	12	
McNaught J.	8	
Morris T.	29	3
Murray	8	
O'Hagen	14	5
Stansfield H.	23	5
Swann	2	
Tait A.	24	1
Walton J.	19	6
Warner A.	10	6
Watson J.	25	
Williams C.	7	
Woodward V.	20	7
Own Goal		1

Southern League 1904–05

1 Bristol Rvs	34	20	8	6	74:36	48
5 TOTTENHAM	34	15	8	11	53:34	38

Western League 1904–05

1 Plymouth	20	13	4	3	52:18	30
8 TOTTENHAM	20	5	6	9	20:28	16

SEASON 1905/1906

2 Sep	SLge	A	Reading	D	1-1
4 Sep	WLge	H	Reading	W	5-1
9 Sep	SLge	H	Watford	W	1-0
11 Sep	WLge	A	QPR	D	1-1
16 Sep	SLge	A	Brighton	L	0-2
23 Sep	SLge	H	West Ham	W	2-0
25 Sep	WLge	H	Bristol Rvs	L	0-1
30 Sep	SLge	A	Fulham	D	0-0
2 Oct	WLge	H	Plymouth	L	0-2
7 Oct	SLge	H	QPR	W	2-1
11 Oct	WLge	A	Reading	D	0-0
14 Oct	SLge	A	Bristol Rvs	W	2-0
16 Oct	WLge	H	Fulham	W	1-0
21 Oct	SLge	H	N/Brompton	W	6-0
23 Oct	WLge	H	Millwall	W	5-0
28 Oct	WLge	A	Portsmouth	D	0-0
4 Nov	SLge	H	Swindon	W	2-1
6 Nov	WLge	A	West Ham	L	1-4
8 Nov	SCC	H	QPR	W	2-0
11 Nov	SLge	A	Millwall	L	1-2
13 Nov	WLge	H	Brentford	L	2-3
18 Nov	SLge	H	Luton	W	1-0
20 Nov	WLge	A	Fulham	W	3-0
25 Nov	SLge	H	Northampton	W	2-0
27 Nov	F	H	Camb Univ	W	2-1
2 Dec	SLge	A	Brentford	W	3-0
9 Dec	F	H	Corinthians	W	3-1
16 Dec	SLge	A	Plymouth	L	1-2
23 Dec	SLge	H	Southampton	W	5-0
25 Dec	SLge	H	Portsmouth	W	3-1
26 Dec	SLge	A	Southampton	L	0-1
30 Dec	SLge	H	Reading	W	1-0
6 Jan	SLge	A	Watford	D	0-0
13 Jan	FC	H	Burnley	W	2-0
20 Jan	SLge	H	Brighton	W	3-1
24 Jan	F	A	Camb Univ	L	1-4
27 Jan	SLge	A	West Ham	W	1-0
29 Jan	WLge	H	QPR	L	1-2
3 Feb	FC	H	Reading	W	3-2
10 Feb	SLge	A	QPR	D	0-0
12 Feb	SLge	H	Fulham	L	0-1
17 Feb	SLge	A	Bristol Rvs	D	2-2
19 Feb	WLge	A	Millwall	D	1-1
24 Feb	FC	H	Birmingham	D	1-1
26 Feb	WLge	H	Brentford	W	1-0
28 Feb	FCr	A	Birmingham	L	0-2
3 Mar	WLge	H	Portsmouth	D	1-1
5 Mar	SLge	H	N/Brompton	L	0-1
10 Mar	SLge	A	Swindon	L	0-2

17 Mar	SLge	A	Millwall	W	3-1
19 Mar	WLge	H	Bristol Rvs	D	0-0
21 Mar	WLge	A	Plymouth	D	0-0
24 Mar	SLge	A	Luton	L	0-2
26 Mar	WLge	A	West Ham	W	1-0
31 Mar	SLge	H	Northampton	D	0-0
7 Apr	SLge	A	Brentford	W	4-1
13 Apr	SLge	H	Southampton	D	1-1
14 Apr	SLge	H	Norwich	L	1-4
16 Apr	SLge	A	Portsmouth	L	0-1
17 Apr	SLge	A	Norwich	W	3-0
21 Apr	SLge	H	Plymouth	L	0-1
23 Apr	SCCsf	H	Woolwich Asnl	D	0-0
25 Apr	WLge	H	Southampton	L	0-1
28 Apr	SCCsfr	A	Woolwich Asnl	L	0-5

Player	SL App	Goals
Berry	4	1
Brearley H.	16	1
Bull W.	30	2
Burton O.	6	
Carrick C.	15	4
Chaplin	2	
Chapman H.	28	11
Darnell J.	10	
Eggett	34	
Freeborough	1	
George	1	
Glen A.	14	2
Hughes E.	22	
Kyle	25	8
Leach-Lewis A.	2	2
Morris T.	32	2
Murray	13	
O'Hagan	7	
Page G.	1	
Shackleton	3	1
Stansfield H.	7	1
Tait A.	27	1
Walton J.	21	5
Watson J.	33	
Whyman A.	7	
Woodward V.J.	12	5

Southern League 1905–06

1 Fulham	34	19	12	3	44:15	50
5 TOTTENHAM	34	16	7	11	46:29	39

Western League 1905–06

1 QPR	20	11	4	5	33:27	26
4 TOTTENHAM*	20	7	7	6	28:17	21v

SEASON 1906/07

1 Sep	SLge	H	West Ham	L	1-2
3 Sep	WLge	H	Plymouth	D	0-0
5 Sep	SLge	A	Watford	D	1-1
8 Sep	SLge	A	Bristol Rvs	L	2-3
10 Sep	WLge	H	Southampton	L	2-3
13 Sep	F	H	London Cal	W	6-4
15 Sep	SLge	A	Swindon	D	0-0
17 Sep	F	H	Ilford	D	4-4
22 Sep	SLge	H	Norwich	D	2-2
24 Sep	SLge	H	Fulham	W	5-1
29 Sep	SLge	A	Luton	L	0-2
3 Oct	WLge	A	Southampton	L	0-2
6 Oct	SLge	H	C. Palace	W	3-0
8 Oct	WLge	A	West Ham	L	0-5
13 Oct	SLge	A	Brentford	D	2-2
20 Oct	WLge	H	Millwall	W	1-0
22 Oct	SCC	H	West Ham	W	2-0
27 Oct	SLge	A	Leyton	D	1-1
29 Oct	SLge	A	Fulham	L	1-2
3 Nov	SLge	H	Portsmouth	D	1-1
7 Nov	WLge	A	Portsmouth	L	0-1
10 Nov	SLge	A	N/Brompton	W	1-0
12 Nov	F	H	Camb Univ	W	4-2
14 Nov	F	A	Corinthians	L	1-6
19 Nov	F	H	Oxford Univ	W	2-1
24 Nov	SLge	A	Brighton	W	2-0
26 Nov	WLge	H	Portsmouth	W	4-2
1 Dec	SLge	H	Reading	W	2-0
8 Dec	F	H	Corinthians	W	5-0
12 Dec	WLge	H	Plymouth	D	2-2*
12 Dec	SLge	H	Plymouth	W	4-2*
15 Dec	SLge	H	Northampton	W	6-0

22 Dec	SLge	A	QPR	L	1-3
25 Dec	SLge	H	Millwall	W	3-1
26 Dec	SLge	A	Southampton	L	1-2
29 Dec	SLge	A	West Ham	L	2-4
5 Jan	SLge	H	Bristol Rvs	W	4-0
12 Jan	FC	H	Hull City	D	0-0
17 Jan	FCr	A	Hull City	D	0-0
19 Jan	SLge	H	Swindon	W	3-0
21 Jan	FCr	H	Hull City	W	1-0
26 Jan	SLge	A	Norwich	L	0-5
2 Feb	FC	H	Blackburn	D	1-1
7 Feb	FCr	A	Blackburn	D	1-1
9 Feb	SLge	A	C. Palace	W	1-0
11 Feb	FCr	§	Blackburn	W	1-0
16 Feb	SLge	H	Brentford	W	2-1
23 Feb	FC	A	Notts Co	L	0-4
2 Mar	SLge	H	Leyton	D	0-0
9 Mar	SLge	A	Portsmouth	L	1-3
16 Mar	SLge	H	N/Brompton	W	2-0
23 Mar	SLge	A	Plymouth	D	0-0
25 Mar	SLge	H	Luton	L	1-2
29 Mar	SLge	H	Southampton	W	2-0
30 Mar	SLge	H	Brighton	W	3-0
1 Apr	SLge	A	Millwall	L	0-2
2 Apr	F	H	Spurs 1901 XI	L	1-4†
3 Apr	SCC	H	QPR	W	4-0
6 Apr	SLge	A	Reading	L	0-2
8 Apr	WLge	H	West Ham	W	4-2
13 Apr	SLge	H	Watford	D	0-0
15 Apr	F	H	W. Browns XI	W	2-1
20 Apr	SLge	A	Northampton	L	0-2
22 Apr	WLge	A	Millwall	D	0-0
27 Apr	SLge	H	QPR	W	2-0
29 Apr	SCCF	A	Southampton	W	2-0
26 May	F	A	Ostend Club	W	8-1‡
27 May	F	A	Fulham	W	2-1‡

* Spurs played Plymouth twice on the same day in both Southern and Western Leagues. The reserves played the Western League match
† Charity match: current Spurs side v 1901 side. Benefit for S. Mountford
‡ Played in Ostend, Belgium
§ Played at Villa Park

Player	SL App	Goals
Badenoch	1	
Berry	1	
Bull W.	27	2
Burton O.	4	
Brearley H.	18	
Chaplin J.	34	
Chapman H.	11	3
Darnell	2	
Dow	9	3
Eames	7	2
Eggett	5	
Hewitt	31	11
Hughes E.	25	
Jones W.H.	9	
McDiarmid	7	
Morris T.	33	2
Pickett A.	15	4
Reid	26	16
Reilly C.H.	1	
Reilly G.	19	
Stansfield H.	10	2
Steel D.	6	
Tait A.	24	
Walker	9	
Walton J.	34	9
Watson J.	12	
Whitbourne J.	14	
Whyman A.	3	1
Wilkinson	2	
Woodward V.J.	19	8

Southern League 1906–07

1 Fulham	38	20	13	5	58:32	53
6 TOTTENHAM	38	17	9	12	63:45	43

Western League 'B' 1906–07

1 West Ham	10	7	1	2	25:14	15
4 TOTTENHAM	10	3	3	4	13:15	9

SEASON 1907/08

2 Sep	SLge	A	QPR	D	3-3
7 Sep	SLge	A	West Ham	D	1-1
9 Sep	WLge	H	Bristol Rvs	W	10-0
14 Sep	SLge	H	QPR	W	3-2
18 Sep	WLge	A	Bristol Rvs	L	1-2
21 Sep	SLge	H	N/Brompton	W	2-1
23 Sep	WLge	A	Millwall	L	0-2
28 Sep	SLge	A	Swindon	L	0-1
30 Sep	SCC	H	Millwall	L	0-1
2 Oct	WLge	A	Reading	W	2-1
5 Oct	SLge	H	C. Palace	L	1-2
7 Oct	WLge	H	West Ham	W	2-1
12 Oct	SLge	A	Luton	L	1-3
14 Oct	WLge	A	Reading	L	0-2
19 Oct	SLge	H	Brighton	D	1-1
21 Oct	F	H	Ilford	W	10-0
23 Oct	WLge	A	C. Palace	L	0-2
26 Oct	SLge	A	Portsmouth	W	2-1
28 Oct	F	H	Clapton	W	2-0
2 Nov	SLge	H	Bradford PA	D	0-0
4 Nov	WLge	A	West Ham	W	3-1
9 Nov	WLge	A	Millwall	W	2-1
16 Nov	SLge	H	Brentford	W	1-0
18 Nov	SCC	A	Millwall	L	1-2
23 Nov	SLge	A	Bristol Rvs	D	0-0
25 Nov	WLge	H	Millwall	L	0-3
30 Nov	SLge	A	Leyton	W	1-0
2 Dec	WLge	H	C. Palace	W	1-0
7 Dec	SLge	A	Reading	L	1-3
v9 Dec	WLge	A	Luton	W	5-1
14 Dec	SLge	H	Watford	W	5-0
16 Dec	WLge	H	Luton	W	2-0
21 Dec	SLge	H	Norwich	W	3-0
25 Dec	SLge	H	Northampton	W	2-0
26 Dec	SLge	A	Southampton	D	1-1
28 Dec	SLge	A	Northampton	L	1-2
4 Jan	SLge	H	West Ham	W	3-2
11 Jan	FC	A	Everton	L	0-1
18 Jan	SLge	A	N/Brompton	W	2-1
20 Jan	SLge	A	Plymouth	L	0-1
25 Jan	SLge	H	Swindon	W	1-0
1 Feb	F	H	Woolwich Asnl	L	0-1
8 Feb	SLge	H	Luton	L	1-2
12 Feb	SLge	A	C. Palace	W	2-0
15 Feb	SLge	A	Brighton	L	0-2
22 Feb	F	A	Chelsea	D	1-1
29 Feb	SLge	A	Bradford PA	W	2-1
7 Mar	SLge	H	Millwall	L	1-2
14 Mar	SLge	A	Brentford	L	0-3
21 Mar	SLge	H	Bristol Rvs	L	1-2
28 Mar	SLge	A	Leyton	W	5-2
4 Apr	SLge	H	Reading	W	2-0
6 Apr	SLge	A	Portsmouth	L	2-3
11 Apr	SLge	A	Watford	D	2-2
17 Apr	SLge	H	Southampton	W	3-0
18 Apr	SLge	A	Norwich	L	1-2
20 Apr	SLge	A	Plymouth	L	0-1
30 Apr	F	A	Clapton	L	0-2

Player	SL App	Goals
Brewster	1	
Bull W.	21	3
Burton O.	31	
Chaplin J.	30	
Coquet E.	6	
Cousins	2	
Darnell J.	22	
Dixon A.	5	
Gray	15	
Hughes E.	1	
McNair W.	15	6
Manning G.	33	
Middlemiss H.	25	8
Minter W.J.	9	4
Morris T.	32	
Pass J.E.	18	5
Payne G.	6	3
Pickett A.E.	13	2
Reid	11	2
Seeburg M.P.	15	4
Stansfield H.	8	1
Steel D.	25	1
Tait A.	1	
Walker R.H.	11	2
Walton J.	21	1
Watson J.	3	

Player	Lg App	Goals
Whitbourne J.G.	5	
Whyman A.	8	
Woodruff C.L.	5	3
Woodward V.J.	20	10
Own Goals		4

Southern League 1907–08

1 QPR	38	21	9	8	82:57	51
7 TOTTENHAM	**38**	**17**	**7**	**14**	**59:48**	**41**

Western League 'B' 1907–08

1 Millwall	12	9	2	1	31:15	20
2 TOTTENHAM	**12**	**7**	**0**	**5**	**26:13**	**14**

SEASON 1908/09

1 Sep	Lge	H	Wolves	W	3-0
5 Sep	Lge	A	Leeds	L	0-1
12 Sep	Lge	A	Barnsley	W	4-0
19 Sep	Lge	H	Bolton	W	2-1
26 Sep	Lge	A	Hull	L	0-1
3 Oct	Lge	H	Derby	D	0-0
5 Oct	LCC	H	QPR	W	1-0
10 Oct	Lge	A	Blackpool	D	1-1
17 Oct	Lge	H	Chesterfield	W	4-0
24 Oct	Lge	A	Glossop	D	1-1
31 Oct	Lge	A	Stockport	D	0-0
2 Nov	LPCF	H	Clapton	D	1-1
7 Nov	Lge	A	WBA	L	0-3
14 Nov	Lge	H	Birmingham	W	4-0
21 Nov	Lge	A	Gainsbro'	W	2-0
28 Nov	Lge	A	Grimsby	W	2-0
30 Nov	LCC	A	West Ham	W	2-0
5 Dec	Lge	A	Fulham	W	3-2
12 Dec	Lge	H	Burnley	W	4-2
19 Dec	Lge	A	Bradford PA	W	2-0
25 Dec	Lge	A	Oldham	L	0-1
26 Dec	Lge	H	Oldham	W	3-0
28 Dec	Lge	A	Wolves	L	0-1
2 Jan	Lge	H	Leeds	W	3-0
9 Jan	Lge	A	Barnsley	D	1-1
16 Jan	FC	A	Man City	W	4-3
23 Jan	Lge	A	Bolton	W	1-0
30 Jan	Lge	H	Hull	D	0-0
6 Feb	FC	H	Fulham	W	1-0
13 Feb	Lge	H	Blackpool	W	4-1
20 Feb	FC	H	Burnley	D	0-0
24 Feb	FCr	A	Burnley	L	1-3
27 Feb	Lge	H	Glossop	D	3-3
6 Mar	Lge	A	Stockport	W	3-1
8 Mar	Lge	A	Chesterfield	W	3-1
13 Mar	Lge	H	WBA	L	1-3
20 Mar	Lge	A	Birmingham	D	3-3
22 Mar	LCC	A	Millwall	L	0-2
27 Mar	Lge	H	Gainsbro'	D	1-1
3 Apr	Lge	A	Grimsby	W	2-1
9 Apr	Lge	H	Clapton	L	0-1
10 Apr	Lge	H	Fulham	W	1-0
12 Apr	Lge	A	Clapton	D	0-0
17 Apr	Lge	A	Burnley	W	2-1
24 Apr	Lge	H	Bradford PA	W	3-0
28 Apr	Lge	A	Derby	D	1-1
29 Apr	Lge	A	Clapton	W	3-2
5 Jun	F	*	Everton	D	2-2
10 Jun	F	*	Uruguay Lge	W	8-0
13 Jun	F	*	Argentinos	W	1-0
16 Jun	F	*	Liga Argentina	W	4-1
19 Jun	F	*	Everton	L	0-4
20 Jun	F	*	Rosario	W	9-0
24 Jun	F	*	Alumini	W	5-0

* Tour of Uruguay and Argentina

Player	Lg App	Goals
Boreham F.	8	
Brough J.	1	
Bull W.	12	
Burton O.	33	
Coquet E.	37	
Curtis J.	2	1
Darnell J.	37	
Hewitson R.	30	
Leslie T.	2	
MacFarlane D.	16	2
Massey F.J.	1	
Middlemiss H.	38	14
Minter W.J.	34	14

Player	Lg App	Goals
Morris T.	24	1
Morton J.	2	
Seeburg M.P.	1	
Steel R.	37	12
Steel D.	38	1
Watson J.	24	2
Wilkes F.	6	
Woodruff C.L.	8	1
Woodward V.J.	27	19

Final table for Second Division

1 Bolton	38	24	4	10	59:28	52
2 TOTTENHAM	**38**	**20**	**11**	**7**	**67:32**	**51**

SEASON 1909/10

1 Sep	Lge	A	Sunderland	L	1-3
4 Sep	Lge	A	Everton	L	2-4
11 Sep	Lge	A	Man Utd	D	2-2
18 Sep	Lge	A	Brad City	L	1-5
20 Sep	LCC	A	Nunhead	W	9-0
25 Sep	Lge	H	Sheff Wed	W	3-0
29 Sep	F	A	Reading	W	3-2
2 Oct	Lge	A	Bristol C	D	0-0
9 Oct	Lge	H	Bury	W	1-0
11 Oct	LCC	H	Croydon	W	7-1
16 Oct	Lge	H	Middlesbro	L	1-3
30 Oct	Lge	H	Notts Co	L	1-3
1 Nov	LPCF	H	Arsenal	W	3-0
6 Nov	Lge	A	Newcastle	L	0-1
8 Nov	LCCsf	*	QPR	D	0-0
13 Nov	Lge	H	Liverpool	W	1-0
15 Nov	LCCsfr	†	QPR	W	4-1
20 Nov	Lge	A	Aston Villa	L	2-3
22 Nov	Lge	A	Preston	L	1-4
27 Nov	Lge	H	Sheff Utd	W	2-1
4 Dec	Lge	A	Arsenal	L	0-1
6 Dec	LCCf	*	Fulham	L	1-4
11 Dec	Lge	H	Bolton	D	1-1
18 Dec	Lge	A	Chelsea	L	1-2
25 Dec	Lge	H	Nottm For	D	2-2
27 Dec	Lge	A	Nottm For	D	2-2
1 Jan	Lge	A	Blackburn	L	0-2
8 Jan	Lge	H	Everton	W	3-0
15 Jan	FC	A	Plymouth	D	1-1
19 Jan	FCr	H	Plymouth	W	7-1
22 Jan	Lge	A	Man Utd	L	0-5
29 Jan	Lge	H	Bradford C	D	0-0
5 Feb	FC	A	Chelsea	W	1-0
12 Feb	Lge	H	Bristol C	W	3-2
19 Feb	FC	A	Swindon	L	2-3
26 Feb	Lge	A	Middlesbro	L	3-4
5 Mar	Lge	H	Preston	W	2-1
12 Mar	Lge	A	Notts Co	L	0-3
14 Mar	Lge	H	Sheff Utd	D	1-1
19 Mar	Lge	H	Newcastle	L	0-4
25 Mar	Lge	H	Sunderland	W	5-1
26 Mar	Lge	A	Liverpool	L	0-2
29 Mar	Lge	H	Blackburn	W	4-0
2 Apr	Lge	H	Aston Villa	D	1-1
9 Apr	Lge	A	Sheff Utd	D	1-1
16 Apr	Lge	H	Arsenal	D	1-1
20 Apr	Lge	A	Bury	L	1-3
23 Apr	Lge	A	Bolton	W	2-0
30 Apr	Lge	H	Chelsea	W	2-1

Player	Lg App	Goals
Bentley F.W.	19	
Boreham F.	12	
Brown D.C.	1	
Brown I.	8	
Burton O.	4	
Coquet E.	27	
Curtis J.	37	3
Darnell J.	25	
Drabble F.	1	
Elkin R.H.	8	
Harris W.	7	
Humphreys P.	20	13
Joyce J.W.	23	
Kennedy J.J.	2	
Kerry A.H.G.	1	
Leslie T.	7	
Lunn T.H.	2	
Lyle A.	1	
MacFarlane D.	5	
Middlemiss H.	36	9

Player	Lg App	Goals
Minter W.J.	38	15
Morris T.	26	1
Newman E.	1	
Steel A.	1	
Steel D.	36	2
Steel R.	38	9
Tull W.D.	7	1
Wilkes F.	23	
Woodruff C.L.	2	

Final table for First Division

1 Aston Villa	38	23	7	8	84:42	53
15 TOTTENHAM	**38**	**11**	**10**	**17**	**53:69**	**32**

SEASON 1910/11

1 Sep	Lge	A	Everton	L	0-2
3 Sep	Lge	H	Sheff Wed	W	3-1
10 Sep	Lge	A	Bristol C	W	2-0
17 Sep	Lge	H	Newcastle	L	1-2
19 Sep	LCC	H	Clapton	W	1-0
24 Sep	Lge	A	Oldham	L	0-2
1 Oct	Lge	A	Middlesbrough	L	0-2
3 Oct	LPCF	A	Chelsea	W	3-0
8 Oct	Lge	H	Preston	D	1-1
10 Oct	LCC	H	Chelsea	W	3-0
15 Oct	Lge	A	Notts Co	L	0-1
22 Oct	Lge	H	Man Utd	D	2-2
29 Oct	Lge	A	Liverpool	L	1-2
5 Nov	Lge	H	Bury	W	5-0
7 Nov	LCCsf	A	Millwall	D	2-2*
12 Nov	Lge	A	Sheff Utd	L	0-3
19 Nov	Lge	H	Aston Villa	L	1-2
21 Nov	LCCsfr	A	Millwall	W	2-0*
26 Nov	Lge	A	Sunderland	L	0-4
3 Dec	Lge	H	Arsenal	W	3-1
5 Dec	LCCf	†	Fulham	W	2-1
10 Dec	Lge	A	Brad City	L	0-3
17 Dec	Lge	H	Blackburn	D	2-2
24 Dec	Lge	A	Nottm Forest	W	2-1
26 Dec	Lge	H	Nottm Forest	L	1-4
27 Dec	Lge	H	Man City	D	1-1
31 Dec	Lge	A	Sheff Wed	L	1-2
3 Jan	Lge	A	Man City	L	1-2
7 Jan	Lge	A	Bristol City	W	3-2
14 Jan	FC	H	Millwall	W	2-1
21 Jan	Lge	A	Newcastle	D	1-1
4 Feb	FC	A	Blackburn	D	0-0
9 Feb	FCr	H	Blackburn	L	0-2
11 Feb	Lge	A	Preston	L	0-1
13 Feb	Lge	H	Middlesbrough	W	6-2
18 Feb	Lge	H	Notts Co	W	3-0
25 Feb	Lge	A	Aston Villa	L	0-4
4 Mar	Lge	H	Liverpool	W	1-0
11 Mar	Lge	A	Bury	L	1-2
15 Mar	Lge	A	Man Utd	L	2-3
18 Mar	Lge	H	Sheff Wed	W	2-1
27 Mar	Lge	H	Oldham	W	2-0
1 Apr	Lge	H	Sunderland	D	1-1
8 Apr	Lge	A	Arsenal	L	0-2
15 Apr	Lge	H	Brad City	W	2-0
17 Apr	Lge	H	Everton	L	0-1
22 Apr	Lge	H	Blackburn	L	0-3
7 May	F	‡	Nth German XI	W	4-1
13 May	F	‡	Preussen	W	7-0
14 May	F	‡	Hertha	W	4-1
20 May	F	‡	Wacker	W	8-1
21 May	F	‡	Eintracht F.	W	4-1
25 May	F	‡	Kickers Vict	W	6-0

* Played at Leyton
† Final played at Stamford Bridge
‡ German tour

Player	Lg App	Goals
Bentley F.W.	16	
Birnie E.L.	4	1
Brown I.	4	
Bulling E.	2	
Collins T.	25	
Coquet E.	13	
Crompton E.	5	
Curtis J.	30	1
Darnell J.	38	2
Elkin R.H.	17	
Foreman T.	2	1
Gosnell A.A.	5	
Humphreys P.	24	10

Player	Lg App	Goals
Joyce J.W.	4	
Kennedy J.J.	7	1
Leslie T.	1	
Lunn T.H.	34	
McTavish J.K.	7	
McTavish R.	11	2
Middlemiss H.	30	4
Minter W.J.	38	19
Morris T.	11	
Newman E.	2	1
Rance C.S.	11	
Steel D.	26	
Steel R.	29	9
Tull W.D.	3	1
Wilkes F.	19	

Final table for First Division

1 Manchester U.	38	22	8	8	72:40	52
15 TOTTENHAM	**38**	**13**	**6**	**19**	**52:63**	**32**

SEASON 1911/12

2 Sep	Lge	A	Everton	D	2-2
4 Sep	Lge	H	Sheff Wed	W	3-1
9 Sep	Lge	H	WBA	W	1-0
16 Sep	Lge	A	Sunderland	D	1-1
18 Sep	LCC	A	Brentford	L	1-4
23 Sep	Lge	A	Blackburn	L	0-2
30 Sep	Lge	A	Sheff Wed	L	0-4
7 Oct	Lge	H	Bury	W	2-1
14 Oct	Lge	A	Middlesbro	L	0-2
21 Oct	Lge	A	Notts Co	D	2-2
23 Oct	LPCF	H	Fulham	W	3-0
28 Oct	Lge	H	Preston	W	6-2
4 Nov	Lge	A	Man Utd	W	2-1
11 Nov	Lge	A	Liverpool	W	2-1
18 Nov	Lge	A	Aston Villa	D	2-2
25 Nov	Lge	H	Newcastle	L	1-2
2 Dec	Lge	A	Sheff Utd	W	2-1
9 Dec	Lge	H	Oldham	W	4-0
16 Dec	Lge	A	Bolton	L	0-1
23 Dec	Lge	H	Bradford C	L	2-3
25 Dec	Lge	H	Woolwich A.	W	5-0
26 Dec	Lge	A	Woolwich A.	L	1-3
30 Dec	Lge	H	Everton	L	0-1
13 Jan	FC	A	WBA	L	0-3
20 Jan	Lge	A	Sunderland	D	0-0
27 Jan	Lge	A	Blackburn	D	0-0
3 Feb	F	H	C. Orient	W	3-2
10 Feb	Lge	A	Bury	L	1-2
17 Feb	Lge	H	Middlesbro	W	2-1
24 Feb	Lge	A	Newcastle	D	2-2
2 Mar	Lge	A	Preston	W	1-0
13 Mar	Lge	A	WBA	L	0-2
16 Mar	Lge	A	Liverpool	W	2-1
23 Mar	Lge	H	Aston Villa	W	2-1
30 Mar	Lge	A	Newcastle	L	0-2
5 Apr	Lge	A	Man City	L	1-2
6 Apr	Lge	H	Sheff Utd	D	1-1
8 Apr	Lge	H	Man City	L	0-2
9 Apr	Lge	A	Man United	D	1-1
13 Apr	Lge	A	Oldham	L	1-2
18 Apr	F	†	Northampton	L	0-2
20 Apr	Lge	H	Bolton	W	1-0
27 Apr	Lge	A	Bradford C	L	0-3
29 Apr	F	*	Woolwich A.	L	0-3
12 May	F	†	Hull City	L	0-2
16 May	F	‡	Bewegungs	W	3-1
20 May	F	‡	Sport Vienna	W	5-3
24 May	F	‡	Woolwich A.	L	0-4
27 May	F	‡	Varosi Torna	W	4-1
28 May	F	‡	Olympic XI	D	2-2
30 May	F	‡	Olympic XI	W	4-3
2 Jun	F	‡	Olympic XI	L	0-3

* Titanic fund charity match at Shepherd's Bush (QPR ground)
† Bedekker Cup match in Brussels
‡ Tour of Leipzig (first game) and Vienna (remaining six games)

Player	Lg App	Goals
Bentley F.W.	1	
Bliss H.	5	1
Bowering G.	7	
Brittan R.C.	26	
Collins T.	33	

Player	Lg App	Goals
Crompton E.	3	
Curtis J.	9	
Darnell J.	34	1
Elliot J.	5	2
Foreman T.	6	
Grimsdell A.	2	
Humphreys P.	1	
Joyce J.W.	4	
Kennedy J.J.	4	
Lightfoot E.J.	21	
Lunn T.H.	34	
McTavish J.K.	30	3
Mason T.L.	7	1
Middlemiss H.	32	11
Minter W.J.	35	18
Morris T.	9	
Newman E.	19	6
Rance C.S.	17	
Steel D.	29	
Steel R.	30	7
Tattersall W.	2	
Webster F.	6	
Wilkes F.	9	
Young A.	5	3

Final table for First Division

1 Blackburn	38	20	9	9	60:43	49
12 TOTTENHAM	**38**	**14**	**9**	**15**	**53:53**	**37**

SEASON 1912/13

Date	Comp		Opponent		Result
2 Sep	Lge	H	Everton	L	0-2
7 Sep	Lge	H	Sheff Wed	L	2-4
14 Sep	Lge	A	Blackburn	L	1-6
21 Sep	Lge	H	Derby	L	1-2
23 Sep	LCC	H	Bromley	W	3-0
28 Sep	Lge	A	Sunderland	D	2-2
5 Oct	Lge	A	Middlesbro	D	1-1
14 Oct	LPCF	A	Fulham	L	0-1
19 Oct	Lge	A	Man Utd	L	0-2
26 Oct	Lge	H	Aston Villa	D	3-3
28 Oct	LCC	H	C. Palace	D	3-3
2 Nov	Lge	A	Liverpool	L	1-4
4 Nov	Lge	H	Notts Co.	L	0-3
9 Nov	Lge	H	Bolton	L	0-1
11 Nov	LCC	A	C. Palace	L	1-4
16 Nov	Lge	A	Sheff Utd	L	0-4
23 Nov	Lge	H	Newcastle	W	1-0
30 Nov	Lge	A	Oldham	L	1-4
7 Dec	Lge	H	Chelsea	W	1-0
14 Dec	Lge	A	Woolwich A.	W	3-0
21 Dec	Lge	H	Bradford C.	W	2-1
25 Dec	Lge	A	Man City	D	2-2
26 Dec	Lge	H	Man City	W	4-0
28 Dec	Lge	A	Sheff Wed	L	1-2
1 Jan	Lge	A	Everton	W	2-1
4 Jan	Lge	H	Blackburn	L	0-1
11 Jan	FC	H	Blackpool	D	1-1
16 Jan	FCr	*	Blackpool	W	6-1
18 Jan	Lge	A	Derby	L	0-5
25 Jan	Lge	H	Sunderland	L	1-2
1 Feb	FC	A	Reading	L	0-1
8 Feb	Lge	A	Middlesbro	W	5-3
15 Feb	Lge	A	Notts Co.	W	1-0
22 Feb	Lge	H	Sheff Utd	W	1-0
1 Mar	Lge	A	Aston Villa	L	0-1
8 Mar	Lge	H	Liverpool	W	1-0
15 Mar	Lge	A	Bolton	L	0-2
21 Mar	Lge	H	WBA	W	3-1
24 Mar	Lge	A	WBA	L	1-4
29 Mar	Lge	A	Newcastle	L	0-3
31 Mar	Lge	H	Man Utd	D	1-1
5 Apr	Lge	H	Oldham	W	1-0
9 Apr	F	A	Watford	D	0-0
12 Apr	Lge	A	Chelsea	L	0-1
19 Apr	Lge	H	Woolwich A.	D	1-1
26 Apr	Lge	A	Bradford C.	L	1-3
1 May	F	‡	Red Star	W	4-1
4 May	F	‡	French XI	W	9-0

‡ Played in Paris
* Blackpool sold home advantage; game played at White Hart Lane

Player	Lg App	Goals
Bliss H.	18	7
Brittan R.C.	14	
Cantrell J.	25	12

Player	Lg App	Goals
Collins T.	28	1
Curtis J.	4	
Darnell J.	4	
Elliott J.	6	1
Grimsdell A.	25	
Jones G.	7	
Joyce J.W.	20	
Lightfoot E.J.	15	
Lunn T.H.	16	
Middlemiss H.	38	8
Minter W.J.	37	11
Newman E.	3	
Rance C.S.	32	
Steel R.	19	1
Tate J.A.	2	
Tattersall W.	30	3
Upton S.	2	
Walden F.	1	
Webster F.	34	
Weir F.	34	1
Young C.	4	

Final table for First Division

1 Sunderland	38	25	4	9	86:43	54
17 TOTTENHAM	**38**	**3**	**12**	**23**	**26:74**	**18**

SEASON 1913/14

Date	Comp		Opponent		Result
1 Sep	Lge	A	Sheff Utd	W	4-1
6 Sep	Lge	A	Chelsea	W	3-1
8 Sep	Lge	H	Sheff Utd	W	2-1
13 Sep	Lge	A	Derby	D	1-1
20 Sep	Lge	A	Oldham	L	0-3
22 Sep	LCC	H	Metrogas	W	11-2
27 Sep	Lge	H	Man City	W	3-1
4 Oct	Lge	A	Man Utd	L	1-3
11 Oct	Lge	H	Bradford C.	D	0-0
14 Oct	LCC	A	Fulham	W	2-0
18 Oct	Lge	A	Burnley	L	1-3
25 Oct	Lge	H	Blackburn	D	3-3
27 Oct	LPCF	H	C. Palace	L	1-2
1 Nov	Lge	A	Preston	W	2-1
8 Nov	Lge	H	Sunderland	L	1-4
10 Nov	LCCsf	*	Arsenal	W	2-1
15 Nov	Lge	A	Newcastle	L	0-2
22 Nov	Lge	H	Everton	W	4-1
29 Nov	Lge	A	Liverpool	L	1-2
6 Dec	Lge	H	WBA	W	3-0
8 Dec	LCCf	†	C. Palace	W	2-0
13 Dec	Lge	A	Aston Villa	D	3-3
20 Dec	Lge	H	Sheff Wed	D	1-1
26 Dec	Lge	H	Middlesbro	L	0-1
27 Dec	Lge	H	Chelsea	L	1-2
1 Jan	Lge	A	Bolton	L	0-3
3 Jan	Lge	A	Derby	L	0-4
10 Jan	FC	A	Leicester	D	5-5
15 Jan	FCr	H	Leicester	W	2-0
17 Jan	Lge	H	Oldham	W	3-1
24 Jan	Lge	A	Man City	L	1-2
31 Jan	FC	A	Man City	L	1-2
7 Feb	Lge	H	Man Utd	W	2-1
14 Feb	Lge	A	Bradford C	L	1-2
21 Feb	Lge	H	Burnley	W	2-0
28 Feb	Lge	A	Blackburn	D	1-1
5 Mar	F	H	Mus. Hall Arts	W	3-0
7 Mar	F	H	Preston	W	1-0
14 Mar	Lge	A	Sunderland	L	0-2
21 Mar	Lge	H	Newcastle	D	0-0
28 Mar	Lge	A	Everton	D	1-1
4 Apr	Lge	H	Liverpool	D	0-0
10 Apr	Lge	H	Bolton	W	3-0
11 Apr	Lge	A	WBA	D	1-1
13 Apr	Lge	A	Middlesbro	L	0-6
18 Apr	Lge	H	Aston Villa	L	0-2
25 Apr	Lge	A	Sheff Wed	L	0-2
3 May	F	‡	Hanover	W	6-3
6 May	F	‡	Nuremburg	D	1-1
9 May	F	‡	Bayern FC	W	6-0
10 May	F	‡	Furth	D	2-2
13 May	F	‡	Milan	W	5-0
17 May	F	‡	Zurich	W	6-0
21 May	F	‡	St Gallen	W	3-0
23 May	F	‡	Pforzheim	W	5-0
24 May	F	‡	Stuttgart	W	1-0

* Played at Stamford Bridge
† Played at Highbury
‡ Tour of Germany and Switzerland

Player	Lg App	Goals
Banks J.A.	5	

Player	Lg App	Goals
Banks J.A.	12	
Bauchop J.R.	10	6
Bliss H.	29	6
Bowler G.	3	
Cantrell J.	33	15
Cartwright W.	13	
Clay T.	15	
Collins T.	15	
Crowl S.R.	1	
Darnell J.	1	
Elliott J.E.	1	
Fleming J.B.M.	8	1
Grimsdell A.	37	1
Joyce J.W.	17	1
King A.	19	
Lightfoot E.J.	2	1
Middlemiss H.	34	4
Minter W.J.	16	5
Newman E.	5	
Oliver W.	2	
Sparrow H.	3	4
Steel R.	37	
Tate J.A.	2	
Tattersall W.	7	
Walden F.	30	5
Webster F.	33	
Weir F.	33	
Own Goal		1

Final table for First Division

1 Blackburn	38	20	11	7	78:42	51
17 TOTTENHAM	**38**	**12**	**10**	**16**	**50:62**	**34**

SEASON 1914/15

Date	Comp		Opponent		Result
22 Aug	WRF	H	Arsenal	L	1-5
2 Sep	Lge	H	Everton	L	1-3
5 Sep	Lge	H	Chelsea	D	1-1
12 Sep	Lge	A	Bradford C.	D	2-2
19 Sep	Lge	A	Burnley	L	1-3
21 Sep	LCC	A	Nunhead	W	2-1
26 Sep	Lge	A	Man City	L	1-2
28 Sep	Lge	H	WBA	W	2-0
3 Oct	Lge	A	Newcastle	L	0-4
10 Oct	Lge	H	Middlesbro	D	3-3
15 Oct	F	A	Chelsea	D	1-1
17 Oct	Lge	A	Sheff Utd	D	1-1
19 Oct	LCC	A	C. Palace	L	1-3
24 Oct	Lge	A	Aston Villa	L	0-2
28 Oct	LPCF	A	C. Palace	D	2-2
31 Oct	Lge	A	Liverpool	L	2-7
7 Nov	Lge	H	Bradford PA	W	3-0
14 Nov	Lge	A	Oldham	L	1-4
21 Nov	Lge	H	Man Utd	W	2-0
28 Nov	Lge	A	Bolton	L	2-4
5 Dec	Lge	H	Blackburn	L	0-4
12 Dec	Lge	H	Notts Co.	W	2-1
19 Dec	Lge	H	Sunderland	L	0-6
25 Dec	Lge	A	Sheff Wed	L	2-3
26 Dec	Lge	H	Sheff Wed	W	6-1
1 Jan	Lge	A	Everton	D	1-1
2 Jan	Lge	A	Chelsea	D	1-1
9 Jan	FC	H	Sunderland	W	2-1
16 Jan	Lge	H	Bradford C.	D	0-0
23 Jan	Lge	A	Burnley	L	1-3
30 Jan	FC	A	Norwich	L	2-3
6 Feb	F	H	Fulham	D	2-2
13 Feb	Lge	A	Middlesbro	L	5-7
20 Feb	Lge	H	Notts Co	W	2-0
27 Feb	Lge	A	Aston Villa	L	1-3
6 Mar	Lge	H	Liverpool	L	0-1
13 Mar	Lge	A	Bradford PA	L	1-5
15 Mar	Lge	H	Man City	D	2-2
20 Mar	Lge	H	Oldham	W	1-0
27 Mar	Lge	A	Man Utd	D	1-1
2 Apr	Lge	H	Newcastle	D	0-0
3 Apr	Lge	H	Bolton	W	4-2
6 Apr	Lge	A	WBA	L	2-3
10 Apr	Lge	A	Blackburn	L	1-4
17 Apr	F	H	Cameron High.	L	1-2
19 Apr	Lge	H	Sheff Utd	D	1-1
24 Apr	Lge	A	Sunderland	L	0-5

Player	Lg App	Goals
Bliss H.	33	21
Cantrell J.	26	14
Clay T.	38	4
Collins T.	12	
Darnell J.	11	
Eadon J.	5	
Fleming J.B.M.	11	2
Grimsdell A.	8	
Jacques W.	28	
Joyce J.W.	5	
Lightfoot E.J.	23	1
Lowe H.	2	
Middlemiss H.	33	3
Minter W.J.	26	5
Pearson J.	17	
Rance C.S.	3	
Sparrow H.	15	3
Steel R.	36	2
Tattersall W.	5	
Walden F.	38	1
Webster F.	9	
Weir F.	29	1

Final table for First Division

1 Everton	38	19	8	11	76:47	46
20 TOTTENHAM	**38**	**8**	**12**	**18**	**57:90**	**28**

SEASON 1915/16

Date	Comp		Opponent		Result
4 Sep	Lge	A	Arsenal	L	0-2
11 Sep	Lge	H	Brentford	D	1-1
18 Sep	Lge	A	West Ham	D	1-1
25 Sep	Lge	A	Chelsea	L	1-3
2 Oct	Lge	H	C. Palace	L	2-4
9 Oct	Lge	A	QPR	W	4-0
16 Oct	Lge	H	Fulham	W	3-1
23 Oct	Lge	A	C. Orient	D	0-0
30 Oct	Lge	H	Watford	W	3-0
6 Nov	Lge	A	Millwall	L	2-3
13 Nov	Lge	H	Arsenal	D	3-3
20 Nov	Lge	A	Brentford	D	1-1
27 Nov	Lge	H	West Ham	W	3-0
4 Dec	Lge	A	Chelsea	L	1-8
11 Dec	Lge	A	C. Palace	L	2-4
18 Dec	Lge	H	QPR	W	2-1
25 Dec	Lge	H	Croydon Comm	W	3-0
27 Dec	Lge	A	Croydon Comm	D	0-0
1 Jan	Lge	A	Fulham	W	2-0
8 Jan	Lge	H	C. Orient	D	1-1
15 Jan	Lge	A	Watford	W	1-0
22 Jan	Lge	A	Millwall	D	2-2
29 Jan	F	H	C. Orient	L	0-1
5 Feb	LSupp	A	West Ham	L	0-2
12 Feb	LSupp	H	Croydon Comm	W	1-0
19 Feb	LSupp	A	Fulham	L	1-3
26 Feb	LSupp	A	Luton	W	7-4
4 Mar	LSupp	A	Arsenal	W	3-0
11 Mar	LSupp	H	QPR	D	0-0
18 Mar	LSupp	A	Croydon	D	3-3
25 Mar	LSupp	H	Fulham	W	4-0
1 Apr	LSupp	A	Luton	W	2-1
8 Apr	LSupp	H	Arsenal	W	3-2
15 Apr	LSupp	A	QPR	W	3-1
21 Apr	LSupp	H	C. Palace	W	3-1
24 Apr	LSupp	A	C. Palace	L	0-4
26 Apr	F	A	Norwich	D	1-1
29 Apr	LSupp	H	West Ham	D	1-1
6 May	F	A	C. Orient	L	2-3

Player	Lg App	Goals
Banks J.	17	7
Barton P.	29	1
Bassett E.	28	9
Bliss H.	33	23
Chaplin A.	4	
Clay T.	32	4
Darnell J.	15	
Doyle J.	1	
Elliott J.	33	
Fricker F.	1	
Glen P.	1	1
Hopkins T.	3	1
Jacques W.	18	
Joyce J.	17	

Player	War Lg App	Goals
Knighton T.	4	2
Lloyd H.	12	6
Minter A.	3	1
Morris J.	35	3
Page J.	1	
Page R.	3	
Ralston A.	17	
Rance C.	36	4
Steel R.	29	6
Thomas D.	9	1
Travers G.	3	
Watkins W.	1	
Weir F.	1	
Wilson A.	10	

London Combination 1915–16

1 Chelsea	22	17	3	2	71:18	37
6 TOTTENHAM	**22**	**8**	**8**	**6**	**38:35**	**24**

Supplementary Tournament Group 1915–16

1 Chelsea	14	10	1	3	50:15	21
2 TOTTENHAM	**14**	**8**	**3**	**3**	**31:22**	**19**

SEASON 1916/17

2 Sep	Lge	H	Chelsea	L	0-2
9 Sep	Lge	A	Arsenal	D	1-1
16 Sep	Lge	*	Luton	L	2-3
23 Sep	Lge	A	Reading	W	4-2
30 Sep	Lge	†	Millwall	L	1-4
7 Oct	Lge	A	Watford	W	2-0
14 Oct	Lge	A	C. Orient	W	4-2
21 Oct	Lge	A	Fulham	L	1-2
28 Oct	Lge	†	QPR	L	4-5
4 Nov	Lge	A	West Ham	L	1-5
11 Nov	Lge	A	Southampton	L	0-1
18 Nov	Lge	*	C. Palace	W	3-1
25 Nov	Lge	A	Chelsea	W	4-2
2 Dec	Lge	*	Arsenal	W	4-1
9 Dec	Lge	A	Luton	W	3-1
16 Dec	Lge	*	Portsmouth	W	1-0‡
23 Dec	Lge	A	Millwall	D	3-3
25 Dec	Lge	A	Brentford	W	5-1
26 Dec	Lge	†	Brentford	W	5-2
30 Dec	Lge	*	Watford	W	3-0
6 Jan	Lge	A	C. Orient	W	2-1
13 Jan	Lge	†	Fulham	W	1-0
20 Jan	Lge	A	QPR	D	1-1
27 Jan	Lge	*	West Ham	D	0-0
3 Feb	Lge	*	Southampton	W	3-1
10 Feb	Lge	A	C. Palace	W	1-0
17 Feb	Lge	A	Portsmouth	W	4-2
24 Feb	Lge	*	C. Palace	W	4-1
3 Mar	Lge	*	Luton	W	3-2
10 Mar	Lge	A	Southampton	W	4-2
17 Mar	Lge	*	C. Orient	W	5-2
24 Mar	Lge	A	West Ham	L	0-3
31 Mar	Lge	*	Portsmouth	W	10-0
6 Apr	Lge	†	Arsenal	D	0-0
7 Apr	Lge	A	C. Palace	W	3-0
9 Apr	Lge	A	Arsenal	L	2-3
10 Apr	Lge	*	Portsmouth	W	2-1
14 Apr	Lge	A	Luton	L	4-5
21 Apr	Lge	†	Southampton	W	4-0
28 Apr	Lge	A	C. Orient	W	8-0
5 May	F	A	West Ham	D	3-3

* White Hart Lane commissioned by War Office. Home games played at Highbury
† Home games played at Homerton, ground of Clapton Orient
‡ Abandoned

Player	War Lg App	Goals
Banks J.	31	30
Barton P.	37	5
Bassett J.	36	26
Bearman F.	1	
Bliss H.	26	19
Caldwell T.	1	
Clay T.	30	3
Clayton A.	1	
Croft F.	2	
Croft W.	2	

Crossley J.	1	
Crowl S.	12	1
Darnell J.	14	2
Elliott J.	36	3
Grimes W.	3	1
Hannaford C.	1	1
Hawkins W.	9	2
Hoad S.	4	
Hunt K.	1	
Jacques W.	38	
Lloyd H.	23	1
McVey J.	2	
Middlemiss H.	2	1
Morris J.	4	1
Potter H.	13	4
Powell H.	1	
Ralston A.	37	
Rance C.	23	1
Slade H.	1	
Smith J.	1	
Thwaites W.	9	3
Travers G.	3	1
Walden F.	30	6
Watkin W.	1	
Weir F.	3	
Williamson E.	1	
Own Goal		1

London Combination 1916–17

1 West Ham	40	30	5	5	110:45	65
4 TOTTENHAM	**40**	**24**	**5**	**11**	**112:62**	**53**

* Took over record of Reading who had played and lost 7 games with 8 goals for and 34 against. Note C. Palace v Luton, QPR v Watford, Southampton v C. Palace were never played. Each team played the others twice and then played any 7 of their rivals according to fixture availability.

SEASON 1917/18

1 Sep	Lge	A	C. Palace	W	4-2
8 Sep	Lge	*	Chelsea	L	0-4
15 Sep	Lge	A	Brentford	L	2-5
22 Sep	Lge	*	Arsenal	L	1-2
29 Sep	Lge	A	West Ham	L	0-1
6 Oct	Lge	*	Fulham	W	1-0
13 Oct	Lge	A	QPR	W	3-2
20 Oct	Lge	†	C. Orient	W	2-1
27 Oct	Lge	*	C. Palace	W	1-0
3 Nov	Lge	A	Chelsea	D	0-0
10 Nov	Lge	*	Brentford	W	6-1
17 Nov	Lge	†	Arsenal	W	1-0
24 Nov	Lge	*	West Ham	W	2-0
1 Dec	Lge	A	Fulham	L	3-4
8 Dec	Lge	†	QPR	L	0-1
15 Dec	Lge	A	C. Orient	W	4-2
22 Dec	Lge	A	C. Palace	W	3-2
25 Dec	Lge	A	Millwall	W	5-0
26 Dec	Lge	†	Millwall	L	0-1
29 Dec	Lge	*	Chelsea	W	2-0
5 Jan	Lge	A	Brentford	W	3-2
12 Jan	Lge	A	Arsenal	W	4-1
19 Jan	Lge	A	West Ham	D	2-2
26 Jan	Lge	*	Fulham	L	0-1
2 Feb	Lge	A	QPR	W	7-2
9 Feb	Lge	†	Millwall	W	4-2
16 Feb	Lge	*	C. Palace	W	8-0
23 Feb	Lge	A	Chelsea	L	0-3
2 Mar	Lge	*	Brentford	W	3-0
9 Mar	Lge	A	Arsenal	L	1-4
16 Mar	Lge	*	West Ham	L	0-5
23 Mar	Lge	A	Fulham	W	3-0
29 Mar	Lge	A	C. Orient	W	3-2
30 Mar	Lge	†	QPR	L	1-2
1 Apr	Lge	†	C. Orient	W	5-2
6 Apr	Lge	A	Millwall	W	1-0
13 Apr	L Supp	A	Chelsea	D	1-1
20 Apr	L Supp	*	Chelsea	L	0-1
27 Apr	L Supp	A	Fulham	L	0-3
4 May	L Supp	‡	Fulham	L	2-3

* Home games played at Highbury
† Home games played at Homerton
‡ Played at Upton Park

Player	War Lg App	Goals
Ayres	2	

Baldwin	1	
Banks J.	33	21
Barnard	1	2
Barton P.	4	
Bassett E.	7	1
Beaton	2	
Bird	1	
Bliss H.	2	
Brown R.	2	
Clay T.	20	
Coomber G.	14	2
Crosswell T.	11	
Crowl S.	1	
Darnell J.	20	
Elliott J.	36	1
Fleming J.	1	
Goldthorpe	7	5
Halle W.	1	
Hawkins W.	36	10
Hill	2	
Hoffman	1	
Jack	6	4
Jacques W.	29	
Laurence A.	5	1
Lightfoot E.	2	
Lindsay A.	8	
Lindsay D.	5	2
Lloyd H.	1	
Middlemiss H.	6	2
Minter W.	3	4
Nuttall J.	18	9
Peake	15	7
Potter H.	5	
Ralston A.	36	
Rance C.	36	3
Robinson	1	
Saunders	1	1
Spencer	1	1
Thomas D.	7	1
Thwaites W.	2	
Tomkin	12	
Walden F.	33	7
Wren	1	
Own Goal		1

London Combination 1917–18

1 Chelsea	36	21	8	7	82:39	50
4 TOTTENHAM	**36**	**22**	**2**	**12**	**85:55**	**46**

SEASON 1918/19

31 Aug	F	A	RAMC XI	D	1-1
7 Sep	Lge	A	Fulham	D	2-2
14 Sep	Lge	†	Brentford	D	1-1
21 Sep	Lge	A	West Ham	W	1-0
28 Sep	Lge	†	C. Orient	W	2-0
5 Oct	Lge	*	Chelsea	W	2-1
12 Oct	Lge	A	Arsenal	L	0-3
19 Oct	Lge	*	C. Palace	W	2-0
26 Oct	Lge	A	Millwall	W	2-0
2 Nov	Lge	†	Fulham	W	1-0
9 Nov	Lge	A	Brentford	L	1-7
16 Nov	Lge	†	West Ham	L	1-4
23 Nov	Lge	A	C. Orient	W	3-0
30 Nov	Lge	A	Chelsea	L	1-3
7 Dec	Lge	*	Arsenal	W	1-0
14 Dec	Lge	A	C. Palace	L	3-6
21 Dec	Lge	†	Millwall	L	0-3
25 Dec	Lge	A	QPR	D	1-1
26 Dec	Lge	†	QPR	D	0-0
28 Dec	Lge	A	Fulham	L	1-3
4 Jan	Lge	*	Brentford	D	1-1
11 Jan	Lge	A	West Ham	L	0-2
18 Jan	Lge	†	C. Orient	L	2-4
25 Jan	Lge	*	Chelsea	D	1-1
1 Feb	Lge	A	Arsenal	W	3-2
8 Feb	Lge	*	C. Palace	W	4-2
15 Feb	Lge	A	QPR	L	1-7
22 Feb	Lge	†	Fulham	L	0-2
1 Mar	Lge	A	Brentford	L	1-4
8 Mar	Lge	†	West Ham	L	0-1
15 Mar	Lge	A	C. Orient	W	2-1
22 Mar	Lge	A	Chelsea	W	2-1
29 Mar	Lge	*	Arsenal	L	0-1
5 Apr	Lge	A	C. Palace	D	2-2
12 Apr	Lge	*	QPR	L	2-3
18 Apr	Lge	*	Millwall	D	2-2

19 Apr	VC	‡	Fulham	L	0-2
21 Apr	Lge	A	Millwall	W	4-2
26 Apr	F	A	C. Orient	L	1-6

* Home games at Highbury
† Home games at Homerton
‡ Played at Stamford Bridge

Player	War Lg App	Goals
Banks J.	27	5
Barnard	7	2
Barton	14	
Beaton S.	6	
Bennett	4	1
Blake H.	1	
Bliss H.	2	2
Bowlier	1	
Brown R.	1	
Buley	1	
Cain	1	1
Cantrell J.	2	
Chester	2	
Clay T.	24	
Couchman	1	
Darnell J.	21	
Dockray	11	
Duncan	1	
Eaden	1	
Elliott J.	18	1
Fraser	1	
Freeman	2	
Gee	2	
Goldthorpe	10	4
Grimsdell A.	9	
Haydn-Price	9	3
Harbridge	2	
Hawkins	21	
Hoffman	1	
Jack	13	3
Jacques W.	16	
Jennings	1	
Lindsay A.	16	
Lindsay C.	3	
Lindsay D.	14	4
Lloyd	1	
McCalmont	1	1
McIver	3	
Middlemiss H.	4	3
Minter W.	9	9
Parsons	1	
Patterson	1	
Peake	4	1
Potter	2	
Ralston A.	10	
Rance C.	24	3
Simmons	3	2
Smith E.	4	
Smith J.	5	1
Thomas	8	4
Tomkins	21	
Walden F.	4	1
Walters C.	1	
Williams C.	3	1
Worral	11	

London Combination 1918–19

1 Brentford	36	20	9	7	94:46	49
8 TOTTENHAM	**36**	**13**	**8**	**15**	**52:72**	**34**

SEASON 1919/20

30 Aug	Lge	A	Coventry	W	5-0
1 Sep	Lge	H	Leicester	W	4-0
6 Sep	Lge	A	Coventry	W	4-1
11 Sep	Lge	A	Leicester	W	4-2
13 Sep	Lge	H	Sth Shields	W	2-0
20 Sep	Lge	A	Sth Shields	W	3-0
22 Sep	LnC	H	Millwall	W	6-0
27 Sep	Lge	H	Lincoln	W	6-1
29 Sep	F	A	Arsenal	W	1-0
4 Oct	Lge	A	Lincoln	D	1-1
6 Oct	LnC	A	C. Palace	L	2-3
11 Oct	Lge	H	C. Orient	W	2-1
18 Oct	Lge	A	C. Orient	W	4-0
27 Oct	Lge	A	Port Vale	W	1-0
1 Nov	Lge	H	Port Vale	W	1-0
8 Nov	Lge	A	Bury	L	1-2
15 Nov	Lge	H	Bury	W	2-1

Date	Comp	H/A	Opponent	Result	Score
22 Nov	Lge	A	Nottm Forest	D	1-1
29 Nov	Lge	H	Nottm Forest	W	5-2
6 Dec	Lge	A	Fulham	W	4-1
13 Dec	Lge	H	Fulham	W	4-0
15 Dec	F	H	Corinthians	W	4-1
20 Dec	Lge	A	Barnsley	L	0-3
25 Dec	Lge	H	Hull City	W	4-0
26 Dec	Lge	A	Hull City	W	3-1
27 Dec	Lge	H	Barnsley	W	4-0
3 Jan	Lge	A	Stockport	W	2-1
10 Jan	FC	A	Bristol Rvs	W	4-1
17 Jan	Lge	H	Stockport	W	2-0
24 Jan	Lge	A	Huddersfield	D	1-1
31 Jan	FC	H	West Stanley	W	4-0
7 Feb	Lge	A	Blackpool	W	1-0
14 Feb	Lge	H	Blackpool	D	2-2
16 Feb	Lge	H	Huddersfield	W	2-0
21 Feb	FC	H	West Ham	W	3-0
25 Feb	Lge	A	Bristol City	W	2-1
28 Feb	Lge	H	Bristol City	W	2-0
6 Mar	FC	H	Aston Villa	L	0-1
13 Mar	Lge	A	West Ham	L	1-2
20 Mar	Lge	H	Rotherham	W	2-0
22 Mar	Lge	H	West Ham	W	2-0
27 Mar	Lge	A	Rotherham	D	1-1
2 Apr	Lge	H	Wolves	W	4-2
3 Apr	Lge	H	Stoke	W	2-0
5 Apr	Lge	A	Wolves	W	3-1
10 Apr	Lge	A	Stoke	W	3-1
17 Apr	Lge	H	Grimsby	W	3-1
19 Apr	F	A	Mid Rhondda	D	0-0*
24 Apr	Lge	A	Grimsby	L	0-2
26 Apr	Lge	A	Birmingham	D	0-0
1 May	Lge	A	Birmingham	W	1-0
8 May	LCC	A	Norwich	W	4-0
15 May	CS	H	WBA	L	0-2

*Abonded after 25 minutes

Player	War Lg App	Goals
Archibald J.	13	
Banks J.A.	19	2
Bliss H.	42	31
Brown R.S.	20	
Cantrell J.	30	19
Castle S.R.	2	
Chipperfield J.	15	6
Clay T.	27	2
Dimmock J.H.	27	5
Elliott J.E.	1	
Goodman A.A.	16	1
Grimsdell A.	37	14
Jacques W.	42	
Lindsay A.F.	3	
Lorimar H.H.	4	
Lowe H.	1	
McDonald R.J.	1	
Middlemiss H.	3	
Minter W.J.	19	7
Pearson J.	21	
Rance C.S.	26	
Sage W.	1	
Seed J.M.	5	1
Skinner J.F.	3	
Smith B.	40	2
Walden F.	32	4
Walters C.	1	
Wilson C.	11	7
Own Goal		1

Final table for Second Division

1 TOTTENHAM	42	32	6	4	102:32	70

SEASON 1920/21

Date	Comp	H/A	Opponent	Result	Score
28 Aug	Lge	H	Blackburn	L	1-2
30 Aug	Lge	A	Derby	D	2-2
4 Sep	Lge	A	Blackburn	D	1-1
6 Sep	Lge	H	Derby	W	2-0
11 Sep	Lge	A	Aston Villa	L	2-4
18 Sep	Lge	H	Aston Villa	L	1-2
25 Sep	Lge	A	Man Utd	W	1-0
2 Oct	Lge	H	Man Utd	W	4-1
9 Oct	Lge	H	Chelsea	W	5-0
11 Oct	LCC	A	Barking	W	4-1
16 Oct	Lge	A	Chelsea	W	4-0
23 Oct	Lge	H	Burnley	L	1-2
25 Oct	LPCF	H	Arsenal	W	2-0

Date	Comp	H/A	Opponent	Result	Score
30 Oct	Lge	A	Burnley	L	0-2
1 Nov	LCC	H	Arsenal	W	3-1
6 Nov	Lge	H	Oldham	W	5-1
13 Nov	Lge	A	Oldham	W	5-2
18 Nov	F	A	Oxford Univ	L	0-1
20 Nov	Lge	H	Preston	L	1-2
27 Nov	Lge	A	Preston	L	1-4
4 Dec	Lge	H	Sheff Utd	W	4-1
11 Dec	Lge	A	Sheff Utd	D	1-1
18 Dec	Lge	H	Boston	W	5-2
25 Dec	Lge	A	Newcastle	D	1-1
27 Dec	Lge	H	Newcastle	W	2-0
1 Jan	Lge	A	Bolton	L	0-1
8 Jan	FC	H	Bristol Rvs	W	6-2
15 Jan	Lge	H	Arsenal	W	2-1
22 Jan	Lge	A	Arsenal	L	2-3
29 Jan	FC	H	Bradford C	W	4-0
3 Feb	Lge	A	Bradford PA	W	2-0
5 Feb	Lge	H	Bradford PA	D	1-1
12 Feb	Lge	H	Man City	W	2-0
19 Feb	FC	A	Southend	W	4-1
23 Feb	Lge	A	West Brom	L	1-3
26 Feb	Lge	H	West Brom	W	1-0
5 Mar	FC	H	Aston Villa	W	1-0
9 Mar	Lge	A	Man City	L	0-2
12 Mar	Lge	H	Everton	W	2-0
19 Mar	FCsf	*	Preston	W	2-1
25 Mar	Lge	A	Liverpool	D	1-1
26 Mar	Lge	H	Sunderland	W	1-0
28 Mar	Lge	H	Liverpool	W	1-0
2 Apr	Lge	H	Sunderland	D	0-0
9 Apr	Lge	A	Bradford C	L	0-1
11 Apr	LCC	†	C. Orient	L	1-2
16 Apr	Lge	H	Bradford C	W	2-0
23 Apr	FCf	‡	Wolves	W	1-0
25 Apr	Lge	A	Huddersfield	L	0-2
27 Apr	Lge	A	Everton	D	0-0
30 Apr	Lge	H	Huddersfield	W	1-0
2 May	Lge	A	Middlesbrough	L	0-1
7 May	Lge	H	Middlesbrough	D	2-2
14 May	F	A	Fulham	W	4-0
16 May	CS	H	Burnley	W	2-0

* at Hillsborough
† at Highbury
‡ at Stamford Bridge

Player	Lg App	Goals
Archibald J.	6	1
Banks J.A.	20	3
Bliss H.	36	17
Brown R.S.	2	
Cantrell J.	23	7
Castle S.R.	3	
Clay T.	35	1
Dimmock J.H.	41	9
Forester M.	7	
Grimsdell A.	38	3
Hunter A.C.	11	
Jacques W.	30	
Lindsay A.F.	5	
Lowe H.	5	
McDonald R.J.	36	
Pearson J.	5	
Rance C.S.	14	
Seed J.M.	37	12
Skinner J.F.	2	
Smith B.	36	3
Thompson A.	3	
Walden F.	22	5
Walters C.	25	
Wilson C.	20	9

Final table for First Division

1 Burnley	42	23	13	6	79:36	59
6 TOTTENHAM	42	19	9	14	70:48	47

SEASON 1921/22

Date	Comp	H/A	Opponent	Result	Score
27 Aug	Lge	A	Cardiff	W	1-0
29 Aug	Lge	H	Bolton	L	1-2
3 Sep	Lge	H	Cardiff	W	4-1
5 Sep	Lge	A	Bolton	L	0-1
10 Sep	Lge	H	Middlesbro	L	2-4
12 Sep	LPCF	A	West Ham	L	0-1
17 Sep	Lge	H	Middlesbro	D	0-0
19 Sep	F	A	Partick This.	L	1-3
22 Sep	F	A	Inverness Cale.	L	3-6

Date	Comp	H/A	Opponent	Result	Score
24 Sep	Lge	H	Aston Villa	W	3-1
1 Oct	Lge	A	Aston Villa	L	1-2
6 Oct	F	H	Corinthians	W	2-1
8 Oct	Lge	H	Man Utd	D	2-2
15 Oct	Lge	A	Man Utd	L	1-2
17 Oct	LCC	H	London Cal	W	5-0
22 Oct	Lge	H	Liverpool	L	0-1
29 Oct	Lge	A	Liverpool	D	1-1
31 Oct	LCC	H	Brentford	D	1-1
5 Nov	Lge	H	Newcastle	W	4-0
7 Nov	LCCr	H	Brentford	W	3-2
12 Nov	Lge	A	Newcastle	W	2-0
14 Nov	LCCsf	*	Arsenal	D	0-0
19 Nov	Lge	H	Burnley	D	1-1
21 Nov	LCCsfr	†	Arsenal	L	1-2
26 Nov	Lge	A	Burnley	L	0-1
1 Dec	F	A	Oxford Univ	W	1-0
3 Dec	Lge	H	Sheff Utd	W	2-1
10 Dec	Lge	A	Sheff Utd	L	0-1
17 Dec	Lge	H	Chelsea	D	0-0
24 Dec	Lge	A	Chelsea	W	2-1
26 Dec	Lge	H	Bradford C.	W	1-0
27 Dec	Lge	A	Bradford C.	W	4-0
31 Dec	Lge	H	Preston	W	5-0
7 Jan	FC	A	Brentford	W	2-0
14 Jan	Lge	A	Preston	W	2-1
21 Jan	Lge	A	WBA	L	0-3
28 Jan	FC	H	Watford	W	1-0
30 Jan	Lge	A	WBA	W	2-0
4 Feb	Lge	A	Man City	D	3-3
11 Feb	Lge	H	Man City	W	3-1
13 Feb	F	H	Oxford Univ	W	4-3
18 Feb	FC	H	Man City	W	2-1
25 Feb	Lge	H	Everton	W	2-0
4 Mar	FC	A	Cardiff	D	1-1
9 Mar	FCr	H	Cardiff	W	2-1
11 Mar	Lge	A	Sunderland	W	1-0
15 Mar	Lge	A	Everton	D	0-0
18 Mar	Lge	H	Huddersfield	W	1-0
25 Mar	FCsf	‡	Preston	L	1-2
27 Mar	Lge	A	Huddersfield	D	1-1
1 Apr	Lge	H	Birmingham	W	3-0
5 Apr	Lge	A	Sunderland	L	0-2
8 Apr	Lge	H	Birmingham	W	2-1
14 Apr	Lge	H	Oldham	W	3-1
15 Apr	Lge	H	Arsenal	W	2-0
17 Apr	Lge	A	Oldham	L	0-1
22 Apr	Lge	A	Arsenal	L	0-1
29 Apr	Lge	H	Blackburn	W	2-1
6 May	Lge	A	Blackburn	D	1-1
16 May	F		††Chelsea	D	1-1

* at Stamford Bridge † at Homerton ‡ at Hillsborough ∆†† at Camberley

Player	Lg App	Goals
Archibald J.	5	
Banks J.A.	11	1
Blake H.E.	8	
Bliss H.	23	7
Cantrell J.	13	3
Clay T.	37	8
Dimmock J.H.	42	7
Forster M.	4	
Grimsdell A.	35	3
Handley C.H.J.	1	
Hunter A.C.	12	
Jacques W.	22	
Lindsay A.F.	16	3
Lorimer H.H.	1	
Lowe H.	12	
McDonald R.J.	40	
Pearson J.	3	
Seed J.M.	36	10
Skinner J.F.	16	2
Smith B.	25	
Thompson A.	18	6
Walden F.	28	2
Walters C.	33	
Wilson C.	21	11
Own Goals		2

Final table for First Division

1 Liverpool	42	22	13	7	63:36	57
2 TOTTENHAM	42	21	9	12	65:39	51

SEASON 1922/23

Date	Comp	H/A	Opponent	Result	Score
26 Aug	Lge	H	Cardiff	D	1-1
2 Sep	Lge	A	Cardiff	W	3-2
4 Sep	Lge	H	Everton	W	2-0
9 Sep	Lge	A	Burnley	L	1-3
11 Sep	F	A	Corinthians	W	2-1
16 Sep	Lge	A	Burnley	W	1-0
23 Sep	Lge	H	Arsenal	L	1-2
30 Sep	Lge	A	Arsenal	W	2-0
2 Oct	LPCF	H	West Ham	W	2-1
7 Oct	Lge	A	Aston Villa	L	0-2
14 Oct	Lge	H	Aston Villa	L	1-2
16 Oct	F	A	Llanelli	L	1-2
21 Oct	Lge	H	WBA	W	3-1
23 Oct	LCC	A	Arsenal	L	2-3
28 Oct	Lge	A	WBA	L	1-5
4 Nov	Lge	H	Liverpool	L	2-4
11 Nov	Lge	A	Liverpool	D	0-0
16 Nov	F	H	Camb Univ	W	5-1
18 Nov	Lge	H	Newcastle	L	0-1
25 Nov	Lge	A	Newcastle	D	1-1
30 Nov	F	A	Oxford Univ	W	3-0
2 Dec	Lge	H	Nottm Forest	W	2-1
9 Dec	Lge	A	Nottm Forest	W	1-0
16 Dec	Lge	A	Chelsea	D	0-0
23 Dec	Lge	H	Chelsea	W	3-1
25 Dec	Lge	H	Sheff Utd	W	2-1
26 Dec	Lge	A	Sheff Utd	L	0-2
30 Dec	Lge	A	Middlesbrough	L	0-2
1 Jan	Lge	A	Everton	L	1-3
6 Jan	Lge	H	Middlesbrough	W	2-0
13 Jan	FC	A	Worksop Town	D	0-0*
15 Jan	FCr	H	Worksop Town	W	9-0
20 Jan	Lge	A	Oldham	W	3-0
27 Jan	Lge	H	Oldham	W	3-0
3 Feb	FC	H	Man Utd	W	4-0
10 Feb	Lge	A	Blackburn	L	0-1
14 Feb	Lge	H	Blackburn	W	2-0
17 Feb	Lge	H	Bolton	L	0-1
19 Feb	F	H	Oxford Univ	L	1-2
24 Feb	FC	H	Cardiff	W	3-2
3 Mar	Lge	H	Man City	W	3-1
10 Mar	FC	H	Derby	L	0-1
14 Mar	Lge	A	Man City	L	0-3
17 Mar	Lge	A	Stoke	D	0-0
24 Mar	Lge	H	Stoke	W	3-1
30 Mar	Lge	H	Preston	W	3-1
31 Mar	Lge	A	Sunderland	L	0-2
2 Apr	Lge	A	Preston	L	0-2
7 Apr	Lge	H	Sunderland	L	0-1
11 Apr	Lge	A	Bolton	W	2-0
14 Apr	Lge	A	Birmingham	L	1-2
21 Apr	Lge	H	Birmingham	W	2-0
28 Apr	Lge	H	Huddersfield	L	0-1
5 May	Lge	A	Huddersfield	D	0-0
7 May	F	H	West Ham	W	5-2

* Worksop agreed to play first match at White Hart Lane

Player	Lg App	Goals
Banks J.A.	2	
Barnett F.W.	2	
Blake H.E.	36	
Bliss H.	8	3
Brooks S.	7	1
Brown R.S.	12	
Cantrell J.	10	4
Clay T.	34	3
Dimmock J.H.	42	6
Forster M.	12	
Grimsdell A.	40	21
Handley C.H.J.	30	5
Hartley F.	1	
Jacques W.	1	
Lindsay A.F.	34	11
Lowe H.	14	
McDonald R.J.	17	
Maddison G.	5	
Pearson J.	1	
Ross J.	6	
Seed J.M.	36	9
Sharp B.	2	
Skinner J.F.	15	1
Smith B.	32	2
Thompson A.	2	
Walden F.	30	3
Walters C.	29	

Wilson C.   2

Final table for First Division

| 1 Liverpool | 42 26 8 8 70:31 60 |
| **12 TOTTENHAM** | **42 17 7 18 50:50 41** |

SEASON 1923/24

Date	Comp		Opponent	Res	Score
25 Aug	Lge	H	Preston	W	2-0
27 Aug	Lge	A	Chelsea	W	1-0
1 Sep	Lge	A	Preston	D	2-2
3 Sep	Lge	H	Chelsea	L	0-1
8 Sep	Lge	H	Middlesbrough	W	2-1
15 Sep	Lge	A	Middlesbrough	W	1-0
22 Sep	Lge	H	Bolton	D	0-0
29 Sep	Lge	A	Bolton	L	1-3
6 Oct	Lge	A	Notts Co	D	0-0
8 Oct	LPCF	H	Clapton O.	L	1-3
13 Oct	Lge	H	Notts Co	L	1-3
20 Oct	Lge	A	Sunderland	L	0-1
22 Oct	LCC	A	C. Palace	D	1-1
25 Oct	F	A	Norwich	W	3-2
27 Oct	Lge	H	Sunderland	D	1-1
29 Oct	LCC	H	C. Palace	W	2-1
3 Nov	Lge	A	Nottm Forest	D	0-0
5 Nov	LCC	A	Clapton O.	L	0-2
10 Nov	Lge	H	Nottm Forest	W	3-0
15 Nov	F	A	Camb Univ	W	6-5
17 Nov	Lge	A	Arsenal	D	1-1
24 Nov	Lge	H	Arsenal	W	3-0
1 Dec	Lge	H	WBA	D	0-0
4 Dec	F	A	Oxford Univ	W	5-0
8 Dec	Lge	A	WBA	L	1-4
15 Dec	Lge	H	Blackburn	W	2-1
22 Dec	Lge	A	Blackburn	W	1-0
25 Dec	Lge	H	Huddersfield	W	1-0
26 Dec	Lge	A	Huddersfield	L	1-2
29 Dec	Lge	H	Birmingham	D	1-1
1 Jan	Lge	A	Man City	L	0-1
5 Jan	Lge	A	Birmingham	L	2-3
12 Jan	FC	A	C. Palace	L	0-2
19 Jan	Lge	H	Newcastle	W	2-0
26 Jan	Lge	A	Newcastle	D	2-2
2 Feb	F	A	Chelsea	D	0-0
9 Feb	Lge	A	West Ham	D	0-0
16 Feb	Lge	H	Cardiff	D	1-1
18 Feb	F	H	Oxford Univ	W	8-1
23 Feb	F	A	West Ham	D	1-1
1 Mar	Lge	H	Sheff Utd	L	1-2
8 Mar	Lge	A	Sheff Utd	L	2-6
15 Mar	Lge	A	Aston Villa	D	0-0
17 Mar	F	A	West Ham	D	1-1
22 Mar	Lge	H	Aston Villa	L	2-3
29 Mar	Lge	A	Liverpool	L	0-1
5 Apr	Lge	H	Liverpool	D	1-1
7 Apr	Lge	A	Cardiff	L	1-2
12 Apr	Lge	H	Everton	L	2-5
16 Apr	F	H	Inter Varsities	W	7-1
19 Apr	Lge	A	Everton	D	1-1
21 Apr	Lge	H	Man City	W	4-1
22 Apr	Lge	H	West Ham	L	0-1
26 Apr	Lge	A	Burnley	D	2-2
3 May	Lge	H	Burnley	W	1-0

Player	Lg App	Goals
Barnett F.W.	2	
Blake H.E.	7	
Brooks S.	3	
Brown R.S.	3	
Clay T.	40	1
Dimmock J.H.	25	2
Elkes J.E.	37	11
Forster M.	35	
Grimsdell A.	27	1
Handley C.H.J.	22	5
Hargreaves H.	7	3
Lindsay A.F.	39	19
Lowe H.	22	
McDonald R.J.	3	
Maddison G.	35	
Osborne F.R.	12	1
Poynton C.	10	1
Ross J.	1	
Sage W.	7	
Seed J.M.	21	2
Skinner J.F.	2	
Smith B.	41	1

Player		
Thompson A.	7	1
Walden F.	34	1
Walters C.	15	
White S.E.	5	
Own Goal		1

Final table for First Division

| 1 Huddersfield | 42 23 11 8 60:33 57 |
| **15 TOTTENHAM** | **42 12 14 16 50:56 38** |

SEASON 1924/25

Date	Comp		Opponent	Res	Score
30 Aug	Lge	H	Bolton	W	3-0
3 Sep	Lge	A	Birmingham	W	2-0
6 Sep	Lge	A	Notts Co.	D	0-0
8 Sep	Lge	A	WBA	L	0-2
13 Sep	Lge	H	Everton	D	0-0
20 Sep	Lge	A	Sunderland	L	1-4
22 Sep	Lge	H	WBA	L	0-1
27 Sep	Lge	H	Cardiff	D	1-1
4 Oct	Lge	A	Preston	W	3-0
11 Oct	Lge	H	Burnley	D	1-1
18 Oct	Lge	A	Leeds Utd	L	0-1
25 Oct	Lge	A	Arsenal	L	0-1
27 Oct	LCC	H	Fulham	W	5-1
1 Nov	Lge	H	Aston Villa	L	1-3
3 Nov	LPCF	A	C. Orient	L	1-2†
6 Nov	F	A	Oxford Univ	W	2-1
8 Nov	Lge	A	Huddersfield	W	2-1
10 Nov	Lge	H	Man City	W	2-1
15 Nov	Lge	H	Blackburn	W	5-0
17 Nov	LCC	H	Kingstonians	W	5-0
22 Nov	Lge	A	West Ham	D	1-1
24 Nov	LCC	*	C. Orient	L	1-2
29 Nov	Lge	H	Sheff Utd	W	4-1
6 Dec	Lge	A	Newcastle	D	1-1
13 Dec	Lge	H	Liverpool	D	1-1
20 Dec	Lge	A	Nottm Forest	L	0-1
25 Dec	Lge	H	Bury	D	1-1
27 Dec	Lge	A	Bolton	L	0-3
1 Jan	Lge	H	Bury	L	2-5
3 Jan	Lge	H	Notts Co.	D	1-1
10 Jan	FC	H	Northampton	W	3-0
17 Jan	Lge	A	Everton	L	0-1
24 Jan	Lge	H	Sunderland	W	1-0
31 Jan	FC	H	Bolton	D	1-1
3 Feb	FCr	A	Bolton	W	1-0
7 Feb	Lge	H	Preston	W	2-0
14 Feb	Lge	A	Burnley	W	4-1
21 Feb	FC	H	Blackburn	D	2-2
26 Feb	FCr	A	Blackburn	L	1-3
28 Feb	Lge	H	Arsenal	W	2-0
7 Mar	Lge	A	Aston Villa	W	1-0
9 Mar	Lge	A	Leeds Utd	W	2-1
14 Mar	Lge	H	Huddersfield	L	1-2
18 Mar	Lge	A	Cardiff	W	2-0
21 Mar	Lge	A	Blackburn	D	1-1
28 Mar	Lge	H	West Ham	D	1-1
4 Apr	Lge	A	Sheff Utd	L	0-2
10 Apr	Lge	H	Birmingham	L	0-1
11 Apr	Lge	H	Newcastle	W	3-0
18 Apr	Lge	A	Liverpool	L	0-1
25 Apr	Lge	H	Nottm Forest	W	1-0
2 May	Lge	A	Man City	L	0-1
9 May	F	A	Basel Old Boys	W	3-0
10 May	F	A	Zurich	W	2-0
17 May	F	A	Winterthur	W	4-0
18 May	F	A	Lausanne	W	6-1
20 May	F	A	La Cheux de Fonds	W	8-1
21 May	F	A	Bern	W	5-0
24 May	F	A	Basel	W	1-0

† abandoned after 70 minutes
* at Highbury

Player	Lg App	Goals
Clay T.	21	2
Dimmock J.H.	29	5
Elkes J.E.	33	10
Forster M.	21	
Grimsdell A.	14	
Handley C.H.J.	14	3
Hargreaves H.	20	3
Hinton F.	42	
Lane W.H.C.	17	6
Lindsay A.F.	18	2
Lowe H.	6	

Player		
McDonald R.J.	12	
Osborne F.R.	23	
Poynton C.	24	
Sage W.	1	
Seed J.M.	41	17
Sharp B.	1	
Skinner J.F.	34	
Skitt H.	27	
Smith B.	37	1
Thompson A.	20	3
Walters C.	22	
White S.E.	5	

Final table for First Division

| 1 Huddersfield | 42 21 18 5 69:28 58 |
| **12 TOTTENHAM** | **42 15 12 15 52:43 42** |

SEASON 1925/26

Date	Comp		Opponent	Res	Score
29 Aug	Lge	A	Arsenal	W	1-0
31 Aug	Lge	A	Sheff Utd	W	3-2
3 Sep	F	H	Real Madrid	W	4-0
5 Sep	Lge	H	Man City	W	1-0
7 Sep	Lge	H	Sheff Utd	W	3-2
12 Sep	Lge	A	Everton	D	1-1
14 Sep	Lge	H	Cardiff	L	1-2
15 Sep	LCC	H	Brentford	L	1-2
19 Sep	Lge	H	Huddersfield	D	5-5
21 Sep	Lge	A	Cardiff	W	1-0
26 Sep	Lge	A	Sunderland	L	0-3
3 Oct	Lge	H	Blackburn	W	4-2
10 Oct	Lge	A	Bury	L	0-3
17 Oct	Lge	A	Man Utd	D	0-0
22 Oct	F	A	Norwich	L	2-3*
24 Oct	Lge	H	Liverpool	W	3-1
31 Oct	Lge	A	Leicester	L	3-5
7 Nov	Lge	H	West Ham	W	4-2
12 Nov	F	A	Camb Univ	L	1-2
14 Nov	Lge	A	Newcastle	L	1-3
16 Nov	LPCF	H	QPR	W	1-0
21 Nov	Lge	H	Bolton	L	2-3
26 Nov	F	H	Oxford Univ	W	4-1
28 Nov	Lge	A	Notts Co	L	2-4
5 Dec	Lge	H	Aston Villa	D	2-2
12 Dec	Lge	H	Burnley	W	2-1
19 Dec	Lge	H	Leeds	W	3-2
25 Dec	Lge	A	Birmingham	L	1-3
26 Dec	Lge	H	Birmingham	W	2-1
2 Jan	Lge	H	Arsenal	D	1-1
9 Jan	FC	H	West Ham	W	5-0
16 Jan	Lge	A	Man City	D	0-0
23 Jan	Lge	H	Everton	D	1-1
30 Jan	FC	H	Man Utd	D	2-2
3 Feb	FCr	A	Man Utd	L	0-2
6 Feb	Lge	H	Sunderland	L	0-2
13 Feb	Lge	A	Blackburn	L	2-4
20 Feb	Lge	H	Bury	W	4-2
27 Feb	Lge	H	Man Utd	L	0-1
3 Mar	Lge	A	Huddersfield	L	0-2
6 Mar	Lge	A	Liverpool	D	0-0
13 Mar	Lge	H	Leicester	L	1-3
20 Mar	Lge	A	West Ham	L	1-3
25 Mar	Lge	A	Newcastle	W	1-0
27 Mar	F	A	Hull	L	0-5
2 Apr	Lge	H	WBA	W	3-2
3 Apr	Lge	A	Bolton	D	1-1
5 Apr	Lge	A	WBA	L	0-1
10 Apr	Lge	H	Notts Co	W	4-0
17 Apr	Lge	A	Aston Villa	L	0-3
24 Apr	Lge	H	Burnley	L	0-2
1 May	Lge	A	Leeds	L	1-4
3 May	F	A	West Ham	D	1-1

Player	Lg App	Goals
Bann W.	8	
Britton J.	9	
Clay T.	34	2
Dimmock J.H.	40	14
Elkes J.E.	31	11
Forster M.	42	
Grimsdell A.	13	
Handley C.H.J.	2	
Hargreaves H.	8	1
Hinton I.F.	15	
Kaine W.E.	11	
Lane W.H.C.	5	
Lindsay A.F.	23	2

Player		
Lowe H.	2	
Osborne F.R.	39	25
Roe T.W.	4	1
Sage W.	3	
Seed J.M.	30	6
Skinner J.F.	17	
Skitt H.	35	
Smith B.	38	
Smith J.	7	
Thompson A.	35	4
Walters C.	1	
White S.E.	10	

Final table for First Division

| 1 Huddersfield | 42 23 11 8 92:60 57 |
| **15 TOTTENHAM** | **42 15 9 18 66:79 39** |

SEASON 1926/27

Date	Comp		Opponent	Res	Score
28 Aug	Lge	H	Everton	W	2-1
30 Aug	Lge	H	Sheff Wed	W	7-3
4 Sep	Lge	A	Blackburn	L	0-1
6 Sep	Lge	H	Leicester	D	2-2
11 Sep	Lge	H	Huddersfield	D	3-3
13 Sep	Lge	A	Leicester	D	2-2
18 Sep	Lge	A	Sunderland	L	2-3
20 Sep	F	H	Bohemians	W	1-0
25 Sep	Lge	H	WBA	W	3-0
27 Sep	LCC	A	Millwall	L	2-5
2 Oct	Lge	A	Bury	D	0-0
9 Oct	Lge	A	Birmingham	W	6-1
16 Oct	Lge	H	Sheff Utd	W	3-1
23 Oct	Lge	A	Derby	L	1-4
30 Oct	Lge	H	Bolton	W	1-0
4 Nov	F	H	Camb Univ	W	3-2
6 Nov	Lge	A	Aston Villa	W	3-2
8 Nov	LPCF	A	C. Orient	W	3-1
11 Nov	F	A	Oxford Univ	W	7-0
13 Nov	Lge	H	Cardiff	W	4-1
20 Nov	Lge	A	Burnley	L	0-5
27 Nov	Lge	H	Newcastle	L	1-3
29 Nov	F	A	Corinthians	W	2-0
4 Dec	Lge	A	Leeds	D	1-1
11 Dec	Lge	H	Liverpool	L	1-2
18 Dec	Lge	A	Arsenal	W	4-2
25 Dec	Lge	H	Man Utd	D	1-1
27 Dec	Lge	A	Man Utd	L	1-2
28 Dec	Lge	A	Sheff Wed	L	1-3
8 Jan	FC	A	West Ham	L	2-3
15 Jan	Lge	A	Everton	W	2-1
22 Jan	Lge	A	Blackburn	D	1-1
29 Jan	Lge	A	Huddersfield	L	0-2
5 Feb	Lge	H	Sunderland	L	0-2
12 Feb	Lge	A	WBA	L	0-5
19 Feb	Lge	H	Bury	W	1-0
26 Feb	Lge	A	Birmingham	L	0-1
5 Mar	Lge	A	Sheff Utd	D	3-3
12 Mar	Lge	H	Derby	W	3-2
19 Mar	Lge	H	Bolton	D	2-2
26 Mar	Lge	H	Aston Villa	L	0-1
2 Apr	Lge	A	Cardiff	W	2-1
9 Apr	Lge	H	Burnley	W	4-1
15 Apr	Lge	H	West Ham	L	1-3
16 Apr	Lge	A	Newcastle	L	2-3
18 Apr	Lge	A	West Ham	W	2-1
23 Apr	Lge	H	Leeds	W	4-1
30 Apr	Lge	A	Liverpool	L	0-1
7 May	Lge	H	Arsenal	L	0-4

Player	Lg App	Goals
Barnett F.W.	1	
Bellamy W.R.	1	
Blair J.G.	24	10
Britton J.	18	
Clay T.	16	
Dimmock J.H.	41	19
Elkes J.E.	40	2
Forster M.	35	
Grimsdell A.	2	
Handley C.H.J.	24	10
Lane W.H.C.	4	1
Lindsay A.F.	37	
Lowe H.	1	
Nicholls J.H.	1	
O'Callaghan E.	13	5
Osborne F.R.	34	9
Poynton C.	31	

Player	Lg App	Goals
Richardson J.	2	
Roe T.W.	3	3
Sanders A.W.	12	7
Seed J.M.	23	7
Skitt H.	22	
Smith B.	24	
Smith J.	23	
Thompson A.	30	3

Final table for First Division

1	Newcastle	42 25 6 11	96:58	56
13	**TOTTENHAM**	**42 16 9 17**	**76:78**	**41**

SEASON 1927/28

27 Aug	Lge	H	Birmingham	W	1-0
31 Aug	Lge	A	Middlesbrough	L	1-3
3 Sep	Lge	A	Newcastle	L	1-4
10 Sep	Lge	H	Huddersfield	D	2-2
12 Sep	Lge	H	Middlesbrough	W	4-2
17 Sep	Lge	A	Portsmouth	L	0-3
22 Sep	Lge	H	Leicester	W	2-1
24 Sep	Lge	A	Man Utd	L	0-3
1 Oct	Lge	H	Everton	L	1-3
8 Oct	Lge	A	Cardiff	L	1-2
13 Oct	F	A	Norwich	D	1-1
15 Oct	Lge	H	Blackburn	D	1-1
17 Oct	LCC	A	Fulham	L	2-5
22 Oct	Lge	H	Sunderland	W	3-1
26 Oct	F	A	Reading	W	5-2
29 Oct	Lge	A	Derby	D	1-1
3 Nov	F	A	Camb Univ	L	1-2
5 Nov	Lge	H	West Ham	W	5-3
7 Nov	LPCF	H	Clapton O.	W	4-3
10 Nov	F	A	Oxford Univ	W	5-2
12 Nov	Lge	A	Aston Villa	W	2-1
19 Nov	Lge	H	Sheff Utd	D	2-2
3 Dec	Lge	H	Burnley	W	5-0
5 Dec	F	H	West Ham	D	1-1
10 Dec	Lge	A	Bury	W	2-1
17 Dec	Lge	H	Liverpool	W	3-1
24 Dec	Lge	A	Leicester	L	1-6
26 Dec	Lge	A	Bolton	L	1-4
31 Dec	Lge	A	Birmingham	L	2-3
2 Jan	Lge	A	Arsenal	D	1-1
7 Jan	Lge	H	Newcastle	W	5-2
14 Jan	FC	A	Bristol C.	W	2-1
21 Jan	Lge	A	Huddersfield	L	2-4
28 Jan	FC	A	Oldham	W	3-0
4 Feb	Lge	A	Man Utd	W	4-1
6 Feb	Lge	H	Bolton	L	1-2
11 Feb	Lge	A	Everton	W	5-2
18 Feb	FC	A	Leicester	W	3-0
25 Feb	Lge	A	Blackburn	L	1-2
3 Mar	FC	A	Huddersfield	L	1-6
5 Mar	Lge	H	Cardiff	W	1-0
10 Mar	Lge	H	Derby	L	1-2
17 Mar	Lge	A	West Ham	D	1-1
19 Mar	Lge	A	Portsmouth	L	0-3
26 Mar	Lge	H	Aston Villa	W	2-1
28 Mar	Lge	A	Sunderland	D	0-0
31 Mar	Lge	A	Sheff Utd	L	1-3
6 Apr	Lge	H	Sheff Wed	L	1-3
7 Apr	Lge	H	Arsenal	W	2-0
10 Apr	Lge	A	Sheff Wed	L	2-4
14 Apr	Lge	A	Burnley	D	2-2
21 Apr	Lge	H	Bury	L	1-4
23 Apr	F	A	Norwich	L	0-3
25 Apr	F	A	Ebbw Vale	W	7-3
28 Apr	Lge	A	Liverpool	L	0-2
6 May	F	A	Olympic XI	W	5-2
9 May	F	A	Den Haag	W	6-2
13 May	F	A	All Holland XI	W	3-0
16 May	F	A	Rotterdam	W	3-0

Player	Lg App	Goals
Armstrong J.W.	11	4
Austin P.	1	
Barnett F.W.	5	
Bellamy W.R.	4	
Blair J.G.	5	4
Britton J.	13	
Clay T.	16	
Dimmock J.H.	38	12
Elkes J.E.	22	5
Evans A.A.	3	
Forster M.	32	

Player	Lg App	Goals
Grimsdell A.	35	2
Handley C.H.J.	27	4
Hartley F.	2	
Helliwell S.	2	
Lowdell A.	34	
Lindsay A.F.	18	3
Nicholls J.H.	3	
O'Callaghan E.	42	19
Osborne F.R.	31	18
Poynton C.	14	
Richardson J.	24	
Sanders A.W.	1	
Skitt H.	38	
Smith B.	8	
Spiers C.H.	26	
Thompson A.	4	
Townley J.C.	3	2
Own Goal		1

Final table for First Division

1	Everton	42 20 13 9	102:66	53
21	**TOTTENHAM**	**42 15 8 19**	**74:86**	**38**

SEASON 1928/29

25 Aug	Lge	H	Oldham	W	4-1
27 Aug	Lge	H	Middlesbrough	L	2-5
1 Sep	Lge	A	Southampton	D	1-1
8 Sep	Lge	H	Wolves	W	3-2
15 Sep	Lge	A	Notts Co	L	0-2
22 Sep	Lge	H	Millwall	W	2-1
29 Sep	Lge	A	Port Vale	L	1-2
4 Oct	F	A	Norwich	W	4-2
6 Oct	Lge	H	Hull	W	4-1
13 Oct	Lge	A	Bradford	L	1-4
15 Oct	LCC	H	London Cal	W	2-1
20 Oct	Lge	H	Grimsby	W	2-1
27 Oct	Lge	A	Stoke	L	0-2
29 Oct	LCC	A	QPR	D	1-1
3 Nov	Lge	H	Clapton O.	W	2-1
5 Nov	LCC	H	QPR	W	3-1
10 Nov	Lge	A	Swansea	L	0-4
15 Nov	F	H	Camb Univ	W	12-3
17 Nov	Lge	H	Nottm Forest	W	2-1
21 Nov	F	A	Oxford Univ	W	4-2
24 Nov	Lge	A	Bristol City	L	1-2
26 Nov	LCCsf	*	Charlton	W	5-3
1 Dec	Lge	H	Barnsley	W	2-0
3 Dec	LPCF	A	Clapton O.	W	4-2
8 Dec	Lge	A	Chelsea	D	1-1
15 Dec	Lge	H	Blackpool	L	1-2
22 Dec	Lge	A	West Brom	L	2-3
25 Dec	Lge	H	Reading	D	2-2
26 Dec	Lge	A	Reading	L	3-4
29 Dec	Lge	A	Oldham	L	1-3
1 Jan	Lge	A	Middlesbrough	L	0-3
5 Jan	Lge	H	Southampton	W	3-2
12 Jan	FC	A	Reading	L	0-2
19 Jan	Lge	A	Wolves	L	2-4
26 Jan	Lge	H	Notts Co	W	3-0
2 Feb	Lge	A	Millwall	L	1-5
9 Feb	Lge	H	Port Vale	W	4-2
23 Feb	Lge	H	Bradford	W	3-2
2 Mar	Lge	A	Grimsby	L	0-2
9 Mar	Lge	H	Stoke	W	1-0
16 Mar	Lge	A	C. Orient	W	3-2
23 Mar	Lge	H	Swansea	D	1-1
29 Mar	Lge	A	Preston	D	2-2
30 Mar	Lge	A	Nottm Forest	D	2-2
1 Apr	Lge	H	Preston	W	2-0
6 Apr	Lge	H	Bristol City	D	1-1
13 Apr	Lge	A	Barnsley	L	1-4
15 Apr	Lge	A	Hull City	D	1-1
20 Apr	Lge	H	Chelsea	W	4-1
27 Apr	Lge	A	Blackpool	D	2-2
4 May	Lge	H	WBA	W	2-0
6 May	LCCf	†	Millwall	W	5-1
11 May	F	A	Sliema	W	7-1
12 May	F	A	Valletta	W	2-1
16 May	F	A	British Army	W	5-0
18 May	F	A	British Army	W	1-0
19 May	F	A	Floriana	W	2-1
21 May	F	A	Pick/Malta XI	W	5-1

* at Upton Park † at Highbury

Player	Lg App	Goals
Armstrong J.W.	12	3

Player	Lg App	Goals
Bann W.E.	4	
Barnett F.W.	6	1
Bellamy W.R.	9	
Cable T.H.	2	
Clay T.	5	
Crompton A.	8	1
Dimmock J.H.	30	11
Elkes J.E.	27	10
Evans A.A.	2	
Forster M.	33	
Galloway R.	3	2
Grimsdell A.	11	
Handley C.H.J.	1	
Harper E.C.	11	11
Hartley F.	3	1
Helliwell S.	6	
Herod E.R.B.	13	
Knight J.G.	1	
Lindsay A.F.	6	
Lowdell A.	39	
Nicholls J.	11	
O'Callaghan E.	36	10
Osborne F.R.	33	16
Poynton C.	23	1
Richardson J.	12	
Roberts W.T.	4	2
Scott J.	12	4
Skitt H.	29	
Smith B.	10	
Smy J.	4	
Spiers C.H.	31	
Thompson A.	13	1
Wilding H.T.	12	1

Final table for Second Division

1	Middlesbrough	42 22 11 9	92:57	55
10	**TOTTENHAM**	**42 17 9 16**	**75:81**	**43**

SEASON 1929/30

31 Aug	Lge	A	Bradford PA	L	1-2
2 Sep	Lge	A	Millwall	W	5-2
7 Sep	Lge	H	Barnsley	W	2-1
14 Sep	Lge	A	Blackpool	L	2-3
21 Sep	Lge	H	Bury	D	2-2
23 Sep	Lge	A	Millwall	D	1-1
28 Sep	Lge	A	Chelsea	L	0-3
5 Oct	Lge	H	Nottm Forest	D	1-1
9 Oct	Lge	H	Stoke	W	3-1
10 Oct	F	A	Norwich	L	0-1
12 Oct	Lge	A	Oldham	L	0-2
13 Oct	LCC	A	C. Orient	L	1-2
19 Oct	Lge	A	Wolves	L	0-3
26 Oct	Lge	H	Bradford C	D	1-1
2 Nov	Lge	A	Swansea	W	1-0
4 Nov	LPCF	H	Crystal P.	W	5-0
9 Nov	Lge	H	Cardiff	L	1-2
16 Nov	Lge	A	Preston	L	0-4
23 Nov	Lge	A	Bristol C.	W	2-1
30 Nov	Lge	A	Notts Co.	L	0-2
7 Dec	Lge	H	Reading	D	0-0
14 Dec	Lge	A	Charlton	L	0-1
21 Dec	Lge	H	Hull City	D	2-2
25 Dec	Lge	A	Southampton	W	3-2
26 Dec	Lge	H	Southampton	L	0-1
28 Dec	Lge	H	Bradford PA	D	1-1
4 Jan	Lge	A	Barnsley	L	0-2
11 Jan	FC	H	Man City	D	2-2
14 Jan	FCr	A	Man City	L	1-4
18 Jan	Lge	H	Blackpool	W	6-1
25 Jan	Lge	A	Bury	L	1-2
1 Feb	Lge	H	Chelsea	D	3-3
8 Feb	Lge	A	Nottm Forest	D	0-0
15 Feb	Lge	H	Oldham	W	2-1
22 Feb	Lge	H	Wolves	W	4-2
1 Mar	Lge	A	Bradford C	W	2-0
8 Mar	Lge	H	Swansea	W	3-0
15 Mar	Lge	A	Cardiff	L	0-1
22 Mar	Lge	H	Preston	W	1-0
29 Mar	Lge	A	Bristol C	L	0-1
5 Apr	Lge	A	Notts Co	W	2-0
12 Apr	Lge	A	Reading	L	0-3
18 Apr	Lge	H	WBA	L	0-2
19 Apr	Lge	H	Charlton	W	3-0
21 Apr	Lge	A	WBA	L	3-4
26 Apr	Lge	A	Hull City	L	0-2
1 May	F	A	Yeovil + Peters	W	6-4
3 May	Lge	A	Stoke City	L	0-1

Player	Lg App	Goals
Armstrong J.W.	5	
Bellamy W.R.	12	2
Cable W.R.	34	
Cook G.W.	32	9
Crompton A.	7	1
Davies W.	14	2
Dimmock J.H.	32	6
Evans T.	3	
Harper E.C.	19	14
Hartley F.	1	
Forster M.	15	
Herod E.R.B.	41	
Illingworth J.	9	
Lindsay A.F.	10	
Lowdell A.	13	
Meads T.	33	2
O'Callaghan E.	10	4
Osborne F.R.	32	9
Poynton C.	16	1
Reddish J.	3	
Rowley R.W.M.	9	4
Scott J.	5	
Skitt H.	37	
Smy J.	7	2
Spiers C.H.	42	
Thompson A.	21	2
Own Goal		1

Final table for Second Division

1	Blackpool	42 27 4 11	98:67	58
12	**TOTTENHAM**	**42 15 9 18**	**59:61**	**39**

SEASON 1930/31

30 Aug	Lge	H	Reading	W	7-1
1 Sep	Lge	H	Burnley	W	8-1
6 Sep	Lge	A	Wolves	L	1-3
8 Sep	Lge	A	Preston	L	1-2
13 Sep	Lge	H	Bradford PA	W	3-2
15 Sep	Lge	H	Preston	D	0-0
20 Sep	Lge	A	Stoke	L	1-2
27 Sep	Lge	H	Millwall	W	4-1
4 Oct	Lge	A	Oldham	W	2-1
11 Oct	Lge	H	Nottm Forest	W	2-1
13 Oct	LCC	H	Charlton	W	6-0
18 Oct	Lge	H	Bury	W	3-1
25 Oct	Lge	A	Everton	L	2-4
27 Oct	LCC	A	Chelsea	W	2-1
30 Oct	F	A	Oxford Univ	W	3-0
1 Nov	Lge	H	Charlton	W	5-0
3 Nov	LPCF	A	C. Palace	D	2-2
8 Nov	Lge	A	Bradford C	L	0-2
13 Nov	F	H	Camb Univ	W	8-0
15 Nov	Lge	H	Swansea	D	1-1
17 Nov	LCCsf	*	Ilford	W	8-1
22 Nov	Lge	A	WBA	W	2-0
29 Nov	Lge	H	Port Vale	W	5-0
6 Dec	Lge	A	Plymouth	L	0-2
8 Dec	F	A	West Ham	W	2-1
13 Dec	Lge	H	Bristol C	W	4-1
20 Dec	Lge	A	Barnsley	W	1-0
25 Dec	Lge	H	Southampton	L	1-3
26 Dec	Lge	A	Southampton	W	3-0
27 Dec	Lge	A	Reading	W	2-1
3 Jan	Lge	H	Wolves	W	1-0
10 Jan	FC	H	Preston	W	3-1
17 Jan	Lge	A	Bradford PA	L	1-4
24 Jan	FC	A	WBA	D	0-0
26 Jan	Lge	H	Stoke City	W	3-0
31 Jan	Lge	A	Millwall	W	3-2
7 Feb	Lge	H	Oldham	W	4-0
14 Feb	Lge	A	Nottm Forest	D	0-2
21 Feb	Lge	A	Bury	L	0-2
28 Feb	F	H	Huddersfield	L	2-4
7 Mar	Lge	A	Charlton	L	0-1
14 Mar	Lge	H	Bradford C	W	3-1
16 Mar	Lge	H	Everton	W	1-0
21 Mar	Lge	A	Swansea	W	2-1
28 Mar	Lge	H	WBA	D	2-2
3 Apr	Lge	A	Cardiff	D	2-2
4 Apr	Lge	A	Port Vale	L	0-3
6 Apr	Lge	A	Cardiff	D	0-0
11 Apr	Lge	H	Plymouth	D	1-1
18 Apr	Lge	A	Bristol C	L	1-2
25 Apr	Lge	H	Barnsley	W	4-2
2 May	Lge	A	Burnley	L	0-1

4 May LCCf † Arsenal L 1-2
* at Upton Park † at Stamford Bridge

Player	Lg App	Goals
Alsford W.J.	14	
Bellamy W.R.	17	4
Cable T.H.	4	
Cook G.W.	31	12
Davies W.	42	4
Dimmock J.H.	13	4
Harper E.C.	30	36
Herod E.R.B.	3	
Hodgkinson H.	39	
Howe L.	3	
Hunt G.S.	9	4
Lyons A.	37	2
Meads T.	41	
Messer A.T.	39	2
O'Callaghan E.	37	10
Osborne F.R.	6	
Poynton C.	5	
Rowley R.W.M.	8	3
Scott J.	1	
Skitt H.	24	
Smailes J.	11	3
Smy J.	6	4
Spiers C.H.	42	

Final table for Second Division

1 Everton	42	28	5	9	121:66	61
3 TOTTENHAM	**42**	**22**	**7**	**13**	**88:55**	**51**

SEASON 1931/32

29 Aug	Lge	A	Wolves	L	0-4
31 Aug	Lge	H	Preston	W	4-0
5 Sep	Lge	H	Bradford PA	D	3-3
7 Sep	Lge	A	Southampton	L	1-2
12 Sep	Lge	A	Man Utd	D	1-1
14 Sep	Lge	H	Southampton	W	5-2
19 Sep	Lge	H	Barnsley	W	4-2
26 Sep	Lge	A	Nottm Forest	L	1-3
3 Oct	Lge	A	Chesterfield	L	2-4
10 Oct	Lge	H	Burnley	D	1-1
11 Oct	LCC	H	Brentford	W	4-1
17 Oct	Lge	A	Notts Co	L	1-3
24 Oct	Lge	A	Plymouth	L	0-1
28 Oct	LCC	A	Kingstonian	W	3-1
31 Oct	Lge	A	Bristol C	D	1-1
5 Nov	F	A	Camb Univ	W	9-3
7 Nov	Lge	H	Swansea	W	6-2
14 Nov	Lge	A	Bury	D	1-1
16 Nov	LCC	‡	C. Palace	L	0-2
19 Nov	F	H	Oxford Univ	D	5-5
21 Nov	Lge	H	Port Vale	W	9-3
28 Nov	Lge	A	Millwall	W	2-1
5 Dec	Lge	H	Bradford C	L	1-5
12 Dec	Lge	A	Leeds	L	0-1
19 Dec	Lge	H	Oldham	W	3-2
25 Dec	Lge	H	Charlton	L	0-1
26 Dec	Lge	A	Charlton	W	5-2
2 Jan	Lge	H	Wolves	D	3-3
9 Jan	FC	H	Sheff Wed	D	2-2
13 Jan	FCr	A	Sheff Wed	L	0-3
16 Jan	Lge	A	Bradford PA	L	1-2
23 Jan	Lge	H	Man Utd	W	4-1
30 Jan	Lge	A	Barnsley	L	2-3
6 Feb	Lge	A	Nottm Forest	W	3-1
13 Feb	Lge	H	Chesterfield	D	3-3
20 Feb	Lge	A	Burnley	L	0-2
27 Feb	Lge	H	Notts Co	W	2-0
5 Mar	Lge	A	Plymouth	L	1-4
12 Mar	Lge	H	Bristol C	W	2-1
19 Mar	Lge	A	Swansea	D	1-1
25 Mar	Lge	H	Stoke	D	3-3
26 Mar	Lge	H	Bury	D	0-0
28 Mar	Lge	A	Stoke	D	2-2
2 Apr	Lge	A	Port Vale	W	3-1
9 Apr	Lge	H	Millwall	W	1-0
16 Apr	Lge	A	Bradford C	L	0-2
23 Apr	Lge	H	Leeds	W	3-1
30 Apr	Lge	A	Oldham	W	2-1
7 May	Lge	A	Preston	W	2-1
12 May	F	A	Guernsey XI	W	2-1
16 May	F	A	Jersey XI	W	9-0

‡ Played at Upton Park. After this date, Tottenham no longer put out their first team in London Challenge Cup matches

Player	Lg App	Goals
Alsford W.J.	10	
Bellamy W.R.	12	3
Brain J.	32	8
Cable T.H.	2	
Colquhoun D.M.	36	1
Davies W.	38	12
Evans T.	12	3
Evans W.	28	5
Felton W.	10	
Greenfield G.	12	5
Harper E.C.	3	1
Hodgkinson H.	17	
Hunt G.S.	37	25
Lyons A.	17	1
Marshall W.H.	1	
Meads T.	27	3
Messer A.T.	11	
Moran J.	12	
Nicholls J.H.	2	
O'Callaghan E.	34	16
Poynton C.	25	
Reddish J.	3	
Rowe A.S.	29	
Rowley R.W.M.	7	3
Smailes J.	5	
Spiers C.H.	17	
Taylor A.	23	
Own Goal		

Final table for Second Division

1 Wolverhampton	42	24	8	10	115:49	56
8 TOTTENHAM	**42**	**16**	**11**	**15**	**87:78**	**43**

SEASON 1932/33

27 Aug	Lge	H	Charlton	W	4-1
29 Aug	Lge	A	Nottm Forest	L	1-3
3 Sep	Lge	A	Stoke	L	0-2
5 Sep	Lge	H	Nottm Forest	W	0-0
10 Sep	Lge	H	Man Utd	W	6-1
17 Sep	Lge	A	Bury	L	0-1
24 Sep	Lge	A	Grimsby	L	2-3
1 Oct	Lge	H	Oldham	D	1-1
8 Oct	Lge	A	Preston	W	6-2
15 Oct	Lge	H	Burnley	W	4-1
22 Oct	Lge	H	Southampton	W	5-0
27 Oct	F	A	Oxford Univ	W	6-0
29 Oct	Lge	A	Millwall	W	4-1
3 Nov	F	H	Camb Univ	D	3-3
5 Nov	Lge	H	Port Vale	W	4-0
12 Nov	Lge	A	Lincoln	D	2-2
19 Nov	Lge	H	Chesterfield	W	4-1
26 Nov	Lge	A	Bradford C.	W	1-0
3 Dec	Lge	A	Swansea	W	7-0
10 Dec	Lge	A	Fulham	D	2-2
17 Dec	Lge	H	West Ham	D	2-2
24 Dec	Lge	A	Notts Co.	L	0-3
26 Dec	Lge	A	Bradford PA	D	3-3
27 Dec	Lge	H	Bradford PA	W	2-0
31 Dec	Lge	A	Charlton	W	3-0
7 Jan	Lge	H	Stoke City	W	3-2
14 Jan	FC	H	Oldham	W	6-0
21 Jan	Lge	A	Man Utd	L	1-2
28 Jan	FC	A	Luton	L	0-2
1 Feb	Lge	H	Bury	W	2-1
4 Feb	Lge	A	Grimsby	W	4-3
11 Feb	Lge	H	Oldham	W	5-1
18 Feb	Lge	H	Preston	D	1-1
4 Mar	Lge	A	Southampton	D	1-1
11 Mar	Lge	H	Millwall	W	2-1
18 Mar	Lge	A	Port Vale	D	1-1
25 Mar	Lge	H	Lincoln	W	2-1
1 Apr	Lge	A	Chesterfield	D	1-1
8 Apr	Lge	H	Bradford C	D	1-1
14 Apr	Lge	A	Plymouth	D	0-0
15 Apr	Lge	A	Swansea	W	2-0
17 Apr	Lge	H	Plymouth	D	2-2
22 Apr	Lge	H	Fulham	D	0-0
24 Apr	Lge	A	Burnley	D	1-1
29 Apr	Lge	H	West Ham	L	0-1
6 May	Lge	H	Notts Co	W	3-1
11 May	F	A	Chanl Ilse XI	W	6-0
13 May	F	A	Guernsey XI	W	8-0
18 May	F	A	Jersey XI	W	5-1

Player	Lg App	Goals
Allen A.	1	1
Alsford W.J.	2	
Bellamy W.R.	3	
Brain J.	12	2
Colquhoun D.	29	1
Davies W.	15	1
Evans T.	16	1
Evans W.	42	28
Felton W.	41	
Greenfield G.	13	6
Hall G.W.	21	1
Lowe L.	18	7
Hunt G.S.	41	32
Levene L.	5	
McCormick J.	9	
Meads T.	35	
Morrison J.A.	1	1
Nicholls J.H.	37	
O'Callaghan E.	32	15
Poynton C.	4	
Rowe A.S.	41	
Taylor A.	5	
Whatley W.J.	39	

Final table for Second Division

1 Stoke	42	25	6	11	78:39	56
2 TOTTENHAM	**42**	**20**	**15**	**7**	**96:51**	**55**

SEASON 1933/34

26 Aug	Lge	A	Sheff Utd	D	0-0
28 Aug	Lge	H	Wolves	W	4-0
2 Sep	Lge	H	Aston Villa	W	3-2
4 Sep	Lge	A	Wolves	L	0-1
9 Sep	Lge	H	Leicester	W	3-1
16 Sep	Lge	H	Arsenal	D	1-1
23 Sep	Lge	H	Liverpool	L	0-3
30 Sep	Lge	A	Chelsea	W	4-0
7 Oct	Lge	H	Sunderland	W	3-1
14 Oct	Lge	A	Portsmouth	W	1-0
21 Oct	Lge	A	Everton	D	1-1
28 Oct	Lge	H	Middlesbrough	W	2-0
2 Nov	F	A	Oxford Univ	W	3-1
4 Nov	Lge	A	WBA	W	2-1
11 Nov	Lge	H	Newcastle	W	4-0
18 Nov	Lge	A	Leeds	D	0-0
23 Nov	F	A	Camb Univ	W	6-0
25 Nov	Lge	A	Derby	L	1-2
2 Dec	Lge	H	Man City	L	0-2
9 Dec	Lge	H	Birmingham	W	3-2
16 Dec	Lge	A	Sheff Wed	L	1-2
23 Dec	Lge	A	Blackburn	W	4-1
25 Dec	Lge	H	Huddersfield	L	1-3
26 Dec	Lge	H	Huddersfield	L	0-2
30 Dec	Lge	H	Sheff Utd	W	4-1
1 Jan	Lge	A	Blackburn	L	0-1
6 Jan	Lge	A	Aston Villa	W	5-1
13 Jan	FC	H	Everton	W	3-0
20 Jan	Lge	H	Leicester	L	0-1
27 Jan	FC	H	West Ham	W	4-1
31 Jan	Lge	A	Arsenal	W	3-1
3 Feb	Lge	A	Liverpool	L	1-3
10 Feb	Lge	H	Chelsea	W	2-1
17 Feb	FC	H	Aston Villa	L	0-1
21 Feb	Lge	A	Sunderland	L	0-6
24 Feb	Lge	H	Portsmouth	D	0-0
3 Mar	Lge	H	Everton	W	3-0
5 Mar	F	H	The Army	W	4-1
10 Mar	Lge	A	Middlesbrough	D	1-1
17 Mar	Lge	H	WBA	W	2-1
24 Mar	Lge	A	Newcastle	W	3-1
30 Mar	Lge	A	Stoke	D	0-0
31 Mar	Lge	H	Leeds	W	5-1
2 Apr	Lge	A	Stoke	L	0-2
7 Apr	Lge	A	Derby	L	3-4
14 Apr	Lge	H	Man City	W	5-1
21 Apr	Lge	A	Birmingham	L	0-2
28 Apr	Lge	H	Sheff Wed	W	4-3
30 Apr	F	A	Luton	D	2-2
2 May	SLS	H	Corinthians	W	7-4

Player	Lg App	Goals
Alsford W.J.	13	
Bellamy W.R.	5	
Bolan L.A.	1	
Channell F.C.	22	
Colquhoun D.M.	13	
Day A.	3	
Evans T.	26	
Evans W.	36	16
Hall B.A.C.	2	
Hall G.W.	42	3
Hedley F.	1	
Howe L.	10	6
Hunt G.S.	40	32
Felton W.	22	1
McCormick J.	40	9
Meads J.	30	1
Nicholls J.H.	42	
O'Callaghan E.	32	11
Rowe A.S.	42	
Whatley W.J.	40	

Final table for First Division

1 Arsenal	42	25	9	8	75:47	59
3 TOTTENHAM	**42**	**21**	**7**	**14**	**79:56**	**49**

SEASON 1934/35

25 Aug	Lge	H	Everton	D	1-1
27 Aug	Lge	H	Preston	L	1-2
1 Sep	Lge	A	Huddersfield	D	0-0
3 Sep	Lge	A	Preston	L	0-1
8 Sep	Lge	H	Wolves	W	3-1
15 Sep	Lge	A	Chelsea	W	3-1
22 Sep	Lge	A	Aston Villa	L	0-2
29 Sep	Lge	A	Derby	L	1-2
6 Oct	Lge	H	Leicester	D	2-2
13 Oct	Lge	A	Sunderland	W	2-1
20 Oct	Lge	A	Arsenal	L	1-5
27 Oct	Lge	H	Portsmouth	W	4-1
1 Nov	F	A	Oxford Univ	W	4-3
3 Nov	Lge	A	Man City	L	1-3
7 Nov	SLS	H	Corinthians	W	7-2
10 Nov	Lge	H	Middlesbrough	W	3-1
14 Nov	F	H	Camb Univ	W	4-0
17 Nov	Lge	A	WBA	L	0-4
24 Nov	Lge	H	Sheff Wed	W	3-2
1 Dec	Lge	A	Birmingham	L	1-2
8 Dec	Lge	H	Stoke	W	3-2
15 Dec	Lge	H	Liverpool	L	1-4
22 Dec	Lge	H	Leeds	D	1-1
25 Dec	Lge	A	Grimsby	L	0-3
26 Dec	Lge	H	Grimsby	W	3-0
29 Dec	Lge	A	Everton	L	2-5
1 Jan	Lge	A	Blackburn	L	0-2
5 Jan	Lge	H	Huddersfield	D	0-0
12 Jan	FC	H	Man City	W	1-0
19 Jan	Lge	A	Wolves	L	2-6
26 Jan	FC	H	Newcastle	W	2-0
30 Jan	Lge	H	Chelsea	L	1-3
2 Feb	Lge	A	Aston Villa	L	0-1
9 Feb	Lge	H	Derby	D	2-2
16 Feb	FC	H	Bolton	D	1-1
20 Feb	FCr	A	Bolton	D	1-1
23 Feb	Lge	H	Sunderland	D	1-1
25 Feb	FCr	*	Bolton	L	0-2
6 Mar	Lge	H	Arsenal	L	0-6
9 Mar	Lge	A	Portsmouth	D	1-1
16 Mar	Lge	H	Man City	D	0-0
23 Mar	Lge	A	Middlesbrough	L	1-3
28 Mar	Lge	A	Leicester	L	0-6
30 Mar	Lge	H	WBA	L	0-1
6 Apr	Lge	A	Sheff Wed	L	0-4
13 Apr	Lge	H	Birmingham	D	1-1
19 Apr	Lge	H	Blackburn	W	1-0
20 Apr	Lge	A	Stoke	L	0-1
24 Apr	F	A	Burton Town	D	2-2
27 Apr	Lge	H	Liverpool	W	5-1
4 May	Lge	A	Leeds	L	3-4
16 May	F	A	Chanl Isle XI	W	5-0
18 May	F	A	Guernsey XI	W	5-0

* Played at Villa Park

Player	Lg App	Goals
Alsford W.J.	21	
Bell S.	8	2
Bellamy W.R.	7	1
Bolan L.A.	9	3
Brain J.	1	
Burgon A.	4	
Channell F.C.	41	1

Colquhoun D.M.	3	
Day A.	9	
Duncan A.	6	
Evans T.	28	
Evans W.	32	12
Fullwood J.	2	
Goldsmith G.	1	
Greenfield G.	6	
Hall A.G.	12	3
Hall G.W.	18	3
Hedley F.	3	1
Hooper P.G.	3	
Howe L.F.	32	2
Hunt D.A.	12	4
Hunt G.S.	30	10
Illingworth J.	1	
Jones C.	8	
King E.F.	1	
Levene D.	3	
Meads T.	18	
McCormick J.	28	6
Morrison J.A.	2	1
Nicholls J.H.	21	
O'Callaghan E.	16	4
Phypers E.	2	
Rowe A.S.	18	
Sargent F.A.	1	
Taylor A.	18	
Whatley W.J.	37	
Own Goal		1

Final table for First Division

1 Arsenal	42 23 12 7	115:46 58
22 TOTTENHAM	**42 10 10 22**	**54:93 30**

SEASON 1935/36

31 Aug	Lge	A	Bradford C.	W	1-0
2 Sep	Lge	H	Hull	W	3-1
7 Sep	Lge	H	Newcastle	L	1-2
9 Sep	Lge	A	Hull	L	0-1
14 Sep	Lge	A	Sheff Utd	D	1-1
16 Sep	Lge	H	Barnsley	W	3-0
21 Sep	Lge	A	Man Utd	D	0-0
28 Sep	Lge	H	Port Vale	W	5-2
5 Oct	Lge	A	Fulham	W	2-1
12 Oct	Lge	H	Burnley	W	5-1
19 Oct	Lge	H	Bradford	W	4-0
26 Oct	Lge	A	Leicester	L	1-4
2 Nov	Lge	H	Swansea	W	7-2
9 Nov	Lge	A	West Ham	D	2-2
16 Nov	Lge	H	Bury	W	4-3
21 Nov	F	H	Oxford Univ	W	4-2
23 Nov	Lge	A	Southampton	L	0-2
28 Nov	F	A	Camb Univ	L	0-1
30 Nov	Lge	H	Blackpool	W	3-1
7 Dec	Lge	A	Nottm Forest	L	1-4
14 Dec	Lge	H	Norwich	W	2-1
21 Dec	Lge	A	Doncaster	L	1-4
25 Dec	Lge	H	Plymouth	L	1-2
26 Dec	Lge	A	Plymouth	L	1-2
28 Dec	Lge	H	Bradford C	W	4-0
4 Jan	Lge	A	Newcastle	W	4-1
11 Jan	FC	H	Southend	D	4-4
15 Jan	FCr	A	Southend	W	2-1
18 Jan	Lge	H	Sheff Utd	D	1-1
25 Jan	FC	H	Huddersfield	W	1-0
1 Feb	Lge	A	Port Vale	W	5-1
5 Feb	Lge	H	Man Utd	D	0-0
8 Feb	Lge	H	Fulham	D	2-2
15 Feb	FC	A	Bradford PA	D	0-0
17 Feb	FCr	H	Bradford PA	W	2-1
22 Feb	Lge	A	Bradford PA	W	5-2
29 Feb	FC	A	Sheff Utd	L	1-3
4 Mar	Lge	H	Nottm Forest	D	1-1
7 Mar	Lge	A	Bury	D	1-1
14 Mar	Lge	H	West Ham	L	1-3
21 Mar	Lge	A	Swansea	D	1-1
28 Mar	Lge	H	Southampton	W	8-0
4 Apr	Lge	A	Blackpool	W	4-2
10 Apr	Lge	H	Charlton	D	1-1
11 Apr	Lge	H	Leicester	D	1-1
13 Apr	Lge	A	Charlton	L	1-2
18 Apr	Lge	A	Newcastle	L	0-1
20 Apr	Lge	A	Burnley	D	0-0
25 Apr	Lge	H	Doncaster	W	3-1
2 May	Lge	A	Barnsley	D	0-0

Player	Lg App	Goals
Alsford W.J.	14	
Bell S.	5	3
Buckingham V.F.	16	
Channell F.C.	32	
Day A.	1	
Duncan A.	24	6
Edrich W.J.	9	1
Evans T.	8	
Evans W.	33	15
Fullwood J.	12	1
Grice F.	7	
Hall A.E.	1	
Hall A.G.	4	
Hall G.W.	32	6
Hooper P.G.	21	
Howe L.	33	6
Hunt D.A.	4	2
Hunt G.S.	15	11
Jones C.	10	
McCormick J.	21	3
Meek J.	10	5
Morrison J.A.	32	25
Nicholls J.H.	7	
Phypers E.	26	
Rowe A.S.	28	
Sargent F.A.	16	5
Taylor A.	14	
Ward R.A.	8	
Whatley W.J.	19	
Own Goals		2

Final table for Second Division

1 Manchester U.	42 22 12 8	85:43 56
5 TOTTENHAM	**42 18 13 11**	**91:55 49**

SEASON 1936/37

29 Aug	Lge	A	West Ham	L	1-2
31 Aug	Lge	A	Blackpool	D	0-0
5 Sep	Lge	H	Norwich	L	2-3
12 Sep	Lge	A	Newcastle	W	1-0
14 Sep	Lge	H	Leicester	W	4-2
19 Sep	Lge	H	Bradford	W	5-1
21 Sep	Lge	H	Blackpool	L	1-2
26 Sep	Lge	A	Barnsley	L	0-1
3 Oct	Lge	H	Sheff Utd	D	2-2
10 Oct	Lge	A	Burnley	L	1-3
17 Oct	Lge	H	Southampton	W	4-0
24 Oct	Lge	A	Swansea	L	1-2
31 Oct	Lge	H	Bradford C	W	5-1
7 Nov	Lge	A	Aston Villa	D	1-1
14 Nov	Lge	H	Chesterfield	W	5-1
16 Nov	F	H	Corinthians	W	5-1
19 Nov	F	A	Oxford Univ	W	2-0
26 Nov	F	A	Camb Univ	W	6-2
28 Nov	Lge	H	Plymouth	L	1-3
5 Dec	Lge	A	Coventry	L	0-1
12 Dec	Lge	H	Doncaster	W	2-0
19 Dec	Lge	A	Fulham	D	3-3
25 Dec	Lge	A	Blackburn	W	4-0
26 Dec	Lge	H	West Ham	L	2-3
28 Dec	Lge	H	Blackburn	W	5-1
2 Jan	Lge	A	Norwich	W	3-2
9 Jan	Lge	H	Newcastle	L	0-1
16 Jan	FC	A	Portsmouth	W	5-0
23 Jan	Lge	A	Bradford	L	2-3
30 Jan	FC	H	Plymouth	W	1-0
3 Feb	Lge	H	Barnsley	W	3-0
6 Feb	Lge	A	Sheff Utd	L	2-3
13 Feb	Lge	H	Burnley	W	3-0
20 Feb	FC	A	Everton	D	1-1
22 Feb	FCr	H	Everton	W	4-3
24 Feb	Lge	A	Southampton	L	0-1
27 Feb	Lge	H	Swansea	W	3-1
6 Mar	FC	A	Preston	L	1-3
10 Mar	Lge	A	Bradford C	D	2-2
13 Mar	Lge	H	Aston Villa	D	2-2
20 Mar	Lge	A	Chesterfield	W	3-1
26 Mar	Lge	A	Bury	L	3-5
27 Mar	Lge	H	Nottm Forest	W	2-1
29 Mar	Lge	H	Bury	W	2-0
3 Apr	Lge	A	Plymouth	D	2-2
10 Apr	Lge	H	Coventry	W	3-1
17 Apr	Lge	A	Doncaster	D	1-1
21 Apr	Lge	A	Nottm Forest	L	0-3
24 Apr	Lge	H	Fulham	D	1-1

1 May	Lge	A	Leicester	L 1-4

Player	Lg App	Goals
Alexander S.	9	1
Alsford W.J.	7	
Bell S.	2	1
Blyth J.	11	
Brown J.	4	
Buckingham V.F.	25	
Duncan A.	29	9
Edrich W.J.	11	3
Evans T.	1	
Evans W.	7	2
Fullwood J.	5	
Grice F.	22	
Hall A.E.	1	
Hall G.W.	19	1
Hall J.	39	
Cooper P.G.	3	
Howe L.	28	
Hunt D.A.	1	
Hunt G.S.	13	10
Ludford G.A.	1	
McCormick J.	35	8
Meek J.	28	9
Miller L.	23	12
Morrison J.A.	32	29
Page A.E.	15	
Phypers E.	2	
Ringrose A.	10	
Rowe A.S.	15	
Ward R.A.	32	3
Whatley W.J.	32	

Final table for Second Division

1 Leicester	42 24 8 10	89:57 56
1 TOTTENHAM	**42 17 9 16**	**88:66 43**

SEASON 1937/38

28 Aug	Lge	H	Coventry	D	0-0
30 Aug	Lge	H	Burnley	W	4-0
4 Sep	Lge	A	Nottm Forest	L	1-3
6 Sep	Lge	A	Burnley	L	1-2
11 Sep	Lge	H	Newcastle	D	2-2
16 Sep	Lge	A	Sheff Wed	W	3-0
18 Sep	Lge	A	Luton	W	4-2
25 Sep	Lge	H	Barnsley	W	3-0
2 Oct	Lge	A	Stockport	L	2-3
9 Oct	Lge	H	Man Utd	L	0-1
16 Oct	Lge	A	Fulham	L	1-3
23 Oct	Lge	H	Plymouth	W	3-2
30 Oct	Lge	A	Chesterfield	D	2-2
6 Nov	Lge	H	Swansea	W	2-0
13 Nov	Lge	A	Norwich	L	1-2
18 Nov	F	H	Oxford Univ	W	3-2
20 Nov	Lge	H	West Ham	W	2-0
25 Nov	F	A	Camb Univ	L	2-3
27 Nov	Lge	A	Bradford PA	W	2-1
4 Dec	Lge	H	Aston Villa	W	2-1
11 Dec	Lge	A	Southampton	L	1-2
18 Dec	Lge	H	Blackburn	W	3-1
25 Dec	Lge	A	Bury	W	2-1
26 Dec	Lge	H	Bury	L	1-3
1 Jan	Lge	A	Coventry	L	1-2
8 Jan	FC	H	Blackburn	W	3-2
15 Jan	Lge	H	Nottm Forest	W	3-0
22 Jan	FC	A	N/Brighton	D	0-0
26 Jan	FCr	H	N/Brighton	W	5-2
29 Jan	Lge	H	Luton	W	3-0
2 Feb	Lge	A	Newcastle	L	0-1
5 Feb	Lge	A	Barnsley	D	1-1
12 Feb	FC	A	Chesterfield	D	2-2
16 Feb	FCr	H	Chesterfield	W	2-1
19 Feb	Lge	A	Man Utd	W	1-0
23 Feb	Lge	H	Stockport	W	2-0
26 Feb	Lge	H	Fulham	D	1-1
7 Mar	FC	H	Sunderland	L	0-1*
9 Mar	Lge	A	Plymouth	D	2-2
12 Mar	Lge	H	Chesterfield	W	2-0
19 Mar	Lge	A	Swansea	L	2-3
26 Mar	Lge	H	Norwich	W	4-0
2 Apr	Lge	A	West Ham	W	3-1
9 Apr	Lge	H	Bradford PA	W	2-1
15 Apr	Lge	H	Sheff Utd	L	1-2
16 Apr	Lge	A	Aston Villa	L	0-2
18 Apr	Lge	A	Sheff Utd	L	0-1

23 Apr	Lge	H	Southampton	W	5-0
30 Apr	Lge	A	Blackburn	L	1-2
7 May	Lge	H	Sheff Wed	L	1-2

* Tottenham's record attendance (75,038)

Player	Lg App	Goals
Buckingham V.F.	29	
Duncan A.	13	2
Fullwood J.	15	
Gibbons A.H.	27	13
Grice F.	17	1
Hall A.E.	6	
Hall G.W.	30	4
Hall J.	12	
Hitchins A.W.	10	
Hooper P.G.	30	
Howe L.	33	4
Jeffrey G.	1	1
Ludford G.A.	1	
Lyman C.C.	24	4
McCormick J.	3	
Meek J.	7	1
Miller L.	16	5
Morrison J.A.	39	23
Page A.E.	23	
Rowe A.S.	9	
Sargent F.A.	42	14
Spelman I.	8	
Ward R.A.	42	4
Whatley W.J.	25	

Final table for Second Division

1 Aston Villa	42 25 7 10	73:35 57
5 TOTTENHAM	**42 19 6 17**	**76:54 44**

SEASON 1938/39

20 Aug	J†	A	Arsenal	W	2-0
27 Aug	Lge	A	Southampton	W	2-1
29 Aug	Lge	H	Sheff Wed	D	3-3
3 Sep	Lge	A	Coventry	W	2-1
10 Sep	Lge	A	Nottm Forest	L	1-2
12 Sep	Lge	H	Sheff Utd	D	2-2
17 Sep	Lge	H	Newcastle	W	1-0
24 Sep	Lge	A	WBA	L	3-4
1 Oct	Lge	A	Norwich	W	4-1
8 Oct	Lge	A	Luton	D	0-0
15 Oct	Lge	H	Fulham	W	1-0
22 Oct	Lge	A	Blackburn	L	1-3
29 Oct	Lge	H	West Ham	W	2-1
5 Nov	Lge	A	Man City	L	0-2
12 Nov	Lge	H	Bradford PA	D	2-2
19 Nov	Lge	A	Swansea	D	1-1
26 Nov	Lge	H	Chesterfield	D	2-2
3 Dec	Lge	A	Tranmere	W	2-0
10 Dec	Lge	H	Millwall	W	4-0
17 Dec	Lge	A	Bury	L	1-3
24 Dec	Lge	H	Southampton	D	1-1
26 Dec	Lge	A	Burnley	L	0-1
27 Dec	Lge	H	Burnley	W	1-0
31 Dec	Lge	A	Coventry	L	0-4
7 Jan	FC	H	Watford	W	7-1
14 Jan	Lge	H	Nottm Forest	W	4-1
21 Jan	FC	A	West Ham	D	3-3
28 Jan	Lge	H	WBA	D	2-2
30 Jan	FCr	H	West Ham	D	1-1
2 Feb	FCr	*	West Ham	L	1-2
4 Feb	Lge	A	Norwich	W	2-1
11 Feb	Lge	H	Luton	L	0-1
18 Feb	Lge	A	Fulham	L	0-1
25 Feb	Lge	H	Blackburn	W	4-3
1 Mar	Lge	A	Newcastle	W	1-0
4 Mar	Lge	H	West Ham	W	2-0
11 Mar	Lge	H	Man City	L	2-3
18 Mar	Lge	A	Bradford PA	D	0-0
25 Mar	Lge	H	Swansea	W	3-0
1 Apr	Lge	A	Chesterfield	L	1-3
7 Apr	Lge	H	Plymouth	W	1-0
8 Apr	Lge	H	Tranmere	W	3-1
10 Apr	Lge	A	Plymouth	W	1-0
15 Apr	Lge	A	Millwall	L	0-2
29 Apr	Lge	H	Bury	W	4-3
29 Apr	Lge	A	Sheff Wed	L	0-1
6 May	Lge	A	Sheff Utd	L	1-6

* Played at Highbury
J† Jubilee Trust Fun

211

Player	Lg App	Goals
Buckingham V.F.	41	1
Burgess W.A.R.	17	1
Cox F.J.A.	9	2
Duncan A.	21	5
Grice F.	1	
Hall A.E.	24	10
Hall G.W.	40	9
Hall J.	2	
Hitchins A.W.	25	1
Cooper P.G.	40	
Howe L.	8	1
Ludford G.A.	10	6
Lyman C.C.	22	6
McCormick J.	1	
Miller L.	17	5
Morrison J.A.	27	9
Nicholson W.E.	8	
Page A.E.	17	
Sargent F.A.	34	4
Spelman I.	20	2
Sproston B.	9	
Tomkin A.H.	2	
Ward R.A.	33	3
Whatley W.J.	34	2

Second Division 1938–39

1 Blackburn	42 25	5 12	94:60	55
8 TOTTENHAM	**42 19**	**9 14**	**67:62**	**47**

SEASON 1939/40

19 Aug	J†	H	Arsenal	L	0-1
26 Aug	Lge*	H	Birmingham	D	1-1
31 Aug	Lge*	A	Newport	D	1-1
2 Sep	Lge*	A	WBA	W	4-3
23 Sep	F	A	Chelmsford	L	2-4
30 Sep	F	A	Chelsea	L	2-4
7 Oct	F	H	West Ham	L	0-2
21 Oct	Lge	A	Southend	W	2-1
28 Oct	Lge	H	Millwall	W	3-0
4 Nov	Lge	A	West Ham	L	1-2
11 Nov	Lge	H	Watford	W	8-2
18 Nov	Lge	A	Arsenal	L	1-2
25 Nov	Lge	H	Charlton	W	4-2
2 Dec	Lge	A	C. Orient	L	1-2
9 Dec	Lge	H	C. Palace	L	1-3
16 Dec	Lge	A	Norwich	L	2-5
23 Dec	Lge	H	Southend	L	3-4‡
25 Dec	Lge	A	Millwall	L	1-5
26 Dec	Lge	H	West Ham	L	0-1
30 Dec	Lge	A	Watford	L	1-6
13 Jan	Lge	A	Charlton	W	5-1
17 Jan	Lge	H	Southend	L	2-4
20 Jan	Lge	H	C. Orient	L	2-3
25 Jan	Lge	A	Arsenal	L	0-1
10 Feb	Lge	A	West Ham	L	0-2
17 Feb	Lge	H	Charlton	W	2-0
24 Feb	Lge	A	Chelsea	W	2-0
28 Feb	Lge	A	C. Palace	D	1-1
2 Mar	Lge	H	Southampton	W	4-1
9 Mar	Lge	H	Brentford	D	1-1
16 Mar	Lge	A	Portsmouth	W	2-1
22 Mar	Lge	H	Millwall	L	1-2
23 Mar	Lge	A	Fulham	W	3-2
25 Mar	Lge	A	Millwall	D	1-1
30 Mar	Lge	H	Arsenal	D	1-1
6 Apr	Lge	H	West Ham	L	2-6
10 Apr	Lge	A	Fulham	W	3-1
13 Apr	Lge	A	Charlton	W	4-2
20 Apr	CUP	A	C. Palace	L	1-4
24 Apr	Lge	A	Arsenal	W	4-2
27 Apr	CUP	H	C. Palace	W	2-1
4 May	Lge	A	Brentford	W	3-2
11 May	Lge	H	Portsmouth	W	4-1
18 May	Lge	A	Southampton	D	3-3
25 May	Lge	H	Chelsea	W	3-2
27 May	Lge	H	Norwich	D	2-2

J† Football League Jubilee match
* Three Football League fixtures which were played before the season was abandoned. Other League matches this season were in the two Regional Leagues South.   ‡ Match abandoned and replayed on 17 Jan.

Player	Lg App	Goals
Buckingham V.F.	3	
Burgess W.A.R.	3	1
Dix R.W.	3	1
Hall G.W.	3	
Hitchins A.W.	2	
Hooper P.G.	3	
Ludford G.A.	2	
Lyman C.C.	1	
Morrison J.A.	1	3
Nicholson W.E.	3	
Page A.E.	1	
Sargent F.A.	3	1
Tomkin A.H.	2	
Ward R.A.	3	

Player	War Lg App	Goals
Bennett L.	11	6
Buckingham V.	14	
Burchell	1	
Burgess R.	14	2
Cox F.	10	1
Ditchburn E.	2	
Dix R.	14	6
Dorling	12	
Dowers	2	
Duncan A.	16	4
Evans	1	
Hall A.E.	4	2
Hall G.W.	26	4
Hitchens	32	
Hooper P.	33	
Howe L.	31	5
Hunt D.	2	2
Ludford G.	11	7
Lyman C.	6	1
McCormick J.	6	
McEwan	3	
Medley L.	23	10
Morrison J.	29	21
Ottewell*	1	
Page A.	7	
Piper	1	
Sargent F.	15	5
Spelman I.	11	
Stephens	1	
Tomkin A.	1	2
Ward R.	21	2
Whatley G.	33	
Wilbert G.	1	

* Guest

Second Division 1939–40

1 Luton	3 2 1 0	7:1	5
7 TOTTENHAM	**3 1 2 0**	**6:5**	**4**

Regional League South 'A' 1939–40

1 Arsenal	18 13 4 1	62:22	30
9 TOTTENHAM	**18 5 2 11**	**37:43**	**12**

Regional League South 'C' 1939–40

1 TOTTENHAM	**18 11 4 3**	**43:30**	**26**

SEASON 1940/41

31 Aug	Lge	H	West Ham	L	2-3
7 Sep	Lge	A	West Ham	W	4-1*
14 Sep	Lge	H	Chelsea	W	3-2*
21 Sep	Lge	A	Chelsea	L	1-4
28 Sep	Lge	H	Charlton	L	1-3
5 Oct	Lge	A	QPR	D	1-1
12 Oct	Lge	H	QPR	L	2-3*
19 Oct	Lge	A	Charlton	L	0-4
26 Oct	Lge	H	Portsmouth	L	1-2
2 Nov	Lge	A	Luton	D	1-1
16 Nov	Lge	A	Arsenal	D	1-1
23 Nov	Lge	H	Luton	W	2-1*
30 Nov	Lge	A	Southend	L	2-3†
7 Dec	Lge	H	QPR	L	2-3
21 Dec	Lge	H	C. Orient	W	9-0
25 Dec	Lge	H	Millwall	D	3-3
28 Dec	Lge	A	C. Orient	W	7-0
4 Jan	LCup	H	C. Orient	W	3-0
11 Jan	LCup	A	C. Orient	W	9-1
18 Jan	LCup	A	Millwall	W	3-1
25 Jan	LCup	H	Millwall	W	4-0
1 Feb	LCup	H	West Ham	L	1-2
8 Feb	LCup	A	West Ham	L	2-3
15 Feb	LGC	H	Bournemouth	W	4-1
22 Feb	LGC	A	Bournemouth	W	6-1
1 Mar	LGC	H	Northampton	W	4-0
8 Mar	LGC	A	Northampton	W	3-1
15 Mar	Lge	H	Millwall	L	0-1
22 Mar	LGC	H	Cardiff	D	3-3
29 Mar	LGC	A	Cardiff	W	3-2
5 Apr	LGC	A	Arsenal	L	1-2
12 Apr	LGC	H	Arsenal	D	1-1
14 Apr	LCup	H	Reading	D	2-2
19 Apr	LCup	A	Reading	D	2-2
26 Apr	Lge	A	Aldershot	W	3-2
3 May	LCup	H	Arsenal	D	3-3
10 May	Lge	H	C. Palace	D	1-1
17 May	Lge	A	Leicester	W	2-1
21 May	LCup	A	Arsenal	W	3-0
24 May	Lge	H	Leicester	W	3-0
31 May	LCupsf	H	Brentford	L	0-2
7 Jun	Lge	H	Fulham	W	2-1

* Matches abandoned
† Played at Chelmsford

Player	War Lg App	Goals
Arnold*	1	
Bennett L.	5	
Broadis I.	4	2
Brown J.	1	
Buckingham V.	14	
Burdett	1	
Burgess R.	9	8
Duncan A.	17	5
Flack*	5	
Gibbons A.	8	9
Goodman*	1	
Hall G.W.	15	3
Henley*	1	
Hitchens	22	
Hooper P.	14	
Howe L.	4	2
Ludford G.	23	11
McCarthy	1	
McCormick J.	2	
Medley L.	6	2
Newman A.	1	
O'Callaghan F.	8	1
Paton*	4	
Piper	3	
Sainsbury	1	
Sargent F.	6	1
Saunders*	3	
Skinner	3	1
Sperrin J.	4	2
Sperrin W.	8	3
Wallace J.	1	
Wallis J.	2	
Ward R.	22	2
Whatley W.	20	
White R.	13	
Own Goal		1

* Guest

Regional League South 1940–41

1 C. Palace	27 16 4 7	86:44 1.954	
10 TOTTENHAM	**23 9 5 9**	**53:41 1.292**	

Final placings were decided solely on goal average.

SEASON 1941/42

30 Aug	Lge	H	Watford	W	5-0
6 Sep	Lge	A	Aldershot	L	2-3
13 Sep	Lge	H	Millwall	W	3-0
20 Sep	Lge	A	Arsenal	L	0-3
27 Sep	Lge	H	QPR	W	3-1
4 Oct	Lge	A	Reading	D	1-1
11 Oct	Lge	H	Brighton	L	1-2
18 Oct	Lge	A	Brentford	W	4-1
25 Oct	Lge	H	C. Palace	D	1-1
1 Nov	Lge	A	Fulham	D	2-2
8 Nov	Lge	H	C. Orient	W	2-0
15 Nov	Lge	A	Portsmouth	W	2-1
22 Nov	Lge	A	Chelsea	D	1-1
29 Nov	Lge	A	Charlton	L	1-2
6 Dec	Lge	H	West Ham	D	1-1
13 Dec	Lge	A	Watford	W	2-1
20 Dec	Lge	H	Aldershot	D	1-1
25 Dec	Lge	A	Millwall	W	2-1
27 Dec	Lge	H	Arsenal	L	1-2
3 Jan	Lge	A	QPR	L	0-1
10 Jan	Lge	H	Reading	W	2-1
17 Jan	Lge	A	Brighton	L	2-5
31 Jan	Lge	A	C. Palace	D	2-2
14 Feb	Lge	A	C. Orient	W	3-2
21 Feb	Lge	H	Portsmouth	D	1-1
28 Feb	Lge	H	Chelsea	W	2-0
7 Mar	Lge	H	Charlton	W	2-0
14 Mar	Lge	A	West Ham	W	3-2
21 Mar	CUP	A	Reading	W	2-1
28 Mar	CUP	H	Watford	W	5-2
4 Apr	CUP	A	Reading	W	2-1
6 Apr	CUP	A	Watford	D	0-0
11 Apr	CUP	H	Charlton	L	0-3
18 Apr	CUP	A	Charlton	L	0-4
25 Apr	Lge	H	Brentford	W	2-1
2 May	Lge	H	Fulham	W	7-1
25 May	F	A	C. Palace	W	5-3

Player	War Lg App	Goals
Bennett F.	4	
Bennett L.	1	1
Broadis I.	29	11
Buckingham V.	1	
Burgess R.	5	2
Cox F.	2	
Ditchburn E.	10	
Duncan A.	24	3
Edwards R.	1	
Finch*	1	
Fitzgerald*	1	
Gibbons A.	23	18
Gilberg H.	2	
Hall G.W.	29	1
Hitchens	26	
Hooper P.	16	
Howe L.	4	1
Joliffe	1	
Ludford G.	24	15
Mannion W.*	4	
McCormick J.	1	
Noble*	6	3
Pearson*	2	
Revell*	1	1
Sainsbury	3	
Sibley	3	1
Sperrin J.	3	
Sperrin W.	8	
Stevens	1	2
Tickridge	30	
Trailer	1	
Ward R.	30	
Whatley W.	5	
White R.	24	2
Williams*	3	
Woodward	1	

* Guest

London League 1941–42

1 Arsenal	30 23 2 5	108:43	48
5 TOTTENHAM	**30 15 8 7**	**61:41**	**38**

SEASON 1942/43

29 Aug	Lge	H	C. Palace	L	1-3
5 Sep	Lge	A	QPR	W	1-0
12 Sep	Lge	H	Charlton	W	6-1
19 Sep	Lge	A	West Ham	L	1-3
26 Sep	Lge	H	Southampton	D	1-1
3 Oct	Lge	H	Aldershot	W	4-0
10 Oct	Lge	H	Millwall	W	2-1
17 Oct	Lge	A	Reading	W	6-2
24 Oct	Lge	A	Portsmouth	L	0-1
31 Oct	Lge	H	Chelsea	D	1-1
7 Nov	Lge	A	Arsenal	W	1-0
14 Nov	Lge	A	Luton	D	3-3
21 Nov	Lge	H	Watford	W	6-0
28 Nov	Lge	A	C. Palace	D	0-0
5 Dec	Lge	H	QPR	W	6-0
12 Dec	Lge	A	Charlton	W	3-0
19 Dec	Lge	H	West Ham	W	2-0

25 Dec	Lge	H	Brentford	D	1-1
26 Dec	Lge	A	Brentford	L	1-2
2 Jan	Lge	A	Southampton	L	1-2
9 Jan	Lge	A	Aldershot	W	3-1
16 Jan	Lge	A	Millwall	W	3-0
23 Jan	Lge	H	Reading	D	2-2
30 Jan	Lge	H	Portsmouth	W	5-2
6 Feb	Lge	A	Chelsea	W	1-0
13 Feb	Lge	A	Arsenal	L	0-1
20 Feb	Lge	H	Luton	W	4-1
27 Feb	Lge	A	Watford	W	3-0
6 Mar	CUP	H	Chelsea	W	2-0
13 Mar	CUP	A	Reading	D	1-1
20 Mar	CUP	H	Millwall	W	5-0
27 Mar	CUP	A	Chelsea	W	2-0
3 Apr	CUP	H	Reading	L	1-2
10 Apr	CUP	A	Millwall	W	1-0
17 Apr	F	A	QPR	D	1-1
24 Apr	F	H	Charlton	W	2-1
26 Apr	F	H	Fulham	W	3-0
1 May	F	H	C. Orient	W	4-3
8 May	F	H	Arsenal	L	1-2

Player	War Lg App	Goals
Barron	1	
Beasley*	21	10
Bennett L.	1	
Briggs*	2	
Broadis I.	9	2
Browne	3	
Burgess R.	4	
Chapman*	1	
Chisholm	28	
Cox F.	3	2
Ditchburn E.	9	
Dix R.	1	
Duncan A.	1	
Eastham*	1	
Edwards R.	3	1
Finlay	3	
Gibbons A.	23	17
Gurr	1	
Hall G.W.	25	6
Hares*	1	
Hooper P.	16	
Howe L.	16	
Jackson*	2	
Ludford G.	23	15
Maeshall	1	
Martin*	19	6
McCormick J.*	2	
Muir	1	
Nicholson W.	1	
O'Callaghan E.	6	2
Pattison*	12	3
Sainsbury	1	
Sargent	1	1
Sperrin W.	3	2
Staley*	1	
Ward R.	26	1
Whatley W.	11	
White R.	25	
* Guest		

Football League South 1942–43

1 Arsenal	28	21	1	6	102:40	43
2 TOTTENHAM	**28**	**16**	**6**	**6**	**68:28**	**38**

SEASON 1943/44

28 Aug	Lge	H	C. Palace	D	1-1
4 Sep	Lge	A	QPR	L	0-1
11 Sep	Lge	H	Charlton	W	4-2
18 Sep	Lge	A	West Ham	D	3-3
25 Sep	Lge	H	Southampton	D	2-2
2 Oct	Lge	A	Aldershot	W	5-2
9 Oct	Lge	H	Brighton	W	2-0
16 Oct	Lge	A	Reading	W	3-2
23 Oct	Lge	A	Luton	L	2-4
30 Oct	Lge	H	Chelsea	W	5-1
6 Nov	Lge	A	Brentford	W	2-0
13 Nov	Lge	A	C. Orient	W	4-0
20 Nov	Lge	H	Watford	W	4-2
27 Nov	Lge	A	C. Palace	L	0-3
4 Dec	Lge	H	QPR	D	2-2
11 Dec	Lge	A	Charlton	W	2-0
18 Dec	Lge	H	Arsenal	W	2-1

25 Dec	Lge	H	Fulham	W	2-0
27 Dec	Lge	A	Fulham	W	2-0
1 Jan	Lge	H	West Ham	W	1-0
8 Jan	Lge	H	Brentford	W	1-0
15 Jan	Lge	A	Southampton	W	3-2
22 Jan	Lge	A	Aldershot	W	1-0
29 Jan	Lge	A	Brighton	W	2-0
5 Feb	Lge	H	Reading	D	2-2
12 Feb	Lge	H	Luton	W	8-1
19 Feb	CUP	*	Millwall	W	1-0
26 Feb	CUP	H	Portsmouth	W	1-0
4 Mar	CUP	A	Aldershot	L	1-2
11 Mar	CUP	H	Millwall	W	1-0
18 Mar	CUP	A	Portsmouth	W	2-1
25 Mar	CUP	H	Aldershot	W	2-0
1 Apr	CUPsf	†	Charlton	L	0-3
8 Apr	F	A	Chelsea	D	1-1
10 Apr	F	A	Millwall	D	0-0
22 Apr	Lge	A	Arsenal	D	3-3
29 Apr	Lge	H	C. Orient	W	1-0
6 May	Lge	A	Watford	D	1-1

* Played at Selhurst Park
† Played at Stamford Bridge

Player	War Lg App	Goals
Adams	4	
Beasley	28	11
Bennett L.	1	1
Briggs*	1	
Browne	2	
Bryant	3	1
Buckingham V.	6	
Burgess R.	19	7
Chisholm	24	
Clayton*	2	1
Cox F.	9	1
Davie*	1	
Ditchburn E.	21	
Dix R.	2	
Downer*	1	
Edwards R.	2	
Flack*	2	
Gibbins	1	
Gilberg H.	1	
Hall G.W.	6	
Harris*	1	
Hooper P.	8	
Howe L.	5	1
Jones*	16	7
Ludford G.	13	1
Manley*	1	
Martin*	14	3
Mogford*	4	
Mosley	3	1
O'Callaghan E.	2	
O'Donnell*	11	7
Page	2	
Rowley*	18	19
Sainsbury	1	
Smith T.*	2	1
Walters	9	4
Ward R.	30	1
Whatley W.	21	
Whent	2	1
White R.	22	1
Willis	6	
Wilson*	1	
Young*	2	
Own Goals		2
* Guest		

Football League South 1943–44

1 TOTTENHAM	**30**	**19**	**8**	**3**	**71:36**	**46**

SEASON 1944/45

19 Aug	F	A	Coventry	L	1-3
26 Aug	Lge	H	West Ham	D	2-2
2 Sep	Lge	H	Arsenal	W	4-0
9 Sep	Lge	A	Reading	D	0-0
16 Sep	Lge	H	Portsmouth	D	1-1
23 Sep	Lge	A	Southampton	W	3-1
30 Sep	Lge	H	Charlton	W	2-1
7 Oct	Lge	A	C. Palace	W	3-1
14 Oct	Lge	H	Chaelsea	L	1-5
21 Oct	Lge	A	Luton	W	9-1
28 Oct	Lge	H	Brentford	D	2-2

4 Nov	Lge	H	Aldershot	W	7-0
11 Nov	Lge	A	Millwall	W	4-3
18 Nov	Lge	A	C. Orient	W	2-0
25 Nov	Lge	H	Fulham	W	2-1
2 Dec	Lge	A	West Ham	W	1-0
9 Dec	Lge	A	Arsenal	W	3-2
16 Dec	Lge	H	Reading	W	3-2
23 Dec	Lge	A	QPR	D	0-0
25 Dec	Lge	H	QPR	W	4-2
30 Dec	Lge	A	Portsmouth	D	0-0
6 Jan	Lge	H	Southampton	W	4-0
13 Jan	Lge	A	Charlton	W	2-1
20 Jan	Lge	H	C. Palace	W	3-1
27 Jan	Lge	A	Chelsea	W	2-1
3 Feb	CUP	H	QPR	D	1-1
10 Feb	CUP	A	West Ham	L	0-1
17 Feb	CUP	A	Aldershot	W	6-1
24 Feb	CUP	A	QPR	L	0-1
3 Mar	CUP	H	West Ham	W	4-0
10 Mar	CUP	A	Aldershot	W	2-0
24 Mar	Lge	A	Brentford	W	2-0
1 Apr	Lge	A	Aldershot	W	1-0
7 Apr	F	A	C. Palace	L	1-3
14 Apr	Lge	H	Millwall	W	4-0
21 Apr	Lge	H	C. Orient	W	4-0
28 Apr	Lge	A	Fulham	W	4-2
5 May	Lge	H	Luton	W	1-0
19 May	F	H	Arsenal	W	4-0
26 May	F	H	Fulham	D	2-2

Player	War Lg App	Goals
Adams	4	
Anderson*	1	
Beasley	24	9
Boulton*	1	
Broadis	6	2
Brown	3	
Burgess R.	23	10
Burke*	10	
Burnett*	1	2
Chisholm	6	
Dix	1	
Duke*	2	
Dunn*	1	
Flavell*	11	
Foreman*	5	8
Gibbons A.	11	10
Gilberg H.	8	6
Goodman	1	
Hall A.E.	5	2
Hall F.*	14	
Henley*	1	1
Howe L.	5	1
Hughes*	21	
Jackson*	2	
Ludford G.	12	5
Martin*	1	
Medley L.	7	1
Mogford	3	
Muir*	1	
Oakes*	1	
O'Donnell*	2	1
Page	3	
Pryde*	1	
Rowley*	2	2
Smith K.*	1	
Stevens	11	5
Swift	1	
Wallis	4	
Walters	30	8
Ward R.	30	5
Whatley W.	1	
White R.	24	
Whittingham*	1	1
Willis	27	
Own Goals		2
* Guest		

Football League South 1944–45

1 TOTTENHAM	**30**	**23**	**6**	**1**	**81:30**	**52**

SEASON 1945/46

25 Aug	Lge	H	Wolves	L	1-4
1 Sep	Lge	A	Wolves	L	2-4
8 Sep	Lge	A	West Ham	D	1-1
12 Sep	Lge	H	Leicester	W	6-2

15 Sep	Lge	H	West Ham	L	2-3
22 Sep	Lge	A	West Brom	L	0-5
29 Sep	Lge	H	West Brom	W	4-2
6 Oct	Lge	A	Birmingham C	L	0-8
13 Oct	Lge	A	Birmingham C	L	0-1
20 Oct	Lge	A	Swansea	L	2-4
27 Oct	Lge	H	Swansea	W	3-1
3 Nov	Lge	H	Brentford	W	1-0
10 Nov	Lge	A	Brentford	W	3-1
17 Nov	Lge	A	Chelsea	W	2-1
24 Nov	Lge	H	Chelsea	W	3-2
1 Dec	Lge	H	Millwall	W	5-1
8 Dec	Lge	A	Millwall	L	2-3
15 Dec	Lge	A	Southampton	L	2-3
22 Dec	Lge	H	Southampton	W	4-3
25 Dec	Lge	H	Derby	L	2-5
26 Dec	Lge	A	Derby	L	0-2
29 Dec	Lge	H	Leicester	L	0-4
5 Jan	FC	H	Brentford	D	2-2
10 Jan	FC	A	Brentford	L	0-2*
12 Jan	Lge	A	Luton	L	1-3
19 Jan	Lge	H	Luton	L	2-3
26 Jan	Lge	H	Coventry	W	2-0
2 Feb	Lge	A	Aston Villa	L	1-5
9 Feb	Lge	A	Arsenal	D	1-1
16 Feb	Lge	H	Arsenal	W	2-0
20 Feb	Lge	H	Aston Villa	W	3-0
23 Feb	Lge	H	Charlton	W	2-1
2 Mar	F	H	Chelsea	W	4-2
9 Mar	Lge	A	Fulham	D	1-1
16 Mar	Lge	H	Fulham	L	1-3
23 Mar	Lge	H	Plymouth	W	2-0
30 Mar	Lge	A	Plymouth	W	1-0
6 Apr	Lge	A	Portsmouth	W	1-0
13 Apr	Lge	H	Portsmouth	W	2-0
17 Apr	Lge	A	Charlton	L	0-1
19 Apr	Lge	H	Nottm Forest	W	3-2
20 Apr	Lge	A	Newport	W	4-1
22 Apr	Lge	A	Nottm Forest	W	2-0
27 Apr	Lge	H	Newport	W	1-0
4 May	Lge	A	Coventry	W	1-0
7 May	F	H	FA XI	W	4-1†

* Second leg, not a replay
†Willie Hall testimonial

Player	War Lg App	Goals
Acquroff J.*	2	2
Adams	1	
Baily E.	1	
Beasley	2	
Bennett L.	11	
Blair J.	2	1
Boradis I.	9	5
Buckingham V.	19	
Burgess R.	37	7
Chisholm	1	
Cox F.	1	
Ditchburn E.	2	
Dix R.	26	4
Duquemin L.	1	
Ferrier*	1	
Fletcher	1	
Ford*	3	
Foreman G.	10	13
Garwood L.	1	
Gibbons A.	21	14
Gilberg H.	1	
Hall A.E.	24	5
Hall F.	6	
Hall J.	9	
Howe L.	1	
Howshall*	1	
Hughes W.	27	
Jinks J.*	1	2
Joslin	4	
Ludford G.	30	3
Lyman G.	21	7
McCormick J.	3	1
Medley L.	17	3
Morrison J.	1	
Nicholson W.	11	
Page	16	
Rundle C.	4	
Sargent	2	
Skinner G.	11	2
Smith	4	
Stevens L.	13	1
Walters W.	2	

Player		
Ward R.	26	4
Whitchurch C.	17	4
White A.	1	
White R.	24	
Willis A.	32	
Young*	1	

* Guest

Football League South 1945–46

1 Birmingham	42 28 5 9	96:45	61
9 TOTTENHAM	**42 22 3 17**	**78:81**	**47**

SEASON 1946/47

31 Aug	Lge	H	Birmingham	L	1-2
7 Sep	Lge	A	WBA	L	2-3
9 Sep	Lge	H	Southampton	W	2-1
14 Sep	Lge	H	Newcastle	D	1-1
19 Sep	Lge	A	Newport	W	4-2
21 Sep	Lge	A	Swansea	W	2-0
28 Sep	Lge	H	Man City	D	0-0
5 Oct	Lge	H	Burnley	D	1-1
7 Oct	Lge	H	Newport	W	3-1
12 Oct	Lge	A	Barnsley	W	3-1
19 Oct	Lge	A	West Ham	D	2-2
26 Oct	Lge	H	Sheff Wed	W	2-0
31 Oct	F	A	Oxford Univ	W	2-0
2 Nov	Lge	A	Fulham	D	1-1
9 Nov	Lge	H	Bury	W	2-1
16 Nov	Lge	A	Luton	L	2-3
20 Nov	F	A	Camb Univ	L	3-4
23 Nov	Lge	H	Plymouth	W	2-1
30 Nov	Lge	A	Leicester	D	1-1
7 Dec	Lge	H	Chesterfield	L	3-4
14 Dec	Lge	A	Millwall	W	3-0
21 Dec	Lge	H	Bradford PA	D	3-3
25 Dec	Lge	A	Coventry	L	1-3
26 Dec	Lge	H	Coventry	D	0-0
28 Dec	Lge	A	Birmingham	L	0-1
4 Jan	Lge	H	WBA	W	2-0
11 Jan	FC	H	Stoke	D	2-2
15 Jan	FCr	A	Stoke	L	0-1
18 Jan	Lge	A	Newcastle	L	0-1
25 Jan	F	H	Arsenal	W	2-0
27 Jan	Lge	H	Swansea	W	3-1
1 Feb	Lge	A	Man City	L	0-1
18 Feb	Lge	A	Burnley	W	1-0
1 Mar	Lge	A	Sheff Wed	L	1-5
8 Mar	Lge	H	Fulham	D	1-1
22 Mar	Lge	H	Luton	W	2-1
29 Mar	Lge	A	Plymouth	W	4-3
4 Apr	Lge	H	Nottm Forest	W	2-0
5 Apr	Lge	H	Leicester	W	2-1
7 Apr	Lge	A	Nottm Forest	D	1-1
12 Apr	Lge	A	Chesterfield	D	0-0
19 Apr	Lge	H	Millwall	W	2-1
26 Apr	Lge	A	Bradford PA	L	1-2
3 May	Lge	A	Bury	W	2-1
10 May	Lge	A	Southampton	L	0-1
12 May	F	H	Norwich	W	2-0
17 May	F	H	West Ham	D	0-0
7 Jun	Lge	H	Barnsley	D	1-1
13 Jun	F	A	Marseille	L	1-2
15 Jun	F	A	Toulouse	L	1-2
19 Jun	F	A	Montpelier	W	1-0
21 Jun	F	A	St Etienne	W	2-0

Player	Lg App	Goals
Baily E.F.	1	
Bennett L.D.	38	14
Buckingham V.F.	27	
Burgess W.A.R.	40	5
Cox F.J.A.	25	5
Ditchburn E.G.	41	
Dix R.W.	31	5
Foreman G.A.	36	15
Gilberg H.	1	
Hall A.E.	8	
Hughes W.A.	1	
Jones W.E.A.	1	
Jospeh L.	1	
Medley L.D.	10	4
Nicholson W.E.	39	
Rundle C.R.	18	10
Skinner G.	1	
Stevens L.W.J.	30	1
Ludford G.A.	41	2

Player		
Tickridge S.	14	
Trailor C.H.	1	
Walters W.E.	1	1
Whitchurch C.H.	8	2
Willis A.	37	
Woodward H.J.	11	
Own Goal		1

Final table for Second Division

1 Manchester C.	42 26 10 6	78:35	62
6 TOTTENHAM	**42 17 14 11**	**65:53**	**48**

SEASON 1947/48

23 Aug	Lge	A	WBA	L	0-1
27 Aug	Lge	A	Bury	L	0-2
30 Aug	Lge	H	Sheff Wed	W	5-1
1 Sep	Lge	H	Bury	D	2-2
6 Sep	Lge	A	Cardiff	W	3-0
8 Sep	Lge	A	West Ham	D	1-1
13 Sep	Lge	H	Bradford PA	W	3-1
15 Sep	Lge	H	West Ham	D	2-2
20 Sep	Lge	A	Nottm Forest	L	0-1
27 Sep	Lge	H	Doncaster	W	2-0
4 Oct	Lge	A	Southampton	D	1-1
11 Oct	Lge	A	Barnsley	L	1-2
18 Oct	Lge	H	Plymouth	W	2-0
25 Oct	Lge	A	Luton	D	0-0
30 Oct	F	A	Oxford Univ	W	4-1
1 Nov	Lge	H	Brentford	W	4-0
8 Nov	Lge	A	Leicester	W	3-0
15 Nov	Lge	H	Leeds	W	3-1
22 Nov	Lge	A	Fulham	W	2-0
29 Nov	Lge	H	Coventry	W	2-1
6 Dec	Lge	A	Newcastle	L	0-1
13 Dec	Lge	A	Birmingham	L	1-2
20 Dec	Lge	H	WBA	D	1-1
25 Dec	Lge	H	Chesterfield	W	3-0
27 Dec	Lge	A	Chesterfield	L	1-3
3 Jan	Lge	A	Sheff Wed	L	0-1
10 Jan	FC	A	Bolton	W	2-0
17 Jan	Lge	H	Cardiff	W	2-1
24 Jan	FC	H	WBA	W	3-1
31 Jan	Lge	A	Bradford	W	2-0
7 Feb	FC	H	Leicester	W	5-2
14 Feb	Lge	A	Doncaster	D	1-1
21 Feb	Lge	H	Southampton	D	0-0
28 Feb	FC	A	Southampton	W	1-0
6 Mar	Lge	A	Plymouth	D	1-1
13 Mar	FCsf	*	Blackpool	L	1-3
15 Mar	Lge	H	Barnsley	L	0-3
20 Mar	Lge	A	Brentford	L	0-2
26 Mar	Lge	A	Millwall	D	0-0
27 Mar	Lge	H	Leicester	D	0-0
29 Mar	Lge	H	Millwall	W	3-2
3 Apr	Lge	A	Leeds	W	3-1
5 Apr	Lge	H	Luton	L	0-1
10 Apr	Lge	H	Fulham	L	0-2
12 Apr	Lge	H	Nottm Forest	L	0-3
17 Apr	Lge	A	Coventry	D	1-1
24 Apr	Lge	H	Newcastle	D	1-1
1 May	Lge	A	Birmingham	D	0-0
12 May	F	A	Jersey	W	3-0
15 May	F	A	Guernsey	W	7-0

* Semi-final played at Villa Park

Player	Lg App	Goals
Baily E.F.	22	5
Bennett L.D.	36	8
Buckingham V.F.	42	
Burgess W.A.R.	31	2
Chisholm J.R.	2	
Cox F.J.A.	34	4
Ditchburn E.G.	41	
Dix R.W.	5	
Duquemin L.S.	36	16
Flint K.	5	1
Gilberg H.	1	
Hughes W.A.	1	
Jones W.E.A.	19	3
Jordan J.W.	23	10
Ludford G.A.	8	
Medley L.D.	2	
Nicholson W.E.	38	
Rundle C.R.	6	1
Stevens L.W.J.	22	4
Tickridge S.	39	

Player		
Trailor C.H.	9	
Walters W.E.	1	
Willis A.	3	
Withers C.F.	1	
Woodward H.J.	35	1
Own Goal		1

Final table for Second Division

1 Birmingham	42 22 15 5	55:24	59
8 TOTTENHAM	**42 15 14 13**	**56:43**	**44**

SEASON 1948/49

21 Aug	Lge	H	Sheff Wed	W	3-2
23 Aug	Lge	A	Coventry	L	0-2
28 Aug	Lge	A	Lincoln	D	0-0
30 Aug	Lge	H	Coventry	W	4-0
4 Sep	Lge	H	Chesterfield	W	4-0
8 Sep	Lge	A	Leeds	D	0-0
11 Sep	Lge	A	WBA	D	2-2
13 Sep	Lge	H	Leeds	D	2-2
18 Sep	Lge	H	Bury	W	3-1
20 Sep	F	A	Chelmsford	W	5-1
25 Sep	Lge	A	West Ham	L	0-1
2 Oct	Lge	H	Blackburn	W	4-0
9 Oct	Lge	A	Cardiff	W	1-0
16 Oct	Lge	H	QPR	W	1-0
23 Oct	Lge	A	Luton	D	1-1
28 Oct	F	A	Oxford Univ	W	7-0
30 Oct	Lge	H	Bradford PA	W	5-1
6 Nov	Lge	A	Southampton	L	1-3
13 Nov	Lge	H	Barnsley	W	4-1
20 Nov	Lge	A	Grimsby	D	1-1
25 Nov	F	A	Camb Univ	W	4-1
4 Dec	Lge	A	Fulham	D	1-1
11 Dec	Lge	H	Plymouth	W	3-0
18 Dec	Lge	A	Sheff Wed	L	1-3
25 Dec	Lge	A	Leicester	W	2-1
27 Dec	Lge	H	Leicester	D	1-1
1 Jan	Lge	H	Lincoln	L	1-2
8 Jan	FC	A	Arsenal	L	0-3
15 Jan	Lge	A	Chesterfield	L	0-1
22 Jan	Lge	H	WBA	W	2-0
29 Jan	F	H	Middlesbrough	W	4-1
5 Feb	Lge	A	Bury	D	1-1
12 Feb	Lge	H	Nottm Forest	D	1-1
19 Feb	Lge	H	West Ham	D	1-1
26 Feb	Lge	A	Blackburn	D	1-1
5 Mar	Lge	H	Cardiff	L	0-1
12 Mar	Lge	H	QPR	D	0-0
19 Mar	Lge	A	Luton	W	2-1
26 Mar	Lge	A	Bradford PA	D	1-1
2 Apr	Lge	H	Southampton	L	0-1
9 Apr	Lge	A	Barnsley	L	1-4
15 Apr	Lge	H	Brentford	W	2-0
16 Apr	Lge	H	Grimsby	W	5-2
18 Apr	Lge	A	Brentford	D	1-1
23 Apr	Lge	A	Nottm Forest	D	2-2
25 Apr	F	H	Hibernian	L	2-5
30 Apr	Lge	A	Fulham	D	1-1
7 May	Lge	A	Plymouth	W	5-0
9 May	F	A	Crnwall Co XI	W	2-0

Player	Lg App	Goals
Baily E.F.	41	11
Bennett L.D.	42	19
Buckingham V.F.	25	
Burgess W.A.R.	40	3
Clarke H.A.	10	
Cox F.J.A.	31	4
Ditchburn E.G.	42	
Duquemin L.S.	37	15
Garwood L.F.	2	
Jones W.E.A.	35	12
Ludford G.A.	10	
Medley L.D.	6	3
Nicholson W.E.	41	2
Rundle C.R.	4	1
Stevens L.W.J.	2	
Tickridge S.	41	
Toulouse C.H.	2	
Walters W.E.	12	1
Willis A.	10	
Withers C.F.	12	
Woodward H.J.	17	
Own Goal		1

Final table for Second Division

1 Fulham	42 24 9 9	77:37	57
5 TOTTENHAM	**42 17 16 9**	**72:44**	**50**

SEASON 1949/50

20 Aug	Lge	A	Brentford	W	4-1
22 Aug	Lge	H	Plymouth	W	4-1
27 Aug	Lge	H	Blackburn	L	2-3
31 Aug	Lge	A	Plymouth	W	2-0
3 Sep	Lge	A	Cardiff	W	1-0
5 Sep	Lge	H	Sheff Wed	W	1-0
10 Sep	Lge	H	Leeds	W	2-0
17 Sep	Lge	H	Bury	W	3-1
24 Sep	Lge	A	Leicester	W	2-1
1 Oct	Lge	H	Bradford	W	5-0
8 Oct	Lge	A	Southampton	D	1-1
15 Oct	Lge	H	Coventry	W	3-1
22 Oct	Lge	H	Luton	D	1-1
27 Oct	F	A	Camb Univ	L	2-3
29 Oct	Lge	H	Barnsley	W	2-0
5 Nov	Lge	A	West Ham	W	1-0
10 Nov	F	A	Oxford Univ	W	3-1
12 Nov	Lge	A	Sheff Utd	W	7-0
19 Nov	Lge	A	Grimsby	W	3-2
26 Nov	Lge	H	QPR	W	3-0
3 Dec	Lge	A	Preston	W	3-1
10 Dec	Lge	H	Swansea	W	3-1
17 Dec	Lge	H	Brentford	D	1-1
24 Dec	Lge	A	Blackburn	W	2-1
26 Dec	Lge	H	Chesterfield	W	1-0
27 Dec	Lge	A	Chesterfield	D	1-1
31 Dec	Lge	H	Cardiff	W	2-0
7 Jan	FC	A	Stoke	W	1-0
14 Jan	Lge	A	Leeds	L	0-3
21 Jan	Lge	A	Bury	W	2-1
28 Jan	FC	H	Sunderland	W	5-1
4 Feb	Lge	H	Leicester	L	0-2
11 Feb	FC	A	Everton	L	0-1
18 Feb	Lge	A	Bradford	W	3-1
25 Feb	Lge	H	Southampton	W	4-0
4 Mar	Lge	A	Coventry	W	1-0
11 Mar	Lge	H	Luton	D	0-0
18 Mar	Lge	A	Barnsley	L	0-2
25 Mar	Lge	H	West Ham	W	4-1
1 Apr	Lge	H	QPR	W	2-0
7 Apr	Lge	A	Hull	D	0-0
8 Apr	Lge	H	Preston	W	3-2
10 Apr	Lge	A	Hull	L	0-1
15 Apr	Lge	A	Sheff Utd	L	1-2
22 Apr	Lge	H	Grimsby	L	1-2
24 Apr	F	A	Chelmsford	W	4-0
29 Apr	Lge	A	Swansea	L	0-1
1 May	F	A	Hibernian	L	0-1
6 May	Lge	A	Sheff Wed	D	0-0
8 May	F	A	Norwich	D	2-2
14 May	F	A	Hanover	W	3-0
18 May	F	A	Tennis- Borussia	W	2-0
21 May	F	A	Wacker Innsbruck	W	5-2
24 May	F	A	Borussia- Dortmund	W	4-0
27 May	F	A	Ryl Beerschot	L	1-2

Player	Lg App	Goals
Baily E.F.	40	8
Bennett L.D.	35	14
Burgess W.A.R.	39	
Clarke H.A.	42	
Cook R.	3	
Ditchburn E.G.	42	
Duquemin L.S.	40	16
Ludford G.A.	4	
Marchi A.V.	2	
Medley L.D.	42	18
Nicholson W.E.	39	2
Ramsey A.E.	41	4
Rees W.	11	3
Scarth J.	4	2
Tickridge S.	1	
Walters W.E.	35	14
Willis A.	2	
Withers C.F.	40	

Final table for Second Division

1 TOTTENHAM	42 27 7 8 81:35 61

SEASON 1950/51

19 Aug	Lge	H	Blackpool	L	1-4
23 Aug	Lge	A	Bolton	W	4-1
26 Aug	Lge	A	Arsenal	D	2-2
28 Aug	Lge	H	Bolton	W	4-2
2 Sep	Lge	A	Charlton	D	1-1
6 Sep	Lge	A	Liverpool	L	1-2
9 Sep	Lge	H	Man Utd	W	1-0
16 Sep	Lge	A	Wolves	L	1-2
18 Sep	F	H	Lovells Ath.	W	8-0
23 Sep	Lge	H	Sunderland	D	1-1
30 Sep	Lge	A	Aston Villa	W	3-2
7 Oct	Lge	H	Burnley	W	1-0
14 Oct	Lge	A	Chelsea	W	2-0
21 Oct	Lge	H	Stoke	W	6-1
28 Oct	Lge	A	WBA	W	2-1
4 Nov	Lge	H	Portsmouth	W	5-1
9 Nov	F	A	Camb Univ	W	2-1*
9 Nov	F	A	Oxford Univ	D	1-1*
11 Nov	Lge	A	Everton	W	2-1
18 Nov	Lge	H	Newcastle	W	7-0
25 Nov	Lge	A	Huddersfield	L	2-3
2 Dec	Lge	H	Middlesbro	D	3-3
9 Dec	Lge	A	Sheff Wed	D	1-1
16 Dec	Lge	A	Blackpool	W	1-0
23 Dec	Lge	H	Arsenal	W	1-0
25 Dec	Lge	A	Derby	D	1-1
26 Dec	Lge	H	Derby	W	2-1
30 Dec	Lge	H	Charlton	W	1-0
6 Jan	FC	A	Huddersfield	L	0-2
13 Jan	Lge	A	Man Utd	L	1-2
20 Jan	Lge	H	Wolves	W	2-1
27 Jan	F	A	Cardiff	W	3-2
3 Feb	Lge	A	Sunderland	D	0-0
6 Feb	F	A	Standard Liege	W	4-1
17 Feb	Lge	H	Aston Villa	W	3-2
24 Feb	Lge	A	Burnley	L	0-2
3 Mar	Lge	H	Chelsea	W	2-1
10 Mar	Lge	A	Stoke	D	0-0
17 Mar	Lge	H	WBA	W	5-0
23 Mar	Lge	A	Fulham	W	1-0
24 Mar	Lge	A	Portsmouth	D	1-1
26 Mar	Lge	H	Fulham	W	2-1
31 Mar	Lge	H	Everton	W	3-0
7 Apr	Lge	A	Newcastle	W	1-0
14 Apr	Lge	A	Huddersfield	L	0-2
21 Apr	Lge	A	Middlesbro	D	1-1
23 Apr	F	A	Hibernian	D	0-1
28 Apr	Lge	H	Sheff Wed	D	1-0
30 Apr	F	A	Chelmsford	W	7-3
5 May	Lge	H	Liverpool	W	3-1
7 May	F	H	FC Austria	L	0-1
10 May	F	A	Scunthorpe	D	0-0
12 May	F	H	Bor. Dortmund	W	2-1
14 May	F	†	Arsenal	D	0-0
16 May	F	A	Racing Club Paris	W	4-2
29 May	F	A	Danish XI	W	4-2
30 May	F	A	Danish XI	D	2-2
31 May	F	A	Danish XI	W	2-0

* Half first team played at Oxford, half at Cambridge. At the time Oxford were being coached by Vic Buckingham and Cambridge by Bill Nicholson. † Festival of Britain match played at Selhurst P.

Player	Lg App	Goals
Baily E.F.	40	12
Brittan C.	8	
Bennett L.D.	25	7
Burgess W.A.R.	35	2
Clarke H.A.	42	
Ditchburn E.G.	42	
Duquemin L.S.	33	14
McClellan S.B.	7	3
Medley L.D.	35	11
Murphy P.	25	9
Nicholson W.E.	41	1
Ramsey A.E.	40	4
Scarth J.	1	
Tickridge S.	1	
Uphill D.E.	2	1
Walters W.E.	40	15

Willis A.	39	
Withers C.F.	4	
Wright A.M.	2	1
Own Goals		2

Final table for First Division

1 TOTTENHAM	42 25 10 7 82:44 60

SEASON 1951/52

18 Aug	Lge	A	Middlesbro'	L	1-2
20 Aug	Lge	H	Fulham	W	1-0
25 Aug	Lge	H	WBA	W	3-1
29 Aug	Lge	A	Fulham	W	2-1
1 Sep	Lge	A	Newcastle	L	2-7
3 Sep	Lge	A	Burnley	D	1-1
8 Sep	Lge	H	Bolton	W	2-1
10 Sep	Lge	H	Burnley	D	1-1
15 Sep	Lge	A	Stoke C.	W	6-1
22 Sep	Lge	H	Man Utd	W	2-0
24 Sep	CS	H	Newcastle	W	2-1
29 Sep	Lge	A	Arsenal	D	1-1
6 Oct	Lge	A	Man City	W	2-1
10 Oct	F	H	Copenhagen XI	W	2-1
13 Oct	Lge	A	Derby	L	2-4
20 Oct	Lge	H	Aston Villa	W	2-0
27 Oct	Lge	A	Sunderland	W	1-0
3 Nov	Lge	H	Wolves	W	4-2
10 Nov	Lge	A	Huddersfield	D	1-1
17 Nov	Lge	H	Chelsea	W	3-2
24 Nov	Lge	A	Portsmouth	L	0-2
1 Dec	Lge	H	Liverpool	L	2-3
8 Dec	Lge	A	Blackpool	L	0-1
15 Dec	Lge	H	Middlesbro'	W	3-1
22 Dec	Lge	A	WBA	L	1-3
25 Dec	Lge	A	Charlton	W	3-0
26 Dec	Lge	H	Charlton	L	2-3
29 Dec	Lge	H	Newcastle	W	2-1
5 Jan	Lge	A	Bolton	D	1-1
12 Jan	FC	A	Scunthorpe	W	3-0
19 Jan	Lge	H	Stoke	W	2-0
26 Jan	Lge	A	Man Utd	L	0-2
2 Feb	FC	H	Newcastle	L	0-3
9 Feb	Lge	H	Arsenal	L	1-2
16 Feb	Lge	A	Man City	D	1-1
23 Feb	Lge	H	Preston	W	1-0
1 Mar	Lge	H	Derby	W	5-0
8 Mar	Lge	A	Aston Villa	W	3-0
15 Mar	Lge	H	Sunderland	W	2-0
22 Mar	Lge	A	Wolves	D	1-1
26 Mar	F	A	FC Austria	D	2-2
2 Apr	Lge	H	Huddersfield	W	1-0
12 Apr	Lge	H	Portsmouth	W	3-1
14 Apr	Lge	A	Preston	D	1-1
19 Apr	Lge	A	Liverpool	D	1-1
23 Apr	F	A	Hibernian	L	1-2
26 Apr	Lge	H	Blackpool	W	2-0
30 Apr	Lge	A	Chelsea	W	2-0
3 May	F	A	Racing, Paris	W	2-1
5 May	F	A	Ipswich	D	2-2
11 May	F	A	Crittalls Ath.	W	8-1
22 May	F		Toronto	W	7-0*
26 May	F		Saskathewan	W	18-1*
31 May	F		British Col.	W	9-2*
2 Jun	F		Victoria	W	7-0*
4 May	f		British Col.	W	8-2*
7 May	F		Alberta	W	11-0*
9 May	F		Manitoba	W	5-0*
14 May	F		Man Utd	W	5-0*
15 May	F		Man Utd	W	7-1*
18 May	F		Quebec	W	8-0*

* End of season tour to Canada

Player	Lg App	Goals
Adams C.J.	5	1
Baily E.F.	30	4
Bennett L.D.	35	19
Brittan C.	6	
Burgess W.A.R.	40	
Clarke H.A.	33	
Ditchburn E.G.	42	
Duquemin L.S.	25	12
Farley B.R.	1	
Harmer T.C.	13	3
King D.A.	2	
McClellan S.B.	12	3
Medley L.D.	34	8

Murphy P.	13	5
Nicholson W.E.	37	1
Ramsey A.E.	38	5
Robb G.W.	1	1
Robshaw H.K.	1	
Scarth J.W.	2	1
Uphill D.E.	2	
Walters W.E.	37	11
Wetton R.	7	
Willis A.	17	
Withers C.F.	29	
Own Goals		2

Final table for First Division

1 Manchester U.	42 23 11 8 95:52 57
2 TOTTENHAM	42 22 9 11 76:51 53

SEASON 1952/53

23 Aug	Lge	H	WBA	L	3-4
27 Aug	Lge	A	Man City	W	1-0
30 Aug	Lge	A	Newcastle	D	1-1
1 Sep	Lge	H	Man City	D	3-3
6 Sep	Lge	H	Cardiff	W	2-1
10 Sep	Lge	A	Liverpool	L	1-2
13 Sep	Lge	A	Sheff Wed	L	0-2
15 Sep	Lge	H	Liverpool	W	3-1
20 Sep	Lge	A	Arsenal	L	1-3
27 Sep	Lge	H	Burnley	W	2-1
4 Oct	Lge	A	Preston	L	0-1
11 Oct	Lge	A	Derby	D	0-0
18 Oct	Lge	H	Blackpool	W	4-0
25 Oct	Lge	A	Chelsea	L	1-2
27 Oct	F	A	Gloucester	L	1-2
1 Nov	Lge	H	Man Utd	L	1-2
5 Nov	F	A	Oxford Univ	W	3-0
6 Nov	F	A	Camb Univ	D	2-2
8 Nov	Lge	A	Portsmouth	L	1-2
15 Nov	Lge	H	Bolton	D	1-1
22 Nov	Lge	A	Aston Villa	W	3-0
29 Nov	Lge	H	Sunderland	D	2-2
6 Dec	Lge	A	Wolves	D	0-0
13 Dec	Lge	H	Charlton	W	2-0
20 Dec	Lge	A	WBA	L	1-2
25 Dec	Lge	H	Middlesbro'	W	7-1
27 Dec	Lge	A	Middlesbro'	W	4-0
3 Jan	Lge	A	Newcastle	W	3-2
10 Jan	FC	A	Tranmere	D	1-1
12 Jan	FCr	H	Tranmere	W	9-1
17 Jan	Lge	A	Cardiff	D	0-0
24 Jan	FC	A	Sheff Wed	W	2-1
31 Jan	FC	A	Preston	D	2-2
4 Feb	FCr	H	Preston	W	1-0
7 Feb	Lge	A	Arsenal	L	0-4
14 Feb	FC	A	Halifax	W	3-0
17 Feb	Lge	A	Burnley	L	2-3
21 Feb	Lge	H	Preston	D	4-4
28 Feb	FC	A	Birmingham	D	1-1
4 Mar	FCr	H	Birmingham	D	2-2
7 Mar	Lge	A	Blackpool	L	0-2
9 Mar	FCr	*	Birmingham	W	1-0
12 Mar	Lge	H	Derby	W	5-2
14 Mar	Lge	H	Chelsea	L	2-3
21 Mar	FCsf	†	Blackpool	L	1-2
25 Mar	Lge	A	Man Utd	L	2-3
28 Mar	Lge	H	Portsmouth	D	3-3
3 Apr	Lge	H	Stoke	W	1-0
4 Apr	Lge	A	Bolton	W	3-2
6 Apr	Lge	A	Stoke	L	0-2
11 Apr	Lge	H	Aston Villa	D	1-1
16 Apr	F	A	West Ham	L	1-2
18 Apr	Lge	A	Sunderland	D	1-1
20 Apr	F	A	Reading	W	4-0
25 Apr	Lge	A	Wolves	W	3-2
30 Apr	Lge	A	Charlton	L	2-3
4 May	F	A	Arsenal	W	2-0
11 May	‡	A	Hibernian	D	1-1
12 May	‡	A	Hibernian	D	1-1
15 May	F	A	Hearts	L	0-2
30 May	F	A	Racing, Paris	D	1-1

* Second replay at Molineux
† Semi-final at Villa Park ‡ Coronation Cup

Player	Lg App	Goals
Adams C.J.	1	
Baily E.F.	30	6
Baker P.R.B.	1	

Bennett L.D.	30	14
Brittan C.	9	
Brooks J.	1	
Burgess W.A.R.	30	2
Clarke H.A.	31	
Ditchburn E.G.	42	
Duquemin L.S.	38	18
Dicker L.R.	10	2
Gibbins E.	1	
Groves V.G.	3	2
Grubb A.J.	2	
Harmer T.C.	17	4
Hollis R.W.	3	1
Hopkins M.	2	
King P.A.	10	
McClellan S.B.	17	8
Marchi A.V.	5	
Medley L.D.	21	1
Nicholson W.E.	31	
Ramsey A.E.	37	6
Robb G.W.	6	2
Stokes A.F.	2	1
Uphill D.E.	2	1
Walters W.E.	26	8
Wetton R.	12	
Willis A.	27	1
Withers C.F.	15	
Own Goal		1

Final table for First Division

1 Arsenal	42 21 12 9 97:64 54
10 TOTTENHAM	42 15 11 16 78:69 41

SEASON 1953/54

19 Aug	Lge	H	Aston Villa	W	1-0
22 Aug	Lge	A	Sheff Wed	L	1-3
26 Aug	Lge	H	Charlton	W	3-1
29 Aug	Lge	H	Middlesbrough	W	4-1
3 Sep	Lge	A	Charlton	W	1-0
5 Sep	Lge	A	WBA	L	0-3
7 Sep	Lge	H	Burnley	L	2-4
12 Sep	Lge	H	Liverpool	W	2-1
16 Sep	Lge	H	Burnley	L	2-3
19 Sep	Lge	A	Newcastle	W	3-1
21 Sep	F	A	Hibernian	D	1-1
26 Sep	Lge	H	Man Utd	D	1-1
29 Sep	F	H	Racing Club	W	5-3
3 Oct	Lge	A	Bolton	L	0-2
10 Oct	Lge	H	Arsenal	L	1-4
17 Oct	Lge	H	Cardiff	L	0-1
19 Oct	F	A	Millwall	W	2-0
24 Oct	Lge	H	Man City	W	3-0
28 Oct	F	H	FC Austria	W	3-2
31 Oct	Lge	A	Sunderland	L	3-4
7 Nov	Lge	H	Chelsea	W	2-1
14 Nov	Lge	A	Blackpool	L	0-1
21 Nov	Lge	H	Huddersfield	W	1-0
28 Nov	Lge	A	Sheff Utd	L	2-5
5 Dec	Lge	H	Wolves	L	2-3
12 Dec	Lge	A	Aston Villa	W	2-1
19 Dec	Lge	H	Sheff Wed	W	3-1
25 Dec	Lge	H	Portsmouth	D	1-1
26 Dec	Lge	A	Portsmouth	D	1-1
2 Jan	Lge	A	Middlesbrough	L	0-3
9 Jan	FC	A	Leeds	D	3-3
13 Jan	FCr	H	Leeds	W	1-0
16 Jan	Lge	H	WBA	L	0-1
23 Jan	Lge	A	Liverpool	D	2-2
30 Jan	FC	A	Man City	W	1-0
6 Feb	Lge	H	Newcastle	W	3-0
13 Feb	Lge	A	Man Utd	L	0-2
20 Feb	FC	A	Hull	D	1-1
24 Feb	FCr	H	Hull	W	2-0
27 Feb	Lge	A	Arsenal	W	3-0
3 Mar	Lge	H	Bolton	W	3-2
6 Mar	Lge	H	Cardiff	L	0-1
13 Mar	FC	A	WBA	L	0-3
17 Mar	Lge	A	Man City	L	1-4
20 Mar	Lge	H	Sunderland	L	0-3
27 Mar	Lge	A	Chelsea	L	0-1
3 Apr	Lge	H	Blackpool	D	2-2
5 Apr	F	A	Hibernian	W	3-2
10 Apr	Lge	A	Huddersfield	W	5-2
16 Apr	Lge	A	Preston	L	1-2
17 Apr	Lge	H	Sheff Utd	W	2-1
19 Apr	Lge	H	Preston	L	2-6
24 Apr	Lge	A	Wolves	L	0-2

215

28 Apr F   A Austria Select L 0-2
1 May   F   A Stuttgart   L 1-3
5 May   F   A Eintracht   L 0-1
7 May   F   A Hamburg SV   D 2-2

Player	Lg App	Goals
Baily E.F.	33	5
Baker P.R.B.	4	1
Bennett L.D.	26	4
Brittan C.	3	1
Brooks J.	18	2
Burgess W.A.R.	24	
Clarke H.A.	41	
Ditchburn E.G.	39	
Dunmore D.G.I.	10	2
Duquemin L.S.	27	9
Groves V.G.	1	1
Harmer T.C.	6	2
Hopkins M.	2	
Hutchinson G.H.	5	1
King D.A.	2	
Marchi A.V.	8	1
McClellan S.B.	5	
Nicholson W.E.	30	
Owen A.W.	1	
Ramsey A.E.	37	2
Reynolds R.S.M.	3	
Robb G.W.	37	16
Stokes A.F.	2	1
Walters W.E.	37	14
Wetton R.	21	
Willis A.	9	
Withers C.F.	31	
Own Goals		3

Final table for First Division

1 Wolverhampton 42 25 7 10 96:56 57
16 TOTTENHAM   42 16 5 21 65:76 37

SEASON 1954/55

14 Aug F   A Lille Olym   D 1-1
21 Aug Lge A Aston Villa   W 4-2
25 Aug Lge H Wolves   W 3-2
28 Aug Lge H Sunderland   L 0-1
30 Aug Lge A Wolves   L 2-4
4 Sep   Lge A Arsenal   L 0-2
8 Sep   Lge H Man Utd   L 0-2
11 Sep Lge A Sheff Wed   D 2-2
15 Sep Lge A Man Utd   L 1-2
18 Sep Lge H Portsmouth   D 1-1
25 Sep Lge A Blackpool   L 1-5
2 Oct   Lge H Charlton   L 1-4
9 Oct   Lge H WBA   W 3-1
11 Oct F   A QPR   L 1-2
16 Oct Lge A Newcastle   D 4-4
18 Oct F   H Sptklub Vienna   L 1-2
23 Oct Lge H Preston   W 3-1
30 Oct Lge A Sheff Utd   L 1-4
2 Nov   F   H Essen Rot
                Weiss   W 4-2
6 Nov   Lge H Cardiff   L 0-2
13 Nov Lge A Chelsea   L 1-2
15 Nov F   H Finchley   D 2-2
20 Nov Lge H Leicester   W 5-1
27 Nov Lge A Burnley   W 2-1
29 Nov F   A Accrington St.   D 0-0
4 Dec   Lge H Everton   L 1-3
11 Dec Lge A Man City   D 0-0
18 Dec Lge H Aston Villa   D 1-1
25 Dec Lge A Bolton   W 2-1
27 Dec Lge H Bolton   W 2-0
1 Jan   Lge A Sunderland   D 1-1
8 Jan   FC   A Gateshead   W 2-0
15 Jan Lge H Arsenal   L 0-1
22 Jan Lge H Sheff Wed   W 7-2
29 Jan FC   H Port Vale   W 4-2
5 Feb   Lge A Portsmouth   W 3-0
12 Feb Lge H Blackpool   W 3-2
19 Feb FC   A York   L 1-3
2 Mar   F   H Arsenal   L 1-4
5 Mar   Lge H Man City   D 2-2
9 Mar   F   H Racing, Paris   W 6-0
12 Mar Lge A Preston   L 0-1
14 Mar F   A Hibernian   D 1-1
19 Mar Lge H Sheff Utd   W 5-0
26 Mar Lge A Cardiff   W 2-1

30 Mar F   H FC Servette   W 5-1
2 Apr   Lge H Chelsea   L 2-4
9 Apr   Lge A Everton   L 0-1
11 Apr Lge A Huddersfield   D 1-1
12 Apr Lge H Huddersfield   L 0-1
16 Apr Lge H Burnley   L 0-3
23 Apr Lge A Leicester   L 0-2
27 Apr Lge A WBA   W 2-1
30 Apr Lge H Newcastle   W 2-1
5 May   Lge A Charlton   W 2-1
11 May F   A FC Austria   L 2-6
15 May F   A Kinizi, Hungary L 1-4
18 May F   A Vegas, Hun.   L 2-4
19 May F   A Pecs Doza   W 1-0
25 May F   A Racing, Paris   D 0-0

Player	Lg App	Goals
Baily E.F.	41	12
Baker P.R.B.	8	
Bennett L.D.	6	2
Blanchflower R.D.	22	
Brittan C.	10	7
Brooks J.	31	
Clarke H.A.	36	
Ditchburn E.G.	16	
Dowsett G.J.	1	1
Dunmore D.G.I.	22	7
Duquemin L.S.	19	8
Dyson T.K.	1	13
Gavin J.T.	29	
Harmer T.C.	5	
Henry R.P.	1	
Hopkins M.	32	
King D.A.	5	
McClellan S.B.	11	8
Marchi A.V.	32	
Nicholson W.E.	10	
Ramsey A.E.	33	3
Reynolds R.S.M.	26	
Robb G.W.	36	8
Walters W.E.	7	2
Wetton R.	5	
Withers C.F.	11	
Woods A.E.	6	
Own Goal		1

Final table for First Division

1 Chelsea   42 20 12 10 81:57 52
16 TOTTENHAM   42 16 8 18 72:73 40

SEASON 1955/56

20 Aug Lge H Burnley   L 0-1
24 Aug Lge A Man Utd   D 2-2
27 Aug Lge A Luton   L 1-2
31 Aug Lge H Man Utd   L 1-2
3 Sep   Lge H Charlton   L 2-3
5 Sep   Lge A Sheff Utd   L 0-2
10 Sep Lge H Arsenal   W 3-1
17 Sep Lge A Everton   L 1-2
24 Sep Lge H Newcastle   W 3-1
25 Sep F   A Aarhus   W 4-3
1 Oct   Lge A Birmingham   L 0-3
8 Oct   Lge H Bolton   L 0-3
12 Oct F   H FC Vasas   L 1-2
15 Oct Lge A Chelsea   L 0-2
22 Oct Lge H Sunderland   L 2-3
24 Oct F   H Plymouth   D 0-0
29 Oct Lge A Portsmouth   L 1-4
5 Nov   Lge H Cardiff   D 1-1
12 Nov Lge A Man City   W 2-1
14 Nov F   A Partick Thistle L 0-1
19 Nov Lge H Wolves   W 2-1
26 Nov Lge A Aston Villa   W 2-0
3 Dec   Lge H Blackpool   D 1-1
6 Dec   F   H Swansea   W 4-1
10 Dec Lge A Huddersfield   L 0-1
17 Dec Lge A Burnley   L 0-2
24 Dec Lge H Luton   W 2-1
26 Dec Lge H WBA   W 4-1
27 Dec Lge A WBA   L 0-1
31 Dec Lge A Charlton   W 2-1
7 Jan   FC   H Boston Utd   W 4-0
14 Jan Lge A Arsenal   W 1-0
21 Jan Lge H Everton   D 1-1
28 Jan FC   H Middlesbrough   W 3-1
4 Feb   Lge A Newcastle   W 2-1

11 Feb Lge H Birmingham   L 0-1
18 Feb FC   A Doncaster   W 2-0
25 Feb Lge H Chelsea   W 4-0
3 Mar   FC   H West Ham   D 3-3
8 Mar   FCr A West Ham   W 2-1
10 Mar Lge H Portsmouth   D 1-1
17 Mar FCsf † Man City   L 0-1
21 Mar Lge A Bolton   L 2-3
24 Mar Lge H Man City   W 2-1
30 Mar Lge H Preston   L 0-4
31 Mar Lge A Sunderland   L 2-3
2 Apr   Lge A Preston   D 3-3
7 Apr   Lge H Aston Villa   W 4-3
14 Apr Lge A Blackpool   W 2-0
18 Apr Lge A Wolves   L 1-5
21 Apr Lge H Huddersfield   L 1-2
23 Apr Lge A Cardiff   D 0-0
28 Apr Lge H Sheff Utd   W 3-0
† at Villa Park

Player	Lg App	Goals
Baily E.F.	18	1
Baker P.R.B.	5	
Blanchflower R.D.	1	
Brittan C.	39	10
Brooks J.	39	4
Clarke H.A.	14	
Ditchburn E.G.	6	
Dulin M.C.	10	1
Dunmore D.G.I.	17	5
Duquemin L.S.	3	
Dyson T.K.	3	
Gavin J.T.	3	2
Harmer T.C.	10	5
Henry R.P.	1	
Hopkins M.	41	
McClellan S.B.	16	7
Marchi A.V.	42	1
Norman M.	27	1
Reynolds R.S.M.	41	7
Robb G.W.	3	1
Ryden JJ	3	1
Smith R.A.	21	10
Stokes A.E	11	5
Walters W.E.	21	10
Wetton R.	11	5
Whalley E	2	
Withers C.F.	2	
Woods A.E.	14	1
Own Goal		10

Final table for Second Division

1 Manchester U. 42 25 10 7 83:51 60
18 TOTTENHAM   42 15 7 20 61:71 37

SEASON 1956/57

18 Aug Lge A Preston   W 4-1
22 Aug Lge A Man City   D 2-2
25 Aug Lge H Leeds   W 5-1
29 Aug Lge H Man City   W 3-2
1 Sep   Lge A Bolton   L 0-1
3 Sep   Lge A Blackpool   L 1-4
8 Sep   Lge A Wolves   W 4-1
11 Sep F   H Racing, Paris   W 2-0
15 Sep Lge A Aston Villa   W 4-2
17 Sep F   A Hibernian   W 5-1
22 Sep Lge H Luton   W 5-0
26 Sep F   H Partick Thistle W 4-1
29 Sep Lge A Sunderland   W 2-1
6 Oct   Lge A Chelsea   W 4-2
13 Oct Lge H Cardiff   W 5-0
15 Oct F   A Hearts   L 2-3
20 Oct Lge A Arsenal   L 1-3
27 Oct Lge H Burnley   W 2-0
31 Oct F   H Hibernian   D 3-3
3 Nov   Lge A Portsmouth   W 3-2
10 Nov Lge H Newcastle   W 3-1
12 Nov F   H Hearts   W 4-2
17 Nov Lge A Sheff Wed   L 1-4
24 Nov Lge H Man Utd   D 2-2
26 Nov F   A Partick Thistle L 0-2
1 Dec   Lge A Birmingham   D 0-0
3 Dec   F   H Red Banner   W 7-1
8 Dec   Lge H WBA   D 2-2
15 Dec Lge H Preston   D 1-1
25 Dec Lge H Everton   W 6-0
26 Dec Lge A Everton   D 1-1

29 Dec Lge H Bolton   W 4-0
5 Jan   FC   H Leicester   W 2-0
12 Jan Lge A Wolves   L 0-3
19 Jan Lge H Aston Villa   W 3-0
26 Jan FC   H Chelsea   W 4-0
2 Feb   Lge A Luton   W 3-1
9 Feb   Lge H Sunderland   W 5-2
16 Feb FC   A Bournemouth   L 1-3
20 Feb Lge H Chelsea   L 3-4
2 Mar   Lge A Leeds Utd   D 1-1
9 Mar   Lge A WBA   D 1-1
13 Mar Lge A Arsenal   L 1-3
16 Mar Lge H Portsmouth   W 2-0
19 Mar F   A Comb.
                Antwerp   W 2-1
23 Mar Lge A Newcastle   D 2-2
30 Mar Lge H Sheff Wed   D 1-1
6 Apr   Lge A Man Utd   D 0-0
13 Apr Lge H Birmingham   W 5-1
19 Apr Lge A Charlton   D 1-1
20 Apr Lge A Cardiff   W 3-0
22 Apr Lge H Charlton   W 6-2
27 Apr Lge H Blackpool   W 2-1
29 Apr Lge A Burnley   L 0-1
19 May F   Celtic   W 4-3*
22 May F   Essex Co. XI   W 8-1*
25 May F   Ontario All
                Stars   W 7-0*
29 May F   Alberta   W 6-1*
1 Jun   F   Celtic   W 6-3*
3 Jun   F   British Col.   L 0-2*
4 Jun   F   Manitob All
                Stars   W12-0*
8 Jun   F   Celtic   W 3-1*
9 Jun   F   Celtic   L 0-1*
* Canadian tour

Player	Lg App	Goals
Baker P.R.B.	38	
Blanchflower R.D.	39	1
Brittan C.	1	
Brooks J.	23	11
Clarke H.A.	21	
Ditchburn E.G.	29	
Dulin M.C.	1	
Dunmore D.G.I.	5	3
Duquemin L.S.	2	1
Dyson T.K.	8	3
Harmer T.C.	42	17
Henry R.P.	1	
Hopkins M.	35	
Marchi A.V.	42	
Medwin T.C.	37	14
Norman M.	16	
Reynolds R.S.M.	13	
Robb G.W.	37	14
Ryden J.J.	15	
Stokes A.F.	21	18
Smith R.A.	33	18
Whalley E.	2	
Wilkie R.M.	1	
Own Goals		4

Final table for First Division

1 Manchester U. 42 28 8 6 103:54 64
2 TOTTENHAM   42 22 12 8 104:56 56

SEASON 1957/58

3 Aug   F   A IFB Stuttgart   D 2-2
24 Aug Lge H Chelsea   D 1-1
28 Aug Lge A Portsmouth   L 1-5
31 Aug Lge A Newcastle   L 3-5
4 Sep   Lge H Portsmouth   L 3-5
7 Sep   Lge H Burnley   W 3-1
11 Sep Lge A Birmingham   D 0-0
14 Sep Lge A Preston   L 1-3
18 Sep Lge H Birmingham   W 7-1
21 Sep Lge H Sheff Wed   W 4-2
28 Sep Lge A Man City   L 1-5
2 Oct   Lge A Wolves   L 0-4
5 Oct   Lge H Nottm Forest   L 2-3
12 Oct Lge H Arsenal   W 3-1
14 Oct F   A Hibernian   L 2-5
19 Oct Lge A Bolton   L 2-3
23 Oct F   A Swiss Nat. XI   W 5-4
26 Oct Lge H Leeds   W 2-0

2 Nov	Lge	A	Sunderland	D 1-1
6 Nov	F	A	Bristol C.	L 3-4
9 Nov	F	H	Everton	W 3-1
11 Nov	F	H	IFB Stuttgart	W 3-2
16 Nov	Lge	A	Aston Villa	D 1-1
23 Nov	Lge	H	Luton	W 3-1
30 Nov	Lge	A	Man Utd	W 4-3
7 Dec	Lge	H	Leicester	L 1-4
14 Dec	Lge	A	Blackpool	W 2-0
21 Dec	Lge	A	Chelsea	W 4-2
26 Dec	Lge	H	Wolves	W 1-0
28 Dec	Lge	H	Newcastle	D 3-3
4 Jan	FC	H	Leicester	W 4-0
11 Jan	Lge	A	Burnley	L 0-2
18 Jan	Lge	H	Preston	D 3-3
25 Jan	FC	H	Sheff Utd	L 0-3
1 Feb	Lge	A	Sheff Wed	L 0-2
8 Feb	Lge	H	Man City	W 5-1
15 Feb	Lge	A	Nottm Forest	W 2-1
22 Feb	Lge	A	Arsenal	D 4-4
1 Mar	F	H	Partick Thistle	W 4-1
8 Mar	Lge	A	Leeds U.	W 2-1
12 Mar	Lge	H	Bolton	W 4-1
15 Mar	Lge	H	Sunderland	L 0-1
22 Mar	Lge	A	Luton	D 0-0
27 Mar	F	A	Rotterdam XI	W 4-1
29 Mar	Lge	H	Aston Villa	W 6-2
4 Apr	Lge	H	WBA	D 0-0
5 Apr	Lge	A	Everton	W 4-3
7 Apr	Lge	A	WBA	W 2-0
12 Apr	Lge	H	Man Utd	W 1-0
14 Apr	F	H	Hibernian	W 4-0
19 Apr	Lge	A	Leicester	W 3-1
24 Apr	F	H	Canto de Rio	W 4-1
26 Apr	Lge	H	Blackpool	W 2-1

Player	Lg App	Goals
Baker P.R.B.	18	
Bing T.E.	1	
Blanchflower R.D.	40	
Brittan C.	3	
Brooks J.	25	10
Clayton E.	5	3
Ditchburn E.G.	26	
Dulin M.C.	3	2
Dunmore D.G.I.	5	2
Dyson T.K.	12	2
Harmer T.C.	40	9
Henry R.P.	15	
Hills J.R.	21	
Hopkins M.	26	
Iley J.	19	
Ireland J.J.C.	1	
Jones C.W.	10	1
Medwin T.C.	39	14
Norman M.	33	1
Reynolds R.S.M.	16	
Robb G.W.	15	3
Ryden J.J.	35	
Smith R.A.	38	36
Stokes A.F.	15	8
Walley E.	1	
Own Goals		2

Final table for First Division

1 Wolverhampton	42	28	8	6	103:47	64
3 TOTTENHAM	42	21	9	12	93:77	51

SEASON 1958/59

23 Aug	Lge	H	Blackpool	L 2-3
27 Aug	Lge	A	Chelsea	L 1-2
30 Aug	Lge	A	Blackburn	L 0-5
3 Sep	Lge	H	Chelsea	W 4-0
6 Sep	Lge	H	Newcastle	L 1-3
10 Sep	Lge	H	Nottm Forest	D 1-1
13 Sep	Lge	A	Arsenal	L 1-3
17 Sep	Lge	A	Nottm Forest	W 1-0
20 Sep	Lge	A	Man Utd	D 2-2
27 Sep	Lge	H	Wolves	W 2-1
4 Oct	Lge	A	Portsmouth	D 1-1
11 Oct	Lge	H	Everton	W10-4
14 Oct	F	H	Bella Vista	W 3-1
18 Oct	Lge	A	Leicester	W 4-3
25 Oct	Lge	H	Leeds Utd	L 2-3
1 Nov	Lge	A	Man City	L 1-5
8 Nov	Lge	H	Bolton	D 1-1

10 Nov	F	H	Hibernian	W 5-2
15 Nov	Lge	A	Luton	W 2-1
22 Nov	Lge	H	Birmingham	L 0-4
29 Nov	Lge	A	WBA	L 3-4
6 Dec	Lge	H	Preston	L 1-2
8 Dec	F	H	Bucharest Sel.	W 4-2
13 Dec	Lge	A	Burnley	L 1-3
20 Dec	Lge	A	Blackpool	D 0-0
25 Dec	Lge	A	West Ham	L 1-2
26 Dec	Lge	H	West Ham	L 1-4
3 Jan	Lge	H	Blackburn	W 3-1
10 Jan	FC	H	West Ham	W 2-0
17 Jan	Lge	A	Newcastle	W 2-1
24 Jan	FC	H	Newport	W 4-1
31 Jan	Lge	H	Arsenal	L 1-4
7 Feb	Lge	A	Man Utd	L 1-3
14 Feb	FC	H	Norwich	D 1-1
18 Feb	FCr	A	Norwich	L 0-1
21 Feb	Lge	H	Portsmouth	D 4-4
28 Feb	Lge	A	Everton	L 1-2
2 Mar	F	A	Wolves	D 1-1
7 Mar	Lge	H	Leicester	W 6-0
14 Mar	Lge	A	Leeds	L 1-3
21 Mar	Lge	H	Man City	W 3-1
27 Mar	Lge	A	Aston Villa	W 3-2
28 Mar	Lge	A	Bolton	L 1-4
30 Mar	Lge	A	Aston Villa	D 1-1
4 Apr	Lge	H	Luton	W 3-0
8 Apr	Lge	H	Burnley	D 2-2
11 Apr	Lge	A	Birmingham	L 1-5
18 Apr	Lge	H	WBA	W 5-0
25 Apr	Lge	A	Preston	D 2-2
27 May	F	A	Moscow Torpedo	W 1-0
1 Jun	F	A	Dynamo Kiev	W 2-1
4 Jun	F	A	Com Russian XI	L 1-3

Player	Lg App	Goals
Baker P.R.B.	36	
Blanchflower R.D.	36	1
Brooks J.	25	3
Clayton E.	11	4
Ditchburn E.G.	2	
Dodge W.C.	5	
Dunmore D.G.I.	13	6
Dyson T.K.	7	
Harmer T.C.	35	4
Henry R.P.	8	
Hills J.R.	7	
Hollowbread J.F.	40	
Hopkins M.	34	
Iley J.	34	1
Ireland J.J.C.	2	
Jones C.W.	22	5
Mackay D.C.	4	1
Medwin T.C.	35	14
Norman M.	35	3
Ryden J.J.	10	1
Robb G.W.	9	2
Sharpe F.C.	2	1
Smith R.A.	36	32
Stokes A.F.	14	7

Final table for First Division

1 Wolverhampton	42	28	5	9	110:49	61
18 TOTTENHAM	42	13	10	19	85:95	36

SEASON 1959/60

22 Aug	Lge	A	Newcastle	W 5-1
26 Aug	Lge	H	WBA	D 2-2
29 Aug	Lge	H	Birmingham	D 0-0
2 Sep	Lge	A	WBA	W 2-1
5 Sep	Lge	A	Arsenal	D 1-1
9 Sep	Lge	H	West Ham	D 2-2
12 Sep	Lge	A	Man Utd	W 5-1
14 Sep	Lge	A	West Ham	W 2-1
19 Sep	Lge	H	Preston	W 5-1
26 Sep	Lge	A	Leicester	D 1-1
3 Oct	Lge	H	Burnley	D 1-1
10 Oct	Lge	H	Wolves	W 5-1
17 Oct	Lge	A	Sheff Wed	L 1-2
21 Oct	F	A	Reading	W 5-2
24 Oct	Lge	H	Nottm Forest	W 2-1
31 Oct	Lge	A	Man City	W 2-1
7 Nov	Lge	H	Bolton	L 0-2

14 Nov	Lge	A	Luton	L 0-1
16 Nov	F	H	Moscow Torpedo	W 3-2
21 Nov	Lge	H	Everton	W 3-0
28 Nov	Lge	A	Blackpool	D 2-2
5 Dec	Lge	H	Blackburn	W 2-1
12 Dec	Lge	A	Fulham	D 1-1
19 Dec	Lge	H	Newcastle	W 4-0
26 Dec	Lge	A	Leeds	W 4-2
28 Dec	Lge	H	Leeds	L 1-4
2 Jan	Lge	A	Birmingham	W 1-0
v9 Jan	FC	A	Newport	W 4-0
16 Jan	Lge	H	Arsenal	W 3-0
23 Jan	Lge	H	Man Utd	W 2-1
30 Jan	FC	A	Crewe	D 2-2
3 Feb	FCr	H	Crewe	W13-2
v6 Feb	Lge	A	Preston	D 1-1
13 Feb	Lge	H	Leicester	L 1-2
20 Feb	FC	H	Blackburn	L 1-3
27 Feb	Lge	A	Blackburn	W 4-1
1 Mar	Lge	A	Burnley	L 0-2
v5 Mar	Lge	H	Sheff Wed	W 4-1
12 Mar	Lge	A	Nottm Forest	W 3-1
19 Mar	Lge	H	Fulham	D 1-1
26 Mar	Lge	A	Bolton	L 1-2
2 Apr	Lge	H	Luton	D 1-1
9 Apr	Lge	A	Everton	L 1-2
15 Apr	Lge	A	Chelsea	W 3-1
16 Apr	Lge	H	Man City	L 0-1
18 Apr	Lge	H	Chelsea	L 0-1
23 Apr	Lge	A	Wolves	W 3-1
30 Apr	Lge	H	Blackpool	W 4-1
2 May	F	A	C. Palace	D 2-2
25 May	F	A	Juventus	L 0-2

Player	Lg App	Goals
Allen L.W.	15	7
Baker P.R.B.	41	
Blanchflower R.D.	40	2
Brooks J.	4	2
Brown W.D.F.	40	
Clayton E.	1	
Dodge W.C.	1	
Dunmore D.G.I.	10	2
Dyson T.K.	6	
Henry R.P.	25	
Hills J.R.	1	
Hollowbread J.F.	2	
Hopkins M.	14	
Harmer T.C.	37	3
Jones C.W.	38	20
Mackay D.C.	38	11
Marchi A.V.	14	1
Medwin T.C.	26	4
Norman M.	39	
Smith J.	1	
Smith R.A.	40	25
White J.A.	28	5
Worley L.F.	1	
Own Goals		4

Final table for First Division

1 Burnley	42	24	7	11	85:61	55
3 TOTTENHAM	42	21	11	10	86:50	53

THE DOUBLE SEASON – 1960/61

20 Aug	Lge	H	Everton	W 2-0
22 Aug	Lge	A	Blackpool	W 3-1
27 Aug	Lge	A	Blackburn	W 4-1
31 Aug	Lge	H	Blackpool	W 3-1
3 Sep	Lge	H	Man Utd	W 4-1
7 Sep	Lge	A	Bolton	W 2-1
10 Sep	Lge	A	Arsenal	W 3-2
14 Sep	Lge	H	Bolton	W 3-1
17 Sep	Lge	A	Leicester	W 2-1
24 Sep	Lge	H	Aston Villa	W 6-2
1 Oct	Lge	A	Wolves	W 4-0
10 Oct	Lge	A	Man City	D 1-1
15 Oct	Lge	A	Nottm Forest	W 4-0
24 Oct	F	H	Army XI	L 3-5
29 Oct	Lge	A	Newcastle	W 4-3
2 Nov	Lge	H	Cardiff	W 3-2
5 Nov	Lge	H	Fulham	W 5-1
12 Nov	Lge	A	Sheffield Wed	L 1-2
14 Nov	F	H	Dinamo Tbilisi	W 5-2

19 Nov	Lge	H	Birmingham	W 6-0
26 Nov	Lge	A	WBA	W 3-1
3 Dec	Lge	H	Burnley	D 4-4
10 Dec	Lge	A	Preston	W 1-0
17 Dec	Lge	A	Everton	W 3-1
24 Dec	Lge	H	West Ham	W 2-0
26 Dec	Lge	A	West Ham	W 3-0
31 Dec	Lge	H	Blackburn	W 5-2
7 Jan	FC	H	Charlton	W 3-2
16 Jan	Lge	A	Man Utd	L 0-2
21 Jan	Lge	H	Arsenal	W 4-2
28 Jan	FC	H	Crewe	W 5-1
4 Feb	Lge	H	Leicester	L 2-3
11 Feb	Lge	A	Aston Villa	W 2-1
18 Feb	FC	A	Aston Villa	W 2-0
22 Feb	Lge	H	Wolves	D 1-1
25 Feb	Lge	A	Man City	W 1-0
4 Mar	FC	A	Sunderland	D 1-1
8 Mar	FCr	H	Sunderland	W 5-0
11 Mar	Lge	A	Cardiff	L 2-3
18 Mar	FCsf	†	Burnley	W 3-0
22 Mar	Lge	H	Newcastle	L 1-2
25 Mar	Lge	A	Fulham	D 0-0
31 Mar	Lge	H	Chelsea	W 4-2
1 Apr	Lge	H	Preston	W 5-0
3 Apr	Lge	A	Chelsea	W 3-2
18 Apr	Lge	A	Birmingham	W 3-2
17 Apr	Lge	H	Sheffield Wed	W 2-1
22 Apr	Lge	A	Burnley	L 2-4
26 Apr	Lge	H	Nottm Forest	W 1-0
29 Apr	Lge	A	WBA	L 1-2
6 May	FCf	*	Leicester	W 2-0
15 May	F	A	Feijenoord	W 2-1
17 May	F	A	Amsterdam XI	W 3-0
* At Wembley			† At Villa Park	

Player	Lg App	Goals
ALLEN	42	22
BAKER	41	1
BARTON	1	
BL'FLOWER	42	6
BROWN	41	
DYSON	40	12
HENRY	42	
HOLLOWB'D	1	
JONES	29	15
MACKEY	37	4
MARCHI	6	
MEDWIN	14	5
NORMAN	41	4
SAUL	6	3
J. SMITH	1	
R. SMITH	36	28
WHITE	42	13
Own Goals		4

Final Table for First Division

1 TOTTENHAM	42	31	4	7	115:55	66

SEASON 1961/62

12 Aug	CS	H	England Sel. XI	W 3-2
19 Aug	Lge	A	Blackpool	W 2-1
23 Aug	Lge	H	West Ham	D 2-2
26 Aug	Lge	H	Arsenal	W 4-3
28 Aug	Lge	A	West Ham	L 1-2
2 Sep	Lge	H	Cardiff	W 3-2
4 Sep	Lge	A	Sheff Utd	D 1-1
9 Sep	Lge	A	Man Utd	L 0-1
13 Sep	EC	A	Gornik	L 2-4
16 Sep	Lge	H	Wolves	W 1-0
20 Sep	EC	H	Gornik	W 8-1
23 Sep	Lge	A	Nottm Forest	L 0-2
30 Sep	Lge	A	Aston Villa	W 1-0
9 Oct	Lge	A	Bolton	W 2-1
14 Oct	Lge	H	Man City	W 2-0
21 Oct	Lge	A	Ipswich	L 2-3
28 Oct	Lge	H	Burnley	W 4-2
1 Nov	EC	A	Feijenoord	W 3-1
4 Nov	Lge	A	Everton	L 0-3
11 Nov	Lge	H	Fulham	W 4-2
15 Nov	EC	H	Feijenoord	D 1-1
18 Nov	Lge	H	Sheff Wed	D 0-0
25 Nov	Lge	H	Leicester	L 1-2
2 Dec	Lge	A	WBA	W 4-2
9 Dec	Lge	H	Birmingham	W 3-1
16 Dec	Lge	H	Blackpool	W 5-2

Date	Comp	H/A	Opponent	Result
23 Dec	Lge	A	Arsenal	L 1-2
26 Dec	Lge	H	Chelsea	W 2-0
30 Dec	Lge	A	Chelsea	W 5-2
6 Jan	FC	A	Birmingham	D 3-3
10 Jan	FCr	H	Birmingham	W 4-2
13 Jan	Lge	A	Cardiff	D 1-1
20 Jan	Lge	H	Man Utd	D 2-2
27 Jan	FC	A	Plymouth	W 5-1
3 Feb	Lge	A	Wolves	L 1-3
10 Feb	Lge	H	Nottm Forest	W 4-2
14 Feb	EC	A	Dukla Prague	L 0-1
17 Feb	FC	A	WBA	W 4-2
21 Feb	Lge	A	Aston Villa	D 0-0
24 Feb	Lge	H	Bolton	D 2-2
26 Feb	EC	H	Dukla Prague	W 4-2
3 Mar	Lge	A	Man City	L 2-6
10 Mar	FC	H	Aston Villa	W 2-0
14 Mar	Lge	A	Ipswich	L 1-3
17 Mar	Lge	H	Burnley	D 2-2
21 Mar	ECsf	A	Benfica	L 1-3
24 Mar	Lge	H	Everton	W 3-1
31 Mar	FCsf	*	Man Utd	W 3-1
5 Apr	ECsf	H	Benfica	W 2-1
7 Apr	Lge	H	Sheff Wed	W 4-0
9 Apr	Lge	H	Sheff Utd	D 3-3
17 Apr	Lge	A	Fulham	D 1-1
20 Apr	Lge	A	Blackburn	W 4-1
21 Apr	Lge	H	WBA	L 1-2
23 Apr	Lge	A	Blackburn	W 1-0
28 Apr	Lge	A	Birmingham	W 3-2
30 Apr	Lge	A	Leicester	W 3-2
5 May	FCf	†	Burnley	W 3-1
26 May	F	A	Tel Aviv Select	W 2-1
30 May	F	A	Haifa Select	W 5-0

* Semi-final at Hillsborough
† Final at Wembley

Player	Lg App	Goals
Allen L.W.	23	9
Baker P.R.B.	36	
Barton K.R.	2	
Blanchflower R.D.	39	2
Clayton E.	7	3
Brown W.D.F.	35	
Collins J.	2	
Dyson T.K.	23	6
Greaves J.P.	22	21
Henry R.P.	41	
Hollowbread J.F.	7	
Hopkins M.	5	
Jones C.W.	38	16
Mackay D.C.	26	8
Marchi A.V.	21	
Medwin T.C.	20	5
Norman M.	40	
Saul F.L.	8	3
Smith J.	5	
Smith R.A.	26	6
White J.A.	36	8
Own Goal		1

Final table for First Division

1 Ipswich	42 24 8 10	93:67 56
3 TOTTENHAM	**42 21 10 11**	**88:69 52**

SEASON 1962/63

Date	Comp	H/A	Opponent	Result
11 Aug	CS	A	Ipswich	W 5-1
18 Aug	Lge	H	Birmingham	W 3-0
20 Aug	Lge	A	Aston Villa	L 1-2
25 Aug	Lge	A	West Ham	W 6-1
29 Aug	Lge	H	Aston Villa	W 4-2
1 Sep	Lge	H	Man City	W 4-2
8 Sep	Lge	A	Blackpool	W 2-1
12 Sep	Lge	H	Wolves	L 1-2
15 Sep	Lge	H	Blackburn	W 4-1
19 Sep	Lge	A	Wolves	D 2-2
22 Sep	Lge	A	Sheff Utd	L 1-3
29 Sep	Lge	H	Nottm Forest	W 9-2
6 Oct	Lge	H	Arsenal	D 4-4
13 Oct	Lge	A	WBA	W 2-1
20 Oct	Lge	H	Man Utd	W 6-2
27 Oct	Lge	A	Leyton Orient	W 5-1
31 Oct	ECWC	H	Rangers	W 5-2
3 Nov	Lge	H	Leicester	W 4-0
10 Nov	Lge	A	Fulham	W 2-0
14 Nov	F	A	Zamalek	W 7-3

Date	Comp	H/A	Opponent	Result
17 Nov	Lge	H	Sheff Wed	D 1-1
24 Nov	Lge	A	Burnley	L 1-2
1 Dec	Lge	H	Everton	D 0-0
8 Dec	Lge	A	Bolton	L 0-1
11 Dec	ECWC	A	Rangers	W 3-2
15 Dec	Lge	A	Birmingham	W 2-0
22 Dec	Lge	H	West Ham	D 4-4
26 Dec	Lge	H	Ipswich	W 5-0
16 Jan	FC	A	Burnley	L 0-3
19 Jan	Lge	H	Blackpool	W 2-0
26 Jan	F	H	Arsenal	W 2-0
2 Feb	F	A	Portsmouth	W 3-2
23 Feb	Lge	A	Arsenal	W 3-2
2 Mar	Lge	H	WBA	W 2-1
5 Mar	ECWC	A	Slovan Bratislava	L 0-2
9 Mar	Lge	A	Man Utd	W 2-0
14 Mar	ECWC	H	Slovan Bratislava	W 6-0
16 Mar	Lge	A	Ipswich	W 4-2
23 Mar	Lge	A	Leicester	D 2-2
27 Mar	Lge	H	Leyton Orient	W 2-0
30 Mar	Lge	D	Burnley	D 1-1
8 Apr	Lge	A	Sheff Wed	L 1-3
12 Apr	Lge	A	Liverpool	L 2-5
13 Apr	Lge	H	Fulham	D 1-1
15 Apr	Lge	H	Liverpool	W 7-2
20 Apr	Lge	A	Everton	L 0-1
24 Apr	ECWCsf	A	OFK Belgrade	W 2-1
27 Apr	Lge	H	Bolton	W 4-1
1 May	ECWCsf	H	OFK Belgrade	W 3-1
4 May	Lge	H	Sheff Utd	W 4-2
11 May	Lge	A	Man City	L 0-1
15 May	ECWCf	†	Atletico Madrid	W 5-1
18 May	Lge	A	Nottm Forest	D 1-1
20 May	Lge	A	Blackburn Rvs	L 0-3
31 May	F	*	NSAFL XI	W 5-1
5 Jun	F	*	NFL XI	W 5-2
8 Jun	F	*	S Africa XI	W 3-1

† European Cup Winners Cup final played in Rotterdam
* Tour of S Africa

Player	Lg App	Goals
Allen L.W.	25	5
Baker P.R.B.	33	
Blanchflower R.D.	24	3
Brown W.D.F.	40	
Clayton E.	3	
Dyson T.K.	13	2
Greaves J.P.	41	37
Henry R.P.	42	
Hollowbread J.F.	2	
Hopkins M.	9	
Jones C.W.	37	20
Mackay D.C.	37	6
Marchi A.V.	22	3
Medwin T.C.	26	9
Norman M.	38	1
Piper R.D.	1	
Saul F.P.	10	4
Smith J.	7	1
Smith R.A.	15	8
White J.A.	37	8
Own Goals		4

Final table for First Division

1 Everton	42 25 11 6	84:42 61
2 TOTTENHAM	**42 23 9 10**	**111:62 55**

SEASON 1963/64

Date	Comp	H/A	Opponent	Result
24 Aug	Lge	A	Stoke City	L 1-2
28 Aug	Lge	A	Wolves	W 4-1
31 Aug	Lge	H	Nottm Forest	W 4-1
4 Sep	Lge	H	Wolves	W 4-3
7 Sep	Lge	A	Blackburn	L 2-7
14 Sep	Lge	H	Blackpool	W 6-1
16 Sep	Lge	A	Aston Villa	W 4-2
21 Sep	Lge	A	Chelsea	W 3-0
28 Sep	Lge	H	West Ham	W 3-0
2 Oct	Lge	H	Birmingham	W 6-1
5 Oct	Lge	A	Sheff Utd	D 3-3
15 Oct	Lge	A	Arsenal	D 4-4
19 Oct	Lge	H	Leicester	D 1-1
26 Oct	Lge	A	Everton	L 0-1

Date	Comp	H/A	Opponent	Result
2 Nov	Lge	H	Fulham	W 1-0
9 Nov	Lge	A	Man Utd	L 1-4
16 Nov	Lge	H	Burnley	W 3-2
23 Nov	Lge	A	Ipswich	W 3-2
30 Nov	Lge	H	Sheff Wed	D 1-1
3 Dec	ECWC	H	Man Utd	W 2-0
7 Dec	Lge	A	Bolton	W 3-1
10 Dec	ECWC	A	Man Utd	L 1-4
14 Dec	Lge	H	Stoke	W 2-1
21 Dec	Lge	A	Nottm Forest	W 2-1
26 Dec	Lge	A	WBA	D 4-4
28 Dec	Lge	H	WBA	L 0-2
5 Jan	FC	A	Chelsea	D 1-1
8 Jan	FCr	H	Chelsea	L 0-2
11 Jan	Lge	H	Blackburn	W 4-1
18 Jan	Lge	A	Blackpool	W 2-0
25 Jan	Lge	H	Aston Villa	W 3-1
1 Feb	Lge	H	Chelsea	L 1-2
8 Feb	Lge	A	West Ham	L 0-4
15 Feb	Lge	H	Sheff Utd	D 0-0
22 Feb	Lge	H	Arsenal	W 3-1
29 Feb	Lge	A	Birmingham	W 2-1
7 Mar	Lge	H	Everton	L 2-4
21 Mar	Lge	H	Man Utd	L 2-3
27 Mar	Lge	H	Liverpool	L 1-3
28 Mar	Lge	A	Fulham	D 1-1
30 Mar	Lge	A	Liverpool	L 1-3
4 Apr	Lge	H	Ipswich	W 6-3
13 Apr	Lge	A	Sheff Wed	L 0-2
18 Apr	Lge	H	Bolton	W 1-0
21 Apr	Lge	A	Burnley	L 2-7
25 Apr	Lge	A	Leicester	W 2-1
28 Apr	F	A	Coventry	W 6-5

Player	Lg App	Goals
Allen L.W.	8	1
Beal P.	16	
Baker P.R.B.	35	1
Barton K.R.	1	
Blanchflower R.D.	15	
Brown L.	9	1
Brown W.D.F.	27	
Clayton E.	1	
Dyson T.K.	39	11
Greaves J.P.	41	35
Henry R.P.	29	
Hollowbread J.F.	15	
Hopkins M.	19	
Jones C.W.	39	14
Mackay D.C.	17	3
Marchi A.V.	21	1
Mullery A.P.	9	1
Norman M.	42	3
Possee D.J.	1	1
Robertson J.	3	1
Saul F.L.	2	
Smith J.	7	
Smith R.A.	26	13
White J.A.	40	6
Own Goals		5

Final table for First Division

1 Liverpool	42 26 5 11	92:45 57
4 TOTTENHAM	**42 22 7 13**	**97:81 51**

SEASON 1964/65

Date	Comp	H/A	Opponent	Result
5 Aug	F	A	Glasgow Sel	L 2-4
8 Aug	F	A	Feijenoord	L 3-4
22 Aug	Lge	A	Sheff Utd	W 2-0
25 Aug	Lge	A	Burnley	D 2-2
29 Aug	Lge	A	Everton	L 1-4
2 Sep	Lge	H	Burnley	W 4-1
5 Sep	Lge	A	Birmingham	W 4-1
9 Sep	Lge	A	Stoke	L 0-2
12 Sep	Lge	H	West Ham	L 2-3
17 Sep	Lge	H	Stoke	W 2-1
19 Sep	Lge	H	WBA	W 2-1
23 Sep	F	A	Copenhagen XI	L 1-2
26 Sep	Lge	A	Man Utd	L 1-4
28 Sep	Lge	A	Blackpool	D 1-1
5 Oct	Lge	H	Fulham	W 3-0
10 Oct	Lge	H	Arsenal	W 3-1
17 Oct	Lge	A	Leeds	L 1-3
24 Oct	Lge	H	Chelsea	D 1-1
31 Oct	Lge	A	Leicester	L 2-4
7 Nov	Lge	H	Sunderland	W 3-0

Date	Comp	H/A	Opponent	Result
11 Nov	*	H	Scotland XI	L 2-6
14 Nov	Lge	A	Wolves	L 1-3
21 Nov	Lge	A	Aston Villa	W 4-0
28 Nov	Lge	A	Liverpool	D 1-1
5 Dec	Lge	H	Sheff Wed	W 3-2
8 Dec	F	A	Leytonstone	W 5-0
12 Dec	Lge	A	Sheff Utd	D 3-3
19 Dec	Lge	A	Everton	D 2-2
26 Dec	Lge	A	Nottm Forest	W 2-1
28 Dec	Lge	H	Nottm Forest	W 4-0
2 Jan	Lge	A	Birmingham	L 0-1
9 Jan	FC	D	Torquay Utd	D 3-3
16 Jan	Lge	H	West Ham	W 3-2
18 Jan	FCr	H	Torquay Utd	W 5-1
23 Jan	Lge	A	WBA	L 0-2
30 Jan	FC	H	Ipswich	W 5-0
6 Feb	Lge	H	Man Utd	W 1-0
13 Feb	Lge	A	Fulham	L 1-4
20 Feb	FC	A	Chelsea	L 0-1
23 Feb	Lge	A	Arsenal	L 1-3
27 Feb	Lge	A	Leeds Utd	D 0-0
10 Mar	Lge	A	Chelsea	L 1-3
13 Mar	Lge	H	Blackpool	W 4-1
20 Mar	Lge	A	Sunderland	L 1-2
27 Mar	Lge	H	Wolves	W 7-4
3 Apr	Lge	A	Aston Villa	L 0-1
9 Apr	Lge	H	Liverpool	W 3-0
16 Apr	Lge	H	Blackburn	W 5-2
17 Apr	Lge	A	Sheff Wed	L 0-1
19 Apr	Lge	A	Blackburn	L 1-3
24 Apr	Lge	H	Leicester	W 6-2
27 Apr	F	A	Anderlecht	L 2-4
29 Apr	F	A	Coventry	W 3-0
18 May	F	A	DWS Amsterdam	L 0-1
22 May	F	A	Telstar	W 3-2
21 Jun	F	A	Hakoah	W 3-1†
24 Jun	F	A	Maccabi Sel	W 3-2†

* John White testimonial match
† Tour of Israel

Player	Lg App	Goals
Allen L.W.	6	2
Baker P.	3	
Beal P.	8	
Brown L.	16	1
Brown W.D.F.	19	
Clayton E.	15	1
Dyson T.K.	32	5
Gilzean A.J.	20	11
Greaves J.P.	41	29
Henry R.P.	41	1
Jennings P.A.	23	
Jones C.W.	39	13
Knowles C.B.	38	
Low A.R.	6	1
Marchi A.V.	17	
Mullery A.P.	42	2
Norman M.	30	1
Possee D.J.	1	
Robertson J.G.	36	7
Saul F.L.	23	11
Weller K.	6	
Own Goals		2

Final table for First Division

1 Manchester U.	42 26 9 7	89:39 61
6 TOTTENHAM	**42 19 7 16**	**87:71 45**

SEASON 1965/66

Date	Comp	H/A	Opponent	Result
14 Aug	F	A	Valencia	W 2-1
15 Aug	F	A	Standard Liege	W 1-0
25 Aug	Lge	H	Leicester	W 4-2
27 Aug	Lge	H	Blackpool	W 4-0
1 Sep	Lge	A	Leicester	D 2-2
4 Sep	Lge	A	Fulham	W 2-0
8 Sep	Lge	H	Leeds	W 3-2
11 Sep	Lge	H	Arsenal	D 2-2
15 Sep	Lge	A	Leeds	L 0-2
18 Sep	Lge	H	Liverpool	W 2-1
22 Sep	F	A	Walton & Hersham	W 8-1
25 Sep	Lge	A	Aston Villa	L 2-3
6 Oct	Lge	H	Sunderland	W 3-0
9 Oct	Lge	A	Everton	L 1-3
16 Oct	Lge	H	Man Utd	W 5-1
23 Oct	Lge	A	Newcastle	D 0-0

218

Date	Comp		Opponent		Result
30 Oct	Lge	H	WBA	W	2-1
6 Nov	Lge	A	Nottm Forest	L	0-1
13 Nov	Lge	H	Sheff Wed	L	2-3
18 Nov	F	H	Hungarian Sel	W	4-0
20 Nov	Lge	A	Northampton	W	2-0
27 Nov	Lge	H	Stoke	D	2-2
4 Dec	Lge	A	Burnley	D	1-1
11 Dec	Lge	H	Chelsea	W	4-2
18 Dec	Lge	A	Man Utd	L	1-5
27 Dec	Lge	H	Sheff Utd	W	1-0
28 Dec	Lge	A	Sheff Utd	W	3-1
1 Jan	Lge	H	Everton	D	2-2
8 Jan	Lge	A	Chelsea	L	1-2
15 Jan	Lge	H	Newcastle	D	2-2
22 Jan	FC	H	Middlesbrough	W	4-0
29 Jan	Lge	H	Blackburn	W	4-0
5 Feb	Lge	A	Blackpool	D	0-0
12 Feb	FC	H	Burnley	W	4-3
19 Feb	Lge	H	Fulham	W	4-3
5 Mar	FC	A	Preston	L	1-2
8 Mar	Lge	A	Arsenal	D	1-1
12 Mar	Lge	H	Liverpool	L	0-1
19 Mar	Lge	H	Aston Villa	D	5-5
26 Mar	Lge	A	Sunderland	L	0-2
2 Apr	Lge	H	Nottm Forest	L	2-3
8 Apr	Lge	H	West Ham	L	1-4
9 Apr	Lge	A	Sheff Wed	D	1-1
16 Apr	Lge	H	Northampton	D	1-1
23 Apr	Lge	A	Stoke City	W	1-0
25 Apr	Lge	A	West Ham	L	0-2
30 Apr	Lge	H	Burnley	L	0-1
3 May	F	A	Legia Warsaw	L	0-2
7 May	Lge	A	WBA	L	1-2
9 May	Lge	A	Blackburn	W	1-0
15 May	F	A	Sarpsborg	W	3-0
19 May	F	A	Bermuda Sel	W	3-2*
21 May	F	A	Celtic	L	0-1*
25 May	F	A	Hartford USA XI	W	3-0*
29 May	F	A	Bologna	L	0-1*
1 Jun	F	A	Celtic	L	1-2*
4 Jun	F	A	Celtic	D	1-1*
8 Jun	F	A	Vancouver Sel	W	3-0*
12 Jun	F	A	Mexico Sel	W	1-0*
15 Jun	F	A	Mexico Americano	W	2-0*
17 Jun	F	A	Bayern Munich	W	3-0*
19 Jun	F	A	Bayern Munich	D	1-1*

* North American tour matches

Player	Lg App		Goals
Beal P.	21		
Brown L.	27		1
Brown W.D.F.	20		
Clayton E.	38		9
Collins J.L.	2		
Gilzean A.J.	40		12
Greaves J.P.	29		15
Henry R.P.	1		
Hoy R.E.	5		
Jennings P.A.	22		
Johnson N.	10	(1)	1
Jones C.W.	9		8
Kinnear J.P.	8		
Knowles C.B.	41		3
Low A.R.	1	(1)	
Mackay D.C.	41		6
Mullery A.P.	40		1
Norman M.	16		1
Pitt S.W.	1		
Possee D.J.	17		3
Robertson J.G.	33		6
Saul F.L.	26		8
Venables T.	1		
Weller K.	5		1

Note: First season using substitutes, with appearances as sub in brackets. League apps include occasions when player came on as sub

Final table for First Division

1 Liverpool	42	26	9	7	79:34	61
8 TOTTENHAM	**42**	**16**	**12**	**14**	**75:66**	**44**

SEASON 1966/67

14 Aug	F	A	Malaga	W	2-1
15 Aug	F	A	Benfica	W	2-1
20 Aug	Lge	H	Leeds	W	3-1

Date	Comp		Opponent		Result
24 Aug	Lge	A	Stoke	L	0-2
27 Aug	Lge	A	Newcastle	W	2-0
31 Aug	Lge	H	Stoke	W	2-0
3 Sep	Lge	H	Arsenal	W	3-1
6 Sep	Lge	A	Sheff Utd	L	1-2
10 Sep	Lge	A	Man Utd	W	2-1
14 Sep	FLC	A	West Ham	L	0-1
17 Sep	Lge	A	Burnley	D	2-2
24 Sep	Lge	H	Nottm Forest	W	2-1
1 Oct	Lge	A	Fulham	W	4-3
8 Oct	Lge	A	Man City	W	2-1
10 Oct	F	A	Dundee	W	3-2
15 Oct	Lge	H	Blackpool	L	1-3
26 Oct	Lge	A	Chelsea	L	0-3
29 Oct	Lge	H	Aston Villa	L	0-1
5 Nov	Lge	A	Blackpool	D	2-2
12 Nov	Lge	H	West Ham	L	3-4
19 Nov	Lge	A	Sheff Wed	L	0-1
23 Nov	F	H	Polish Sel XI	W	2-1
26 Nov	Lge	A	Southampton	W	3-0
3 Dec	Lge	A	Sunderland	W	1-0
10 Dec	Lge	H	Leicester	W	2-0
17 Dec	Lge	A	Leeds	L	2-3
26 Dec	Lge	A	WBA	L	0-3
27 Dec	Lge	H	WBA	D	0-0
31 Dec	Lge	H	Newcastle	W	4-0
7 Jan	Lge	A	Arsenal	W	2-0
14 Jan	Lge	A	Man Utd	L	0-1
21 Jan	Lge	H	Burnley	W	2-0
28 Jan	FC	A	Millwall	D	0-0
1 Feb	FCr	H	Millwall	W	1-0
4 Feb	Lge	A	Nottm Forest	D	1-1
11 Feb	Lge	H	Fulham	W	4-2
18 Feb	FC	H	Portsmouth	W	3-1
25 Feb	Lge	H	Man City	D	1-1
4 Mar	Lge	H	Aston Villa	D	3-3
11 Mar	FC	A	Bristol City	W	2-0
18 Mar	Lge	H	Chelsea	D	1-1
22 Mar	Lge	A	Everton	W	1-0
25 Mar	Lge	A	Leicester	W	1-0
27 Mar	Lge	H	Everton	W	2-0
1 Apr	Lge	H	Liverpool	W	2-1
8 Apr	FC	A	Birmingham	D	0-0
12 Apr	FCr	H	Birmingham	W	6-0
15 Apr	Lge	H	Sheff Wed	W	2-1
22 Apr	Lge	A	Southampton	W	1-0
29 Apr	FCsf	*	Nottm Forest	W	2-1
3 May	Lge	H	Sunderland	W	1-0
6 May	Lge	A	Liverpool	D	0-0
9 May	Lge	A	West Ham	W	2-0
13 May	Lge	H	Sheff Utd	W	2-0
20 May	FCf	†	Chelsea	W	2-1
30 May	F	A	FC Zurich	W	2-0
1 Jun	F	A	Yng Boys Bern	W	3-2
7 Jun	F	A	Servette	W	4-1

* Semi-final played at Hillsborough † Final played at Wembley

Player	Lg Ap		Goals
Beal P.	26		
Bond D.	1	(1)	
Brown W.D.F.	1		
Clayton E.	9	(3)	
England M.	42		1
Gilzean A.J.	40		18
Greaves J.P.	38		23
Jennings P.A.	41		
Jones C.W.	20		6
Kinnear J.P.	20	(1)	
Knowles C.B.	42		1
Low A.R.	1	(1)	
Mackay D.C.	39		3
Mullery A.P.	39		5
Robertson J.G.	40		6
Saul F.L.	22	(2)	4
Venables T.	41		3
Weller K.	10	(2)	
Own Goal			1

Final table for First Division

1 Manchester U.	42	24	12	6	84:45	60
3 TOTTENHAM	**42**	**24**	**8**	**10**	**71:48**	**56**

SEASON 1967/68

5 Aug	F	A	Celtic	D	3-3
12 Aug	CS	A	Man utd	D	3-3

Date	Comp		Opponent		Result
19 Aug	Lge	A	Leicester	W	3-2
23 Aug	Lge	H	Everton	D	1-1
26 Aug	Lge	H	West Ham	W	5-1
29 Aug	Lge	A	Everton	W	1-0
2 Sep	Lge	A	Burnley	L	1-5
6 Sep	Lge	A	Wolves	W	2-1
9 Sep	Lge	H	Sheff Wed	W	2-1
16 Sep	Lge	A	Arsenal	L	0-4
20 Sep	ECWC	A	Hajduk Split	W	2-0
23 Sep	Lge	H	Man Utd	L	1-3
27 Sep	ECWC	H	Hajduk Split	W	4-3
30 Sep	Lge	H	Sunderland	W	3-0
7 Oct	Lge	H	Sheff Utd	D	1-1
14 Oct	Lge	A	Coventry	W	3-2
25 Oct	Lge	A	Nottm Forest	D	1-1
28 Oct	Lge	A	Stoke	L	1-2
4 Nov	Lge	H	Liverpool	D	1-1
11 Nov	Lge	A	Southampton	W	2-1
18 Nov	Lge	A	Chelsea	W	2-0
25 Nov	Lge	A	WBA	L	0-2
29 Nov	ECWC	A	Olymp. Lyon	L	0-1
2 Dec	Lge	H	Newcastle	D	1-1
9 Dec	Lge	A	Man City	L	1-4
13 Dec	ECWC	H	Olymp. Lyon	W	4-3
16 Dec	Lge	A	Leicester	L	0-1
23 Dec	Lge	A	West Ham	L	1-2
26 Dec	Lge	H	Fulham	D	2-2
30 Dec	Lge	A	Fulham	W	2-1
17 Jan	Lge	A	Sheff Wed	W	2-1
20 Jan	Lge	H	Arsenal	W	1-0
28 Jan	FC	A	Man Utd	D	2-2
31 Jan	FCr	H	Man Utd	W	1-0
3 Feb	Lge	A	Man Utd	L	1-2
10 Feb	Lge	A	Sunderland	W	1-0
17 Feb	FC	H	Preston	W	3-1
26 Feb	Lge	A	Sheff Utd	L	2-3
1 Mar	Lge	H	WBA	D	0-0
9 Mar	FC	A	Liverpool	D	1-1
12 Mar	FCr	H	Liverpool	L	1-2
16 Mar	Lge	A	Nottm Forest	D	0-0
23 Mar	Lge	H	Stoke	W	3-0
30 Mar	Lge	H	Burnley	W	5-0
6 Apr	Lge	H	Southampton	W	6-1
12 Apr	Lge	H	Leeds	W	2-1
13 Apr	Lge	A	Chelsea	L	0-2
17 Apr	Lge	A	Leeds	L	0-1
20 Apr	Lge	A	Coventry	W	4-2
27 Apr	Lge	A	Newcastle	W	3-1
29 Apr	Lge	A	Liverpool	D	1-1
4 May	Lge	H	Man City	L	1-3
11 May	Lge	A	Wolves	L	1-2
15 May	F	A	Panathinaikos	D	2-2
19 May	F	A	Anorthosis	W	5-0
22 May	F	A	AEL	W	7-1
25 May	F	A	Cyprus XI	W	3-0
29 May	F	A	Apoel	W	3-0

Player	Lg App		Goals
Beal P.	35	(1)	
Bond D.	6	(1)	
Chivers M.	18		7
Clayton E.	2	(1)	
England M.	31		3
Gilzean A.J.	34	(2)	8
Greaves J.P.	39		23
Hoy R.E.	5		
Jennings P.A.	42		
Jones C.W.	30	(3)	12
Kinnear J.P.	30	(1)	1
Knowles C.B.	42		
Mackay D.C.	29		1
Mullery A.P.	41		2
Robertson J.G.	34	(1)	5
Saul F.L.	19	(2)	4
Venables T.	36	(1)	2
Want A.G.	2		
Own Goals			2

Final table for First Division

1 Manchester C.	42	26	6	10	86:43	58
7 TOTTENHAM	**42**	**19**	**9**	**14**	**70:59**	**47**

SEASON 1968/69

31 Jul	F	H	Rangers	W	3-1
3 Aug	F	A	FK Austria	D	2-2
10 Aug	Lge	H	Arsenal	L	1-2

Date	Comp		Opponent		Result
17 Aug	Lge	A	Everton	W	2-0
21 Aug	Lge	H	WBA	D	1-1
24 Aug	Lge	A	Sheff Wed	L	1-2
28 Aug	Lge	A	Man Utd	L	1-3
31 Aug	Lge	A	Chelsea	D	2-2
4 Sep	FLC	H	Aston Villa	W	4-1
7 Sep	Lge	H	Burnley	W	7-0
14 Sep	Lge	A	West Ham	D	2-2
17 Sep	Lge	A	Coventry	W	2-1
21 Sep	Lge	H	Nottm Forest	W	2-1
25 Sep	FLC	H	Exeter	W	6-3
28 Sep	Lge	A	Newcastle	W	2-1
5 Oct	Lge	H	Leicester	W	3-2
9 Oct	Lge	H	Man Utd	D	2-2
12 Oct	Lge	A	Man City	L	0-4
16 Oct	FLC	A	Peterborough	W	1-0
19 Oct	Lge	H	Liverpool	W	2-1
26 Oct	Lge	A	Ipswich	W	1-0
30 Oct	FLC	H	Southampton	W	1-0
2 Nov	Lge	H	Stoke	D	1-1
9 Nov	Lge	A	Leeds	D	0-0
16 Nov	Lge	H	Sunderland	W	5-1
20 Nov	FLCsf	A	Arsenal	L	0-1
23 Nov	Lge	A	Southampton	L	1-2
4 Dec	FLCsf	H	Arsenal	D	1-1
7 Dec	Lge	A	Wolves	L	0-2
14 Dec	Lge	H	Man City	D	1-1
21 Dec	Lge	A	Liverpool	L	0-1
4 Jan	FC	H	Walsall	W	1-0
11 Jan	Lge	H	Stoke	D	1-1
18 Jan	Lge	H	Leeds	D	0-0
25 Jan	FC	H	Wolves	W	2-1
29 Jan	Lge	H	QPR	W	3-2
1 Feb	Lge	A	Sunderland	D	0-0
12 Feb	FC	H	Aston Villa	W	3-2
15 Feb	Lge	A	QPR	D	1-1
22 Feb	Lge	H	Wolves	D	1-1
1 Mar	FC	A	Man City	L	0-1
8 Mar	Lge	H	Everton	D	1-1
18 Mar	Lge	H	Ipswich	D	2-2
22 Mar	Lge	H	Chelsea	W	1-0
24 Mar	Lge	A	Arsenal	L	0-1
29 Mar	Lge	H	Burnley	D	2-2
2 Apr	Lge	H	Newcastle	L	0-1
4 Apr	Lge	H	Coventry	W	2-0
7 Apr	Lge	A	WBA	L	3-4
12 Apr	Lge	H	Nottm Forest	W	2-0
19 Apr	Lge	H	West Ham	W	1-0
22 Apr	Lge	H	Southampton	W	2-1
29 Apr	Lge	A	Leicester	L	0-1
12 May	Lge	H	Sheff Wed	D	0-0
15 May	F	A	West Ham	W	4-3*
17 May	F	A	Aston Villa	D	2-2*
28 May	F	A	Fiorentina	L	0-3*
1 Jun	F	A	Rangers	W	4-3*

* Games played on tour of North America; West Ham in Baltimore, Villa in Atlanta, Fiorentina and Rangers in Toronto

Player	Lg App		Goals
Beal P.	39		1
Bond D.	2		
Chivers M.	10		3
Collins J.L.	1		
Collins P.	24	(3)	
England M.	36		3
Evans R.	6	(1)	
Gilzean A.J.	37		7
Greaves J.P.	42		27
Jenkins D.	11	(1)	2
Jennings P.A.	42		
Johnson N.	16	(3)	3
Jones C.W.	7	(1)	5
Kinnear J.P.	24		
Knowles C.B.	37	(1)	2
Morgan R.	13		3
Mullery A.P.	41		1
Pearce J.	27	(3)	3
Pratt J.	9	(1)	
Robertson J.G.	11	(3)	1
Venables T.	37		
Want A.G.	8	(1)	

Final table for First Division

1 Leeds	42	27	13	2	66:26	67
6 TOTTENHAM	**42**	**14**	**17**	**11**	**61:51**	**45**

SEASON 1969/70

Date	Comp		Opponent		Score
2 Aug	F	A	Hearts	D	1-1
4 Aug	F	A	Rangers	W	1-0
9 Aug	Lge	A	Leeds	L	1-3
13 Aug	Lge	H	Burnley	W	4-0
16 Aug	Lge	H	Liverpool	L	0-2
19 Aug	Lge	A	Burnley	W	2-0
23 Aug	Lge	A	Crystal P.	W	2-0
27 Aug	Lge	H	Chelsea	D	1-1
30 Aug	Lge	H	Ipswich	W	3-2
3 Sep	FLC	A	Wolves	L	0-1
6 Sep	Lge	A	West Ham	W	1-0
13 Sep	Lge	H	Man City	L	0-3
16 Sep	Lge	A	Arsenal	W	3-2
20 Sep	Lge	A	Derby	L	0-5
27 Sep	Lge	H	Sunderland	L	0-1
4 Oct	Lge	A	Southampton	D	2-2
7 Oct	Lge	A	Liverpool	D	0-0
11 Oct	Lge	H	Wolves	L	0-1
18 Oct	Lge	H	Newcastle	W	2-1
25 Oct	Lge	A	Stoke	D	1-1
1 Nov	Lge	H	Sheff Wed	W	1-0
8 Nov	Lge	A	Nottm Forest	D	2-2
15 Nov	Lge	H	WBA	W	2-0
22 Nov	Lge	A	Man Utd	L	1-3
6 Dec	Lge	A	Coventry	L	2-3
13 Dec	Lge	A	Man City	D	1-1
17 Dec	Lge	H	Everton	D	0-0†
20 Dec	Lge	H	West Ham	L	0-2
26 Dec	Lge	H	Crystal P.	W	2-0
27 Dec	Lge	A	Ipswich	L	0-2
3 Jan	FC	A	Bradford C	D	2-2
7 Jan	FCr	H	Bradford C	W	5-0
10 Jan	Lge	H	Derby	W	2-1
17 Jan	Lge	A	Sunderland	L	1-2
24 Jan	FC	H	Crystal P.	D	0-0
28 Jan	FCr	A	Crystal P.	L	0-1
31 Jan	Lge	H	Southampton	L	0-1
7 Feb	Lge	A	Wolves	D	2-2
14 Feb	Lge	H	Leeds	D	1-1
21 Feb	Lge	H	Stoke	W	1-0
28 Feb	Lge	A	Newcastle	W	2-1
11 Mar	Lge	H	Everton	L	0-1
14 Mar	Lge	A	Everton	L	2-3
21 Mar	Lge	H	Coventry	L	1-2
27 Mar	Lge	H	Nottm Forest	W	4-1
28 Mar	Lge	A	WBA	D	1-1
30 Mar	Lge	A	Sheff Wed	W	1-0
4 Apr	Lge	A	Chelsea	L	0-1
13 Apr	Lge	H	Man Utd	W	2-1
2 May	Lge	H	Arsenal	W	1-0
13 May	F	A	Valletta	W	3-0
16 May	F	A	Sliema Wand	W	2-1
17 May	F	A	Malta Sel	L	0-1

† Match abandoned after 29 minutes due to floodlight failure.

Player	Lg App		Goals
Beal P.	31	(2)	
Bond D.	12		1
Chivers M.	31	(4)	11
Collins P.	18	(2)	2
England M.	36		1
Evans R.	16	(1)	
Gilzean A.J.	36	(2)	10
Greaves J.P.	28		8
Hancock K.	1		
Jenkins D.	3	(2)	
Jennings P.A.	41		
Johnson N.	5		1
Kinnear J.P.	9		
Knowles C.B.	33		
Morgan R.	37		4
Mullery A.P.	41		4
Naylor T.	3		
Pearce J.	31	(6)	7
Perryman S.	23		1
Peters M.	7		2
Pratt J.	12		1
Want A.G.	29	(3)	
Woolcott R.	1		
Own Goal			1

Final table for First Division

1 Everton	42	29	8	5	72:34	66
11 TOTTENHAM	**42**	**17**	**9**	**16**	**54:55**	**43**

SEASON 1970/71

Date	Comp		Opponent		Score
3 Aug	F	H	Rangers	W	2-0
7 Aug	F	A	IFC Koln	L	0-1
8 Aug	F	A	Atletico Mad.	L	0-1
15 Aug	Lge	H	West Ham	D	2-2
19 Aug	Lge	H	Leeds	L	0-2
22 Aug	Lge	A	Wolves	W	3-0
25 Aug	Lge	A	Southampton	D	0-0
29 Aug	Lge	H	Coventry	W	1-0
1 Sep	Lge	H	Huddersfield	D	1-1
5 Sep	Lge	A	Arsenal	L	0-2
9 Sep	FLC	H	Swansea	W	3-0
12 Sep	Lge	H	Blackpool	W	3-0
16 Sep	TEX	H	Dunfermline	W	4-0
19 Sep	Lge	A	Crystal P.	W	3-0
26 Sep	Lge	H	Man City	W	2-0
29 Sep	TEX	A	Dunfermline	W	3-0
3 Oct	Lge	A	Derby	D	1-1
7 Oct	FLC	H	Sheff Utd	W	2-1
10 Oct	Lge	H	Liverpool	W	1-0
17 Oct	Lge	A	West Ham	D	2-2
21 Oct	TEX	H	Motherwell	W	3-2
24 Oct	Lge	A	Stoke	W	3-0
28 Oct	FLC	A	WBA	W	5-0
31 Oct	Lge	A	Nottm Forest	W	1-0
3 Nov	TEX	A	Motherwell	L	1-3
7 Nov	Lge	H	Burnley	W	4-0
14 Nov	Lge	A	Chelsea	W	2-0
18 Nov	FLC	H	Coventry	W	4-1
21 Nov	Lge	H	Newcastle	L	1-2
28 Nov	Lge	A	Everton	D	0-0
5 Dec	Lge	H	Man Utd	D	2-2
12 Dec	Lge	A	WBA	L	1-3
16 Dec	FLCsf	A	Bristol City	D	1-1
19 Dec	Lge	H	Wolves	D	0-0
23 Dec	FLCsf	H	Bristol City	W	2-0
2 Jan	FC	H	Sheff Wed	W	4-1
9 Jan	Lge	A	Leeds	W	2-1
16 Jan	Lge	H	Southampton	L	1-3
23 Jan	FC	A	Carlisle	W	3-2
30 Jan	Lge	H	Everton	W	2-1
6 Feb	Lge	A	Man Utd	L	1-2
13 Feb	FC	H	Nottm Forest	W	2-1
17 Feb	Lge	H	WBA	D	2-2
20 Feb	Lge	A	Newcastle	L	0-1
27 Feb	FLCf	*	Aston Villa	W	2-0
6 Mar	FC	A	Liverpool	D	0-0
10 Mar	Lge	H	Nottm Forest	L	0-1
13 Mar	Lge	H	Chelsea	W	2-1
16 Mar	FCr	H	Liverpool	L	0-1
20 Mar	Lge	A	Burnley	D	0-0
23 Mar	Lge	A	Ipswich	W	2-1
3 Apr	Lge	A	Coventry	D	0-0
7 Apr	Lge	H	Derby	W	2-1
10 Apr	Lge	H	Ipswich	W	2-0
12 Apr	Lge	H	Blackpool	D	0-0
17 Apr	Lge	A	Liverpool	D	0-0
24 Apr	Lge	H	C. Palace	W	2-0
28 Apr	Lge	H	Huddersfield	D	1-1
1 May	Lge	A	Man City	W	1-0
3 May	Lge	H	Arsenal	L	0-1
5 May	Lge	A	Stoke	W	1-0
29 May	F	A	All Japan XI	W	6-0
3 Jun	F	A	All Japan XI	W	7-2
9 Jun	F	A	All Japan XI	W	3-0

* Played at Wembley

Player	Lg App		Goals
Beal P.	32		
Bond D.	2	(1)	
Chivers M.	42		21
Collins P.	26		
England M.	22		1
Evans R.	7		
Gilzean A.J.	38		9
Hancock K.	2		
Jennings P.A.	40		
Johnson N.	3	(3)	
Kinnear J.P.	35		
Knowles C.B.	38		
Morgan R.	8		1
Mullery A.P.	41		6
Naylor T.	4	(1)	
Neighbour J.	17	(5)	
Pearce J.	32	(10)	2
Perryman S.	42		3
Peters M.	42		9
Pratt J.	7	(2)	
Want A.G.	4		
Own Goals			2

Final table for First Division

1 Arsenal	42	29	7	6	71:29	65
3 TOTTENHAM	**42**	**19**	**14**	**9**	**54:33**	**52**

SEASON 1971/72

Date	Comp		Opponent		Score
7 Aug	F	A	Hearts	L	1-2
9 Aug	F	A	Rangers	L	0-1
14 Aug	Lge	A	Wolves	D	2-2
18 Aug	Lge	H	Newcastle	D	0-0
21 Aug	Lge	H	Huddersfield	W	4-1
25 Aug	Lge	A†	Leeds	D	1-1
28 Aug	Lge	A	Man City	L	0-4
1 Sep	*	A	Torino	W	1-0
4 Sep	Lge	H	Liverpool	W	2-0
8 Sep	FLC	A	WBA	W	1-0
11 Sep	Lge	H	Sheff Utd	D	2-2
14 Sep	UEFA	H	Keflavik	W	6-1
18 Sep	Lge	H	C. Palace	W	3-0
22 Sep	*	H	Torino	W	2-0
25 Sep	Lge	A	Coventry	L	0-1
28 Sep	UEFA	A	Keflavik	W	9-0
2 Oct	Lge	H	Ipswich	W	2-1
6 Oct	FLC	A	Torquay	W	4-1
9 Oct	Lge	A	Derby	D	2-2
16 Oct	Lge	H	Wolves	W	4-1
20 Oct	UEFA	A	Nantes	D	0-0
23 Oct	Lge	H	Nottm Forest	W	6-1
27 Oct	FLC	H	Preston	D	1-1
30 Oct	Lge	A	Stoke	L	0-2
2 Nov	UEFA	H	Nantes	W	1-0
6 Nov	Lge	H	Everton	W	3-0
8 Nov	FLCr	A	Preston	W	2-1
13 Nov	Lge	A	Man Utd	L	1-3
17 Nov	FLC	H	Blackpool	W	2-0
20 Nov	Lge	H	WBA	W	3-2
24 Nov	Lge	H	Arsenal	D	1-1
27 Nov	Lge	A	Chelsea	L	0-1
4 Dec	Lge	A	Southampton	W	1-0
8 Dec	UEFA	A	Rapid Bucarest	W	3-0
11 Dec	Lge	A	Leicester	D	2-2
15 Dec	UEFA	H	Rapid Bucarest	W	2-0
18 Dec	Lge	H	Liverpool	D	0-0
22 Dec	FLCsf	A	Chelsea	L	2-3
27 Dec	Lge	H	West Ham	L	0-1
1 Jan	Lge	H	Crystal P.	D	1-1
5 Jan	FLCsf	H	Chelsea	D	2-2
8 Jan	Lge	H	Man City	D	1-1
15 Jan	FC	A	Carlisle	D	1-1
18 Jan	FCr	H	Carlisle	W	3-1
22 Jan	Lge	A	Newcastle	L	1-3
29 Jan	Lge	H	Leeds U.	W	1-0
5 Feb	FC	H	Rotherham	W	2-0
12 Feb	Lge	A	Nottm Forest	W	1-0
19 Feb	Lge	H	Stoke	W	2-0
26 Feb	FC	A	Everton	W	2-0
1 Mar	Lge	A	Everton	D	1-1
4 Mar	Lge	H	Man Utd	W	2-0
7 Mar	UEFA	H	UT Arad	W	2-0
11 Mar	Lge	H	Derby	L	0-1
18 Mar	FC	A	Leeds	L	1-2
21 Mar	UEFA	A	UT Arad	D	1-1
25 Mar	Lge	H	Sheff Utd	D	0-0
28 Mar	Lge	H	Huddersfield	D	1-1
31 Mar	Lge	H	Coventry	W	1-0
1 Apr	Lge	A	West Ham	L	0-2
3 Apr	Lge	A	Ipswich	L	1-2
5 Apr	UEFAsf	H	AC Milan	W	2-1
8 Apr	Lge	A	WBA	D	1-1
15 Apr	Lge	H	Chelsea	W	3-0
19 Apr	UEFAsf	A	AC Milan	D	1-1
22 Apr	Lge	A	Southampton	D	0-0
29 Apr	Lge	H	Leicester	W	4-3
3 May	UEFAf	A	Wolves	W	2-1
11 May	Lge	A	Arsenal	W	2-0
17 May	UEFAf	H	Wolves	D	1-1
7 Jun	F	A	Maccabi	W	3-2

* Anglo-Italian League Cup Winners Cup (two legs) † Played at Boothferry Park

Player	Lg App		Goals
Beal P.	32		
Chivers M.	39		25
Coates R.	32		2
Collins P.	7	(1)	
Daines B.	1		
England M.	38		2
Evans R.	22		
Gilzean A.	38		11
Holder P.	6	(2)	
Jennings P.A.	41		
Kinnear J.P.	21	(1)	
Knowles C.B.	34		2
Morgan R.	10	(2)	
Mullery A.	18		3
Naylor T.	12		
Neighbour J.	14	(2)	1
Pearce J.	15	(6)	5
Perryman S.	40	(1)	
Peters M.	35		10
Pratt J.	23		1
Want A.G.	7		
Own Goal			1

Final table for First Division

1 Derby	42	24	10	8	69:33	58
6 TOTTENHAM	**42**	**19**	**13**	**10**	**63:42**	**51**

SEASON 1972/73

Date	Comp		Opponent		Score
29 Jul	F	A	Bournemouth	W	4-2
2 Aug	F	A	Aston Villa	D	0-0
7 Aug	F	A	Celtic	L	0-1
12 Aug	Lge	H	Coventry	W	2-1
16 Aug	Lge	A	WBA	W	1-0
19 Aug	Lge	A	Wolves	L	2-3
23 Aug	Lge	H	Birmingham	W	2-0
26 Aug	Lge	A	Leeds Utd	D	0-0
30 Aug	Lge	H	Newcastle	W	1-0
2 Sep	Lge	A	Ipswich	D	1-1
6 Sep	FLC	H	Huddersfield	W	2-1
9 Sep	Lge	H	C. Palace	W	2-1
13 Sep	UEFA	A	Lyn Oslo	W	6-3
16 Sep	Lge	A	Man City	L	1-2
23 Sep	Lge	H	West Ham	W	1-0
27 Sep	UEFA	H	Lyn Oslo	W	6-0
30 Sep	Lge	A	Derby	L	1-2
3 Oct	FLC	A	Middlesbrough	D	1-1
7 Oct	Lge	H	Stoke	W	4-3
11 Oct	FLCr	H	Middlesbrough	D	0-0
14 Oct	Lge	A	Norwich	L	1-2
17 Oct	*	H	Feyenoord	W	2-1
21 Oct	Lge	A	Chelsea	L	0-1
25 Oct	UEFA	H	Olympiakos	W	4-0
28 Oct	Lge	A	Man Utd	W	4-1
30 Oct	FLCr	H	Middlesbrough	W	2-1
1 Nov	FLC	A	Millwall	W	2-0
4 Nov	Lge	A	Birmingham	D	0-0
8 Nov	UEFA	A	Olympiakos	L	0-1
11 Nov	Lge	H	WBA	D	1-1
18 Nov	Lge	A	Leicester	W	1-0
25 Nov	Lge	H	Liverpool	L	1-2
29 Nov	UEFA	H	Red Star	W	2-0
2 Dec	Lge	A	Southampton	D	1-1
4 Dec	FLC	H	Liverpool	D	1-1
6 Dec	FLCr	H	Liverpool	W	3-1
9 Dec	Lge	H	Arsenal	L	1-2
13 Dec	UEFA	A	Red Star	L	0-1
16 Dec	Lge	A	Everton	L	1-3
20 Dec	FLCsf	A	Wolves	W	2-1
23 Dec	Lge	H	Sheff Utd	W	2-0
26 Dec	Lge	A	West Ham	D	2-2
30 Dec	FLCsf	H	Wolves	D	2-2
6 Jan	Lge	A	Leeds	L	1-2
13 Jan	FC	A	Margate	W	6-0
20 Jan	Lge	H	Ipswich	L	0-1
27 Jan	Lge	A	C. Palace	D	0-0
3 Feb	FC	A	Derby	D	1-1
7 Feb	FCr	H	Derby	L	3-5
10 Feb	Lge	H	Man City	L	2-3
17 Feb	Lge	H	Coventry	W	1-0
24 Feb	Lge	H	Everton	W	3-0
3 Mar	FLCf	†	Norwich	W	1-0
7 Mar	UEFA	H	Vitoria Setubal	W	1-0
10 Mar	Lge	H	Norwich	W	3-0
14 Mar	Lge	A	Stoke	D	1-1
21 Mar	UEFA	A	Vitoria Setubal	L	1-2
24 Mar	Lge	H	Man Utd	D	1-1
31 Mar	Lge	A	Liverpool	D	1-1
3 Apr	Lge	A	Chelsea	W	1-0
7 Apr	Lge	H	Southampton	L	1-2

10 Apr	UEFAsf	A	Liverpool	L 0-1
14 Apr	Lge	A	Arsenal	D 1-1
18 Apr	Lge	H	Derby	W 1-0
21 Apr	Lge	H	Leicester	D 1-1
25 Apr	UEFAsf	H	Liverpool	W 2-1
28 Apr	Lge	A	Newcastle	W 3-2
30 Apr	Lge	H	Wolves	D 2-2
2 May	Lge	A	Sheff Utd	L 2-3

* Jimmy Greaves testimonial
† Played at Wembley

Player	Lg App		Goals
Beal P.	24		
Chivers M.	38		17
Clarke R.	1	(1)	
Coates R.	32	(3)	2
Collins P.	7		2
Daines B.	2		
Dillon M.	8		
England M.	31		1
Evans R.	24	(1)	
Gilzean A.	35		5
Jennings P.	40		
Kinnear J.	24		1
Knowles C.	35		
Naylor T.	16	(2)	
Neighbour J.	7	(1)	1
Pearce J.	35	(8)	4
Perryman S.	41		2
Peters M.	41		15
Pratt J.	38	(1)	5
Own Goals			3

Final table for First Division

1 Liverpool	42	25 10 7	72:42	60
8 TOTTENHAM	**42**	**16 13 13**	**58:48**	**45**

SEASON 1973/74

8 Aug	F	A	Ajax	L 1-4
11 Aug	F	A	Cardiff	W 3-1
18 Aug	F	A	Sunderland	W 1-0
25 Aug	Lge	A	Coventry	L 0-1
28 Aug	Lge	A	Birmingham	W 2-1
1 Sep	Lge	H	Leeds	L 0-3
5 Sep	Lge	H	Burnley	L 2-3
8 Sep	Lge	A	West Ham	W 1-0
11 Sep	Lge	A	Burnley	D 2-2
15 Sep	Lge	H	Sheff Utd	L 1-2
19 Sep	UEFA	A	Grasshoppers	W 5-1
22 Sep	Lge	A	Liverpool	L 2-3
29 Sep	Lge	H	Derby	W 1-0
3 Oct	UEFA	H	Grasshoppers	W 4-1
6 Oct	Lge	A	Ipswich	D 0-0
8 Oct	FLC	A	QPR	L 0-1
13 Oct	Lge	H	Arsenal	W 2-0
20 Oct	Lge	A	Norwich	D 1-1
24 Oct	UEFA	A	Aberdeen	D 1-1
27 Oct	Lge	H	Newcastle	L 0-2
3 Nov	Lge	A	Everton	D 1-1
7 Nov	UEFA	H	Aberdeen	W 4-1
10 Nov	Lge	H	Man Utd	W 2-1
17 Nov	Lge	A	Southampton	D 1-1
24 Nov	Lge	H	Wolves	L 1-3
28 Nov	UEFA	A	Dinamo Tbilisi	D 1-1
1 Dec	Lge	A	Leicester	L 0-3
3 Dec	*	H	Bayern Munich	D 2-2
8 Dec	Lge	H	Stoke	L 2-3
12 Dec	UEFA	H	Dinamo Tbilisi	W 5-1
15 Dec	Lge	H	Man City	L 0-2
22 Dec	Lge	A	Derby	L 0-2
26 Dec	Lge	H	QPR	D 0-0
29 Dec	Lge	H	West Ham	W 2-0
1 Jan	Lge	A	Leeds	D 1-1
5 Jan	FC	A	Leicester	L 0-1
12 Jan	Lge	A	Sheff Utd	D 2-2
19 Jan	Lge	H	Coventry	W 2-1
2 Feb	Lge	A	Man City	D 0-0
6 Feb	Lge	H	Birmingham	W 4-2
16 Feb	Lge	A	Arsenal	W 1-0
23 Feb	Lge	H	Ipswich	D 1-1
2 Mar	Lge	A	QPR	L 1-3
6 Mar	UEFA	A	IFC Koln	W 2-1
16 Mar	Lge	H	Norwich	D 0-0
20 Mar	UEFA	H	IFC Koln	W 3-0
23 Mar	Lge	A	Man Utd	W 1-0
30 Mar	Lge	H	Everton	L 0-2

3 Apr	Lge	H	Chelsea	L 1-2
6 Apr	Lge	A	Wolves	D 1-1
10 Apr	UEFAsf	A	Locomotiv Leipzig	W 2-1
13 Apr	Lge	H	Southampton	W 3-1
15 Apr	Lge	A	Chelsea	D 0-0
20 Apr	Lge	A	Stoke	L 0-1
24 Apr	UEFAsf	H	Lokomotiv Leipzig	W 2-0
27 Apr	Lge	H	Leicester	W 1-0
8 May	Lge	H	Liverpool	D 1-1
11 May	Lge	H	Newcastle	W 2-0
21 May	UEFAf	H	Feyenoord	D 2-2
29 May	UEFAf	A	Feyenoord	L 0-2
8 Jun	F	A	Mauritius XI	W 5-0
13 Jun	F	A	Mauritius XI	W 6-3
16 Jun	F	A	Mauritius XI	W 6-0

* Testimonial for Phil Beal

Player	Lg App		Goals
Beal P.	41		
Chivers M.	40	(1)	17
Coates R.	36		3
Daines B.	5		
Dillon M.	16	(3)	1
England M.	33		
Evans R.	40		2
Gilzean A.	25	(4)	3
Holder P.	7	(2)	1
Jennings P.	36		
Kinnear J.	7	(4)	
Knowles C.	20		2
Lee T.	1		
McGrath C.	25	(3)	5
McNab N.	1	(1)	
Naylor T.	28	(1)	
Neighbour J.	14	(3)	
Osgood K.	1	(1)	
Perryman S.	39		1
Peters M.	35		6
Pratt J.	35		4

Final table for First Division

1 Leeds	42	24 14 4	66:31	62
11 TOTTENHAM	**42**	**14 14 14**	**45:50**	**42**

SEASON 1974/75

3 Aug	F	A	Hearts	D 1-1
7 Aug	F	A	Portsmouth	W 2-0
10 Aug	F	A	Fulham	W 1-0
17 Aug	Lge	H	Ipswich	L 0-1
21 Aug	Lge	A	Man City	L 0-1
24 Aug	Lge	A	Carlisle	L 0-1
28 Aug	Lge	H	Man City	L 1-2
31 Aug	Lge	H	Derby	W 2-0
7 Sep	Lge	A	Liverpool	L 2-5
11 Sep	FLC	H	Middlesbrough	L 0-4
14 Sep	Lge	H	West Ham	W 2-1
21 Sep	Lge	A	Wolves	W 3-2
28 Sep	Lge	H	Middlesbrough	L 1-2
5 Oct	Lge	H	Burnley	L 2-3
12 Oct	Lge	A	Chelsea	L 0-1
16 Oct	Lge	A	Carlisle	D 1-1
19 Oct	Lge	H	Arsenal	W 2-0
26 Oct	Lge	A	Luton	D 1-1
2 Nov	Lge	A	Stoke	D 2-2
9 Nov	Lge	H	Everton	D 1-1
16 Nov	Lge	A	Leicester	W 2-1
23 Nov	Lge	H	Birmingham	D 0-0
27 Nov	*	H	Red Star	W 2-0
30 Nov	Lge	A	Sheff Utd	L 1-2
4 Dec	Lge	A	Leeds	L 1-2
7 Dec	Lge	H	Newcastle	W 3-0
14 Dec	Lge	A	Ipswich	L 0-4
21 Dec	Lge	H	QPR	L 1-2
26 Dec	Lge	A	West Ham	D 1-1
28 Dec	Lge	H	Coventry	D 1-1
4 Jan	FC	A	Nottm Forest	D 1-1
8 Jan	FCr	H	Nottm Forest	L 0-1
11 Jan	Lge	A	Newcastle	W 5-2
18 Jan	Lge	H	Sheff Utd	L 1-3
24 Jan	F	A	Watford	W 3-2
27 Jan	F	A	Enfield	W 2-1
1 Feb	Lge	A	Everton	L 0-1
8 Feb	Lge	H	Stoke	L 0-2
15 Feb	Lge	A	Coventry	D 1-1

18 Feb	Lge	A	Birmingham	L 0-1
22 Feb	Lge	H	Leicester	L 0-3
26 Feb	F	A	Red Star	W 1-0
1 Mar	Lge	A	Derby	L 1-3
15 Mar	Lge	A	Middlesbrough	L 0-3
22 Mar	Lge	H	Liverpool	L 0-2
28 Mar	Lge	H	Wolves	W 3-0
29 Mar	Lge	A	QPR	W 1-0
5 Apr	Lge	H	Luton	W 2-1
12 Apr	Lge	A	Burnley	L 2-3
19 Apr	Lge	H	Chelsea	W 2-0
26 Apr	Lge	A	Arsenal	L 0-1
28 Apr	Lge	H	Leeds	W 4-2

* Testimonial for Alan Gilzean

Player	Lg App		Goals
Beal P.	28		
Chivers M.	28	(1)	10
Coates R.	30	(4)	1
Conn A.	17	(1)	6
Daines B.	1		
Duncan J.	28		12
England M.	31		2
Evans R.	21	(1)	
Jennings P.	41		
Jones C.	16		1
Kinnear J.	17		
Knowles C.	31		4
McAllister D.	8	(1)	
McGrath C.	9	(4)	
McNab N.	2		
Naylor T.	38	(1)	
Neighbour T.	25	(4)	3
Osgood K.	10		
Perryman S.	42		6
Peters M.	29		4
Pratt J.	29	(2)	1
Own Goals			2

Final table for First Division

1 Derby	42	21 11 10	67:49	53
19 TOTTENHAM	**42**	**13 8 21**	**52:63**	**34**

SEASON 1975/76

23 Jul	F	A	Rott Weiss	D 1-1
25 Jul	F	A	Karlsruhe	L 1-2
29 Jul	F	A	Hanover	D 1-1
3 Aug	F	A	NAC Breda	W 1-0
8 Aug	F	A	Bristol Rvs	W 4-1
16 Aug	Lge	H	Middlesbrough	W 1-0
20 Aug	Lge	H	Ipswich	D 1-1
23 Aug	Lge	A	Liverpool	L 2-3
25 Aug	Lge	A	West Ham	L 0-1
30 Aug	Lge	H	Norwich	D 2-2
6 Sep	Lge	A	Man Utd	L 2-3
9 Sep	FLC	A	Watford	W 1-0
13 Sep	Lge	H	Derby	L 2-3
20 Sep	Lge	A	Leeds	D 1-1
27 Sep	Lge	H	Arsenal	D 0-0
29 Sep	F	A	Le Stade Rennais	D 1-1
4 Oct	Lge	A	Newcastle	D 0-0
8 Oct	FLC	A	Crewe	W 2-0
11 Oct	Lge	A	Aston Villa	D 1-1
18 Oct	Lge	H	Man City	D 2-2
22 Oct	*	A	Arsenal	W 3-2
25 Oct	Lge	A	Leicester	W 3-2
27 Oct	Lge	A	Millwall	L 1-3
1 Nov	Lge	H	Wolves	W 2-1
8 Nov	FLC	A	QPR	D 0-0
12 Nov	Lge	H	West Ham	D 0-0
15 Nov	Lge	H	Stoke	D 1-1
22 Nov	FLCr	A	Man City	L 1-2
24 Nov	Lge	A	West Ham	W 2-0
29 Nov	Lge	H	Burnley	W 2-1
3 Dec	FLC	A	Doncaster	W 7-2
6 Dec	Lge	A	Sheff Utd	W 2-1
10 Dec	Lge	H	Everton	D 2-2
13 Dec	Lge	H	Liverpool	L 0-4
20 Dec	Lge	A	Middlesbrough	L 0-1
26 Dec	Lge	H	Birmingham	L 1-3
27 Dec	Lge	A	Coventry	D 2-2
3 Jan	FC	H	Stoke	D 1-1
10 Jan	Lge	A	Derby	W 3-2
14 Jan	FLCsf	H	Newcastle	W 1-0
17 Jan	Lge	H	Man Utd	D 1-1

Player	Lg App		Goals
Brotherston N.	1		
Chivers M.	35	(4)	7
Coates R.	24	(3)	2
Conn A.	8	(1)	
Daines B.	2		
Duncan J.	37	(2)	20
Hoddle G.	7	(1)	1
Jennings P.	40		
Jones C.	34	(9)	5
Kinnear J.	1		
Knowles C.	10		
McAllister D.	35		2
McGrath C.	4	(1)	
McNab N.	15	(4)	
Naylor T.	36		
Neighbour J.	35		3
Osgood K.	42		3
Perryman S.	40		6
Pratt T.	41		10
Robinson M.	2	(1)	1
Smith I.	2		
Stead M.	4		
Walford S.	2	(1)	
Young W.	35		3

Final table for First Division

1 Liverpool	42	23 14 5	66:31	60
9 TOTTENHAM	**42**	**14 15 13**	**63:63**	**43**

SEASON 1976/77

24 Jul	F	A	Osnabruck	W 3-1
28 Jul	F	A	Eintracht	L 1-4
31 Jul	F	A	IFC Koln	L 1-3
4 Aug	F	A	Baunatal	W 2-1
6 Aug	F	A	Bad Honnef	W 2-0
10 Aug	F	A	Swindon	L 1-3
16 Aug	F	A	Ryl Antwerp	D 1-1
21 Aug	Lge	A	Ipswich	L 1-3
25 Aug	Lge	H	Newcastle	L 0-2
28 Aug	Lge	H	Middlesbrough	D 0-0
31 Aug	FLC	A	Middlesbrough	W 2-1
4 Sep	Lge	A	Man Utd	L 2-3
11 Sep	Lge	H	Leeds Utd	W 1-0
18 Sep	Lge	A	Liverpool	L 0-2
22 Sep	FLC	H	Wrexham	L 2-3
25 Sep	Lge	H	Norwich	L 1-2
2 Oct	Lge	A	WBA	L 2-4
9 Oct	F†	A	Arsenal	W 2-1
12 Oct	F	A	Nepredac	L 0-4
16 Oct	Lge	A	Derby	L 2-8
20 Oct	Lge	H	Birmingham	W 1-0
23 Oct	Lge	H	Coventry	L 0-1

21 Jan	FLCsf	A	Newcastle	L 1-3
24 Jan	FCr	A	Stoke	L 1-2
31 Jan	Lge	A	Ipswich	W 2-1
7 Feb	Lge	H	West Ham	D 1-1
14 Feb	Lge	H	QPR	L 0-3
21 Feb	Lge	A	Stoke	W 2-1
24 Feb	Lge	A	Everton	L 0-1
28 Feb	Lge	H	Leicester	D 1-1
6 Mar	Lge	A	Norwich	L 1-3
13 Mar	Lge	H	Aston Villa	W 5-2
16 Mar	Lge	A	Wolves	W 1-0
20 Mar	Lge	A	Burnley	W 2-1
23 Mar	†	A	Brighton	W 6-1
27 Mar	Lge	H	Sheff Utd	W 5-0
3 Apr	Lge	A	Arsenal	W 2-0
10 Apr	Lge	A	Leeds	D 0-0
17 Apr	Lge	A	Birmingham	L 1-3
19 Apr	Lge	H	Coventry	W 4-1
21 Apr	F	A	Nrth Herts XI	L 1-2
24 Apr	Lge	H	Newcastle	L 0-3
27 Apr	F	A	Toronto Metros	W 1-0
1 May	F	A	Fiji Select	W 4-0
3 May	F	A	Auckland XI	W 5-3
5 May	F	A	Wellington XI	W 3-2
9 May	F	A	Victoria	W 3-1
12 May	F	A	N. Sth Wales	W 5-1
16 May	F	A	Australian XI	W 3-2
18 May	F	A	South Aust.	W 5-2
23 May	F	A	Western Aust.	W 4-0

* Testimonial for Cyril Knowles   †
† Testimonial for Joe Kinnear

221

Date	Comp		Opponent	Res	Score
30 Oct	Lge	H	Everton	D	3-3
6 Nov	Lge	A	West Ham	L	3-5
13 Nov	Lge	H	Bristol City	L	0-1
20 Nov	Lge	A	Sunderland	L	1-2
23 Nov	F*	H	Arsenal	W	3-2
27 Nov	Lge	H	Stoke	W	2-0
11 Dec	Lge	H	Man City	D	2-2
18 Dec	Lge	H	Leicester	L	1-2
27 Dec	Lge	H	Arsenal	D	2-2
1 Jan	Lge	H	West Ham	W	2-1
8 Jan	FC	A	Cardiff	L	0-1
11 Jan	Lge	H	QPR	L	1-2
22 Jan	Lge	H	Ipswich	W	1-0
5 Feb	Lge	A	Middlesbrough	L	0-2
12 Feb	Lge	H	Man Utd	L	1-3
19 Feb	Lge	H	Leeds	L	1-2
26 Feb	Lge	A	Newcastle	L	0-2
5 Mar	Lge	A	Norwich	W	3-1
9 Mar	Lge	H	Liverpool	W	1-0
12 Mar	Lge	H	WBA	L	0-2
19 Mar	Lge	A	Birmingham	W	2-1
23 Mar	Lge	H	Derby	D	0-0
26 Mar	Lge	A	Everton	L	0-4
2 Apr	Lge	A	Coventry	D	1-1
9 Apr	Lge	H	QPR	W	3-0
11 Apr	Lge	A	Arsenal	L	0-1
12 Apr	Lge	A	Bristol City	L	0-1
16 Apr	Lge	H	Sunderland	D	1-1
20 Apr	Lge	A	Aston Villa	L	1-2
23 Apr	Lge	A	Stoke	D	0-0
30 Apr	Lge	H	Aston Villa	W	3-1
7 May	Lge	A	Man City	L	0-5
14 May	Lge	H	Leicester	W	2-0
17 May	F	A	Stord	W	5-0
19 May	F	A	Sogndal	W	6-0

* Pat Jennings Testimonial   † Peter Simpson Testimonial

Player	Lg App		Goals
Armstrong G.	21	(1)	3
Coates R.	31	(3)	3
Conn A.	13	(1)	
Daines B.	19		
Duncan J.	9		4
Gorman J.	15		
Hoddle G.	39		4
Holmes J.	10		1
Jennings P.	23		
Jones C.	31		9
Keeley G.	6	(1)	
McAllister D.	12	(2)	1
McNab N.	10	(4)	
Moores I.	17	(1)	2
Naylor T.	40		
Neighbour J.	7		
Osgood K.	42		7
Perryman S.	42		1
Pratt J.	34	(4)	4
Stead M.	8		
Taylor P.	32	(1)	8
Young W.	19		1

Final table for First Division

1	Liverpool	42	23	11	8	62:33	57
22	TOTTENHAM	42	12	9	21	48:72	33

SEASON 1977/78

Date	Comp		Opponent	Res	Score
7 Aug		A	Royale Union	W	2-0*
10 Aug		A	Leicester	W	2-1*
12 Aug		A	Norsjo	W	3-2*
20 Aug	Lge	H	Sheff Utd	W	4-2
24 Aug	Lge	A	Blackburn	D	0-0
27 Aug	Lge	H	Notts Co.	W	2-1
31 Aug	FLC	H	Wimbledon	W	4-0
3 Sep	Lge	A	Cardiff	D	0-0
10 Sep	Lge	H	Fulham	W	1-0
17 Sep	Lge	A	Blackpool	W	2-0
24 Sep	Lge	H	Luton	W	2-0
1 Oct	Lge	A	Orient	D	1-1
4 Oct	Lge	A	Hull	W	2-0
8 Oct	Lge	H	Oldham	W	5-1
15 Oct	Lge	A	Charlton	L	1-4
22 Oct	FLC	H	Coventry	L	2-3
26 Oct	Lge	H	Bristol Rvs	W	9-0
29 Oct	Lge	A	Stoke	W	3-1
5 Nov	Lge	H	Burnley	W	3-0
12 Nov	Lge	A	Crystal P.	W	2-1
19 Nov	Lge	A	Brighton	D	0-0
22 Nov	F	A	Arsenal	W	3-1
26 Nov	Lge	A	Bolton	L	0-1
3 Dec	Lge	H	Southampton	D	0-0
10 Dec	Lge	A	Sunderland	W	3-1
17 Dec	Lge	H	Crystal P.	D	2-2
26 Dec	Lge	A	Millwall	W	3-1
27 Dec	Lge	H	Mansfield	D	1-1
31 Dec	Lge	H	Blackburn	W	4-0
2 Jan	Lge	A	Sheff Utd	D	2-2
7 Jan	FC	H	Bolton	D	2-2
10 Jan	FCr	A	Bolton	L	1-2
14 Jan	Lge	A	Notts Co.	D	3-3
21 Jan	Lge	A	Cardiff	W	2-1
4 Feb	Lge	H	Fulham	D	1-1
11 Feb	Lge	H	Blackpool	D	1-1
22 Feb	Lge	A	Luton	W	2-1
25 Feb	Lge	H	Orient	D	3-2
4 Mar	Lge	A	Oldham	D	3-1
11 Mar	Lge	H	Charlton	W	3-3
18 Mar	Lge	A	Bristol Rvs	W	3-3
22 Mar	Lge	H	Stoke	W	1-2
25 Mar	Lge	A	Mansfield	D	1-0
27 Mar	Lge	A	Millwall	L	1-3
1 Apr	Lge	A	Burnley	L	1-2
8 Apr	Lge	H	Bolton	W	1-0
15 Apr	Lge	A	Brighton	L	1-3
22 Apr	Lge	A	Sunderland	L	2-3
26 Apr	Lge	H	Hull	W	1-0
29 Apr	Lge	A	Southampton	D	0-0
3 May	F	A	Truro City	W	8-2
5 May	F	A	Orient	W	3-1
8 May	F	A	Aleppo Select	W	1-0
10 May	F	A	Syrian Select	W	4-0
12 May	F †	H	Arsenal	L	3-5
15 May	F	A	Hamark'tene	L	0-3
17 May	F	A	FC Kvik	W	2-0
19 May	F	A	Karlstad BK	W	4-1

* Scandinavian tour
† Testimonial for John Pratt

Player	Lg Ap		Goals
Armstrong G.	19	(9)	2
Coates R.	3	(2)	
Daines B.	42		
Duncan J.	27		16
Hoddle G.	41		12
Holmes J.	38		
Jones C.	20		8
Lee C.	25	(2)	11
McAllister D.	25		4
McNab N.	42		3
Moores I.	10	(3)	4
Naylor T.	37		
Osgood K.	18		3
Perryman S.	42		1
Pratt J.	42		7
Robinson M.	4		1
Stead M.	3	(1)	
Taylor P.	41		11

Final table for Second Division

1	Bolton	42	24	10	8	63:33	58
3	TOTTENHAM	42	20	16	6	83:49	56

SEASON 1978/79

Date	Comp		Opponent	Res	Score
5 Aug	F	A	Aberdeen	L	1-3
8 Aug	F	A	Ryl Antwerp	W	3-1
10 Aug	F	A	Venlo	L	0-1
12 Aug	F	A	Bohemians	W	4-0
19 Aug	Lge	A	Nottm Forest	D	1-1
23 Aug	Lge	H	Aston Villa	L	1-4
26 Aug	Lge	H	Chelsea	D	2-2
29 Aug	FLC	A	Swansea	D	2-2
2 Sep	Lge	A	Liverpool	L	0-7
6 Sep	FLCr	H	Swansea	L	1-3
9 Sep	Lge	H	Bristol C.	W	1-0
16 Sep	Lge	A	Leeds	W	2-1
19 Sep	F	A	Aldershot	D	1-1
23 Sep	Lge	A	Man City	L	0-2
26 Sep	F	A	IFK Gothburg	L	0-1
30 Sep	Lge	H	Coventry	D	1-1
7 Oct	Lge	A	WBA	L	0-1
9 Oct	F	A	Saudi Arab XI	W	4-2
14 Oct	Lge	H	Birmingham	W	1-0
16 Oct	F	A	Wolves	L	1-2
21 Oct	Lge	A	Derby	D	2-2
28 Oct	Lge	H	Bolton	W	2-0
4 Nov	Lge	A	Norwich	D	2-2
11 Nov	Lge	H	Nottm Forest	L	1-3
18 Nov	Lge	A	Chelsea	W	3-1
22 Nov	Lge	H	Liverpool	D	0-0
25 Nov	Lge	H	Wolves	W	1-0
4 Dec	F	A	West Ham	L	2-4
9 Dec	Lge	A	Ipswich	D	1-1
16 Dec	Lge	A	Man Utd	L	0-2
18 Dec	F	A	El Nasr	W	1-0
23 Dec	Lge	H	Arsenal	L	0-5
26 Dec	Lge	A	QPR	D	2-2
30 Dec	Lge	H	Everton	D	1-1
10 Jan	FC	H	Altrincham	D	1-1
13 Jan	Lge	A	Bristol C.	D	0-0
16 Jan	FCr	A	Altrincham	W	3-0*
20 Jan	Lge	A	Leeds	L	1-2
3 Feb	Lge	H	Man City	L	0-3
10 Feb	Lge	H	Coventry	W	3-1
12 Feb	FC	H	Wrexham	D	3-3
21 Feb	FCr	A	Wrexham	W	3-2
24 Feb	Lge	A	Birmingham	L	0-1
28 Feb	FC	A	Oldham	W	1-0
3 Mar	Lge	H	Derby	W	2-0
10 Mar	FC	H	Man Utd	D	1-1
14 Mar	FCr	A	Man Utd	L	0-2
17 Mar	Lge	H	Norwich	W	2-0
24 Mar	Lge	H	Aston Villa	W	3-2
28 Mar	Lge	H	Southampton	D	0-0
31 Mar	Lge	A	Middlesbrough	L	0-1
3 Apr	Lge	A	Wolves	L	2-3
7 Apr	Lge	A	Middlesbrough	L	1-2
10 Apr	Lge	A	Arsenal	L	0-1
14 Apr	Lge	H	QPR	D	1-1
16 Apr	F	A	Southampton	D	3-3
21 Apr	Lge	H	Man Utd	D	1-1
24 Apr	F	A	QPR	W	3-1
28 Apr	Lge	A	Ipswich	L	1-2
30 Apr	†	H	West Ham	D	2-2
5 May	Lge	H	Everton	D	1-1
8 May	Lge	A	Bolton	W	3-1
11 May	F	A	Gillingham	W	3-2
14 May	Lge	H	WBA	W	1-0
16 May	F	A	Kuwait Army	W	2-1
23 May	F	A	Selangor Sel	W	4-0
27 May	F	A	Indonesia	W	6-0‡
29 May	F	A	Japan XI	W	2-0‡
31 May	F	A	Fiorentina	D	1-1‡
2 Jun	F	A	San Lorenzo	W	5-3‡
5 Jun	F	A	Dundee Utd	W	2-0‡
6 Jun	F	A	Bermuda Sel	W	3-1

* Played at Maine Road
†Testimonial for Steve Perryman
‡ Games played during 'Japan Cup' tournament

Player	Lg App		Goals
Aleksic M.	5		
Ardiles O.	38		3
Armstrong G.	10	(3)	1
Beavon S.	1		
Daines B.	14		
Duncan J.	2		1
Falco M.	1		1
Galvin T.	1		
Gorman J.	15		
Hoddle G.	35	(1)	7
Holmes J.	33		1
Jones C.	19	(1)	5
Kendall M.	23		
Lacy J.	35		
Lee C.	27	(1)	8
McAllister D.	38		1
McNab N.	2		
Miller P.	7		
Moores I.	2		
Naylor T.	22		
Perryman S.	42		1
Pratt J.	38	(1)	4
Smith G.	2	(1)	
Taylor P.	33	(1)	10
Villa R.	32	(6)	2
Own Goals			3

Final table for First Division

1	Liverpool	42	30	8	4	85:16	68
11	TOTTENHAM	42	13	15	14	48:61	41

SEASON 1979/80

Date	Comp		Opponent	Res	Score
2 Aug	F	A	Gillingham	D	1-1
4 Aug	F	A	Oxford	L	1-2
7 Aug	F	A	Dundee Utd	L	2-3
8 Aug	F	A	Aberdeen	L	0-2
11 Aug	F	A	Orient	L	1-1
18 Aug	Lge	H	Middlesbrough	L	1-3
22 Aug	Lge	A	Norwich	L	0-4
25 Aug	Lge	A	Stoke	L	1-3
29 Aug	FLC	H	Man Utd	W	2-1
1 Sep	Lge	H	Man City	W	2-1
5 Sep	FLC	A	Man Utd	L	1-3
8 Sep	Lge	H	Brighton	W	2-1
15 Sep	Lge	A	Southampton	L	2-5
22 Sep	Lge	H	WBA	D	1-1
29 Sep	Lge	A	Coventry	D	1-1
6 Oct	Lge	A	Crystal P.	D	1-1
10 Oct	Lge	H	Norwich	W	3-2
13 Oct	Lge	H	Derby	W	1-0
20 Oct	Lge	H	Leeds	W	2-1
27 Oct	Lge	H	Nottm Forest	W	1-0
3 Nov	Lge	A	Middlesbrough	D	0-0
6 Nov	F	A	Widad Maroc	W	4-2
10 Nov	Lge	H	Bolton	W	2-0
17 Nov	Lge	A	Liverpool	L	1-2
24 Nov	Lge	A	Everton	D	1-1
1 Dec	Lge	H	Man Utd	L	1-2
8 Dec	Lge	A	Bristol C.	W	3-1
15 Dec	Lge	H	Aston Villa	L	1-2
21 Dec	Lge	A	Ipswich	L	1-3
26 Dec	Lge	A	Arsenal	L	0-1
29 Dec	Lge	H	Stoke	W	1-0
5 Jan	FC	H	Man Utd	D	1-1
9 Jan	FCr	A	Man Utd	W	1-0
12 Jan	Lge	A	Man City	D	1-1
19 Jan	Lge	A	Brighton	W	2-0
26 Jan	FC	A	Swindon	D	0-0
30 Jan	FCr	H	Swindon	W	2-1
2 Feb	Lge	H	Southampton	D	0-0
9 Feb	Lge	A	WBA	L	1-2
16 Feb	FC	H	Birmingham	W	3-1
23 Feb	Lge	A	Derby	L	1-2
27 Feb	Lge	H	Coventry	W	4-3
1 Mar	Lge	H	Leeds	W	2-1
8 Mar	FC	H	Liverpool	L	0-1
11 Mar	Lge	A	Nottm Forest	L	0-4
15 Mar	Lge	A	Crystal P.	W	2-0
22 Mar	Lge	A	Bolton	L	1-2
29 Mar	Lge	H	Liverpool	W	2-0
2 Apr	Lge	H	Ipswich	L	0-2
5 Apr	Lge	A	Wolves	W	2-1
7 Apr	Lge	A	Arsenal	L	1-2
12 Apr	Lge	A	Man Utd	L	1-4
15 Apr	F	A	Crystal P.	W	3-2
19 Apr	Lge	H	Everton	W	3-0
23 Apr	Lge	H	Wolves	D	2-2
26 Apr	Lge	A	Aston Villa	L	0-1
29 Apr	*	H	Crystal P.	L	0-2
3 May	Lge	H	BristolC.	D	0-0
5 May	F	A	Bournemouth	W	2-1
7 May	F	A	Hertford Town	W	4-0
11 May	F	A	Vienna Select	L	0-3
13 May	F	A	Sturm Graz	L	0-2

* Testimonial for Terry Naylor

Player	Lg App		Goals
Aleksic M.	8		
Armstrong G.	30	(2)	4
Ardiles O.	40		3
Beavon S.	3	(1)	
Daines B.	32		
Falco M.	9	(2)	2
Galvin T.	10	(3)	4
Gibson T.	1		
Hazard M.	3		
Hoddle G.	41		19
Hughton C.	39		1
Jones C.	37	(1)	9
Kendall M.	2		
Lacy J.	4		
Lee C.	10	(2)	
McAllister D.	36	(1)	1

Miller P.	27		2
Naylor T.	7	(1)	
Perryman S.	40		1
Pratt J.	24	(5)	2
Smith G.	14		
Southey P.	1		
Taylor P.	9	(2)	
Villa R.	22		4
Yorath T.	33		1

Final table for First Division

1 Liverpool	42	25	10	7	81:30	60
14 TOTTENHAM	**42**	**15**	**10**	**17**	**52:62**	**40**

SEASON 1980/81

28 Jul	F	A	Southend	D	1-1
30 Jul	F	A	Portsmouth	W	2-1
2 Aug	F	A	PSV Eindhoven	L	2-4
4 Aug	F	A	Rangers	L	1-2
5 Aug	F	A	Dundee Utd	L	1-4
8 Aug	F	A	Swansea	L	0-1
16 Aug	Lge	H	Nottm Forest	W	2-0
19 Aug	Lge	A	C. Palace	W	4-3
23 Aug	Lge	H	Brighton	D	2-2
27 Aug	FLC	A	Orient	W	1-0
30 Aug	Lge	A	Arsenal	L	0-2
3 Sep	FLC	H	Orient	W	3-1
6 Sep	Lge	H	Man Utd	D	0-0
13 Sep	Lge	A	Leeds	D	0-0
20 Sep	Lge	H	Sunderland	D	0-0
24 Sep	FLC	H	C. Palace	D	0-0
27 Sep	Lge	A	Leicester	L	1-2
30 Sep	FLCr	A	C. Palace	W	3-1
4 Oct	Lge	A	Stoke	W	3-2
11 Oct	Lge	H	Middlesbrough	W	3-2
18 Oct	Lge	A	Aston Villa	L	0-3
22 Oct	Lge	A	Man City	L	1-3
25 Oct	Lge	H	Coventry	W	4-1
1 Nov	Lge	A	Everton	D	2-2
4 Nov	FLC	H	Arsenal	W	1-0
8 Nov	Lge	H	Wolves	D	2-2
12 Nov	Lge	H	C. Palace	W	4-2
15 Nov	Lge	A	Nottm Forest	W	3-0
17 Nov	F	A	Weymouth	W	6-1
22 Nov	Lge	A	Birmingham	L	1-2
29 Nov	Lge	H	WBA	L	2-3
2 Dec	FLC	A	West Ham	L	0-1
6 Dec	Lge	A	Liverpool	L	1-2
13 Dec	Lge	H	Man City	W	2-1
17 Dec	Lge	H	Ipswich	W	5-3
20 Dec	Lge	A	Middlesbrough	L	1-4
26 Dec	Lge	H	Southampton	D	4-4
27 Dec	Lge	H	Norwich	D	2-2
3 Jan	FC	A	QPR	D	0-0
7 Jan	FCr	H	QPR	W	3-1
10 Jan	Lge	A	Birmingham	W	1-0
17 Jan	Lge	H	Arsenal	W	2-0
24 Jan	FC	H	Hull City	W	2-0
31 Jan	Lge	A	Brighton	W	2-0
2 Feb	F	A	Jersey Sel XI	W	5-0
7 Feb	Lge	H	Leeds	D	1-1
14 Feb	FC	H	Coventry	W	3-1
17 Feb	Lge	A	Man Utd	D	0-0
21 Feb	Lge	H	Leicester	L	1-2
28 Feb	Lge	A	Sunderland	D	1-1
7 Mar	FC	H	Exeter	W	2-0
11 Mar	Lge	H	Stoke	D	2-2
14 Mar	Lge	A	Ipswich	L	0-3
21 Mar	Lge	H	Aston Villa	W	2-0
28 Mar	Lge	A	Coventry	W	1-0
4 Apr	Lge	H	Everton	D	2-2
11 Apr	FCsf	*	Wolves	D	2-2
15 Apr	FCsfr	*	Wolves	W	3-0
18 Apr	Lge	H	Norwich	L	2-3
20 Apr	Lge	A	Southampton	D	1-1
25 Apr	Lge	H	Liverpool	D	1-1
30 Apr	Lge	A	Wolves	L	0-1
2 May	Lge	A	WBA	L	2-4
9 May	FCf	†	Man City	D	1-1
11 May	‡	H	West Ham	D	0-0
14 May	FCfr	†	Man City	W	3-2
24 May	F	A	Bahrain XI	W	3-0
26 May	F	A	Kuwait Army XI	W	2-1
28 May	F	A	Bahrain XI	W	5-3
10 Jun	F	A	Trabzonspor	W	4-0
13 Jun	F	A	Fenerbahce	W	5-1

*First semi-final at Hillsborough, replay at

Highbury
†Cup final and replay at Wembley
‡ Testimonial for Barry Daines

Player	Lg App		Goals
Aleksic M.	10		
Archibald S.	41	(1)	20
Ardiles O.	36		5
Armstrong G.	4	(4)	
Brooke G.	18	(8)	3
Crooks G.	40		16
Daines B.	28		
Falco M.	3		1
Galvin T.	18	(1)	1
Hazard M.	4	(2)	
Hoddle G.	38		12
Hughton C.	34		1
Kendall M.	4		
Lacy J.	31		2
Mazzon G.	2	(1)	
McAllister D.	18		
Miller P.	25	(1)	2
O'Reilly G.	2	(1)	
Perryman S.	42		2
Roberts G.	24	(3)	
Smith G.	20	(2)	1
Taylor P.	8	(3)	1
Villa R.	29	(1)	2
Yorath T.	15	(4)	
Own Goal			1

Final table for First Division

1 Aston Villa	42	26	8	8	72:40	60
10 TOTTENHAM	**42**	**14**	**15**	**13**	**70:68**	**43**

SEASON 1981/82

8 Aug	F	A	Glentoran	D	3-3
10 Aug	F	A	Limerick	W	6-2
12 Aug	F	A	Norwich	D	2-2
16 Aug	F	A	Aberdeen	W	1-0
22 Aug	CS	*	Aston Villa	D	2-2
29 Aug	Lge	A	Middlesbrough	W	3-1
2 Sep	Lge	H	West Ham	L	0-4
5 Sep	Lge	H	Aston Villa	L	1-3
12 Sep	Lge	A	Wolves	W	1-0
16 Sep	ECWC	A	Ajax	W	3-1
19 Sep	Lge	H	Everton	W	3-0
22 Sep	Lge	A	Swansea	L	1-2
26 Sep	Lge	A	Man City	W	1-0
29 Sep	ECWC	H	Ajax	W	3-0
3 Oct	Lge	H	Nottm Forest	W	3-0
7 Oct	FLC	H	Man Utd	W	1-0
10 Oct	Lge	H	Stoke	W	2-0
12 Oct	F	A	Luton	D	2-2
17 Oct	Lge	A	Sunderland	W	2-0
21 Oct	ECWC	A	Dundalk	D	1-1
24 Oct	Lge	H	Brighton	L	0-1
28 Oct	FLC	A	Man Utd	W	1-0
31 Oct	Lge	A	Southampton	W	2-1
4 Nov	ECWC	H	Dundalk	W	1-0
7 Nov	Lge	H	WBA	L	1-2
11 Nov	FLC	H	Wrexham	W	2-0
14 Nov	F	A	Israeli Sel	W	3-2
21 Nov	Lge	H	Man Utd	W	3-1
28 Nov	Lge	A	Notts C	D	2-2
2 Dec	FLC	A	Fulham	W	1-0
5 Dec	Lge	H	Coventry	L	1-2
12 Dec	Lge	A	Leeds	D	0-0
22 Dec	F	A	Plymouth	D	1-1
29 Dec	F	A	Sp Lisbon	L	2-3
2 Jan	FC	A	Arsenal	W	1-0
18 Jan	FLC	H	Nottm Forest	W	1-0
23 Jan	FC	H	Leeds	W	1-0
27 Jan	Lge	A	Middlesbrough	W	1-0
30 Jan	Lge	A	Everton	D	1-1
3 Feb	FLCsf	A	WBA	D	0-0
6 Feb	Lge	H	Wolves	W	6-1
10 Feb	FLCsf	H	WBA	W	1-0
13 Feb	FC	H	Aston Villa	W	1-0
17 Feb	Lge	A	Aston Villa	D	1-1
20 Feb	Lge	H	Man City	W	2-0
22 Feb	F	A	Jersey Sel	W	8-3
27 Feb	Lge	A	Stoke	W	2-0
3 Mar	ECWC	H	Eintrach Fr.	W	2-0
6 Mar	FC	A	Chelsea	W	3-2
9 Mar	Lge	A	Brighton	W	3-1

---

13 Mar	FLCf	*	Liverpool	L	1-3
17 Mar	ECWC	A	Eintrach Fr.	L	1-2
20 Mar	Lge	H	Southampton	W	3-2
23 Mar	Lge	A	Birmingham	D	0-0
27 Mar	Lge	A	WBA	L	0-1
29 Mar	Lge	H	Arsenal	D	2-2
3 Apr	FCsf	†	Leicester	W	2-0
7 Apr	ECWCsf	H	Barcelona	D	1-1
10 Apr	Lge	H	Ipswich	W	1-0
12 Apr	Lge	A	Arsenal	W	3-1
14 Apr	Lge	H	Sunderland	D	2-2
17 Apr	Lge	A	Man Utd	L	0-2
21 Apr	ECWCsf	A	Barcelona	L	0-1
24 Apr	Lge	H	Notts Co	W	3-1
28 Apr	Lge	H	Birmingham	D	1-1
1 May	Lge	A	Coventry	D	0-0
3 May	Lge	H	Liverpool	D	2-2
5 May	Lge	H	Swansea	W	2-1
8 May	Lge	H	Leeds	W	2-1
10 May	Lge	A	West Ham	D	2-2
12 May	Lge	A	Nottm Forest	L	0-2
15 May	Lge	A	Liverpool	L	1-3
17 May	Lge	A	Ipswich	L	1-2
22 May	FCf	*	QPR	D	1-1
27 May	FCfr	*	QPR	W	1-0

* at Wembley   † at Villa Park

Player	Lg App		Goals
Aleksic M.	2		
Archibald S.	27	(1)	6
Ardiles O.	26		2
Brooke G.	16	(4)	4
Clemence R.	38		
Corbett P.	4	(1)	1
Crook I.	4	(1)	
Crooks G.	27		13
Dick A.	1		
Falco M.	21		5
Galvin A.	32		3
Gibson T.	1		
Hazard M.	28	(2)	5
Hoddle G.	34		10
Hughton C.	37		2
Jones C.	7	(4)	
Lacy J.	12	(5)	
Miller P.	35		
O'Reilly G.	4		
Parks A.	2		
Perryman S.	42		1
Price P.	21	(3)	
Roberts G.	37	(2)	6
Smith G.	2	(1)	
Villa R.	27	(1)	8
Own Goal			1

Final table for First Division

1 Liverpool	42	26	9	7	80:32	87
4 TOTTENHAM	**42**	**20**	**11**	**11**	**67:48**	**71**

SEASON 1982/83

3 Aug	F	A	Scunthorpe	W	5-0
6 Aug	F	A	Lausanne	L	0-3
8 Aug	F	A	Rangers	W	1-0
13 Aug	F	A	Ajax	L	2-3[1]
15 Aug	F	A	Cologne	D	0-0[1]
21 Aug	CS	*	Liverpool	L	0-1
28 Aug	Lge	H	Luton	D	2-2
31 Aug	Lge	A	Ipswich	W	2-1
4 Sep	Lge	A	Everton	L	1-3
8 Sep	Lge	H	Southampton	W	6-0
11 Sep	Lge	H	Man City	L	1-2
15 Sep	ECWC	A	Coleraine	W	3-0
18 Sep	Lge	A	Sunderland	W	1-0
20 Sep	F	A	Barnet	L	1-2[2]
25 Sep	Lge	H	Nottm Forest	W	4-1
29 Sep	ECWC	H	Coleraine	W	4-0
2 Oct	Lge	A	Swansea	L	0-2
6 Oct	FLC	H	Brighton	D	1-1
9 Oct	Lge	H	Coventry	W	4-0
16 Oct	Lge	A	Norwich	D	0-0
20 Oct	ECWC	H	Bayern Munich	D	1-1
23 Oct	Lge	H	Notts County	W	4-2
26 Oct	FLC	A	Brighton	W	1-0
30 Oct	Lge	A	Aston Villa	L	0-4
3 Nov	ECWC	A	Bayern Munich	L	1-4
6 Nov	Lge	H	Watford	L	0-1

---

9 Nov	FLC	A	Gillingham	W	4-2
13 Nov	Lge	A	Man Utd	L	0-1
20 Nov	Lge	H	West Ham	W	2-1
27 Nov	Lge	A	Liverpool	L	0-3
1 Dec	FLC	H	Luton	W	1-0
4 Dec	Lge	H	WBA	D	1-1
11 Dec	Lge	A	Stoke	L	0-2
18 Dec	Lge	H	Birmingham	W	2-1
20 Dec	F	A	Borussia Moen	L	0-2[3]
22 Dec	F	A	Israel Nat. Team	D	2-2[3]
27 Dec	Lge	A	Arsenal	L	0-2
28 Dec	Lge	H	Brighton	W	2-0
1 Jan	Lge	A	West Ham	L	0-3
3 Jan	Lge	H	Everton	W	2-1
8 Jan	FC	H	Southampton	W	1-0
15 Jan	Lge	A	Luton	D	1-1
19 Jan	FLC	H	Burnley	L	1-4
22 Jan	Lge	H	Sunderland	D	1-1
29 Jan	FC	H	WBA	W	2-1
5 Feb	Lge	A	Man City	D	2-2
12 Feb	Lge	H	Swansea	W	1-0
19 Feb	FC	A	Everton	L	0-2
26 Feb	Lge	H	Norwich	D	0-0
5 Mar	Lge	A	Notts County	L	0-3
12 Mar	Lge	A	Coventry	D	1-1
19 Mar	Lge	A	Watford	W	1-0
23 Mar	Lge	H	Aston Villa	W	2-0
25 Mar	F	A	Northerners (G.)	W	6-1
2 Apr	Lge	A	Brighton	L	1-2
4 Apr	Lge	A	Arsenal	W	5-0
9 Apr	Lge	A	Nottm Forest	D	2-2
16 Apr	Lge	H	Ipswich	W	3-1
19 Apr	F	A	Bristol Rovers	W	3-2[4]
23 Apr	Lge	A	WBA	W	1-0
30 Apr	Lge	H	Liverpool	W	2-0
3 May	Lge	A	Southampton	W	2-1
7 May	Lge	A	Birmingham	L	0-2
11 May	Lge	H	Man Utd	W	2-0
14 May	Lge	H	Stoke	W	4-1
17 May	F	A	Trinidad Nat. XI	D	2-2
20 May	F	A	A.S.L. Trinidad	W	2-1
23 May	F	A	Charlton	D	4-4[5]
30 May	F	A	Aalesund	W	3-2
4 Jun	F	A	Man Utd	L	1-2
11 Jun	F	A	Man Utd	W	2-0

1. Amsterdam 707 tournament. 2. Brinkman testimonial. 3. In Tel Aviv. 4. Bristol Rovers centenary match. 5. Powell testimonial. 6. Sun international challenge trophy tournament in Swaziland. * at Wembley.

Player	Lg App		Goals
Archibald S.	31		11
Ardiles O.	2		
Brazil A.	12		6
Brooke G.	23	(4)	7
Clemence R.	41		
Corbett P.	1	(1)	
Crook I.	4	(3)	
Crooks G.	26		8
Dick A.	2		
Falco M.	16	(5)	5
Galvin A.	26		2
Gibson T.	16	(2)	4
Hazard M.	18	(3)	1
Hoddle G.	24	(2)	1
Hughton C.	38		3
Lacy J.	22		
Mabbut G.	38		10
Mazzon G.	2		
Miller P.	23		1
O'Reilly G.	26	(1)	
Parks A.	1		
Perryman S.	33	(1)	1
Price P.	16		
Roberts G.	24	(4)	2
Villa R.	23	(1)	2
Webster S.	2	(1)	
Own Goal			1

Final table for First Division

1 Liverpool	42	24	10	8	87:37	82
4 TOTTENHAM	**42**	**20**	**9**	**13**	**65:50**	**69**

SEASON 1983/84

Date	Comp		Opponent	Result
2 Aug	F	A	Hertford Town	W 2-1
3 Aug	F	A	Southall	W 8-0
4 Aug	F	A	Enfield	W 4-1
6 Aug	F	A	Brentford	W 4-2[1]
6 Aug	F	A	Aylesbury	W 4-0[1]
9 Aug	F	A	Portsmouth	W 3-1
10 Aug	F	A	Aldershot	L 0-1
12 Aug	F	A	Brighton	D 0-0
13 Aug	F	A	Lewes	W 6-0
16 Aug	F	A	Celtic	D 1-1
17 Aug	F	A	Dundee Utd	D 1-1[2]
21 Aug	F	H	West Ham	D 1-1[3]
27 Aug	Lge	A	Ipswich	L 1-3
29 Aug	Lge	H	Coventry	D 1-1
3 Sep	Lge	H	West Ham	L 0-2
7 Sep	Lge	A	WBA	D 1-1
10 Sep	Lge	A	Leicester	W 3-0
14 Sep	UEFA	A	Drogheda	W 6-0
17 Sep	Lge	H	Everton	L 1-2
24 Sep	Lge	A	Watford	W 3-2
28 Sep	UEFA	H	Drogheda	W 8-0
2 Oct	Lge	H	Nottm Forest	W 2-1
5 Oct	FLC	A	Lincoln	W 3-1
8 Oct	F	A	Vale Recreation	W 7-2
15 Oct	Lge	A	Wolves	W 3-2
19 Oct	UEFA	H	Feyenoord	W 4-2
22 Oct	Lge	A	Birmingham	W 1-0
26 Oct	FLC	H	Lincoln	L 1-2
29 Oct	Lge	H	Notts County	W 1-0
2 Nov	UEFA	A	Feyenoord	W 2-0
5 Nov	Lge	A	Stoke	D 1-1
9 Nov	FLC	A	Arsenal	L 1-2
12 Nov	Lge	H	Liverpool	D 2-2
19 Nov	Lge	A	Luton	W 4-2
23 Nov	UEFA	A	Bayern Munich	L 0-1
26 Nov	Lge	H	Q.P.R.	W 3-2
3 Dec	Lge	A	Norwich	L 1-2
7 Dec	UEFA	H	Bayern Munich	W 2-0
10 Dec	Lge	H	Southampton	D 0-0
16 Dec	Lge	A	Man Utd	L 2-4
26 Dec	Lge	A	Arsenal	L 2-4
27 Dec	Lge	A	Aston Villa	D 0-0
31 Dec	Lge	A	West Ham	L 1-4
2 Jan	Lge	H	Watford	L 2-3
7 Jan	FC	A	Fulham	D 0-0
11 Jan	FCr	H	Fulham	W 2-0
14 Jan	Lge	H	Ipswich	W 2-0
21 Jan	Lge	A	Everton	L 1-2
28 Jan	FC	H	Norwich	D 0-0
1 Feb	FCr	A	Norwich	L 1-2
24 Feb	Lge	A	Nottm Forest	D 2-2
8 Feb	Lge	H	Sunderland	W 3-0
11 Feb	Lge	H	Leicester	W 3-2
21 Feb	Lge	A	Notts County	W 1-0
25 Feb	Lge	H	Birmingham	L 0-t
3 Mar	Lge	H	Stoke	W 1-0
7 Mar	UEFA	H	F.K. Austria	W 2-0
10 Mar	Lge	A	Liverpool	L 1-3
17 Mar	Lge	H	WBA	L 0-1
21 Mar	UEFA	A	F.K. Austria	D 2-2
24 Mar	Lge	A	Coventry	W 4-2
26 Mar	F	A	Wimbledon	W 5-0[4]
31 Mar	Lge	H	Wolves	W 1-0
7 Apr	Lge	A	Sunderland	D 1-1
11 Apr	UEFAsf	A	Hajduk Split	L 1-2
14 Apr	Lge	H	Luton	W 2-1
18 Apr	Lge	H	Aston Villa	W 2-1
21 Apr	Lge	A	Arsenal	L 2-3
25 Apr	UEFAsf	H	Hajduk Split	W 1-0
28 Apr	Lge	A	Q.P.R.	L 1-2
5 May	Lge	H	Norwich	W 2-0
7 May	Lge	A	Southampton	L 0-5
9 May	UEFAf	A	Anderlecht	D 1-1
12 May	Lge	H	Man Utd	D 1-1
18 May	F	A	West Ham	L 1-4[5]
23 May	UEFAf	H	Anderlecht	D 1-1[6]
29 May	F	H	England XI	D 2-2[7]
2 Jun	F	A	Liverpool	L 2-5[8]
9 Jun	F	A	Liverpool	D 1-1[8]

1. Half the first team played in each match. 2. McAlpine testimonial. 3. Nicholson testimonial 4. Bassett testimonial. 5. Holland testimonial. 6. Spurs won 4-3 on penalties 7. Burkinshaw testimonial. 8. Sun international challenge trophy tournament in Swaziland.

Player	LgApp		Goals
Archibald S.	32	(1)	21
Ardiles O.	9	(1)	
Bowen M.	7	(1)	
Brace R.	1	(1)	
Brazil A.	19	(2)	3
Brooke G.	12	(5)	
Clemence R.	26		
Cockram A.	2		
Cooke R.	9		(1)
Crook I.	3		
Crooks G.	10	(4)	1
Culverhouse	2	(1)	
Dick A.	11	(1)	2
Falco M	36	(4)	13
Galvin A.	30		1
Hazard M.	11	(2)	2
Hoddle G.	24		4
Hughton C.	34		3
Mabbutt G.	21		2
Millar P.	21	(1)	
O'Reilly G.	12	(3)	
Parks A.	16		
Perryman S.	41		
Price P.	2	(1)	
Roberts G.	35		6
Stevens G.	40	(3)	4
Thomas D.	27	(1)	
Webster S.	1		

Final table for First Division

1 Liverpool	42	22 14	6	73:32	80
8 TOTTENHAM	42	17 10 15		64:65	61

SEASON 1984/85

Date	Comp		Opponent	Result
27 Jul	F	A	Jordal Blink	W 9-0
29 Jul	F	A	Ostersund	W 4-0
31 Jul	F	A	Viking	W 1-0
4 Aug	F	A	Enfield	W 7-0
6 Aug	F	A	OGC Nice	D 2-2
11 Aug	F	A	Brentford	W 3-0
16 Aug	F	A	Man City	W 2-0
18 Aug	F	A	Sheff Utd	W 3-0
20 Aug	F	H	Fulham	W 3-1[1]
25 Aug	Lge	A	Everton	W 4-1
27 Aug	Lge	H	Leicester	D 2-2
1 Sep	Lge	H	Norwich	W 3-1
4 Sep	Lge	A	Sunderland	L 0-1
8 Sep	Lge	H	Sheff Wed	L 1-2
12 Sep	F	A	Real Madrid	L 0-1[2]
15 Sep	Lge	H	QPR	W 5-0
19 Sep	UEFA	H	SC Braga	W 3-0
22 Sep	Lge	H	Aston Villa	W 1-0
26 Sep	FLC	A	Halifax	W 5-1
29 Sep	Lge	H	Luton	W 4-2
3 Oct	UEFA	H	SC Braga	W 6-0
6 Oct	Lge	A	Southampton	L 0-1
9 Oct	FLC	H	Halifax	W 4-0
12 Oct	Lge	H	Liverpool	W 1-0
14 Oct	F	A	Malta Natl XI	W 1-0
20 Oct	Lge	A	Man Utd	L 0-1
24 Oct	UEFA	A	FC Bruges	L 1-2
27 Oct	Lge	H	Stoke	W 4-0
31 Oct	FLC	A	Liverpool	W 1-0
3 Nov	Lge	A	WBA	L 2-3
7 Nov	UEFA	H	FC Bruges	H 3-0
10 Nov	Lge	A	Nottm Forest	A 2-1
13 Nov	F	A	Sutton Utd	W 5-3[3]
17 Nov	Lge	A	Ipswich	A 3-0
21 Nov	FLC	A	Sunderland	D 0-0
24 Nov	Lge	H	Chelsea	D 1-1
28 Nov	UEFA	H	Bohemians	W 2-0
1 Dec	Lge	A	Coventry	D 1-1
5 Dec	FLC	H	Sunderland	L 1-2
8 Dec	Lge	H	Newcastle	W 3-1
12 Dec	UEFA	A	Bohemians	D 1-1
15 Dec	Lge	A	Watford	W 2-1
22 Dec	Lpe	A	Norwich	W 2-1
26 Dec	Lge	H	West Ham	D 2-2
29 Dec	Lge	H	Sunderland	W 2-0
1 Jan	Lge	A	Arsenal	W 2-1
5 Jan	FC	H	Charlton	D 1-1
12 Jan	FC	A	QPR	D 2-2
23 Jan	FC	H	Charlton	W 2-1
27 Jan	FC	A	Liverpool	L 0-1
2 Feb	Lge	A	Luton	D 2-2

(continued)

Date	Comp		Opponent	Result
23 Feb	Lge	A	WBA	W 1-0
2 Mar	Lge	A	Stoke	W 1-0
6 Mar	UEFA	H	Real Madrid	L 0-1
8 Mar	F	+	Kuwait Natl XI	W 1-0
12 Mar	Lge	H	Man Utd	L 1-2
16 Mar	Lge	A	Liverpool	W 1-0
20 Mar	UEFA	A	Real Madrid	D 0-0
23 Mar	Lge	H	Southampton	W 5-1
30 Mar	Lge	H	Aston Villa	L 0-2
3 Apr	Lge	H	Everton	L 1-2
6 Apr	Lge	A	West Ham	L 1-2
8 Apr	F	A	Guernsey XI	W 5-0
13 Apr	Lge	A	Leicester	W 2-1
17 Apr	Lge	H	Arsenal	L 0-2
20 Apr	Lge	H	Ipswich	L 2-3
27 Apr	Lge	A	Chelsea	D 1-1
29 Apr	F	A	Bristol Rovers	W 6-2[4]
4 May	Lge	H	Coventry	W 4-2
6 May	Lge	A	Newcastle	W 3-2
8 May	F	A	Arsenal	W 3-2[5]
11 May	Lge	H	Watford	L 1-5
14 May	Lge	H	Sheff Wed	W 2-0
17 May	Lge	H	Nottm Forest	W 1-0
23 May	F	A	Seiko	W 4-0
29 May	F		Australia Natl XI	L 1-6
1 Jun	F		Udinese	L 0-2[6]
5 Jun	F		Vasco da Gama	D 1-1[6]
9 Jun	F		Udinese	W 4-1[6]

+ At Amman, Jordan 1.Peter Southey Memorial 2. Benito testimonial 3. Pritchard testimonial 4. Bristol Cancer Fund Match 5. Pat Jennings farewell 6. Australian international tournament at Melbourne, Sydney and Adelaide.

Player	LgApp		Goals
Allen C.	13	(1)	7
Ardiles O.	11	(1)	2
Bowen M.	6		
Brooke G.	4	(3)	1
Chiedozie J.	34	(3)	5
Clemence R.	42		
Crook I.	5	(3)	1
Crooks G.	22		10
Dick A.	2		
Falco M.	42		22
Galvin A.	38		4
Hazard M.	23	(8)	4
Hoddle G.	28	(2)	8
Hughton C.	31	(2)	1
Leworthy D.	6		3
Mabbutt G.	25	(10)	2
Miler P.	39		
Perryman S.	42		1
Roberts G.	40		7
Stevens G.	28		
Thomas D.	16	(2)	

Final table for First Division

1 Everton	42	28 6	8	88:43	90
3 TOTTENHAM	42	23 8 11		78:51	77

SEASON 1985/86

Date	Comp		Opponent	Result
24 Jul	F	A	Chesterfield	W 4-2
27 Jul	F	A	Bournemouth	W 3-0
31 Jul	F	A	Plymouth	L 0-1
3 Aug	F	A	Exeter	D 2-2
4 Aug	F	H	Arsenal	D 1-1[1]
10 Aug	F	A	Norwich	D 1-1
17 Aug	Lge	H	Watford	W 4-0
21 Aug	Lge	A	Oxford	D 1-1
24 Aug	Lge	A	Ipswich	L 0-1
26 Aug	Lge	H	Everton	L 0-1
31 Aug	Lge	A	Man City	L 1-2
4 Sep	Lge	H	Chelsea	W 4-1
7 Sep	Lge	A	Newcastle	W 5-1
10 Sep	F	A	Fareham Town	W 6-3
14 Sep	Lge	H	Nottm Forest	W 1-0
21 Sep	Lge	H	Sheff Wed	W 5-1
23 Sep	FLC	A	Orient	L 0-2
28 Sep	Lge	A	Liverpool	L 1-4
2 Oct	SSSC	H	Southampton	W 2-1
5 Oct	Lge	A	WBA	D 1-1
14 Oct	F	A	Maidstone Utd	W 2-1[2]

2 Oct	Lge	A	Coventry	W 3-2
26 Oct	Lge	H	Leicester	L 1-3
30 Oct	FLC	H	Orient	W 4-0
2 Nov	Lge	A	Southampton	L 0-1
6 Nov	FLC	H	Wimbledon	W 2-0
9 Nov	Lge	H	Luton	L 1-3
16 Nov	Lge	A	Man Utd	D 0-0
20 Nov	FLC	H	Portsmouth	D 0-0
23 Nov	Lge	H	QPR	D 1-1
27 Nov	FLC	A	Portsmouth	D 0-0
30 Nov	Lge	A	Aston Villa	W 2-1
3 Dec	SSSC	A	Liverpool	L 0-2
7 Dec	Lge	H	Oxford	W 5-1
10 Dec	FLC	A	Portsmouth	L 0-1
14 Dec	Lge	A	Watford	L 0-1
17 Dec	SSSC	A	Southampton	W 3-1
21 Dec	Lge	H	Ipswich	W 2-0
26 Dec	Lge	H	West Ham	W 1-0
28 Dec	Lge	A	Chelsea	L 0-2
1 Jan	Lge	A	Arsenal	D 0-0
4 Jan	FC	A	Oxford	D 1-1
8 Jan	FC	H	Oxford	W 2-1
11 Jan	Lge	H	Nottm Forest	L 0-3
14 Jan	SSSC	H	Liverpool	L 0-3
18 Jan	Lge	H	Man City	L 0-2
25 Jan	FC	A	Notts County	D 1-1
29 Jan	FC	H	Notts County	W 5-0
1 Feb	Lge	A	Everton	L 0-1
5 Feb	SSSC	H	Everton	D 0-0
8 Feb	F	A	Coventry	L 0-1
10 Feb	F	A	Jersey FAXI	W 7-0
22 Feb	Lge	A	Sheff Wed	W 2-1
2 Mar	Lge	H	Liverpool	L 1-2
4 Mar	FC	A	Everton	L 1-2
8 Mar	Lge	A	WBA	W 5-0
15 Mar	Lge	A	Birmingham	W 2-1
19 Mar	SSSC	A	Everton	L 1-3
22 Mar	Lge	A	Newcastle	D 2-2
29 Mar	Lge	A	Arsenal	W 1-0
31 Mar	Lge	A	West Ham	L 1-2
5 Apr	Lge	A	Leicester	W 4-1
6 Apr	F	A	Rangers	W 2-0
12 Apr	Lge	A	Luton	D 1-1
16 Apr	Lge	H	Birmingham	W 2-0
19 Apr	Lge	H	Man Utd	D 0-0
22 Apr	F	A	Chelmsford	W 8-23
26 Apr	Lge	A	QPR	W 5-2
1 May	F	A	Inter Milan	W 2-1[4]
3 May	Lge	H	Aston Villa	W 4-2
5 May	Lge	H	Southampton	W 5-3
9 May	F	A	Brentford	L 3-4[5]
12 May	F	A	West Ham	L 1-5[6]

1. Glenn Hoddle testimonial 2. Thompson testimonial 3. Johnson testimonial 4. Ossie Ardiles benefit 5. Salman testimonial 6. Ampofo benefit

Player	LgApp		Goals
Allen C.	19	(3)	9
Allen P	33	(4)	1
Ardiles O.	23	(3)	1
Bowen M.	2	(1)	1
Chiedozie J.	18	(5)	7
Clemence R.	42		
Cooke R.	2	(2)	2
Crook I.	4	(3)	
Dick A.	1		
Falco M.	40		19
Galvin A.	23		4
Hazard M.	4	(1)	1
Hoddle G.	31		7
Howells D	1		1
Hughton C.	33		1
Leworthy D	5	(3)	
Mabbutt G.	32	(3)	3
Miller P.	29		2
Perryman S.	23	(1)	1
Roberts G.	32		1
Stevens G.	29	(1)	2
Thomas D.	27		1
Waddle C.	39		11

Final table for First Division

1 Liverpool	42	26 10 6		89:37	88
10 TOTTENHAM	42	19 8 15		74:52	65

SEASON 1986/87

Date	Comp		Opponent		Result
2 Aug	F	H	Rangers	D	1-1[1]
4 Aug	F	A	Aldershot	W	3-2
8 Aug	F	A	Brighton	W	4-0[2]
12 Aug	F	A	Gillingham	D	1-1[3]
19 Aug	F	A	PSV Eindhoven	D	1-1[4]
20 Aug	F	A	AC Milan	W	2-1[5]
23 Aug	Lge	A	Aston Villa	W	3-0
25 Aug	Lge	H	Newcastle	D	1-1
30 Aug	Lge	A	Manchester C.	W	1-0
2 Sep	Lge	A	Southampton	L	0-2
6 Sep	Lge	A	Arsenal	D	0-0
13 Sep	Lge	H	Chelsea	L	1-3
20 Sep	Lge	A	Leicester	W	2-1
23 Sep	FLC	A	Barnsley	W	3-2
27 Sep	Lge	H	Everton	W	2-0
4 Oct	Lge	H	Luton	D	0-0
8 Oct	FLC	H	Barnsley	W	5-3
11 Oct	Lge	A	Liverpool	W	1-0
18 Oct	Lge	H	Sheff Wed	D	1-1
25 Oct	Lge	A	QPR	L	0-2
29 Oct	FLC	H	Birmingham	W	5-0
1 Nov	Lge	H	Wimbledon	L	1-2
4 Nov	F	H	SV Hamburg	W	5-1
8 Nov	Lge	A	Norwich	L	1-2
15 Nov	Lge	H	Coventry	W	1-0
22 Nov	Lge	A	Oxford	W	4-2
26 Nov	FLC	A	Cambridge Utd	W	3-1
29 Nov	Lge	H	Nottm Forest	L	2-3
7 Dec	Lge	A	Man Utd	D	3-3
13 Dec	Lge	H	Watford	W	2-1
16 Dec	F	A	Bermuda Natl XI	W	3-1
20 Dec	Lge	A	Chelsea	W	2-0
26 Dec	Lge	H	West Ham	W	4-0
27 Dec	Lge	A	Coventry	L	3-4
1 Jan	Lge	A	Charlton	W	2-0
4 Jan	Lge	H	Arsenal	L	1-2
10 Jan	FC	H	Scunthorpe	W	3-2
20 Jan	F	A	Linfield	W	3-2[6]
24 Jan	Lge	H	Aston Villa	W	3-0
27 Jan	FLC	A	West Ham	D	1-1
31 Jan	FC	H	Crystal P	W	4-0
2 Feb	FLC	H	West Ham	W	5-0
8 Feb	FLC	A	Arsenal	W	1-0
14 Feb	Lge	H	Southampton	W	2-0
21 Feb	FC	H	Newcastle	W	1-0
25 Feb	Lge	H	Leicester	W	5-0
1 Mar	FLCsf	A	Arsenal	L	1-2
4 Mar	FLCsf	H	Arsenal	L	1-2
7 Mar	Lge	A	QPR	W	1-0
15 Mar	FC	A	Wimbledon	W	2-0
22 Mar	Lge	H	Liverpool	W	1-0
25 Mar	Lge	A	Newcastle	D	1-1
28 Mar	Lge	A	Luton	L	1-3
4 Apr	Lge	H	Norwich	W	3-0
7 Apr	Lge	A	Sheff Wed	W	1-0
11 Apr	FCsf	*	Watford	W	4-1
15 Apr	Lge	A	Man City	D	1-1
18 Apr	Lge	A	Charlton	W	1-0
20 Apr	Lge	A	West Ham	L	1-2
22 Apr	Lge	A	Wimbledon	D	2-2
25 Apr	Lge	H	Oxford	W	3-1
2 May	Lge	A	Nottm Forest	L	0-2
4 May	Lge	H	Man Utd	W	4-0
9 May	Lge	A	Watford	L	0-1
11 May	Lge	A	Everton	L	0-1
16 May	FCf	+	Coventry	L	2-3
29 May	F	A	Millonarios	L	0-1[7]

* at Villa Park + at Wembley 1. Paul Miller testimonial 2. Ryan testimonial 3. Weatherley testimonial 4. Gamper Tournament, Barcelona lost 3-4 on pens 5. Gamper Tournament, Barcelona 6. Coyle testimonial 7. at Miami

Player	LgApp		Goals
Allen C	39	(1)	33
Allen P	37	(3)	3
Ardiles O	25	(9)	
Bowen M	2	(1)	1
Chiedozie J.	1		
Claesen N.	26	(8)	8
Clemence R.	40		
Close S.	2	(1)	
Falco M.	6	(1)	
Galvin A.	24	(4)	1
Gough R	40		2
Gray P.	1		
Hoddle G.	35	(1)	3
Hodge S.	19		4
Howells D.	1		
Hughton C.	9		
Mabbutt G.	37		1
Miller P	2		
Moncur J.	1		
Moran P.	1		
O'Shea T.	2	(1)	
Parks A.	2		
Polston J.	6		
Roberts G.	17		1
Ruddock N.	4		
Samways V.	2	(1)	
Stevens G.	20		
Stimson M.	1		
Thomas D.	17	(4)	
Thomas M.	39		4
Waddle C.	39		6
Own Goal			1

Final table for First Division

1 Everton	42	26	8	8	76:31	86
3 TOTTENHAM	**42**	**21**	**8**	**13**	**68:43**	**71**

SEASON 1987/88

Date	Comp		Opponent		Result
23 Jul	F	A	Exeter	W	1-0
25 Jul	F	A	Bournemouth	D	4-4
30 Jul	F	A	Orebro SK	L	1-3
1 Aug	F	A	Lansi Uudenmaan XI	W	7-2
3 Aug	F	A	Vasteras XI	W	4-2
5 Aug	F	A	Marsta IK	W	5-0
6 Aug	F	A	Div 1 North XI	L	0-1
10 Aug	F	H	Arsenal	W	3-1[1]
15 Aug	Lge	A	Coventry	L	1-2
19 Aug	Lge	H	Newcastle	W	3-1
22 Aug	Lge	H	Chelsea	W	1-0
29 Aug	Lge	A	Watford	D	1-1
1 Sep	Lge	H	Oxford	W	3-0
5 Sep	Lge	A	Everton	D	0-0
12 Sep	Lge	H	Southampton	W	2-1
19 Sep	Lge	A	West Ham	W	1-0
23 Sep	FLC	A	Torquay	L	0-1
26 Sep	Lge	A	Man Utd	L	0-1
3 Oct	Lge	H	Sheff Wed	W	2-0
7 Oct	FLC	H	Torquay	W	3-0
10 Oct	Lge	A	Norwich	L	1-2
18 Oct	Lge	H	Arsenal	L	1-2
20 Oct	F	H	West Ham	D	2-2[2]
24 Oct	Lge	A	Nottm Forest	L	0-3
28 Oct	FLC	A	Aston Villa	L	1-2
31 Oct	Lge	H	Wimbledon	L	0-3
4 Nov	Lge	A	Portsmouth	D	0-0
10 Nov	F	A	St. Albans	W	6-0
14 Nov	Lge	H	QPR	D	1-1
21 Nov	Lge	A	Luton	L	0-2
28 Nov	Lge	H	Liverpool	L	0-2
5 Dec	F	A	Brentford	D	0-0
13 Dec	Lge	H	Charlton	L	0-1
20 Dec	Lge	A	Derby	W	2-1
26 Dec	Lge	A	Southampton	L	1-2
28 Dec	Lge	H	West Ham	W	2-1
1 Jan	Lge	H	Watford	W	2-1
2 Jan	Lge	A	Chelsea	D	0-0
9 Jan	FC	H	Oldham	W	4-2
16 Jan	Lge	H	Coventry	D	2-2
23 Jan	Lge	A	Newcastle	L	0-2
30 Jan	FC	A	Port Vale	L	1-2
13 Feb	Lge	A	Oxford	D	0-0
15 Feb	F	A	AS Monaco	L	0-4
19 Feb	F	A	WBA	L	1-4[3]
23 Feb	Lge	H	Man Utd	D	1-1
27 Feb	Lge	A	Sheff Wed	W	3-0
1 Mar	Lge	H	Derby	D	0-0
6 Mar	Lge	A	Arsenal	L	1-2
9 Mar	Lge	H	Everton	W	2-1
12 Mar	Lge	H	Norwich	L	1-3
19 Mar	Lge	A	Wimbledon	L	0-3
26 Mar	Lge	H	Nottm Forest	L	1-2
28 Mar	F	H	Man Utd	L	2-3[4]
2 Apr	Lge	H	Portsmouth	L	0-1
4 Apr	Lge	A	QPR	L	0-2
15 Apr	F	A	Hull	L	1-2[5]
23 Apr	Lge	A	Liverpool	L	0-1
26 Apr	F	A	Crystal P.	D	3-3[6]
2 May	Lge	A	Charlton	D	1-1
4 May	Lge	H	Luton	W	2-1
6 May	F	A	Barnet	W	2-1[7]
10 May	F	A	Euskadi	L	0-4[8]

1. Chris Hughton testimonial 2. Tony Galvin testimonial 3. Brown benefit 4. Danny Thomas benefit 5. Radcliff testimonial 6. Cannon testimonial 7. Millett testimonial 8. at Bilbao

Player	LgApp		Goals
Allen C.	34	(3)	11
Allen P.	39		3
Ardiles O.	28	(2)	
Claesen N.	24	(5)	10
Clemence R.	11		
Close S.	7	(5)	
Fairclough C.	40		4
Fenwick T.	17		
Gough R.	9		
Gray P.	1	(1)	
Hodge S.	26	(1)	3
Howells D.	11	(8)	
Hughton C.	13	(1)	
Mabbutt G.	37		2
Metgod J.	12	(7)	
Mimms R.	13		
Moncur J.	5	(2)	
Moran P.	13	(4)	1
O'Shea T.	1	(1)	
Parks A.	16		
Polston J.	2	(2)	
Ruddock N.	5	(2)	
Samways V.	26	(5)	
Statham B.	18	(4)	
Stevens G.	18		
Thomas M.	36	(1)	
Waddle C.	22	(1)	2
Walsh P.	11		1
Own Goal			1

Final table for First Division

1 Liverpool	40	26	12	2	87:24	90
13 TOTTENHAM	**40**	**12**	**11**	**17**	**38:48**	**47**

SEASON 1988/89

Date	Comp		Opponent		Result
5 Jul	F	A	Vederslov & DIF	W	4-1
28 Jul	F	A	Trelleborgs FF	W	3-0
31 Jul	F	A	GAIS	D	1-1
2 Aug	F	A	Jonkopings Sodra	D	1-1
7 Aug	F	A	Dundee Utd	D	1-1[1]
10 Aug	F	A	Reading	L	1-2[2]
13 Aug	F	*	Arsenal	L	0-4
14 Aug	F	*	AC Milan	L	1-2
16 Aug	F	A	Chelsea	D	0-0[3]
21 Aug	F	A	West Ham	L	0-2[4]
3 Sep	Lge	A	Newcastle	D	2-2
6 Sep	F	A	Swansea	W	3-0[5]
10 Sep	Lge	H	Arsenal	L	2-3
17 Sep	Lge	A	Liverpool	D	1-1
24 Sep	Lge	H	Middlesbrough	W	3-2
27 Sep	FLC	A	Notts Co.	D	1-1
1 Oct	Lge	H	Man Utd	D	2-2
8 Oct	Lge	A	Charlton	D	2-2
11 Oct	FLC	H	Notts Co.	W	2-1
18 Oct	F	A	Home Farm	W	4-0
22 Oct	Lge	A	Norwich	L	1-3
25 Oct	Lge	H	Southampton	L	1-2
29 Oct	Lge	A	Aston Villa	L	1-2
1 Nov	FLC	H	Blackburn	D	0-0
5 Nov	Lge	H	Derby	L	1-3
9 Nov	FLC	H	Blackburn	W	2-1
12 Nov	Lge	H	Wimbledon	W	3-2
20 Nov	Lge	A	Sheff Wed	W	2-0
23 Nov	Lge	H	Coventry	D	1-1
26 Nov	Lge	H	QPR	D	2-2
30 Nov	FLC	A	Southampton	L	1-2
3 Dec	Lge	A	Everton	L	0-1
10 Dec	Lge	H	Millwall	W	2-0
17 Dec	Lge	A	West Ham	W	2-0
26 Dec	Lge	A	Luton	D	0-0
31 Dec	Lge	H	Newcastle	W	2-0
2 Jan	Lge	A	Arsenal	L	0-2
7 Jan	FC	A	Bradford City	L	0-1
15 Jan	Lge	H	Nottm Forest	L	1-2
17 Jan	F	A	AS Monaco	L	1-3
21 Jan	Lge	A	Middlesbrough	D	2-2

Player	LgApp		Goals
Allen P.	37	(2)	1
Bergsson G.	8		
Butters G.	28	(1)	1
Fairclough C.	20		1
Fenwick T.	34		8
Gascoigne P.	32	(1)	6
Gray P.	1	(1)	
Howells D.	27	(15)	3
Hughton C.	21	(1)	
Mabbutt G.	38		1
Mimms R.	20		
Moncur J.	1	(1)	
Moran P.	8	(4)	
Nayim	11	(3)	2
Polston J.	3	(3)	
Robson M.	5	(2)	
Samways V.	19	(7)	3
Statham B.	6		
Stevens G.	5		
Stewart P.	30	(1)	12
Stimson M.	1	(1)	
Thomas M.	25	(3)	1
Thorstvedt E.	18		
Waddle C.	38		14
Walsh P.	33	(5)	6
Own Goal			1

Final table for First Division

1 Arsenal	38	22	10	6	73:36	76
6 TOTTENHAM	**38**	**15**	**12**	**11**	**60:46**	**57**

SEASON 1989/90

Date	Comp		Opponent		Result
19 Jul	F	H*	Fulham	W	3-1
23 Jul	F	A	Bohemians	W	2-0
25 Jul	F	A	Cork City	W	3-0
28 Jul	F	H*	Bournemouth	W	6-0
1 Aug	F	H*	Swindon	L	0-1
6 Aug	F	A	Rangers	L	0-1
8 Aug	F	A	Viking	W	5-1
10 Aug	F	A	Brann	W	2-0
11 Aug	F	+	Dinamo Bucharest	L	1-3
13 Aug	F	+	Atletico Madrid	L	0-1
19 Aug	Lge	H	Luton	W	2-1
22 Aug	Lge	A	Everton	L	1-2
28 Aug	Lge	A	Man City	D	1-1
9 Sep	Lge	A	Aston Villa	L	0-2
16 Sep	Lge	H	Chelsea	L	1-4
20 Sep	FLC	H	Southend	W	1-0
23 Sep	Lge	A	Norwich	D	2-2
30 Sep	Lge	H	QPR	W	3-2
4 Oct	FLC	A	Southend	L	2-3
14 Oct	Lge	A	Charlton	W	3-1
18 Oct	Lge	H	Arsenal	W	2-1
21 Oct	Lge	H	Sheff Wed	W	3-0
25 Oct	FLC	A	Man Utd	W	3-0
29 Oct	Lge	A	Liverpool	L	0-1
31 Oct	F	A*	SM Caen	D	1-1
4 Nov	Lge	A	Southampton	D	1-1
6 Nov	F	A	Leicester	W	5-2[1]
11 Nov	Lge	H	Wimbledon	L	0-1
18 Nov	Lge	A	Crystal P.	W	3-2
22 Nov	FLC	A	Tranmere	D	2-2

* Wembley International Tournament
1. Narey testimonial 2. Hicks testimonial 3. Pates testimonial 4. Martin testimonial 5. Hughes benefit 6. Gritt testimonial

5 Feb Lge A Man Utd L 0-1
11 Feb Lge H Charlton D 1-1
21 Feb Lge H Norwich W 2-1
25 Feb Lge A Southampton W 2-0
1 Mar Lge H Aston Villa W 2-0
4 Mar F H Bordeaux L 1-2
11 Mar Lge A Derby D 1-1
18 Mar Lge A Coventry W 1-0
22 Mar Lge A Nottm Forest W 2-1
26 Mar Lge H Liverpool L 1-2
28 Mar Lge A Luton W 3-1
1 Apr Lge H West Ham W 3-0
4 Apr F A Charlton L 3-4[6]
12 Apr Lge H Sheff Wed D 0-0
15 Apr Lge A Wimbledon W 2-1
22 Apr Lge H Everton W 2-1
29 Apr Lge A Millwall W 5-0
13 May Lge A QPR L 0-1

Date	Comp		Opponent	Res	Score
2 Dec	Lge	A	Luton	D	0-0
9 Dec	Lge	H	Everton	W	2-1
16 Dec	Lge	A	Man Utd	W	1-0
26 Dec	Lge	H	Millwall	W	3-1
30 Dec	Lge	H	Nottm Forest	L	2-3
1 Jan	Lge	A	Coventry	D	0-0
6 Jan	FC	H	Southampton	L	1-3
13 Jan	Lge	H	Man City	D	1-1
17 Jan	FLC	A	Nottm Forest	D	2-2
20 Jan	Lge	A	Arsenal	L	0-1
24 Jan	FLC	H	Nottm Forest	L	2-3
26 Jan	F	A	Plymouth	W	3-0[2]
4 Feb	Lge	A	Norwich	W	4-0
10 Feb	Lge	A	Chelsea	W	2-1
21 Feb	Lge	H	Aston Villa	L	0-2
24 Feb	Lge	A	Derby	L	1-2
3 Mar	Lge	H	Crystal P.	L	0-1
10 Mar	Lge	H	Charlton	W	3-0
17 Mar	Lge	A	QPR	L	1-3
21 Mar	Lge	H	Liverpool	W	1-0
31 Mar	Lge	A	Sheff Weds	W	4-2
3 Apr	F	A	Brighton	W	3-0[3]
7 Apr	Lge	A	Nottm Forest	W	3-1
14 Apr	Lge	H	Coventry	W	3-2
16 Apr	Lge	A	Millwall	W	1-0
21 Apr	Lge	H	Man Utd	W	2-1
23 Apr	F	A	Valerengen	D	1-1
28 Apr	Lge	A	Wimbledon	L	0-1
1 May	F	H	N. Ireland XI	W	2-1[4]
5 May	Lge	H	Southampton	W	2-

1H* At Chase Lodge + Villa Tournament, Madrid A* At Cherborg
1. Ramsey testimonial 2. Crudgington testimonial 3. Moseley testimonial
4. Danny Blanchflower benefit

Player	LgApp		Goals
Allen P.	32	(3)	6
Bergsson G.	18	(1)	
Butters G.	7		
Fenwick T.	10		
Gascoigne P.	34		6
Howells D.	34	(1)	5
Hughton C.	8		
Lineker G.	38		24
Mabbutt G.	36		
Mimms R.	4		
Moncur J.	5	(3)	1
Moran P.	5	(5)	1
Nayim	19	(1)	
Polston A.	1	(1)	
Polston J.	13	(2)	1
Robson M.	3	(3)	
Samways V.	23	(5)	3
Sedgley S.	32	(1)	
Stevens G.	7	(3)	
Stewart P.	28	(4)	8
Thomas M.	26	(9)	1
Thorstvedt E.	34		
Van den Hauwe P.	31		
Walsh P.	26	(14)	2
Own Goal			1

Final table for First Division

1 Liverpool	38	23	10	5	78:40	79
3 TOTTENHAM	**38**	**19**	**6**	**13**	**60:47**	**63**

SEASON 1990/91

Date	Comp		Opponent	Res	Score
27 Jul	F	H*	Ipswich	W	3-0
30 Jul	F	H*	Maidstone	L	0-1
1 Aug	F	A	Shelbourne	W	3-0
3 Aug	F	A	Derry City	W	3-0
7 Aug	F	A	Brann	W	1-0
9 Aug	F	A	Viking	D	1-1
11 Aug	F	A	Sogndal	W	1-0
13 Aug	F	A	Hearts	W	1-0
17 Aug	F	H	West Ham	W	4-1[1]
20 Aug	F	A	Southend	W	4-1
25 Aug	Lge	H	Man City	W	3-1
28 Aug	Lge	A	Sunderland	D	0-0
1 Sep	Lge	A	Arsenal	D	0-0
8 Sep	Lge	H	Derby	W	3-0
15 Sep	Lge	A	Leeds	W	2-0
22 Sep	Lge	H	Crystal P.	D	1-1
26 Sep	FLC	H	Hartlepool	W	5-0
29 Sep	Lge	H	Aston Villa	W	2-1

Date	Comp		Opponent	Res	Score
6 Oct	Lge	A	QPR	D	0-0
9 Oct	FLC	A	Hartlepool	W	2-1
13 Oct	F	A	Arsenal	W	5-2[2]
20 Oct	Lge	H	Sheff Utd	W	4-0
27 Oct	Lge	A	Nottm Forest	W	2-1
30 Oct	FLC	H	Bradford City	W	2-1
4 Nov	Lge	A	Liverpool	L	1-3
10 Nov	Lge	H	Wimbledon	W	4-2
12 Nov	F	A	West Ham	L	3-4[3]
18 Nov	Lge	A	Everton	D	1-1
24 Nov	Lge	H	Norwich	W	2-1
27 Nov	FLC	H	Sheff Utd	W	2-0
1 Dec	Lge	A	Chelsea	L	2-3
8 Dec	Lge	H	Sunderland	D	3-3
15 Dec	Lge	A	Man City	L	1-2
22 Dec	Lge	H	Luton	W	2-1
26 Dec	Lge	A	Coventry	L	0-2
29 Dec	Lge	A	Southampton	L	0-3
1 Jan	Lge	H	Man Utd	L	1-2
5 Jan	FC	A	Blackpool	W	1-0
9 Jan	Lge	A	Arsenal	D	0-0
16 Jan	FLC	A	Chelsea	D	0-0
20 Lge	A		Derby	W	1-0
23 Jan	FLC	H	Chelsea	L	0-3
26 Jan	FC	H	Oxford	W	4-2
2 Feb	Lge	H	Leeds	D	0-0
16 Feb	FC	A	Portsmouth	W	2-1
23 Feb	Lge	A	Wimbledon	L	1-5
2 Mar	Lge	H	Chelsea	D	1-1
10 Mar	FC	H	Notts Co.	W	2-1
16 Mar	Lge	A	Aston Villa	L	2-3
23 Mar	Lge	H	QPR	D	0-0
30 Mar	Lge	H	Coventry	D	2-2
1 Apr	Lge	A	Luton	D	0-0
6 Apr	Lge	H	Southampton	W	2-0
10 Apr	Lge	A	Norwich	L	1-2
14 Apr	FCsf	*	Arsenal	W	3-1
17 Apr	Lge	A	Crystal P.	L	0-1
20 Apr	Lge	A	Sheff Utd	D	2-2
24 Apr	Lge	H	Everton	D	3-3
4 May	Lge	H	Nottm Forest	D	1-1
11 May	Lge	A	Liverpool	L	0-2
18 May	FCf	*	Nottm Forest	W	2-1
20 May	Lge	A	Man Utd	D	1-1
2 Jun	F	A*	Vasco Da Gama	D	0-0
5 Jun	F	A*	Thailand Natl XI	W	2-1
9 Jun	F	A*	Japan Natl XI	L	0-4

* At Wembley   A* at Kirin Cup at Kobe, Nagoya & Tokyo   H* at Chase Lodge
1. Ray Clemence benefit 2. Rix testimonial 3. Bonds testimonial

Player	LgApp		Goals
Allen P.	36	(2)	3
Bergsson G.	12	(3)	1
Edinburgh J.	16	(2)	1
Fenwick T.	4		
Garland P.	1	(1)	
Gascoigne P.	26		7
Gray P.	6	(3)	
Hendon I.	2	(2)	
Hendry J.	4	(2)	2
Howells D.	29		4
Lineker G.	32		15
Mabbutt G.	35		2
Moncur J.	9	(5)	
Moran P.	1	(1)	
Nayim	33	(1)	5
Samways V.	23	(9)	1
Sedgley S.	34	(1)	
Stewart P.	35		3
Thomas M.	31	(8)	
Thorstvedt E.	37		
Tuttle D.	6	(2)	
Van den Hauwe P.	32	(1)	
Walker I.	1		
Walsh P.	29	(13)	7

Final table for First Division

1 Arsenal	38	24	13	1	74:18	83
							*1
10 TOTTENHAM	**38**	**11**	**16**	**11**	**51:50**	**49**

*1 Two Points deducted

SEASON 1991/92

Date	Comp		Opponent	Res	Score
23 Jul	F	A	Sligo Rovers	W	4-0
25 Jul	F	A	Drogheda Utd	W	2-0
27 Jul	F	A	Shelbourne	W	3-1
30 Jul	F	A	Brann	D	1-1
1 Aug	F	A	Bryne	L	0-4
4 Aug	F	A	Celtic	L	0-1
10 Aug	CS	*	Arsenal	D	0-0
11 Aug	F	A*	AC Messina	L	0-2
13 AUR	F	A*	US Catanzaro	W	1-0
17 Aug	Lge	A	Southampton	W	3-2
21 Aug	ECWC	A	SV Stockerau	W	1-0
24 Aug	Lge	H	Chelsea	L	1-3
28 Aug	Lge	A	Nottm Forest	W	3-1
31 Aug	Lge	A	Norwich	W	1-0
4 Sep	ECWC	H	SV Stockerau	W	1-0
7 Sep	Lge	A	Aston Villa	D	0-0
14 Sep	Lge	H	QPR	W	2-0
17 Sep	ECWC	H	Hajduk Split	L	0-1[1]
21 Sep	Lge	A	Wimbledon	W	5-3
25 Sep	FLC	A	Swansea	L	0-1
28 Sep	Lge	H	Man Utd	L	1-2
2 Oct	ECWC	H	Hajduk Split	W	2-0
5 Oct	Lge	A	Everton	L	1-3
9 Oct	FLC	H	Swansea	W	5-1
19 Oct	Lge	H	Man City	W	0-1
23 Oct	ECWC	H	FC Porto	W	3-1
26 Oct	Lge	A	West Ham	L	1-2
29 Oct	FLC	A	Grimsby	W	3-0
2 Nov	Lge	H	Sheff Wed	D	0-0
7 Nov	ECWC	A	FC Porto	D	0-0
10 Nov	F	H	Spurs 81-2	D	2-2[2]
16 Nov	Lge	H	Luton	W	4-1
23 Nov	Lge	H	Sheff Utd	W	0-1
1 Dec	Lge	A	Arsenal	L	0-2
4 Dec	FLC	A	Coventry	W	2-1
7 Dec	Lge	H	Notts Co.	W	2-1
14 Dec	Lge	A	Leeds	D	1-1
18 Dec	Lge	A	Liverpool	L	1-2
22 Dec	Lge	A	Crystal P.	W	2-1
26 Dec	Lge	H	Nottm Forest	L	1-2
28 Dec	Lge	H	Norwich	W	3-0
1 Jan	Lge	A	Coventry	W	2-1
5 Jan	FC	A	Aston Villa	D	0-0
8 Jan	FLC	H	Norwich	W	2-1
11 Jan	Lge	A	Chelsea	L	0-2
14 Jan	FC	A	Aston Villa	L	0-1
18 Jan	Lge	H	Southampton	L	1-2
25 Jan	Lge	H	Oldham	D	0-0
1 Feb	Lge	A	Man City	L	0-1
9 Feb	FLCsf	A	Nottm Forest	D	1-1
16 Feb	Lge	H	Crystal P.	L	1-2
22 Feb	Lge	H	Arsenal	D	1-1
1 Mar	FLCsf	H	Nottm Forest	L	1-2
4 Mar	ECWC	A	Feyenoord	L	0-1
7 Mar	Lge	A	Leeds	L	1-3
11 Mar	Lge	A	Luton	D	0-0
14 Mar	Lge	H	Sheff Wed	L	0-2
18 Mar	ECWC	H	Feyenoord	D	0-0
21 Mar	Lge	A	Liverpool	L	1-2
28 Mar	Lge	H	Coventry	W	4-3
1 Apr	Lge	H	West Ham	W	3-0
4 Lge	H		Aston Villa	L	2-5
7 Apr	LRe	A	Notts County	W	2-0
11 Apr	Lge	A	QPR	W	2-1
14 Apr	Lge	A	Sheff Utd	L	0-2
18 Apr	Lge	H	Wimbledon	W	3-2
20 Apr	Lge	A	Oldham	L	0-1
25 Apr	Lge	H	Everton	D	3-3
2 May	Lge	A	Man Utd	L	1-3
5 May	F	A	Cardiff	W	2-0[3]
8 May	F	A	Hull City	W	6-2[4]

* At Wembley   A* Ceravolo Tournament at Catanzaro
1. At Linz 2. Cyril Knowles Memorial 3. Parsons testimonial 4. Roberts testimonial

Player	LgApp		Goals
Allen P.	39	(1)	3
Bergsson G.	28	(11)	1
Cundy J.	10		
Durie G.	31		7
Edinburgh J.	23	(1)	
Fenwick T.	23	(1)	
Gray A.	14		1
Hendon I.	2	(2)	
Hendry J.	5	(4)	1

Player	LgApp		Goals
Houghton S.	10	(10)	2
Howells D.	31	(4)	1
Lineker G.	35		28
Mabbutt G.	40		2
Minton J.	2		1
Nayim	31	(9)	1
Samways V.	27	(1)	1
Sedgley S.	34	(13)	
Stewart P.	38		5
Thorstvedt E.	24		
Tuttle D.	2		
Van den Hauwe P.	18	(5)	
Walker I.	18		
Walsh P.	29	(12)	3
Own Goal			1

Final table for First Division

1 Leeds	42	22	16	4	74:37	82
15 TOTTENHAM	**42**	**15**	**7**	**20**	**58:63**	**52**

SEASON 1992/93

Date	Comp		Opponent	Res	Score
20 Jul	F	H*	Reading	W	3-1
21 Jul	F	H*	Gillingham	W	2-0
25 Jul	F	A	Hearts	W	2-1
29 Jul	F	A	Brighton	D	1-1
1 Aug	F	A	Glenavon	W	1-0
3 Aug	F	A	WBA	W	2-0
5 Aug	F	A	Sunderland	W	3-0[1]
8 Aug	F	A	Watford	W	1-0
10 Aug	F	A	Portsmouth	L	2-4
15 Aug	Lge	A	Southampton	D	0-0
19 Aug	Lge	H	Coventry	L	0-2
22 Aug	Lge	H	Crystal P.	D	2-2
25 Aug	Lge	A	Leeds	L	0-5
30 Aug	Lge	A	Ipswich	D	1-1
2 Sep	Lge	H	Sheff Utd	W	2-0
5 Sep	Lge	H	Everton	W	2-1
14 Sep	Lge	A	Coventry	L	0-1
19 Sep	Lge	A	Man Utd	D	1-1
21 Sep	FLC	A	Brentford	W	3-1
23 Sep	F	A	SS Lazio	L	0-3[2]
27 Sep	Lge	A	Sheff Wed	L	0-2
3 Oct	Lge	H	QPR	L	1-4
7 Oct	FLC	A	Brentford	W	4-2
17 Oct	Lge	H	Middlesbrough	D	2-2
20 Oct	F	H	SS Lazio	L	0-2[2]
25 Oct	Lge	A	Wimbledon	D	1-1
28 Oct	FLC	A	Man City	W	1-0
31 Oct	Lge	H	Liverpool	W	2-0
7 Nov	Lge	A	Blackburn	W	2-0
10 Nov	F	A	Swansea	D	3-3[3]
21 Nov	Lge	H	Aston Villa	D	0-0
28 Nov	Lge	A	Man City	W	1-0
2 Dec	FLC	A	Nottm Forest	L	0-2
5 Dec	Lge	H	Chelsea	L	1-2
12 Dec	Lge	H	Arsenal	W	1-0
19 Dec	Lge	A	Oldham	L	1-2
26 Dec	Lge	A	Norwich	D	0-0
28 Dec	Lge	H	Nottm Forest	W	2-1
2 Jan	FC	A+	Marlow	W	5-1
9 Jan	Lge	A	Man Utd	L	1-4
16 Jan	Lge	H	Sheff Wed	L	0-2
24 Jan	FC	A	Norwich	W	2-0
27 Jan	Lge	H	Ipswich	L	0-2
30 Jan	Lge	A	Crystal P.	W	3-1
7 Feb	Lge	H	Southampton	W	4-3
10 Feb	Lge	A	Everton	W	2-1
14 Feb	FC	H	Wimbledon	W	3-2
20 Feb	Lge	H	Leeds	W	4-0
27 Feb	Lge	H	QPR	W	3-2
2 Mar	Lge	A	Sheff Utd	L	0-6
7 Mar	FC	A	Man City	W	4-2
10 Mar	Lge	A	Aston Villa	D	0-0
20 Mar	Lge	A	Chelsea	D	1-1
24 Mar	Lge	H	Man City	W	3-1
28 Mar	F	A	Crystal P.	D	3-3[4]
4 Apr	FCsf	*	Arsenal	L	0-1
9 Apr	Lge	H	Norwich	W	5-1
12 Apr	Lge	A	Nottm Forest	L	1-2
17 Apr	Lge	H	Oldham	W	4-1
20 Apr	Lge	A	Middlesbrough	L	0-3
23 Apr	F	A	Real Zaragoza	L	0-2
27 Apr	F	H	Real Madrid	L	0-1[5]
27 Apr	F	H	Inter Milan	D	0-0*
1 May	Lge	H	Wimbledon	D	1-1
5 May	Lge	H	Blackburn	L	1-2
8 May	Lge	A	Liverpool	L	2-6

| 11 May | Lge | A | Arsenal | W 3-1 |
| 14 May | F | A | Enfield | W 5-1[6] |

H* At Chase Lodge   * At Wembley   A+
Played at White Hart Lane
1. City Celebration match 2. Capital Cup 3.
Woolacott testimonial 4. Allison testimonial
5. Fiorucci Cup Tournament 5+ Lost 6-5 on
penalties 6. Eddie Baily testimonial

Player	LgApp		Goals
Allen P.	38		3
Anderton D.	34	(2)	6
Austin D.	34	(1)	
Barmby N.	22	(5)	6
Bergsson G.	5	(5)	
Campbell S.	1	(1)	1
Cundy J.	15	(2)	1
Dearden K.	1	(1)	
Durie G.	17		3
Edinburgh J.	32	(1)	
Fenwick T.	5	(2)	
Gray A.	17	(8)	1
Hendry J.	5	(2)	2
Hill D.	4	(2)	
Hodges L.	4	(4)	
Howells D.	18	(2)	1
Mabbutt G.	29		2
McDonald D.	2		
Moran P.	3	(3)	
Nayim	18	(3)	3
Nethercott S.	5	(2)	
Ruddock N.	38		3
Samways V.	34		
Sedgley S.	22	(2)	3
Sheringham E.	38		21
Thorstvedt E.	27	(2)	
Turner A.	18	(11)	3
Tuttle D.	5	(1)	
Van den Hauwe P.	18	(5)	
Walker I.	17		
Watson K.	5	(1)	
Own Goal			1

Final table for FA Premier League

1 Manchester U.	42 24 12 6	66:31 84
8 TOTTENHAM	**42 16 11 15**	**60:66 59**

SEASON 1993/94

16 Jul	F	A	Shelbourne	W 4-2
18 Jul	F	A	Drogheda Utd	W 3-1
23 Jul	F	A	Team Nord Trond.	W 1-0
25 Jul	F	A	Lyn Oslo	D 0-0[1]
27 Jul	F	A	Team Porsgrunn	W 5-4
31 Jul	F	H	SS Lazio	W 3-2[2]
1 Aug	F	H	Chelsea	L 0-4[2]
6 Aug	F	A	Brentford	D 0-0[3]
9 Aug	F	A	Peterborough	W 2-1
14 Aug	Lge	A	Newcastle	W 1-0
16 Aug	Lge	H	Arsenal	L 0-1
21 Aug	Lge	H	Man City	W 1-0
25 Aug	Lge	A	Liverpool	W 2-1
28 Aug	Lge	A	Aston Villa	L 0-1
1 Sep	Lge	H	Chelsea	D 1-1
11 Sep	Lge	A	Sheff Utd	D 2-2
18 Sep	Lge	H	Oldham	W 5-0
22 Sep	FLC	A	Burnley	D 0-0
26 Sep	Lge	A	Ipswich	D 2-2
3 Oct	Lge	H	Everton	W 3-2
6 Oct	FLC	H	Burnley	W 3-1
11 Oct	F	A	Brann	L 0-2
16 Oct	Lge	A	Man Utd	L 1-2
19 Oct	F	A	Hartlepool	W 3-1[4]
23 Oct	Lge	H	Swindon	D 1-1
27 Oct	FLC	A	Derby	W 1-0
30 Oct	Lge	A	Blackburn	L 0-1
6 Nov	Lge	A	Southampton	L 0-1
20 Nov	Lge	H	Leeds	D 1-1
24 Nov	Lge	H	Wimbledon	D 1-1
27 Nov	Lge	A	QPR	D 1-1
1 Dec	FLC	A	Blackburn	W 1-0
4 Dec	Lge	H	Newcastle	L 1-2
6 Dec	Lge	A	Arsenal	D 1-1
11 Dec	Lge	A	Man City	W 2-0
18 Dec	Lge	H	Liverpool	D 3-3
27 Dec	Lge	H	Norwich	L 1-3
28 Dec	Lge	A	West Ham	W 3-1

1 Jan	Lge	H	Coventry	L 1-2
3 Jan	Lge	A	Sheff Wed	L 0-1
8 Jan	FC	A	Peterborough	D 1-1
12 Jan	FLC	H	Aston Villa	L 1-2
15 Jan	Lge	H	Man Utd	L 0-1
19 Jan	FC	H	Peterborough	D 1-1[5]
22 Jan	Lge	A	Swindon	L 1-2
29 Jan	FC	A	Ipswich	L 0-3
5 Feb	Lge	H	Sheff Wed	L 1-3
12 Feb	Lge	H	Blackburn	L 0-2
15 Feb	F	A+Atletico Madrid	W 2-1
27 Feb	Lge	A	Chelsea	L 3-4
2 Mar	Lge	H	Aston Villa	D 1-1
5 Mar	Lge	H	Sheff Utd	D 2-2
19 Mar	Lge	A	Ipswich	D 1-1
26 Mar	Lge	A	Everton	W 1-0
2 Apr	Lge	A	Norwich	W 2-1
4 Apr	Lge	H	West Ham	L 1-4
9 Apr	Lge	A	Coventry	L 0-1
17 Apr	Lge	A	Leeds	L 0-2
23 Apr	L8e	H	Southampton	W 3-0
30 Apr	Lge	A	Wimbledon	L 1-2
5 May	Lge	A	Oldham	W 2-0
7 May	Lge	H	QPR	L 1-2

A+ Played at Jerez

1. Sundby testimonial 2. Makita International
Tournament 3. Millen testimonial 4. Cyril
Knowles Tribute 5. Won 5-4 on penalties

Player	LgApp		Goals
Allen P.	1	(1)	
Anderton D.	37	(2)	6
Austin D.	23	(3)	
Barmby N.	27		5
Calderwood C.	26		
Campbell S.	34	(7)	
Carr S.	1		
Caskey D.	25	(9)	4
Dozzell J.	32	(4)	8
Durie G.	10		1
Edinburgh J.	25	(1)	
Gray A.	2	(2)	1
Hazard M.	17	(4)	2
Hendry J.	3	(3)	
Hill D.	3	(2)	
Howells D.	18	(3)	1
Kerslake D.	17	(1)	
Mabbutt G.	29		
Mahorn P.	1		
Moran P.	5	(5)	
Nethercott S.	10	(1)	
Robinson S.	2	(1)	
Rosenthal R.	15	(4)	2
Samways V.	39		3
Scott K.	12		1
Sedgley S.	42		6
Sheringham E.	19	(2)	13
Thorstvedt E.	32		
Turner A.	1	(1)	
Walker I.	11	(1)	
Own Goal			1

Final table for FA Premier League

1 Manchester U.	42 27 11 4	80:38 92
15 TOTTENHAM	**42 11 12 19**	**54:59 45**

SEASON 1994/95

22 Jul	F	A	Bournemouth	W 5-0
25 Jul	F	A	Cambridge	W 3-0
29 Jul	F	A	Bristol City	W 3-0
2 Aug	F	A	Brighton	W 3-0
6 Aug	F	A	Watford	D 1-1
9 Aug	F	A	Shelbourne	W 3-0
20 Aug	Lge	A	Sheff Wed	W 4-3
24 Aug	Lge	H	Everton	W 2-1
27 Aug	Lge	H	Man Utd	L 0-1
30 Aug	Lge	A	Ipswich	W 3-1
12 Sep	Lge	H	Southampton	L 1-2
17 Sep	Lge	A	Leicester	L 1-3
21 Sep	FLC	A	Watford	W 6-3
24 Sep	Lge	H	Nottm Forest	L 1-4
1 Oct	Lge	A	Wimbledon	W 2-1
4 Oct	FLC	A	Watford	L 2-3
8 Oct	Lge	H	QPR	D 1-1
15 Oct	Lge	A	Leeds	D 1-1

22 Oct	Lge	A	Man City	L 2-5
26 Oct	FLC	A	Notts County	W 0-3
29 Oct	Lge	H	West Ham	W 3-1
5 Nov	Lge	A	Blackburn	L 0-2
11 Nov	F	A	Reading	D 1-1
19 Nov	Lge	H	Aston Villa	L 3-4
23 Nov	Lge	A	Chelsea	D 0-0
26 Nov	Lge	A	Liverpool	D 1-1
3 Dec	Lge	H	Newcastle	W 4-2
10 Dec	Lge	H	Sheff Wed	W 3-1
17 Dec	Lge	A	Everton	D 0-0
26 Dec	Lge	A	Norwich	W 2-0
27 Dec	Lge	H	Crystal P.	D 0-0
31 Dec	Lge	A	Coventry	W 4-0
2 Jan	Lge	H	Arsenal	W 1-0
7 Jan	FC	A	Altrincham	W 3-0
14 Jan	Lge	A	West Ham	W 2-1
25 Jan	Lge	A	Aston Villa	L 0-1
29 Jan	FC	H	Sunderland	W 4-1
5 Feb	Lge	A	Blackburn	W 3-1
11 Feb	Lge	H	Chelsea	D 1-1
18 Feb	FC	H	Southampton	D 1-1
25 Feb	Lge	H	Wimbledon	L 1-2
1 Mar	FC	A	Southampton	W 6-2
4 Mar	Lge	A	Nottm Forest	D 2-2
8 Mar	Lge	H	Ipswich	W 3-0
11 Mar	FC	A	Liverpool	W 2-1
15 Mar	Lge	A	Man Utd	D 0-0
18 Mar	Lge	H	Leicester	W 1-0
22 Mar	Lge	H	Liverpool	D 0-0
2 Apr	Lge	A	Southampton	L 3-4
9 Apr	FCsf	*Everton	L 1-4
11 Apr	Lge	H	Man City	W 2-1
14 Apr	Lge	A	Crystal P.	D 1-1
17 Apr	Lge	H	Norwich	W 1-0
29 Apr	Lge	A	Arsenal	D 1-1
3 May	Lge	A	Newcastle	D 3-3
6 May	Lge	A	QPR	L 1-2
9 May	Lge	H	Coventry	L 1-3
14 May	Lge	H	Leeds	D 1-1
21 May	F	A	Kitchee/Eastern	W 7-2[2]
24 May	F	A	Guangzhou	W 2-1[2]
26 May	F	A	Singapore Lions	D 1-1[2]

* at Elland Road
1. Richard Cooke testimonial 2. Tour to Hong
Kong, China and
Singapore

Player	LgApp		Goals
Anderton D.	37		5
Austin D.	24	(1)	
Barmby N.	38	(1)	9
Calderwood C.	36	(1)	2
Campbell S.	30	(1)	
Caskey D.	4	(3)	
Dozzell J.	7	(1)	
Dumitrescu I.	13	(2)	4
Edinburgh J.	31	(2)	
Hazard M.	11	(9)	
Hill D.	3	(2)	
Howells D.	26		1
Kerslake D.	18	(2)	
Klinsmann J.	41		20
Mabbutt G.	36	(3)	
McMahon G.	2		
Nethercott S.	17	(9)	
Popescu G.	23		3
Rosenthal R.	20	(6)	
Scott K.	4		
Sheringham E.	42	(1)	18
Thorstvedt E.	1		
Turner A.	1		
Walker I.	41		
Own goals			4

Final table for FA Premier League

1 Blackburn	42 27 8 7	80:39 89
7 TOTTENHAM	**42 16 14 12**	**66:58 62**

SEASON 1995/96

22 Jul	F	A	Silkeborg	L 1-3[1]
23 Jul	F	A	Halmstads BK	L 1-2[1]
24 Jul	F	A	IFK Gothenburg	W 2-0[1]
26 Jul	F	A	IFK Hassleholm	L 1-3[1]
29 Jul	F	A	Sampdoria	D 0-2[2]
30 Jul	F	A	Steau Bucharest	L 2-3[2]

2 Aug	F	A	Derby	L 0-1
5 Aug	F	A	Watford	W 2-0
12 Aug	F	H	Newcastle	L 0-2[3]
19 Aug	Lge	A	Man City	D 1-1
23 Aug	Lge	H	Aston Villa	L 0-1
26 Aug	Lge	H	Liverpool	L 1-3
30 Aug	Lge	A	West Ham	D 1-1
9 Sep	Lge	H	Leeds	W 2-1
16 Sep	Lge	H	Sheff Wed	W 3-1
20 Sep	FLC	H	Chester	W 4-0
25 Sep	Lge	A	QPR	W 3-2
30 Sep	Lge	A	Wimbledon	W 3-1
4 Oct	FLC	A	Chester City	W 3-1
14 Oct	Lge	H	Nottm Forest	L 0-1
22 Oct	Lge	A	Everton	D 1-1
25 Oct	FLC	A	Coventry	L 2-3
29 Oct	Lge	H	Newcastle	D 1-1
4 Nov	Lge	A	Coventry	W 3-2
18 Nov	Lge	H	Arsenal	W 2-1
21 Nov	Lge	A	Middlesbrough	W 1-0
25 Nov	Lge	A	Chelsea	D 0-0
2 Dec	Lge	H	Everton	D 0-0
9 Dec	Lge	H	QPR	W 1-0
16 Dec	Lge	A	Wimbledon	W 1-0
23 Dec	Lge	H	Bolton	D 2-2
26 Dec	Lge	A	Southampton	D 0-0
30 Dec	Lge	A	Blackburn	L 1-2
1 Jan	Lge	H	Man Utd	W 4-1
6 Jan	FC	H	Hereford	D 1-1
13 Jan	Lge	H	Man City	W 1-0
17 Jan	FCr	H	Hereford	W 5-1
21 Jan	Lge	A	Aston Villa	L 1-2
27 Jan	FC	A	Wolves	D 1-1
3 Feb	Lge	A	Liverpool	D 0-0
7 Feb	FC	A	Wolves	W 2-0
12 Feb	Lge	H	West Ham	L 0-1
19 Feb	FC	A	Nottm Forest	D 4
24 Feb	FC	H	Sheff Wed	W 1-0
28 Feb	FC	A	Nottm Forest	D 2-2
2 Mar	Lge	H	Southampton	W 1-0
9 Mar	FC	H	Nottm Forest	D 1-1[5]
16 Mar	Lge	H	Blackburn	L 2-3
20 Mar	Lge	H	Bolton	W 3-2
24 Mar	Lge	A	Man Utd	L 0-1
30 Mar	Lge	H	Coventry	W 3-1
6 Apr	Lge	A	Nottm Forest	L 1-2
8 Apr	Lge	H	Middlesbrough	D 1-1
15 Apr	Lge	A	Arsenal	D 0-0
27 Apr	Lge	H	Chelsea	D 1-1
2 May	Lge	A	Leeds	W 3-1
5 May	Lge	A	Newcastle	D 1-1

1 Tour of Denmark and Sweden 2 Ibrox
International Tournament 3 Gary Mabbutt
testimonial 4 Match abandoned after 15 minutes due to snow blizzard 5 Lost 3-1 on
penalties

Player	LgApp		Goals
Anderton D.	8	(2)	2
Armstrong C.	36		15
Austin D.	28		
Calderwood C.	29	(3)	
Campbell S.	31		1
Caskey D.	3		
Cundy J.	1	(1)	
Dozzell J.	28	(4)	3
Dumitrescu I.	5		
Edinburgh J.	22	(7)	
Fox R.	26		6
Howells D.	29		3
Kerslake D.	2		
Mabbutt G.	32		
McMahon G.	14	(7)	
Nethercott S.	13	(4)	
Rosenthal R.	33	(7)	1
Scott K.	2	(2)	
Sheringham E.	38		16
Sinton A.	5	(1)	
Slade S.	5	(4)	
Walker I.	38		
Wilson C.	28		
Own goals			3

Final table for FA Premier League

1 Man Utd	38 25 7 6	87:39 82
8 TOTTENHAM	**38 16 13 9**	**50:38 61**

SEASON 1996/97

23 Jul	F	A	Ham-Kam	W	2-0[1]	
25 Jul	F	A	Odd Grenland	L	1-2[1]	
26 Jul	F	A	Raufoss	D	0-0[1]	
31 Jul	F	A	Brentford	W	3-0	
3 Aug	F	A	Reading	W	1-0	
7 Aug	F	A	Southend	W	3-1	
10 Aug	F	A	Charlton	W	3-1[2]	
17 Aug	Lge	A	Blackburn	W	2-0	
21 Aug	Lge	H	Derby	D	1-1	
24 Aug	Lge	H	Everton	D	0-0	
4 Sep	Lge	A	Wimbledon	L	0-1	
7 Sep	Lge	H	Newcastle	L	1-2	
14 Sep	Lge	A	Southampton	W	1-0	
17 Sep	FLC	A	Preston	D	1-1	
22 Sep	Lge	H	Leicester	L	1-2	
25 Sep	FLC	H	Preston	W	3-0	
29 Sep	Lge	A	Man Utd	L	0-2	
12 Oct	Lge	H	Aston Villa	W	1-0	
19 Oct	Lge	A	Middlesbrough	W	3-0	
23 Oct	FLC	H	Sunderland	W	2-1	
26 Oct	Lge	A	Chelsea	L	1-3	
2 Nov	Lge	H	West Ham	W	1-0	
16 Nov	Lge	H	Sunderland	W	2-0	
24 Nov	Lge	A	Arsenal	L	1-3	
27 Nov	FLC	A	Bolton	L	1-6	
2 Dec	Lge	H	Liverpool	L	0-2	
7 Dec	Lge	A	Coventry	W	2-1	
14 Dec	Lge	A	Leeds	D	0-0	
21 Dec	Lge	H	Sheff Wed	D	1-1	
26 Dec	Lge	H	Southampton	W	3-1	
28 Dec	Lge	A	Newcastle	L	1-7	
5 Jan	FC	A	Man Utd	L	0-2	
12 Jan	Lge	H	Man Utd	L	1-2	
19 Jan	Lge	A	Nottm Forest	L	1-2	
29 Jan	Lge	H	Blackburn	W	2-1	
1 Feb	Lge	H	Chelsea	L	1-2	
15 Feb	Lge	H	Arsenal	D	0-0	
24 Feb	Lge	A	West Ham	L	3-4	
1 Mar	Lge	H	Nottm Forest	L	0-1	
4 Mar	Lge	A	Sunderland	W	4-0	
15 Mar	Lge	H	Leeds	W	1-0	
19 Mar	Lge	A	Leicester	D	1-1	
22 Mar	Lge	A	Derby	L	2-4	
5 Apr	Lge	H	Wimbledon	W	1-0	
9 Apr	Lge	A	Sheff Wed	L	1-2	
12 Apr	Lge	A	Everton	L	0-1	
19 Apr	Lge	A	Aston Villa	D	1-1	
24 Apr	Lge	H	Middlesbrough	W	1-0	
3 May	Lge	A	Liverpool	L	1-2	
11 May	Lge	H	Coventry	L	1-2	

1. Tour of Norway 2. Walsh testimonial

Player	LgApp		Goals
Allen R.	12	(3)	2
Anderton D.	16	(2)	3
Armstrong C.	12		5
Austin D.	15	(2)	
Baardsen E.	2	(1)	
Calderwood C.	34	(1)	
Campbell S.	38		
Carr S.	26	(2)	
Clapham J.	1	(1)	
Dozzell J.	17	(7)	2
Edinburgh J.	24	(3)	
Fenn N.	4	(4)	
Fox R.	25	(6)	1
Howells D.	32		2
Iversen S.	16		6
Mabbutt G.	1		
McVeigh P.	3	(1)	1
Nethercott S.	9	(7)	
Nielsen A.	29	(1)	6
Rosenthal R.	20	(16)	1
Scales J.	12	(2)	
Sheringham E.	29		7
Sinton A.	33	(1)	6
Vega R.	8		1
Walker I.	37		
Wilson C.	26	(3)	1

Final table for FA Premier League

1	Man Utd	38	21	12	5	76:44	75
10	**TOTTENHAM**	**38**	**13**	**7**	**18**	**44:51**	**46**

228

Index

(Page numbers in italics refer to captions and illustrations)

AC Milan 101, 110, 118, *121*, 190, 196
Aberdeen FC 123, 135
Adams, Tony *166*, 167, *175*, 176
Adamson, Jimmy *124*
Agana, Tony *183*
Agboola, Reuben *153*
Albion 29
Ajax Amsterdam 140
Aleksic, Milija 132, 137, 138, 139, 140
Alexandra Palace *13*
Alexiou, Douglas 152, *173*
Allen, Bradley 173
Allen, Clive 109, 148, 152, 155, *156*, 157, *158*, 159, 160, *161*
Allen, Jack 31
Allen, Les 83, 85, *86*, 88, 91, *93*, *97*, 99, 109, *113*, 116, 148, 157
Allen, Malcolm 159
Allen, Paul 157, 159, 166, 168, *171*, *175*, *175*, 179, 180
Allen Ronnie1 140
Allen, Rory 195
Altrincham FC 185, 186
Amateur Cup 19, 62
Amateur Football Alliance 17
Amokachi, Daniel 189
Amos, R. 9, *13*
Anderlecht 110, *148*, 152, 153, 154, 156
Anderson, J. and T. 11
Anderson, Jimmy 61, 72, 74, 76, 77, *77*, *78*, 79, 114
Anderson, John *13*
Anderton, Darren 176, 177, 178, *179*, *181*, 182, 185, 187, 191, 191, 192, 193, 194, 195, 197
Andrews, Eamonn 179
Anfield *122*, 145, 155, *186*, 189
Angus, John *101*
Antwerp 161
'Arbee' 32
Archibald, Steve 123, 135, 137, 138, *139*, 140, 143, 145, *145*, 148, *148*, 149, *149*, 152, 154
Ardiles, Osvaldo 127, *127*, 128, *128*, 129, 129, 130, 132, 134, 137, 138, 139, 140, *142*, 142, 143, 145, 146, 147, 148, *150*, 151, 152, 153, 155, 158, 159, 160, 161, *177*, 180, *182*, 183, 184, *184*, 185, 186, 188, 190, 194
Armstrong, Chris 190, *190*, 191, 192, 193, 194, 195, 196, 197
Armstrong, George 118
Armstrong, Gerry 123, *123*
Armstrong, Robert 153
Arsenal (Royal Woolwich) 15, 16, 17, 18, 22, 31, 39, 40, 44, 46, 57, 60, 66, 72, 74, 101, 118, 123, 124, 125, *135*, 137, 138, 142, 143, 145, 149, 152, 159, 160. *162*, *162*, 165, 166, *166*, 167, *167*, 176, 177, *184*, 191, 197
Aston Villa 17, 20, 30, 32, 33, 46, 50, 74, 79, 84, 90, 96, 118, *118*, 132, *135*, *140*, 142, 143, *145*, 149, 155, 159, 161, *163*, 164, 175, 178, 185, 196
Atlético Madrid 84 101, 103, 106, 106, 146
Austin, Dean 176, 178, 184, 190, *191*, 194
Austria Viennna 152, 194

Baardsen Espen 192, 193, 194, 196, 197
Bailey Gary 135, 155
Baily, Eddie *59*, 60, *61*, 62, 63, 66, 68, 71, 72, 74, 75, 106, 107, 109, 121, 123
Baker, Joe 112
Baker, Peter *77*, 81, *82*, 86, 88, *91*, 109, *113*
Bangor Town FC 123
Banks, Gordon 91, *105*
Banks, John 40, *43*, 44, *45*, 49, *49*
Barcelona 145, 146, 152, 160
Barclay, Patrick 140
Barmby, Nick 176, 177, 178, 184, 187, 188, 190
Barnes, John 159
Bates, Ken 160
Bayern Munich 152, 189, *189*, 192

Bayne, A. *13*
Beal, Phil 118
Beardsley, Peter 176, 185
Bearman, Fred *58*, 86, *91*, 106
Beasant, Dave *179*
Beaven, E. 11
Beckwith's Nursery 22
Bedford Town 82
Beeston FC 19
Benfica 84, 97, 99, 101, *103*, 156
Bennett, Dave 150
Bennett, Les 58, *59*, 60, 62, 154
Bennett, William 30, 31
Bergkamp, Dennis *192*
Bergsson, Gudni 176
Berry, George 137
Berry, Tony *173*, 174
Bingham Billy 132
Birmingham City 72, 112, 124, 132
Blackburn Rovers 9, 14, *36*, *65*, 161, 143, *145*, 161, 162, 178, 187, 191, 194, 197
Blackpool FC 39, 60, 64, 66, 74, 109, 112, 147
Blair, Tony 195
Blake, Herbert *51*
Blanchflower, Danny *72*, 74, *77*, 101, *101*, 103, *105*, 106, 107, 110, 113, *113*, 114, 121, 122, 140, 147, 148, *178*, 179
Bliss, Bert 41, *43*, 46, 47, 49, 50, 52
Bloor, Alan *117*
Bobroff, Paul 151, 163, 167, 171, 172
Bolton Wanderers 26, 38, 39, 66, 126, 196, 197
Bond, John 123, 138, 139
Bonetti, Peter *105*, 113
Book, Tony 109
Bordeaux 161, 190
Bosman Ruling 193
Bosnich, Mark 196
Boston United 77
Bould, Steve 167
Boyle, John *105*
Bradford City *45*, 49, 162
Bradford fire disaster 156
Bradford Park Avenue 35
Bradshaw, Paul 137
Brazil, Alan 152
Bremner, Billy 135
Bremner, Des *149*
Brentford FC 65, *147*, 193
Brettell, Frank 28
Briggs, Stanley *18*, 20
Brighton and Hove Albion 126
Bristol City 20, 28, 29, 111, 118
Bristol Rovers 20, 33, 49,
Brøndby 192
Brook, Eric 68
Brooke, Gary *130*, 137, 138, 145, *153*
Brooking, Trevor 138
Brooks, Johnny 77, 82, 83
Brown, Alexander ('Sandy') 21, 24, *24*, 25, 26, 27, 28, 29, 31, *31*
Brown, Bill *78*, *79*, 82, *85*, *86*, 88, *99*, 103, *106*, 109, *113*
Brown, Deryk *86*, 112
Brown, L. *13*
Buckingham, Vic 62, 68
Buckle, Bobby 9, 11, *13*, 14, *14*
Bull, Hedley 9, *10*, *13*, 14
Bull, Walter *18*
Buller, Sir Redvers *23*, 31
Bullock, Ralph 20, *28*
Bullock, Robert 22
Bum Kun Cha 145
Bumberry, T.W. 9, *13*
Burden Park 31
Burge, Ken *183*
Burgess, Ronald 58, *59*, 60, 62, 65, *66*, 68, *68*, *70*, 71, 74, 113
Burkinshaw, Keith 116, 123, 124, 125, 126, 127, 128, *128*, 129, 129, *130*, 132, 134, *135*, 137, 138, 140, 145, 146, 147, 148, 151, 152, 153, 154, 155, 158, 177
Burnley FC 44, 46, 66, 84, 85, 87, 88, 91, 97, *101*, *124*, 178
Burt, G. *13*
Burtenshaw, Norman *109*
Bury FC 28, 29
Busby, Mark 71, 116, 127, 138
Bush, G. *13*
Butcher, Terry 159

Cadman, Morton , Mr and Mrs 28
Calderwood, Colin 177, 178, 182, 184, 188, *193*, 194, 195, 196
California 192

Cameron, John 21, 24, *24*, 25, 26, 27
Campbell, Kevin 166, 167
Campbell, Sol 182, 187, 191, *192*, 193, 194, 195
Camsell, George 68
Cantrell, Jimmy 41, *43*, *45*, 46, 49, *49*, *50*
Cardiff City 50, 51, 52, 78, 124
Carr, Stephen 197
Carr, Willie 137
Casey, L. 11
Casey, L.R. 11
Casey, Sam (Ham) 9, 11, *13*, 14
Caskey, Darren 178, 191
Casuals, The 15, 16, 17, 19
Caton, Tommy 138, *139*, 140, *140*
Chalmers, Len 91, 92, *105*, 147
Chapman, Herbert 41, 44
Charity Shield 93, 99, 140, 146
Charles, Gary 168, *168*
Charles, Mel 81
Charlton Athletic 44, 66, *133*, 155, 161, 193
Charrington's Brewery 22, 24
Chelmsford City 61, 70
Chelsea FC 34, 36, 39, *39*, 40, 50, 106, 110, 112, 113, 135, 143, 146, *156*, 158, 159, 165, 175, 176, 177, 179, 193, 196, 197
Chesham 19
Chester City FC 190
Chiedozie, John 152, 155, 158
Chivers, Martin 117, 118, *118*, 120, *120*, 121, 123, 124
City Ramblers 19
Claesen, Nico 159, 160, 161
Clapham Rovers 19
Clapton Orient 34, 44
Clarke, Harry *59*, 60, 66, 68, *70*
Clawley, George 24, *24*, 27, 28
Clay, Tommy 40, 44, 46, *46*, 47
Clayton, Eddie *101*, 112, *113*
Clemence, Ray 118, *135*, 140, 142, 143, 145, 146, 148, 153, 155, *156*, 159, 160, 161, 176, 177, *177*
Clough, Brian 167, 168, 177
Clough, Nigel 170, *171*
Coates, Ralph 111, *118*, 120, *124*, *126*, 128
Coca-Cola Cup *see Football League Cup*
Cockburn, Henry 61
Cockerel symbol 34, 38, *39*, 77
Coldstream Guards *14*
Collins, Bobby 81
Collins, Tom *37*, *39*
Conn, Alfie 121, 123, 128
Connelly, John 88
Copeland, David 24, *24*, 28
Coppell, Steve 162, 176
Copping, Wilf 68
Corinthians 15, 18
Corrigan Joe 136, 138, *139*, 139, 140, *140*
Costa Pereira 101, *103*
Cottrell, Frank 9, *13*
Coventry City *132*, 137, 156, 160, 162, *164*, *171*, 185, 190, 196, 197
Cowans Gordon *130*
Craggs, John *135*
Crawford, Ray 93
Crewe Alexandra 85, 90
Crooks, Garth *123*, 135, 138, *139*, 139, 140, 142, 145, *145*, 147, 148, 152, 155, 165, 180
Crossley, Mark *168*, 169, *170*
Crump, Charles 32
Cruyff, Johan 152, 160
Cruyff, Jordi 194
Crystal Palace (club) 117, 124, *126*, 137, 147, 159, 162, 176, 190, 193
Crystal Palace (ground) 21, 22, 28
Cullis, Stan 84, *86*, 87, 113
Cundy, Jason 176
Currie, Tony 147, 148, 149
Czerniatinski, Alex 175

Daily Express 148
Daily Mail 129, 140, 153, 161, 182
Daily Mirror 180
Daines, Barry 125, 126, 138
Dalglish, Kenny 145, 194
Darlington FC *122*
Davies, Hunter 118
Dawes, Tommy 88
Day, Chris 193
Day, Taffy *54*, *58*
Deacock T. 28
Dean, William 'Dixie' 52
Deeley, Norman 99

Delano, Captain 9, *11*, 22
Denaby United *130*
Denmark 194
Dennis, Mike 182
Denyer, Charlie 11
Derby County 28, 38, 109, 120, 124, *126*, 165, 178, 194
Dexter, Fred 11, 13
Di Matteo, Roberto 193
Dick, Ally 153
Dimmock, Jimmy *43*, 46, 47, 49, *49*, 59, 51, 56
Dinamo Tbilisi 145
Ditchburn, Ted 58, *59*, 60, 62, 64, *64*, 65, 66, 68, *70*, *125*
Dixon, Wilf 123
Docherty, Tommy 106, 110
Doncaster Rovers 49, 77
Dozzell, Jason 177, 178, 197
Drewry, Arthur 71
Drogheda *149*, 152
Dukla, Prague 99
Dulin, Mickey 77
Dumitrescu, Ilie 181, 183, *183*, 184, *184*, 185, 189, 191
Duncan, John 122, 124, 126
Dundee United 159
Dunlop, Albert 81, *91*
Dunmore, Dave 77
Dunn, Arthur 15
Dunn, Joe 88
Dunn, John *118*
Duquemin, Len *59*, 60, *61*, 68, 70, *70*, 71, 72, 74, 76, 82
Durie, Gordon *174*, 175, 176, 178
Dyson, Geoff 113
Dyson, Terry *77*, 78 85, *86*, 88, 91, *93*, *97*, *97*, 99, *101*, *105*, 106, *106*, 109, *113*

East End Cup 15
Eastern Counties League 90
Edennote 180
Edinburgh, Justin *175*, 176, *177*, 182, 195
Edmonton *15*
Eintracht Frankfurt 161, 164
Elder, Alex *101*
Ellis, Arthur *62*
Elm Park 28, 193
Else, Fred *80*, 88
England, Mike *109*, 110, 112, 118, *118*, 122, 123, *124*
Erentz, Harry 24, *24*, 26
European Championships 192
European Champions' League 192, 196
European Cup 84, 85, 91, 96, 97, 99, *99*, *103*, 110, 164, 195
European Cup Winners' Cup 84, 99, 101, *105*, 106, *106*, 113, *113*, 140, 142, 145, 155, *174*, 176
Evans, Allan 155
Evans, David 85
Evans, Ray 120
Evans, Willie 55
Everton 13, 24, 38, 52, *57*, 66, 70, 80, 81, 101, 155, 157, 159, 161, 164, *164*, 176, 179, 183, *187*, 189, 194, 195
Ewood Park 194

FA Cup 14, 15, 19, 21, *23*, 24, 27, 28, 29, 30, 31, 32, 36, 40, 41, *43*, 49, 50, 51, 52, *57*, 60, 67, 76, 84, 85, 90, 92, 97, 101, *101*, *105*, 109, 111, *111*, 117, 118, 120, 124, 132, *136*, 137, 138, 142, *142*, 143, *145*, 146, 155, *156*, *158*, 159, 160, 165, 166, 167, 168, *168*, 169, 170, *170*, 175, 176, 180, 185, *186*, 191, *195*, 197
FA Cup winners medal *24*
FC Cologne 110, 120
Fairclough, Chris 160, 162, 180
Fairhurst, Dave 68
Falco, Mark 140, 142, 143, 145, *145*, *150*, 152, 154, 155, 158, 159
Fantham, John 87
Fashanu, John 178, 179
FC Köln 120
Felton, Frank 57
Fenwick, Terry *147*, 148, 149, 161, 163
Feola, Vicente 101
Ferdinand, Les 190
Ferguson, Alec 135
Feyenoord 99, 103, 120, *149*, 152, 161, *174*, 176
Fillery, Mike 143
Finney, Tom *33*, 36, 81